Lossless Information
Hiding in Images

Lossless Information Hiding in Images

Zhe-Ming Lu

Professor, School of Aeronautics and Astronautics
Zhejiang University
Hangzhou, P.R. China

Shi-Ze Guo

Professor, School of Computer Science
Beijing University of Posts and Communications
Beijing, China

ZHEJIANG UNIVERSITY PRESS
浙江大学出版社

ELSEVIER

AMSTERDAM • BOSTON • HEIDELBERG • LONDON
NEW YORK • OXFORD • PARIS • SAN DIEGO
SAN FRANCISCO • SINGAPORE • SYDNEY • TOKYO

Syngress is an imprint of Elsevier

SYNGRESS.

Syngress is an imprint of Elsevier
50 Hampshire Street, 5th Floor, Cambridge, MA 02139, United States

Notices
Knowledge and best practice in this field are constantly changing. As new research and experience broaden our understanding, changes in research methods, professional practices, or medical treatment may become necessary.

Practitioners and researchers must always rely on their own experience and knowledge in evaluating and using any information, methods, compounds, or experiments described herein. In using such information or methods they should be mindful of their own safety and the safety of others, including parties for whom they have a professional responsibility.

To the fullest extent of the law, neither the Publisher nor the authors, contributors, or editors, assume any liability for any injury and/or damage to persons or property as a matter of products liability, negligence or otherwise, or from any use or operation of any methods, products, instructions, or ideas contained in the material herein.

Library of Congress Cataloging-in-Publication Data
A catalog record for this book is available from the Library of Congress

British Library Cataloguing-in-Publication Data
A catalogue record for this book is available from the British Library

ISBN: 978-0-12-812006-4

For information on all Syngress publications
visit our website at https://www.elsevier.com/

Working together
to grow libraries in
developing countries

www.elsevier.com • www.bookaid.org

Publisher: Todd Green
Acquisition Editor: Simon Tian
Editorial Project Manager: Naomi Robertson
Production Project Manager: Priya Kumaraguruparan
Cover Designer: Mark Rogers

Typeset by TNQ Books and Journals

Contents

Preface

The enormous popularity of the World Wide Web in the early 1990s demonstrated the commercial potential of offering multimedia resources through digital networks. Representation of media in digital format facilitates its access. Digital media includes text, digital audio, images, video, and software. The recent growth of networked multimedia systems has increased the need for the protection of digital media. Since commercial interests seek to use the digital networks to offer digital media for profit, it is particularly important for the protection and enforcement of intellectual property rights, and they have a strong interest in protecting their ownership rights. On the other hand, the age of digital multimedia has brought many advantages in the creation and distribution of information. Representation of media in digital format enhances the accuracy, efficiency, and portability of existence of data. The powerful multimedia manipulation software has made it possible to edit and alter the media's content seamlessly. Since the ease of copying and editing decreases the credibility of multimedia, a secure authentication system is needed to verify data integrity and trustworthiness. Furthermore, the rapid development of the Internet requires confidential information that needs to be protected from the unauthorized users. Thus, the standard and concept of "what you see is what you get (WYSIWYG)," which we encounter sometimes while printing images or other materials, is no longer precise and would not fool a steganographer as it does not always hold true. Images can be more than what we see with our human visual system (HVS); hence, they may convey more than merely 1000 words. For decades, people strove to develop innovative methods for secret communication.

Under these circumstances, many approaches have been presented to protect the digital media itself or utilize the digital media to protect other important information. These approaches can be mainly classified into two categories, i.e., cryptography and information hiding. In conventional cryptographic systems, the sender generates a digital signature for an image in advance using a public key cryptography system such as the Rivest–Shamir–Adleman system. The sender then transmits both the digital signature and the corresponding image to the receiver. Later, the receiver can verify the integrity and authenticity of the received image by using the corresponding digital signature. The cryptographic system permits only valid keyholders access to encrypted data, but once such data is decrypted there is no way to track its reproduction or retransmission. Information hiding, which is also known as data hiding, is distinct from cryptography as it aims to make the embedded data unrecoverable and inviolateable. Information hiding is a method of hiding secret messages into a cover medium so that an unintended observer will not be aware of the existence of the hidden messages.

Information hiding techniques can be classified into three techniques, i.e., steganography, watermarking, and fingerprinting. These techniques are quite difficult to tease apart especially for people coming from different disciplines. The term steganography is retrieved from the Greek words *stegos* means *cover* and *grafia* meaning *writing*, defining it as *covered writing*. The similarity between steganography and cryptography is that both are used to conceal information. However, the difference is that steganography does not reveal any suspicion about the hidden information to the user. Therefore the attackers will not try to decrypt information. There are other two techniques that seem to be same as steganography. They are watermarking and fingerprinting. Both these techniques sounds to be the same and provide the same end goals, but both are very different in the way they work. Watermarking allows a person to provide hidden copyright notices or other verification licenses, whereas fingerprinting uses each copy of the content and makes it unique to the receiver. Watermarking is usually a signature to identify the origin, and all the copies are marked in the same way. However, in fingerprinting different unique copies are embedded for distinct copies. Digital watermarking has also been proposed as a possible solution for data authentication and tamper detection. The invisible authenticator, sensitive watermark is inserted using the visual redundancy of HVS and is altered or destroyed when the host image is modified by various linear or nonlinear transformations. The changes of authentication watermark can be used to determine the modification of the marked image, and even locate the tampered area. Because the watermark is embedded in the content of image, it can exert its efficiency in the whole lifecycle.

Today, there is a huge volume of literature on information hiding techniques. However, most of the existing information hiding schemes distort the original image irreversibly; then, the challenge becomes one of minimizing distortion relative to capacity. In several applications, such as medical or military imaging, any distortion is intolerable. In such cases, lossless information hiding schemes are the only recourse. To meet this need, the concept of distortion-free embedding has become a very important issue, especially in sensitive images. Lossless information hiding, also called reversible information hiding or reversible data hiding, allows a sender to embed invisible information into an original image in a reversible manner. Then, the receiver can extract the embedded data and restore the original image. Lossless information hiding in images is gaining more attention in the past few years because of its increasing applications in military communication, health care, and law enforcement.

Lossless information hiding can be used in many applications. A possible application is to use lossless reversible watermarking algorithms to achieve the lossless watermark authentication, supporting completely accurate authentication for the cover media, which is actually the original intention of reversible watermarking schemes. In some applications, people are more concerned about the quality of the cover media itself. In this type of application, the common requirements are that the watermarking algorithm and the watermark embedding process do not introduce permanent distortion to the cover media. A special class of application that we are most likely to think of is the special accuracy requirement for special media, such as medical images, military images, remote sensing images, legal evidence images, secret documents, precious works of art, and science experimental images. For this type of application, even 1-bit permanent loss in the original cover media is not allowed, so the data embedding algorithms must be reversible. Since reversible watermark embedding algorithms can remove the embedding distortion completely, they can be referred to as data embedding styles with 100% fidelity. Another application is to restore the image modification operations. In some image processing applications, the process is completed by a few simple adjustments. If the image processing operator worries about the fact that the users are not satisfied with the image processing results, he can treat the parameters as a watermark and reversibly embed it in the cover image and in the future restore the image to its original state or its approximate state, thus you do not have to store a lot of original images.

Lossless information hiding algorithms for images can be classified into three categories, i.e., the spatial domain−based, the transform domain−based, and the compressed domain−based schemes. Transform domain−based lossless information hiding methods can be classified into two categories, i.e., integer discrete cosine transform (DCT)−based schemes and integer discrete wavelet transform (DWT)−based schemes. Here, the transform used in reversible information hiding should be in the category of invertible mapping. Nowadays, since more and more images are being stored in compressed formats such as JPEG and JPEG2000 or transmitted based on vector quantization (VQ) and block truncation coding (BTC), more and more efforts are being focused on developing the compressed domain information hiding approaches. Here, we view the compressed image as the cover image, and reversibility means that after extracting the secret data from the unattacked stego image, we can recover the original compressed image losslessly.

In general, payload capacity, stego image quality, and complexity of the data embedding algorithm are the three major criteria used to evaluate lossless information hiding. Payload capacity means how much secret information can be embedded in an image. The quality of a stego image is measured by the peak signal-to-signal ratio (PSNR): a higher PSNR value can guarantee less distortion caused in the cover image. Moreover, the complexity of the data embedding algorithm should be as simple as it is effective. In practice, high payload capacity and low distortion are conflicting requirements: the larger the capacity created by a reversible embedding technique, the higher is the distortion introduced by embedding.

Based on this background, this book is devoted to lossless information hiding techniques for images. This book is suitable for researchers in the field of information hiding. Our aim is to recommend a relatively novel monograph to cover recent progress of research hotspots in the area of lossless information hiding such that the researchers can refer to this book to have a comprehensive understanding and carry out in-depth research in their own directions. This book consists of six chapters. Chapter 2 discusses the lossless information techniques in the spatial domain. In this chapter, we first overview the spatial domain−based lossless schemes. Then, we discuss some typical spatial domain lossless information hiding methods. Chapter 3 discusses transform domain−based lossless schemes. In this chapter, we first introduce some related concepts and requirements for lossless information hiding in transform domains. Then we give a brief overview of transform domain−based information hiding. Next we introduce two types of transform domain−based lossless information hiding methods. Chapter 4 focuses on the VQ-based lossless information hiding schemes. We first review the schemes related to VQ-based information hiding. Then, we mainly focus on three kinds of VQ-based lossless information hiding schemes. Chapter 5 discusses the topic of embedding data in BTC-compressed images with lossless hiding techniques. First, we introduce the block truncation coding technique. Then, we review the schemes related to BTC-based information hiding. Then, we focus on two topics, i.e., lossless information hiding schemes for BTC-compressed grayscale images and color images. Chapter 6 first introduces JPEG and JPEG2000 compression techniques in brief, together with the embedding challenges. Then, we introduce the lossless information hiding schemes for JEPG- and JPEG2000-compressed images.

This book is a monograph in the area of information hiding. It focuses on one branch of the field of information hiding, i.e., lossless information hiding. Furthermore, it focuses on the most popular media, images. This book embodies the following characteristics. (1) Novelty: This book introduce many state-of-the-art lossless hiding schemes, most of that come from the authors' publications in the past 5 years. The content of this book covers the research hotspots and their recent progress in the field of lossless information hiding. After reading this book, readers can immediately grasp the status, the typical algorithms, and the trend in the field of lossless information hiding. For example, in Chapter 6, reversible data hiding in JPEG2000 images is a very new research branch. (2) All roundedness: In this book, lossless information hiding schemes for images are classified into three categories, i.e., spatial domain−based, transform domain−based, and compressed−domain based schemes. Furthermore, the compressed domain−based methods are classified into VQ-based, BTC-based, and JPEG/JPEG2000-based methods. Especially, the lossless information hiding in JPEG images is very useful since most of the images are stored in the JPEG format. Therefore, the classification of lossless hiding schemes covers all kinds of methods. (3) Theoretical: This book embodies many theories related to lossless information hiding, such as image compression, integer transforms, multiresolution analysis, VQ, BTC, JPEG, and JPEG2000. For example, in Chapter 3, several definitions related to invertible mappings and integer DCT transforms are introduced in detail to understand the content of later chapters easily. (4) Practical: It is suitable for all researchers, students, and teachers in the fields of information security, image processing, information hiding, and communications. It can guide the engineers to design a suitable hiding scheme for their special purpose, such as copyright protection, content authentication, and secret communication in the fields of military, medicine, and law.

This book is completely written by Prof. Zhe-Ming Lu. The research fruits of this book are based on the work accumulation of the author for over a decade, most of which comes from the fruits of PhD and master students supervised by Prof. Lu. For example, Dr. Zhen-Fei Zhao and Dr. Hao Luo carried out the research work on reversible secret sharing−based lossless information hiding schemes supervised by Prof. Lu. Dr. Bian Yang, who was a former masters and PhD student, cosupervised by Prof. Lu, carried out the research work in Germany on lossless information hiding schemes based on integer DCT/DWT transforms as the main part of his thesis topic. Dr. Yu-Xin Su, who was a former masters student, supervised by Prof. Lu, carried out the research work on lossless information hiding schemes for BTC-compressed color images as part of his thesis topic. Mr. Xiang Li, who was a former masters student, supervised by Prof. Lu, carried out the research work on lossless information hiding in JPEG/JPEG2000-compressed images as part of his thesis topic. We would like to show our great appreciation of the assistance from other teachers and students at the Institute of Astronautics Electronics Engineering of Zhejiang University. Part of research work in this book was supported by the National Scientific Foundation of China under the grants 61171150 and 61003255 and the Zhejiang Provincial Natural Science Foundation of China under the grants R1110006 and RLY14F020024. Owing to our limited knowledge, it is inevitable that errors and defects will appear in this book, and we adjure readers to criticize.

Zhe-Ming Lu
Hangzhou, China
June 2016

Introduction

1

1.1 BACKGROUND

1.1.1 DEFINITION OF IMAGES

1.1.1.1 Images

An *image* is a visual representation of something that depicts or records visual perception. For example, a picture is similar in appearance to some subject, which provides a depiction of a physical object or a person. Images may be captured by either optical devices, such as cameras, mirrors, lenses, and telescopes, or natural objects and phenomena, such as human eyes or water surfaces. For example, in a film camera works the lens focuses an image onto the film surface. The color film has three layers of emulsion, each layer being sensitive to a different color, and the (slide) film records on each tiny spot of the film to reproduce the same color as the image projected onto it, the same as the lens saw. This is an *analog image*, the same as our eyes can see, so we can hold the developed film up and look at it.

Images may be two-dimensional, such as a photograph, or three-dimensional, such as a statue or a hologram. An image in a broad sense also refers to any two-dimensional figure such as a map, a graph, a pie chart, or an abstract painting. In this sense, images can also be rendered manually, such as by drawing, painting, carving; can be rendered automatically by printing or computer graphics technology; or can be developed by a combination of methods, especially in a pseudophotograph. In photography, visual media, and the computer industries, the phrase "still image" refers to a single static image that is distinguished from a kinetic or moving image (often called video), which emphasizes that one is not talking about movies. The phrase "still image" is often used in very precise or pedantic technical writing such as an image compression standard.

In this book, we consider two-dimensional still images in a broad sense. Thus, an *analog image (physical image)* **I** defined in the "real world" is considered to be a function of two real variables as follows:

$$\mathbf{I} = \{I(x,y) \in [0,\ B] | 0 \le x \le X,\ 0 \le y \le Y\} \tag{1.1}$$

where $I(x,y)$ is the amplitude (e.g., brightness or intensity) of the image at the real coordinate position (x,y), B is the possible maximum amplitude, and X and Y define the maximum coordinates. An image may be considered to contain subimages sometimes referred to as *regions*. This concept reflects the fact that images frequently contain collections of *objects*, each of which can be the basis for a region.

1.1.1.2 Digital Images

A *digital image* is the numeric representation of an analog image (physical image). Any image from a scanner, from a digital camera, or in a computer is a digital image. Depending on whether the image resolution is fixed or not, it may be of vector or raster type. *Raster images* are created through the process of scanning source artwork or "painting" with a photo editing or paint program such as Corel Photo-PAINT or Adobe PhotoShop. A raster image is a collection of dots called *pixels*. Pixel is a computer word formed from PICture ELement, because a pixel is a tiny colored square that is the smallest element of the digital image. Scanned images and web images [Joint Photographic Experts Group (JPEG) and graphics interchange format (GIF) files] are the most common forms of raster images. *Vector images* are created through the process of drawing with vector illustration programs such as CorelDRAW or Adobe Illustrator. The word "vector" is a synonym for line. A vector image is a collection of connected lines and curves that produce objects. When creating a vector image in a vector illustration program, node or drawing points are inserted and lines and curves connect the nodes together. Sometimes, both raster and vector elements will be combined in one image, for example, in the case of a billboard with text (vector) and photographs (raster). By itself, the term "digital image" usually refers to *raster images*.

In this book, we mainly consider two-dimensional still raster images. Raster images can be created by a variety of input devices and techniques, such as digital cameras, scanners, coordinate-measuring machines, seismographic profiling, and airborne radar. A digital camera creates a digital picture with a charge-coupled device or complementary metal oxide semiconductor chip behind the lens. The lens focuses the physical image onto the digital sensor, which is constructed with a grid of many tiny light-sensitive cells, or sensors, arranged to divide the total picture area into rows and columns composed of a huge number of very tiny subareas called pixels, as shown in Fig. 1.1. Each sensor inspects and remembers the color of the tiny area. A digital camera remembers the color by digitizing the analog color into three digital values representing the color (i.e., three components, red, green, and blue,

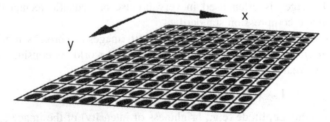

FIGURE 1.1

Digitalization of the Physical Image by Pixels.

called RGB), or sometimes one digital value representing the brightness of the color. Similarly, a scanner has a one-row array of similar cells, and a carriage motor moves this row of sensors down the page, making columns in many rows to form the full image grid. Both scanners and cameras generate images composed of pixels, and a pixel contains the digital RGB color data or brightness of one tiny surface area. This process is called *digitization*. Printers and video screens are digital devices too, and their only purpose in life is to display pixels.

From these descriptions, we come to know that a digital image contains a fixed number of rows and columns of pixels. Pixels are the smallest individual element in a digital image, holding quantized values that represent the brightness of a given color at any specific point. Typically, the pixels are stored in computer memory as a raster image or raster map, a two-dimensional array of small integers. Thus, a digital image **I** can be defined as an array, or a matrix, of square pixels arranged in columns and rows as follows:

$$\mathbf{I} = \{I(m,n) | 0 \leq m \leq M - 1, \quad 0 \leq n \leq N - 1\} \tag{1.2}$$

where $I(m,n)$ is the color data or brightness value of the pixel at the mth column and nth row, and M and N define the width (number of columns) and height (number of rows) of the digital image.

According to the range of $I(m,n)$, we can classify digital images into *binary images*, *grayscale images,* and *color images*, and three examples are shown in Fig. 1.2. In color images, each pixel's color sample has three numerical RGB components to represent the color of that tiny area, i.e., $I(m,n)$ is denoted by (R, G, B) with R$\in$ [0, 255], G$\in$ [0, 255], and B$\in$ [0, 255]. Typically, for each pixel, its three RGB components are three 8-bit numbers. These 3 bytes (1 byte for each RGB) compose a 24-bit color. Each byte can have 256 possible values, ranging from 0 to 255. In the RGB system, we know red and green make yellow. Thus (255, 255, 0) means both red and green are fully saturated (255 is as large as an 8-bit value can be), with no

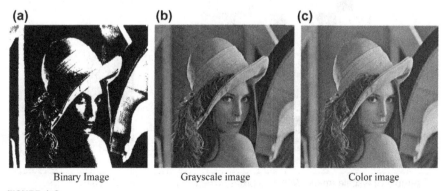

(a)	(b)	(c)
Binary Image	Grayscale image	Color image

FIGURE 1.2

The (a) Binary, (b) Grayscale, and (c) Color Images of Lena.

blue (zero), resulting in the color yellow. However, three values like (250, 165, 0), meaning (red = 250, green = 165, blue = 0), can denote one orange pixel.

A grayscale image is what people normally call a black-and-white image, but the name emphasizes that such an image will also include many shades of gray. In an 8-bit grayscale image, each picture element has an assigned intensity that ranges from 0 to 255, i.e., $I(m,n) \in [0, 255]$. A gray has the property of having equal RGB values. For example, black is an RGB value of (0, 0, 0) and white is (255, 255, 255), (220, 220, 220) is a light gray (near white), and (40, 40, 40) is a dark gray (near black). Since gray has equal values in RGB, a grayscale image only uses 1 byte per pixel instead of 3 bytes. The byte still holds values 0 to 255, to represent 256 shades of gray. Fig. 1.3 shows an enlarged grayscale image with 100 pixels of different grayscales.

A binary image is a digital image that has only two possible values for each pixel, i.e., $I(m,n) \in \{0, 1\}$. Typically the two colors used for a binary image are black and white, although any two colors can be used. Binary images are also called bilevel or two level. This means that each pixel is stored as a single bit, i.e., 0 or 1. Binary images often arise in digital image processing as masks or as a result of certain operations such as segmentation, thresholding, and dithering. Some input/output devices, such as laser printers, fax machines, and bilevel computer displays, can only handle bilevel images. A binary image can be stored in memory as a bitmap, a packed array of bits, i.e., every 8 bits is packed into 1 byte.

1.1.2 IMAGE PROCESSING AND IMAGE ANALYSIS

1.1.2.1 Image Processing in a Broad Sense

In a broad sense, *image processing* is any form of signal processing for which the input is an image, such as a photograph or video frame; the output of image

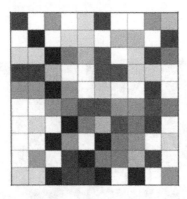

FIGURE 1.3

An Example Grayscale Image With 100 pixels, Where Each Pixel Has a Value From 0 (Black) to 255 (White), and the Possible Range of the Pixel Values Depends on the Color Depth of the Image, Here 8 bits = 256 tones or Grayscales.

processing may be either an image or a set of characteristics or parameters related to the image. Most image processing techniques involve treating the image as a two-dimensional signal and applying standard signal processing techniques to it.

Image processing usually refers to digital image processing, but optical and analog image processing also are possible. In electrical engineering and computer science, *analog image processing* is any image processing task conducted on two-dimensional analog signals by analog means as opposed to digital image processing. *Digital image processing* is the use of computer algorithms to perform image processing on digital images. As a subcategory or field of digital signal processing, digital image processing has many advantages over analog image processing. It allows a much wider range of algorithms to be applied to the input data and can avoid problems such as the buildup of noise and signal distortion during processing. Since images are defined over two dimensions (perhaps more), digital image processing may be modeled in the form of multidimensional systems.

In this book, we only discuss digital image processing. Digital image processing refers to the processing of a 2D/3D image by a computer. Digital image processing systems require that the images be available in the digitized form. For digitization, the given analog image is sampled on a discrete grid and each sample or pixel is quantized using a finite number of bits. The digitized image then can be processed by a computer. Modern digital technology has made it possible to manipulate multidimensional signals with systems that range from simple digital circuits to advanced parallel computers. The goal of this manipulation can be divided into three categories: (1) *image processing in a narrow sense,* where the input is an image and the output is also an image; (2) *image analysis*, where the input is an image, whereas the outputs are some measurements of the image; and (3) *image understanding*, where the input is an image, whereas the outputs are some high-level descriptions of the image.

An image may be considered to contain subimages sometimes referred to as regions of interest, or simply regions. This concept reflects the fact that images frequently contain collections of objects each of which can be the basis for a region. In a sophisticated image processing system, it should be possible to apply specific image processing operations to selected regions. Thus one part of an image (region) might be processed to suppress motion blur, whereas another part might be processed to improve color rendition.

Two concepts closely related to image processing are *computer graphics* and *computer vision*. In computer graphics, images are manually made from physical models of objects, environments, and lighting, instead of being acquired (via imaging devices such as cameras) from natural scenes, as in most animated movies. *Computer vision*, on the other hand, is often considered high-level image processing out of which a machine/computer/software intends to decipher the physical contents of an image or a sequence of images (e.g., videos or 3D full-body magnetic resonance scans).

In modern sciences and technologies, images also gain much broader scopes due to the ever-growing importance of *scientific visualization* (of often large-scale complex scientific/experimental data). Examples include microarray data in genetic research, or real-time multiasset portfolio trading in finance.

1.1.2.2 Image Processing in a Narrow Sense

In this section, we consider image processing in a narrow sense, that is, the study of any algorithm that takes an image as input and returns an image as output. Before processing an image, it is converted into a digital form. Digitization includes sampling of an image and quantization of the sampled values. After converting the image into bit information, the following processing steps are performed. Three main traditional processing techniques are *image enhancement, image restoration,* and *image compression,* which are briefly described as follows.

1.1.2.2.1 Image Enhancement

The goal of image enhancement is to improve the usefulness of an image for a given task such as providing a more subjectively pleasing image for human viewing. In image enhancement, little or no attempt is made to estimate the actual image degradation process, and the techniques are often ad hoc. This process does not increase the inherent information content in data. It is a subjective process. It includes gray level and contrast manipulation, noise reduction, edge sharpening, filtering, interpolation and magnification, and pseudocoloring. Image enhancement techniques can be divided into two categories: frequency domain methods and spatial domain methods. The former process the image as a two-dimensional signal and enhance the image based on its two-dimensional Fourier transform. The low-pass filter—based method can remove noise from the image, whereas using high-pass filtering, we can enhance the edge, which is a kind of high-frequency signal, and make the blurred image clear. Typical spatial domain—based algorithms are the local mean filtering—based method and median filtering (take intermediate pixel value of the local neighborhood)—based method, which can be used to remove or weaken the noise.

1.1.2.2.2 Image Restoration

Images are often degraded during the data acquisition process. The degradation may involve motion blurring, information loss due to sampling, camera misfocus, quantization effects, and various sources of noise. The purpose of image restoration is to estimate the original image from the degraded data. It is concerned with filtering the observed image to minimize the effect of degradations. Effectiveness of image restoration depends on the extent and accuracy of the knowledge of the degradation process as well as on filter design. Image restoration is different from image enhancement in that the latter is designed to emphasize features of the image that make the image more pleasing to the observer, but not necessarily to produce realistic data from a scientific point of view. Image enhancement techniques use no a priori model of the process that created the image.

1.1.2.2.3 Image Compression

The objective of image compression is to reduce irrelevance and redundancy of the image data to be able to store or transmit data in an efficient form. It is concerned with minimizing the number of bits required to represent an image. Image compression may be lossy or lossless. Lossless compression is preferred for archival purposes and often for medical imaging, technical drawings, clip art, or comics. Lossy compression methods, especially when used at low bit rates, introduce compression artifacts. Lossy methods are especially suitable for natural images such as photographs in applications in which minor (sometimes imperceptible) loss of fidelity is acceptable to achieve a substantial reduction in bit rate. The lossy compression that produces imperceptible differences may be called visually lossless. We will provide an overview of image compression methods in Section 1.3.

Besides these three techniques, in fact, we can view the process of information embedding in cover images as a special kind of digital image processing, since both its input and output are digital images.

1.1.2.3 Image Analysis

Image analysis is the extraction of meaningful information from images, mainly from digital images by means of digital image processing techniques. Image analysis tasks can be as simple as reading bar coded tags or as sophisticated as identifying a person based on faces. There are many different techniques used in automatically analyzing images. Each technique may be useful for a small range of tasks; however, there are still no known methods of image analysis that are generic enough for wide ranges of tasks, compared with the abilities of a human's image-analyzing capabilities. Examples of image analysis techniques in different fields include: 2D and 3D object recognition, image segmentation, motion detection (e.g., single particle tracking), video tracking, optical flow, medical scan analysis, 3D pose estimation, automatic number plate recognition, and so on.

Digital image analysis is the process in which a computer or electrical device automatically studies an image to obtain useful information from it. Note that the device is often a computer, but it may also be an electrical circuit, a digital camera, or a mobile phone. The applications of digital image analysis are continuously expanding through all areas of science and industry, including medicine, such as detecting cancer in an MRI scan; microscopy, such as counting the germs in a swab; remote sensing, such as detecting intruders in a house and producing land cover/land use maps; astronomy, such as calculating the size of a planet; materials science, such as determining if a metal weld has cracks; machine vision, such as automatically counting items in a factory conveyor belt; security, such as detecting a person's eye color or hair color; robotics, such as avoiding steering into an obstacle; optical character recognition, such as detecting automatic license plate; assay microplate reading, such as detecting where a chemical was manufactured; and metallography, such as determining the mineral content of a rock sample.

Computers are indispensable for the analysis of large amounts of data, for tasks that require complex computation, or for the extraction of quantitative information. *Computer image analysis* largely involves the fields of computer or machine vision, and medical imaging, and makes heavy use of pattern recognition, digital geometry, and signal processing. It is the quantitative or qualitative characterization of 2D or 3D digital images. Two-dimensional images are usually analyzed in computer vision, whereas 3D images in are analyzed in medical imaging. On the other hand, the human visual cortex is an excellent image analysis apparatus, especially for extracting higher level information, and for many applications—including medicine, security, and remote sensing—human analysts still cannot be replaced by computers. For this reason, many important image analysis tools such as edge detectors and neural networks are inspired by human visual perception models.

In fact, we can view the process of information extracting from *stego images* as a special kind of digital image analysis, since its input is an image and its output is the secret information or the conclusion whether the stego image is authentic or watermarked. Thus, the topic of information hiding in images is closely related to digital image processing and analysis, and many traditional image processing and analysis techniques can be used in information hiding.

1.1.3 NETWORK INFORMATION SECURITY

With the rapid development of computer technology, the *information network* has become an important guarantee of social development. An information network involves national governments, military, cultural, educational, and other fields, and the information it transmits, stores, and processes is related to the government's macrocontrol policies, business and economic information, bank money transfer information, important information in stocks and bonds, energy and resource data, and research data. There is a lot of sensitive information, or even a state secret, so it will inevitably attract the attack from a variety of people around the world (such as information leakage, information theft, data tampering, data deletion, and appending, computer viruses). Often, in crime using computers, it is difficult to leave evidences of a crime, which greatly stimulates the occurrence of high-tech computer crime cases. The rapid increase in computer crimes causes computer systems of all countries, especially network systems, to face a serious threat, and it has become one of the serious social problems.

Network information security is an important issue related to national security and sovereignty, social stability, and ethnic and cultural inheritance. It becomes more and more important with the accelerated pace of global information. Network information security is a comprehensive discipline involving computer science, network technology, communication technology, *cryptography*, information security technology, applied mathematics, number theory, information theory, and other disciplines. It mainly refers to the fact that the hardware, software, and data in the network system are protected from destruction, alteration, and disclosure due to accidental or malicious reasons; that the network system can run continuously and reliably; and that the network service is not interrupted.

Network information security consists of four aspects, i.e., the security problems in information communication, the security problems in storage, the audit of network information content, and authentication. To maintain the security of data transmission, it is necessary to apply data encryption and integrity identification techniques. To guarantee the security of information storage, it is necessary to guarantee database security and terminal security. Information content audit is to check the content of the input and output information from networks, so as to prevent or trace the possible whistle-blowing. User identification is the process of verifying the principal part in the network. Usually there are three kinds of methods to verify the principal part identity. One is that only the secret known by the principal part is available, e.g., passwords or keys. The second is that the objects carried by the principal part are available, e.g., intelligent cards or token cards. The third is that only the principal part's unique characteristics or abilities are available, e.g., fingerprints, voices, or retina or signatures. The technical characteristics of the network information security mainly embody the following aspects. (1) *Integrity*: It means the network information cannot be altered without authority; it is against active attacks, guaranteeing data consistence and preventing data from being modified and destroyed by illegal users. (2) *Confidentiality*: It is the characteristic that the network information cannot be leaked to unauthorized users; it is against passive attacks so as to guarantee that the secret information cannot be leaked to illegal users. (3) *Availability*: it is the characteristics that the network information can be visited and used by legal users if needed. It is used to prevent information and resource usage by legal users from being rejected irrationally. (4) *Nonrepudiation*: It means all participants in the network cannot deny or disavow the completed operations and promises; the sender cannot deny the already sent information, while the receiver also cannot deny the already received information. (5) *Controllability*: It is the ability of controlling the network information content and its prevalence, namely, it can monitor the network information security.

The coming of the network information era also proposes a new challenge to copyright protection. *Copyright* is also called author right. It is a general designation (http://dict.iciba.com/be) called by a joint name/of spirit right based on a special production and the economic right which completely dominates this production and its interest. With the continuous enlargement of the network scope and the gradual maturation of digitalization techniques, the quantity of various digitalized books, magazines, pictures, photographs, music, songs, and video products has increased rapidly. These digitalized products and services can be transmitted by the network without the limitation of time and space, even without logistic transmission. After the trade and payment completed, they can be efficiently and quickly provided for clients by the network. On the other hand, the network openness and resource sharing will cause the problem of how to validly protect the digitalized network products' copyright. There must be some efficient techniques and approaches for the prevention of digitalized products' alteration, counterfeit, plagiarism and embezzlement, etc.

Information security protection methods are also called *security mechanisms*. All security mechanisms are designed for some types of security attack threats. They can be used individually or in combination in different manners. The commonly used network security mechanisms are as follows. (1) *Information encryption and hiding mechanism*. Encryption makes an attacker unable to understand the message content, and thus the information is protected. On the contrary, hiding is to conceal the useful information in other information, and thus the attacker cannot find it. It not only realizes information secrecy but also protects the communication itself. So far, information encryption is the most basic approach in information security protection, whereas information hiding is a new direction in information security areas. It draws more and more attention in the applications of digitalized productions' copyright protection. (2) *Integrity protection*. It is used for illegal alteration prevention based on the cipher theory. Another purpose of integrity protection is to provide nonrepudiation services. When information source's integrity can be verified but cannot be simulated, the information receiver can verify the information sender. Digital signatures can provide methods for us. (3) *Authentication mechanism*. The basic mechanism of network security, namely, network instruments should authenticate each other so as to guarantee the right operations and audit of a legal user. (4) *Audit*. It is the foundation of preventing inner criminal offenses and taking evidence after accidents. Through the records of some important events, errors can be localized and reasons of successful attacks can be found when mistakes appear in the system or it is attacked. Audit information should prevent illegal deletion and modification. (5) *Power control and access control*. It is the requisite security means of host computer systems. Namely, the system endows suitable operation power to a certain user according to the right authentication and thus makes him not exceed his authority. Generally, this mechanism adopts the role management method, that is, aiming at system requirements, to define various roles, e.g., manager, and accountant, and then to endow them different executive powers. (6) *Traffic padding*. It generates spurious communications or data units to disguise the amount of real data units being sent. Typically, useless random data are sent out in vacancy and thus enhance the difficulty to obtain information through the communication stream. Meanwhile, it also enhances the difficulty to decipher the secret communications. The sent random data should have good simulation performance and thus can mix the false with the genuine. This book focuses on applying *digital watermarking* techniques to solve the *copyright protection* and *content authentication* problems for images, involving the first three security mechanisms.

1.1.4 IMAGE PROTECTION AND IMAGE AUTHENTICATION

With the rapid development of *digital image processing* techniques and popularization of the *Internet*, *digital images* are being more and more widely used in a number of applications from medical imaging and law enforcement to banking and daily consumer use. They are much more convenient in editing, copying, storing, transmitting, and utilizing. However, unfortunately, at the same time, digital images are facing the problems of protection and authentication as follows.

1.1.4.1 Image Protection

Image protection mainly includes copyright protection, *copy control*, and source tracing for digital images. Both companies and private individuals have access to networks with an ever-growing bandwidth and network infrastructure. Lack of sufficiently strong copyright protection and copy control is one of the hindrances for increased use of the Internet for publishing images where protection of copyright is a requirement and for distribution of images where copy control is a requirement. Source tracing refers to tracing the source of the pirated image and telling us who the pirate is.

It is important that there be a level of control on what one of the parties is doing with the image received or made available from the other. One example of this kind of transaction is purchase of the image downloaded via the Internet in digital representation and therefore easily manipulated and duplicated with computers or other devices that can read, copy, and transform the received image unless there is some mechanism that controls what the user can do with the image. Often there will be an intellectual property right and a commercial issue connected to the image, and the publisher and distributor therefore need to have influence and control over what the buyer is doing with the delivered digital image.

Another important area is when the image is not delivered from one part to the other but is published on the Internet available for anybody with access to the Internet. Still there may be connected intellectual property rights to the published image, so the publisher needs to be able to trace and prove that the pirate violates the intellectual property rights and copyrights.

What does a potential publisher of images on the Internet or a potential distributor of images over the Internet have to assess before he can decide which techniques, methods, and security products he should employ to ensure protection of copyrights of published images and control over copying of distributed images? There are mainly two approaches used to ensure security and control when distributing and publishing images where intellectual right protection and copy control are major concerns: (1) use of information hiding for copyright protection of images published on the Internet and (2) establishing *digital right management* systems (DRMS) for copy control of distributed information.

In Section 1.4, we will give an overview of information hiding in images and describe how different applications of information hiding can be used to protect intellectual property rights when distributing and publishing images. For example, the *robust image watermarking* technique can be used to embed copyright information in the cover image; then if it is required we can extract the copyright information from the watermarked image, or even the attacked version, to verify the ownership of the image. Furthermore, description of systems that are used for distribution of images when copy control is of critical importance are discussed. These systems are often referred to as DRMS.

Besides copyright protection and copy control, information hiding can be also applied to source tracing. A watermark can be embedded into a digital image at each point of distribution. If a copy of the image is found later, then the watermark may be retrieved from the copy and the source of the distribution is known. This technique can be used to detect the source of illegally copied images or movies.

1.1.4.2 Image Authentication

With the development of network, multimedia information such as books, music, images, and videos has been widespread because of its ease of access and of copying, which has greatly enriched people's lives. However, digital images, in the case of absence of protection, are vulnerable to be tampered or forged, thereby their authenticity and integrity are damaged. When a digital image is used as an evidence, its authenticity and integrity is particularly important. For example, in medicine, the accuracy and integrity of the medical image is very important to diagnosis; in court, the authenticity of provided photographs has an important effect on the nature of the evidence. Therefore, there is an urgent need to develop a technique to protect the authenticity and integrity of multimedia information, especially for images.

Image authentication is a technology emerging in the context of the aforementioned applications, which has been rapidly developed, and its purpose is to identify and detect the authenticity and integrity of the image. Image authentication methods currently implemented can be mainly divided into two categories:

The first category is *digital signature*—based image authentication schemes, which simply add the signature information after the original image. The authentication is realized by recalculating the signature information in the input image and comparing it with the original additional signature information to detect possible image tampering. Although this kind of algorithm is simple in ideas and easy to be implemented, its biggest drawback is that during verification we require additional signature information, and thus we cannot fulfill the blind authentication where we cannot use any additional information.

The second category is digital watermarking—based image authentication schemes, which overcome the deficiencies of the signature-based schemes. The authentication information hidden in the original image without the need for additional signature information is the main advantage of this type of approach. In fact, the whole book mainly focuses on this type of image authentication algorithm. Authentication watermarks can be generally divided into *fragile watermarks* and *semifragile watermarks*. Utilizing the fragility of watermarks, the tampering operations on the watermarked image will also affect the embedded watermark, and therefore the extracted watermark can be used to determine if the image has been tampered with or not. The fragile watermark is sensitive to all operations, that is, any modification operation on the watermarked image will change the extracted watermark. As long as the detected watermark has subtle changes, it shows that the original watermarked image has been altered. The semifragile watermark is robust to some well-intentioned operations but fragile to other malicious operations. The semifragile watermarking—based authentication system can allow certain operations such as image compression and format conversion, but not other malicious operations like pruning.

1.2 OVERVIEW OF INFORMATION HIDING

Digital equipment and computer technologies provide a great convenience for production and access to multimedia information such as audio, images, video, animation, text, and 3D models. Meanwhile, with the growing popularity of the Internet, multimedia information exchange has reached unprecedented breadth and depth. People can now publish their works through the Internet, communicate important information, or perform network trade. However, as a result, some very serious problems also emerge: it becomes easier to infringe the rights of digital works and violate the privacy of people, it becomes more convenient to tamper and forge the digital works, and the malicious attacks become more rampant. Therefore, the problem of how to effectively protect intellectual properties and ensure network information security has attracted people's attention. In addition, modern warfare is a multidimensional war where multiple arms perform cooperative combats; in a way it is a kind of electronic warfare, information warfare, and network warfare and it has been transformed from traditional electronic warfare into information confrontation. Under these circumstances, an emerging interdisciplinary, information hiding, was officially born. Today, as a primary means of secret communication, intellectual property protection, content authentication, and other areas, information hiding is widely studied and applied.

To combat the crime of piracy and ensure network information security, on the one hand, we need to strengthen the protection of intellectual property and network information through legislation; on the other hand we must use advanced techniques to ensure the implementation of the law. Although cryptography can be used to solve some of these problems, there are three disadvantages. (1) It clearly tells the attackers where the important information is, it is easy to cause the attacker's curiosity and attention, and the encrypted information may be cracked by attackers. (2) Once the encrypted file is cracked, its content will be completely transparent. (3) In the case that an attacker failed to decipher the information, he might destroy the information, so that even a legitimate recipient cannot read the message content. In the early 1990s, information hiding technology, with its unique advantages of solving some deficiencies in cryptography, has begun to attract people's attention, and various applications of information hiding have attracted concern and attention from different research groups. The first International Symposium on Information Hiding held in the United Kingdom in May 1996 make these independent research groups come together to achieve consensus on some basic concepts and terminologies of information hiding. The main purpose of this section is to overview the information hiding technique, including basic concepts, models, research branches, properties, and applications of information hiding, together with the classification of information hiding schemes.

1.2.1 BASIC CONCEPTS RELATED TO INFORMATION HIDING

Since the emergence of human culture, human beings have the idea of protecting the information. The two words cryptography and *steganography* officially appeared in the mid-17th century, and both are derived from the Greek, where steganography means "covered writing." In fact, the concept of information hiding can be dated back to ancient Greece times. Information hiding is also known as *data hiding*. Broadly speaking, there are a variety of meanings for information hiding; the first means the message is not visible, the second means the existence of information is hidden, the third means the information recipient and sender are hidden, and the four means the transmission channels are hidden. Information hiding is the process of hiding the secret information in another open carrier so as to not draw the examiner's attention. Here, the carrier may be an image, a video sequence, an audio clip, a channel, or even a coding system or a cryptographic system. Thus, cryptography only hides the content of information, whereas information hiding technology hides not only the content of information but also the existence of information. In the broad sense, information hiding technology includes steganography, digital watermarking, *digital fingerprinting, covert channel, subliminal channel, low-probability intercept communication, and anonymous communication*. From the narrow point of view, information hiding is to hide a secret message in another public information and then to pass secret information through transmitting public information. Information hiding in the narrow sense usually refers to steganography and digital watermarking (including digital fingerprinting).

There are two reasons why information can be used to hide in the multimedia data. (1) There is a big redundancy in multimedia information. From the perspective of information theory, the coding efficiency of uncompressed multimedia information is very low, so the process of embedding the secret information into the multimedia information for confidential transmission is feasible and will not affect the transmission and use of multimedia information. (2) The human eye or ear itself has a masking effect; for example, the resolution of the human eye has only a few dozen gray levels, and human eyes are insensitive to the information near edges. By utilizing these human features, we can very well hide the information to make it unnoticed.

Typically, both hiding and encryption techniques should be based on keys to protect the information. However, information hiding is different from traditional cryptography. Cryptography is to study how to encode the special secret information to form a *ciphertext* that cannot be identified, whereas information hiding is to study how to hide the secret information into other carriers and then pass the secret information through transmitting these public carriers. For encryption-based communication, the possible monitors or illegal interceptors can intercept the ciphertexts and decipher them, or destroy them before sending them, thus affecting the security of confidential information. However, for information hiding, it is difficult for the possible monitors or illegal interceptors to determine the existence of secret information based on the public carriers, thus it is difficult to intercept the confidential information, which can ensure the security of confidential information. For increasing the difficulty of deciphering, we can also combine cryptography and information hiding, that is, the information to be embedded is encrypted to be ciphertexts and then the ciphertexts are hidden into the *cover object*. Thus, the traditional cryptography-based information security and hiding-based information security are not conflicting or competing but complementary.

Under the broad concept of information hiding, here are some terms given in the first International Conference on Information Hiding. The object to be secretly hidden in other media is known as the *embedded object*, which is the secret information (secret message) for a particular purpose. The carrier used to hide the embedded object is called the *cover object*. It should be noted that, here, the object can refer to a message, a text, an image, a video sequence, an audio clip, a cryptographic protocol, or a coding system. The output of embedding an embedded object into a cover object is called *stego object*, because it has no perceivable difference from the cover object. The process of adding the embedded object to the cover object is called *information embedding*, whereas the algorithm used in the embedding process is referred to as *embedding algorithm*. The inverse process of information embedding, i.e., the process of extracting the embedded object from the stego object, is called *information extracting*. Similarly, the algorithm used in the extraction process is referred to as *extracting algorithm*. The organization or individual who performs the embedding process and the extraction process are referred to as the *embeddor* and *extractor*, respectively.

In the information hiding system, people often need to use some additional secret information to control the embedding and extraction processes that only its holder can operate; we call the secret information *stego key*. The key used in the embedding process is referred to as the *embedding key*, whereas in the extraction process the key is called the *extracting key*. Usually the embedding key is the same as the extracting key, and the corresponding information hiding technique is called *symmetric information hiding*; if the keys are not the same, it is called *asymmetric information hiding*.

Similar to cryptography, the research on information hiding can be divided into steganography and *stegoanalysis*. The former focuses on how to add the embedded object to the cover object. The latter focuses on how to break out from the stego object the embedded information, or destroy the embedded information or prevent information detection through processing the stego object. Similarly, we can call the person who researches or implements the hiding technology as a *hider*, whereas the attacker or analyzer of the hiding system is called a *stegoanalyst*.

Note that in different branches of information hidden, the aforementioned terms may correspond to different terminologies.

1.2.2 PROPERTIES AND REQUIREMENTS OF INFORMATION HIDING

Information hiding is different from traditional cryptography, since its purpose is not to restrict normal access to the stego object, but rather to ensure that the secret information will not be violated and discovered. Therefore, the information hiding technology must consider the threat caused by the normal operation of the information, i.e., to make the embedded object (secret information) immune to normal data manipulation techniques. The key of this immunity is to make the part where we embed information not easy to be destroyed by normal data manipulations (such as normal operations of signal conversion or data compression). According to different purposes and technical requirements of information hiding, this technology has the following characteristics or requirements:

1. Transparency (imperceptibility)

   The *transparency* property requires that, based on the characteristics of the human visual system or the human auditory system, through a series of hidden processing, the stego object does not have obvious degradation phenomena compared with the cover object, and the embedded object cannot be seen or heard artificially. Of course, very few applications may need to use *visible watermarking* technologies.

2. Robustness

   Robustness refers to the ability of extracting the embedded object when the stego object is subject to some signal processing operations. Here, signal processing operations include the common information processing (such as data compression, low-pass filtering, image enhancement, subsampling, requantization, A/D and D/A conversion), geometric transformation and geometric distortion (e.g., cropping, scaling, translation, and rotation), adding noise, filtering operations, printing, scanning, and multiple watermarking. After these changes, robust information hiding algorithms should be able to extract the embedded secret information from the stego object.

3. Security

   Security refers to the ability of resisting malicious attacks, i.e., the stego object should be able to withstand intentional attacks to a certain degree, while ensuring that the embedded object is not destroyed. In addition, similar to encryption, the information hiding technique requires that protecting the secret information eventually relies on protecting keys. Thus, the basic requirements of cryptography on keys is also applicable to the information hiding techniques, that is, there must be a large enough key space. In designing an information hiding system, key generation, distribution, and management must also be synthetically considered.

4. Undetectability

   Undetectability requires that the stego object and the cover object have consistent characteristics, such as a consistent statistical noise distribution, so that the analyst cannot determine whether the embedded object is hidden in the stego object.

5. Self-recoverability

   After certain operations or transformations, the stego object may be greatly damaged. If we can recover the embedded object from only a fragment of the stego object, and the recovery process does not require the cover object, then the algorithm has high *self-recoverability*. Of course, not all applications require self-recoverability.

6. Hiding capacity

   The cover object should be able to hide as much information as possible. In fact, if the stego object would not be subject to any disturbance, people could hide more information in the cover object without being noticed. Of course, under the condition of guaranteeing the transparency, the more information we hide, the worse the robustness is.

In fact, the three most important factors of information hiding are transparency, robustness, and hiding capacity; it is difficult to simultaneously achieve them optimally, and we must focus on different factors according to different scenarios. The performance of the entire information hiding system is the result of balancing these three major factors. For example, the research focus of steganography is to hide secret information, thus transparency and hiding capacity must be guaranteed first. However, for digital watermarking technology, the main purpose is to protect the cover object; we need to consider the robustness requirement against all possible attacks.

1.2.3 INFORMATION HIDING MODELS

In the research course of information hiding techniques, different models have been proposed to explain the information hiding. These models can be roughly divided into the prisoner model, the general model, and the communication-based models. Among them, the prisoner model is a classic model of information hiding, the general model gives the algorithm flow of embedding-based information hiding schemes using the cover object, and communication-based models from the perspective of information theory study the model of information hiding and hiding capacity. These models are briefly introduced in the following sections.

1.2.3.1 Prisoner's Model

The *prisoner's model* is a classic model of information hiding as shown in Fig. 1.4. The model is based on the *prisoner's problem* proposed by Simmons in 1983. Alice and Bob were arrested and detained in different cells. Now they want to plan to escape; unfortunately, all communications between them should be carried out in the surveillance of the *warden* Wendy. Wendy does not allow them to carry out encryption-based communications, and if she notices any suspicious communications, she will put them both into single prisons and prohibit any individual information exchange. Therefore, both sides must communicate in a secretive way, to avoid Wendy's suspicion. To this end, they have to create a subliminal channel. A practical approach is to hide useful information in some seemingly ordinary information. In this scenario, Alice and Bob, respectively, correspond to the embeddor and extractor in the information hiding system, whereas the warden Wendy is the stegoanalyst, i.e., attacker. The embeddor Alice uses an information hiding system to transmit the secret information to the extractor such that the warden Wendy cannot find the embedded object in the stego object, because Wendy may modify the stego object, and forward the modified stego object to Bob. Therefore, to let the secret information still pass to Bob, the system should be robust to small modifications.

1.2.3.2 General Model

The prisoner's model summarizes the main idea of most information hiding techniques from the ancient times to nowadays, where the covert communication process between Alice and Bob can be described using a more general model. The *general*

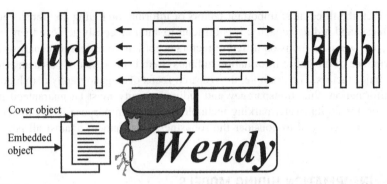

FIGURE 1.4

The Prisoner Model Proposed by Simmons.

model is used to describe the system structure of the embedding flow of information hiding. In fact, according to the terminology introduced in Section 1.2.1, we can get a general model as shown in Fig. 1.5.

1.2.3.3 Communication-Based Models

In essence, information hiding is a kind of communication that passes secret messages between the embeddor and extractor. In the background of digital watermarking technology, Cox proposed three communication-based models for information hiding [1]. The difference between these three models lies in how the cover object is introduced into the traditional communication model. In the first basic model, as shown in Figs. 1.6 and 1.7, the cover object is solely viewed as noise. In the second model, the cover object is still regarded as a noise, but the noise as *the side information* is input to the channel encoder. In the third model, the cover object is not regarded as noise, but as the second information, and this information together with the secret message is transmitted in a multiplexed form. These three communication models have the following obvious flaws. (1) They do not take the features of information hiding into account, namely, the information hiding system makes

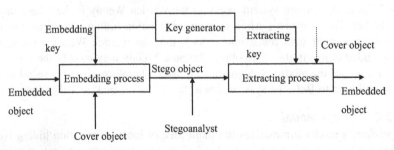

FIGURE 1.5

The General Model of Information Hiding Systems.

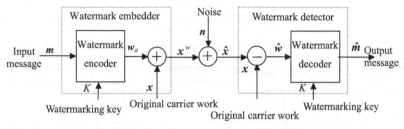

FIGURE 1.6

Nonblind Watermarking System Described by a Communication-Based Model.

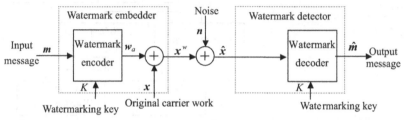

FIGURE 1.7

Blind Watermarking System Described by a Communication-Based Model.

use of the human perceptual model to embed secret messages in the most inconspicuous places of the cover object, and at the same time, the cover object cannot be completely viewed as noise. (2) The robustness is not considered, where robustness means the ability of making the so-called secret message embedded with redundancy, and resistant to signal processing, lossy compression, and geometric attacks.

1.2.4 RESEARCH BRANCHES OF INFORMATION HIDING

Information hiding is an emerging interdisciplinary, and it has broad application prospects in the fields of computers, communications, cryptology, and so on. Information hiding studies involve many fields including cryptography, image processing, pattern recognition, mathematics, and computer science. According to different purposes and different kinds of cover objects, information hiding can be divided into many branches, as shown in Fig. 1.8. The following subsections briefly introduce several major branches of information hiding.

1.2.4.1 Steganography

The research work on information security includes not only the study of cryptography but also the study of channel security, whose essence lies in hiding the existence of information. The application of information hiding in this area is an important branch called steganography. The word "steganography" is derived from the Greek word "στεγανω," which literally means "covert writing," i.e., hiding

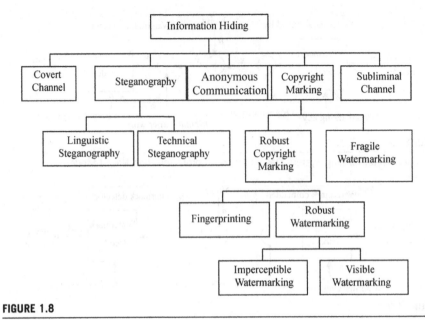

FIGURE 1.8

Main Research Branches of Information Hiding.

secret messages in other messages. The main purpose of steganography is to hide important information and transmit and store it unobtrusively. Therefore, in the steganographic system, the embedded object is the secret message, which is the main body to be protected, whereas the cover object may be any cover data that can be used to achieve the purpose of concealment. Under normal circumstances, we need to consider two factors, *stego capacity* and the imperceptibility of the steganography results when selecting a cover object. Steganography can be broadly divided into two types, one is to record the secret message to be transmitted and then send it out through other media, namely, *technical steganography*; another is to hide the behavior of recording itself, where the message consists of the language or language forms used in covert writing, namely, *linguistic steganography*. For example, induction ink, diminished image, and spread spectrum communication technologies are technical steganography, whereas linguistic steganography includes *semagram, open code, null cipher,* and so on.

1.2.4.2 Copyright Marking

Adding an inconspicuous but distinguishable mark to the digital work is an effective scheme of copyright protection, which is called copyright marking technique. The mark can be a trademark, serial number, or a label preventing unauthorized users to directly copy. According to the content and purpose of labeling, copyright marking techniques can be divided into digital watermarking technology and digital fingerprinting technology. In the digital watermarking system, the *digital watermark* is used to represent the identity of the author. This information must be registered and accredited by management agencies, and a number of digital works can be embedded with the same watermark. On the contrary, in the digital fingerprinting system, *digital fingerprint* is used to represent the identity of the purchaser; it is required to embed different fingerprints in the same work to distinguish different buyers. Note that this book views copyright marking as digital watermarking in a broad sense. In the digital watermarking and digital fingerprint system, the analyst is often called pirate and traitor, respectively.

1.2.4.3 Covert Channel

The so-called covert channel refers to a channel that allows information delivery in the state of violation of safety rules, or allows interprocess communication in the operating system in the state of violation of legitimate security policies. There are two kinds of covert channels, i.e., *covert storage channels* and *covert timing channels*. Covert storage channel includes directly or indirectly writing a memory address by one process, while reading by another process. In a covert timing channel, a process sends a message to another process by adjusting its usage of the system resources (such as CPU time). This treatment also affects the observed actual response time of the second process. The concepts in covert channels are similar to many concepts in steganography, but in covert channel, the cover object is the entire process of a system, rather than specific information media.

1.2.4.4 Subliminal Channel

In 1978, Simmons discovered the fatal flaw existing in the supervision agreement of the SALT II treaty signed between the Soviet Union and the United States, and thus proposed the concept of subliminal channel. Subliminal channel refers to the overt channel created in an implementation of covert communication. The subliminal channel in cryptographic protocols refers to the mathematical structure that is adopted to transmit secret messages in a variety of coding systems and cryptographic protocols. Some research work shows that a vast majority of digital signature schemes contain subliminal communication channels, whose greatest feature is that the subliminal message has no impact on the digital signature and verification processes. Even if the monitor knows what to look for, he cannot find the usage of the channel and get subliminal messages being sent, because the characteristics of subliminal channels determine their security and confidentiality, which are either unconditional or computationally unbreakable.

1.2.4.5 Anonymous Communication

Anonymous communication is the process of looking for ways to hide the sender and receiver of information, whose main techniques include anonymous retransmission and network proxy technologies. This technique can be used in wired telephone networks and satellite telephone networks, and it applies not only to the military but also for business and has been widely used in e-mail, Web browsing, and remote registration. Web applications emphasize the anonymity of the recipient, and e-mail users are concerned about the anonymity of the sender. In addition, the anonymous communication technology can also be used in electronic voting and electronic cash scheme to ensure that the identity of the voter or purchase is not leaked.

1.2.5 CLASSIFICATION OF INFORMATION HIDING TECHNOLOGIES

In addition to the classification way of information hiding based on research branches (or the object to be protected) in Section 1.2.4, information hiding techniques can also be classified according to various other ways, such as the types of cover objects, the symmetry of the keys, and the embedding domains. The following subsections briefly describe the various classification schemes.

1.2.5.1 Classification According to the Types of Cover Objects

According to different types of cover objects, information hiding techniques can be divided into information hiding techniques for text, images, audio, video, 3D models and animations, and so on. Information hiding techniques in text realize the information embedding process by changing the text mode or some of the basic characteristics of the text, which introduces some changes in the document, but the human visual is insensitive to this change. Image-based information hiding techniques view digital images as cover objects and embed the secret information in digital images based on a certain algorithm. Audio-based information hiding techniques embed secret information in the cover audio imperceptibly to achieve copyright protection, covert communication, and other functions. In the information hiding system for video, based on the visual characteristics of the human eyes' limitations on the resolution and sensitivity, the secret information is embedded in the perception redundant of the carrier signal.

1.2.5.2 Classification According to the Symmetry of Keys

According to the keys used in the embedding and extraction processes, information hiding techniques can be divided into *keyless information hiding, symmetric information hiding (private key information hiding), and asymmetric information hiding (public key information hiding)*.

If an information hiding system does not require prearranged keys, we call it keyless information hiding system. Mathematically, the information hiding process can be described as a mapping $Em: C \times M \rightarrow S$, where C is the set of all possible cover objects, M is the set of all possible secret messages, and S is the set of all stego objects. The information extraction process can also be viewed as a mapping $Ex: S \rightarrow M$, which extracts the confidential information from the stego object.

To improve the security of keyless information hiding technology, the secret information can be encrypted before hiding, thus the information is protected by two layers, one is based on cryptograph, and the other is based on information hiding, so that it is more secure than single layer—based schemes. If the embedding and extracting keys are the same, then the system is called symmetric information hiding (private key information hiding), otherwise known as asymmetric information hiding (public key information hiding).

1.2.5.3 Classification According to the Embedding Domains

According to the embedded domains, information hiding methods can be divided into the original domain–based, transform domain–based, and compressed domain–based methods. Original domain–based methods refer to a class of information hiding method that directly modifies the original data of the cover object according to certain rules, e.g., replacing the redundant portion of the cover object with the secret information. Original domain–based schemes can be further divided into spatial, temporal, and spatiotemporal domain–based schemes.

Transform domain–based information hiding algorithms first perform a transformation, such as *fast Fourier transform* (FFT), *discrete cosine transform* (DCT), and *discrete wavelet transform* (DWT), on the original cover signal to obtain the transform coefficients and then embed the secret information by modifying the transform coefficients. With the research progress of multimedia compression technologies, many cover objects are usually stored in a compressed format, so the method of embedding the secret information directly in the compressed domain has become the focus of scholars' attention. The compressed domain–based information hiding technique combines the information hiding process and the compression process, which can effectively prevent attacks that come from perceptual coding. For example, during the JPEG image compression process, we can embed the secret information by modifying the transform coefficients and the quantization factor, thus it can be effectively robust to JPEG decompression and recompression attacks.

1.2.5.4 Classification Based on Other Ways

In addition to above three ways of classification, there are several other classification ways as follows.

According to the situation whether the original cover object is required during the extraction of secret information, information hiding techniques can be divided into nonblind hiding (private hiding) and blind hiding (public hiding) schemes. If the original cover object is not required during the extraction of secret information, it is a blind hiding scheme. On the contrary, if the original cover object is required during the extraction of secret information, then it is a nonblind scheme. Clearly, the use of original cover object can facilitate the detection and extraction of the secret information. However, in the fields of data monitoring and tracking, we cannot get the original cover object. So blind schemes are the focus of research scholars.

According to the reversibility, information hiding techniques can be divided into reversible and irreversible information hiding schemes. For reversible information hiding schemes, if the stego object is not subject to modifications, we can not only decode the secret information from the stego object but also recover the original cover object. For irreversible information hiding schemes, we can only decode the secret information from the stego object, but cannot recover the original cover object.

According to the robustness, information hiding techniques can be divided into robust information hiding schemes, fragile information hiding schemes, and semifragile information hiding schemes. For robust information hiding systems, under the condition that the attacked stego object is visually similar to the cover object, the secret information can be still extracted from the stego object that is attacked by a variety of inadvertent and malicious attacks. For fragile information hiding systems, by contrast, under a variety of unintentional and malicious attacks, the hidden secret information will be lost. For semifragile information hiding systems, they are robust to certain attacks but fragile to other attacks.

1.2.6 APPLICATIONS OF INFORMATION HIDING TECHNIQUES

The application fields of information hiding techniques are very wide. There are mainly the following nine categories: covert communication, broadcast monitoring, owner identification, ownership verification, transaction tracking, content authentication, annotation, copy control, and device control. Each application is concretely introduced in the following sections.

1.2.6.1 Covert Communication

In the modern society with network globalization and economic globalization, every day a large amount of data are sent over the network, some of which involve the important information related to political, military, commercial, financial, and personal privacy. Once the information is illegally intercepted, it will lead to incalculable consequences. Since information hiding techniques have the role of keeping the confidentiality of information, they can protect the information. Covert communication is mainly used for secure communication of confidential information; it protects the information that is embedded in the cover object, where usually we adopt the multimedia information as the cover object. Due to the huge amount of multimedia information online, the secret information is hard to be detected by an eavesdropper.

1.2.6.2 Broadcast Monitoring

The advertiser hopes that his advertisements can be aired completely in the airtime that is bought from the broadcaster, whereas the broadcaster hopes that he can obtain advertisement dollars from the advertiser. To realize broadcast monitoring, we can hire some people to directly survey and monitor the aired content. However, this method costs a lot, and it is also easy to make mistakes. We can also use the dynamic monitoring system to put recognition information outside the area of broadcast signal, e.g., vertical blanking interval; however, there are some compatibility problems to be solved. The watermarking technique can encode recognition information, and it is a good method to replace dynamic monitoring technique. It uses the characteristic of embedding itself in content and requires no special fragments of the broadcast signal. Thus it is completely compatible with the installed analog or digital broadcast device.

1.2.6.3 Owner Identification

There are some limitations in using the text copyright announcement for product owner recognition. First, during the copying process, this announcement is very easy to be removed, sometimes accidentally. For example, when a professor copies several pages of a book, the copyright announcement in topic pages is probably neglected to be copied. Another problem is that it may occupy some parts of the image space, destroying the original image, and it is easy to be cropped. As watermark is not only invisible but also cannot be separated from the watermarked product, it is more beneficial than text announcement in owner identification. If the product user has a watermark detector, he can recognize the watermarked product's owner. Even if the watermarked product is altered by the method that can remove the text copyright announcement, the watermark can still be detected.

1.2.6.4 Ownership Verification

Besides identification of the copyright owner, applying watermarking techniques for copyright verification is also a particular concern. Conventional text announcement is extremely easy to be tampered with and counterfeited, and thus it cannot be used to solve this problem. A solution for this problem is to construct a central information database for digital product registration. However, people may not register their products because of the high cost. To save the registration fee, people may use watermarks to protect copyright. And to achieve a certain level of security, the granting of detectors may need to be restricted. If the attacker has no detector, it is quite difficult to remove watermarks. However, even if the watermark cannot be removed, the attacker also may use his own watermarking system. Thus people may feel there is also attacker's watermark in the same digital product. Therefore, it is not necessary to directly verify the copyright with the embedded watermark. On the contrary, the fact that an image is obtained from another image must be proved. This kind of system can indirectly prove that this disputed image may be owned by the owner instead of the attacker because the copyright owner has the original image. This verification manner is similar to the case that the copyright owner can take out the negative, whereas the attacker can only counterfeit the negative of the disputed image. It is impossible for the attacker to counterfeit the negative of the original image to pass the examination.

1.2.6.5 Transaction Tracking

The watermark can be used to record one or several trades for a certain product copy. For example, the watermark can record each receiver who has been legally sold and distributed with a product copy. The product owner or producer can embed different watermarks in different copies. If the product is misused (e.g., disclosed to the press or illegally promulgated), the owner can find the people who are responsible for it.

1.2.6.6 Content Authentication

Nowadays, it becomes much easier to tamper with digital products in an inconspicuous manner. Research on the message authentication problem is relatively mature in cryptography. *Digital signature* is the most popular encryption scheme. It is essentially an encrypted message digest. If we compare the signature of a suspicious message with the original signature and find that they do not match, then we can conclude that the message must have been changed. All these signatures are source data and must be transmitted together with the product to be verified. Once the signature is lost, this product cannot be authenticated. It may be a good solution to embed the signature in products with watermarking techniques. This kind of embedded signature is called authentication mark. If a very small change can make the authentication mark invalid, we call this kind of mark "fragile watermark."

1.2.6.7 Annotation

Annotation refers to the additional data that are embedded in the digital works; such information may be details about the work, notes, and so on. This hiding-based annotation requires no additional bandwidth, and the annotation data are not easily lost. This technique is often used in the maintenance of medical images; when the patient's medical staff finish shooting X-ray films or photographic films, we can embed the patient's name, doctor's name, and medical history in the image data, to avoid the case that we cannot find the right medical records when the connection between the patient and doctor is lost.

1.2.6.8 Copy Control

Most of the aforementioned watermarking techniques take effect only after the illegal behavior has happened. For example, in the broadcast monitoring system, only when the broadcaster does not broadcast the paid advertisement can we regard the broadcaster dishonest, whereas in the transaction tracking system, only when the opponent has distributed the illegal copy can we identify the opponent. It is obvious that we had better design the system to prevent the behavior of illegal copying. In copy control, people aim to prevent the protected content from being illegally copied. The primary defense of illegal copying is encryption. After encrypting the product with a special key, the product completely cannot be used by those without this key. Then this key can be provided to legal users in a secure manner such that the key is difficult to be copied or redistributed. However, people usually hope that the media data can be viewed, but cannot be copied by others. At this time, people can embed watermarks in content and play it with the content. If each recording device is installed with a watermark detector, the device can forbid copying when it detects the watermark "copy forbidden."

1.2.6.9 Device Control

In fact, copy control belongs to a larger application category called device control. Device control means that the device can react when the watermark is detected. For example, the "media bridge" system of Digimarc can embed watermark in printed images such as magazines, advertisements, parcels, and bills. If this image is captured by a digital camera again, the "media bridge" software and recognition unit in the computer will open a link to related websites.

1.3 OVERVIEW OF IMAGE CODING AND COMPRESSION TECHNIQUES

1.3.1 SOURCE CODING AND DATA COMPRESSION

In computer science and information theory, *data compression* or *source coding* is the process of encoding information with fewer bits than an unencoded representation would use based on specific encoding schemes. As with any communication, compressed data communication only works when both the sender and receiver of the information understand the encoding scheme. Similarly, compressed data can only be understood if the decoding method is known by the receiver. Compression is useful because it helps reduce the consumption of expensive resources, such as the hard disk space or the transmission bandwidth. On the downside, compressed data must be decompressed to be used, and this extra processing may be detrimental to some applications. The design of data compression schemes therefore involves trade-offs among various factors, including the degree of compression, the amount of distortion introduced, and the computational resources required.

Lossless compression algorithms usually exploit statistical redundancy in such a way as to represent the sender's data more concisely without error. Lossless compression is possible because most real-world data possess statistical redundancy. For example, in English text, the letter "e" is much more common than the letter "z," and the probability that the letter "q" will be followed by the letter "z" is very small. Another kind of compression, called *lossy data compression*, is possible if some loss of fidelity is acceptable. Generally, a lossy data compression will be guided by research on how people perceive the data in question. For example, the human eye is more sensitive to subtle variations in luminance than it is to variations in color. JPEG image compression works in part by "rounding off" some of this less-important information. Lossy data compression provides a way to obtain the best fidelity for a given amount of compression.

1.3.2 LOSSLESS IMAGE CODING TECHNIQUES

Image compression is the application of data compression on digital images. The objective is to reduce redundancy of the image data to be able to store or transmit data in an efficient form. Image compression can be lossy or lossless. Lossless compression is sometimes preferred for artificial images such as technical drawings, icons, or comics. This is because lossy compression methods, especially when used at low bit rates, introduce compression artifacts. Lossless compression methods may also be preferred for high value content, such as medical imagery or image scans made for archival purposes. Lossy methods are especially suitable for natural images such as photographs in applications where minor loss of fidelity is acceptable to achieve a substantial reduction in bit rate. The lossy compression that produces imperceptible differences can be called visually lossless. Typical methods for lossless image compression are as follows.

1.3.2.1 Run-Length Encoding

Run-length encoding (RLE) is used as a default method in PCX and as one of possible method in BMP, TGA, and TIFF. RLE is a very simple form of data compression in which runs of data are stored as a single data value and its count, rather than as the original run. This is most useful for data that contain many such runs, for example, relatively simple graphic images such as icons, line drawings, and animations. It is not recommended for use with files that do not have many runs as it could potentially double the file size.

1.3.2.2 Differential Pulse-Code Modulation and Predictive Coding

Differential pulse-code modulation (DPCM) was invented by C. Chapin Cutler at Bell Labs in 1950, and his patent includes both methods. DPCM is a signal encoder that uses the baseline of PCM but adds some functionality based on the prediction of the samples of the signal. The input can be an analog signal or a digital signal. If the input is a continuous-time analog signal, it needs to be sampled first so that a discrete-time signal is the input to the DPCM encoder. There are two options. The first one is to take the values of two consecutive samples; the difference between the first one and the next is calculated and the difference is further entropy coded. The other one is, instead of taking a difference relative to a previous input sample, the difference relative to the output of a local model of the decoder process is taken, and in this option, the difference can be quantized, which allows a good way to incorporate controlled loss in the encoding.

1.3.2.3 Entropy Encoding

In information theory, *entropy encoding* is a lossless data compression scheme that is independent of the specific characteristics of the medium. One of the main types of entropy coding creates and assigns a unique prefix code to each unique symbol that occurs in the input. These entropy encoders then compress data by replacing each fixed-length input symbol by the corresponding variable-length prefix codeword. The length of each codeword is approximately proportional to the negative logarithm of the probability. Therefore, the most common symbols use the shortest codes. According to Shannon's source coding theorem, the optimal code length for a symbol is $\log_b P$, where b is the number of symbols used to make output codes and P is the probability of the input symbol. Two most commonly used entropy encoding techniques are Huffman coding and arithmetic coding. If the approximate entropy characteristics of a data stream are known in advance, a simpler static code may be useful.

1.3.2.4 Adaptive Dictionary Algorithms

Adaptive dictionary algorithms are used in GIF and TIFF, and the typical one is the LZW algorithm. It is a universal lossless data compression algorithm created by Lempel, Ziv, and Welch. It was published by Welch in 1984 as an improved implementation of the LZ78 algorithm published by Lempel and Ziv in 1978. The algorithm is designed to be fast to implement but is not usually optimal because it performs only limited analysis of the data.

1.3.2.5 Deflation

Deflation is used in portable network graphics (PNG), MNG, and TIFF. It is a lossless data compression algorithm that uses a combination of the LZ77 algorithm and Huffman coding. It was originally defined by Phil Katz for version 2 of his PKZIP archiving tool, and was later specified in RFC 1951. Deflation is widely thought to be free of any subsisting patents, and at a time before the patent on LZW (which is used in the GIF file format) expired, this has led to its use in gzip compressed files and PNG image files, in addition to the ZIP format for which Katz originally designed it.

1.3.3 LOSSY IMAGE CODING TECHNIQUES

Typical methods for lossy image compression are as follows.

1.3.3.1 Color Space Reduction

The main idea of *color space reduction* is to reduce the color space to the most common colors in the image. The selected colors are specified in the color palette in the header of the compressed image. Each pixel just references the index of a color in the color palette. This method can be combined with dithering to avoid posterization.

1.3.3.2 Chroma Subsampling

Chroma subsampling takes advantage of the fact that the eye perceives spatial changes in brightness more sharply than those in color, by averaging or dropping some of the chrominance information in the image. It is used in many video encoding schemes, both analog and digital, and also in JPEG encoding. Because the human visual system is less sensitive to the position and motion of color than luminance, bandwidth can be optimized by storing more luminance detail than color detail. At normal viewing distances, there is no perceptible loss incurred by sampling the color detail at a lower rate.

1.3.3.3 Transform Coding

Transform coding is the most commonly used method. Transform coding is a type of data compression for "natural" data like audio signals or photographic images. The transformation is typically lossy, resulting in a lower quality copy of the original input. A Fourier-related transform such as DCT or the wavelet transform is applied, followed by quantization and entropy coding. In transform coding, knowledge of the application is used to choose information to be discarded, thereby lowering its bandwidth. The remaining information can then be compressed via a variety of methods. When the output is decoded, the result may not be identical to the original input, but is expected to be close enough for the purpose of the application. The JPEG format is an example of transform coding, one that examines small blocks of the image and "averages out" the color using a DCT to form an image with far fewer colors in total.

1.3.3.4 Fractal Compression

Fractal compression is a lossy image compression method using fractals to achieve high compression ratios. The method is best suited for photographs of natural scenes such as trees, mountains, ferns, and clouds. The fractal compression technique relies on the fact that in certain images parts of the image resemble other parts of the same image. Fractal algorithms convert these parts, or more precisely, geometric shapes into mathematical data called "fractal codes," which are used to re-create the encoded image. Fractal compression differs from pixel-based compression schemes such as JPEG, GIF, and MPEG since no pixels are saved. Once an image has been converted into fractal code, its relationship to a specific resolution has been lost and it becomes resolution independent. The image can be re-created to fill any screen size without the introduction of image artifacts or loss of sharpness that occurs in pixel-based compression schemes. With fractal compression, encoding is extremely computationally expensive because of the search used to find the self-similarities. However, decoding is quite fast. At common compression ratios, up to about 50:1, - fractal compression provides similar results to DCT-based algorithms such as JPEG. At high compression ratios, fractal compression may offer superior quality.

The following four subsections focus on two famous block-based lossy image compression schemes and two famous image coding standards.

1.3.4 VECTOR QUANTIZATION

Vector quantization (VQ) is an attractive block-based encoding method for image compression [2]. It can achieve a high compression ratio. In environments such as image archival and one-to-many communications, the simplicity of the decoder makes VQ very efficient. In brief, VQ can be defined as mapping from k-dimensional Euclidean space R^k into a finite subset $C = \{c_i| \ i = 0, 1, \ldots, M-1\}$, which is generally called a codebook, where c_i is a codeword and M is the codebook size, as shown in Fig. 1.9. VQ first generates a representative codebook from a number of training vectors using, for example, the well-known iterative clustering algorithm that is often referred to as the generalized Lloyd algorithm. In VQ, as shown in Fig. 1.10, the image to be encoded is first decomposed into vectors and then sequentially encoded vector by vector. In the encoding phase, each k-dimensional input vector $x = (x_1, x_2, \ldots, x_k)$ is compared with the codewords in the codebook $C = \{c_0, c_1, \ldots, c_{M-1}\}$ to find the best matching codeword $c_i = (c_{i1}, c_{i2}, \ldots, c_{ik})$ satisfying the following condition:

$$d(x, c_i) = \min_{0 \le j \le N-1} d(x, c_j) \qquad (1.3)$$

That is, the distance between x and c_i is the smallest, where $d(x, c_j)$ is the distortion of representing the input vector x by the codeword c_j, which is often measured by the squared Euclidean distance, i.e.,

$$d(x, c_j) = \sum_{l=1}^{k} (x_l - c_{jl})^2 \qquad (1.4)$$

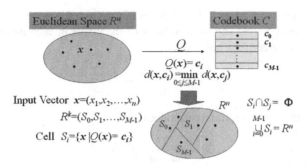

FIGURE 1.9

The Principle of VQ.

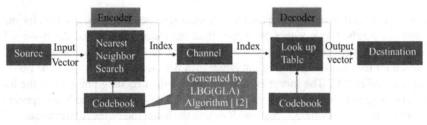

FIGURE 1.10

The Encoding and Decoding Processes of VQ.

And then the index i of the best matching codeword assigned to the input vector x is transmitted over the channel to the decoder. The decoder has the same codebook as the encoder. In the decoding phase, for each index i, the decoder merely performs a simple table lookup operation to obtain c_i and then uses c_i to reconstruct the input vector x. Compression is achieved by transmitting or storing the index of a codeword rather than the codeword itself. The compression ratio is determined by the code-book size and the dimension of the input vectors, and the overall distortion depends on the codebook size and the selection of codewords.

1.3.5 BLOCK TRUNCATION CODING

Block truncation coding (BTC) [3] is a simple and efficient lossy image compression technique, which has the advantage of being easy to implement when compared with other block-based compression techniques such as transform coding and VQ. Its simplicity, performance, and channel error resisting capability make it attractive in the real-time image transmission. Essentially, BTC is a 1-bit adaptive moment-preserving quantizer that preserves certain statistical moments of small blocks of the input image in the quantized output. The principle of the original BTC method is to preserve the block mean and the block standard deviation (STD). Lema and Mitchell present absolute moment BTC (AMBTC) [4] that preserves the higher and the lower means of a block. In the AMBTC method, the image is divided into blocks of size $m = 4 \times 4$. The mean value $\bar{x}$ of the pixels in each block x is taken as the one-bit quantizer threshold, i.e.,

$$\bar{x} = \frac{1}{m} \sum_{i=1}^{m} x_i \tag{1.5}$$

The two output quantization level values are

$$\bar{x}_L = \frac{1}{m-q} \sum_{x_i <= \bar{x}} x_i \tag{1.6}$$

$$\bar{x}_H = \frac{1}{q} \sum_{x_i > \bar{x}} x_i \tag{1.7}$$

where $\bar{x}_L$ and $\bar{x}_H$ denote the lower and higher means, respectively and q stands for the number of pixels whose values are larger than the mean value. Then the two-level quantization is performed for the pixels in the block to form a bit plane so that "0" is stored for the pixels with values not larger than the mean, and the rest of the pixels are presented by "1." The image is reconstructed at the decoding phase from the bit plane by assigning the value $\bar{x}_L$ to "0" and $\bar{x}_H$ to "1." Thus a compressed block appears as a triple $(\bar{x}_L, \bar{x}_H, B)$, where $\bar{x}_L, \bar{x}_H$, and B denote the lower mean, the higher mean, and the bit plane, respectively. Fig. 1.11 shows an example of a compressed image block.

AMBTC is very fast, requires no extra memory, is easy to implement, and has low computational demands. It preserves the quality of the reconstructed image and retains the edges. However, in the AMBTC, the lower and higher means are coded separately with 8 bits each, and the bit plane needs 16 bits, so the bit rate of AMBTC is $\frac{8+8+16}{16} = 2$ bits/pixel.

1.3.6 JPEG

The JPEG standard is a collaboration among the International Telecommunication Union (ITU), International Organization for Standardization (ISO), and International Electrotechnical Commission (IEC). Its official names are "ISO/IEC 10918-1 Digital compression and coding of continuous-tone still image," and "ITU-T Recommendation T.81." JPEG has the following modes of operations. (1) *Lossless mode*: The image is encoded to guarantee exact recovery of every pixel of original image, even though the compression ratio is lower than those of the lossy modes. (2) *Sequential mode:* It compresses the image in a single left-to-right, top-to-bottom scan. (3) *Progressive mode:* It compresses the image in multiple scans. When transmission time is long, the image will display from indistinct to clear appearance. (4) *Hierarchical mode*: The image is compressed at multiple resolutions so that the lower resolution of the image can be accessed first without decompressing the whole resolution of the image.

The last three DCT-based modes are lossy compressions because precision limitation to compute DCT and the quantization process introduce distortion in the

Original				Bit-plane				Reconstructed			
2	9	12	15	0	1	1	1	3	12	12	12
2	11	11	9	0	1	1	1	3	12	12	12
2	3	12	15	0	0	1	1	3	3	12	12
3	3	4	14	0	0	0	1	3	3	3	12

$$\bar{x} = 7.94 \qquad q = 9 \qquad \bar{x}_L = 3 \quad \bar{x}_H = 12$$

FIGURE 1.11

AMBTC by the Triple $(\bar{x}_L, \bar{x}_H, B)$.

reconstructed image. The lossless mode uses predictive method and does not have quantization process. The hierarchical mode can use DCT-based coding or predictive coding optionally. The most widely used mode in practice is called the baseline JPEG system, which is based on sequential mode, DCT-based coding, and Huffman coding for entropy encoding. Fig. 1.12 is the block diagram of baseline system.

The baseline encoding process can be briefly described as follows:

Step 1: The representation of the colors in the image is converted from RGB to YC_bC_r, consisting of one luma component (Y), representing brightness, and two chroma components, (Cb and Cr), representing color. The advantage of converting the image into luminance-chrominance color space is that the luminance and chrominance components are very much decorrelated between each other. This step is sometimes skipped. The transformation from RGB to YC_bC_r is based on the following mathematical expression:

$$\begin{bmatrix} Y \\ C_b \\ C_r \end{bmatrix} = \begin{bmatrix} 0.299000 & 0.587000 & 0.114000 \\ -0.168736 & -0.331264 & 0.500002 \\ 0.500000 & -0.418688 & -0.081312 \end{bmatrix} \begin{bmatrix} R \\ G \\ B \end{bmatrix} + \begin{bmatrix} 0 \\ 128 \\ 128 \end{bmatrix} \qquad (1.8)$$

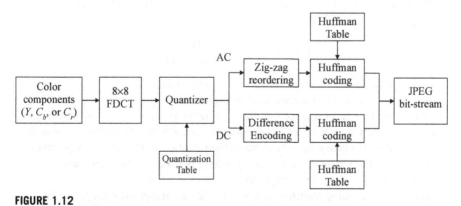

FIGURE 1.12

Baseline JPEG Encoder.

Step 2: The resolution of the chroma data is reduced, usually by a factor of 2 or 3. This reflects the fact that the eye is less sensitive to fine color details than to fine brightness details.

Step 3: The image is split into blocks of 8×8 pixels, and for each block, each of the Y, CB, and CR data undergo DCT. A DCT is similar to a Fourier transform in the sense that it produces a kind of spatial frequency spectrum. The forward DCT block $F(u,v)$ of the input block $f(x,y)$ is defined as

$$F(u, v) = \frac{1}{4} C(u)C(v) \sum_{x=0}^{7} \sum_{y=0}^{7} f(x, y) \cos \left[\frac{\pi(2x + 1)u}{16} \right] \cos \left[\frac{\pi(2y + 1)v}{16} \right]$$

for $u = 0, ..., 7$ and $v = 0, ..., 7$ (1.9)

$$\text{where } C(k) = \begin{cases} 1/\sqrt{2} \text{ for } k = 0 \\ 1 \quad \text{otherwise} \end{cases}$$

and the inverse DCT of $F(u,v)$ is defined as

$$f(x, y) = \frac{1}{4} \sum_{u=0}^{7} \sum_{v=0}^{7} C(u)C(v)F(u, v) \cos \left[\frac{\pi(2x + 1)u}{16} \right] \cos \left[\frac{\pi(2y + 1)v}{16} \right]$$

for $x = 0, ..., 7$ and $y = 0, ..., 7$ (1.10)

Step 4: The amplitudes of the frequency components are quantized. Here, each of the 64 DCT coefficients are uniformly quantized. The 64 quantization step-size parameters for uniform quantization of the 64 DCT coefficients form an 8×8 quantization matrix. The JPEG standard does not define any fixed quantization matrix. It is the prerogative of the user to select a quantization matrix. Each element in the quantization matrix is an integer between 1 and 255. Each DCT coefficient $F(u,v)$ is divided by the corresponding quantizer step-size parameter $Q(u,v)$ in the quantization matrix and rounded to the nearest integer as

$$F_q(u, v) = Round \left(\frac{F(u, v)}{Q(u, v)} \right)$$ (1.11)

Human vision is much more sensitive to small variations in color or brightness over large areas than to the strength of high-frequency brightness variations. Therefore, the magnitudes of the high-frequency components are stored with lower accuracy than those of low-frequency components. The quality setting of the encoder affects to what extent the resolution of each frequency component is reduced. If an excessively low-quality setting is used, the high-frequency components are discarded altogether.

Step 5: The resulting data for all 8×8 blocks are traversed zigzag, like in Fig. 1.13 (the reason for this zigzag traversing is that we traverse the 8×8 DCT

0	1	5	6	14	15	27	28
2	4	7	13	16	26	29	42
3	8	12	17	25	30	41	43
9	11	18	24	31	40	44	53
10	19	23	32	39	45	52	54
20	22	33	38	46	51	55	60
21	34	37	47	50	56	59	61
35	36	48	49	57	58	62	63

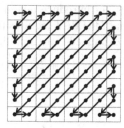

FIGURE 1.13

Zigzag Reordering Matrix.

coefficients in the order of increasing the spatial frequencies) and further compressed with a lossless algorithm, a variant of Huffman encoding.

The decoding process reverses these steps, except the quantization because it is irreversible.

1.3.7 JPEG2000

JPEG 2000 is an image compression standard and coding system. It was created by the Joint Photographic Experts Group committee in 2000 with the intention of superseding their original DCT-based JPEG standard created in 1992 with a newly designed, wavelet-based method. The standardized filename extension is .jp2 for ISO/IEC 15444-1—conforming files and .jpx for the extended part-2 specifications, published as ISO/IEC 15444-2. The aim of JPEG 2000 is not only improving compression performance over JPEG but also adding or improving features such as scalability and editability. The improvement of JPEG 2000 in compression performance relative to the original JPEG standard is actually rather modest and should not ordinarily be the primary consideration for evaluating the design. Very low and very high compression rates are supported in JPEG 2000. The ability of the design to handle a very large range of effective bit rates is one of the strengths of JPEG 2000, e.g., to reduce the number of bits for a picture below a certain amount; the advisable thing to do with the first JPEG standard is to reduce the resolution of the input image before encoding. This is unnecessary when using JPEG2000, because it already does this automatically by its multiresolution decomposition structure. The following subsections describe the algorithm of JPEG 2000.

1.3.7.1 Color Component Transformation

Similar to JPEG, initially the images have to be transformed from the RGB color space to another color space, leading to three components that are handled separately. For JPEG2000, there are two possible choices. (1) *Irreversible color transform* uses the well-known YCbCr color space as given in JPEG. It is called "irreversible" because it has to be implemented in floating or fix-point and causes round-off errors. (2) *Reversible color transform* (RCT) uses a modified YUV color space that does not introduce quantization errors, so it is fully reversible. Proper implementation of the RCT requires that numbers are rounded by a special method that cannot be expressed exactly in the matrix form. The transformation is:

$$Y = \left\lfloor \frac{R + 2G + B}{4} \right\rfloor ; C_b = B - G; C_r = R - G \qquad (1.12)$$

and

$$G = Y - \left\lfloor \frac{C_b + C_r}{4} \right\rfloor ; R = C_r + G; B = C_b + G \qquad (1.13)$$

The chrominance components can be, but do not necessarily have to be, downscaled in resolution; in fact, since the wavelet transform already separates images into scales, downsampling is more effectively handled by dropping the finest wavelet scale. This step is called multiple component transformation in the JPEG 2000 language since its usage is not restricted to the RGB color model.

1.3.7.2 Tiling

After color transformation, the image is split into the so-called tiles, rectangular regions of the image that are transformed and encoded separately. Tiles can be any size, and it is also possible to consider the whole image as one single tile. Once the size is chosen, all the tiles will have the same size (except optionally those on the right and bottom borders). Dividing the image into tiles is advantageous in that the decoder will need less memory to decode the image and it can opt to decode only selected tiles to achieve a partial decoding of the image. The disadvantage of this approach is that the quality of the picture decreases due to a lower peak signal-to-noise ratio (PSNR). Using many tiles can create a blocking effect similar to the older JPEG standard.

1.3.7.3 Wavelet Transform

The tiles obtained are then wavelet transformed to an arbitrary depth, in contrast to JPEG 1992, which uses an 8×8 block size DCT. JPEG 2000 uses two different wavelet transforms. (1) Irreversible: the CDF 9/7 wavelet transform. It is said to be "irreversible" because it introduces quantization noise that depends on the precision of the decoder. (2) Reversible: a rounded version of the biorthogonal CDF 5/3 wavelet transform. It uses only integer coefficients, so the output does not require rounding (quantization), and so it does not introduce any quantization noise. It is used in lossless coding. The wavelet transforms are implemented by the lifting scheme or by convolution.

1.3.7.4 Quantization

After wavelet transform, the coefficients are scalar-quantized to reduce the number of bits to represent them, at the expense of quality. The output is a set of integer numbers that have to be encoded bit by bit. The parameter that can be changed to set the final quality is the quantization step: the greater the step, the greater is the compression and the loss of quality. With a quantization step that equals 1, no quantization is performed, which is used in lossless compression.

1.3.7.5 Coding

The result of the previous process is a collection of subbands that represent several approximation scales. A subband is a set of coefficients—real numbers that represent aspects of the image associated with a certain frequency range as well as a spatial area of the image. The quantized subbands are split further into precincts, rectangular regions in the wavelet domain. They are typically selected in a way that the coefficients within them across the subbands form approximately spatial blocks in the image domain, although this is not a requirement. Precincts are split further into code blocks. Code blocks are located in a single subband and have equal sizes—except those located at the edges. The encoder has to encode the bits of all quantized coefficients of a code block, starting with the most significant bits and progressing to less significant bits by a process called the Embedded Block Coding with Optimal Truncation (EBCOT) scheme. In this encoding process, each bit plane of the code block gets encoded in three so-called coding passes, first encoding bits (and signs) of insignificant coefficients with significant neighbors (i.e., with 1 bit in higher bit planes), then refinement bits of significant coefficients, and finally coefficients without significant neighbors. The three passes are called significance propagation, magnitude refinement, and Cleanup pass, respectively. Clearly, in lossless mode all bit planes have to be encoded by the EBCOT, and no bit planes can be dropped. The bits selected by these coding passes then get encoded by a context-driven binary arithmetic coder, namely, the binary MQ coder. The context of a coefficient is formed by the state of its nine neighbors in the code block.

The result is a bit-stream that is split into packets where a packet groups selected passes of all code blocks from a precinct into one indivisible unit. Packets are the key to quality scalability. Packets from all subbands are then collected in the so-called layers. The way the packets are built up from the code-block coding passes, and thus which packets a layer will contain, is not defined by the JPEG 2000 standard, but, in general, a codec will try to build layers in such a way that the image quality will increase monotonically with each layer, and the image distortion will shrink from layer to layer. Thus, layers define the progression by image quality within the code stream. The problem is now to find the optimal packet length for all code blocks that minimizes the overall distortion in a way that the generated target bit rate equals the demanded bit rate.

Although the standard does not define a procedure as to how to perform this form of rate-distortion optimization, the general outline is given in one of its many appendices: For each bit encoded by the EBCOT coder, the improvement in image quality, defined as the mean square error (MSE), gets measured; this can be implemented by an easy table lookup algorithm. Furthermore, the length of the resulting code stream gets measured. This forms for each code block a graph in the rate-distortion plane, giving image quality over bit-stream length. The optimal selection for the truncation points, and thus for the packet buildup points, is then given by defining critical slopes of these curves and picking all those coding passes whose curve in the rate-distortion graph is steeper than the given critical slope. This method can be seen as a special application of the method of Lagrange multiplier, which is used for optimization problems under constraints. The Lagrange multiplier, typically denoted by λ, turns out to be the critical slope, the constraint is the demanded target bit rate, and the value to optimize is the overall distortion.

Packets can be reordered almost arbitrarily in the JPEG 2000 bit-stream; this gives the encoder as well as image servers a high degree of freedom. Already encoded images can be sent over networks with arbitrary bit rates by using a layer-progressive encoding order. On the other hand, color components can be moved back in the bit-stream; lower resolutions (corresponding to low-frequency subbands) could be sent first for image previewing. Finally, spatial browsing of large images is possible through appropriate tile and/or partition selection. All these operations do not require any reencoding but only byte-wise copy operations.

1.4 OVERVIEW OF INFORMATION HIDING TECHNIQUES FOR IMAGES

In this section, we provide an overview the information hiding techniques for images. That is, the cover object is a digital image, and after we embed the secret information into the cover image, we can get the stego image. According to different purposes and applications, we can mainly classify information hiding techniques into four categories, i.e., robust watermarking for copyright protection, fragile watermarking for content authentication, fingerprinting for transaction tracking, and steganography for covert communication. For these four categories, we do not care regarding the recoverability of the cover image after extracting the secret information in the stego image. For some areas, it is required that the cover image should be recovered after removing the secret information from the stego image, thus we have a new category named *lossless information hiding*, and this category is mainly used for content authentication for special images, such as military images, law images, and medical images.

1.4.1 ROBUST IMAGE WATERMARKING

1.4.1.1 Background

Because of the fast and extensive growth of network technology, digital information can be distributed with no quality loss, low cost, and nearly instantaneous delivery. Protection of multimedia content has become an important issue because of the consumers' insufficient cognizance of the ownership of intellectual property. Many research groups around the world are working toward the highly ambitious technological goal of protecting the ownership of digital contents, which would dramatically protect inventions represented in the digital form for being vulnerable to illegal possession, duplication, and dissemination [5]. Digital watermarking [6] is the process of embedding digital information called watermark into a multimedia product, and then the embedded data can later be extracted or detected from the watermarked product, for protecting digital content copyright and ensuring tamper resistance, which is indiscernible and hard to remove by unauthorized persons. Copyright protection appears to be one of the first applications for which digital watermarking was targeted. The metadata in this case contains information about the copyright owner. It is imperceptibly embedded as a watermark in the cover work to be protected. If users of digital content (music, images, and video) have easy access to watermark detectors, they should be able to recognize and interpret the embedded watermark and identify the copyright owner of the watermarked content.

1.4.1.2 Definitions

Essentially, watermarking is defined as the process of embedding the watermark within the cover signal. A cover signal is a raw digital audio, image, or video signal that will be used to contain a watermark. A watermark itself is loosely defined as a set of data, usually in binary form, that will be stored or transmitted through a cover signal. The watermark may be as small as a single bit or as large as the number of samples in the cover signal itself. It may be a copyright notice, a secret message, or any other information. It is important to realize that a watermark is not transmitted in addition to a digital signal, but rather as an integral part of the signal samples. The value of watermarking comes from the fact that regular sideband data may be lost or modified when the digital signal is converted between formats, but the samples of the digital signal are (typically) unchanged [7]. Finally, a key may be necessary to embed a watermark into a cover signal, and it may be needed to extract the watermark data afterward [6].

1.4.1.3 Image Watermarking System

Digital watermarking systems typically include two primary components: the encoder and the decoder. To combine a watermark with a digital document, for example, images, you need an image (C_O), a watermark (W) that contains the watermarking information, a security key (K), and an encoding algorithm (E) to create a watermarked image (C_W). The encoder takes the signature and the cover document and generates the watermarked image, which is described as a function

$$C_W = E(C_O, W, K) \tag{1.14}$$

In this case, secret or public keys and other parameters can be used to extend the watermarking encoder. The watermark is considered to be robust if it is embedded in such a way that the watermark can survive even if the watermarked data C_W go through severe distortions.

A watermark extractor or detector involves a two-step process. Watermark retrieval is the first step that applies some scrambling algorithms to extract a sequence referred to as retrieved watermarks. Then, in the second step, the embedded watermarks are detected and extracted from a suspected signal of containing watermarks. The second step normally requires the analysis and comparison of the unreliable watermark with the original one, and the consequences could be several kinds of confidence assessment displaying the similarity between the extracted watermark and the original one. The watermark detection procedure is depicted as follows:

$$W' = D(C_W, K, ...) \tag{1.15}$$

where $D(.)$ is the detection algorithm and C and W are the optional inputs for the detection function. In this case, the decoder loads the watermarked, normal or corrupted image C_W and extracts the hidden signature W. Using nonblind and blind watermarking techniques in Figs. 1.6 and 1.7, the decoder D loads an additional image C_O, which is often the original image, to extract the watermarking information by correlation.

1.4.1.4 Characteristics

It is essential to define the criteria for evaluating a watermarking system. Generally, there are five important issues that are usually considered in the most practical application.

1. Imperceptibility

   There are two main reasons why it is important to keep the imperceptibility of the cover media after the encoding with watermark data. First, the presence or absence of a watermark cannot be distinguished from the primary purpose of the original media, if the watermarked media is so badly distorted that its value is lost. In addition, suspicious perceptible artifacts may introduce a watermark, perhaps its precise location being detected from the cover media. This information may provide accesses for distorting, substituting, or removing the watermark data maliciously.

2. Robustness

   One of the most commonly measured properties is that watermark signals must be reasonably resilient to various attacks and common signal processing operations in digital watermarking systems. For the digital watermarking of images, the good watermarking method is likely to resist against noise addition; filtering processing; geometrical transformations such as scaling, translation, and rotation; and also JPEG compression.

3. Capacity

   Capacity is defined using the largest quantity of information that inserted watermarks are capable of hiding, and embedded watermarks can be extracted credibly for the purposes of copyright safeguards. For images, the capacity refers to the amount of embedded bits into pixels or patterns of the images.

4. Security

   All existing watermarking algorithms that are not secure cannot be used for copyright protection. The watermarking algorithm is safe and robust, if the attacker, using watermarking procedures and knowledge, does not know the key used for watermarking digital content. In addition, the complexity of the watermark process may be safety related. To improve the security of the algorithm, it can enlarge the embedded space and increase the size of the keys split into small pieces of cover image.

5. False-positive

   There are two subtle distinctive ways to describe this probability. In the first explanation, the false-positive probability is the possibility that for a preconditioned settled cover image and arbitrarily chosen watermarks, the detector will state that a watermark exists in that image. In the second definition, the false-positive possibility is that for randomly chosen images and a preconditioned settled watermark, the detector will retrieve that watermark in an image.

Note that the conditions of imperceptibility, robustness, and capability are conflicted and limited by each other. One may want to increase the watermarking strength to increase the robustness, but this results in a more perceptible watermark. On the other hand, under the condition of imperceptibility, a watermark would have to be created with the maximum possible separation to avoid a situation where a small corruption of the watermarked image would lead to erroneous watermark detection. Similarly, one can increase the data payload by decreasing the number of samples allocated to each hidden bit, but this is counterbalanced by a loss of robustness. In other words, for any watermarking scheme, it is impossible to meet these three requirements simultaneously. As a result, a good trade-off among these requirements has to be achieved.

1.4.1.5 Overview of Techniques

Up to now, two traditionally used strategies, spatial domain [8] and transform domain [9,10] techniques, have been developed for digital image watermarking. The former category is designed to insert directly a watermark into the original image by a factor, which would lead to fair-quality watermarked images. The latter approach, for taking advantage of perceptual properties, is devised to embed a watermark into the frequency domain of the original images. These types of watermarking schemes have good performances of robustness when compared with the most common signal processing manipulations such as JPEG compression, filtering, and addition of noise [11]. Signal processing operators are applied to watermarked images for removing the watermark or decreasing its energy so that the extracted watermark is unrecognizable or insufficient as the validate evidence. Unfortunately, the ineffectiveness of existing traditional watermarking algorithms is described by the robustness against unintentional or malicious geometric attacks [12]. Geometric attacks induce synchronization errors between the original and the extracted watermark during the detection process. In other words, the watermark still exists in the watermarked image, but its positions have been changed. Therefore, although traditional watermarking systems require the creation of a framework of resilience to geometrical modifications as well as creation and enforcement of synchronization errors of watermarked data, correction of such frameworks is now possible. Besides facilitating more efficient copyrighted protection and robustness against desynchronization, adaptation of geometrically invariant image features can potentially offer a greater robust capacity to detect watermarks without synchronization errors, especially when applied to surviving local distortions such as random bending attacks. Development of such a framework is an essential starting point for organizations that wish to improve or replace currently existing watermarking algorithm—based pixel frequency or other transform coefficients for watermark embedding, and develop a set of means to establish and maintain feature-based watermarking of geometric distortion correction.

Watermarking algorithms robust to the geometrical distortions have been the focus of research [13]. Several approaches to this problem include exhaustive search, synchronization pattern/template, and invariant domain, and implicit synchronization using image features are widely used. The exhaustive search technique [14] performs the process of watermark detection over a training sequence containing each pilot geometrical inverse deformation. The watermark is recovered by searching each hypothetical distortion parameter. The template-based approach performs the watermark retrieval process by asserting the presence of a watermark and estimating and compensating the severe geometric transformation of the watermarked image for accomplishing resynchronization patterns [15]. Another solution consists in embedding the watermark in a geometrical invariant subspace. In Ref. [16] using histogram specification to hide a watermark invariant to geometrical distortions is suggested. Feature-based synchronization watermarking schemes follow the same basic process: detected feature points are localized at the local maxima, whereas nonmaxima suppression eliminates pixels that are not local maxima, and the final set of features is determined by analysis of threshold. Afterward, extracted feature points are applied to identify regions for watermark insertion in the cover image. At the receiver side, the feature points are detectable without synchronization error. The feature-based process can be invariant to local geometrical deformations so that it is an encouraging approach to solve the robustness against geometrical deformations in the watermarking scheme with blind detection. Most of the proposed geometrical transform invariant algorithms are actually only rotation-scaling-translation invariant. Also, the systematic analysis of the watermarking algorithm performance under geometrical distortion has begun to draw great attention. Most of these efforts confine to theoretically analyzing and quantifying the effect of the global affine transform to the performance of the watermarking algorithms. Local distortions are more and more regarded as a necessary test scenario in benchmarking software. However, it is difficult to theoretically analyze its effect on watermark detection due to its complexity.

1.4.2 FRAGILE IMAGE WATERMARKING

1.4.2.1 Background

Digital watermarking has been also proposed as a possible solution for data authentication and tamper detection. The invisible authenticator, sensitive watermark, is inserted using the visual redundancy of human visual system (HVS), and is altered or destroyed when the cover image is modified by various linear or nonlinear transformations. The changes of authentication watermark can be used to determine the modification of the marked image, even locate the tampered area. Because the watermark is embedded in the content of image, it can exert its efficiency in the whole lifecycle.

1.4.2.2 Classification

The authentication watermark can be classified into fragile watermark and semifragile watermark according to its fragility and sensitivity. The fragile watermark is very sensitive and designed to detect every possible change in marked image; so it fits to verify the integrity of data and is viewed as an alternative verification solution to a standard digital signature scheme. However, in most multimedia applications, minor data modifications are acceptable as long as the content is authentic, so the semifragile watermark is developed and widely used in content verifying. Semifragile watermark is robust for acceptable content-preserving manipulations (compression, enhancement, etc.) whereas fragile watermark is robust for malicious distortions such as feature adding or removal. Therefore it is suitable to verify the trustworthiness of data.

1.4.2.3 Requirements

A watermarking-based authentication system can be considered as effective if it satisfies the following requirements:

1. *Invisibility*: The embedded watermark is invisible. It is the basic requirement of keeping the commercial quality of watermarked images. The watermarked image must be perceptually identical to the original one under normal observation.
2. *Tampering detection*: An authentication watermarking system should detect any tampering in a watermarked image. This is the most fundamental property to reliably test image's authenticity.
3. *Security*: The embedded watermark cannot be forged or manipulated. In such systems the marking key is private, the marking key should be difficult to deduce from the detection information, and the insertion of a mark by unauthorized parties should be difficult.
4. *Identification of manipulated area*: The authentication watermark should be able to detect the location of altered areas and verify other areas as authentic. The detector should also be able to estimate what kind of modification had occurred.

1.4.2.4 Watermarking-Based Authentication System

The process of digital watermarking—based authentication is similar to any watermarking system; it is composed of two parts: the embedding of authentication watermark and the extraction and verification of authentication watermark.

1.4.2.4.1 Authentication Watermark Embedding

The general description of watermark embedding is:

$$c' = E(c, a, w, K_{pr}) \tag{1.16}$$

where $E(.)$ is the watermark embedding operator; c and c' are image pixels or coefficients before and after watermark embedding; w is the embedded watermark sample, which is generated by the pseudorandom sequence generator or chaotic sequence; and a is a tuning parameter determining the strength of the watermark to ensure the invisibility. It can be a constant or a JND function proposed by HVS [17]. K_{pr} is the private key that controls the generation of watermark sequence or selects the location for embedding.

1.4.2.4.2 Authentication Watermark Extraction and Verification

The general description of watermark extraction is:

$$w' = D(I_1, K_{pu}) \tag{1.17}$$

where $D(.)$ is the watermark extraction operator, I_1 is the questionable marked image, and K_{pu} is the public key corresponding to K_{pr} [18]. If the Hamming distance between the extracted and original watermarks is less than a predefined threshold, the modification of marked image is acceptable and the image's content is authentic, or the marked image is unauthentic. The tampered area can be located by the differences between the extracted and original watermarks: the watermark differences of the tampered image are most likely concentrated in a particular area, whereas the differences caused by incidental manipulation such as compression are sparse and widely spread over the entire image. So the tampered area can be determined.

1.4.2.5 Overview of Techniques

Many early authenticating watermarking systems embed the mark in the spatial domain of an image. Some watermark schemes can easily detect random changes to an image but fail to detect tampered area. An example is the fragile mark embedded in the least significant bit (LSB) plane of an image [19].

The later authentication watermark schemes are developed in transform domains, such as DCT and wavelet domains. The properties of a transform can be used to characterize how the image has been damaged, and the choice of watermark embedding locations enables us to flexibly adjust the sensitivity of the authentication watermark. For example, if one is only interested in determining whether an image has been tampered with, one could use a special type of signal that can be easily destroyed by slight. modifications, e.g., an encrypted JPEG compressed image file. On the other hand, if one is interested in determining which part of an image has been altered, one should embed the watermark in each DCT block or wavelet detail subband, to find out which part has been modified. Some authentication watermark schemes are developed from the spread spectrum-based robust watermarking algorithms [20,21]. The semifragile watermarks are attached on the middle-low DCT coefficients or the wavelet low-resolution detail subbands as additive white Gaussian noise. At detector, the correlation value between the original watermark sequence and the extracted watermark or marked image is used to determine the authenticity of the test image. Because the influence on middle-low frequency coefficients of incidental manipulations such as compression is small, whereas that of tampering is significant, the algorithms can detect whether the images are tampered or not, but cannot locate the tampered area.

Considering the authentication watermark is sensitive to noise, the quantization technique is widely used in the authentication schemes. As a result, the effect of the noise created by the cover image is concealed. Kundur [22,23] proposed a semifragile watermarking authentication scheme based on the wavelet transform. The image is decomposed using the Haar wavelets. Both the embedding and extraction processes of authentication watermark depend on the quantization process of secret key selected wavelet transform coefficients. The spatial frequency property of wavelet transform helps to locate and characterize the tampered area. Yu et al. [24] developed Kundur's schemes, and modeled the probabilities of watermark errors caused by malicious tampering and incidental distortion as Gaussian distributions with large and small variances, respectively, and computed the best number of coefficients needed to embed watermark at each scale such that the trade-off between robustness and fragility is optimized, so the scheme can detect maliciously tampered areas while tolerating some incidental distortions.

1.4.3 IMAGE FINGERPRINTING
1.4.3.1 Background and Basic Concept
Basically, there are two concepts related to multimedia fingerprinting. First, multimedia fingerprinting is referred to as robust hashing, where fingerprints are perceptual features or short summaries of a multimedia object. This concept is an analogy with cryptographic hash functions, which map arbitrary length data to a small and fixed number of bits. Second, multimedia fingerprinting is regarded as the second application of robust image watermarking technique. Here, a fingerprint is a type of watermark that identifies the recipient of a digital object as well as its owner (i.e., a "serial number" assigned by the vendor to a given purchaser). In this book, we adopt the second concept. As in the applications of copyright protection, the watermark for fingerprinting is used to trace authorized users who violate the license agreement and distribute the copyrighted material illegally. Thus, the information embedded in the content is usually about the customer such as customer's identification number. Additional data embedded by watermark in this application is used to trace the originator or recipients of a particular copy of multimedia file. This is intended to act as a deterrent to illegal redistribution by enabling the owner of the

data object to identify the original buyer of the redistributed copy. For example, watermarks carrying different serial or ID numbers are embedded in different copies of multimedia information before distributing them to a large number of recipients.

1.4.3.2 Differences Between Watermarking and Fingerprinting

Both watermarking and fingerprinting are techniques of embedding hidden data in the multimedia. In watermarking, the hidden data are called a watermark, and it identifies the owner of the multimedia. In fingerprinting, the hidden data are called a fingerprint, and it identifies the purchaser. Watermarking is a technique used to retain the owner's copyright, whereas fingerprinting is used to trace the source of illegal copies. Fingerprints must be embedded in the multimedia in an imperceptible way. This can be done by embedding fingerprints in the image's pixels [25,26], in the DCT domain [25,27–29] or in the wavelet transform domain [30]. An analysis of the fingerprint presenting in the illegal copy will allow to identify the pirate.

1.4.3.3 Requirements

The algorithms implemented in fingerprinting applications need to be invisible and must also be invulnerable to intentional attacks and signal processing modifications such as lossy compression or filtering. It should be assumed that pirates will perform attacks intended to remove fingerprints from their copies to distribute a pirate copy. The greatest threat are organized groups of pirates. In these groups each pirate has fingerprinted copies, and they combine them to produce a pirated copy with a heavily damaged fingerprint. Such attacks are called collusion attacks [31–34]. Fingerprinting should be resistant to the collusion attack, that is, it is impossible to embed more than one ID number in the cover multimedia file; otherwise, a group of users with the same image containing different fingerprints would be able to collude and validate the fingerprint or create a copy without any fingerprint.

Fingerprinting is an active tamper detection technique. In this case the authors of the tampered copy (pirates) are trying to deny that they have distributed this copy. It is known that the copy was tampered with, and the objective is to prove that the pirates were in fact the originators of the tampered copy. A description of passive tamper detection techniques can be found in [35]. In this case the authors of the tampered copy are trying to make changes that look natural and/or want to claim the copyrights. It is not known that the copy was tampered with, and the objective is to verify the copy's integrity and its authors' copyrights. This is contrary to the purpose of digital fingerprinting, thus passive tamper detection techniques will not be discussed in this chapter.

1.4.3.4 Overview of Techniques

There are many fingerprinting methods in literatures, but to the best of our knowledge, none of them are based on quaternion calculus. Therefore, this section focuses on the most representative schemes. Fingerprinting methods can be divided into three groups according to the place where the fingerprints can be embedded.

Transmitter-side fingerprinting: the fingerprints are embedded on the transmitter side, and then copies are sent to the users via unicast transmissions. The most important method is Cox's method [36], which inserts i.i.d. Gaussian sequences into the perceptually most significant components of the data. The watermark is robust against signal processing and against the collusion of five pirates. The method based on Cox's formula is a watermarking scheme that is based on the extreme learning machine [37], which reduces the time of watermark construction to milliseconds.

In-network fingerprinting: the fingerprints are embedded as the data travel through the network. For example, in Ammar's method [38] there are special devices in the network that embed their own watermarks in the transmitted data. Therefore, the user's fingerprint is a composition of embedded watermarks, and it depends on the user's location in the network.

Receiver-side fingerprinting: each user has a unique decryption key that allows to decrypt the data with some unique and imperceptible changes, i.e., fingerprints. The most important method is joint fingerprinting and decryption [28], which encrypts the low-frequency DCT coefficients of the image by reversing their signs, and each user's key can decrypt only a portion of the coefficients. Unfortunately, fingerprint embedding reduces image quality, and the method has very limited robustness against collusion attacks. Another method is called Chameleon [39], which is a stream cipher based on lookup tables. The decryption changes only the LSBs of the image, so the fingerprint does not reduce image quality. However, this method can trace only up to four pirates in a collusion. The next example is the Fingercasting scheme [40,41], which improves Chameleon by using a spread spectrum watermarking scheme. The main drawback is the large size of the lookup table.

1.4.4 IMAGE STEGANOGRAPHY
1.4.4.1 Background and Basic Concept
Over the past two decades, the rapid development of the Internet requires confidential information that needs to be protected from unauthorized users. This is accomplished through data hiding. It is a method of hiding secret messages into a cover medium so that an unintended observer will not be aware of the existence of the hidden messages. This is achieved by steganography. The term steganography is retrieved from the Greek words "stegos" (means cover) and "grafia" (means writing), defining it as covered writing. Steganography is the science that involves communicating secret data in an appropriate multimedia carrier, e.g., image, audio, and video files. The similarity between steganography and cryptography is that both are used to conceal information. However, the difference is that steganography does not reveal any suspicion about the hidden information to the user. Therefore the attackers will not try to decrypt information.

1.4.4.2 Image Steganography System
The graphical representation of a typical image steganography system is shown in Fig. 1.14. Let C denote the cover carrier and C' the stegoimage. Let K represent

an optional key (a seed used to encrypt the message or to generate a pseudorandom noise, which can be set to$\{\Phi\}$ for simplicity) and let M be the message we want to communicate. *Em* is an acronym for embedding and *Ex* for extraction. We can define the processes of embedding and extraction as follows:

$$Em: C \oplus K \oplus M \to C \qquad\qquad (1.18)$$

$$Ex(Em(c,k,m)) \approx m, \text{for any } c \in C, k \in K, m \in M \qquad (1.19)$$

1.4.4.3 Overview of Techniques

This subsection attempts to give an overview of the most important steganographic techniques in digital images. The most popular image formats on the Internet are GIF, JPEG, and to a lesser extent—the PNG. Most of the techniques developed were set up to exploit the structures of these formats with some exceptions in the literature that use the bitmap format (BMP) for its simple data structure. We can classify the existing image steganography schemes into four categories, i.e., steganography exploiting the image format, steganography in the image spatial domain, steganography in the image frequency domain and adaptive steganography.

Steganography can be accomplished by simply appending the secret message in the text file "Message.txt" into the JPEG image file "Cover.jpg" and produces the stego image "Stego.jpg." The message is packed and inserted after the EOF(End of file) tag. When Stego.jpg is viewed using any photo editing application, anything coming after the EOF tag will be ignored. However, when opened in Notepad, for example, the message reveals itself after displaying some messy data. The embedded message does not impair the image quality. Unfortunately, this simple technique would not resist any kind of editing to the stego image nor any attacks by steganalysis experts. Another naive implementation of steganography is to append hidden data into the image's extended file information, which is a standard used by digital camera manufacturers to store information in the image file, which is metadata information about the image and its source located at the header of the file. This method is not a reliable one as it suffers from the same drawbacks as that of the EOF method. Note that it is not always recommended to hide data directly without encrypting as in this example.

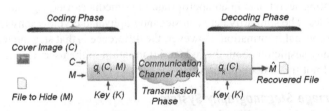

FIGURE 1.14

The Graphical Representation of a Typical Image Steganography System.

In spatial domain methods, a steganographer modifies the secret data and the cover medium in the spatial domain, which involves encoding at the level of the LSBs. Although this method is simpler, it has a larger impact compared to the other three types of methods [42]. Potdar et al. [43] used a spatial domain technique in producing a fingerprinted secret sharing steganography for robustness against image cropping attacks. Shirali-Shahreza and Shirali-Shahreza [44] exploited Arabic and Persian alphabet punctuations to hide messages. Color palette−based steganography exploits the smooth ramp transition in colors as indicated in the color palette. Jung and Yoo [45] downsampled an input image to half of its size, and then used a modified interpolation method, termed the neighbor mean interpolation, to upsample the result back to its original dimensions ready for embedding. Histogram-based data hiding is another commonly used data hiding scheme, which is a lossless scheme that will be discussed in Chapter 2 in detail.

The discovery of the LSB embedding mechanism is actually a big achievement. Although it is perfect in not deceiving the HVS, its weak resistance to attacks left researchers wondering where to apply it next until they successfully applied it within the frequency domain. DCT is used extensively with video and image compression, e.g., JPEG lossy compression. Most of the techniques use JPEG images as carriers to embed their data. For example, Li and Wang [46] presented a steganographic method that modifies the QT and inserts the hidden bits in the middle frequency coefficients. Some famous JPEG steganography schemes are JSteg, F5, and Outguess. According to Raja et al.'s article [47], the FFT-based method introduces round-off errors, thus it is not suitable for covert communication. However, Johnson and Jajodia [48] thought differently and included it among the used transformations in steganography, and McKeon [49] utilized the 2D discrete Fourier transform to generate Fourier-based steganography in movies. As for steganography in the DWT, the reader is directed to some examples in the literature. The DWT-based embedding technique is still in its infancy. Abdelwahab and Hassan [50] proposed a data hiding technique in the DWT domain. Both secret and cover images are decomposed using DWT(first level). Each of this is divided into disjoint 4 × 4 blocks. Blocks of the secret image fit into the cover blocks to determine the best match. Afterward, error blocks are generated and embedded into coefficients of the best matched blocks in the HL subband of the cover image.

Adaptive steganography is a special case of the two former methods. It is also known as "statistics-aware embedding" [51], "masking" [48], or "model-based" [52]. This kind of method takes statistical global features of the image before attempting to interact with its LSB/DCT coefficients. The statistics will dictate where to make the changes [53,54]. It is characterized by a random adaptive selection of pixels depending on the cover image and the selection of pixels in a block with large local STD. The latter is meant to avoid areas of uniform color (smooth areas). This behavior makes adaptive steganography seek images with existing or deliberately added noise and images that demonstrate color complexity.

1.4.5 LOSSLESS INFORMATION HIDING IN IMAGES

1.4.5.1 Background and Basic Concepts

Through suitable watermarking techniques, protection of the data can be ensured and one can know whether the received content has been tampered with or not. However, watermarking can cause damage to the sensitive information present in the cover work, and thus at the receiving end, the exact recovery of cover works may not be possible. In some applications, even the slightest distortion in the cover work is intolerable. For example, in the field of medical imagery, if a medical image is modified using conventional watermarking, the small change may affect the interpretation significantly and a physician may make a wrong diagnosis. Similarly, in case of military application, changes due to embedding of secret information can substantially alter the cover image and therefore, the decision taken may cost considerably. Consequently, there is a strong need to restore the cover work to its original form.

Lossless information hiding, also known as reversible information hiding or reversible watermarking, mainly refers to the technique that has the following property: after information embedding based on this technique, although it may damage the visual quality of the cover image to some extent, if the watermarked image suffers no change in the transmission process, then the legitimate users and authorities can clear the distortion and restore the original image according to the embedded information. That is to say, it allows full extraction of the embedded information along with the complete restoration of the cover work. Reversible watermarking can thus be considered as a special case of watermarking. Due to the unique nature of this technique, reversible watermarking is gaining more attention in the past few years because of its increasing applications in military communication, health care, and law enforcement, that is, it can be applied to areas where there is a high requirement for the quality of the original image. For example, in the commercial area, it can be applied to prevent the digital ticket from being tampered with; in the medical area, it can be used to check if the digital medical images are modified during the transmission; in the military area, it may be used to ensure the integrity of the obtained digitized military satellite images; and in the court, it can be used to verify the authenticity of the digital photographs that are used as evidences.

The principle of lossless information hiding is as follows: for the input digital image signal I, we embed the information W into it by using some kind of nondestructive information embedding methods, obtaining another digital image signal I', and then, the signal I' may be transmitted and communicated publicly. For the authorized user, in the absence of the digital image signal I and the embedded information W, from the obtained signal I', we can obtain the embedded information W through an appropriate extraction method and at the same time completely recover the original digital image signal I. Fig. 1.15 shows the block diagram of a basic reversible watermarking system.

In fact, there is no essential difference in principle between the lossless information hiding and traditional information hiding techniques. However, for the lossless information technique, because of the need to extract the embedded information and then completely recover the original image without any loss, the requirements for embedding information become more stringent:

1. We need to know the embedding order and embedding locations of the data.
2. We need to know each altered value of the original image data.
3. We need to avoid the embedded data information from exceeding the scope of the original image data.

Referring to the general information hiding model, the lossless information hiding model is given in Fig. 1.16, which includes:

1. *The cover media*: It is the carrier used to hide the secret information. Since this book focuses on lossless information hiding methods described on digital images, thus it is specifically referred to as the cover image in our book.
2. *The secret information*: It is one of the inputs for the embedding process, which is referred to as the object to be embedded into the original cover media. It can be called a watermark that is a sequence consisting of a number of randomly generated "0"s and "1"s by, where each bit is called watermark bit.
3. *The embedding process*: Based on the key, this process hides the secret information into the cover media through the lossless embedding model.
4. *The stego media*: It is the output of the embedding process embedded in the output process, referring to the obtained media after embedding secret information. For image media, we often call it the watermarked image.
5. *The extraction process*: Based on the key, this process extracts the hidden information from the stego media or possible attacked stego media and/or recovers the cover media. In this process, the required auxiliary information is generally referred to as side information.
6. *The recovered media*: It is one of the outputs of the extraction process, i.e., the recovered cover media after extracting the secret information from the stego media. For images, it is specifically referred to as the recovered image.

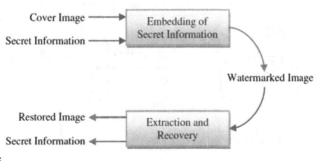

FIGURE 1.15

Basic Reversible Image Watermarking Scheme.

7. *The key*: It is the additional secret information that may be required during the information hiding process. In general, we can generate the key from the important parameters or side information of the embedding process.

8. *The covert attack*: It is located in the transmission channel of stego media. Taking into account the special nature of lossless information hiding, we only study the effects of nonmalicious operations on the watermarked image, e.g., JPEG lossy compression and additive Gaussian noises. However, in the lossless case, it is assumed that there is no influence of covert attacks.

1.4.5.2 Classifications of Schemes

In past, reviews of different reversible watermarking techniques were carried out [55–57]. Feng et al. [56] discussed key requirements of the watermark and classified reversible watermarking schemes into three categories: data compression, difference expansion (DE), and histogram shifting. A single reversible watermarking scheme is discussed in each of these categories. Some major challenges faced by the researchers in this field are also outlined. Pan et al. [57] categorized various reversible watermarking approaches into two classes, additive and substitution, based on the embedding method. Comparison is carried out through empirical analysis of selected reversible watermarking approaches on medical images. Caldelli et al. [55] provided another review that classifies reversible watermarking techniques on the basis of watermarking properties, i.e., into robust, fragile, and semifragile. Caldelli et al. [55] also performed classification according to the watermark embedding domain, i.e., spatial or frequency domain. The aforementioned review articles were quite valuable; however, they cover very limited area and discuss only few of the works in the field of reversible watermarking. The prospective reversible watermarking approaches based on the concept of error expansion have been reported in large numbers, and they mostly outperform other types of reversible watermarking approaches. Most of these new and efficient prediction error–based reversible watermarking techniques are not covered by the aforementioned reviews. Additionally, there has been a rapid increase in the applications of reversible watermarking

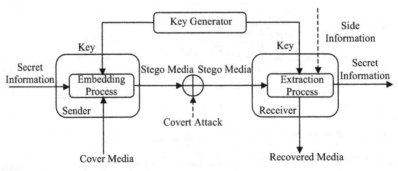

FIGURE 1.16

The Lossless Information Hiding Model.

techniques. Consequently, a review of newly emerging reversible watermarking techniques is highly desirable.

1.4.5.3 Overview of Techniques

One of the first reversible watermarking method was introduced by Honsinger et al. [58]. They utilized modulo addition 256 to achieve reversibility in their watermarking technique. Macq [59] developed a reversible watermarking approach by modifying the patchwork algorithm and using modulo addition 256. Although, Honsinger et al. [58] and Macq [59] proposed reversible techniques, the imperceptibility of their approaches is not impressive. The watermarked images resulting from Honsinger et al. [58] and Macq's [59] techniques suffer from salt-and-pepper noises because of the use of modulo addition 256. A reversible watermarking technique without using modulo addition 256 was then introduced by Fridrich et al. [60]. Fridrich et al. [60] proposed the concept of compressing the LSB plane of cover image to make space for the watermark to be embedded. However, the embedding capacity of this approach was limited. To improve the embedding capacity and imperceptibility of the watermarked image, Fridrich et al. [61] then proposed another approach. Evolution of reversible watermarking started around 2000, and it is now quite difficult to keep up with the development that is going on in this field. Many reversible watermarking algorithms have been developed in the 2000s. A number of new techniques, extensions, or improved versions of the earlier techniques have been proposed afterwards. The improvement is primarily based upon making a good imperceptibility versus capacity trade-off. Zheng et al. reported a comprehensive survey on robust image watermarking algorithms [62]. Guo [63] and Guo et al. [64] reported reversible watermarking techniques for the halftone images. We reviewed newly emerging reversible watermarking techniques and categorized them into four groups, i.e., compression based, histogram modification based, quantization based, and expansion based.

To recover the original image, we need to store the information essential for recovery of the original image along with the watermark. Thus, in case of reversible watermarking, additional data need to be embedded and consequently, we need more space compared with conventional watermarking for data embedding. A simple approach may be compressing a part of cover image for embedding data. Several reversible watermarking schemes are reported using this approach. In 2004, Yang et al. [65] proposed a high-capacity companding technique for image watermarking in the DCT domain. Celik et al. [66] in 2005 proposed a well-known compression-based approach. The intensity values of pixels in the cover image are first quantized by applying L-level scalar quantization. Then, the remainders obtained are compressed using a context-based adaptive lossless image codec, and watermark information is concatenated with it. Xuan et al. [67] developed a reversible watermarking technique using companding function on integer wavelet coefficients. Arsalan et al. [68] utilized Xuan et al. [67] companding function in combination with genetic algorithm to develop a high-capacity reversible watermarking technique.

Many researchers have carried out research in the field of histogram modification—based reversible watermarking. Initially, Vleeschouwer et al. [69] presented circular interpretation—based reversible watermarking. In 2006, Ni et al. [70] developed a novel reversible watermarking approach based on image histogram modification. Before embedding, a pair of peak and zero points is selected from the histogram of the cover image. Only pixels with values between peak and zero points undergo modification during the embedding process. To increase the embedding capacity of histogram-based reversible watermarking techniques, different algorithms are reported. Lin et al. [71] presented a multilevel reversible watermarking approach that utilizes the histogram of difference image for data embedding. In another work, Ni et al. [72] proposed an approach that does not suffer from salt-and-pepper noise. Gao et al. [73] then highlighted the shortcomings of Ni et al.'s approach [72] and improved it. Tsai et al. [74] proposed a subtly different approach from Lin et al. [71]. The difference between a basic pixel and every other pixel in the block is used rather than the difference of adjacent pixels. Kim et al. [75] proposed a novel method that exploits the spatial correlation between subsampled images. Kamran et al. [76] reported a novel approach that utilizes the concept of downsampling for performance improvement.

Quantization-based watermarking techniques are, in general, robust. However, the reversible quantization—based watermarking approaches are mostly fragile in nature. In 2007, Cheung et al. proposed a Sequential Quantization Strategy (SQS) for data embedding [77]. SQS makes the modulation of a pixel value dependent on the previous pixels. A reversible data embedding method is used with SQS to make it more suitable for the authentication purposes. Saberian et al. [78] presented a Weighted Quantization Method (WQM) approach, which can be applied in spatial as well as transform domains. In contrast to other approaches, the distortion caused by this scheme is not payload dependent. It is shown that WQM gives high embedding capacity, when applied to Point-to-Point Graph transform. Lee et al. [79] proposed a VQ-based reversible watermarking technique using histogram modification to achieve high embedding capacity. The conventional quantization index modulation (QIM)—based watermarking techniques are not reversible in general, because of the irreversible distortions caused in the watermarked image due to the quantization process. However, in 2011, Ko et al. [80] developed a nested QIM watermarking algorithm for medical image watermarking systems, which ensures the recovery of the cover image. Ko et al. [81] also presented a reversible watermarking technique for biomedical image using QIM and fractional DCT. This technique outperforms the nested QIM [80].

In 2003, Tian [82] presented a novel approach, named DE. It gave a new direction to the reversible watermarking methods. It achieves high embedding capacity and low computational complexity compared with the preceding techniques. Several improved DE-based watermarking schemes were then proposed over the time. There are mainly three types of expansion-based reversible watermarking techniques: contrast mapping—based reversible watermarking, correlation-based reversible watermarking and interpolation—based reversible watermarking. Their typical schemes are described as follows. In 2007, Coltuc et al. [83] presented their work on contrast mapping—based reversible watermarking. In their technique, they performed transformation of pair of pixels. The transformation is invertible for some pair of pixels, even if the LSBs of transformed pairs are lost. In 2004, Thodi et al. [84] proposed a new reversible watermarking scheme based on the correlation among the neighboring pixels for grayscale images. This correlation is modeled using a predictor, which computes the current pixel intensity. Luo et al. [85] reported a reversible watermarking method using interpolation technique. The watermark bits are first embedded in the nonsample pixels until no nonsample pixel is left. Then, the rest of the watermark bits are inserted into the sample pixels, which are interpolated using neighboring watermarked pixels.

In medical diagnostics, remote sensing and forensic evidence, and other sensitive applications, as an effective means to protect the copyright of digital media, lossless information hiding has received many researchers' attention. However, conventional lossless information hiding methods do not consider the covert attack on the stego media during the transmission process, making it difficult to meet the needs of practical applications. In other words, even if the stego media suffers very slight degradation, the receiver cannot correctly extract the secret information. To solve this problem, robust lossless information hiding has been put forward and has attracted many researchers' interests [86—89].

1.4.5.4 Performance Evaluation Criteria for Lossless Data Hiding Schemes

For particular applications, the performance metrics for a lossless information hiding scheme should reflect if it is really suitable for this particular application. However, for algorithm research, the general performance of some algorithms is still a topic of researchers' concern, since the performance of the algorithm can reflect its adaptation range and accuracy, and also the application potential of an algorithm. For fragile reversible watermarking algorithms, the performance is mainly reflected in the following aspects:

1. The ratio of data capacity to distortion
   Similar to general nonreversible watermarking schemes, the watermark embedding process will definitely cause a change in the carrier medium; we call this difference between the stego media and the cover media as distortion. We always hope that a watermark embedding algorithm can have as much data capacity as possible under certain distortion. Reversible watermarking algorithms also take this as an important performance measure of the algorithm, i.e., the ratio of data capacity to distortion. Also, because there is no robustness requirement for fragile reversible watermarking schemes, the ratio of data capacity to distortion becomes the main criterion to evaluate the performance of a reversible watermarking scheme, and it has also become a focus of reversible watermarking algorithms.

Strictly speaking, the data capacity can be specific as the amount of watermark data that can be completely extracted after they are embedded into a cover media based on a certain reversible watermarking algorithm; we usually use the embedded bits per sample to represent it. For images, it is just denoted as the number of embedded bits per pixel (BPP). On the other hand, the distortion calculation often adopts the Euclidean distance−based MSE, or directly the MSE-based PSNR. Let the size of the cover image be $L_1 \times L_2$; x_{ij} is the pixel value at the position (i,j) $(0 \le i \le L_1-1, 0 \le j \le L_2-1)$, wherein PSNR and MSE are defined as follows:

$$\text{MSE} = \frac{\sum_{i=0}^{L_1-1}\sum_{j=0}^{L_2-1}(x_{ij} - x_{wij})^2}{L_1 \times L_2} \tag{1.20}$$

$$\text{PSNR} = 10 \cdot \text{Log}_{10}\frac{L_1 \times L_1}{\text{MSE}} \tag{1.21}$$

In reversible watermarking, although the original cover media can be fully restored, according to the general requirements for watermarking algorithm, the bigger the PSNR and data capacity (Capacity) the better. In the simulation for a reversible information hiding scheme, we often use the PSNR−BITRATE curve to represent the ratio of data capacity to distortion as shown in Fig. 1.17.

2. Performance stability
   Performance stability has two meanings: one refers to the performance stability of reversible watermarking algorithms with regard to different statistical properties of the image, whereas the other refers to the performance stability of the reversible watermarking algorithm with regard to different ranges of indicators. For a good algorithm, its performance should cover a wider range of BPP on the PSNR−BITRATE curve, and the change of PSNR values in this range should be as smooth as possible.

3. Performance fineness
   Performance fineness refers to the density of the sampling points that can be achieved on the performance curve. In an algorithm whose performance curve is actually connected or fitted by a plurality of performance points, if the density of performance points is high, then the fineness is high. For users, the high fineness means the adjustability or controllability of the algorithm performance is high.

4. Computational complexity
   The complexity of an algorithm consists of two main aspects: one is the time complexity of the algorithm, represented by the required time for reversible watermark embedding and extraction/recovery processes; the other is the spatial complexity of the algorithm, represented by the required extra space for reversible watermark embedding and extraction processes. A good algorithm

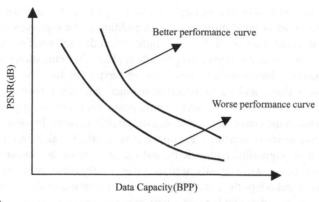

FIGURE 1.17

PSNR–BPP Reversible Watermarking Performance Curve.

should have low time complexity and less additional information utilized, that too without taking up extra storage space.

5. The security of the algorithm

Algorithm security, on the one hand, refers to the fact that the watermark content and the storage locations of the additional information are kept secret for the reversible watermarking algorithm, which can be achieved by using encryption; on the other hand, it refers to the fact that the watermarking algorithm itself is imperceptible (undetectability), that is, the algorithm satisfies the requirements of steganography.

1.5 APPLICATIONS OF LOSSLESS INFORMATION HIDING IN IMAGES

Lossless information hiding in images is gaining more attention in the past few years because of its increasing applications in military communication, health care, and law enforcement. Following are some typical application fields.

1.5.1 LOSSLESS HIDING AUTHENTICATION

People can use lossless reversible watermarking algorithms to achieve the lossless watermark authentication, supporting completely accurate authentication for the cover media, which is actually the original intention of reversible watermarking schemes. A more comprehensive and detailed discussion of this aspect can be found in Fridrich's article [60], and we will not repeat them here.

From the idea of the reversible watermarking schemes that embed signature information in cover media, we can know that reversible watermarking algorithms should be able to be used to embeld other information and fully realize exact information authentication. For example, when we perform lossless watermarking authentication on an original military map, in addition to the signature information of the original image, we may also want to hide some other information in the cover media, such as the generation time, the generation place, the generation manner, creator's information, distributor's information, the expected handling manner, the dissemination manner, and the destruction manner. Another possible application is to view the cover media as a covert communication channel; then you can write secret messages in the cover media in a steganographic manner. In these cases, you need to not only perform authentication on the cover media but also perform security authentication of originality, authenticity, and integrity on these metadata or secret messages. Sometimes, we even only need to perform authentication on metadata and secret messages and adopt the cover media as covert communication tools. We call this type of authentication that is mainly performed on the embedded information is *lossless hiding authentication.*

For the applications that need to perform authentication both on the cover media X and the embedded metadata W, we can use reversible watermarking algorithm to embed W reversibly in and generate a signature S based on the resulting watermarked cover media X_W, and then adopt a reversible watermarking algorithm to embed this signature S reversibly in the watermarked media X_W, resulting in the final media X_{WS} embedded with the signature S and metadata W. This authentication scheme can be shown in Fig. 1.18. Obviously, the object that is generated with a signature S is the media X_W that has been already embedded with metadata, thus we can simultaneously perform authentication on the cover media X and the embedded metadata W. Thus, any change in the embedded result X_W will cause the inconformity between the recalculated signature from X_W and the signature extracted from X_{WS}. In addition, since the algorithm that embeds W in X is a reversible watermarking algorithm, X and W can be fully restored.

For the applications that only need to perform authentication on the embedded secret message M, its authentication scheme is similar to the authentication scheme mentioned earlier that is performed on both the cover media X and metadata W, which can be shown in Fig. 1.19. Note that because we only need to perform authentication on the secret message M, the method used to embed W in X does not need to be reversible, but it is should be guaranteed that it can correctly extract the secret message M in the absence of external attack or change. However, according to different applications, we may require that the embedding method for W should satisfy steganography requirements to some extent.

In the two applications shown in Figs. 1.18 and 1.19, since the authentication methods performed on the media embedded with the secret message and the media embedded with the metadata (X_W and X_M) are both based on reversible watermarking algorithms, both them can be completely recovered. Such lossless hiding authentication—based applications extend the lossless watermark authentication—based applications to the authentication applications based on embedding any data, which requires higher data capacity to meet different uses of data embedding and authentication.

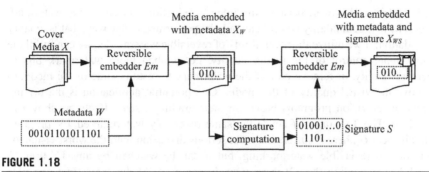

FIGURE 1.18

Embedding of Lossless Hiding Authentication for Host Media and Metadata.

1.5.2 FIDELITY CONTROL FOR COVER MEDIA

In some applications, people are more concerned about the quality of the cover media itself. In this type of application, the common requirements are that the watermarking algorithm and the watermark embedding process do not introduce permanent distortion to the cover media. A special class of application that we are most likely to think of is that there is a special accuracy requirement for special media, such as medical images, military images, remote sensing images, legal evidence images, secret documents, precious works of art, and science experimental images. For this type of application, even only 1 bit permanent loss in the original cover media is not allowed, so the data embedding algorithms must be reversible. Since reversible watermark embedding algorithms can remove the embedding distortion completely, they can referred to as the data embedding style with 100% fidelity.

In some other occasions, people are not demanding a 100% fidelity for the cover media; they just expect the media to possess more fidelity to improve the perceptual effect of the cover media. This gives us an inspiration: we can use the fact that watermark embedding will cause fidelity reduction to achieve the grading control of the

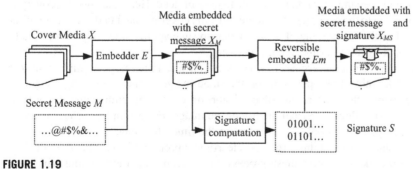

FIGURE 1.19

Embedding of Lossless Hiding Authentication for Secret Messages.

media fidelity. However, because the fidelity reduction caused by the watermark cannot be restored, fidelity control can only be performed in one way, that is, quality degradation; if we utilize the reversibility of reversible watermarks, we can fulfill the bidirectional control of the media fidelity, i.e., embed more watermark bits to decrease fidelity, or remove part of the watermark to restore some of the media to improve the visual quality of the media. One potential application is the pricing model of television programs based on their grading visual effects, as shown in Fig. 1.20: The TV station T sends the same reversibly watermarked TV program P to all users U_i; here P suffers the most serious distortion with the worst visual effects due to reversible watermarking, but it can be watched by any TV user U_i ($i = 1,2,3$) (including the TV users who do not pay). At the same time, the user U_1 possesses a key K_1 to purchase programs from the TV station; through the key K_1, part of the watermark can be removed from the TV program P, and thus the program P is partially restored to obtain a program P_1 with higher visual fidelity. However, the user U_2 may pay with a higher price, and thus more watermark is removed through the key K_2 to obtain a program P_2 with much higher visual fidelity, and the user U_3 does not purchase any key, so he can only watch the program P with the lowest visual fidelity. Obviously, compared with the traditional TV encryption technology, the reversible watermarking technique has the advantage of fine-grading control of media fidelity, and we can freely set the minimum fidelity effect, so that free users can also enjoy the program in low visual quality, to attract the audience's attention. However, the encrypted TV programs cannot be completely watched by free users, which is an apt situation to cause loss of potential users.

As can be seen, the substance of the fidelity control for the cover media is to use the reversibility of the reversible watermarking technology to adjust the media fidelity in two opposite ways, to meet different application needs with different multimedia perceptual quality.

1.5.3 STATUS RECOVERY FOR COVER MEDIA

The reversibility of reversible watermarking systems means the recoverability of the signal status. In some applications, it is desirable to record the steps and parameters of signal processing for signal recovery in case of need. Here, the signal recovery is often not due to the accuracy requirements of the cover media, but due to the requirements of further processing of cover media, so such applications may be referred to as status protection during signal processing.

The most common scenario is the occasion that requires performing multiple watermark embedding operations on the same image; if the embedding method is not reversible, then the accumulated distortion caused by embedding every time may seriously affect the visual quality of the image. For example, during the artificial image generation process, for most of the time, the image is in the state to be modified and edited. In this case, it is clearly inappropriate if we embed nonreversible watermarks to protect these process data, because data embedding will bring permanent distortion to the cover data, which will affect the accuracy of subsequent

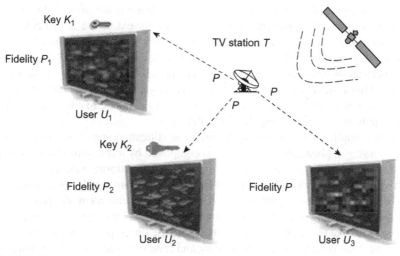

FIGURE 1.20

Visual Quality Scalable Refinement of TV Program.

editing on the image. Furthermore, with the increase in the amount of modification and storage times, the number of embedded watermarks also increases, thus the visual quality of the image is likely damaged due to the accumulated embedding distortion. If we use reversible watermarking schemes to embed data, we can fully restore the status after last editing; thus we can completely avoid the permanent distortion during the embedding process, and we will also be able to avoid affecting the visual quality of the image due to the follow-up processes.

The transfers and transactions of usage rights of digital media products can also adopt the reversible watermarking scheme to restore the original state. For example, a user A wants to transfer a copy of the CD to another user B, but because the content data of CD has been embedded with the user's identity, the corresponding access permissions, and the copy control watermark, direct transfer of the CD from A to B will be viewed as illegal by B's playback device. To proceed with this legal transaction smoothly, the watermark embedding techniques used must be reversible, that is, A allows a legitimate and authorized dealer to erase the identity information in A's CD according to A's key, and then reset B's key and embed the identity and license declarations of B in the CD according to B's key, thus B will be able to legally play this CD. As can be seen, in the case involving the changes of former information embedded in the digital products, reversible watermarking techniques can be conveniently used to achieve the recovery of the original state of the cover media, and can then successfully update the key information and the watermark information.

Another possible application of status recovery is to eliminate the traces of image steganography. After performing data embedding using watermarks, some characteristics introduced by watermarking will be left in different parts of the spatial or transformed image. After using watermarks, these features are often difficult to be removed, so that the image obtained after watermark extraction is difficult to be recovered to the "clean" state in which no watermark is embedded, thus the traces of these watermarking processes can easily be detected by steganalysis. In some cases, permanent retention of such traces will prejudice the security of the whole watermarking system. The reversible watermarking scheme does not have this problem, since it requires complete recovery of the original state of the image, which purges the traces of embedding data completely.

Another application is to restore the image modification operations. In some image processing applications, the process is completed by a few simple adjustments. For example, for gray transform of the image (Log transform, gamma correction, contrast stretching, etc.), histogram modification (histogram equalization, histogram specification, brightness adjustment, etc.), and image enhancement, the goals can be achieved by adjusting a few algorithm parameters. If the image processing operator worries about that the users are not satisfied with the image processing results, he or she can treat the parameters as a watermark and reversibly embed it in the cover image, and in the future restore the image to its original state or its approximate state, thus you do not have to store a lot of original images. If the change is not a simple image processing operation but the local content of the image, then we can adopt a reversible watermarking method to record the changes of such content, and thus we are able to restore the original local content according to this information. This latter application may be suitable for occasions requiring the original image content to be confidential but not to use encryption to attract other people's attention, or the occasion intending to use it as a tool for information deceiving. Here, the modified signal is viewed as an intermediate signal, which can be used to restore the original state of the signal as required at any time.

1.6 MAIN CONTENT OF THIS BOOK

This book focuses on lossless information hiding techniques for images, which are classified into three categories, i.e., spatial domain−based schemes, transform domain−based schemes, and compressed domain−based schemes. For compressed domain−based schemes, we mainly focus on four compressed domains, i.e., VQ, BTC, JPEG, and JPEG2000. Succedent chapters are organized as follows:

Chapter 2 discusses the lossless information techniques in the spatial domain. In this chapter, we first provide an overview the spatial domain−based lossless schemes. Then, we discuss some typical spatial domain lossless information hiding methods, including modulo addition−based schemes, DE-based schemes, histogram modification−based schemes, lossless compression−based schemes, and reversible secret sharing−based schemes.

Chapter 3 discusses transform domain−based lossless schemes. In this chapter, we first introduce some related concepts and requirements for lossless information hiding in transform domains. Then we give a brief overview of transform domain−

based information hiding. Next we introduce two types of transform domain—based lossless information hiding methods, i.e., integer DCT—based schemes and integer DWT—based schemes.

Chapter 4 focuses on the VQ-based lossless information hiding schemes. We first review the schemes related to VQ-based information hiding. Then, we mainly focus on three kinds of VQ-based lossless information hiding schemes, i.e., the modified fast correlation VQ—based scheme, side match VQ—based schemes, and VQ index coding—based schemes.

Chapter 5 discusses the topic of embedding data in BTC compressed images with lossless hiding techniques. First, we introduce the BTC technique. Then, we review the schemes related to BTC-based information hiding. Then, we focus on two topics, i.e., lossless information hiding schemes for BTC compressed grayscale images and for color images. With regard to the schemes in the first topic, we classify them into bitplane flipping—based and mean coding—based schemes. With regard to the schemes in the second topic, we first introduce the problem of BTC compression for color images and then introduce and discuss two algorithms proposed by us.

Chapter 6 first introduces JPEG and JPEG2000 compression techniques in brief, together with the embedding challenges. Then, we introduce the lossless information hiding schemes for JEPG compressed images and JPEG2000 compressed images. For each kind of compressed image, we first overview the existing schemes and then introduce some typical schemes in detail.

REFERENCES

[1] I.J. Cox, Digital Watermarking and Steganography, Morgan Kaufmann, Burlington, MA, USA, 2008.
[2] Y. Linde, A. Buzo, R.M. Gray, An algorithm for vector quantizer design, IEEE Transactions on Communications 28 (1) (1980) 84—95.
[3] E.J. Delp, O.R. Mitchell, Image compression using block truncation coding, IEEE Transactions on Communications 27 (9) (1979) 1335—1342.
[4] M.D. Lema, O.R. Mitchell, Absolute moment block truncation coding and its application to color images, IEEE Transactions on Communications 32 (10) (1984) 1148—1157.
[5] H.Y. Liang, C.H. Cheng, C.Y. Yang, K.F. Zhang, A blind data hiding technique with error correction abilities and a high embedding payload, Journal of Applied Research and Technology 11 (2013) 259—271.
[6] I.J. Cox, M.L. Miller, A review of watermarking and the importance of perceptual modeling, in: Proc. SPIE Electronic Imaging '97, Storage and Retrieval for Image and Video Databases, 3016, 1997.
[7] S. Vukmirović, A. Erdeljan, L. Imre, D. Čapko, Optimal workflow scheduling in critical infrastructure systems with neural networks, Journal of Applied Research and Technology 10 (2) (2012) 114—121.
[8] A. Takahashi, R. Nishimura, Y. Suzuki, Multiple watermarks for stereo audio signals using phase-modulation techniques, IEEE Transactions on Signal Processing 53 (2005) 806—815.

[9]   T.Y. Kim, H. Choi, K. Lee, T. Kim, An asymmetric watermarking system with many embedding watermarks corresponding to one detection watermark, IEEE Signal Processing Tellers 2 (2004) 375–377.

[10] C. Cruz-Ramos, R. Reyes-Reyes, M. Nakano-Miyatake, H. Pérez-Meana, A blind video watermarking scheme robust to frame attacks combined with MPEG2 compression, Journal of Applied Research and Technology 8 (3) (2010) 323–337.

[11] J. Prado-Molina, A. Peralta-Higuera, J.L. Palacio-Prieto, R. Sandoval, Airborne high-resolution digital imaging system, Journal of Applied Research and Technology 4 (1) (2010) 3–23.

[12] V. Licks, R. Jordan, Geometric attacks on image watermarking systems, IEEE Multimedia Magazine 12 (3) (2005) 68–78.

[13] E. Elbaşı, Robust MPEG watermarking in DWT four bands, Journal of Applied Research and Technology 10 (2) (2012) 87–93.

[14] M. Kutter, F. Jordan, F. Bossen, Digital watermarking of color images using amplitude modulation, Journal of Electronic Imaging 7 (2) (1998) 326–332.

[15] W. Lu, H.T. Lu, F.L. Chung, Feature based watermarking using watermark template match, Applied Mathematics Computing 177 (1) (2006) 377–386.

[16] D. Coltuc, P. Bolon, Robust watermarking by histogram specification, Proceedings of IEEE International Conference on Image Processing 2 (1999) 236–239.

[17] J. Fridrich, M. Goljan, Images with self-correcting capabilities, in: Proceedings of IEEE International Conference on Image Processing, Kobe, Japan, October 1999, pp. 792–796.

[18] P.W. Wong, A public key watermark for image verification and authentication, Proceedings of IEEE International Conference on Image Processing vol. I (1998) 455–459.

[19] R.B. Wolfgang, E.J. Delp, A watermark for digital images, Proceedings of IEEE International Conference on Image Processing 3 (1996) 219–222.

[20] E.T. Lin, C.I. Podilchuk, E.J. Delp, Detection of image alterations using semi-fragile watermarks, in: Proceedings of SPIE International Conference on Security and Watermarking of Multimedia Contents 11, vol. 3971, January 23–28, 2000, San Jose, CA, 2000, pp. 152–163.

[21] L. Xie, G.R. Arce, A blind wavelet based digital signature for image authentication, in: Proceedings of EUSIPCO-98-Signal Processing IX Theories and Applications, vol. I, 1998, pp. 21–24.

[22] D. Kundur, D. Hatzinakos, Towards a telltale watermarking technique for tamper-proofing, in: Proceedings of IEEE International Conference on Image Processing, 1998, pp. 409–413.

[23] D. Kundur, D. Hatzinakos, Digital watermarking for telltale tamper proofing and authentication, Proceedings of IEEE 87 (7) (1999) 1167–1180.

[24] G.J. Yu, C.S. Lu, H.Y. Mark Liao, J.P. Sheu, Mean quantization blind watermarking for image authentication, in: Proceedings of IEEE International Conference on Image Processing, Vancouver, Canada, vol. III, 2000, pp. 706–709.

[25] Y. Wang, A. Pearmain, Blind image data hiding based on self reference, Pattern Recognition Letters 25 (15) (2004) 1681–1689.

[26] C.C. Chang, Y.S. Hu, T.C. Lu, A watermarking-based image ownership and tampering authentication scheme, Pattern Recognition Letters 27 (5) (2006) 439–446.

[27] N. Ahmed, T. Natarajan, K.R. Rao, Discrete cosine transform, IEEE Transactions on Computer 32 (1974) 90–93.

[28] D. Kundur, K. Karthik, Video fingerprinting and encryption principles for digital rights management, Proceedings of the IEEE 92 (6) (2004) 918−932.

[29] S. Suthaharan, S.W. Kim, H.K. Lee, S. Sathananthan, Perceptually tuned robust watermarking scheme for digital images, Pattern Recognition Letters 21 (2) (2000) 145−149.

[30] S. Maity, M. Kundu, T. Das, Robust SS watermarking with improved capacity, Pattern Recognition Letters 28 (3) (2007) 350−356.

[31] K.J.R. Liu, W. Trappe, Z.J. Wang, M. Wu, Collusion-resistant fingerprinting for multimedia, IEEE Signal Processing Magazine 21 (2004) 15−27.

[32] K.J.R. Liu, W. Trappe, Z.J. Wang, M. Wu, H. Zhao, Multimedia fingerprinting forensics for traitor tracing, in: EURASIP Book Series on Signal Processing and Communication, vol. 4, Hindawi Publishing Corporation, 2005.

[33] K.J.R. Liu, Z.J. Wang, M. Wu, H. Zhao, Forensic analysis of nonlinear collusion attacks for multimedia fingerprinting, IEEE Transactions on Image Processing 14 (5) (2005) 646−661.

[34] S. He, M. Wu, Joint coding and embedding techniques for multimedia fingerprinting, IEEE Transactions on Information Forensics and Security 1 (2) (2006) 231−247.

[35] J. Goodwin, G. Chetty, Blind video tamper detection based on fusion of source features, in: Proceedings of 2011 International Conference Digital Image Computing: Techniques and Applications (DICTA), 2011, pp. 608−613.

[36] I.J. Cox, J. Kilian, F.T. Leighton, T.G. Shamoon, Secure spread spectrum watermarking for multimedia, IEEE Transactions on Image Processing 6 (12) (1997) 1673−1687.

[37] A. Mishra, A. Goel, R. Singh, G. Chetty, L. Singh, A novel image watermarking scheme using extreme learning machine, in: Proceedings of 2012 International Joint Conference on Neural Networks (IJCNN), 2012, pp. 10−15.

[38] M. Ammar, P. Judge, WHIM: watermarking multicast video with a hierarchy of intermediaries, in: Proceedings of 10th International Workshop on Network and Operating Systems Support for Digital Audio and Video (NOSSDAV'00), Chapel Hill, USA, 2000, pp. pp.699−712.

[39] R. Anderson, C. Manifavas, Chameleon-a new kind of stream cipher, in: E. Biham (Ed.), Lecture Notes in Computer Science, Fast Software Encryption, Springer-Verlag, Heidelberg, Germany, 1997, pp. 107−113.

[40] A. Adelsbach, U. Huber, A.R. Sadeghi, Fingercasting-joint fingerprinting and decryption of broadcast messages, in: Proceedings of 11th Australasian Conference Information Security Privacy, vol. 4058, 2006, pp. 136−147.

[41] S. Katzenbeisser, B. Skoric, M. Celik, A.R. Sadeghi, Combining Tardos fingerprinting codes and fingercasting information hiding, in: T. Furon, F. Cayre, et al. (Eds.), Lecture Notes in Computer Science, vol. 4567, Springer, Berlin/Heidelber, Germany, 2007, pp. 294−310.

[42] P. Alvarez, Using extended file information (EXIF) file headers in digital evidence analysis, International Journal of Digital Evidence, Economic Crime Institute (ECI) 2 (3) (2004) 1−5.

[43] V.M. Potdar, S. Han, E. Chang, Fingerprinted secret sharing steganography for robustness against image cropping attacks, in: Proceedings of IEEE Third International Conference on Industrial Informatics (INDIN), Perth, Australia, August 10−12, 2005, pp. 717−724.

[44] M.H. Shirali-Shahreza, M. Shirali-Shahreza, A new approach to Persian/Arabic text steganography, in: Proceedings of Fifth IEEE/ACIS International Conference on

Computer and Information Science (ICIS-COMSAR 2006), July 10–12, 2006, pp. 310–315.

[45] K.H. Jung, K.Y. Yoo, Data hiding method using image interpolation, Computer Standards and Interfaces 31 (2) (2009) 465–470.

[46] X. Li, J. Wang, A steganographic method based upon JPEG and particle swarm optimization algorithm, Information Sciences 177 (15) (2007) 3099–3109.

[47] K.B. Raja, C.R. Chowdary, K.R. Venugopal, L.M. Patnaik, A secure image steganography using LSB, DCT and compression techniques on raw images, in: Proceedings of IEEE 3rd International Conference on Intelligent Sensing and Information Processing, ICISIP'05, Bangalore, India, December 14–17, 2005, pp. 170–176.

[48] N.F. Johnson, S. Jajodia, Exploring steganography: seeing the unseen, IEEE Computer 31 (2) (1998) 26–34.

[49] R.T. McKeon, Strange Fourier steganography in movies, in: Proceedings of the IEEE International Conference on Electro/Information Technology (EIT), May 17–20, 2007, pp. 178–182.

[50] A.A. Abdelwahab, L.A. Hassan, A discrete wavelet transform based technique for image data hiding, in: Proceedings of 25th National Radio Science Conference, NRSC 2008, Egypt, March 18–20, 2008, pp. 1–9.

[51] N. Provos, P. Honeyman, Hide and seek: an introduction to steganography, IEEE Security and Privacy 1 (3) (2003) 32–44.

[52] P. Sallee, Model-based steganography, in: Proceedings of the Second International Workshop on Digital Watermarking, Seoul, Korea, October 20–22, 2003, Lecture Notes in Computer Science, vol. 2939, 2003, pp. 254–260.

[53] M. Kharrazi, H.T. Sencar, N. Memon, Performance study of common image steganography and steganalysis techniques, Journal of Electrical Imaging 15 (4) (2006) 1–16.

[54] R. Tzschoppe, R. Baum, J. Huber, A. Kaup, Steganographic system based on higher-order statistics, in: Proceedings of SPIE, Security and Watermarking of Multimedia Contents V. Santa Clara, California, USA vol. 5020, 2003, pp. 156–166.

[55] R. Caldelli, F. Filippini, R. Becarelli, Reversible watermarking techniques: an overview and a classification, EURASIP Journal of Information Security 2010 (2010) 1–19.

[56] J. Feng, I. Lin, C. Tsai, Y. Chu, Reversible watermarking: current status and key issues, International Journal of Network Security 2 (3) (2006) 161–170.

[57] W. Pan, G. Coatrieux, J. Montagner, N. Cuppens, F. Cuppens, C. Roux, Comparison of some reversible watermarking methods in application to medical images, in: International Conference of the IEEE Engineering in Medicine and Biology Society, Minneapolis, USA, 2009, pp. 2172–2175.

[58] C.W. Honsinger, P.W. Jones, M. Rabbani, J.C. Stoffel, Lossless recovery of an original image containing embedded data, 2001. U.S. Patent No. 6,278,791.

[59] B. Macq, Lossless multiresolution transform for image authenticating watermarking, in: Proc. EUSIPCO, 2000, pp. 533–536.

[60] J. Fridrich, M. Goljan, R. Du, Invertible authentication, in: Proceedings of the SPIE Security and Watermarking of Multimedia Content, San Jose, USA, 2001, pp. 197–208.

[61] J. Fridrich, M. Goljan, R. Du, Lossless data embedding-new paradigm in digital watermarking, EURASIP Journal on Advances in Signal Processing 2 (2002) 185–196.

[62] D. Zheng, Y. Liu, J. Zhao, A. El Saddik, A survey of RST invariant image watermarking algorithms, ACM Computing Surveys 39 (2) (2007). Article 5.

[63] J.M. Guo, Watermarking in dithered halftone images with embeddable cells selection and inverse halftoning, Signal Processing 88 (6) (2008) 1496–1510.

[64] J.M. Guo, J.J. Tsai, Reversible data hiding in low complexity and high quality compression scheme, Digital Signal Processing 22 (5) (2012) 776–785.

[65] B. Yang, M. Schmucker, W. Funk, C. Busch, S. Sun, Integer DCT-based reversible watermarking for images using companding technique, in: E.J. Delp III, P.W. Wong (Eds.), Proceedings of the SPIE, Security, Steganography, and Watermarking of Multimedia Contents VI, 2004, pp. 405–415.

[66] M.U. Celik, G. Sharma, A.M. Tekalp, E. Saber, Lossless generalized-LSB data embedding, IEEE Transactions on Image Processing 14 (2) (2005) 253–266.

[67] G. Xuan, C. Yang, Y. Zhen, Y.Q. Shi, Z. Ni, Reversible data hiding using integer wavelet transform and companding technique, in: Lecture Notes in Computer Science, Digital Watermarking, vol. 3304, Springer, Berlin, Heidelberg, 2005, pp. 115–124.

[68] M. Arsalan, S.A. Malik, A. Khan, Intelligent reversible watermarking in integer wavelet domain for medical images, Journal of System and Software 85 (4) (2012) 883–894.

[69] C. De Vleeschouwer, J.E. Delaigle, B. Macq, Circular interpretation of histogram for reversible watermarking, in: IEEE Fourth Workshop on Multimedia Signal Processing, 2001, pp. 345–350.

[70] Z. Ni, Y. Shi, N. Ansari, W. Su, Reversible data hiding, IEEE Transactions on Circuits System for Video Technology 16 (3) (2006) 354–362.

[71] C.C. Lin, W.-L. Tai, C.-C. Chang, Multilevel reversible data hiding based on histogram modification of difference images, Pattern Recognition 41 (12) (2008) 3582–3591.

[72] Z. Ni, Y.Q. Shi, N. Ansari, W. Su, Q. Sun, X. Lin, Robust lossless image data hiding designed for semi-fragile image authentication, IEEE Transactions on Circuits System 18 (4) (2008) 497–509.

[73] X. Gao, L. An, X. Li, D. Tao, Reversibility improved lossless data hiding, Signal Processing 89 (10) (2009) 2053–2065.

[74] P. Tsai, Y.-C. Hu, H.-L. Yeh, Reversible image hiding scheme using predictive coding and histogram shifting, Signal Processing 89 (6) (2009) 1129–1143.

[75] K.-S. Kim, M.-J. Lee, H.-Y. Lee, H.-K. Lee, Reversible data hiding exploiting spatial correlation between sub-sampled images, Pattern Recognition 42 (11) (2009) 3083–3096.

[76] Kamran, A. Khan, S.A. Malik, A high capacity reversible watermarking approach for authenticating images: exploiting down-sampling, histogram processing, and block selection, Information Sciences 256 (2014) 162–183.

[77] Y. Cheung, S. Member, H. Wu, S. Member, A sequential quantization strategy for data embedding and integrity verification, IEEE Transactions on Circuits Systems for Video Technology 17 (8) (2007) 1007–1016.

[78] M.J. Saberian, M.A. Akhaee, F. Marvasti, An invertible quantization based watermarking approach, in: IEEE International Conference on Acoustics, Speech and Signal Processing, Las Vegas, USA, 2008, pp. 1677–1680.

[79] J. Lee, Y. Chiou, J. Guo, S. Member, Reversible data hiding based on histogram modification of SMVQ indices, IEEE Transactions on Information Forensics and Security 5 (4) (2010) 638–648.

[80] L.T. Ko, J.E. Chen, Y.S. Shieh, H.C. Hsin, T.Y. Sung, Nested quantization index modulation for reversible watermarking and its application to healthcare information management systems, Computational and Mathematical Methods 2012 (2012) 1–8.

[81] L.T. Ko, J.E. Chen, Y.S. Shieh, M. Scalia, T.Y. Sung, A novel fractional discrete cosine transform based reversible watermarking for healthcare information management systems, Mathematical Problems in Engineering 2012 (2012) 1–17.

[82] J. Tian, Reversible data embedding using a difference expansion, IEEE Transactions on Circuits Systems 13 (8) (2003) 890–896.

[83] D. Coltuc, J. Chassery, Very fast watermarking by reversible contrast mapping, IEEE Signal Processing Letters 14 (4) (2007) 255–258.

[84] D.M. Thodi, J.J. Rodriguez, Prediction-error based reversible watermarking, in: International Conference on Image Processing, 2004, pp. 1549–1552.

[85] L. Luo, Z. Chen, M. Chen, X. Zeng, Z. Xiong, Reversible image watermarking using interpolation technique, IEEE Transactions on Information Forensics and Security 5 (1) (2010) 187–193.

[86] C. De Vleeschouwer, J. Delaigle, B. Macq, Circular interpretation of bijective transformmions in lossless watermarking for media asset management, IEEE Transactions on Multimedia 5 (1) (2003) 97–105.

[87] Z. Ni, Y. Shi, N. Ansari, et al., Robust lossless image data hiding, in: Proceeding of IEEE International Conference on Multimedia and Expo, 3, 2004, pp. 2199–2202.

[88] D. Zou, Y. Shi, Z. Ni, A semi-fragile lossless digital watermarking scheme based on integer wavelet transform, in: Proceedings of IEEE 6th Workshop Multimedia Signal Processing, 2004, pp. 195–198.

[89] D. Zou, Y. Shi, Z. Ni, et al., A semi-fragile lossless digital watermarking scheme based on integer wavelet transform, IEEE Transcations on Circuits Systems for Video Technology 16 (10) (2006) 1294–1300.

Lossless Information Hiding in Images on the Spatial Domain

2.1 OVERVIEW OF SPATIAL DOMAIN—BASED INFORMATION HIDING

At present, the vast majority of reversible information hiding algorithms are focused on the spatial domain, and most algorithms select an image as the carrier signal. Pixels are chosen for the hidden information carrier mainly because the image pixel value is an integer in a certain range without any error. Thus, the spatial domain—based algorithms are relatively abundant and early developed. Currently, researchers have devised a number of spatial domain lossless information hiding methods, which are classified from different angles. Depending on the embedding model, these methods can be divided into four categories, i.e., modulo addition—based, compression-based, difference expansion (DE)—based and histogram-based approaches.

In the early years, modulo addition—based methods were first put forward, which use modulo 256 operations to achieve lossless watermark embedding [1—4]. However, the modulo operation brings the pixel flipping problem, which makes such methods result in a watermarked image with salt-and-pepper noise.

Subsequently, Fridrich et al. [5,6] proposed a reversible authentication framework, which embeds the watermark into the host image through compressing bit-planes. When compressed bit-planes are too many, although the capacity has increased, the visual quality of the watermarked image will drop dramatically. To this end, Celik et al. [7,8] developed this idea, and proposed a method based on generalized least significant bit (G-LSB) plane compression, in pursuit of a better trade-off between the capacity and the quality of the watermark image. Despite the fact that the compression-based method overcomes the salt-and-pepper noise in the watermarked image, its performance is still affected by the compression efficiency largely.

To this end, Tian and Tiara [9,10] proposed a method based on DE; it divides the pixels of the host image into two types, i.e., expandable and nonexpandable pixels, and uses the DE and least significant bit (LSB) replacing manners for embedding. To mark the type of the pixel pair, the location map after compression together with the watermark is embedded into the host image, which reduces the net capacity to some extent. Alattar et al. [11] used the pixel vector instead of the pixel pair to improve the performance of Tian's method. Kamstra et al. [12] used a low-pass image to predict the expandable difference, which greatly reduced the space of the location map. Subsequently, Kim et al. [13] further simplified the location map design and introduced a new definition of expandability. Thodi and Rodriguez [14] improved the capacity of Tian's method by expanding the prediction error. But the compressibility of the location map is still one of the factors that affect the performance of this method. Therefore, Hu et al. [15] proposed a new idea to utilize the sparse location map to improve the capacity. Wang et al. [16] applied the DE technique to content protection of two-dimensional vector maps. Thereafter, still many researchers have proposed new methods that are based on DE [17–21].

At the same time, the histogram-based methods were also proposed. Depending on whether the transmission process considers the impact of covert attacks or not, such methods can be divided into two types, i.e., fragile and robust methods. Ni et al. [22] first proposed the embedding model based on histogram shifting, whose core idea is to find a pair of peak and zero points in the histogram of the host image and to perform watermark embedding by shifting the neighboring histogram column of the peak point forward the zero histogram column. Because the peak point and the zero position information needs to be transmitted to the receiver to extract the watermark and recover the host image, Hwang et al. [23] designed the location map and proposed a two-way iterative embedding method. Then, Kuo et al. [24] further improved the location map. Fallahpour [25] and Tai et al. [26], respectively, utilized the gradient adjustable prediction error histogram and difference histogram to improve the performance.

Unlike the fragile methods that emphasize the capacity and visual quality of the watermarked image, robust lossless information hiding approaches focus on the robustness under the covert attack. De Vleeschouwer presented the first robust lossless information hiding scheme [27,28], which first divides the host image into nonoverlapping blocks of the same size, randomly divides the pixels of each block into two subregions of the same size, maps their histograms onto the circle, and finally embeds the watermark by rotating the centroid vectors of the two regions. Experiments show that the method is robust to JPEG compression, but due to the modulo 256 addition operation, which is used to avoid overflow pixels, there are a large number of salt-and-pepper noisy pixels in the watermarked image, greatly reducing the visual quality of the watermarked image. To solve this problem, Ni et al. [29–32] proposed an idea to embed information by modifying the statistical features of the image with constraints according to the histogram distribution of the host image. Although they overcome the salt-and-pepper noise and improve the visual quality of the watermarked image, due to the use of the error correction code, it faces the problems of low capacity, unreliable robustness, and so on. Then, Zeng et al. [33] further enhanced the performance of the method in [29] by introducing dual thresholds and a new embedding model.

So far, the research on lossless information hiding is still in full swing, and new research results continue to emerge [34–36]. Nevertheless, the actual needs of the application environment, improvement in the performance of lossless information hiding methods, and enhancement of their applicability are still challenges that the information hiding field faces.

2.2 MODULO ADDITION–BASED SCHEME

The modulo addition–based robust reversible watermarking algorithm first appeared in the patent of Eastman Kodak Company applied by Honsinger et al. [4]; then Fridrich et al. [6] extended this idea to the DCT transform domain. The modulo addition idea can achieve reversibility, because the nonadaptive watermark signal can be directly subtracted from the pixel value without any loss, as long as we know the possible embedded watermark pattern and the pixel value overflow problem does not appear, and this modulo addition operation is completely reversible. In Refs. [4,6], this modulo addition mode is used for embedding authentication information into the carrier media. The watermark embedding and authentication process can be shown in Fig. 2.1 as follows:

2.2.1 EMBEDDING PROCESS

The embedding process can be described as follows:

Step 1: Let X be the original image to be authenticated; compute its hash value $H(X)$.

Step 2: Select an addition nonadaptive robust watermarking technique, and generate a watermark pattern W through a secret key K making the payload of W be $H(X)$, where the watermark pattern W is the function of the secret key K and the payload $H(X)$, i.e., $W = W(K, H(X))$.

Step 3: Using the modulo addition operation $\oplus$, add the watermark pattern W to X, generating the image to be generated, i.e., $X_W = X \oplus \alpha W$, where α is the embedding strength coefficient.

2.2.2 AUTHENTICATION PROCESS

Step 1: Extract the watermark bit string H'(payload) from X_W.

Step 2: Generate the watermark pattern $W' = W(K, H')$ through the secret key K and the extracted bit string H'.

Step 3: Subtract W' from X_W, obtaining $X' = X_W - \alpha W'$.

Step 4: Compute the hash value $H(X')$, and compare it with the preextracted hash value H'. If they coincide, the image is authentic, that is, X' is the original image without modification. Otherwise, it is nonauthentic, i.e., the cover image is subject to modification.

2.2.3 EXPLANATION OF THE MODULO ADDITION OPERATION

In the aforementioned watermark embedding and authentication processes, the modulo addition operation is defined as follows:

$$i \oplus k = C \lfloor i/C \rfloor + \mod(i + k, C) \qquad (2.1)$$

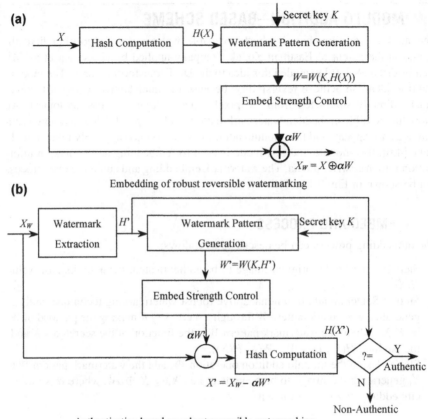

(a)

Embedding of robust reversible watermarking

(b)

Authentication based on robust reversible watermarking

FIGURE 2.1

(a) Robust reversible watermark embedding process and (b) corresponding authentication process.

where i and k are two integers involved in the addition modulo operation, $\lfloor \cdot \rfloor$ is the rounding operation, C is the modulo, and $\mathrm{mod}(.,.)$ is the operation to get the remainder. Through this modulo addition operation, if $i + k$ is just integer times the modulo C, then $\mathrm{mod}(i + k, C) = 0$, thus the absolute difference D between the modulo addition result $i \oplus k = C\lfloor i/C \rfloor$ and $i + k$ is just one modulo C, i.e.,

$$D = |i + k - C\lfloor i/C \rfloor| = |C(\lfloor i/C \rfloor \pm 1) - C\lfloor i/C \rfloor| = C \qquad (2.2)$$

For example, if $C = 16$, assume that the dynamic range of i is $[0,255]$ and $k = 1$, then we have the modulo addition result $0 \to 1$, $1 \to 2$, ..., $15 \to 0$, $16 \to 17$, $17 \to 18$, ..., $31 \to 16$, and so on. Obviously, the smaller the modulo C is, the less distortion this operation introduces near the boundary (i.e., the case that $i + k$ is just integer times C). However, on the other hand, the smaller the modulo C is, the more distorted pixels there are in the whole dynamic range (e.g., the dynamic range of an 8-bit gray-scale image is [0,255]). For a given image, to reduce the distortion introduced by the modulo addition operation, it is required to choose C according to concrete conditions: if k is small and the number of pixels near the boundary (the pixel value near 0 or 255) is small, then we can use a big C, e.g., 256; otherwise, a small value of C should be adopted to avoid severe visual distortion like the salt-and-pepper noise. In addition, note that in the first step of authentication, the method used in watermark extraction is the correlation operation with the noise sequence, thus the robustness of the watermark extraction operation can be guaranteed.

2.3 DIFFERENCE EXPANSION—BASED SCHEMES
2.3.1 TIAN'S SCHEME

The DE technique for reversible data hiding was first proposed by Tian and Tiara [9,10]. It is a high-capacity approach based on expanding the pixel difference value between neighboring pixels. His method allows one bit to be embedded in every pair of pixels. Given a pair of 256-grayscale image pixel values (x, y), $0 \leq x, y \leq 255$, their integer average c and difference d are computed as

$$c = \left\lfloor \frac{x+y}{2} \right\rfloor, d = x - y \qquad (2.3)$$

where $\lfloor z \rfloor$ denotes the floor function that seeks the greatest integer less than or equal to z. The inverse transform of Eq. (2.3) is

$$x = c + \left\lfloor \frac{d+1}{2} \right\rfloor, y = c - \left\lfloor \frac{d}{2} \right\rfloor \qquad (2.4)$$

The reversible transforms denoted by Eqs. (2.3) and (2.4) are called the integer Haar wavelet transform, or the S transform. Tian and Tiara [9,10] shifted d to the left one unit and appended the watermarking bit b in LSB according to the following rule:

$$d' = 2d + b \qquad (2.5)$$

This reversible data-embedding operation given in Eq. (2.5) is called DE. To prevent overflow and underflow problems, that is, to restrict x and y in the range of [0,255], d must satisfy the condition in Eq. (2.6). Here the inverse transform is computed as

$$|d| \leq \min(2 \cdot (255 - c), 2c + 1) \qquad (2.6)$$

The authors classify difference values into four disjoint sets according to the following definitions.

1. The first set, EZ, contains all the expandable $d = 0$ and the expandable $d = -1$.
2. The second set, EN, contains all the expandable $d \notin$ EZ.

3. The third set, CN, contains all the changeable d, which are not in EZ$\cup$EN.
4. The fourth set, NC, contains the rest of d, which are not able to be changed.

Definition 2.1: A difference value d is expandable under the integer average value c if $|2d + b| \leq \min(2 \cdot (255 - c), 2c + 1)$ for both $b = 0$ and 1.

Definition 2.2: A difference value d is changeable under the integer average value c if $|2 \cdot \lfloor \frac{d}{2} \rfloor + b| \leq \min(2 \cdot (255 - c), 2c + 1)$ for both $b = 0$ and $b = 1$.

From Definitions 2.1 and 2.2, it can be proved that:

1. A changeable difference value d remains changeable even after modifying its LSB.
2. An expandable difference value d is changeable.
3. After DE, the expanded difference value d' is changeable.
4. If $d = 0$ or -1, the conditions for expandable and changeable are equivalent.

At the receiving end, to extract embedding data and restore the original image, the expandable, changeable, and nonchangeable sets must be identified. Since an expanded difference value via the DE d' and a changeable difference value with its modified LSB are both changeable after embedding, which is mentioned earlier. All difference values in NC (not changeable) can be unambiguously identified during extraction using the condition in Eq. (2.6). It is necessary to know which difference value has been selected for the DE. That is, some additional information (AI) needs to be used to further identify all the expanded difference values via the DE from all the changeable values. The authors create a binary location map, which contains the location information of all selected expandable difference values, as an overhead for later reconstruction of the original image.

To achieve the payload capacity limit, they select all expandable differences that are in the range of $[-255, 255]$ for the DE, but the peak signal-to-noise ratio (PSNR) value is generally very low and the visual quality degradation of the watermarked image is almost perceptible. To build a balance between the PSNR value and payload size, they present two selection methods to reduce the payload size, which is less than the payload capacity limit, and consequently improve the PSNR value. The first method is described as follows.

They select d with small magnitudes for the DE. That is, they choose a threshold value T, $d \in [-T, T]$, and partition EN into EN_1 and EN_2. Using $EN_1 = \{d \in EN: |d| \leq T\}$, $EN_2 = \{d \in EN: |d| > T\}$. For a payload whose size is equal to the payload capacity limit $EN_1 = EN$, $EN_2 = \Phi$. For a d in EZ$\cup EN_1$, a value of "1" is assigned in the location map; for a value of d in $EN_2 \cup CN \cup NC$, a value of "0" is assigned. Hence a value of "1" indicates the selected expandable difference values.

The embedding process is generalized as follows. After creating the location map, it is compressed without loss using a JBIG2 compression or an arithmetic compression coding to form a bitstream L. For every d in $EN_2 \cup CN$, LSB(d) is stored in a bitstream C. The payload P, including an authentication hash of the original image (for example, MD5) and the bitstreams L and C are concatenated to form the final binary bitstream B. They then embed B into LSBs of one bit left-shifted versions of difference values in EZ∪EN$_1$ and also into LSBs of difference values in EN$_2$∪CN. In the embedding process, the difference values in NC is kept intact. The data embedding by replacement is illustrated in Table 2.1. After all bits in B are embedded, they then apply the inverse transform in Eq. (2.4) to obtain the embedded image.

In the DE method, data embedding and extraction rely on expendable and changeable differences. The expandable differences provide space for data embedding and the changeable differences are used to guarantee blind data extraction. All difference values in the difference image are classified into three categories: expandable, changeable but nonexpandable, and nonchangeable. For a pure payload (the secret bits to be hidden), a number of expandable differences should be selected and their locations should be stored into a binary-type location map, which can be losslessly compressed by run-length coding. All the LSBs of changeable but nonexpandable differences are recorded as an original bitstream. The compressed location map, the original bitstream, and the pure payload are embedded into the difference image together.

The secret data extraction process is simple. The LSBs of all changeable differences in the image compose a bitstream, from which we can extract the location map, the original bitstream, and the pure payload. To restore the image, all previous expandable differences divide by two integrally. The LSBs of all changeable but not expandable differences are reset with the original bitstream. The extraction process starts by calculating the average value c' and the difference value d' of pixel pairs (x', y') by scanning the watermarked image in the same order used during embedding. Referring to Table 2.1, they divide pixel pairs into two sets CH (changeable) and NC (not changeable) using the condition given in Eq. (2.6). They extracts all LSBs of d' for each pair in CH to form a bitstream B, which is identical to that formed during embedding. The extracted bitstream B is decompressed to restore the location map by a JBIG2 decoder. Hence, all expanded pixel pairs after the DE in CH are identified. By identifying an end of message symbol at its end for a JBIG2, the bitstream C including the original LSBs of the changeable difference in EN$_2$∪CN and the payload is retrieved. The original values of differences are restored as follows. For d' in EZ∪EN$_1$, they restore the original values of d' as follows:

$$d = \left\lfloor \frac{d'}{2} \right\rfloor \tag{2.7}$$

Table 2.1 Embedding on Difference Values

Category	Original Set	Original Value	Location Map Value	New Value	New Set
Changeable	EZ or EN$_1$	D	1	$2d + b$	CH
	EN$_2$ or CN	D	0	$2 \cdot \left\lfloor \frac{d}{2} \right\rfloor + b$	
Nonchangeable	NC	D	0	d	NC

For d' in $EN_2 \cup CN$, they restore the original values of according to Eq. (2.8)

$$d = 2 \times \left\lfloor \frac{d'}{2} \right\rfloor + b_1 \quad b_1 \in C \tag{2.8}$$

Finally, they apply the inverse transform given in Eq. (2.4) to retrieve the original image. They then compare the retrieved authentication hash with the hash function of the restored image. If the two hash functions match exactly, the image content is authentic and the restored image is exactly the same as the original image.

Tian implemented the DE method and tested it on various standard grayscale images. Tian also implemented the regular-singular (RS) lossless data-embedding method in Ref. [37] and the lossless G-LSB data-embedding method in Ref. [7] to compare the results among the three methods using 512×512, 8 bits per pixel (bpp) grayscale Lena. From the comparison results described in Ref. [38], Tian achieves the highest embedding capacity, while keeping the lowest distortion. Except for images with many smooth regions, the payload capacity limit of the G-LSB method does not exceed 1 bpp. The DE method could easily embed more than 1 bpp. The payload capacity limit of the RS method is lower than those of the G-LSB and DE methods. By embedding a payload of the same bit length, the embedded Lena image by the DE method is about 2−3 dB higher than those obtained by the G-LSB and RS methods.

2.3.2 ALATTER'S SCHEME

Alatter [11] presented a high-capacity, data hiding algorithm. The proposed algorithm is based on a generalized, reversible, integer transform (GRIT), which calculates the average and pairwise differences between the elements of a vector extracted from the pixels of the image. Several conditions are derived and used in selecting the appropriate difference values. Either the watermark bits are embedded into the LSBs of selected differences or alternatively the LSBs are 1 bit left-shifted versions of selected differences. Derived conditions can identify which difference is selected after embedding to ensure that the new vector computed from the average and embedded difference has grayscale values. To ensure the reversibility, the locations of shifted differences and the original LSBs must be embedded before embedding the payload. The proposed algorithm can embed $N-1$ bits in every vector with a size of $N \times 1$. The proposed algorithm is based on a GRIT. We will now introduce the theorem for GRIT.

Theorem 2.1: For $Du = [a, d_1, d_2, ..., d_{N-1}]^T$, if $v = \lfloor Du \rfloor$, then $u = \lceil D^{-1} \lfloor v \rfloor \rceil$. v and u form a GRIT pair, where D is an $N \times N$ full-rank matrix with an inverse D^{-1}, u is an $N \times 1$ integer column vector, a is the weighted average value of the elements of u, and $d_1, d_2, ..., d_{N-1}$ are the independent pairwise differences between the elements of u. Here, $\lceil . \rceil$ and $\lfloor . \rfloor$, respectively, indicate round up or down to the nearest integer.

The proof is given by Alatter [11]. Alatter generalized the algorithm based on GRIT to vectors of length more than 3. Alatter uses an example in which $N = 4$. One possible value of D is given by

$$D = \begin{bmatrix} a_0/c & a_1/c & a_2/c & a_3/c \\ -1 & 1 & 0 & 0 \\ 0 & -1 & 1 & 0 \\ 0 & 0 & -1 & 1 \end{bmatrix} \tag{2.9}$$

where $c = a_0 + a_1 + a_2 + a_3$ and,

$$D = \begin{bmatrix} 1 & -(c-a_0)/c & -(a_2+a_3)/c & -a_3/c \\ 1 & a_0/c & -(a_2+a_3)/c & -a_3/c \\ 1 & a_0/c & (a_0+a_1)/c & -a_3/c \\ 1 & a_0/c & (a_0+a_1)/c & (c-a_3)/c \end{bmatrix} \tag{2.10}$$

Using this theorem, for the vector $q = (u_0, u_1, u_2, u_3)$, the appropriate GRIT may be defined as

$$\begin{cases} v_0 = \left\lfloor \dfrac{a_0 u_0 + a_1 u_1 + a_2 u_2 + a_3 u_3}{a_0 + a_1 + a_2 + a_3} \right\rfloor \\ v_1 = u_1 - u_0 \\ v_2 = u_2 - u_1 \\ v_3 = u_3 - u_2 \end{cases} \tag{2.11}$$

$$\begin{cases} u_0 = v_0 - \left\lfloor \dfrac{(a_0+a_1+a_2)v_1 + (a_2+a_3)v_2 + a_3 v_3}{a_0 + a_1 + a_2 + a_3} \right\rfloor \\ u_1 = v_1 + u_0 \\ u_2 = v_2 + u_1 \\ u_3 = v_3 + u_2 \end{cases} \tag{2.12}$$

To describe the reversible algorithm in detail and unambiguously, we choose quads to introduce the embedding and detection processes. A quad is a 1×4 vector formed from four pixel values chosen from four different locations each having the same component according to a predetermined order. Each quad is assembled from 2×2 adjacent pixel values in Alatter's algorithm (Fig. 2.2). Each pixel quad of the original image is classified into three groups according to the following definitions.

1. The first group, S_1 contains all expandable quads having $v_1 \leq T_1$, $v_2 \leq T_2$, and $v_3 \leq T_3$. Here, T_1, T_2, and T_3 are predefined thresholds.
2. The second group, S_2, contains all changeable pairs that are not in S_1.
3. The third group, S_3, contains the rest of the pairs, and these are not changeable.

Definition 2.3: The quad $q = (u_0, u_1, u_2, u_3)$ is said to be expandable if for all values of b_1, b_2, and $b_3 \in \{0, 1\}$.

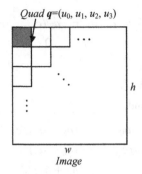

Quad q=(u₀, u₁, u₂, u₃)

h

w
Image

FIGURE 2.2

Quads in an image.

$$0 \le v'_0 - \left\lfloor \frac{(a_0 + a_1 + a_2)v'_1 + (a_2 + a_3)v'_2 + a_3 v'_3}{a_0 + a_1 + a_2 + a_3} \right\rfloor \le 255$$

$$0 \le v'_1 + u_0 \le 255$$
$$0 \le v'_2 + u_1 \le 255 \qquad (2.13)$$
$$0 \le v'_3 + u_2 \le 255$$

where

$$v'_1 = 2v_1 + b_1$$
$$v'_2 = 2v_2 + b_2 \qquad (2.14)$$
$$v'_3 = 2v_3 + b_3$$

Definition 2.4: The quad $q = (u_0, u_1, u_2, u_3)$ is said to be changeable if for all values of b_1, b_2, and $b_3 \in \{0, 1\}$, v'_1, v'_2, and v'_3 are given by Eq. (2.15) and satisfy Eq. (2.13). Here

$$v'_1 = 2 \times \left\lfloor \frac{v_1}{2} \right\rfloor + b_1, v'_2 = 2 \times \left\lfloor \frac{v_2}{2} \right\rfloor + b_2, v'_3 = 2 \times \left\lfloor \frac{v_3}{2} \right\rfloor + b_3 \qquad (2.15)$$

Each of v_1, v_2, and v_3 in S_1 was shifted left by 1 bit to form v'_1, v'_2, and v'_3. Watermark bits b_1, b_2, and b_3 are, respectively, appended in the LSBs of v'_1, v'_2, and v'_3. The conditions in Eq. (2.13) ensure that the new quad is computed using v'_0, v'_1, v'_2, and v'_3 according to the inverse transform with grayscale values in [0, 255]. v_1, v_2, and v_3 in S_2 are the same as v'_1, v'_2, and v'_3 with replaced LSBs with watermark bits. A changeable quad after LSB has been modified is still changeable. An expandable quad is also changeable.

The locations of all the quads in S_1 are indicated by 1's in a binary location map. The JBIG algorithm is used to compress the map to produce the bitstream B_1. The LSBs of v_1, v_2, and v_3 of all the quads in S_2 are now extracted into a bitstream B_2. The payload P, including the authentication hash (MD5) of original image, bitstream B_1

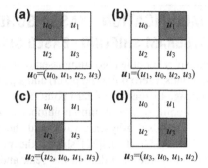

FIGURE 2.3

Quads configuration in an image.

and B_2, are concatenated to form B. Finally, the bitstream B is embedded into LSBs of one-bit left-shifted versions of difference values in S_1. For any quad in S_2, a bit is embedded in the difference by replacing the LSB.

Since the embedding process is completely reversible, the algorithm can be applied to the image recursively to embed more data. However, the difference between the original image and the embedded image increases with every application of the algorithm. Fig. 2.3 depicts four different structures that can be used to permute a quad that is a 1×4 vector.

The retrieval process starts by identifying all the changeable quads in the embedded image using the conditions in Eq. (2.14). The LSBs of the difference values of all the changeable quads are collected to form a bitstream B. The JBIG algorithm is then used to decompress bitstream B to retrieve the location map. By use of the location map, all expandable quads are separated from the changeable quads. The original image can be restored by dividing each difference in the expandable quads by 2 and replacing the LSBs of each difference in the changeable quads with the retrieved original bits. The retrieved authentication hash is compared with the hash function of the restored image. If they match exactly, the image content is authentic and the restored image will be exactly the same as the original image.

Alatter tested the quad-based algorithm on several test images, i.e., Fruits, Lena, and Baboon. The experimental results indicate that the achievable embedding capacity depends on the nature of the image. The algorithm performs much better with Fruits and Lena than with Baboon. It performs slightly better with Fruits than with Lena. With Fruits, the algorithm is able to embed 982 kB (3.74 bits/pixel) with an image quality of 28.42 dB. It is also able to embed 296 kB (0.77 bits/pixel) with a high image quality of 39.05 dB. With Baboon the algorithm is able to embed 808 kB (3.08 bits/pixel) at 20.18 dB and 130 kB (0.50 bits/pixel) at 32.62 dB. Alatter compared the performance of the quad-based algorithm [39] with that of Tian's method described in Ref. [38] using grayscale Lena and Barbara images. The results indicate that the quad-based algorithm outperforms Tian's method at a PSNR value higher than 35 dB. Tian's algorithm marginally outperforms Alatter's algorithm at lower values of PSNR.

2.4 HISTOGRAM MODIFICATION–BASED SCHEMES
2.4.1 ORIGINAL HISTOGRAM SHIFTING–BASED SCHEME

Ni et al. [22] proposed a novel reversible algorithm based on histogram shifting techniques. The algorithm first finds a zero point (no pixel) and a peak point (a maximum number of pixels) of the image histogram. If zero point does not exist for some image histogram, a minimum point with a minimum number of pixels is treated as a zero point by memorizing the pixel grayscale value and the coordinates of those pixels as overhead information. Ni et al. [22] shifted the peak point toward the zero point by one unit and embedded the data in the peak and neighboring points. Note that the original peak point after embedding disappears in the histogram. Hence, to ensure the reversible restoration, the embedding algorithm needs to memorize the zero and peak points as part of the overhead information. The algorithm can embed a significant amount of data (5 kbits to 80 kbits for a $512 \times 512 \times 8$ grayscale image) while keeping a very high visual quality for all natural images. Specifically, the PSNR of the marked image versus the original image is guaranteed to be higher than 48 dB.

Assume that x represents the pixel value and $H(x)$ represents the occurrence frequency of x. Find the maximum $H(x_{Hmax})$ and minimum $H(x_{Hmin})$. Shift all the bars between x_{Hmax} and x_{Hmin} (x_{Hmax} and x_{Hmin} are not included) to x_{Hmin}, and the shift distance is 1. Assume that $x_{Hmax} < x_{Hmin}$. The meaning of the shifting operation is just adding 1 to all the pixels whose value x_i is between x_{Hmax} and x_{Hmin}. After the shifting operation, $H(x_{Hmax}+1) = 0$. Traverse all the pixels in order. If $x_i = x_{Hmax}$, check the secret to be embedded. If it is 0, do not change x_i; otherwise, add 1 to x_i, and then search the next pixel whose value equals x_{Hmax} and embed the next secret data. So we can know the hiding capacity of this scheme is $H(x_{Hmax})$. During the extracting process, just check the pixel values in order. If $x_i = x_{Hmax}$, then the hiding data is 0; otherwise, if $x_i = x_{Hmax} + 1$, then the hiding data is 1. After the extraction, all the pixel values can be recovered. If $x_{Hmax} > x_{Hmin}$, the shifting operation means that 1 should be subtracted from all the pixels with values $x_i \in (x_{Hmax}, x_{Hmin})$. The mechanism of the histogram modification algorithm is shown in Fig. 2.4, where we take the case $x_{Hmax} < x_{Hmin}$ as an example.

2.4.2 ADJACENT PIXEL DIFFERENCE–BASED SCHEME

Li et al. [40] proposed a reversible data hiding method named adjacent pixel difference (APD) based on the neighbor pixel differences modification. In this method, an inverse "S" order is adopted to scan the image pixels. As shown in Fig. 2.5, a 3×3 image block is used to illustrate this principle. The scan direction is marked as the *blue line*, and the block can be rearranged into a pixel sequence as $p_1, p_2, \ldots, p_9$.

Suppose the host image I is an 8-bit gray level image sized as $M \times N$. Then a pixel sequence $p_1, p_2, \ldots, p_{M \times N}$ is obtained via the inverse "S" order scan. The differences of adjacent pixels are computed as

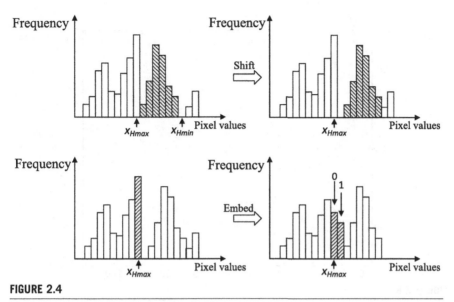

FIGURE 2.4

The histogram modification algorithm for the case $x_{Hmax} < x_{Hmin}$.

p_1	p_2	p_3
p_6	p_5	p_4
p_7	p_8	p_9

FIGURE 2.5

Inverse "S" scan of a 3 × 3 image block.

$$d_i = \begin{cases} p_1 & i = 1 \\ p_{i-1} - p_i & 2 \leq i \leq M \times N \end{cases} \tag{2.16}$$

Considering the similarity of pixel values between p_{i-1} and p_i, a large quantity of d_i ($2 \leq i \leq M \times N$) is equal or close to 0. The difference histogram is constructed based on these $M \times N - 1$ difference statistics. Suppose the histogram bins from left to right are denoted by $b(-255)$, $b(-254)$, ..., $b(-1)$, $b(0)$, $b(1)$, ..., $b(254)$, and $b(255)$. Fig. 2.6 shows the 512 × 512 Lena image's difference histogram. Obviously most differences are concentrated around $b(0)$. When the curve spreads

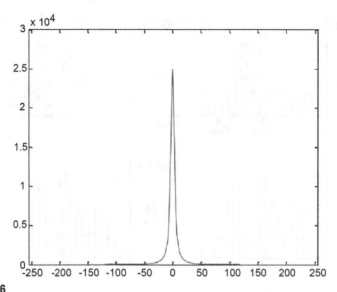

FIGURE 2.6

The difference histogram of 512 × 512 Lena image.

away to both sides, it drops dramatically, and no differences fall into those bins far from $b(0)$.

Basically, APD selects one pair of bins $b(p_1)$ and $b(z_1)$ (suppose $p_1 < z_1$) where $b(p_1)$ and $b(z_1)$ denote the peak and zero points, respectively. Then the bins between $[b(p_1 + 1), b(z_1-1)]$ are shifted rightward one level. Thus $b(p_1 + 1)$ are emptied for data embedding. That is, if a secret bit "1" is embedded, the differences equaling p_1 are added by 1. If "0" is embedded, they are not changed.

To enhance the capacity, APD can also select two pairs of peak–zero points, e.g. $[b(p_1), b(z_1)]$ and $[b(z_2), b(p_2)]$ (suppose $p_1 < z_1$ and $z_2 < p_2$). Then the bins between $[b(p_1 + 1), b(z_1-1)]$ are shifted rightward one level, and those between $[b(z_2 + 1), b(p_2-1)]$ are shifted leftward one level. Thus $b(p_1 + 1)$ and $b(p_2-1)$ are emptied for data embedding. The secret bits modulation is similar as that in one pair of peak–zero points embedding. Note the ranges of $[b(p_1), b(z_1)]$ and $[b(z_2), b(p_2)]$ must not be overlapped.

2.4.3 MULTILEVEL HISTOGRAM MODIFICATION–BASED SCHEME

The disadvantage of the APD method is that the provided capacity is not very high due to only two pairs of peak–zero points at most are employed for data hiding. This limits its scope of application where a large quantity of data is to be embedded. In fact, more pairs of peak–zero points can be utilized. Motivated from this, we designed a multilevel histogram modification mechanism for large capacity data hiding [41], which can be described in detail as follows.

2.4.3.1 Data Embedding

In our scheme, the inverse "S" order is adopted to scan the image pixels for difference generation. The secret data are binary sequences produced by a pseudo random number generator. In the data-embedding stage, a multilevel histogram modification strategy is utilized. An integer parameter called embedding level EL (EL $\geq$ 0) is involved to control the hiding capacity. A larger EL indicates that more secret data can be embedded. As the embedding operations for EL > 0 are more complicated than those of EL $= 0$, we describe them for EL $= 0$ and EL > 0 separately.

Step 1. Inverse "S" scan the image I into a pixel sequence $p_1, p_2, \ldots, p_{M \times N}$.
Step 2. Compute the differences d_i ($1 \leq i \leq M \times N$) according to Eq. (2.16) and construct a histogram based on d_i ($2 \leq i \leq M \times N$).
Step 3. Select an EL. If EL $= 0$, execute Step 4. If EL > 0, go to Step 5.
Step 4. Data embedding for EL $= 0$.
  Step 4.1. Shift the right bins of $b(0)$ rightward one level as:

$$d'_i = \begin{cases} p_1 & \text{if} & i = 1 \\ d_i & \text{if} & d_i \leq 0, 2 \leq i \leq M \times N \\ d_i + 1 & \text{if} & d_i > 0, 2 \leq i \leq M \times N \end{cases} \qquad (2.17)$$

  Step 4.2. Examine $d'_i = 0$ ($2 \leq i \leq M \times N$) one by one. Each difference equaling 0 can be used to hide one secret bit. If the current processing secret bit $w = 0$, it is not changed. If $w = 1$, it is added by 1. The operation is as:

$$d''_i = \begin{cases} p_1 & \text{if} & i = 1 \\ d'_i + w & \text{if} & d'_i = 0, 2 \leq i \leq M \times N \\ d'_i & \text{if} & d'_i \neq 0, 2 \leq i \leq M \times N \end{cases} \qquad (2.18)$$

The histogram modification strategy for EL $= 0$ is shown in Fig. 2.7a–d where the *red and blue arrows* indicate embedding "0" and "1," respectively. After that, go to Step 6.
Step 5. Data embedding for EL > 0.
  Step 5.1. Shift the right bins of $b(\text{EL})$ rightward EL $+ 1$ levels, and shift the left bins of $b(-\text{EL})$ leftward EL levels as:

$$d'_i = \begin{cases} p_1 & \text{if} & i = 1 \\ d_i & \text{if} & -\text{EL} \leq d_i \leq \text{EL}, 2 \leq i \leq M \times N \\ d_i + \text{EL} + 1 & \text{if} & d_i > \text{EL}, 2 \leq i \leq M \times N \\ d_i - \text{EL} & \text{if} & d_i < -\text{EL}, 2 \leq i \leq M \times N \end{cases} \qquad (2.19)$$

  Step 5.2. Examine $d'_i = 0$ ($2 \leq i \leq M \times N$) in the range of $[-\text{EL}, \text{EL}]$ one by one. The multilevel data-embedding strategy is described as follows.

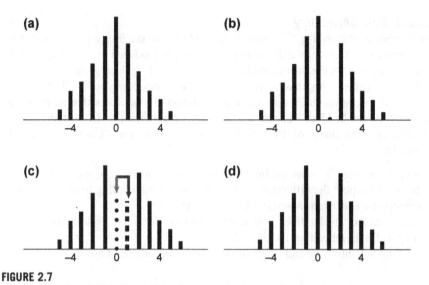

FIGURE 2.7

Histogram modification for EL = 0.

Step 5.2.1. Embed the secret data as:

$$d''_i = \begin{cases} p_1 & \text{if} & i = 1 \\ d'_i & \text{if} & -EL \le d'_i \le EL, 2 \le i \le M \times N \\ 2 \times EL + w & \text{if} & d'_i = EL, 2 \le i \le M \times N \\ -2 \times EL - w + 1 & \text{if} & d'_i = -EL, 2 \le i \le M \times N \end{cases} \tag{2.20}$$

Step 5.2.2. EL is decreased by 1.
Step 5.2.3. If EL $\ne$ 0, execute Steps 5.2.1 and 5.2.2 repeatedly. If EL = 0, execute Eq. (2.21) and then go to Step 6:

$$d''_i = \begin{cases} p_1 & \text{if} & i = 1 \\ d'_i + w & \text{if} & d'_i = 0, 2 \le i \le M \times N \\ d'_i & \text{if} & d'_i \ne 0, 2 \le i \le M \times N \end{cases} \tag{2.21}$$

The histogram modification strategy for EL = 2 is shown in Fig. 2.8a–h, where the *red and blue arrows* correspond to embedding "0" and "1," respectively.
Step 6. Generate the marked pixels sequence p' as:

$$p'_i = \begin{cases} p_1 & i = 1 \\ p_{i-1} - d''_i & 2 \le i \le M \times N \end{cases} \tag{2.22}$$

Step 7. Rearrange p', and the marked image I' is obtained.

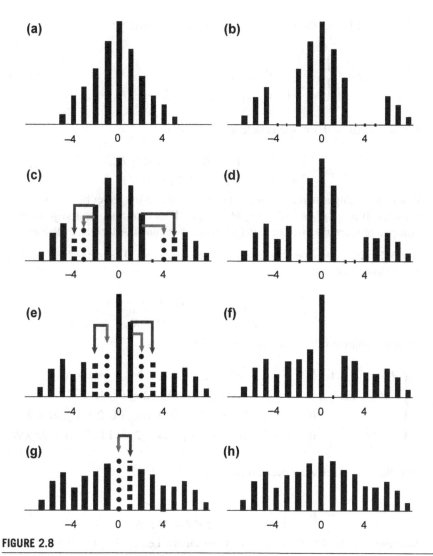

FIGURE 2.8

Histogram modification for EL = 2.

2.4.3.2 Data Extraction and Image Recovery

The data extraction and image recovery is the inverse process of data embedding, and the details are as follows.

> Step 1. Inverse "S" scan the image I' into a pixel sequence p'_i ($1 \le i \le M \times N$).
> Step 2. Receive the EL parameter from the encoder via a secure channel. If EL $= 0$, then execute Steps 3 and 4. If EL > 0, execute Steps 5 and 6.

Step 3. For EL $= 0$, the host image pixels are recovered as:

$$p_i = \begin{cases} p'_1 & \text{if} & i = 1 \\ p'_i & \text{if} & p_{i-1} - p'_i \le 0, 2 \le i \le M \times N \\ p'_i + 1 & \text{if} & p_{i-1} - p'_i \ge 1, 2 \le i \le M \times N \end{cases} \qquad (2.23)$$

Step 4. For EL $= 0$, the secret data is extracted as:

$$w = \begin{cases} 0 & p_{i-1} - p'_i = 0, 2 \le i \le M \times N \\ 1 & p_{i-1} - p'_i = 1, 2 \le i \le M \times N \end{cases} \qquad (2.24)$$

That is, if coming across $p_{i-1} - p'_i = 0$ $(2 \le i \le M \times N)$, a secret bit "0" is extracted. If $p_{i-1} - p'_i = 1$ $(2 \le i \le M \times N)$, a "1" is extracted. Rearrange these extracted bits, and the original secret sequence is obtained. After that, go to Step 7.

Step 5. For EL > 0, obtain the first host pixel as $p_1 = p'_1$. The marked differences are computed as

$$d''_i = \begin{cases} p'_1 & i = 1 \\ p_{i-1} - p'_i & 2 \le i \le M \times N \end{cases} \qquad (2.25)$$

Then the original differences are obtained as

$$d_i = \begin{cases} d''_i - \text{EL} - 1 & \text{if} & d''_i > 2 \times \text{EL} + 1, 2 \le i \le M \times N \\ d''_i + \text{EL} & \text{if} & d''_i \le -2 \times \text{EL}, 2 \le i \le M \times N \\ r & \text{if} & d''_i \in \{2r, 2r + 1\}, r = 0, 1, ..., \text{EL}, 2 \le i \le M \times N \\ -r & \text{if} & d''_i \in \{-2r, -2r + 1\}, r = 1, 2, ..., \text{EL}, 2 \le i \le M \times N \end{cases} \qquad (2.26)$$

Next the host pixel sequence is recovered as

$$p_i = \begin{cases} p'_1 & i = 1 \\ p'_{i-1} - d_i & 2 \le i \le M \times N \end{cases} \qquad (2.27)$$

Note Eqs. (2.23)–(2.25) are executed repeatedly, i.e., p_i $(2 \le i \le M \times N)$ is recovered in advance, and then p_{i+1} is recovered with the aid of p_i. In other words, a sequential recovery strategy is utilized.

Step 6. For EL > 0, the secret data extraction is associated with EL $+ 1$ rounds. First set the round index $R = 1$.

Step 6.1. Extract the data as:

$$w_R = \begin{cases} 0 & \text{if} & d''_i = 2 \times \text{EL}, 2 \le i \le M \times N \\ 0 & \text{if} & d''_i = -2 \times \text{EL} + 1, 2 \le i \le M \times N \\ 1 & \text{if} & d''_i = 2 \times \text{EL} + 1, 2 \le i \le M \times N \\ 1 & \text{if} & d''_i = -2 \times \text{EL}, 2 \le i \le M \times N \end{cases} \qquad (2.28)$$

Step 6.2. EL is decreased by 1 and R is increased by 1.

Step 6.3. If EL $\neq$ 0, execute Steps 6.1 and 6.2 repeatedly. If EL $= 0$, execute Eq. (2.29) as

$$w_R = \begin{cases} 0 & d''_i = 0, 2 \leq i \leq M \times N \\ 1 & d''_i = 1, 2 \leq i \leq M \times N \end{cases} \tag{2.29}$$

In Eq. (2.29), R is increased as EL $+ 1$.

Step 6.4. Rearrange and concatenate the extracted data w_R $(1 \leq R \leq \text{EL} + 1)$ as

$$w = cat(w_1, w_2, ..., w_{EL+1}) \tag{2.30}$$

Hence, the hidden secret bits are obtained, and then go to Step 7.

Step 7. Rearrange the recovered sequence p_i $(1 \leq i \leq M \times N)$ into the host image I.

2.4.3.3 Examples

Two examples for EL $= 0$ and EL $= 2$ are given to explain these principles with a 3×3 block investigated.

2.4.3.3.1 EL $= 0$

1. *Data embedding*. The data-embedding principle for EL $= 0$ is shown in Fig. 2.9. First, the 3×3 block is inverse "S" scanned and the difference histogram is constructed. Next, the histogram shifting is performed. Suppose the secret bits are "10." Thus the "1" can be hidden by changing the first difference 0 to 1 and the "0" is hidden by keeping the second difference 0 unchanged (marked as *red*). In this way, each marked pixel can be produced by its left neighbor

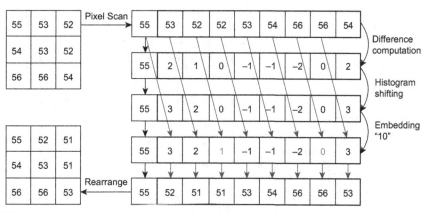

FIGURE 2.9

Example of data embedding for EL $= 0$.

subtracting the modified difference, as indicated by the *blue arrows*. Finally, these marked pixels can be rearranged into the marked block.

2. *Data extraction and image recovery.* As shown Fig. 2.10, the marked block is also inverse "S" scanned into a sequence first. As the first pixel is not changed during embedding, we have $p_1 = p'_1 = 55$. Second, the difference $d''_2 = p_1 - p'_2 = 3$. Obviously, its counterpart $d'_2 = 2$. Thus the original pixel associated with p'_2 is $p_2 = p_1 - d'_2 = 53$. Next, we obtain $d''_3 = p_2 - p'_3 = 2$, and its counterpart $d'_3 = 1$. Then $p_3 = p_2 - d'_3 = 52$. Repeat these operations for the remaining marked pixels, and all the host pixels are recovered. In this example, p_1 is obtained first, and then p_2; p_3, ..., p_9 are recovered consecutively. As marked *red* in Fig. 2.10, 1 bit secret data "1" is extracted from $p_3 - p'_4 = 1$, and a "0" is extracted from $p_7 - p'_8 = 0$.

2.4.3.3.2 EL = 2

1. *Data embedding.* As shown in Fig. 2.11, EL is set as 2 to describe the data-embedding operations for EL > 0. The inverse "S" scan and the difference histogram construction are the same as those in EL = 0. Next, the histogram is shifted as follows: as EL = 2, 3 is added to those differences that are larger than 2 (i.e., EL + 1) and 2 is subtracted from those that are smaller than −2 (i.e., EL). For example, $d'_2 = d_2 + 3 = 7$, $d'_5 = d_5 - 2 = -6$.

Now the secret data can be embedded. Suppose the secret bits are "01101." In the first round, only $d'_6 = -2$ and $d'_8 = 2$ are investigated for falling into [−2, 2] (i.e., [−EL, EL]). As "0" and "1" are embedded in d'_6 and d'_8, respectively, we obtain the marked differences $d''_6 = -2 - 1 = -3$ and $d''_8 = 2 + 3 = 5$. In the second round, only $d'_7 = -1$ and $d'_9 = 1$ are investigated for falling into [−1, 1] (i.e., [−EL + 1, EL−1]). As "1" and "0" are embedded in d'_7 and d'_9, respectively, we obtain $d''_7 = -1 - 1 = -2$ and $d''_9 = 1 + 1 = 2$. In the third round, only d'_4 is investigated

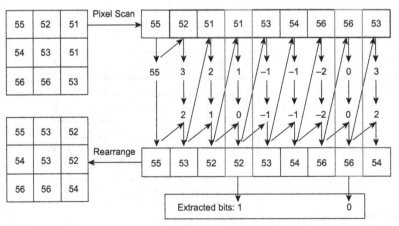

FIGURE 2.10

Example of data extraction and image recovery for EL = 0.

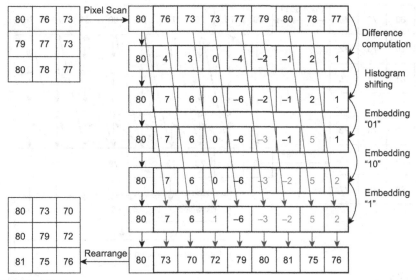

FIGURE 2.11

Example of data embedding for EL = 2.

for equaling 0. As "1" is embedded in d'_4, we obtain $d''_4 = 0 + 1 = 1$. All the marked differences are marked as *red*. Now each marked pixel can be produced by its left neighbor host pixel subtracting the modified difference, as indicated by the *blue arrows*. That is, as $d'' = [80, 7, 6, 1, -6, -3, -2, 5, 2]$ are produced, the marked pixels are obtained as $p'_1 = p_1$, $p'_2 = p_1 - d''_2 = 80 - 7 = 73$, $p'_3 = p_2 - d''_2 = 76 - 6 = 70, ..., p'_9 = p_8 - d''_9 = 78 - 2 = 76$. At last, the marked block is obtained by rearranging these marked pixels.

2. *Data extraction and image recovery.* The image pixel recovery for EL = 2 is shown in Fig. 2.12. The marked block is also inverse "S" scanned into a sequence first. Obviously, the first pixel is not changed during embedding. Second, the difference $d''_2 = p_1 - p'_2 = 80 - 73 = 7$. Its counterpart $d'_2 = 7 - (EL + 1) = 4$. Thus the second host pixel is recovered as $p_2 = p_1 - d'_2 = 76$. Next, we obtain $d''_3 = p_2 - p'_3 = 6$, and its counterpart $d'_3 = 3$. Then $p_3 = p_2 - d'_3 = 73$. Sequentially these operations are repeated for the remaining marked pixels, and all the host pixels are recovered.

For EL = 2, the secret data are extracted with three (i.e., EL + 1) rounds. In the first round, EL is set as 2. As $p_5 - p'_6 = -2 \times EL + 1 = -3$, a secret bit "0" is extracted from p_5 and p'_6. Besides, as $p_7 - p'_8 = 2 \times EL + 1 = 5$, a "1" is extracted from p_7 and p'_8. These two secret bits $w_1 = $ " 01" = are indicated as *bold*.

In the second round, EL is decreased by one and thus EL = 1. As $p_6 - p'_7 = -2 \times EL = -2$, a "1" is extracted from p_6 and p'_7. Besides, as

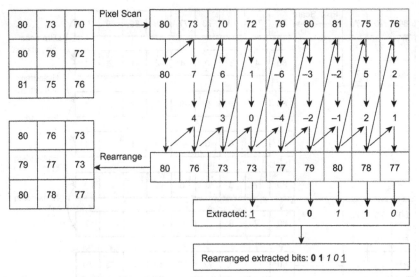

FIGURE 2.12

Example of data extraction and image recovery for EL = 2.

$p_8 - p'_9 = 2 \times$ EL $= 2$, a "0" is extracted from p_8 and p'_9. The $w_2 = $ "10" $=$ are indicated as *italic*.

In the third round, EL is further decreased by 1 and thus EL $= 0$. As $p_3 - p'_4 = 1$, a "1" is extracted from p_3 and p'_4. The $w_3 = $ "1" $=$ is indicated as underlined.

The last step is to rearrange all the extracted bits as $w = cat(w_1, w_2, w_3) = $ "01101". It is exactly the same as the original secret data.

2.4.3.4 Discussion
2.4.3.4.1 Capacity Estimation
The embedding capacity of our scheme is determined by two factors, the embedding level and the peak points around $b(0)$. If no overflow or underflow occurs, the capacity Cap (bit) can be computed as

$$
\text{Cap} = \begin{cases} b(0) & \text{EL} = 0 \\ \sum_{k=-\text{EL}}^{\text{EL}} b(k) & \text{EL} > 0 \end{cases} \tag{2.31}
$$

2.4.3.4.2 Overflow and Underflow Prevention
Given a large EL, the operations of histogram bins empty and shifting may cause overflow (i.e., $p' > 255$) or underflow (i.e., $p' < 0$). Actually, we can predict when they appear. The overflow or underflow first appears on the pixels with values near 255 or 0. In particular, suppose p_{max} and p_{min} represent the maximum and

minimum of the pixel values in I, respectively. In the worst case, the distortions on $p_{\max}$ and $p_{\min}$ can be computed as

$$\begin{cases} p'_{\max} = p_{\max} + \text{EL} + 1 \\ p'_{\min} = p_{\min} - \text{EL} \end{cases} \tag{2.32}$$

where $p'_{\max}$ and $p'_{\min}$ represent the marked pixels. When $p'_{\max} \le 255$ and $p'_{\min} \ge 0$, no overflow or underflow occurs, and consequently EL must be set as

$$\text{EL} \le \min(254 - p_{\max}, p_{\min}) \tag{2.33}$$

That is, EL should be no larger than the minimum of $254 - p_{\max}$ and $p_{\min}$. In other words, if a host pixel has value belonging to [0, EL−1], underflow may appear on it. If belonging to [255−EL, 255], overflow may appear.

In this work, the embedding level is tested as integers that are less than 10. This is because with the EL increasing, the overflow and underflow problems becomes increasingly prevalent. As a result, a lot of pixels with boundary values (i.e., near 255 or 0) in the cover image cannot be used for data embedding. Hence the capacity will not be enhanced any longer. Moreover, the length of the compressed location map is increased at the same time. As the compressed location map is also hiding the cover image, the valid capacity for confidential data hiding is also decreased. Actually, EL selection depends on the cover image content. According to the experimental results, EL can be set as an integer less than 10 on the average for providing a maximum value of valid capacity. In our work, an $M \times N$ location map LM is used for overflow and underflow prevention. Before data embedding, I is preprocessed. If a pixel has value falling into [0, EL−1] or [255−EL, 255], it is excluded for data embedding and a "1" is recorded in the LM, otherwise a "0" is recorded. After all pixels are processed, a binary LM is generated. Obviously, a larger EL corresponds to more "1"s and fewer "0"s in it. Next, the LM is losslessly compressed. In our case, the arithmetic coding is used for its high efficiency. The compressed map LM_c can be also hidden in I. In particular, I is segmented into two parts, I_1 and I_2, for embedding w and LM_c, respectively. That is, some pixels in I_2 are selected according to a secret key, their LSB are replaced by LM_c, and these LSB bits are hidden in I_1 concatenated with w. In decoder, the same key is used to retrieve the selected pixels' LSB bits in I_2 and thus LM_c is reconstructed. After lossless decompression, LM is further obtained. Then we can extract w and the original LSB bits of the selected pixels in I_2. Finally, the host image can be recovered by removing w from I_1 and replacing LSB bits of the selected pixels in I_2 with the latter part of data extracted from I_1.

2.4.3.5 Experimental Results and Comparison With Other Schemes

As shown in Fig. 2.13, six 512×512 gray level images are selected as test images. Table 2.2 lists the capacity (bit) and PSNR (dB) values of the proposed scheme with various ELs. From Table 2.2, we find that a larger EL leads to a larger capacity. Even for EL = 9, the average PSNR is higher than 30 dB. As human eyes are not sensitive to distortions when PSNR > 30 dB, the marked images' visual qualities are acceptable.

FIGURE 2.13

Test images, Lena, Barbara, Aerial, Goldhill, Airplane, Car (from left to right, from top to bottom).

Our scheme is compared with two state-of-the-art methods proposed by Li et al.'s method [40] and Kim et al.'s method [42]. The reason to compare with the method in Ref. [40] is that both methods are based on inverse scan order. That is, the difference histogram is exactly the same, whereas a multilevel histogram modification strategy is

Table 2.2 Performance Comparison of Li et al.'s Method [40] and Our Scheme

Method		Lena		Barbara		Aerial	
		Cap	PSNR	Cap	PSNR	Cap	PSNR
APD1	[40]	24,976	51.14	16,845	51.14	9247	51.13
APD2	[40]	48,383	48.55	33,113	48.41	18,110	48.28
Our	EL=0	24,976	51.14	16,845	51.14	9247	51.15
	EL=1	71,727	44.84	49,062	44.61	27,183	44.40
	EL=2	111,629	41.38	78,018	40.90	44,532	40.49
	EL=3	143,182	39.20	102,547	38.49	60,684	37.87
	EL=4	167,336	37.68	122,019	36.74	75,864	35.95
	EL=5	185,073	36.56	137,108	35.38	90,160	34.45
	EL=6	198,326	35.68	148,842	34.28	103,499	33.23
	EL=7	208,079	34.97	157,873	33.34	115,700	32.21
	EL=8	215,528	34.37	165,031	32.54	126,803	31.35
	EL=9	221,413	33.85	170,783	31.82	137,316	30.60

used in our scheme. Hence the performance improvement achieved by this novel strategy is validated in our work. In addition, the reason to compare with the method of Ref. [42] is that both methods adopt similar multilevel histogram modification strategies. However, as our scheme is based on a pixelwise differential mechanism instead of blockwise processing in Ref. [42], the capacity and the quality of marked images are enhanced simultaneously as proved in the following experimental results. First, our scheme is compared with Li et al.'s method [40] for both are based on APD histogram modification. In Ref. [40], only two cases, APD1 and APD2, are provided for data embedding. Here APD_1 and APD_2 denote that one and two pairs of peak—zero points are used, respectively. The comparison results are also given in Table 2.2. Our scheme can provide a higher capacity than Li et al.'s method with good marked images quality.

Next, our scheme is compared with Kim et al.'s method [42]. Although both are based on multilevel histogram modification, the histogram construction mechanisms are different. In general, the capacity of difference histogram modification is jointly affected by the total number of differences and their concentricity to b(0). In Ref. [42], the differences are computed based on subimages' correlation, and hence the number of differences is determined by the number of subimages. For example, if a 512×512 host image is subsampled into 16 equal-sized subimages, there are $512 \times 512 \times 15/16 = 245,760$ differences produced. In contrast, there are $512 \times 512-1 = 262,143$ differences produced in our scheme. The histogram bins belonging to $[b(-30), b(30)]$ obtained by Ref. [42] and our scheme are shown in Fig. 2.14. Obviously, more differences in our histograms are concentrated around $b(0)$. As a result, a larger capacity can be provided in our scheme than in Ref. [42]. Moreover, $b(-1)$ is emptied after embedding in Ref. [42] because the leftward shift is one level farther than that in our scheme, and consequently the introduced distortions are more serious.

The performance comparisons of our scheme (marked as *blue*) and Kim et al.'s method (marked as *red*) are shown in Figs. 2.15—2.20. The horizontal axis denotes that the EL set from 0 to 9. The vertical axes of capacity and PSNR are normalized as [0, 1.0] bpp and [30,55] dB, respectively. In these experiments, the host images are partitioned into 16 equal-sized subimages in Ref. [42]. All these results demonstrate that not only the capacity but also the PSNR is improved. In other words, even though more secret data are embedded in our scheme, the quality of marked images is still better than the qualities of those in Ref. [42].

2.4.4 HYBRID PREDICTION AND INTERLEAVING HISTOGRAM MODIFICATION—BASED SCHEME

In the conventional histogram shifting—based scheme [43], the histogram of the cover image pixel values is constructed in advance. Then, one or several pairs of peak—zero points of the histogram are found and exploited to insert confidential data. However, as the height of peak points are image dependent, the capacity obtained in this prototype is relatively low. Hereafter, efforts focus on how to construct

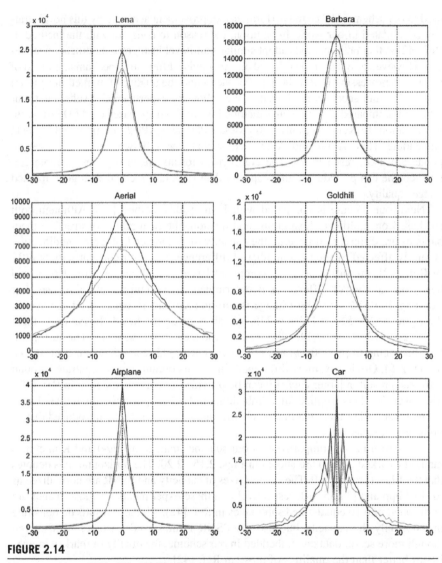

FIGURE 2.14

Histogram bins of [$b(-30)$, $b(30)$] obtained by Kim et al.'s scheme [42] (marked as *red* Gray in print versions) and our scheme (*blue* Black in print versions) on Lena, Barbara, Aerial, Goldhill, Airplane, and Car.

a histogram with higher peak points. One efficient solution is based on prediction [44]. In particular, the histogram is constructed based on the statistics of prediction errors, and the histogram shifting is reduced to the task of modifying them. To further enhance the capacity, a multilevel histogram mechanism is applied in Ref. [42]. To overcome the disadvantages, we proposed a reversible data hiding

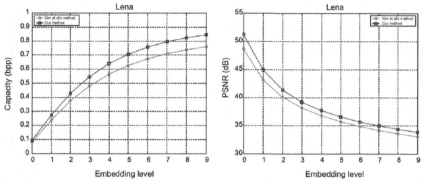

FIGURE 2.15

Comparison of Kim et al.'s scheme [42] and our scheme on Lena image.

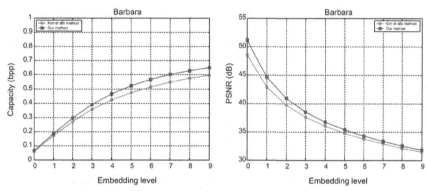

FIGURE 2.16

Comparison of Kim et al.'s scheme [42] and our scheme on Barbara image.

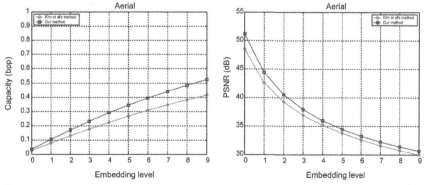

FIGURE 2.17

Comparison of Kim et al.'s scheme [42] and our scheme on Aerial image.

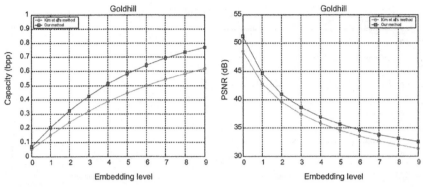

FIGURE 2.18

Comparison of Kim et al.'s scheme [42] and our scheme on Goldhill image.

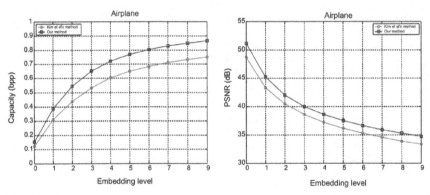

FIGURE 2.19

Comparison of Kim et al.'s scheme [42] and our scheme on Airplane image.

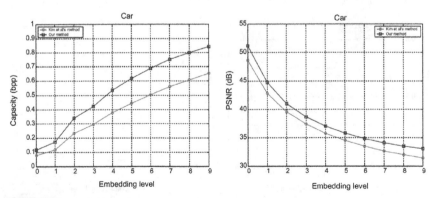

FIGURE 2.20

Comparison of Kim et al.'s scheme [42] and our scheme on Car image.

scheme based on the prediction in Ref. [45]. The cover image with the exception of a seed pixel is partitioned into four segments. Then, a hybrid prediction strategy is employed to predict the approximate values with different predictors. A histogram is constructed based on the prediction errors, and an interleaving histogram modification mechanism is designed for data embedding. In this way, a good trade-off can be achieved between a high capacity and an acceptable quality of marked images.

In prediction-based reversible data hiding methods, the capacity jointly depends on the number of errors and the concentricity of them around zero. Motivated by this, it is necessary to reduce the number of seeds, and meanwhile, to yield errors equaling or close to zero with a high frequency of occurrence. The prediction in our scheme is triggered by a single seed pixel and then spreads all over the cover image.

As shown in Fig. 2.21 (left), the cover image I is partitioned into five disjoint segments (S, A, B, C, and D for short). The prediction of the current processing pixel p can be explained with a 3×3 image block as shown in Fig. 2.21 (right), where p is disposed in the center surrounded by eight neighbors n_1, n_2, ..., n_8. Some of these neighbors are used for engendering the approximate value p_c of p via various predictors. Specifically, the pixels in A and B are predicted with one neighbor as

$$p_c = \begin{cases} n_4 & \text{if} \quad p_c \in A \\ n_2 & \text{if} \quad p_c \in B \end{cases} \tag{2.34}$$

The pixel in C is predicted by the median edge detection predictor [46] as

$$p_c = \begin{cases} \min(n_2, n_4) & \text{if} \quad n_1 \geq \max(n_2, n_4) \\ \max(n_2, n_4) & \text{if} \quad n_1 \geq \min(n_2, n_4) \\ n_2 + n_4 - n_1 & \text{otherwise} \end{cases} \tag{2.35}$$

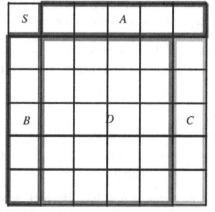

FIGURE 2.21

Five-segment partition of an image (*left*) and a 3×3 image block (*right*).

The pixel in D is predicted with four neighbors as

$$p_c = \text{round}((2n_2 + 2n_4 + n_1 + n_3)/6) \tag{2.36}$$

where "round($\bullet$)" means rounding off its element to the nearest integer. Note the predicted value of p_s is set as itself. In this way, as all pixels of I are predicted, a predicted image I_p can be obtained. The prediction error e is calculated as

$$e = p_c - p \tag{2.37}$$

2.4.4.1 Data Embedding

Given a cover image I and confidential data W, the procedures are as follows.

Step 1. Partition I into S, A, B, C, and D, and generate a prediction error image.
Step 2. Construct a histogram according to these errors with the exception of the left and topmost one. Suppose the histogram bins (corresponding heights) from left to right are denoted as $b_{-255}(h_{-255})$, ..., $b_0(h_0)$, ..., $b_{255}(h_{255})$. An integer parameter termed embedding level (EL for short) is introduced that is established depending on the size of confidential data. Here, we initialize EL $= 1$. Let F denote the flooring operation. Assume r_{em} denotes the embedding round index and $r_{em} = F(\text{EL}/2)$.
Step 3. Compute the capacity Cap as

$$\text{Cap} = \begin{cases} \displaystyle\sum_{k=-F(\text{EL}/2)}^{F(\text{EL}/2)} h_k & \text{if} \quad \text{EL mod } 2 = 1 \\[4mm] \displaystyle\sum_{k=-F((\text{EL}-1)/2)}^{F(\text{EL}/2)} h_k & \text{if} \quad \text{EL mod } 2 = 0 \end{cases} \tag{2.38}$$

Step 4. If Cap is larger than the size of W, then go to Step 5. Otherwise EL increase by 1 and return to Step 3.
Step 5. Empty the associated histogram bins for data embedding. Now EL is finally determined. If it is an odd, the error e is modified into e' as

$$e' = \begin{cases} e + F(\text{EL}/2) & \text{if} \quad e > F(\text{EL}/2) \\ e - F((\text{EL}+1)/2) & \text{if} \quad e < -F(\text{EL}/2) \\ e & \text{otherwise} \end{cases} \tag{2.39}$$

If EL is an even, e is modified as

$$e' = \begin{cases} e + F(\text{EL}/2) & \text{if} \quad e > F(\text{EL}/2) \\ e - F(\text{EL}/2) & \text{if} \quad e < -F((\text{EL}-1)/2) \\ e & \text{otherwise} \end{cases} \tag{2.40}$$

Step 6. Shift peak point bins according to confidential bits. The peak bins from the center to both sides (i.e., b_0, b_1, b_{-1}, b_2, b_{-2}, ...) are interleaving tagged as 1, 2, ..., EL. The bins with odd tags are shifted leftward, whereas those with even tags are shifted rightward. The tagged bin that is farther away from b_0 indicates higher shifting priority. For example, given EL $= 7$, the shifting order is $b_{-3} \rightarrow b_3 \rightarrow b_{-2} \rightarrow b_2 \rightarrow b_{-1} \rightarrow b_1 \rightarrow b_0$. If EL > 1, several rounds are involved in the embedding process. If EL is odd, go to Step 6.1; otherwise go to Step 6.2.

Step 6.1. For an odd EL, a special case of EL $= 1$ must be considered. If EL $= 1$, only one round is required for data embedding and e' is modified as

$$e'' = \begin{cases} e' - w & \text{if} \quad e' = 0 \\ e' & \text{otherwise} \end{cases} \qquad (2.41)$$

where w denotes the current bit to be embedded. If EL > 1, modify e' as

$$e'' = \begin{cases} e' + r_{em} - 1 + w & \text{if} \quad e' = r_{em} \\ e' - r_{em} - w & \text{if} \quad e' = -r_{em} \\ e' & \text{otherwise} \end{cases} \qquad (2.42)$$

Then r_{em} is decreased by 1. If the updated $r_{em} > 0$, execute Eq. (2.42) repeatedly. If the updated $r_{em} = 0$, execute Eq. (2.41) and then go to Step 7.

Step 6.2. For an even EL, e' is modified as

$$e'' = \begin{cases} e' + r_{em} - 1 + w & \text{if} \quad e' = r_{em} \\ e' - r_{em} - w + 1 & \text{if} \quad e' = -r_{em} + 1 \\ e' & \text{otherwise} \end{cases} \qquad (2.43)$$

Then r_{em} is decreased by 1, and execute Eq. (2.43) repeatedly until $r_{em} = 0$. If the updated $r_{em} = 0$, go to Step 7.

Step 7. Generate the marked pixel p_w according to e'' and p_c as

$$p_w = p_c - e'' \qquad (2.44)$$

Step 8. Repeat Steps 5—7 for all the cover pixels, and thus the marked image I_w is obtained. So far the phase of data embedding is completed.

2.4.4.2 Data Extraction and Image Recovery

This phase is to remove the confidential data from the marked images and reconstruct the cover image losslessly. As a whole, the segments A and B are first derived, and then C and D. This is because some pixels of C and D are recovered with the aid of recovered pixels of A and B. Specifically, the pixels of A and B are recovered one by one from left to right and from top to bottom, respectively. The pixels of C and D are recovered with raster scan order. Suppose I_w obtained in the decoder is intact. The details of image recovery and data extraction are described as follows.

Step 1. Obtain the parameter EL from the encoder via a secure channel. Retrieve the seed pixel p_s and partition the rest of I_w into four segments A, B, C, and D.

Step 2. Recover the pixels of A one by one. If the current processing marked pixel p_w belongs to A, initialize the value of $p_c = p_s$, then compute e'' as

$$e'' = p_c - p_w \tag{2.45}$$

If EL is odd, calculate the original error e as

$$e = \begin{cases} e'' - F(\mathrm{EL}/2) & \text{if } e'' > \mathrm{EL} - 1 \\ e'' + F((\mathrm{EL} + 1)/2) & \text{if } e'' < -\mathrm{EL} \\ F((e'' + 1)/2) & \text{if } -\mathrm{EL} \le e'' \le \mathrm{EL} - 1 \end{cases} \tag{2.46}$$

If EL is even, calculate e as

$$e = \begin{cases} e'' - F(\mathrm{EL}/2) & \text{if } e'' > \mathrm{EL} \\ e'' + F(\mathrm{EL}/2) & \text{if } e'' < -\mathrm{EL} + 1 \\ F((e'' + 1)/2) & \text{if } -\mathrm{EL} + 1 \le e'' \le \mathrm{EL} \end{cases} \tag{2.47}$$

Then the recovered pixel p can be obtained as

$$p = p_c - e \tag{2.48}$$

After that, go to process the next marked pixel and repeat the previous steps for all the marked pixels in this segment.

Step 3. Recover the pixels of B as those of A. The only difference is that the prediction value of the current processing pixel is its upper neighbor instead of the left one. Note that the recovery of A and B can be processed in parallel.

Step 4. Recover the pixels of C and D. If the current processing p_w belongs to C, predict its approximate value p_c according to Eq. (2.35). If it belongs to D, obtain the prediction values p_c by means of Eq. (2.36). Then compute e'' with Eq. (2.45). Next, reconstruct e according to Eq. (2.46) or Eq. (2.47). At last, recover the original pixel with Eq. (2.48). All the pixels of C and D are recovered one by one in a sequential order of raster scan.

Step 5. Recover the cover image I by recomposing S, A, B, C, and D.

Step 6. The confidential data extraction is associated with e''. A given EL may correspond to several rounds of data extraction that is opposite to embedding. Initialize the extraction round index $r_{ex} = 1$ and a variable $t = \mathrm{EL}$. If EL is odd, go to Step 6.1, otherwise go to Step 6.2.

Step 6.1 For an odd EL, if $\mathrm{EL} = 1$, one round data extraction is implemented as

$$w_{r_{ex}} = \begin{cases} 1 & \text{if } e'' = -1 \\ 0 & \text{if } e'' = 0 \end{cases} \tag{2.49}$$

If $\mathrm{EL} > 1$, the r_{ex}-th round data extraction is implemented as

$$w_{r_{ex}} = \begin{cases} 1 & \text{if} \quad e'' \in \{t-1, -t\} \\ 0 & \text{if} \quad e'' \in \{t-2, -t+1\} \end{cases} \tag{2.50}$$

Then, t is decreased by 2 and r_{ex} is increased by 1 at the same time. If $t \neq 1$, execute Eq. (2.50) repeatedly. If $t = 1$, execute Eq. (2.49).

Step 6.2 For an even EL, the r_{ex}th round data extraction is implemented as

$$w_{r_{ex}} = \begin{cases} 1 & \text{if} \quad e'' = t \\ 0 & \text{if} \quad e'' = t-1 \end{cases} \tag{2.51}$$

Then, t is decreased by 2 and r_{ex} is increased by 1. If $t \neq 0$, execute Eq. (2.52).

$$w_{r_{ex}} = \begin{cases} 1 & \text{if} \quad e'' \in \{t, -t-1\} \\ 0 & \text{if} \quad e'' \in \{t-1, -t\} \end{cases} \tag{2.52}$$

Then, t is decreased by 2 and r_{ex} is increased by 1. If $t \neq 0$, execute Eq. (2.52) repeatedly. If $t = 0$, execute Eq. (2.49).

In short, no matter what the parity of a positive EL is, the variable t is changed from an odd EL to 1 or an even EL to 0, in steps of two at a time. Therefore, the corresponding extraction round index r_{ex} is changed from 1 to $F(\text{EL}/2) + 1$. Thus, there are also totally $F(\text{EL}/2) + 1$ rounds of extraction processing. That is, symmetry exists between data embedding and extraction.

Step 7. Rearrange and concatenate the extracted data as

$$W = w_1 \big\| w_2 \big\| \cdots \big\| w_{F(\text{EL}/2)+1} \tag{2.53}$$

2.4.4.3 Experimental Results and Comparisons

As shown in Fig. 2.13, a set of 512×512 gray level natural images is selected as test images to evaluate the performance of our scheme. The confidential data are binary sequences produced by a pseudo random number generator. Our scheme is compared with that in Ref. [42] as the results shown in Fig. 2.22. Given an EL, not only the capacities but also the PSNR values of marked images in our scheme are higher than those obtained by Ref. [42] with 4×4 block partition. The improvement is led by more errors concentrated around zero and used for data embedding.

Our scheme is also compared with those in Refs. [40,47] as the results shown in Fig. 2.23. Obviously, our scheme's capacity–PSNR curves are superior to the counterparts of the three predictors in Ref. [47]. Besides, the comparison with Ref. [48] is shown in Table 2.3. On average, the capacity provided by Ref. [48] and our scheme are 40,978 and 47,597 bits, respectively. Nevertheless, the corresponding PSNR values are 48.51 and 48.55 dB, respectively. All the results of our scheme are obtained with EL $= 2$. Clearly both performance indicators are enhanced.

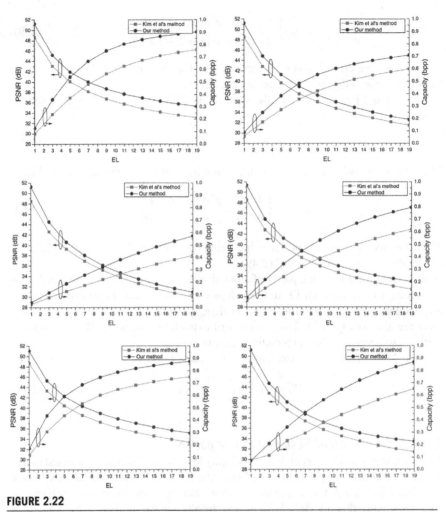

FIGURE 2.22

Comparison of Ref. [42] and our scheme on Lena, Barbara, Aerial, Goldhill, Airplane, and Truck (from *left* to *right*, from *top* to *bottom*).

2.5 LOSSLESS COMPRESSION—BASED SCHEMES

2.5.1 LOSSLESS BIT-PLANE COMPRESSION IN THE SPATIAL DOMAIN

Fridrich's group produced profound research on lossless data hiding techniques and developed a number of algorithms. This group proposed two techniques in this area [6]. The first technique, based on robust spatial additive watermarks, utilizes the modulo addition to embed the hash of the original image. The second technique uses the JBIG Lossless Compression Scheme [49] for losslessly compressing the

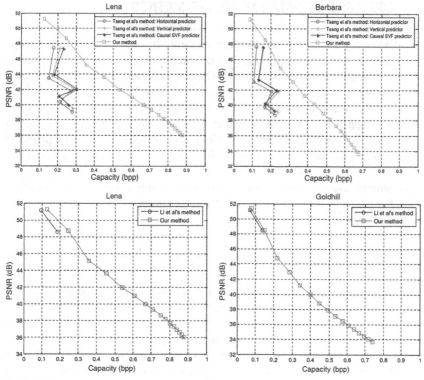

FIGURE 2.23

Comparison of our scheme with Ref. [47] (the *top* two figures) and Ref. [40] (the *bottom* two figures).

Table 2.3 Comparison of Ref. [48] and Our Scheme

	Hong et al.'s Scheme		Our Scheme (EL = 2)	
Image	**Capacity (bit)**	**PSNR (dB)**	**Capacity (bit)**	**PSNR (dB)**
Lena	51,809	48.60	64,348	48.70
Barbara	38,184	48.48	44,356	48.51
Aerial	17,853	48.30	20,586	48.30
Goldhill	35,999	48.46	39,184	48.47
Airplane	65,319	48.73	79,866	48.85
Truck	36,701	48.46	37,243	48.45
Average	40,978	48.51	47,597	48.55

bit-planes to make room for data embedding. To provide sufficient room for data embedding for the second technique, it is usual to compress the high level bit-plane. This mostly leads to visual quality degradation. Since the method aims at authentication, the amount of embedded data is limited.

2.5.2 LOSSLESS RS-DATA EMBEDDING METHOD

Goljan et al. [37] presented the first lossless marking technique suitable for data embedding. They generated loss-free compressible bitstreams using the concepts of invertible noise adding or flipping. Special discrimination or prediction functions were also used on small groups of pixels. The new approach is much more efficient when allowing for large payload with minimal or invertible distortion.

The details are as follows. The pixels in an image with size $M \times N$ are partitioned into nonoverlapped n groups, each of which consist of adjacent pixels $(x_1, x_2,..., x_n)$. For instance, it could be a horizontal block having four consecutive pixels. A discrimination function f is established that assigns a real number $f(x_1, x_2,..., x_n) \in \mathbb{R}$ to each pixel group $G(x_1, x_2,..., x_n)$.

The authors use the discrimination function to capture the smoothness of the groups. For example, the "variation" of the group of pixels $(x_1, x_2,..., x_n)$ can be chosen as the discrimination function $f(\cdot)$:

$$f(x_1, x_2, ..., x_n) = \sum_{i=1}^{n-1} |x_{i+1} - x_i| \qquad (2.54)$$

The purpose of the discrimination function is to capture the smoothness or "regularity" of the group of pixels G. An invertible operation F with the amplitude A can be applied to the groups. It can map a gray level value to another gray level value. It is reversible applying it to a gray level value twice produces the original gray level value. That is, F has the property that $F^2 = $ Identity or $F(F(x)) = x$, for all $x \in P$, where $P = \{0, 1,..., 255\}$, for an 8-bit grayscale image. This invertible operation is called flipping F. The difference between the flipped values and the original values is A.

A suitably chosen discrimination function $f(\cdot)$ and the flipping operation F are utilized to define three types of pixel groups: Regular R, Singular S, and Unusable U.

Regular groups: $G \in R \Leftrightarrow f(F(G)) > f(G)$;
Singular groups: $G \in S \Leftrightarrow f(F(G)) < f(G)$;
Unusable groups: $G \in U \Leftrightarrow f(F(G)) = f(G)$.

From the definitions of the R, S, and U groups, it is apparent that if G is regular, $F(G)$ is singular; if G is singular, $F(G)$ is regular; and if G is unusable, $F(G)$ is unusable. Thus, the R and S groups are flipped into each other using the flipping operation F. The unusable groups U do not change their status. In a symbolic form, $F(R) = S$, $F(S) = R$, and $F(U) = U$.

In the expression $F(G)$, the flipping function F may be applied to all or to selected components of the vector $G(x_1, x_2,..., x_n)$. The noisier the group of pixels $G(x_1, x_2,..., x_n)$ is, the larger the value of the discrimination function becomes. The purpose of the flipping F is to perturb the pixel values in an invertible way by a small amount thus simulating the act of "Invertible Noise Adding." In typical pictures, adding small amount of noise, or flipping by a small amount, will lead to an increase in the discrimination function rather than to a decrease. Although this bias may be small, it will enable us to embed a large amount of information in an invertible manner.

As explained previously, F is a permutation that consists entirely of two cycles. For example, the permutation F_{LSB} is defined as $0 \leftrightarrow 1, 2 \leftrightarrow 3, \ldots, 254 \leftrightarrow 255$ corresponds to flipping or negating the LSB in each gray level. The permutation corresponds to an invertible noise with an amplitude larger than 2. The amplitude A of the flipping permutation F is defined as $0 \leftrightarrow 2, 1 \leftrightarrow 3, \ldots, 253 \leftrightarrow 255$. The average change under the application of F is:

$$A = \frac{1}{|P|} \sum_{x \in P} |x - F(x)| \tag{2.55}$$

For F_{LSB} the amplitude is 1. The other permutation from the previous paragraph has $A = 2$. Larger values of the amplitude A correspond to the action of adding more noise after applying F.

The main idea for lossless embedding is that the image by groups can be scanned according to a predefined order and the status of the image can be losslessly compressed. The bitstream of R and S groups or the RS vector with the U groups may be skipped. This may be considered as the overhead needed to leave room for data embedding. It is not necessary to include the U groups, because they do not change in the process of message embedding and can be all unambiguously identified and skipped during embedding and extraction. The higher a bias between the number of R and S groups, the lower the capacity consumed by the overheads and the higher the real capacity. By assigning a 1 to R and a 0 to S they embed one message bit in each R or S group. If the message bit and the group type do not match, the flipping operation F is applied to the group to obtain a match. The data to be embedded consist of the overhead and the watermark signal.

The extraction starts by partitioning the watermarked image into disjoint groups using the same pattern as used in the embedding. They apply the flipping operation F and discrimination function f to all groups to identify the R, S, and U groups. They then extract the bitstream from all R and S groups ($R = 1, S = 0$) by scanning the image in the same order as embedding. The extracted bitstream is separated into the message and the compressed RS vector C. The bitstream C is decompressed to reveal the original status of all R and S groups. The image is then processed once more, and the status of all groups is adjusted as necessary by flipping the groups back to their original state. Thus, an exact copy of the original image is obtained. The block diagram of the embedding and extracting procedure is given in Fig. 2.24.

Let N_R, N_S, and N_U be, respectively, used to indicate the number of regular, singular, and unusable groups in the image. The sum of N_R, N_S, and N_U is equal to MN/n (the number of all groups). The raw information capacity for this data embedding method is $N_R + N_S = MN/n - N_U$ bits. However, since the compressed bitstream C consumes a large part of the available capacity, the real capacity C_{ap} that can be used for the message is given by

$$C_{\text{ap}} = N_R + N_S - |C| \tag{2.56}$$

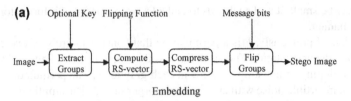

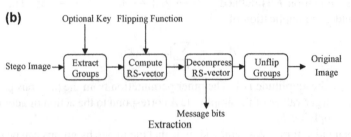

FIGURE 2.24

Diagram for the distortion-free data embedding and extraction algorithm.

where $|C|$ is the length of the bitstream. A theoretical estimate or an upper bound C'_{ap} for the real capacity is

$$C'_{ap} = N_R + N_S + N_R \log\left(\frac{N_R}{N_R + N_S}\right) + N_S \log\left(\frac{N_S}{N_R + N_S}\right) \qquad (2.57)$$

An ideal lossless context-free compression scheme (the entropy coder) would compress the RS vector consisting of $(N_R + N_S)$ bits using $-N_R \log\left(\frac{N_R}{N_R + N_S}\right) -$

$N_S \log\left(\frac{N_S}{N_R + N_S}\right)$ bits.

This estimate for C'_{ap} will be positive whenever there is a bias between the number of R and S groups, or when $N_R = N_S$. This bias is influenced by the size and shape of the group G, the discrimination function f, the amplitude of the invertible noisy permutation F, and the content of the original image. The bias increases with the group size and the amplitude of the permutation F. Smoother and less noisy images lead to a larger bias than images that are highly textured or noisy.

In a practical application, for some natural images, by defining a different discrimination function f, choosing the group size, selecting the number of the pixels that should be flipped, or selecting embedding mask $M = [A_1, A_2, ..., A_n]$, for example, the embedding capacity can be further improved.

The method provides a high embedding capacity while introducing a very small and invertible distortion. A number of experimental results show that the highest capacity was obtained for relatively small groups where n is approximately equal to 4.

2.5.3 LOSSLESS G-LSB DATA EMBEDDING METHOD

Celik et al. [7] presented a high-capacity, low-distortion reversible data hiding technique. A G-LSB modification is proposed as the data embedding method. Lossless recovery of the host signal is achieved by compressing the lowest levels instead of the bit-planes of the signal. The levels chosen were those susceptible to embedding distortion and transmitting the resulting compressed bitstream as part of the embedding payload. The CALIC compression algorithm, which uses the unaltered portions of the host signal as side information, improves the compression efficiency and, thus, the data embedding capacity.

2.5.3.1 G-LSB Embedding

A generalization of LSB-embedded method, namely, G-LSB, is employed by Celik et al. [7]. If the host signal is represented by a vector, G-LSB embedding and extraction can be represented as

$$s_w = Q_L(s) + w \tag{2.58}$$

$$w = s_w - Q_L(s_w) \tag{2.59}$$

where s_w represents the signal containing the embedded information and w represents the embedded payload vector of L-ary symbols. That is, $w_i \in \{0, 1,..., L-1\}$, and

$$Q_L(x) = L \left\lfloor \frac{x}{L} \right\rfloor \tag{2.60}$$

is an L-level scalar quantization function and $\lfloor \cdot \rfloor$ represents the operation of truncation to the integer part.

In the embedding procedure given in Eq. (2.58), for L-ary watermark symbols w_i, it is necessary for them to be converted into binary bitstream, and vice versa, in some practical applications. The following binary to L-ary conversion algorithm can effectively avoid out-of-range sample values produced by the embedding procedure. For instance, in an 8 bpp representation where the range is [0, 255], if operating parameters $L = 6$, $Q_L(s) = 252$, $w = 5$ are used, the output $s_w = 257$ exceeds the range [0, 255].

The binary to L-ary conversion is presented as follows:

The binary input string h is interpreted as the binary representation of a number H in the interval $R = [0, 1]$. That is, $H = .h_0 h_1 h_2...$ and $H \in [0, 1]$. The signal is encoded using integer values between 0 and s_{max}.

1. Given s and s_{max}, determine $Q_L(s)$ and $N = \min(L, s_{max} - Q_L(s))$ the number of possible levels.
2. Divide R into N equal subintervals, R_0 to R_{N-1}.
3. Select the subinterval that satisfies $H \in R_n$.
4. The watermark symbol is $w = n$.
5. Set $R = R_n$ and then go to Step 1, for the next sample.

The conversion process is illustrated in Fig. 2.25. This process involves the following steps.

1. Given s and s_{max}, determine $Q_L(s)$ and $N = \min(L, s_{max} - Q_L(s_w))$ which is the number of possible levels.

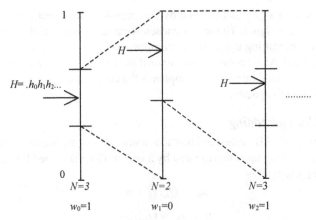

FIGURE 2.25

Binary to L-ary conversion using a variant of arithmetic encoding.

2. Divide R into N equal subintervals, R_0 to R_{N-1}.
3. Set $R = R_w$, where $w = s_w - Q_L(s_w)$ is the current watermark symbol.
4. If there are remaining symbols, go to Step 1. Find the shortest binary string $H \in R$.

The classical LSB modification, which embeds a binary symbol (bit) by over-writing the LSB of a signal sample, is a special case. Here $L = 2$. G-LSB embedding enables the embedding of a noninteger number of bits in each signal sample. Thus, it introduces new operating points along the rate–distortion or capacity–distortion curve.

2.5.3.2 Lossless G-LSB Data Embedding and Extraction

Fig. 2.26 shows a block diagram of the proposed algorithm. In the embedding phase, the host signal is quantized, and the residual is obtained as follows:

$$r = s - Q_L(s) \tag{2.61}$$

Then they adopt the CALIC lossless image compression algorithm. This has the quantized values as side information, to efficiently compress the quantization resid-uals to create high capacity for the payload data. The compressed residual and the payload data are concatenated and embedded into the host signal using the G-LSB modification method. The resulting bitstream is converted to L-ary symbols as mentioned previously. This is then added to the quantized host to form the water-marked signal s_w in Eq. (2.58). Note that the compression block uses the rest of the host signal, $Q_L(s)$, as side information, to facilitate better compression and higher capacity.

In the extraction phase, the watermarked signal s_w is quantized and the water-mark payload h, which is the compressed residual and the payload data, is extracted

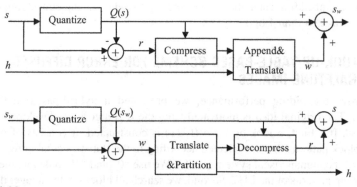

FIGURE 2.26

(Top) Embedding phase and (bottom) extraction phase of the proposed lossless data-embedding algorithm.

in Eq. (2.61). The residual r is decompressed by $Q_L(s_w) = s - Q_L(s)$ as side informa-tion. The original host is reconstructed by replacing the lowest levels of the water-marked signal by the residual as follows:

$$s = Q_L(s) + r = Q_L(s_w) + r \qquad (2.62)$$

The lossless embedding capacity of the system is given by

$$C_{\text{Lossless}} = C_{\text{GLSB}} - C_{\text{residual}} \qquad (2.63)$$

where C_{Lossless} is the raw capacity of G-LSB embedding ($C_{\text{GLSB}} = \log_2(L)$) and C_{residual} is the capacity consumed by the compressed residual. To further improving the lossless embedding capacity, Celik et al. adopt the CALIC lossless image compression algorithm [49,50]. This uses the unaltered portions of the host signal, $Q_L(s)$ as side information, to efficiently compress the residual.

From what is reported in Ref. [7], Celik et al. applied several test images, F-16, Mandrill, and Barbara, to the lossless G-LSB algorithm with its selective embedding extension; Celik et al. compared the results with the RS embedding scheme [37]. The amplitude of the flipping function varied from 1 to 6. The lossless G-LSB algo-rithm at 100% embedding outperforms the RS embedding scheme from a capacity distortion perspective at most points except for the lowest distortion points at $A = 1$ and $L = 2$. The reason is that RS embedding modifies the pixels corresponding to the R and S groups while skipping the U groups. By modifying the embedding extension from 100% to 75%, the lossless G-LSB algorithm slightly surpasses RS embedding at the lowest distortion points. From the aforementioned description, the LGLSB (lossless G-LSB) algorithm can operate at a specified distortion value by flexibly modifying the embedding intensity, or an extension at a given level. The LGLSB also has an advantage over the RS embedding scheme in embedding capacity for a comparable distortion and computational complexity. The LGLSB algorithm can achieve embedding capacities exceeding 1 bpp, whereas the embedding capacity of RS was less than 1 bpp.

2.5.4 LOOK-UP TABLE-BASED SCHEME FOR ERROR DIFFUSED HALFTONE IMAGES

To improve the hiding performance, we presented a hybrid-based method in Ref. [51]. The original idea is motivated from the R-S algorithm developed in Fridrich et al. [6]. First, a look-up table (LUT) is constructed. It consists of pairs of similar block patterns that are selected according to the statistics combining characteristics of the human visual system (HVS). We use "0" and "1" to denote the states of two group patterns of the LUT. Second, we search all blocks in the image: if one is the same as some pattern in the LUT, record its state. Thus a state sequence can be obtained. Third, this sequence is losslessly compressed and the saved space is filled with the hidden data and some *AI*. Here the *AI* refers to extra data aroused by the LUT embedding. Fourth, data is hidden by similar patterns toggling with reference to the new sequence. The last step is to insert the LUT with a secret key, and meanwhile the watermarked halftone image is obtained. In the data extraction stage, the LUT must be re-created first and other procedures are just the inverse process of data hiding. As a reversible technique, the original image can be perfectly recovered if the watermarked version is intact. Furthermore, our approach is also easily extended for halftone image authentication, e.g., hiding a hash sequence. The detailed procedure can be described as follows.

2.5.4.1 Pattern Histogram

The original image is partitioned into a set of nonoverlapping 4×4 blocks. This step aims to choose some appropriate blocks to embed data. Obviously a 4×4 block has totally 2^{16} different patterns. In most cases, a majority of patterns never appear or appear only once in an image. We rearrange a 4×4 block into a binary sequence, and transform it into a decimal integer. Therefore, each pattern is uniquely associated with an integer in the range of $[0, 2^{16} - 1]$, which we call a pattern index (PI). Each PI is associated with a value named the number of appearance times (NAT) of this pattern in the image. The NAT is counted for each PI, and thus the pattern histogram (PH) can be constructed. Fig. 2.27 shows the PHs of six 512×512 halftone images with the x- and y-axes denoting the PI and the NAT, respectively. It is obvious that a small portion of patterns appears many times, whereas others appear rarely. This statistics feature can be employed to insert data.

2.5.4.2 Human Visual System Characteristics

According to the study on the HVS [52], the spatial frequency sensitivity of human eyes is usually estimated as a modulation transfer function. Specifically, the impulse response to a printed image of 300 dpi at a viewing distance of 30 in. is virtually

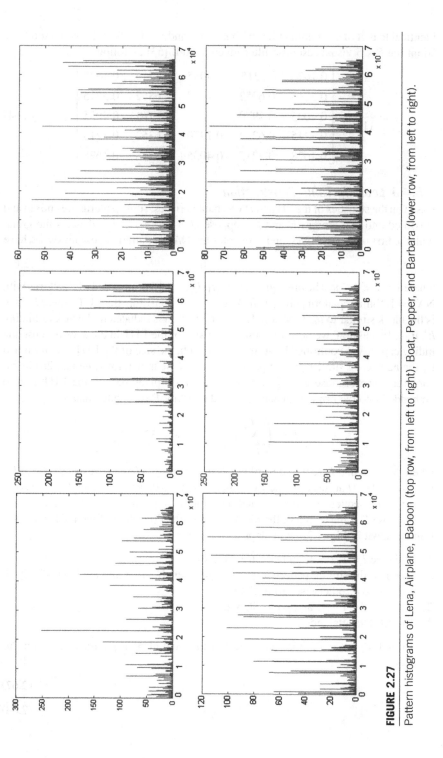

FIGURE 2.27

Pattern histograms of Lena, Airplane, Baboon (top row, from left to right), Boat, Pepper, and Barbara (lower row, from left to right).

identical to that of a Gaussian filter with $\sigma = 1.5$ and $\tau = 0.0095°$. In our method, we adopt the 5×5 visual response filter given in Ref. [53] as follows:

$$f = \frac{1}{11.566} \begin{bmatrix} 0.1628 & 0.3215 & 0.4035 & 0.3215 & 0.1628 \\ 0.3215 & 0.6352 & 0.7970 & 0.6352 & 0.3215 \\ 0.4035 & 0.7970 & 1 & 0.7970 & 0.4035 \\ 0.3215 & 0.6352 & 0.7970 & 0.6352 & 0.3215 \\ 0.1628 & 0.3215 & 0.4035 & 0.3215 & 0.1628 \end{bmatrix} \quad (2.64)$$

2.5.4.3 Look-Up Table Construction
Based on the statistics of the PH and HVS characteristics, some patterns are chosen and classified into two groups, H and L. Suppose $H = \{h_1, h_2, ...,h_u\}$ denotes the group with the first u biggest NATs, and n_i denotes the NAT of pattern h_i; obviously we have

$$n_k \geq n_l \quad (2.65)$$

where $1 \leq k < l \leq u$. The other group $L = \{l_1, l_2,..., l_v\}$ is composed of v patterns with NAT $= 1$. Similar pattern pairs $\{h_i, h'_i\}$ $(1 \leq i \leq u)$ constitute the LUT, where $h'_i \in L$ is the block similar to h_i. Therefore LUT construction is reduced to the task of finding h'_i in L. In addition, we need to compute the size of the LUT in advance because the hiding capacity is controlled by it. In this research, the size of the LUT is determined by the number of similar pattern pairs I, and it can be transformed into a $32I$-bits binary sequence because each pattern contains 4×4 pixels. Since the LUT is also embedded into the original image, the valid capacity P for hidden data is

$$P = \left(\sum_{i=1}^{I} n_i \right) + I - l_{S_c} - 32I \quad (2.66)$$

where $\sum_{i=1}^{I} n_i$ and I are the sums of NATs in the groups H and L, respectively. $32I$ is the size of the AI aroused by the LUT embedding. l_{S_c} denotes the length of the compressed state sequence S; the detailed description is given in the next section.

Suppose D is the length of the hidden data W, the flow chart of the LUT construction is shown in Fig. 2.28 with steps as follows.

1. Initialize $i = 1$, $I = 1$, and construct the PH.
2. Find in L the similar pattern h'_i for h_i, and insert $\{h_i, h'_i\}$ into the LUT. If $P \geq D$, go to Step 4; otherwise, go to Step 3.
3. $i = i + 1$, $I = I + 1$, and go to Step 2.
4. The LUT is attained.

To find h'_i in Step 2, we convolute h_i with f and also all patterns in L with f as follows:

$$h_{f_i} = h_i * f \quad (2.67)$$

$$l_{f_j} = l_j * f \quad (2.68)$$

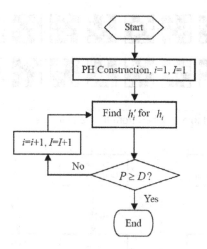

FIGURE 2.28

Flow chart of the LUT construction.

where $j = 1, 2,..., v$. Obviously the size of the convolution results h_{fi} and l_{fj} is 8×8 (the 4×4 matrix convoluted with the 5×5 matrix). Next, the Euclidean distance d_{ij} computed with Eq. (2.69) is used to measure the similarity between h_{fi} and l_{fj}. The l_{fj} with the smallest d_{ij} from h_{fi} is recorded, and the associated pattern in L is selected as the h'_i.

$$d_{ij} = \sum_{u=1}^{8} \sum_{v=1}^{8} \left[h_{fi}(u, v) - l_{fj}(u, v) \right]^2 \qquad (2.69)$$

An example LUT is shown in Fig. 2.29, which is constructed from the 512×512 halftone Lena image. Only the patterns $h_1 - h_{10}$ (the top row) with the first 10 biggest NATs and their similar patterns $h'_1 - h'_{10}$ (the bottom row) are given.

2.5.4.4 Data Hiding

The block diagram of the data hiding process is shown in Fig. 2.30. We use "0" and "1" to denote the states of h_i and h'_i. Once the LUT is created, the process of hiding data is transformed into a simple operation of $h_i - h'_i$ replacement, whose steps are as follows:

1. Partition the original image into nonoverlapping 4×4 blocks.
2. Construct a LUT based on the PH.
3. Search all blocks in the original image. As long as we come across a pattern in the LUT, we record its state based on the following rule: if it belongs to H, "0" is recorded; otherwise if it belongs to L, then "1" is recorded. Thus the state sequence S can be obtained. In fact, suppose l_S denotes the length of S, we have

$$l_S = \left(\sum_{i=1}^{I} n_i \right) + I \qquad (2.70)$$

$h_1\text{-}h_{10}$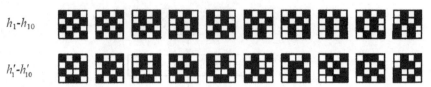

$h'_1\text{-}h'_{10}$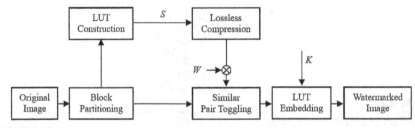

FIGURE 2.29

An example of a look-up table obtained from the Lena image.

FIGURE 2.30

Block diagram of the data hiding process.

4. Compress S into S_c based on certain lossless entropy coding method; in our case, the arithmetic coding algorithm is used. Here the length of S_c is l_{Sc}.
5. Noting that the length of the saved space is $l_S - l_{Sc}$, we fill the space $l_S - l_{Sc} - 32I$ and the space $32I$ with the hidden data W and the AI, respectively, as shown in Fig. 2.31. Thus we get a new state sequence $S' = \{s'_1, s'_2, ..., s'_{ls}\}$. Note that the length of S' is still equal to l_S.
6. Modulate the states of patterns belonging to the LUT to be the states in S' based on the following rule: If s'_k ($1 \le k \le l_s$) equals "0" and the current pattern c_p is exactly the same as h'_i, then we replace h'_i with h_i; Else if s'_k equals "1" and c_p is exactly the same as h_i, then we replace h_i with h'_i. For the other two cases, patterns are unchanged. These operations can be expressed as follows:

$$\begin{cases} h'_i \leftarrow h_i & \text{if } s'_k = 0, c_p = h'_i \\ h_i \leftarrow h_i & \text{if } s'_k = 0, c_p = h_i \\ h'_i \leftarrow h'_i & \text{if } s'_k = 1, c_p = h'_i \\ h_i \leftarrow h'_i & \text{if } s'_k = 1, c_p = h_i \end{cases} \tag{2.71}$$

where $\leftarrow$ means replacing the left pattern with the right one. Hence, data is hidden through the aforementioned similar pair toggling operation.

2.5.4.5 Look-Up Table Embedding
Since different images have different LUTs, no universal table is suitable for all images. Besides, the LUT is also need to be protected. Therefore, the LUT is also embedded in the image in this research, with the steps being as follows. It is rearranged into a $32I$ bits binary sequence. A secret key K is used to generate $32I$ random pixel locations to embed the LUT, noting that these pixels must not fall into the

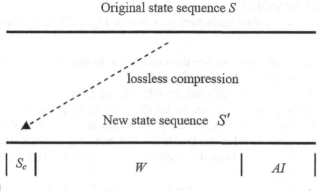

FIGURE 2.31

State sequence lossless compression and the saved space allocation.

blocks in the LUT. We extract the selected pixel values into a $32I$ binary sequence and embed it based on Eq. (2.71). Then we directly replace the selected pixels with the LUT sequence.

This principle is illustrated in Fig. 2.32; the *red blocks* (Gray in print versions) denote the patterns used to extract the state according to the LUT, whereas the *blue points* (Black in print versions) denote the select pixels with K. These pixels values are extracted as AI, and then the rearranged LUT (a binary sequence) is inserted into these locations. For example, if the LUT shown in Fig. 2.32 is to be inserted, we need to select 320 pixel positions (*blue points*) and replace their pixels values using the rearranged LUT, and the original 320 pixels values are hidden by watermark embedding (*red blocks*). More details of the LUT embedding method can be seen in Ref. [54].

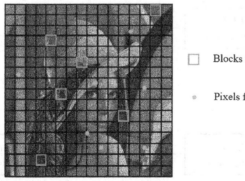

☐   Blocks for similar pair toggling

•   Pixels for LUT embedding

FIGURE 2.32

Look-up table embedding.

2.5.4.6 Data Extraction

The block diagram of data extraction is shown in Fig. 2.33, with steps being as follows.

1. The LUT reconstruction: we use the same key K to find the $32I$ pixel locations and arrange the pixel values into the LUT.
2. The state sequence S' is extracted according to the LUT.
3. Lossless decompression: S' can be divided into three parts: the compressed version of S, the hidden data, and the pixel values selected by K. We use the arithmetic decoding method to decode the first part of S' to get S. Then, the hidden data is extracted from the middle $l_S - l_{Sc} - 32I$ bits. The process is illustrated in Fig. 2.34.
4. *AI* Recovery: We directly extract the last $32I$ bits of S' to recover the pixel values occupied by the LUT.
5. Similar pair toggling: Demodulate the states of patterns belonging to the LUT to be the states in S based on the following rule: If S_k $(1 \le k \le l_s)$ equals "0" and the c_p is exactly the same as h'_i, then we replace h'_i with h_i; Else if S_k equals "1" and the c_p is exactly the same as h_i, then we replace h_i with h'_i. For the other two cases, block patterns are unchanged. These operations can be described as follows:

$$\begin{cases} h_i \leftarrow h'_i & \text{if } s_k = 0, c_p = h'_i \\ h_i \leftarrow h_i & \text{if } s_k = 0, c_p = h_i \\ h'_i \leftarrow h'_i & \text{if } s_k = 1, c_p = h'_i \\ h'_i \leftarrow h_i & \text{if } s_k = 1, c_p = h_i \end{cases} \quad (2.72)$$

2.5.4.7 Experimental Results

Six 512×512 error-diffused halftone images, Lena, Baboon, Airplane, Boat, Pepper, and Barbara, are selected to test the performance of the proposed method, as

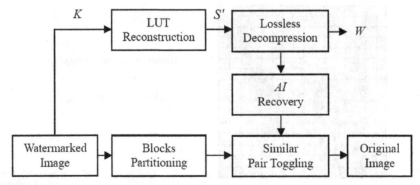

FIGURE 2.33

Block diagram of the data extraction process.

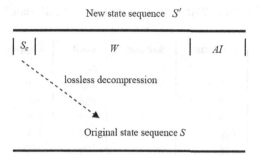

FIGURE 2.34

State sequence lossless decompression for the hidden data extraction and the additional information recovery.

shown in Fig. 2.35. These halftones are obtained by performing Floyd—Steinberg error diffusion filtering on the 8-bit gray level images. The capacities for different images and different sizes of LUT are listed in Table 2.4.

In our experiments, a 1D binary sequence created by a pseudo random number generator is chosen as the hidden data. Fig. 2.36a and b illustrate the original image Lena and its watermarked version, whereas Fig. 2.36c shows the recovered one. To

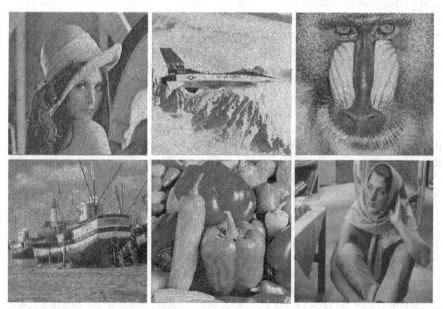

FIGURE 2.35

Six test error—diffused images Lena, Airplane, Baboon (top row, from left to right), Boat, Pepper, and Barbara (bottom row, from left to right).

Table 2.4 Capacity (Bits) With Different Images and Different Sizes of LUT(*l*)

LUT	Lena	Airplane	Baboon	Boat	Pepper	Barbara
$l = 1$	201	195	8	68	152	33
$l = 2$	339	385	21	142	258	73
$l = 3$	432	522	28	204	355	112
$l = 4$	512	635	37	261	429	140
$l = 5$	582	742	41	314	487	165
$l = 6$	641	844	45	366	540	188
$l = 7$	690	936	48	416	582	212
$l = 8$	739	1025	51	464	620	228
$l = 9$	788	1109	52	512	655	241
$l = 10$	831	1191	54	553	685	254

LUT, *look-up table.*

evaluate the introduced distortion, we apply an effective quality metric proposed by Valliappan et al. [55], i.e., weighted signal-to-noise ratio (WSNR). The linear distortion is quantified in Ref. [55] by constructing a minimum mean squared error Weiner filter; in this way the residual image is uncorrelated with the input image. The residual image represents the nonlinear distortion plus additive independent noise. Valliappan et al. [55] spectrally weight the residual by a contrast sensitivity function (CSF) to quantify the effect of nonlinear distortion and noise on quality. A CSF is a linear approximation of the HVS response to a sine wave of a single frequency, and a low-pass CSF assumes that the human eyes do not focus on one point but freely moves the around the image. Since the halftone image is attempted to preserve the useful information of the gray level image, we compare the halftone or watermarked image with the original gray level image. Similar to PSNR, a higher WSNR means a higher quality. In our experiments, the WSNR between the gray level Lena and the halftone Lena is 29.18 dB, whereas the WSNR between the gray level Lena and the watermarked Lena is 28.59 dB. It can be seen that the introduced distortion of the visual quality is slight. Since the WSNR between the gray level Lena and the recovered Lena is 29.18 dB, the recovered version is exactly the same as the original image.

Our method can also be used for halftone image authentication. For example, a hash sequence of the original halftone image can be hidden in the halftone image. We only need to compare the hash extracted from the watermarked image (Hash$_1$) with the hash sequence computed from the recovered image (Hash$_2$). When these two sequences are equal, we can confirm that the watermarked image suffers no alteration. Under no attacks, both of them are certainly equal to the original hash, whereas if the watermarked image is an unauthorized changed, the two sequences are different. The process is illustrated in Fig. 2.37.

(a)   **(b)**   **(c)**

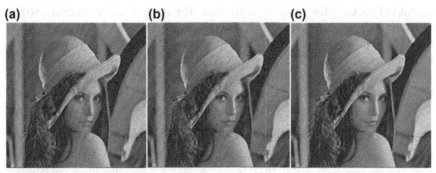

FIGURE 2.36

Data hiding on the halftone Lena. (a) The original Lena, WSNR = 29.18 dB, (b) the watermarked Lena with 831 bits inserted, WSNR = 28.58 dB, (c) the recovered Lena, WSNR = 29.18 dB. *WSNR*, weighted signal-to-noise ratio.

2.6 REVERSIBLE SECRET SHARING—BASED SCHEMES

Secret sharing plays an important role in data encryption. Shamir et al. [56] proposed an (r, n)-threshold prototype based on Lagrange polynomial interpolation. In this model, the secret data are encrypted into n shares. If r or more than r shares are polled, the secret can be decrypted. Otherwise, if $r - 1$ or fewer shares are collected, no meaningful information can be revealed. Thien et al. [57] extended Shamir et al.'s model into image secret sharing, i.e., hiding a secret image in a set of noiselike shadow images. Visual cryptography [58] is another useful technique for image secret sharing. It employs the properties of human visual system and thus maintains the advantage that the secret content can be viewed via stacking a qualified set of shadow images. This stack-to-see mechanism makes it useful in the applications where no computer is available.

More recently, Lin et al. [59,60] proposed two reversible secret sharing schemes based on Lagrange polynomial interpolation. Compared with the available irreversible schemes, Lin et al.'s schemes have two extra advantages. One is that the shadows are meaningful instead of meaningless images. Consequently, much

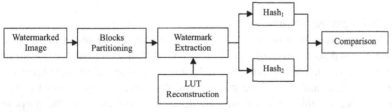

FIGURE 2.37

Application of our scheme in halftone image authentication.

attention of hacker's for attacking is reduced. The other is the reversibility, which means not only the secret image but also the cover image can be recovered accurately. In contrast, the cover image cannot be accurately recovered any longer in irreversible secret sharing.

In this section, we introduces our two high-capacity data hiding schemes during reversible secret sharing.

2.6.1 DATA HIDING IN REVERSIBLE SECRET SHARING

In this section, we introduce our high-capacity data hiding scheme during reversible secret sharing proposed in Ref. [61]. In the encoder, a large quantity of confidential data is embedded and shared along with a secret image in a set of camouflage shadows. In the decoder, the secret and cover images and the confidential data can be precisely recovered simultaneously. This scheme can be used for covert communication, secret image annotation, authentication, etc. Additionally, it is theoretically secure due to the foundation of Lagrange polynomial interpolation.

2.6.1.1 Related Work

In Shamir's model, a prime p is randomly selected and an $r-1$ degree polynomial is constructed as Eq. (2.73) to encrypt a secret integer se into n shares.

$$q(x) = (se + a_1 \cdot x + \dots + a_{r-1} \cdot x^{r-1}) \bmod p \tag{2.73}$$

where the coefficients $a_1, \dots, a_{r-1}$ are randomly chosen positive integers. Both se and $a_1, \dots, a_{r-1}$ belong to $[0, p-1]$. In this way n shares $q(1), \dots, q(n)$ are generated as

$$q(j) = (se + j \cdot a_1 + \dots + j^{r-1} \cdot a_{r-1}) \bmod p \tag{2.74}$$

where $j = 1, 2, \dots, n$. According to Lagrange interpolation, se can be recovered by solving the equation set constructed by any r or more than r shares.

According to Eq. (2.74), it is easy to find that the coefficient a_i is also calculated along with se during decryption. Lin et al.'s method [59] employs all coefficients of the $r-1$ degree polynomial to carry two parts of information, one from the cover image and the other from the secret image. In the encoding stage, the input consists of a secret image S and a cover image C of the same size. The output is composed of a set of shadow images $C_1, \dots, C_n$.

2.6.1.2 Proposed Scheme

Our scheme aims to hide some extra confidential data during secret image sharing with the original advantages of Lin et al.'s method [59] well preserved. A straightforward method is to employ conventional irreversible data hiding techniques on the secret image first, and then share the watermarked secret image using Lin et al.'s method. However, this idea has two shortcomings contradicting the purpose of our method. One is that the limited capacity provided in the conventional data hiding techniques for the visual quality of watermarked images must be carefully considered. Moreover, the host image (i.e., secret image) cannot be recovered accurately in those irreversible methods. Instead, the lossless data hiding is adequate.

As shown in Fig. 2.38, we design a novel high-capacity data hiding method integrated in reversible secret sharing. The key characteristics lie in a double module structure and a lossless data hiding mechanism based on multilevel histogram shifting. In Ref. [59], the same prime p is used for the module processing of S and C. However, in our double module structure, a pair of integers $\{b, p\}$ is adopted. In particular, a prime p and another integer b $(b < p)$ are introduced for C and S processing, respectively. The encoding stage consists of secret image sharing and data hiding, and the decoding stage includes secret image decryption and data extraction.

2.6.1.2.1 Encoding Stage

In this stage, the input includes a cover image C, a secret image S, and a binary sequence confidential data W. Suppose both C and S are $M \times N$ gray level images

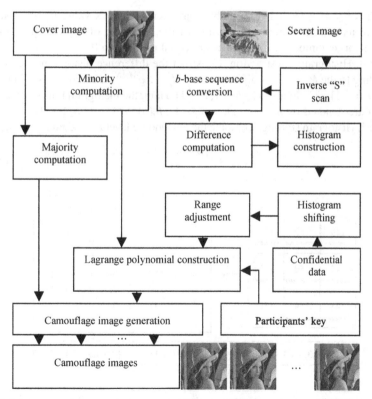

FIGURE 2.38

Block diagram of the proposed method.

and the $\{b, p\}$ pair is predetermined. The output are n shadow images $C_1,\ldots,C_n$. The encoding details are described as follows.

Step 1. Inverse "S" scan. Scan the pixels of S in the inverse "S" order [40] and a pixel sequence $s^1, s^2,\ldots, s^{M\times N}$ is obtained.

Step 2. b-base sequence conversion. Translate each pixel s^i $(1 \leq i \leq M \times N)$ into a b-base sequence $\{s_1^i, s_2^i\ldots, s_v^i\}_b$. Here $v = \lceil \log_b 255 \rceil$ and b is a positive integer smaller than p and not required to be a prime. In this way, there are totally v sequences s_j^i $(1 \leq j \leq v)$ obtained with each containing $M \times N$ elements, i.e.,

$$s_j = \left\{s_j^1, s_j^2, \ldots s_j^{M\times N}\right\}.$$

An example of a 3×3 block inverse "S" scan and b-base sequence conversion is shown in Fig. 2.39, where the scan direction is indicated as the *blue line* (Black in print versions) and $b = 7$.

Step 3. Difference computation. Compute the difference between two adjacent elements of s_j as

$$d_j^i = s_j^{i-1} - s_j^i \tag{2.75}$$

where $2 \leq i \leq M \times N$. It is expectable that each element's value in s_j is usually similar to its adjacent neighbors because of the similarity of adjacent pixels in S. That is, a large number of differences are equal or close to 0.

Step 4. Histogram construction. Construct the difference histogram h_j of s_j according to the $M \times N - 1$ differences $d_j^2, d_j^3, \ldots, d_j^{M\times N}$. Obviously, as s_j^i belongs to $[0, b-1]$, d_j^i belongs to $[-b+1, b-1]$. Here, the histogram bins from left to right are denoted by $h_j(-b+1),\ldots, h_j(-1), h_j(0), h_j(1), \ldots, h_j(b-1)$.

Step 5. Histogram shifting. Compute the embedding level EL according to $\{b, p\}$ as

$$EL = \left\lfloor \left| \frac{p - b - 1}{2} \right| \right\rfloor \tag{2.76}$$

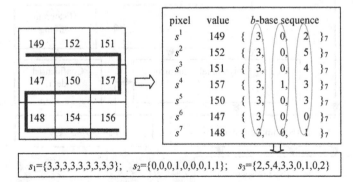

pixel	value	b-base sequence
s^1	149	{ 3, 0, 2 }$_7$
s^2	152	{ 3, 0, 5 }$_7$
s^3	151	{ 3, 0, 4 }$_7$
s^4	157	{ 3, 1, 3 }$_7$
s^5	150	{ 3, 0, 3 }$_7$
s^6	147	{ 3, 0, 0 }$_7$
s^7	148	{ 3, 0, 1 }$_7$

$s_1=\{3,3,3,3,3,3,3,3,3\}$; $s_2=\{0,0,0,1,0,0,0,1,1\}$; $s_3=\{2,5,4,3,3,0,1,0,2\}$

FIGURE 2.39

Inverse "S" scan and b-base sequence conversion of a 3×3 image block.

A larger *EL* indicates that more secret data can be embedded. As the embedding operations of $EL > 0$ are more complicated than those of $EL = 0$, we describe them separately. If $EL = 0$, execute Step 5.1. If $EL > 0$, go to Step 5.2.

Step 5.1 Data embedding for $EL = 0$.

Step 5.1.1 Shift the right bins of $h(0)$ rightward by one level as

$$\bar{d}_j^i = \begin{cases} d_j^i + 1 & \text{if} \quad d_j^i > 0 \\ d_j^i & \text{if} \quad d_j^i \leq 0 \end{cases} \tag{2.77}$$

Step 5.1.2. For the current processing confidential bit *w*, perform the following embedding operation as

$$\tilde{d}_j^i = \begin{cases} \bar{d}_j^i + w & \text{if} \quad \bar{d}_j^i = 0 \\ \bar{d}_j^i & \text{if} \quad \bar{d}_j^i \neq 0 \end{cases} \tag{2.78}$$

After that, go to Step 6.

Step 5.2. Data embedding for $EL > 0$.

Step 5.2.1. Shift the right bins of $h_j(EL)$ rightward by $EL + 1$ levels, and shift the left bins of $h_j(-EL)$ leftward by EL levels as

$$\bar{d}_j^i = \begin{cases} d_j^i + EL + 1 & \text{if} \quad d_j^i > EL \\ d_j^i & \text{if} \quad -EL \leq d_j^i \leq EL \\ d_j^i - EL & \text{if} \quad d_j^i < -EL \end{cases} \tag{2.79}$$

Step 5.2.2. Embed the confidential data *w* as

$$\tilde{d}_j^i = \begin{cases} \bar{d}_j^i & \text{if} \quad \bar{d}_j^i \neq \pm EL \\ 2 \times EL + w & \text{if} \quad \bar{d}_j^i = EL \\ -2 \times EL - w + 1 & \text{if} \quad \bar{d}_j^i = -EL \end{cases} \tag{2.80}$$

Then *EL* is decreased by 1. If $EL \neq 0$, execute Eqs. (2.79) and (2.80) repeatedly until $EL = 0$. If $EL = 0$, execute Eq. (2.81) and then go to Step 6.

$$\tilde{d}_j^i = \begin{cases} \bar{d}_j^i + w & \text{if} \quad \bar{d}_j^i = 0 \\ \bar{d}_j^i & \text{if} \quad \bar{d}_j^i \neq 0 \end{cases} \tag{2.81}$$

Step 6. Generate the watermarked sequence $\tilde{s}_j^i$ as

$$\tilde{s}_j^i = \begin{cases} s_j^i & if & i = 1 \\ s_j^{i-1} - \tilde{d}_j^i & if & 2 \leq i \leq M \times N \end{cases} \tag{2.82}$$

Step 7. Adjust the range according to

$$\tilde{\tilde{s}}_j^i = \tilde{s}_j^i + EL + 1 \tag{2.83}$$

Hence the confidential data embedding is completed. The output $\tilde{\tilde{s}}_j^i$ can be used for the following secret sharing operations.

Step 8. Compute the minority c_{mi} of the current processing pixel c as

$$c_{mi} = c \bmod p \tag{2.84}$$

Step 9. Compute the majority c_{ma} according to c and c_{mi} as

$$c_{ma} = c - c_{mi} \tag{2.85}$$

Step 10. Construct a v-degree polynomial $F(x)$ according to $\tilde{\tilde{s}}_1^i, \tilde{\tilde{s}}_2^i, \dots \tilde{\tilde{s}}_v^i$ and c_{mi} as

$$F(x) = \left(\tilde{\tilde{s}}_1^i + \tilde{\tilde{s}}_2^i \cdot x + \dots + \tilde{\tilde{s}}_v^i \cdot x^{v-1} + c_{mi} \cdot x^v \right) \bmod p \tag{2.86}$$

Step 11. Generate $F(k_m)$ $(m = 1,\dots, n)$ via each participant's key k_m as

$$\begin{cases} F(k_1) = \left(\tilde{\tilde{s}}_1^i + \tilde{\tilde{s}}_2^i \cdot k_1 + \dots + \tilde{\tilde{s}}_v^i \cdot k_1^{v-1} + c_{mi} \cdot k_1^v \right) \bmod p \\ F(k_2) = \left(\tilde{\tilde{s}}_1^i + \tilde{\tilde{s}}_2^i \cdot k_2 + \dots + \tilde{\tilde{s}}_v^i \cdot k_2^{v-1} + c_{mi} \cdot k_2^v \right) \bmod p \\ \qquad\qquad\qquad \dots \\ F(k_n) = \left(\tilde{\tilde{s}}_1^i + \tilde{\tilde{s}}_2^i \cdot k_n + \dots + \tilde{\tilde{s}}_v^i \cdot k_n^{v-1} + c_{mi} \cdot k_n^v \right) \bmod p \end{cases} \tag{2.87}$$

Step 12. Compute c_m according to c_{ma} and $F(k_m)$ as

$$c_m = c_{ma} + F(k_m) \tag{2.88}$$

where c_m corresponds to the current pixel of the shadow image C_m.

Step 13. Repeat Steps 1–12 for all pixels of S and C. In this way, all the shadows images $C_1,\dots,C_n$ are produced.

2.6.1.2.2 Decoding Stage

The input is composed of r or more than r shadow images. If more than r shadows are obtained, we can choose any r different shadows randomly. Besides, suppose the decoder obtains the $\{b, p\}$ via a secure channel. The output consists of the secret image, the cover image, and the confidential data.

Step 1. Suppose $\overline{C}_1, ..., \overline{C}_r$ denote r different shadow images. Obtain the current processing pixels $\overline{c}_l$ and compute $\overline{F}\left(\overline{k}_l\right)$ as

$$\overline{F}\left(\overline{k}_l\right) = \overline{c}_l \mathrm{mod} p \tag{2.89}$$

where $l = 1, 2, ..., r$ and p is the same prime used in the encoder.

Step 2. Construct an equation set as

$$\begin{cases} \overline{F}\left(\overline{k}_1\right) = \left(\widetilde{s}_1^i + \widetilde{s}_2^i \cdot \overline{k}_1 + ... + \widetilde{s}_v^i \cdot \overline{k}_1^{v-1} + c_{mi} \cdot \overline{k}_1^v\right) \mathrm{mod} p \\ \overline{F}\left(\overline{k}_2\right) = \left(\widetilde{s}_1^i + \widetilde{s}_2^i \cdot \overline{k}_2 + ... + \widetilde{s}_v^i \cdot \overline{k}_2^{v-1} + c_{mi} \cdot \overline{k}_2^v\right) \mathrm{mod} p \\ \quad\quad\quad\quad ... \\ \overline{F}\left(\overline{k}_r\right) = \left(\widetilde{s}_1^i + \widetilde{s}_2^i \cdot \overline{k}_r + ... + \widetilde{s}_v^i \cdot \overline{k}_n^{v-1} + c_{mi} \cdot \overline{k}_r^v\right) \mathrm{mod} p \end{cases} \tag{2.90}$$

Thus $\widetilde{s}_1^i, \widetilde{s}_2^i, ... \widetilde{s}_v^i$ and c_{mi} are obtained by solving this equation set.

Step 3. Compute c_{ma} according to $\overline{c}_1$ and $\overline{F}\left(\overline{k}_1\right)$ as

$$c_{ma} = \overline{c}_1 - \overline{F}\left(\overline{k}_1\right) \tag{2.91}$$

Step 4. Recover the cover pixel c according to c_{ma} and c_{mi} as

$$c = c_{ma} + c_{mi} \tag{2.92}$$

Repeat Steps 1–4 for all pixels of $\overline{C}_1, ..., \overline{C}_r$. In this way, the cover image C is reconstructed accurately.

Step 5. Range readjustment. Compute the embedding level as $\mathrm{EL} = \left\lfloor \frac{p-b-1}{2} \right\rfloor$ and obtain the $\widetilde{s}_j^i$ as

$$\widetilde{s}_j^i = \widetilde{s}_j^i - \mathrm{EL} - 1 \tag{2.93}$$

Step 6. If $\mathrm{EL} = 0$, execute Steps 7 and 8. If $\mathrm{EL} > 0$, execute Steps 9 and 10.

Step 7. For $\mathrm{EL} = 0$, s_j^i can be recovered as

$$s_j^i = \begin{cases} \widetilde{s}_j^i & \text{if } s_j^{i-1} - \widetilde{s}_j^i \leq 0 \\ \widetilde{s}_j^i + 1 & \text{if } s_j^{i-1} - \widetilde{s}_j^i \geq 1 \end{cases} \tag{2.94}$$

Step 8. For $\mathrm{EL} = 0$, the current confidential data w is extracted as

$$w = \begin{cases} 0 & \text{if } s_j^{i-1} - \widetilde{s}_j^i = 0 \\ 1 & \text{if } s_j^{i-1} - \widetilde{s}_j^i = 1 \end{cases} \tag{2.95}$$

Rearrange all the extracted bits into the original confidential sequence W. After that, go to Step 11.

Step 9. For EL > 0, obtain $s_j^1 = \tilde{s}_j^1$ and compute $\tilde{\tilde{d}}_j^i$ as

$$\tilde{\tilde{d}}_j^i = s_j^{i-1} - \tilde{s}_j^i \tag{2.96}$$

where $2 \leq i \leq M \times N$. Then d_j^i is obtained as

$$d_j^i = \begin{cases} \tilde{\tilde{d}}_j^i - \text{EL} - 1 & \text{if} & \tilde{\tilde{d}}_j^i > 2 \times \text{EL} + 1 \\ \tilde{\tilde{d}}_j^i + \text{EL} & \text{if} & \tilde{\tilde{d}}_j^i < -2 \times \text{EL} \\ r & \text{if} & \tilde{\tilde{d}}_j^i \in \{2 \times r, 2 \times r + 1\}, r = 0, 1, ..., \text{EL} \\ -r & \text{if} & \tilde{\tilde{d}}_j^i \in \{-2 \times r, -2 \times r + 1\}, r = 1, ..., \text{EL} \end{cases} \tag{2.97}$$

Next, s_j^i is recovered as

$$s_j^i = \tilde{s}_j^{i-1} - d_j^i \tag{2.98}$$

Note Eqs. (2.96)–(2.98) are executed repeatedly, i.e., s_j^i is recovered in advance and then s_j^{i+1} is recovered with the aid of s_j^i. That is, a sequential recovery strategy is utilized.

Step 10. For EL > 0, the confidential data extraction is associated with EL $+ 1$ rounds. First set the round index $R = 1$.

Step 10.1. Retrieve the Rth round confidential data w_R as

$$w_R = \begin{cases} 0 & \text{if} & \tilde{\tilde{d}}_j^i = 2 \times \text{EL} \quad \text{or} \quad \tilde{\tilde{d}}_j^i = -2 \times \text{EL} + 1 \\ 1 & \text{if} & \tilde{\tilde{d}}_j^i = -2 \times \text{EL} \quad \text{or} \quad \tilde{\tilde{d}}_j^i = 2 \times \text{EL} + 1 \end{cases} \tag{2.99}$$

Step 10.2. EL is decreased by 1 and R is increased by 1.

Step 10.3. If EL $\neq 0$, execute Steps 10.1 and 10.2 repeatedly until EL $= 0$. If EL $= 0$, execute

$$w_R = \begin{cases} 0 & \text{if} & \tilde{\tilde{d}}_j^i = 0 \\ 1 & \text{if} & \tilde{\tilde{d}}_j^i = 1 \end{cases} \tag{2.100}$$

Now R is increased as EL $+ 1$.

Step 10.4. Rearrange and concatenate the extracted data w_R ($R = 1$, 2,...,EL $+ 1$) as

$$W = w_1 || w_2 ||, ..., || w_{\text{EL}+1} \tag{2.101}$$

where $||$ represents the concatenation operation. Hence, the hidden confidential data W is extracted, and then go to Step 11.

Step 11. The secret pixel s^i can be losslessly recovered according to

$$s^i = b^{v-1} \times s^i_1 + b^{v-2} \times s^i_2 + \dots + s^i_v \qquad (2.102)$$

Step 12. Perform the inverse "S" scan on the s^i pixels to recover the secret image S.

Hence all the operations in the decoder are completed.

2.6.1.2.3 Example

As shown in Fig. 2.40, an example with $\{b, p\} = \{7, 13\}$ and $s_3 = \{2, 5, 4, 3, 3, 0, 1, 0, 2\}$ produced in Fig. 2.39 is investigated for data embedding. In this case, we can obtain $EL = 2$. Obviously, 6 bits confidential data can be embedded in s_3. Suppose the confidential sequence is "001101." In all sequel operations, the first element of s_3 is kept unchanged because the decoding operations are triggered by it. The preparation procedure includes difference computation and histogram shifting. First, a difference sequence $\{2, -3, 1, 1, 0, 3, -1, 1, -2\}$ is obtained. The next step is the histogram shifting. As $EL = 2$, the shifted results are $\{2, -5, 1, 1, 0, 6, -1, 1, -3\}$. Then the embedding operations are executed with three rounds. In the first round, only the last shifted difference value -2 can be utilized for the first secret bit "0" embedding and it is modified as -3. In the second round, four shifted difference value $\{1, 1, -1, 1\}$ can be utilized for the subsequent secret bits "0110" embedding and they are modified as $\{2, 3, -2, 2\}$. In the third round, only one shifted difference value 0 can be utilized for the last secret bit "1" embedding and it is modified as 1. In this way, the watermarked difference is obtained as $\{2, -5, 2, 3, 1, 6, -2, 2, -3\}$ and those modified differences are marked as *orange* (Gray in print versions) in Fig. 2.39. Then, the watermarked sequence is deduced as $\{2, 7, 3, 1, 2, -3, 2, -1, 3\}$ by subtracting the watermarked differences from the original values of the left neighbor. This processing is indicated as the *blue arrows*. The last operation is range adjustment. As $EL = 2$, 3 is added to each element of $\{2, 7, 3, 1, 2, -3, 2, -1, 3\}$ except the first one (i.e., $EL + 1$) and thus the final watermarked sequence is obtained as $\{2, 10, 6, 4, 5, 0, 5, 2, 6\}$.

The confidential data extraction principle is shown in Fig. 2.41. Suppose the decoder obtained the parameters $\{b, p\} = \{7, 13\}$ and the intact watermarked sequence $\{2, 10, 6, 4, 5, 0, 5, 2, 6\}$. Hence $EL = 2$ can be calculated. The first operation is range readjustment by subtracting $EL + 1$ from $\{2, 10, 6, 4, 5, 0, 5, 2, 6\}$ except the first element and the intermediate result $\{2, 7, 3, 1, 2, -3, 2, -1, 3\}$. Next, the s_3 recovery is triggered by the first element 2. That is, the watermarked difference -5 is computed according to 2 and 7 and its corresponding shifted difference -3 is deduced. According to trigger element 2 and the shifted difference -3, the original element of s_3 is recovered as 5. Repeat this processing with a sequential order, and s_3 can be accurately recovered as $\{2, 5, 4, 3, 3, 0, 1, 0, 2\}$. The confidential data extraction is indicated as orange rectangles also with three rounds involved. Each confidential bit is retrieved by comparing the watermarked elements and their corresponding recovered elements. In the first round, only one secret bit "0" is extracted from the last rectangle for the difference -2 is used in the first round

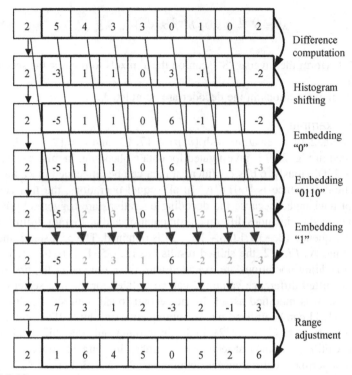

FIGURE 2.40

Example of data embedding for $\{b, p\} = \{7, 13\}$.

data embedding. In the second round, four secret bits "0110" are extracted for the associated differences are used in the second round data embedding. Likewise, one secret bit "1" is extracted in the third round. After that, the original confidential sequence can be obtained by rearranging the extracted results of the three rounds into "001101". These operations prove that s_3 along with the confidential data can be perfectly recovered at the same time. Consequently, the reversibility of secret sharing is still preserved.

2.6.1.3 Experimental Results

As shown in Fig. 2.42, ten 512×512 gray level images are selected as test images to evaluate the average performance of our scheme. The confidential data W in the following experiments are binary sequences produced by a pseudo random number generator. The embedding capacity is jointly determined by the parameters $\{b, p\}$ and the secret image content. Tables 2.5−2.7 show the embedding capacities of 10 images with various $\{b, p\}$, where $EL = 0$, $EL = 1$, and $EL = 2$, respectively. In Table 2.5, the average capacities provided by s_1, s_2, and s_3 are 239,309, 115,524, and 31,098 bits, respectively. In Table 2.6, they are 259,152, 171,483,

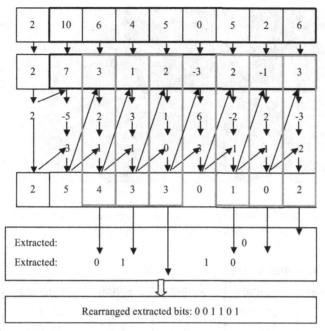

FIGURE 2.41

Example of data extraction for $\{b, p\} = \{7, 13\}$.

and 106,376 bits, respectively. In Table 2.7, they are 261,940, 202,386, and 157,780 bits, respectively. Obviously, a larger difference of b and p (i.e., a larger EL) leads to a higher capacity. Besides, as the similarity among these sequences is $s_1 > s_2 > s_3$, the capacity provided is also $s_1 > s_2 > s_3$. The highest average capacity of 2.37 bpp is achieved when $\{b, p\} = \{7, 13\}$.

Fig. 2.43 shows the capacities with $b = 7$, 8, 9, 10, 11, 12 and $p = 13$. The average highest capacity of 2.37 bpp is achieved when $b = 7$, and the lowest capacity of 1.50 bpp is achieved when $b = 12$. In fact, the distortions on shadow images with various b values are of the same level as long as the same p used. Therefore, it is recommended to set b as 7 to provide the highest capacity.

2.6.2 JOINT SECRET SHARING AND DATA HIDING FOR BLOCK TRUNCATION CODING-COMPRESSED IMAGES

In this subsection, we introduce our secure transmission system for block truncation coding (BTC)-compressed images proposed in Ref. [62]. The application scenario can be described as follows. Given a gray level or color image, we need to compress and transmit it over two independent but not secure channels. Besides transmission security, the following three factors must be considered in the system design. (1) The reconstruction image quality should be preserved, i.e., nearly the same as that in

FIGURE 2.42

Test image Lena, Baboon, Barbara, Airplane, Boat, (top row, from left to right), Bridge, Peppers, Aerial, Truck, and Texture (bottom row, from left to right).

Table 2.5 Capacities With $\{b, p\} = \{11, 13\}$

Secret Image	s_1 (Bit)	s_2 (Bit)	s_3 (Bit)	Total (Bit)	bpp
Lena	250,758	160,164	30,549	441,471	1.68
Baboon	224,799	71,855	24,055	320,709	1.22
Barbara	229,202	119,883	26,838	375,923	1.43
Airplane	253,331	176,023	44,350	473,704	1.81
Boat	246,792	121,672	25,654	394,118	1.50
Bridge	238,091	105,077	56,169	399,337	1.52
Peppers	252,299	142,461	24,842	419,602	1.60
Aerial	224,261	85,253	24,312	333,826	1.27
Truck	242,383	110,903	29,443	382,729	1.46
Texture	231,172	61,950	24,768	317,890	1.21
Average	*239,309*	*115,524*	*31,098*	*385,931*	*1.47*

BTC compression. (2) There should be low-complexity encoding and decoding, thus maintaining the real-time performance of BTC compression. (3) The shares should have a small size. This is essential to save transmission time and channel resources. In fact, in most available secret sharing methods, the sizes of shares are expanded when compared with the original secret data.

In particular, these three advantages are achieved in the proposed system with secret sharing and data hiding well synthesized. The compressed image can be reconstructed as long as both shares are collected. Otherwise, no meaningful information is decrypted. Besides, the encoding/decoding procedures are quite simple and the reconstructed image quality is nearly the same as that in BTC compression. Furthermore, each share is half the size of the compressed image, and thus no extra burden is laid on transmission channels.

Table 2.6 Capacities with $\{b, p\} = \{7, 11\}$

Secret Image	s_1 (Bit)	s_2 (Bit)	s_3 (Bit)	Total (Bit)	bpp
Lena	261,598	211,254	106,052	578,904	2.21
Baboon	256,372	130,972	102,160	489,504	1.87
Barbara	253,467	176,998	102,638	533,103	2.03
Airplane	260,766	219,298	123,758	603,822	2.30
Boat	259,433	178,078	103,649	541,160	2.06
Bridge	259,694	162,935	115,420	538,049	2.05
Peppers	261,048	203,496	101,874	566,418	2.16
Aerial	260,160	142,684	101,711	504,555	1.92
Truck	261,984	170,137	103,376	535,497	2.04
Texture	256,994	118,973	103,122	479,089	1.83
Average	*259,152*	*171,483*	*106,376*	*537,010*	*2.05*

Table 2.7 Capacities with $\{b, p\} = \{7, 13\}$

Secret Image	s_1 (Bit)	s_2 (Bit)	s_3 (Bit)	Total (Bit)	bpp
Lena	262,137	227,737	158,787	648,661	2.47
Baboon	261,998	176,420	155,346	593,764	2.27
Barbara	261,513	202,911	155,811	620,235	2.37
Airplane	261,783	231,767	170,742	664,292	2.53
Boat	261,711	205,501	157,230	624,442	2.38
Bridge	262,066	198,311	154,103	614,480	2.34
Peppers	261,936	224,300	155,516	641,752	2.45
Aerial	262,114	184,628	155,451	602,193	2.30
Truck	262,140	206,147	158,512	626,799	2.39
Texture	261,998	166,141	156,306	584,445	2.23
Average	*261,940*	*202,386*	*157,780*	*622,106*	*2.37*

2.6.2.1 Related Work

The standard BTC compression technique [63] is reviewed in the following discussion. Suppose the original image I is a gray level image. In the encoding stage, I is first partitioned into a set of nonoverlapping $k \times k$ blocks, and the mean value p_m of each block is calculated as

$$p_m = \frac{1}{k \times k} \sum_{x=1}^{k} \sum_{y=1}^{k} p(x, y) \qquad (2.103)$$

where $p(x,y)$ denotes the pixel value in the position (x,y). Next, the block pixels are thresholded as

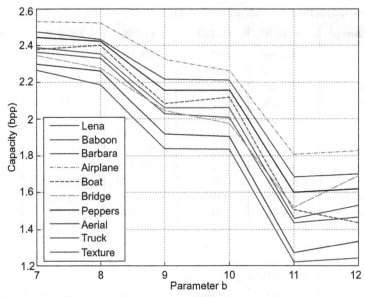

FIGURE 2.43

Capacities with $b = 7, 8, 9, 10, 11, 12$ and $p = 13$.

$$b(x, y) = \begin{cases} 1 & \text{if } p(x, y) > p_m \\ 0 & \text{otherwise} \end{cases} \quad (2.104)$$

resulting in a binary bitmap M, where $b(x,y)$ is the pixel value in the position (x,y) of M. Third, two quantization levels p_h and p_l are computed for each block, i.e., the mean values of those pixels with $p(x,y) > p_m$ and $p(x,y) \le p_m$, respectively. Thus, each block is represented by a pair of integers p_h, p_l in the range of [0, 255] and a $k \times k$ bitmap. The encoding procedure is completed, and the compressed content is transmitted.

In the decoding stage, each block can be approximately recovered with p_h, p_l, and M as

$$p'(x, y) = \begin{cases} p_h & \text{if } b(x, y) = 1 \\ p_l & \text{otherwise} \end{cases} \quad (2.105)$$

where $p'(x,y)$ is the reconstructed pixel value in the position (x,y) of the current decoded block. In this way, the decoded image can be reconstructed by collecting all the reconstructed blocks. In our context, p_m, p_h, and p_l are rounded to their nearest integers.

2.6.2.2 Joint Data Encryption and Data Hiding Model

We start from presenting the joint data encryption and data hiding model. Suppose the secret data is composed of two binary sequences $u = (u_1, u_2, \dots u_K)$ and $v = (v_1, v_2, \dots v_{K-1})$. The main idea of our model is to encrypt u, and meanwhile,

v is also hidden in two shares $m = (m_1, m_2, \ldots m_K)$ and $n = (n_1, n_2, \ldots n_K)$. The encryption strategy of this model is shown in Fig. 2.44.

The encoding procedures are as follows.

Step 1. Encrypt u_1 in m_1 and n_1. Randomly select a "1" or "0" and assign it to m_1, and then n_1 is determined by m_1 and u_1 as

$$n_1 = \begin{cases} m_1 & \text{if } u_1 = 1 \\ 1 - m_1 & \text{if } u_1 = 0 \end{cases} \tag{2.106}$$

Step 2. Hide v_1 in n_1 and m_2. That is, m_2 is determined by n_1 and v_1 as

$$m_2 = \begin{cases} n_1 & \text{if } v_1 = 1 \\ 1 - n_1 & \text{if } v_1 = 0 \end{cases} \tag{2.107}$$

Step 3. Encrypt u_2 in m_2 and n_2. That is, n_2 is determined by m_2 and u_2 as

$$n_2 = \begin{cases} m_2 & \text{if } u_2 = 1 \\ 1 - m_2 & \text{if } u_2 = 0 \end{cases} \tag{2.108}$$

Step 4. Repeat these operations until v_{j-1} is hidden in n_{j-1} and m_j as indicated with the dashed arrow, and u_j is encrypted in m_j and n_j as indicated with the solid arrow.

In this way, the sequence u is encrypted and v is hidden in two produced shares m and n.

In decoding, the sequences u and v can be recovered as

$$u_i = 1 - m_i \oplus n_i \quad 1 \le i \le K \tag{2.109}$$

$$v_i = 1 - m_{i+1} \oplus n_i \quad 1 \le i \le K - 1 \tag{2.110}$$

where $\oplus$ denotes the exclusive-OR operation.

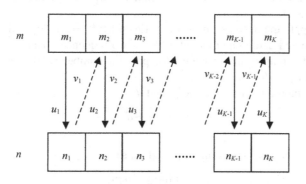

FIGURE 2.44

Encryption strategy of the joint data encryption and data hiding model.

2.6.2.3 Joint Block Truncation Coding and Secret Sharing

In the joint BTC and secret sharing scheme, the standard BTC compression and the joint data encryption and data hiding model are applied. In our case, the original image is partitioned into 4×4 blocks.

In the encoding stage, operations are as follows.

Step 1. Perform the standard BTC encoding on the first block, and its p_m, p_h, and p_l are obtained.

Step 2. Compute the difference d between p_m and p_l as

$$d = p_m - p_l \tag{2.111}$$

Considering in natural images, pixel values change gradually in a 4×4 block; the difference d is small for most natural image blocks as illustrated in Section 2.6.2.4. Therefore, it is reasonable to regard d as an integer that belongs to [0, 127], otherwise we set $d = 127$.

Step3. Translate p_l and d into 8-bit and 7-bit binary sequences, respectively. Concatenate them to form a 15-bit sequence denoted by $v = (v_1, v_2, ..., v_{15})$. Besides, rearrange the bitmap M into a 16-bit binary sequence, represented with $u = (u_1, u_2, ..., u_{16})$.

Step 4. Apply the encoding procedure [Eqs. (2.106)–(2.108)] of the joint data encryption and data hiding model to the block. Thus u is encrypted, and at the same time v is hidden in two produced shares $m = (m_1, m_2, ..., m_{16})$ and $n = (n_1, n_2, ..., n_{16})$.

Step 5. For the first share, translate $(m_1, m_2, ..., m_8)$ and $(m_9, m_{10}, ..., m_{16})$ into two integers in the range of [0, 255], respectively. The similar operations are also performed on n for the second share. In this way, the compressed information of each block corresponds to two shares, each with two "pixels."

Step 6. Repeat these operations for all the other blocks, and the share images S_1 and S_2 are obtained and transmitted independently.

The corresponding operations in the decoding stage are described as follows.

Step 1. Translate the received first two pixels of S_1 and S_2 into two 16-bit binary sequences.

Step 2. Apply the decoding procedure [Eqs. (2.109)–(2.110)] of the joint data encryption and data hiding model to these two sequences. Thus p_l, d, and the associated bitmap M are recovered. Suppose the number of "0"s and "1"s in M are n_l and $n_h = 16-n_l$, respectively.

Step 3. Compute p_m according to p_l and d as

$$p_m = p_l + d \tag{2.112}$$

Step 4. Compute p_h according to p_l and p_m as

$$p_h = \frac{(16p_m - n_l p_l)}{n_h} \tag{2.113}$$

Step 5. Reconstruct the BTC-compressed block based on p_l, p_m, and M according to Eq. (2.105).

Step 6. Repeat Steps 1—5 for all the other received shares' pixels, and thus the BTC-compressed image is reconstructed.

2.6.2.4 Experimental Results

The 512×512 gray level Lena image is selected as the test image, and the related experimental results are shown in Fig. 2.45. Obviously, the two 128×256 share images produced in our scheme look like random noises, thus transmission security of the compressed image can be guaranteed. Furthermore, the total amount of the transmission content is the same as that in the standard BTC compression, i.e., the compression ratio is kept as 4.

Many transmission scenarios, especially wireless transmissions, usually suffer from some abrupt errors such as packet loss [4]. As our scheme is based on a block-wise processing mechanism, these transmission errors of share images only corrupt the associated decrypted blocks. In other words, errors are not diffused to other reconstructed blocks, as illustrated in another experiment shown in Fig. 2.46. Fig. 2.46a and b are the corrupted versions of Fig. 2.45c and d respectively. From Fig. 2.46c, it is easy to find that only the corresponding blocks are corrupted, whereas others are still reconstructed correctly.

It is necessary to note that, compared with the reconstructed image based on the standard BTC, there is a slight quality degradation of the reconstructed image with the two intact shares. This is because the computed p_h for image reconstruction in our scheme is not exactly equal to that directly transmitted in the standard BTC.

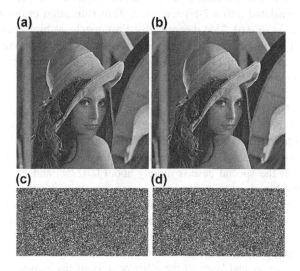

FIGURE 2.45

Experimental results on the Lena image. (a) The original image, (b) the reconstructed image by our scheme, (c) the share image S_1, (d) the share image S_2.

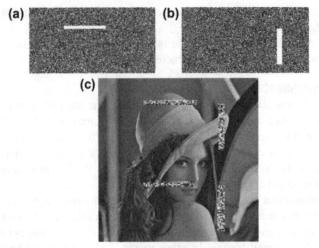

FIGURE 2.46

Experimental results on the received shares suffering transmission errors. (a) the corrupted S_1, (b) the corrupted S_2, and (c) the reconstructed image.

Namely, error is introduced in Eqs. (2.111)–(2.113) when a floating point number is rounded to its nearest integer. A large quantity of experimental results show that this image quality degradation is acceptable. For example, the PSNR of the reconstructed Lena using the standard BTC is 34.00 dB, whereas 33.96 dB is obtained in our scheme.

As mentioned in Section 2.6.2.3, d is set as 127 when it is larger than 127 such that it can be translated into a 7-bit sequence. Thus truncation errors may be produced for the range of d [0, 255] theoretically. Fortunately, as high correlation exist among pixels in natural image blocks, d is small in most cases. Ten 512×512 gray level images (Lena, Baboon, Barbara, Bridge, Boat, F16, Peppers, Elaine, Aerial, Truck) are selected to investigate the statistics of d values. Each image is partitioned into 4×4 blocks, thus totally 163,840 blocks, i.e., 163,840 d values are obtained and examined. The 256-bin histogram of d values is shown in Fig. 2.47. The bins at the high end (bins from 150 to 255) are empty and hence only a part (150 of 256) of the histogram is shown. In this experiment, only 44 d values are larger than 127. In addition, these large d values are in the range of [128, 150]. That is, the percentage of the special case is merely about 0.027%, and thus the possible errors are acceptable in practice.

In addition, there is another special case in our scheme, i.e., all the pixels in an original image block are of the same value. Suppose this value is denoted by p_s. In this case, $p_m = p_s$, $p_l = p_s$, $d = 0$, and all bits in the bitmap M are 0. Obviously, Eq. (2.113) cannot be applied any longer for both its denominator and numerator equal 0. Thus we set $p_h = p_s$, and keep all the other operations unchanged.

Actually, our scheme is also suitable for BTC-compressed color image transmission. Specifically, the original color image is decomposed into *red*, *green*, and *blue*

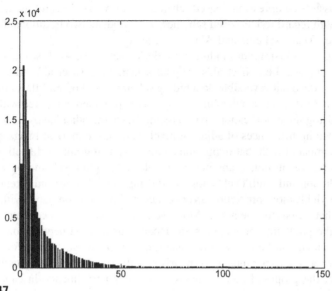

FIGURE 2.47

Statistical histogram of d values.

channels, and each channel is encoded as a gray level image. Finally all encoded channels are recomposed into color noiselike shares.

2.6.2.5 Discussions

Thien and Lin [57] develop a Lagrange interpolation–based (r, t) threshold scheme for image secret sharing. An input image can be encrypted into t random noiselike share images. If r or more than r shares are collected, the original image can be reconstructed. Thien and Lin's scheme is an alternative method to encrypt the BTC-compressed image with $r = t = 2$. For example, a 512×512 input image can be encrypted into two 128×256 shares. However, this is achieved by truncating all compressed "pixel" values (e.g., 4 "pixels" translated from p_h, p_l, and M of a block) from the range [0, 255] to [0, 250] before encryption. In other words, to perfectly reconstruct the BTC-compressed image, the truncation errors must also be encrypted additionally. Consequently, two produced shares are usually larger than 128×256 pixels, resulting in more storage space and transmission time.

2.7 SUMMARY

This chapter discussed the reversible data hiding schemes in the spatial domain. We first provide an overview of the spatial domain–based schemes. Then we discussed five types of spatial domain lossless information hiding methods, i.e., the modulo addition–based scheme, DE-based schemes, histogram modification–based schemes, lossless compression—based schemes, and reversible secret sharing—based schemes. With regard to DE-based schemes, we introduce two traditional DE-based schemes, i.e., Tian's scheme and Alatter's scheme.

With regard to histogram modification—based schemes, we first introduce two traditional schemes, i.e., Ni et al.'s original scheme and Li et al.'s APD method. Then we introduce our reversible data hiding scheme based on multilevel histogram modification. On the one hand, a higher capacity is provided compared with one- or two-level histogram modification—based methods. On the other hands, as secret data are embedded in differences of adjacent pixels values, the marked image quality is improved compared with that in previous multilevel histogram modification—based work. Finally, we introduce another reversible data hiding scheme by means of hybrid prediction and multilevel histogram shifting. As only one seed pixel involved, our scheme yields more prediction errors concentrating at 0 compared with conventional prediction-based methods. Moreover, more errors concentrated around 0 because the prediction precision is enhanced. Our method depends on only one parameter, which can be adjusted to trade the marked image quality for capacity, and vice versa. By experimental comparison with several previous methods, we observe that the proposed method leads to a better performance in capacity and marked image quality simultaneously.

With regard to lossless compression—based schemes, we first introduce two traditional schemes, i.e., the lossless RS data-embedding and lossless G-LSB data embedding methods. Then, we introduce our reversible data hiding method for error diffused halftone images. In this method, the hidden data can be extracted with a secret key and the original image is perfectly recovered. Experimental results show the effectiveness of the method. Since the characteristics of the HVS are exploited, lower degradation is introduced to the visual quality of the image. Our method in this research only focuses on the gray level halftone images, and it is expected to be extended to the color halftone images in the future.

With regard to reversible secret sharing—based schemes, we introduce two of our methods. One is the high-capacity data hiding scheme integrated in reversible secret sharing, where a double module mechanism and a multilevel histogram modification strategy are utilized. Both the secret and cover images can be recovered accurately. In addition, a large quantity of confidential data can be embedded in shadow images during secret sharing and then perfectly retrieved during secret image decryption. As the architecture of our scheme relies on Lagrange interpolation, the security is guaranteed. Experimental results show that the capacity can be achieved as about 2.37 bpp on natural images. Another scheme is a joint secret sharing and data hiding system for BTC-compressed image secure transmission. The compressed content is encrypted and hidden in two share images. Since each share image is half size of the compressed content, the available channel resources are enough for share image transmission. Not only the standard BTC compression properties such as low-encoding/decoding complexity and acceptable reconstructed image quality are still preserved but also transmission security is guaranteed because each block is encrypted individually.

REFERENCES

[1] J. Barton, Method and Apparatus for Embedding Authentication Information Within Digital Data, July 8, 1997. U. S. Patent 5646997.

[2] B. Macq, Lossless multiresolution transform for image authenticating watermarking, The 10th European Signal Processing Conference (2000) 1973–1976.

[3] B. Macq, F. Dewey, Trusted headers for medical images, in: Proceedings of DFG VIII-DII Watermarking Workshop, 1999.

[4] C. Honsinger, P. Jones, M. Rabbani, et al., Lossless Recovery of All Original Image Containing Embedded Data, Auguest 21, 2001. U. S. Patent 6278791 BI.

[5] J. Fridrich, M. Goljan, R. Du, Lossless data embedding for all image formats, Proceedings of SPIE 4675 (2002) 572–583.

[6] J. Fridrieh, M. Goljan, R. Du, Invertible authentication, Proceedings of SPIE 4314 (2001) 197–208.

[7] M. Celik, G. Sharma, A. Tekalp, et al., Reversible data hiding, Proceedings of International Conference on Image Processing 2 (2002) 157–160.

[8] M. Celik, G. Sharma, A. Tekalp, et al., Lossless generalized-LSB data embedding, IEEE Transactions on Image Processing 14 (2) (2005) 253–266.

[9] J. Tian, Reversible watermarking using a difference expansion, Transactions on Circuits and Systems for Video Technology 13 (8) (2003) 890–896.

[10] J. Tiara, High capacity reversible data embedding and content authentication, in: Proceedings of IEEE International Conference on Acoustics, Speech, and Signal Processing 3, 2003, pp. 517–520.

[11] A. Alattar, Reversible watermark using the difference expansion of a generalized integer transform, IEEE Transactions on Image Processing 13 (8) (2004) 1147–1156.

[12] L. Kamstra, H. Heijmans, Reversible data embedding into images using wavelet techniques and sorting, IEEE Transactions on Image Processing 14 (12) (2005) 2082–2090.

[13] H. Kim, V. Sachnev, Y. Shi, et al., A novel difference expansion transform for reversible data embedding, IEEE Transactions on Information Forensics and Security 3 (3) (2008) 456–465.

[14] D. Thodi, J. Rodriguez, Expansion embedding techniques for reversible watermarking, IEEE Transactions on Image Processing 16 (3) (2007) 721–730.

[15] Y. Hu, H. Lee, J. Li, DE-based reversible data hiding with improved overflow location map, IEEE Transactions on Circuits and Systems for Video Technology 19 (2) (2009) 250–260.

[16] X. Wang, C. Shao, X. Xu, et al., Reversible data-hiding scheme for 2-D vector maps based on difference expansion, IEEE Transactions on Information Forensics and Security 2 (3) (2007) 311–320.

[17] Y. Hu, H. Lee, K. Chen, et al., Difference expaansion based reversible data hiding using two embedding directions, IEEE Transactions on Multimedia 10 (8) (2008) 1500–1512.

[18] C. Lee, H. Wu, C. Tsai, et al., Adaptive lossless steganographic scheme with centralized difference expansion, Pattern Recognition 41 (6) (2008) 2097–2106.

[19] D. Wu, G.Z. Wang, Lossless data hiding based on difference expansion and difference shifting, Journal of Jilin University (Engineering and Technology Edition) 40 (4) (2010) 1071–1074.

[20] L. Jiang, X. Guo, H. Yang, et al., Threshold controlled scheme of difference expansion techniques for reversible watermarking, Journal of Shanghai Jiaotong University (Science) 15 (5) (2010) 541–548.

[21] F. Peng, Y. Lei, M. Long, et al., A reversible watermarking scheme for two-dimensional CAD engineering graphics based on improved difference expansion, Computer-Aided Design 43 (8) (2011) 1018–1024.

[22] Z. Ni, Y. Shi, N. Ansari, et al., Reversible data hiding, IEEE Transactions on Circuits and Systems for Video Technology 6 (3) (2006) 354–362.

[23] J. Hwang, J. Kim, J. Choi, A reversible watermarking based on histogram shifting, in: Proceeding of Digital Watermarking 4283, 2006, pp. 348–361. LNCS.

[24] W. Kuo, D. Jiang, Y. Huang, Reversible data hiding based on histogram, in: Proceeding Advanced Intelligent Computing Theories and Application 4682, 2007, pp. 1152–1161. LNCS.

[25] M. Fallahpour, Reversible image data hiding based on gradient adjusted prediction, IEICE Electronic Express 5 (20) (2008) 870–876.

[26] W. Tai, C. Yeh, C. Chang, Reversible data hiding based on histogram modification of pixel differences, IEEE Transactions on Circuits and systems for Video Technology 19 (6) (2009) 906–910.

[27] C. De Vleeschouwer, J. Delaigle, B. Macq, Circular interpretation of bijective transformations in lossless watermarking for media asset management, IEEE Tranctions on Multimedia 5 (1) (2003) 97–105.

[28] C. De Vleeschouwer, J. Delaigle, B. Macq, Circular interpretation of histogram for reversible watermarking, in: Proceedings of IEEE Workshop Multimedia Signal Processing, 2001, pp. 345–350.

[29] Z. Ni, Y. Shi, N. Ansari, et al., Robust lossless image data hiding designed for semi-fragile image authentication, IEEE Transactions on Circuits and systems for Video Technology 18 (4) (2008) 497–509.

[30] Z. Ni, Y. Shi, N. Ansari, et al., Robust lossless image data hiding, in: Proceedings of IEEE International Conference on Multimedia Expo, 3, 2004, pp. 2199–2202.

[31] D. Zou, Y. Shi, Z. Ni, A semi-fragile lossless digital watermarking scheme based on integer wavelet transform, in: Proceedings of IEEE 6th Workshop Multimedia Signal Processing, 2004, pp. 195–198.

[32] D. Zou, Y. Shi, Z. Ni, et al., A semi-fragile lossless digital watermarking scheme based on integer wavelet transform, IEEE Transactions on Circuits and systems for Video Technology 16 (10) (2006) 1294–1300.

[33] X. Zeng, L. Ping, X. Pan, A lossless robust data hiding scheme, Pattern Recognition 43 (4) (2010) 1656–1667.

[34] K. Hayat, W. Puech, G. Gesquiere, Scalable 3-D terrain visualization through reversible JPEG2000-based blind data hiding, IEEE Transactions on Multimedia 10 (7) (2008) 1261–1276.

[35] C. Chang, D. Kieu, Y. Chou, Reversible information hiding for VQ indices based on locally adaptive coding, Journal of Visual Communication and Image Representation 20 (1) (2009) 57–64.

[36] Y. Shi, Q. Xuan, Methods and Apparatus for Lossless Data Hiding, November 2, 2010. U. S. Patent 7 826 638 B2.

[37] M. Goljan, J. Fridrich, R. Du, Distortion-free data embedding for images, in: The 4th Information Hiding Workshop, vol. 2137, LNCS, Springer-Verlag, 2001, pp. 27–41.

[38] J. Tian, Reversible watermarking by difference expansion, Proceedings of Workshop on Multimedia and Security (2002) 19–22.

[39] A.M. Alattar, Reversible watermark using difference expansion of quads, in: Proceedings of IEEE International Conference on Acoustics, Speech, and Signal Processing, vol. 3, 2004, pp. 377−380.

[40] Y.C. Li, C.M. Yeh, C.C. Chang, Data hiding based on the similarity between neighboring pixels with reversibility, Digital Signal Processing 20 (4) (2009) 1116−1128.

[41] Z.F. Zhao, H. Luo, Z.M. Lu, J.S. Pan, Reversible data hiding based on multilevel histogram modification and sequential recovery, AEU—International Journal of Electronics and Communications 65 (10) (2011) 814−826.

[42] K.S. Kim, M.J. Lee, H.Y. Lee, H.K. Lee, Reversible data hiding exploiting spatial correlation between sub-sampled images, Pattern Recognition 42 (11) (2009) 3083−3096.

[43] D. Coltuc, P. Bolon, J.M. Chassery, Exact histogram specification, IEEE Transactions on Image Processing 15 (5) (2006) 1143−1152.

[44] H.C. Wu, H.C. Wang, C.S. Tsai, C.M. Wang, Reversible image steganographic scheme via predictive coding, Displays 31 (1) (2010) 35−43.

[45] H. Luo, F.X. Yu, Z.L. Huang, H. Chen, Z.M. Lu, Reversible data hiding based on hybrid prediction and interleaving histogram modification with single seed pixel recovery, Signal, Image and Video Processing 8 (1) (2014) 813−818.

[46] R.C. Gonzalez, R.E. Woods, Digital Image Processing, Second ed., Prentice Hall, Englewood Cliffs, 2002.

[47] H.W. Tseng, C.P. Hsieh, Prediction-based reversible data hiding, Information Sciences 179 (14) (2009) 2460−2469.

[48] W. Hong, T.S. Chen, C.W. Shiu, Reversible data hiding for high quality images using modification of prediction errors, Journal of Systems and Software 82 (11) (2009) 1833−1842.

[49] X. Wu, N. Memon, Context-based, adaptive, lossless image codec, IEEE Transactions on Communication 45 (1997) 437−444.

[50] X. Wu, Lossless compression of continuous-tone images via context selection, quantization, and modeling, IEEE Transactions on Image Processing 6 (1997) 656−664.

[51] Z.F. Zhao, K.Y. Chau, Z.M. Lu, High capacity data hiding in reversible secret sharing, International Journal of Innovative Computing, Information and Control 7 (11) (2011) 6411−6422.

[52] T.N. Pappas, D.L. Neuhoff, Least-squares model based halftoning, IEEE Transactions on Image Processing 8 (8) (1999) 1102−1116.

[53] S.M. Cheung, Y.H. Chan, A technique for lossy compression of error-diffused halftones, in: Proceedings Of International Conference on Multimedia & Expo, 2004, pp. 1083−1086.

[54] J.S. Pan, H. Luo, Z.M. Lu, A lossless watermarking scheme for halftone image authentication, International Journal of Computer Science and Network Security 6 (2B) (2006) 147−151.

[55] M. Valliappan, B.L. Evans, D.A.D. Tompkins, F. Kossentini, Lossy compression of stochastic halftones with JBIG2, in: Proceedings Of International Conference on Image Processing, 1999, pp. 214−218.

[56] A. Shamir, How to share a secret, Communication of the ACM 22 (11) (1979) 612−613.

[57] C.C. Thien, J.C. Lin, Secret image sharing, Computers and Graphics 26 (5) (2002) 765−770.

[58] M. Naor, A. Shamir, Visual Cryptography. Advances in Cryptology: Eurocrypt'94, Spring-Verlag, Berlin, 1995, pp. 1−12.

[59] P.Y. Lin, J.S. Lee, C.C. Chang, Distortion-free secret image sharing mechanism using modulus operator, Pattern Recognition 42 (2009) 886–895.

[60] P.Y. Lin, C.S. Chan, Invertible secret image sharing with steganography, Pattern Recognition Letters 31 (2010) 1887–1893.

[61] Z.F. Zhao, K.Y. Chau, Z.M. Lu, High capacity data hiding in reversible secret sharing, International Journal of Innovative Computing, Information and Control 7 (11) (2011) 6411–6422.

[62] H. Luo, Z.F. Zhao, Z.M. Lu, Joint secret sharing and data hiding for block truncation coding compressed image transmission, Information Technology Journal 10 (3) (2011) 681–685.

[63] O.R. Mitchell, E.J. Delp, S.G. Carlton, Block truncation coding: a new approach to image compression, in: Proceedings of the IEEE International Conference on Communications, 1978, 12B.1.1–12B.1.4.

Lossless Information Hiding in Images on Transform Domains

3.1 INTRODUCTION

3.1.1 INVERTIBLE MAPPING

Among all the methods suitable for reversible data hiding, transform domain—based methods belong to a category, which are of great significance to value expansion—based reversible watermarking algorithms. Note that during the reversible watermarking process, all the operations should be reversible, including the transform reversibility. The transform used in reversible information hiding should be in the category of invertible mapping, thus we introduce related concepts of functions and invertible mapping.

3.1.1.1 Functions

For a mapping $f: X \rightarrow Y$, it is called a function if it satisfies the following two conditions:

(1) Total: For any $x \in X$, there is at least one $y \in Y$, which makes xfy, that is, x and y hold the relationship f.
(2) Many-to-One: If xfy and xfz, then $y = z$. That is to say, multiple input values can correspond to one output value, but one input value cannot correspond to multiple output values. Note that, many-to-one also involves one-to-one.

For any mapping satisfying these two conditions, we can use a function $y = f(x)$ to denote this mapping.

3.1.1.2 Injection, Surjection, and Bijection

Functions can be classified into three categories, i.e., injection, surjection, and bijection.

(1) Injection, also called one-to-one mapping, maps different arguments x to different images y.
(2) Surjection, also called onto, means for every image y, at least one argument x is mapped on it.
(3) Bijection means for every image y, one and only one argument x is mapped on it. We can prove that if the function $f: X \rightarrow Y$ is a bijection, then its inverse

Lossless Information Hiding in Images. http://dx.doi.org/10.1016/B978-0-12-812006-4.00003-6

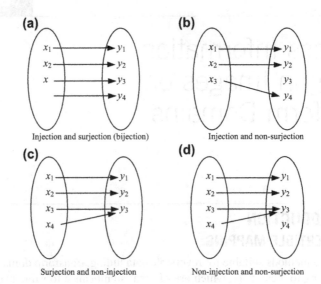

FIGURE 3.1

The combinations of injection and surjection. (a) Injection and surjection (bijection), (b) injection and nonsurjection, (c) surjection and noninjection, (d) noninjection and nonsurjection.

mapping is a function from Y to X denoted as f^{-1} and the function $f^{-1}: Y \rightarrow X$ is also a bijection. Moreover, we also say f is invertible, that is, f is an invertible mapping or invertible function.

Fig. 3.1 gives four combinations related to injection and surjection.

3.1.1.3 Left and Right Inverses
Assume $f: X \rightarrow Y$ and $g: Y \rightarrow X$; if $gf = E_x$, then g is a left inverse for f, and if $fg = E_y$, then g is the right inverse for f. Here, E_x means the identity function on the set X, i.e., the function that leaves its argument unchanged. If we use mappings to denote left and right inverses, for $f: X \rightarrow Y$, we can prove the following conclusions:

(1) f has a left inverse, if and only if f is injective.
(2) f has a right inverse, if and only if f is a surjective.

Obviously, in Fig. 3.1, (a) has both left and right inverses, (b) only has a left inverse but no right inverse, (c) only has a right inverse but no left inverse, and (d) has neither left inverse nor right inverse.

In the design of reversible watermark embedding algorithms, the used transform should be reversible, that is, it has both left and right inverses; in other words, it should be bijective to meet the required reversibility.

3.1.2 REQUIREMENTS OF REVERSIBLE INFORMATION HIDING TO INTEGER TRANSFORMS

The integer transform we refer to is a reversible transform whose input and output are all integers and whose output is not scaled. This integer transform, in fact, is an approximation of float version of corresponding transform. Traditional orthogonal transforms such as discrete cosine transform (DCT) and discrete wavelet transform (DWT) should adopt float versions to guarantee the orthogonality and linearity. But for reversible watermarking systems, the inverse transform of float version will have rounding error. To guarantee the overall reversibility of the algorithm, we need to impose some constraints on the embedding algorithm to avoid the expansion of the rounding error introduced by quantizing the result of inverse transform into integers to guarantee the reversibility of integer transform. For example, the coefficient data C (floats) can be obtained by performing the float DCT forward transform on the image data X (integers):

$$C = \text{DCT}(X) \tag{3.1}$$

If C is not further processed, it can be performed with the direct inverse transform to obtain

$$X' = \text{DCT}^{-1}(C) \tag{3.2}$$

As long as the float precision of the computer or other digital signal processor is sufficiently high, we can guarantee that the rounding result $[X]$ (integers) of the inverse transform X'(floats) is equal to the original input image data X: $[X'] = X$, where [.] is the rounding operation to get the closest integer of a float. However, if we perform other operations on the coefficient C before the inverse transform, for example, the watermark embedding operation, which turns C into C_W, then we can get the inverse transform result X_W:

$$X_W = \text{DCT}^{-1}(C_W) \tag{3.3}$$

After the rounding operation, we can obtain $[X_W]$, thus the error between X_W and $[X_W]$ may result in that the error between the forward DCT transform result C_W' of $[X_W]$:

$$C_W' = \text{DCT}([X_W]) \tag{3.4}$$

and C_W exceeds 2 times of the general rounding error, that is, larger than 1. This will result in the loss of embedded watermark data and the irreversibility of the whole algorithm.

From this discussion, we can see that, unless we impose special requirements on the embedding algorithm, traditional float version transforms cannot guarantee the overall reversibility of the reversible watermarking algorithms. Therefore, for the occasions where we need transform domain–based algorithms, we consider using integer transforms to replace the float versions of the corresponding transforms. These integer transforms should have the following two properties:

(1) The input and output are both integers, that is, integer-to-integer.
(2) The transform is reversible, that is, it is bijective.

In the history, the definitions of integer transforms [1−12] are not so explicit. Some refer to the transforms whose whole conversion process is based on integer arithmetic without rounding error, but the results are often dyadic rational numbers rather than integers in the true sense [1−4]; some refer to the transforms whose input and output are integers, although the intermediate calculations may involve floating points and rounding operations [10−12]. For the latter, there are two cases, one is that the output is subject to scaling operations such as Algorithm B given in Ref. [10], that is, each output is in fact an integer approximation of N times corresponding floating-point real number; the other is that each output is an integer approximation of corresponding floating-point real number without scaling such as Algorithm A given in Ref. [10], which is the true sense of integer approximation of corresponding floating-point conversion.

From the reversibility requirement of reversible watermarking algorithms, i.e., the transform should have both a left and a right inverse, we can see that, among the aforementioned various integer transforms, the integer transforms that are really suitable for reversible watermarking are only those integer-to-integer transforms whose output is an integer approximation of corresponding floating-point real number without scaling. Note that for the integer transform whose conversion result is a dyadic rational number [2−5], its output is not an integer in the true sense; there will be accumulated rounding errors and irreversible problems mentioned earlier; However, for the integer transform whose output is subject to scaling operations such as Algorithm B in Ref. [10], similar to the situation given in Fig. 3.1b, there is no guarantee that it is right invertible, therefore, it cannot guarantee that the overall algorithm is reversible. In this chapter, the integer DCT (IntDCT) we adopt is the 8×8 transform derived from Algorithm A given in Ref. [10] (for the one-dimensional case), whereas the integer DWT we adopt is the integer version of the famous Cohen-Daubechies-Feauveau (CDF) (2,2) wavelet [13] obtained by using the lifting scheme in Ref. [14]. Both integer transforms satisfy the reversibility requirement of reversible watermarking algorithms.

3.2 OVERVIEW OF TRANSFORM-BASED INFORMATION HIDING

In general, transform-based information hiding algorithms are based on spectrum spread. Among various information hiding algorithms, transform domain−based algorithms are the most frequently used information-embedding algorithms. Compared with the spatial domain, transform domain is more complex, but it is robust, even if a lot of payload is embedded, the visual effect is still very good.

Now a widely accepted view is that secret information should be embedded in the middle-frequency coefficients of the transform domain of the host image. This is because the high-frequency part has little effect on the quality of the original image, whereas the low-frequency part can achieve good robustness (after JPEG compression, a large part of the high-frequency components may be quantized to 0), so the middle-frequency part is a good compromise between visibility and robustness. Here we only introduce several kinds of common discrete transform domain–based algorithms.

3.2.1 DISCRETE COSINE TRANSFORM–BASED INFORMATION HIDING

The DCT-based orthogonal transform method proposed by Ahmed et al. [15] is considered to be the best transform domain method for images and speech. For DCT, because the algorithm used in JPEG (image compression standard) is based on two-dimensional 8×8 DCT blocks, it is more robust to compression and filtering operations. The following is the shortcoming of DCT: the main feature of DCT is that after the conversion of an image from the spatial domain to the frequency domain, the image has a good time–frequency property, but this property is not made full use of during the information-embedding process. Although the visual quality of the image obtained is greatly improved, for the image without complex texture, its embedding capacity is still high, however, when the texture is very complex, due to the inability of the algorithm to recognize the texture complexity of the image, there may be a small embedding capacity.

Koch was the first to propose an effective watermarking scheme based on DCT [16]. This scheme first divided the image into 8×8 blocks for further calculation. Then the scheme selected a pair of frequency coefficients from the predetermined 12 pairs of middle-frequency DCT coefficients to embed information.

The DCT-based algorithm proposed by Cox et al. is not based on blocking, but performs DCT on the whole image and adopts the spectrum spreading information hiding technique [17]. By modifying the first N coefficients that perceive most strongly the human visual system (HVS), it achieves the information hiding purpose. Unfortunately, because the embedding strength of the DCT coefficients are different, no further discussion was given in their scheme; however, the algorithm is robust to various image-processing operations, which made a great contribution to improving the robustness of information hiding algorithms.

Tao et al. proposed an adaptive information hiding scheme [18]. This scheme performed data hiding on the alternating current (AC) DCT coefficients. In this scheme, the authors proposed a local classification–based algorithm and adopted the masking effects of HVS to determine the sensitivity to noise. Since this method requires the original image during the watermark extraction, it is a nonblind watermarking scheme.

Compared with the traditional irreversible watermarking algorithms, there are relatively fewer DCT domain reversible watermarking algorithms. Two typical algorithms are Yang et al.'s IntDCT coefficients based histogram modification scheme

[19] and the DCT quantized coefficients based reversible watermarking algorithm proposed by Chen and Kao [20].

3.2.2 DISCRETE FOURIER TRANSFORM–BASED INFORMATION HIDING

Assume we use $f(x_1,x_2)$ to denote an image of size $N_1 \times N_2$, where x_1, x_2 are all integers and $0 \leq x_1 \leq N_1$, $0 \leq x_2 \leq N_2$; then its two-dimensional discrete Fourier transform is as follows:

$$F(k_1, k_2) = \sum_{n_1=0}^{N_1-1} \sum_{n_2=0}^{N_2-1} f(x_1, x_2) e^{-\frac{2\pi x_1 k_1}{N_1} - \frac{2\pi x_2 k_2}{N_2}} \qquad (3.5)$$

and the inverse discrete Fourier transform can be given as follows:

$$f(x_1, x_2) = \frac{1}{N_1 N_2} \sum_{k_1=0}^{N_1-1} \sum_{k_2=0}^{N_2-1} F(k_1, k_2) e^{\frac{2\pi x_1 k_1}{N_1} + \frac{2\pi x_2 k_2}{N_2}} \qquad (3.6)$$

Here, $f(x_1,x_2)$ and $F(k_1,k_2)$ form a DFT pair. In general, the computational load to perform DFT on a natural image is huge.

The basic properties of DFT are as follows:

(1) Translation

If an image is translated in the spatial domain, then its phase will also be translated in the frequency domain, and we have:

$$F(k_1, k_2) = \exp[-j(ak_1 + bk_2)] \leftrightarrow f(x_1 + a, x_2 + b) \qquad (3.7)$$

By using this property of DFT, the energy of an image concentrates on the low-frequency region, after translation, since $f(x_1,x_2)$ and $F(k_1,k_2)$ are periodical functions, the energy of the image will concentrate on the center of the image, which facilitates various operations on the image in the frequency domain and also accord with our visual perception.

(2) Scaling

The scaling effect in the frequency domain is just opposite to that in the spatial domain, which can be described as follows:

$$\frac{1}{\rho} F\left(\frac{k_1}{\rho}, \frac{k_2}{\rho}\right) \leftrightarrow f(\rho x_1, \rho x_2) \qquad (3.8)$$

(3) Rotation

If the image is rotated in the spatial domain by an angle θ, then the corresponding image in the frequency domain is also rotated by an angle θ, which can be described as follows:

$$F(k_1 \cos\theta - k_2 \sin\theta, k_1 \sin\theta + k_2 \cos\theta) \leftrightarrow f(x_1 \cos\theta - x_2 \sin\theta, x_1 \sin\theta + x_2 \cos\theta) \qquad (3.9)$$

Pereira et al. presented a watermarking scheme [21] based on the fast Fourier transform domain [i.e., FFT, which is proposed to reduce the computational complexity of DFT, by using the periodicity and symmetry of the complex exponential $W_N = e^{-j2\pi/N}$ and using the butterfly structure to release the computational burden of DFT, where the complexity is not higher than $N_1N_2 \times \log_2(N_1N_2)$]. The watermark is composed of two parts, one is the template and the other is the spread spectrum signal containing secret information and payload. The template does not contain any information that can be used to detect the watermark information in the DFT-transformed image. If there is a template in the image, then we calibrate the image based on the embedded template, and then extract the watermark information from the calibrated image. This scheme is robust to various image processing operations such as rotation, scaling, and translation; however, the attackers can attack the embedded template by exchanging their own information, which makes the watermark security not easy to guarantee.

3.2.3 DISCRETE WAVELET TRANSFORM—BASED INFORMATION HIDING

With the new JPEG compression standard determining to use the new technology wavelet transform, even though it has not been widely used until now, if you want that your own researched and developed information hiding algorithm has more vitality, you must take into account the wavelet transform. The wavelet transform is developed on the basis of Fourier, and compared with DFT or DCT, its flexibility in the nonstationary signal analysis is stronger, its ability to adapt to the visual characteristics of human eyes is stronger, and it is therefore considered to be a fairly accurate model of the HVS.

Wavelet transform provides a local analysis of time and space frequencies by performing detailed multiresolution analysis on the signal with the scaling and translation operations, which can be focused on any details of the signal, so the wavelet transform is also known as "mathematical microscope."

The wavelet transform can divide the image into a low-resolution approximation image LL and three low-frequency detail images, i.e., HL (horizontal), LH (vertical), and HH (diagonal). After wavelet transform, the image is divided into multiple scales. Fig. 3.2 shows a two-level DWT decomposition of the Lena image.

As can be seen from Fig. 3.2, once every wavelet transform is done, the low-frequency part of it at the same level of resolution is decomposed, whereas the high frequency part is retained, due to the fact that the low-frequency part concentrates most of the energy of the image, whereas the high-frequency part just records some of the edge of the image information. Therefore, in practice, we generally embed data in the high-frequency part, while preserving the low-frequency part of the information as much as possible; otherwise it will affect the quality of the reconstructed image.

FIGURE 3.2

Two-level discrete wavelet transform decomposition of the Lena image.

Corvi et al. proposed one of the first schemes for information hiding in the wavelet transform domain [22]. The scheme randomly generates a spread spectrum sequence as secret information based on a key and then embeds the secret information in the low-frequency part of the wavelet-transformed image. Since the data are embedded in the low-frequency part, the quality of the reconstructed image is not affected; however, this algorithm needs original carrier during the detection and extraction of hidden information.

The watermarking scheme proposed by Kundur utilized the multiresolution property of the wavelet-transformed image together with the human perceptual system (HVS) model [23]. Unlike the scheme proposed by Corvi et al., it embeds secret data in three high-frequency detail components at the same resolution. On the other hand, the selection of secret data is also different from that of Corvi et al.'s scheme; Kundur's scheme uses a binary image as secret information. The specific method is as follows: the host image and the watermark message are both converted from the spatial domain into the wavelet domain, and the host image is independently performed with wavelet transform x times, resulting in $3x$ high-frequency components, whereas the watermark message is performed with wavelet transform only once, resulting in three high-frequency components and a low-frequency component. The selected rectangles from the detail components of each layer of the host image are with the same size of the corresponding components of the watermark message; finally each watermark information is hidden in each rectangle based on the reversible integer wavelet transform—based information hiding scheme. In addition, Xuan et al. [24] proposed an integer wavelet—based histogram gap method, by which the wavelet coefficient histogram continues to form a gap for embedding.

3.3 INTEGER DISCRETE COSINE TRANSFORM—BASED SCHEMES

3.3.1 INTEGER DISCRETE COSINE TRANSFORM

3.3.1.1 One-Dimensional Integer Discrete Cosine Transform and Its Fast Algorithm

Let $x(n)$ $(n = 0, 1, ..., N-1)$ be a real input sequence. We assume that $N = 2^t$, where $t > 0$. The scaled DCT of $x(n)$ is defined as follows:

$$X(k) = \sum_{n=0}^{N-1} x(n)\cos\frac{\pi(2n+1)k}{2N}, \quad k = 0, 1, ..., N-1 \tag{3.10}$$

Let $\mathbf{C}_N$ be the transform matrix of the DCT, that is

$$\mathbf{C}_N = \left\{\cos\frac{\pi(2n+1)k}{2N}\right\}_{k,n=0,1,...,N-1} \tag{3.11}$$

To derive the fast algorithm, we first get a factorization of the transform matrix based on the following lemma [5]:

Lemma 3.1: The transform matrix $\mathbf{C}_N$ can be factored as

$$\mathbf{C}_N = \mathbf{P}_N \begin{bmatrix} \mathbf{I}_{N/2} & \mathbf{0} \\ \mathbf{0} & \mathbf{U}_{N/2} \end{bmatrix} \begin{bmatrix} \mathbf{C}_{N/2} & \mathbf{0} \\ \mathbf{0} & \mathbf{C}_{N/2} \end{bmatrix} \begin{bmatrix} \mathbf{I}_{N/2} & \mathbf{0} \\ \mathbf{0} & \mathbf{D}_{N/2} \end{bmatrix} \begin{bmatrix} \mathbf{I}_{N/2} & \widehat{\mathbf{I}}_{N/2} \\ \mathbf{I}_{N/2} & -\widehat{\mathbf{I}}_{N/2} \end{bmatrix} \tag{3.12}$$

where $\mathbf{I}_{N/2}$ is the identity matrix of order $N/2$, $\widehat{\mathbf{I}}_{N/2}$ is the matrix derived by reversing the rows of $\mathbf{I}_{N/2}$, and $\mathbf{D}_{N/2}$ is a diagonal matrix defined as follows:

$$\mathbf{D}_{N/2} = \mathrm{diag}\left(2\cos\frac{\pi}{2N}, 2\cos\frac{3\pi}{2N}, ..., 2\cos\frac{(N-1)\pi}{2N}\right) \tag{3.13}$$

$$\mathbf{U}_{N/2} = \begin{bmatrix} 0.5 & 0 & 0 & ... & 0 & 0 \\ -0.5 & 1 & 0 & ... & 0 & 0 \\ 0.5 & -1 & 1 & ... & 0 & 0 \\ ... & ... & ... & ... & ... & ... \\ 0.5 & -1 & 1 & ... & 1 & 0 \\ -0.5 & 1 & -1 & ... & -1 & 1 \end{bmatrix} \tag{3.14}$$

$\mathbf{P}_N$ is a permutation matrix defined as follows:

$$\mathbf{P}_N = \begin{bmatrix} 1 & 0 & ... & 0 & 0 & 0 & ... & 0 \\ 0 & 0 & ... & 0 & 1 & 0 & ... & 0 \\ 0 & 1 & ... & 0 & 0 & 0 & ... & 0 \\ 0 & 0 & ... & 0 & 0 & 1 & ... & 0 \\ ... & ... & ... & ... & ... & ... & ... & ... \\ 0 & 0 & ... & 1 & 0 & 0 & ... & 0 \\ 0 & 0 & ... & 0 & 0 & 0 & ... & 1 \end{bmatrix} \tag{3.15}$$

and $\mathbf{C}_{N/2}$ is the transform matrix of the scaled DCT with length $N/2$.

Float-point multiplications are needed for the algorithm when the matrix $\mathbf{D}_{N/2}$ is multiplied by a vector. To avoid float multiplications, we want to turn this matrix into products of lifting matrices and then approximate the elements of the lifting matrices by numbers with the form $\beta/2^\lambda$, where β and λ are integers. To get an IntDCT, we can turn the matrix into $\mathbf{D}_{N/2} = \mathbf{E}_{N/2}\mathbf{F}_{N/2}$, where

$$\mathbf{E}_{N/2} = \text{diag}\left(\sqrt{2}, 1, \dots, 1\right) \tag{3.16}$$

$$\mathbf{F}_{N/2} = \text{diag}\left(\sqrt{2}\cos\frac{\pi}{2N}, 2\cos\frac{3\pi}{2N}, \dots, 2\cos\frac{(N-1)\pi}{2N}\right) \tag{3.17}$$

Lemma 3.2: The determinant of the matrix $\mathbf{F}_{N/2}$ is 1, that is, $\det(\mathbf{F}_{N/2}) = 1$. The matrix $\mathbf{F}_{N/2}$ can be factored into the product of lifting matrices as follows:

$$\mathbf{F}_{N/2} = \left\{ \prod_{k=0}^{N/4-1}\left[\mathbf{L}_{2k,2k+1}(\alpha_{2k}-1)\mathbf{L}_{2k+1,2k}(1) \times \mathbf{L}_{2k,2k+1}\left(\frac{1}{\alpha_{2k}}-1\right)\mathbf{L}_{2k+1,2k}(-\alpha_{2k})\right]\right\} \cdot$$
$$\left\{ \prod_{k=1}^{N/4-1}\left[\mathbf{L}_{2k-1,2k}(\alpha_{2k-1}-1)\mathbf{L}_{2k,2k-1}(1) \times \mathbf{L}_{2k-1,2k}\left(\frac{1}{\alpha_{2k-1}}-1\right)\mathbf{L}_{2k,2k-1}(-\alpha_{2k-1})\right]\right\} \tag{3.18}$$

where $\mathbf{L}_{i,j}(s)$ are lifting matrices with order $N/2$, which is defined as follows:

Definition 3.1: A lifting matrix is a matrix whose diagonal elements are 1s, and only one nondiagonal element is nonzero. If the order of a lifting matrix is N, we use the notation $\mathbf{L}_{i,j}(s)$ $(i \neq j)$ to denote the lifting matrix whose only nonzero element is at the ith row and the jth column $(i, j = 0, 1, \dots, N-1)$ and whose nondiagonal nonzero element is s.

In Eq. (3.18), α_k is defined as follows:

$$\alpha_0 = \sqrt{2}\cos\frac{\pi}{2N}, \alpha_k = 2\alpha_{k-1}\cos\frac{(2k+1)\pi}{2N} \tag{3.19}$$
$$k = 1, 2, \dots, N/2 - 1$$

To avoid float multiplications, we can approximate the nonzero element of the lifting matrices by numbers that are of the form $\beta/2^\lambda$, where β and λ are integers, that is, we replace every nonzero element s by $\text{RB}(s)$ defined as follows:

Definition 3.2: The notation $\text{RB}(s)$ is used to denote a number that is of the form $\beta/2^\lambda$ (dyadic rational number) and approximates to the real number s.

Furthermore, we replace α_j and $1/\alpha_j$ in Eq. (3.18) by $\text{RB}(\alpha_j)$ and $\text{RB}(1/\alpha_j)$ and get an approximating matrix for $\mathbf{F}_{N/2}$ as follows

$$\overline{\mathbf{F}}_{N/2} = \left\{ \prod_{k=0}^{N/4-1}\left[\mathbf{L}_{2k,2k+1}(\text{RB}(\alpha_{2k})-1)\mathbf{L}_{2k+1,2k}(1) \times \mathbf{L}_{2k,2k+1}\left(\text{RB}\left(\frac{1}{\alpha_{2k}}\right)-1\right)\mathbf{L}_{2k+1,2k}(-\text{RB}(\alpha_{2k}))\right]\right\} \cdot$$
$$\left\{ \prod_{k=1}^{N/4-1}\left[\mathbf{L}_{2k-1,2k}(\text{RB}(\alpha_{2k-1})-1)\mathbf{L}_{2k,2k-1}(1) \times \mathbf{L}_{2k-1,2k}\left(\text{RB}\left(\frac{1}{\alpha_{2k-1}}\right)-1\right)\mathbf{L}_{2k,2k-1}(-\text{RB}(\alpha_{2k-1}))\right]\right\} \tag{3.20}$$

We also approximate the matrix $\mathbf{E}_{N/2}$ by

$$\overline{\mathbf{E}}_{N/2} = \mathrm{diag}\left(\mathrm{RB}\left(\sqrt{2}\right), 1, ..., 1\right) \qquad (3.21)$$

Then, the correspondent approximating matrix for the transform matrix $\mathbf{C}_N$ is

$$\overline{\mathbf{C}}_N = \mathbf{P}_N \begin{bmatrix} \mathbf{I}_{N/2} & \mathbf{0} \\ \mathbf{0} & \mathbf{U}_{N/2} \end{bmatrix} \begin{bmatrix} \overline{\mathbf{C}}_{N/2} & \mathbf{0} \\ \mathbf{0} & \overline{\mathbf{C}}_{N/2} \end{bmatrix} \begin{bmatrix} \mathbf{I}_{N/2} & \mathbf{0} \\ \mathbf{0} & \overline{\mathbf{D}}_{N/2} \end{bmatrix} \begin{bmatrix} \mathbf{I}_{N/2} & \widehat{\mathbf{I}}_{N/2} \\ \mathbf{I}_{N/2} & -\widehat{\mathbf{I}}_{N/2} \end{bmatrix} \qquad (3.22)$$

where

$$\overline{\mathbf{D}}_{N/2} = \overline{\mathbf{E}}_{N/2}\mathbf{F}_{N/2} \qquad (3.23)$$

If the same method is used to factor the matrix $\overline{\mathbf{C}}_{N/2}$ recursively until the order is 1, we get the complete factorization of $\overline{\mathbf{C}}_N$. The matrix $\overline{\mathbf{C}}_N$ defines a new transform that does not need float multiplications. Finally, we call it an IntDCT.

Definition 3.3: Assume that $N = 2^t$. The transform matrix of an IntDCT $\overline{\mathbf{C}}_N$ is defined recursively by $\overline{\mathbf{C}}_1 = \{1\}$, and

$$\overline{\mathbf{C}}_{2^j} = \mathbf{P}_{2^j} \begin{bmatrix} \mathbf{I}_{2^{j-1}} & \mathbf{0} \\ \mathbf{0} & \mathbf{U}_{2^{j-1}} \end{bmatrix} \begin{bmatrix} \overline{\mathbf{C}}_{2^{j-1}} & \mathbf{0} \\ \mathbf{0} & \overline{\mathbf{C}}_{2^{j-1}} \end{bmatrix} \begin{bmatrix} \mathbf{I}_{2^{j-1}} & \mathbf{0} \\ \mathbf{0} & \overline{\mathbf{D}}_{2^{j-1}} \end{bmatrix} \begin{bmatrix} \mathbf{I}_{2^{j-1}} & \widehat{\mathbf{I}}_{2^{j-1}} \\ \mathbf{I}_{2^{j-1}} & -\widehat{\mathbf{I}}_{2^{j-1}} \end{bmatrix} \qquad (3.24)$$

The transform is not unique. Actually, any choice of function RB determines a transform. Based on the definition, we get a fast algorithm for the IntDCT as follows.

Algorithm 3.1: Fast Algorithm for IntDCT:

Step 1: Compute

$$\begin{aligned} g(n) &= x(n) + x(N-1-n) \\ h(n) &= x(n) - x(N-1-n), \quad n = 0, 1, ..., N/2-1 \end{aligned} \qquad (3.25)$$

Step 2: Compute $\widehat{\boldsymbol{h}} = \overline{\mathbf{E}}_{N/2}\mathbf{F}_{N/2}\boldsymbol{h}$, where

$$\begin{aligned} \boldsymbol{h} &= (h(0), h(1), ..., h(N/2-1))^{\mathrm{T}} \\ \widehat{\boldsymbol{h}} &= \left(\widehat{h}(0), \widehat{h}(1), ..., \widehat{h}(N/2-1)\right)^{\mathrm{T}} \end{aligned} \qquad (3.26)$$

Step 3: Compute the IntDCT with length $N/2$ for sequences $g(n)$ and $\widehat{h}(n)$, and let the outputs be $G(k)$ and $H(k)$, respectively. Steps 1 and 2 can be used recursively during the computation.

Step 4: Compute

$$\begin{aligned} X(2k) &= G(k), \quad k = 0, 1, ..., N/2-1 \\ X(1) &= H(0)/2 \\ X(2k+1) &= H(k) - X(2k-1), k = 1, 2, ..., N/2-1 \end{aligned} \qquad (3.27)$$

3.3.1.2 Two-Dimensional Integer Discrete Cosine Transform and its Fast Algorithm

This section introduces the 2D-IntDCTs proposed in Ref. [5]. In general, a 2D transform can be generated by simply using the tensor products of the corresponding 1D transform, that is, we can process the 2D input array by implementing the 1D transform along its rows and columns consecutively (also called the row–column method). This method gives a 2D transform that has a separable kernel. In this section, we introduce a nonseparable 2D integer transform by combining the 1D integer transform and the polynomial transform. The 2D transform proposed in Ref. [5] needs far fewer numbers of operations than the row–column 2D transform does.

Let $x(n,m)$ ($n = 0, 1, ..., N-1$; $m = 0, 1, ..., M-1$) be the 2D input sequence. We assume that M and N are powers of 2 and $M \geq N$. Therefore, we can write $N = 2^t$ and $M = 2^J N$, where $t > 0$ and $J \geq 0$, respectively. If $M < N$, the definition can also be used by simply interchanging N and M. The scaled 2D DCT is defined as follows:

$$X(k, l) = \sum_{n=0}^{N-1} \sum_{m=0}^{M-1} x(n, m) \cos \frac{\pi(2n + 1)k}{2N} \cos \frac{\pi(2m + 1)l}{2M},$$

$$k = 0, 1, ..., N - 1; \quad l = 0, 1, ..., M - 1$$

(3.28)

3.3.1.2.1 Two-Dimensional Integer Discrete Cosine Transform

Based on the 1D IntDCT and the polynomial transform, we have the following integer 2D IntDCT [5].

Definition 3.4: The 2D-IntDCT of $x(n,m)$ is $X(k,l)$ ($k = 0, 1,...,N-1$; $l = 0, 1,...,M-1$), which can be computed in the following steps.

Step 1: Compute $y(p,m) = x(q(p,m),m)$, where $q(p,m)$ is defined as follows:

$$q(p, m) = \begin{cases} 2f\left(p, \dfrac{m}{2}\right) & m \text{ is even and } f\left(p, \dfrac{m}{2}\right) < \dfrac{N}{2} \\[2mm] 2N - 1 - 2f\left(p, \dfrac{m}{2}\right) & m \text{ is even and } f\left(p, \dfrac{m}{2}\right) \geq \dfrac{N}{2} \\[2mm] 2f\left(p, M - \dfrac{m+1}{2}\right) & m \text{ is odd and } f\left(p, M - \dfrac{m+1}{2}\right) < \dfrac{N}{2} \\[2mm] 2N - 1 - 2f\left(p, M - \dfrac{m+1}{2}\right) & m \text{ is odd and } f\left(p, M - \dfrac{m+1}{2}\right) \geq \dfrac{N}{2} \end{cases}$$

$$p = 0, 1, ..., N - 1, m = 0, 1, ..., M - 1$$

(3.29)

where $f(p,m) = ((4p + 1)m + p) \bmod N$.

Step 2: Compute the 1D-IntDCT of each row of the array $y(p,m)$, and let the output array be $V(p,l)$.

Step 3: Compute a polynomial transform

$$A_k(z) \equiv \sum_{p=0}^{N-1} V_p(z)\hat{z}^{pk} \mathrm{mod}\left(z^{2M}+1\right), \quad k=0,1,...,N-1 \qquad (3.30)$$

where $V_p(z) = \sum_{l=0}^{M-1} V(p,l)z^l - \sum_{l=M+1}^{2M-1} V(p,2M-l)z^l$; $\hat{z} \equiv z^{2^{J+2}} \mathrm{mod}\, z^{2M}+1$, and then we get

$$B_k(z) \equiv A_k(z)z^{2^J k} \mathrm{mod}\left(z^{2M}+1\right) \qquad (3.31)$$

Step 4: Compute

$$X_k(z) = \sum_{l=0}^{2M-1} X(k,l)z^l \equiv \frac{1}{2}\left(B_k(z) + B_k\left(z^{-1}\right)\right)\mathrm{mod}\left(z^{2M}+1\right) \qquad (3.32)$$

where only $X(k,l)$ ($k = 0, 1, ..., N-1$; $l = 0, 1, ..., M-1$) is needed.

It can be proved that if the IntDCT in Step 2 is replaced by the ordinary DCT, the 2D-IntDCT defined earlier is the scaled version of the ordinary 2D-DCT defined in Eq. (3.28). Therefore, the 2D-IntDCT can also be viewed as the integer approximation to the float-point 2D-DCT. However, it is different from the row—column 2D-IntDCT.

3.3.1.2.2 Reconstruction Algorithm for 2D-Integer Discrete Cosine Transform

The aforementioned 2D-IntDCT is invertible if the 1D-IntDCT used in Step 1 is invertible. In addition, the inverting process can be described as follows.

Algorithm 3.2: Fast Algorithm for Inverse 2D-IntDCT:

Step 1: Generate the polynomials

$$X_k(z) = \sum_{l=0}^{M-1} X(k,l)z^l - \sum_{l=M+1}^{2M-1} X(k,2M-l)z^l, \text{ and compute}$$

$$A_k(z) \equiv \left(X_k(z) + X_{N-k}(z)z^{-M}\right)z^{k2^J}\mathrm{mod}\left(z^{2M}+1\right) \qquad (3.33)$$

Step 2: Compute a polynomial transform

$$V_p(z) \equiv \frac{1}{N}\sum_{k=0}^{N-1} A_k(z)\hat{z}^{pk}\mathrm{mod}\left(z^{2M}+1\right), \quad p=0,1,...,N-1 \qquad (3.34)$$

where the coefficient of $V_p(z)$ is denoted by $V(p,l)$.

Step 3: Compute the inverse 1-D IntDCT of each row of the array $V(p,l)$, and let the output array be $y(p,m)$.

Step 4: Reorder the array $y(p,m)$ to get $x(p,m) = y(r(n,m),m)$, where

$$r(n,m) = \begin{cases} g\left(\dfrac{n}{2},\dfrac{m}{2}\right) & m \text{ and } n \text{ are even} \\[3mm] g\left(N - \dfrac{n+1}{2},\dfrac{m}{2}\right) & m \text{ is even and } n \text{ is odd} \\[3mm] g\left(\dfrac{n}{2}, M - \dfrac{m+1}{2}\right) & n \text{ is even and } m \text{ is odd} \\[3mm] g\left(N - \dfrac{n+1}{2}, M - \dfrac{m+1}{2}\right) & m \text{ and } n \text{ are odd} \end{cases} \quad (3.35)$$

$$n = 0,1,\ldots,N-1, m = 0,1,\ldots,M-1$$

and the function $g(n,m) = ((4m+1)^{-1}(n-m)) \bmod N$.

3.3.1.3 Comparison of Discrete Cosine Transform and Integer Discrete Cosine Transform

IntDCT has at least two advantages over DCT. First, IntDCT needs no floating-point multiplications. The floating-point multiplications are replaced by lifting steps that need only integer operations and shifting. This is very important for applications in mobile devices since it is easier and cheaper (power saving) to realize integer operations than to implement floating-point multiplications. Second, if a sufficient word length is used to represent the intermediate data of IntDCT, the round-off error can be eliminated completely. There is no information lost after the transform even if it is computed in a fixed-point computer. Therefore, it can be used for lossless compression. Furthermore, we can also approximate the lifting step as shown in Fig. 3.3 by using a nonlinear transform, i.e., approximate a DCT by an invertible integer to integer nonlinear transform as follows:

$$\hat{y}(i) = x(i) + \lfloor sx(j) \rfloor, \quad \hat{y}(k) = x(k), \quad k \neq i \quad (3.36)$$

This transform is nonlinear! In addition, it maps integer into integer! The nonlinear transform is invertible, and its inverse is as follows:

$$x(i) = \hat{y}(i) - \lfloor s\hat{y}(j) \rfloor, \quad x(k) = \hat{y}(k), \quad k \neq i \quad (3.37)$$

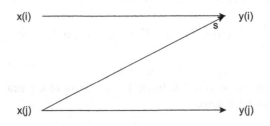

FIGURE 3.3

Flowchart of a lifting step.

Although DCT is also an invertible transform, the round-off error always exists when we approximate the trigonometric functions. It is impossible to perfectly construct the original data. Therefore, it cannot be used for lossless image compression. However, since IntDCT is a new transform, its performance, such as the decorrelation property, remains to be questioned, and more experiments are needed to be done. Generally speaking, the performance of IntDCT is related to the number of bits used for the lifting multipliers. In the aforementioned algorithms, it is equivalent to the accuracy of approximating (α_j) or $(1/\alpha_j)$ by $RB(\alpha_j)$ or $RB(1/\alpha_j)$. It is very difficult to give a theoretical analysis on the accuracy and performance. Fortunately, experiments in Refs. [25] and [26] have shown that even with a very coarse approximation, the performance of eight-point and 16-point IntDCT is still close to that of DCT.

3.3.2 INTEGER DISCRETE COSINE TRANSFORM—BASED LOSSLESS INFORMATION HIDING SCHEME USING COMPANDING TECHNIQUE

As we know, natural images' histogram is shaped differently. And bit-shifts on pixel values will cause much noticeable distortion to images. These two facts make the companding and bit-shift-based approach hard to be suitable for lossless information hiding applications in images, although the capacity performance is quite a desirable advantage of this reversible technique. Yang et al. proposed a 2-dimensional IntDCT—based approach [27] to circumvent these problems and use the bit-shift operation of companding technique successfully in reversible watermarking for images. In 2003, the authors from Philips Research proposed a reversible image watermarking scheme [28], which also exhibits high capacity, but this scheme is not based on bit-shift operations. In this section, we first review some relevant knowledge on the approach proposed in Ref. [29] and integer-to-integer DCT, then introduce Yang et al.'s reversible image watermarking scheme [27], and finally introduce the simulation results given in Ref. [27].

3.3.2.1 Related Knowledge
3.3.2.1.1 The Distribution of 8 × 8 Discrete Cosine Transform Coefficients
With regard to the distribution of 8 × 8 DCT transform coefficients, Lam analyzed it theoretically [30]; the distribution of 8 × 8 DCT coefficients of most natural images can be summarized as a generalized Gaussian distribution, and the higher the image redundancy, the narrower the shape of the distribution (i.e., the larger the number of coefficients with small values is, the better role the bit-shift operation plays). We divide the original gray-scale image of size $M \times N$ into 8 × 8 blocks (assuming the total number of image blocks is S), and perform the 8 × 8 DCT transform on each pixel block B_i ($i = 0, 1, ..., S-1$) to obtain S coefficient blocks C_i ($i = 0, 1, ..., S-1$). Next, for all S coefficient blocks C_i ($i = 0, 1, ..., S-1$), we take all AC coefficients $c_i(p,q)$ at position (p,q) to compose 63 AC coefficient

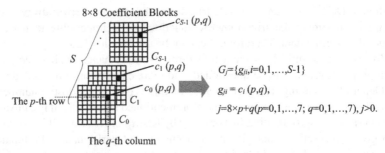

FIGURE 3.4

8 × 8 Discrete cosine transform coefficient grouping.

sets G_j ($j = 1, 2, ..., 63$), as shown in Fig. 3.4. Ref. [30] provided all typical histogram distributions for the direct current (DC)-efficient set and all AC coefficient groups $G_j(j = 1, 2, ...,63)$ as shown in Fig. 3.5. As can be seen from Fig. 3.5, the histogram of DCT coefficient group G_j shows the trend of being gradually concentrated near the value 0 with the AC coefficient tending to be of high frequency, which gives us a revelation: if we perform the bit-shift operation on high-frequency DCT coefficients, we should be able to get the best watermarking performance in terms of peak signal-to-noise ratio (PSNR)-bit-rate curve. However, note that owing to the presence of rounding errors and accumulated errors during the calculation process for floating-point DCT, it is difficult to meet the reversibility requirements for reversible watermarking algorithms; we can only consider the integer transforms that meet the reversibility requirements (discussed in detail in Section 3.1.2).

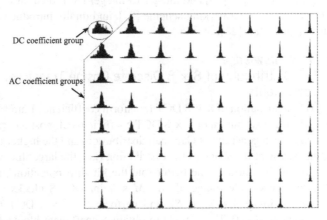

FIGURE 3.5

8 × 8 Discrete cosine transform direct current (DC) and alternating current (AC) coefficient groups' distribution shape.

3.3.2.1.2 Bit-Shift-Based Reversible Watermarking Technique

Assume there is a time discrete signal x of length N: $x \in \{0, 1, ..., 2^m - 1\}^N$, where m is the number of bits used to represent a sample. The bit-shift operation used in the companding technique–based watermarking algorithm [29] can be briefly described as follows.

Note that if x_{max} is not larger than half the maximum possible value, i.e., $x_{max} \leq 2^{m-1} - 1$, it may be amplified by 2 (left shifted by 1 bit) without introducing any overflow in the quantization:

$$y' = 2x \tag{3.38}$$

e.g., $x = 5(101\text{B})$, $y' = 10(1010\text{B})$.

Obviously, the result contains only even-valued samples. So the least significant bit (LSB) of y' is available for embedding a watermark and additional information. This result can be generalized to the case of p bit-shift operations, which allows the embedding of p bits in the LSB of a signal x:

$$y' = 2^p x \tag{3.39}$$

with

$$x_{max} \leq 2^{m-p-1} \quad \text{and} \quad p = 1, 2, ..., m - 1 \tag{3.40}$$

Note that as long as Eq. (3.40) is satisfied, the embedded watermark and additional bits can be retrieved from the LSB of y' and the original signal x can be restored perfectly by one bit-shift operation to the right side.

In some cases, Eq. (3.40) is not satisfied, and an overflow can be prevented by applying a companding function. In this book, a companding process includes the bit-shift operation, a compression function C, and an expansion function E, and C and E are related as follows:

$$EC\, x = I\, x\, (I: \text{identity function}) \tag{3.41}$$

In the digital case, the quantized version of C and E are C_Q and E_Q, where Q reflects a quantization operation. It can be easily seen that, for some n, C_Q may map more than one input $x[n]$ to the same output $x_Q[n]$ and E_Q cannot reconstruct the original signal, i.e.,:

$$x_E[n] = (E_Q C_Q x)[n] \neq I\, x[n] \tag{3.42}$$

Then the companding error can be defined as

$$q[n] = x[n] - (E_Q C_Q x)[n] = x[n] - x_E[n] \tag{3.43}$$

Note that this companding error will not be 0 whenever a non-one-to-one mapping occurs in CQ. To make the embedding process reversible, we must losslessly compress $q[n]$ as a part of the overhead bits embedded in the space saved from the bit-shift operations. While extracting the embedded data and restoring the original signal, the expansion function and inverse bit-shift operations are performed.

(a) (b)

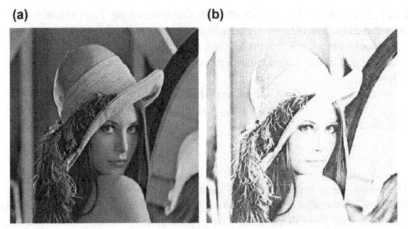

FIGURE 3.6

Comparison between the watermarked Lena image and the original Lena. (a) Original 256 grayscale Lena (b) Watermarked Lena using the companding scheme directly in the spatial domain: Peak signal-to-noise ratio = 6.457 dB, capacity < 0.

The embedding and extracting structures and further details about bit-shift and companding process are presented in Ref. [29].

The reversible watermarking approach proposed in Ref. [29] shows high capacity, which is close to 1 bit per sample for audio signals. However, due to the disadvantage of natural images' histogram, this approach is obviously not suitable for images. We give a watermarked example in Fig. 3.6 as a simulation result from an original 512×512-sized 256 grayscale Lena image by using the companding scheme directly in the spatial domain. We can see from Fig. 3.6b that although the capacity reaches 262,144 (512×512) bits, the quality of the watermarked image is completely unacceptable and the bit cost (1,027,315 bits) for the companding error is even much more than the capacity! In our simulations, although companding functions can be improved to gain a better result in some cases, the bits used to represent companding errors are hard to be less than the saved space.

3.3.2.1.3 Integer Discrete Cosine Transform and Left and Right Invertible Mapping

The problem of histogram shape suggests our searching for a way to modify an image's original histogram to exhibit a "good" shape with as many samples as possible around small values like Laplacian distribution shape. Of course this modification must be a reversible transformation if the reversibility is required. It is easily seen that many integer-to-integer transforms satisfy this condition.

With regard to the energy-concentrating ability, we consider DCTs. Lam and Goodman [30] analyzed the distribution of 2D 8×8 DCT coefficients of 8×8 image blocks and provide a theoretical explanation for the generalized Gaussian distribution—the distribution of the DCT coefficients of most natural images. In many cases, the shape of the generalized Gaussian distribution looks close to the Laplacian distribution, which makes it possible to use the bit-shift scheme in the transformed domain of integer-to-integer version of float-point 2D DCT.

We perform 2D-IntDCT on each 8×8 block and bit-shifts on each coefficient group consisting of coefficients from all coefficient blocks corresponding to the same position in an 8×8 array. For example, if we divide a 512×512 sized image into 8×8 blocks B_{ij} ($i = 0,1,...,4095$; $j = 0,1,...,63$), which corresponds to coefficient blocks C_{ij} ($i = 0, 1, ..., 4095$; $j = 0, 1, ..., 63$), all the coefficients collected from the 4096 blocks in the same position j in each coefficient block constitute a coefficient group G_{ji} ($j = 0, 1, ..., 63$; $i = 0, 1, ..., 4095$) as shown in Fig. 3.4. The histogram of each G_{ji} exhibits a Laplacian-like shape, which can be explained in Fig. 3.5 [30]. Then we can perform the bit-shift operations on all G_{ji} to embed watermarks and other overhead bits as described in Sections 3.3.2.2−3.3.2.5.

Note that the integer data type of outputs in the forward or inverse transform is not sufficient to ensure the reversibility of Yang et al.'s reversible watermarking scheme [27]. Another important factor is that the chosen IntDCT must be both a left-invertible and a right-invertible mapping. For example, when we perform the forward 2D IntDCT on an original image block B, we can obtain the result C, and when we perform the inverse transform on C, we can surely restore B. The process from B to C and back to B can be called left-invertible property of this IntDCT, as in Eq. (3.44), where Int.DCT and Int.$^{-1}$DCT represent forward 2D-IntDCT and its inverse operation.

$$\begin{cases} \text{Int.DCT}(B) = C \\ \text{Int.}^{-1}\text{DCT}(C) = B \end{cases} \tag{3.44}$$

Now suppose we modify C (corresponding to B in the spatial domain) to C' ($C' \neq C$) in the IntDCT domain; the reversibility requires that for any C', the result B' by the inverse transform must not equal the original B. We call this process from C' to B' ($B' \neq B$) and back to C' right-invertible property, as in Eq. (3.45).

$$\begin{cases} \text{Int.}^{-1}\text{DCT}(C') = B' \\ \text{Int. DCT}(B') = C' \end{cases} \tag{3.45}$$

Now if $B = B'$ when $C' \neq C$, Eqs. (3.44) and (3.45) cannot be satisfied at the same time, so this IntDCT does not satisfy the reversibility required for Yang et al.'s scheme. Note that in Refs. [3,4] IntDCTs represent those transforms close to regular DCT but with integer operations and dyadic rationales as resulting coefficients. These IntDCTs can modify the output coefficients to integers by value scaling, but they are absolutely not right-invertible after the scaling operation. If we modify one LSB bit of a coefficient in C, it is hard to ensure that the resulting B' is different, at least 1 bit, from the original B. So we only consider those integer-to-integer DCTs that are both left and right invertible. In Yang et al.'s schemes, they derived a 2D-IntDCT from the 1D version proposed in Ref. [10]

(algorithm A in Ref. [10]) and utilized it to obtain coefficient values for bit-shift operations. This IntDCT is linearly constructed by a very simple lifting matrix and satisfies the requirement of left and right invertible property on the whole integer field.

Another problem we must consider is the pixel value over- and underflow caused by the coefficient modification in the 2D-IntDCT domain. The errors between the original pixels and those modified ones are difficult to estimate due to nonlinearity of IntDCTs. Yang et al. estimated the errors in an indirect way, as described in Section 3.3.2.2.

3.3.2.2 Basic Embedding and Extracting Processes

A basic frame of Yang et al.'s scheme is presented in Fig. 3.7, based on the 2D-IntDCT described in Section 3.3.2.1, where x is an original 8×8 image block; x_W is the watermarked version of x; c and c_W are coefficient blocks of the original image block and the watermarked coefficient block, respectively; and c_{BS} is the coefficient block with those selected AC coefficients' LSB saved by bit-shift operations. *Key* is a secret key to decide which coefficients are to be modified in one coefficient block. The positions tagged with "×" in Fig. 3.7, for example, represent the coefficients selected by *Key* in the coefficient block. *WM* represents the watermark bits. Int.DCT represents 2D-IntDCT and Int.$^{-1}$DCT is the inverse transform.

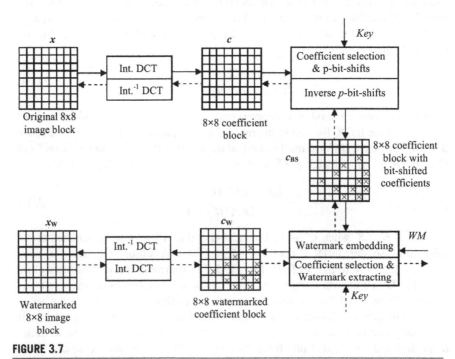

FIGURE 3.7

Embedding and extracting process for one 8×8 image block (*solid arrow*, embedding; *dashed arrow*, extracting).

3.3.2.3 Error Estimation to Prevent Overflow and Underflow

Note that not all 8×8 blocks in the original image are suitable for watermark embedding due to possible overflow (e.g., >255 for 256 grayscale images) and underflow (e.g., <0 for 256 grayscale images) problems. Specifically, overflows and underflows can be caused by two reasons: the first is the bit-shift operation and the second is the embedding of watermark bits in the saved p LSBs.

Overflows and underflows caused by the first reason can be determined correctly simply by applying bit-shift operations over selected coefficients, and it should be sees if the resulting pixels after the inverse IntDCT will overflow or underflow or not. If overflows or underflows occur, the original image block cannot be a candidate for embedding and we can just leave it intact. Otherwise, we proceed to consider the second reason—the embedded watermark bits. Obviously, we cannot predict the specific watermark bits to be embedded, so we must manage to find out those block proof against overflows and underflows under the condition whatever information is embedded. Similar to the preprocessing method in Ref. [31], Yang et al. preset two thresholds TH_l and TH_h ($0 \le TH_l < TH_h \le 255$) in image's pixel scale range [0.255]. Assume x is the original image block, then x' is the restored version of x by IntDCT with selected coefficients bit-shifted but without any watermark or other overhead bits embedded (i.e., all LSB of selected coefficients equal 0). It is expected that any x' with all its 64 pixels' values falling inside the scale range $[TH_l, TH_h]$ can be embedded with any watermark bits embedded in the LSB of selected coefficients without worrying about any overflows or underflows. To calculate the two thresholds TH_l and TH_h, we must estimate the maximum pixel errors caused by the watermark bits embedding in the saved LSB.

However, the IntDCT is not a linear transform and the error estimation based on x' is a complicated task. We can circumvent this problem with a float-point DCT as a bridge. The detailed scheme is shown in Fig. 3.8, where x is the original 8×8 image block, c is the 2D-IntDCT coefficient block of x; c_{BS} is the coefficient block after bit-shift (with all LSB of selected coefficients to be "0"), x_{BSF} is the pixel block restored from c_{BS} by 2-dimensional float-point DCT, w is watermark bits to be embedded in LSB of c_{BS}, c_W is the coefficient block with watermark bits embedded in the LSB plane, x_{wF} is the pixel block restored from c_W by 2D float-point DCT, and x_{wI} is the pixel block restored from c_W by 2D-IntDCT. Int.DCT and Flt.DCT represent

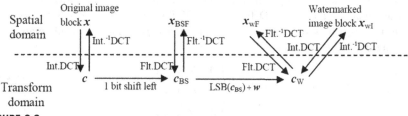

FIGURE 3.8

Pixel value error estimation scheme.

2D-IntDCT and 2D float-point DCT, respectively; $\text{Int.}^{-1}\text{DCT}$ and $\text{Flt.}^{-1}\text{DCT}$ are the corresponding inverse transforms. The details of the error estimation scheme are as follows.

Based on the errors in Ref. [10] between the float-point DCT coefficients and the IntDCT coefficients for the same integer input, we deduce the 8×8 error matrix $T(i,j)$ $(i, j = 0, 1, ..., 7)$, in which each component $t_{ij} > 0$ represents the maximum value error for the pixel in the corresponding position (i,j) in the 8×8 image block. The error matrix $T(i,j)$ is as follows:

$$T(i,j) = \begin{bmatrix} 17.9 & 16.7 & 17.1 & 22.4 & 17.3 & 22.8 & 16.1 & 15.3 \\ 16.3 & 15.2 & 15.5 & 20.3 & 15.7 & 20.7 & 14.6 & 13.8 \\ 16.6 & 15.5 & 15.9 & 20.8 & 16.1 & 21.2 & 14.9 & 14.2 \\ 18.3 & 17.2 & 17.5 & 22.4 & 17.7 & 22.7 & 16.6 & 15.9 \\ 17.7 & 16.5 & 16.9 & 22.2 & 17.1 & 22.6 & 15.8 & 15.1 \\ 18.4 & 17.3 & 17.7 & 22.5 & 17.9 & 22.9 & 16.7 & 16.0 \\ 16.3 & 15.1 & 15.5 & 20.4 & 15.7 & 20.8 & 14.5 & 13.8 \\ 15.7 & 14.7 & 15.0 & 20.0 & 15.2 & 20.2 & 14.0 & 13.3 \end{bmatrix} \quad (3.46)$$

For any fixed x_{wI}, we can obtain

$$|x_{\text{wI}}(i,j) - x_{\text{wF}}(i,j)| < t_{ij} \quad (3.47)$$

where $x_{\text{wI}}(i,j)$ and $x_{\text{wF}}(i,j)$ are pixel values at position (i,j), $0 \le i \le 7, 0 \le j \le 7$, inside x_{wI} and x_{wF}, respectively. In view of the linearity of the transforms $c_{\text{BS}} \leftrightarrow x_{\text{BSF}}$ and $c_{\text{W}} \leftrightarrow x_{\text{wF}}$, we have

$$x_{\text{wF}}(i,j) - x_{\text{BSF}}(i,j) < \sum_{m=0}^{7} \sum_{n=0}^{7} f_p\left(\left[\text{Flt.DCT}^{-1}\left(1_{m,n}\right)\right](i,j)\right) = t_{pij} \quad (3.48)$$

$$x_{\text{wF}}(i,j) - x_{\text{BSF}}(i,j) < \sum_{m=0}^{7} \sum_{n=0}^{7} f_p\left(\left[\text{Flt.DCT}^{-1}\left(1_{m,n}\right)\right](i,j)\right) = t_{nij} \quad (3.49)$$

where $x_{\text{BSF}}(i,j)$ is the pixel value at position, $0 \le i \le 7, 0 \le j \le 7$, inside x_{BSF}, and $1_{m,n}$ is an 8×8 matrix with "1" values for those components whose positions (m,n) $(0 \le m \le 7, 0 \le n \le 7)$ correspond to the positions of all selected coefficients in c_{BS}, and all the other components are set to be "0." We define $\text{Flt.DCT}^{-1}(a)$ as the result matrix of inverse 2D float-point DCT where a is an 8×8 matrix and $[\text{Flt.DCT}^{-1}(a)](i,j)$ is the component at position (i,j) inside the result matrix. f_p and f_n are defined as follows:

$$f_p(x) = \begin{cases} 0 & \text{if } x \le 0 \\ x & \text{if } x > 0 \end{cases} \quad (3.50)$$

$$f_n(x) = \begin{cases} 0 & \text{if } x \ge 0 \\ x & \text{if } x < 0 \end{cases} \quad (3.51)$$

Suppose t_{pij} and t_{nij} $(0 \le i \le 7, 0 \le j \le 7)$ are components at position (i,j) inside the error matrices $\mathbf{T}_p(i,j)$ and $\mathbf{T}_n(i,j)$, then from Eqs. (3.48) to (3.51) we can see that t_{pij} and t_{nij} represent a maximum positive limit and a maximum negative limit for errors caused by the embedded watermark bits for the pixel at position (i,j), respectively. According to Eqs. (3.47)–(3.49), if x_{wI} is required not to be bigger than 255 or less than 0, the safe range of each pixel $x_{BSF}(i,j)$ $(0 \le i \le 7, 0 \le j \le 7)$ can be defined by

$$t_{ij} - t_{nij} \le x_{BSF}(i,j) \le 255 - t_{ij} - t_{pij} \qquad (3.52)$$

Thus we can set $TH_l = t_{ij}-t_{nij}$ and $TH_h = 255-t_{ij}-t_{pij}$. Note that in this indirect estimation scheme, the two thresholds TH_l and TH_h are set on x_{BSF} instead of x'.

For example when $m + n > 0$ in Eqs. (3.48) and (3.49), i.e., the case that all AC coefficients modified, the corresponding error estimation matrices $\mathbf{T}_p(i,j)$ and $\mathbf{T}_n(i,j)$ are calculated as follows:

$$\mathbf{T}_p(i,j) = \begin{bmatrix} 6.9 & 2.4 & 4.1 & 3.1 & 3.8 & 3.3 & 3.6 & 3.5 \\ 2.4 & 3.6 & 3.2 & 3.4 & 3.3 & 3.4 & 3.3 & 3.3 \\ 4.1 & 3.2 & 3.5 & 3.3 & 3.5 & 3.4 & 3.4 & 3.4 \\ 3.1 & 3.4 & 3.3 & 3.4 & 3.3 & 3.7 & 3.3 & 3.4 \\ 3.8 & 3.3 & 3.5 & 3.3 & 3.4 & 3.4 & 3.4 & 3.4 \\ 3.3 & 3.4 & 3.4 & 3.4 & 3.4 & 3.4 & 3.4 & 3.4 \\ 3.6 & 3.3 & 3.4 & 3.3 & 3.4 & 3.4 & 3.4 & 3.4 \\ 3.5 & 3.3 & 3.4 & 3.4 & 3.4 & 3.4 & 3.4 & 3.4 \end{bmatrix} \qquad (3.53)$$

$$\mathbf{T}_n(i,j) = (-1) \cdot \begin{bmatrix} 0.0 & 4.4 & 2.7 & 3.8 & 3.1 & 3.5 & 3.3 & 3.4 \\ 4.4 & 3.2 & 3.7 & 3.4 & 3.6 & 3.5 & 3.6 & 3.5 \\ 2.7 & 3.7 & 3.3 & 3.5 & 3.4 & 3.5 & 3.4 & 3.5 \\ 3.8 & 3.4 & 3.6 & 3.5 & 3.5 & 3.5 & 3.5 & 3.5 \\ 3.1 & 3.6 & 3.4 & 3.5 & 3.4 & 3.5 & 3.5 & 3.5 \\ 3.5 & 3.5 & 3.5 & 3.5 & 3.5 & 3.5 & 3.5 & 3.5 \\ 3.3 & 3.6 & 3.4 & 3.5 & 3.5 & 3.5 & 3.5 & 3.5 \\ 3.4 & 3.5 & 3.5 & 3.5 & 3.5 & 3.5 & 3.5 & 3.5 \end{bmatrix} \qquad (3.54)$$

It can be easily seen that the componentwise errors estimated by the above-mentioned method are quite large. However, in practical experiments, the errors are usually much smaller than these estimated values, depending on different original images.

3.3.2.4 Twice-Try Structures for Block Discrimination

As mentioned earlier, for those blocks suitable for embedding, we can first estimate the pixel value errors and then set the two thresholds to find them out. Once these candidate blocks have been used for embedding, they may no longer be suitable for a second embedding, and therefore cannot be differentiated from those originally ineligible blocks. This problem is unavoidable during the extracting process. Identifying those blocks modified during the embedding process is the key to watermark extraction and image restoration.

One possible solution is to use overhead bits to record the blocks' locations in the original image. This strategy was also employed in Ref. [6] where a location map acts as the indication of pixel pairs used for embedding. Similarly, we use overhead bits to record the block location information. Another problem is where to embed these overhead bits in view of the fact that the embedding positions for these overhead bits should be able to be determined directly by the retrieval algorithm itself without any additional overhead information to indicate. In other words, we must embed the location information in those blocks with some features that are invariant to embedding and can be recognized directly during extraction. Obviously, those blocks, which are proof against overflows and underflows after twice embedding process, should satisfy this condition because they can be easily located by a second embedding test during extraction. Yang et al. call this block discrimination method "twice-try." Yang et al. utilized this method to retrieve those twice-embedding permitted blocks and then identify the location information of other blocks used for embedding (once-embedding permitted blocks).

For the second-embedding process, the error estimation for the last two LSB planes can be calculated, and the safe range of each pixel $x_{\text{BSF}}(i,j)$ $(0 \le i \le 7, 0 \le j \le 7)$ can be defined as:

$$t_{ij} - t'_{nij} \le x_{\text{BSF}}(i,j) \le 255 - t_{ij} - t'_{pij} \tag{3.55}$$

and the two thresholds can be set to $TH'_l = t_{ij} - t'_{nij}$ and $TH'_h = 255 - t_{ij} - t'_{pij}$. For example, when $m + n > 0$ in Eqs. (3.48) and (3.49), i.e., the case that all AC coefficients are modified, the corresponding error estimation matrices $\mathbf{T}'_p(i,j)$ and $\mathbf{T}'_n(i,j)$ of t'_{pij} and t'_{nij} are calculated as follows:

$$\mathbf{T}'_p(i,j) = \begin{bmatrix}
20.6 & 7.2 & 12.4 & 9.3 & 11.3 & 10.0 & 10.8 & 10.4 \\
7.2 & 10.9 & 9.5 & 10.3 & 9.8 & 10.1 & 9.9 & 10.0 \\
12.4 & 9.5 & 10.6 & 9.9 & 10.4 & 10.1 & 10.2 & 10.2 \\
9.3 & 10.3 & 9.9 & 10.2 & 10.0 & 10.1 & 10.0 & 10.1 \\
11.3 & 9.8 & 10.4 & 10.0 & 10.2 & 10.1 & 10.2 & 10.1 \\
10.0 & 10.1 & 10.1 & 10.1 & 10.1 & 10.1 & 10.1 & 10.1 \\
10.8 & 9.9 & 10.2 & 10.0 & 10.2 & 10.1 & 10.1 & 10.1 \\
10.4 & 10.0 & 10.2 & 10.1 & 10.1 & 10.1 & 10.1 & 10.1
\end{bmatrix} \tag{3.56}$$

$$\mathbf{T}'_n(i,j) = (-1) \cdot \begin{bmatrix} 0.0 & 13.3 & 8.2 & 11.3 & 9.2 & 10.6 & 9.8 & 10.2 \\ 13.3 & 9.7 & 11.1 & 10.3 & 10.8 & 10.4 & 10.7 & 10.6 \\ 8.2 & 11.1 & 10.0 & 10.6 & 10.2 & 10.5 & 10.3 & 10.4 \\ 11.3 & 10.3 & 10.6 & 10.4 & 10.6 & 10.5 & 10.5 & 10.5 \\ 9.2 & 10.8 & 10.2 & 10.6 & 10.3 & 10.5 & 10.4 & 10.4 \\ 10.6 & 10.4 & 10.5 & 10.5 & 10.5 & 10.5 & 10.5 & 10.5 \\ 9.8 & 10.7 & 10.3 & 10.5 & 10.4 & 10.5 & 10.4 & 10.4 \\ 10.2 & 10.6 & 10.4 & 10.5 & 10.4 & 10.5 & 10.4 & 10.5 \end{bmatrix} \qquad (3.57)$$

Fig. 3.9 shows the twice-try-based block discrimination structure for the embedding process, by which Yang et al. classified the input 8×8-sized image block x into one of three classes [27]. In Fig. 3.9, Int.DCT and Flt.$^{-1}$DCT represent a 2D-IntDCT

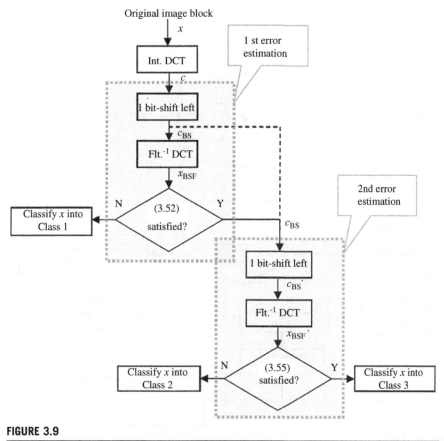

FIGURE 3.9

Twice-try-based block discrimination structure for embedding process.

and an inverse 2D float-point DCT, respectively. Note that Yang at al. utilized the inverse float-point DCT according to the error estimation method discussed in Section 3.3.2.3. The definition of c, c_{BS}, and x_{BSF} are the same as in Fig. 3.8, and c'_{BS} and x'_{BSF} are obtained directly from c_{BS} according to Fig. 3.9. Yang et al. utilized this twice-try structure to find suitable blocks (Class 2 and Class 3) for embedding [27].

Fig. 3.10 shows the twice-try-based block discrimination structure for the extracting process, by which Yang et al. classified the input 8×8-sized watermarked image block x_{wI} (and its original version x) into one of three classes. Note that during extraction, some x_{wBSF} originating from Class 2 in the embedding process may satisfy Eq. (3.52) because errors caused by actual watermark bits embedded in x_{wI} are usually much smaller than the absolute values of t_{ij}, t_{pij}, and t_{nij} in Eq. (3.52), and this makes a portion of x_{wBSF} originally in Class 2 now able to satisfy Eq. (3.52). We define this portion of x_{wBSF} (and their original version x) as Class $2''$ and the remaining x_{wBSF} [those still unable to satisfy Eq. (3.52)]

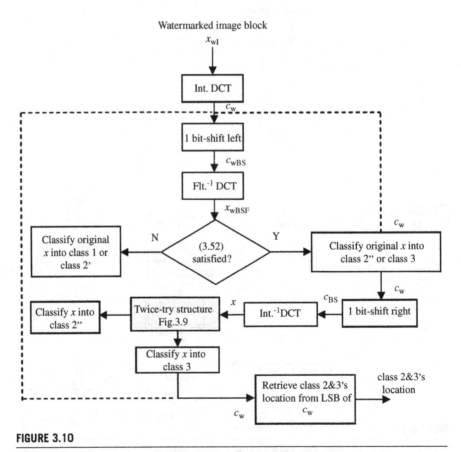

FIGURE 3.10

Twice-try-based block discrimination structure for extracting process.

(and their original version x) as Class $2'$. Obviously, Class 2 is the combination of Class $2'$ and Class $2''$. Now that all x_{wI} in Class 2 and Class 3 are 1-bit-shifted and watermarked versions of x, we can first restore x_{wI} to x and then use the twice-try structure in Fig. 3.9 to discriminate Class $2''$ from Class 3. We can retrieve the location information bits from Class 3 and then discriminate Class $2'$ from Class 1, and finally we can retrieve all embedded bits from c_w in Class 3 and Class 2 and restore the original x perfectly.

Note that in Figs. 3.9 and 3.10, for convenience and simplicity, we suppose the companding process includes only a bit-shift operation.

3.3.2.5 Improved Embedding and Extracting Processes

The embedding process of Yang et al.'s scheme is illustrated in Fig. 3.11, where x is an original image block; Classes 1, 2, and 3 are the classification result of x by the twice-try structure mentioned in Section 3.3.2.4; w is the watermark bit vector formed by the original N (N is the number of coefficients selected in one 8×8 coefficient block) binary watermark bits and other ($64\text{-}N$) "0" bits; l is the vector consisting of location information overhead bits for those blocks to be embedded with data (Classes 2&3) formed by N meaningful bits and other ($64\text{-}N$) "0" bits; and c_w and x_{wI} are the watermarked coefficient block and the image block, respectively. Int.$^{-1}$DCT represents inverse 2D-IntDCT. Note that in this embedding process, Yang et al. first embedded all l bits in the LSB space saved by the bit-shift operation over coefficient blocks of Class 3, which will not cause any overflow and underflow after twice embedding processes, and next Yang et al. embedded real watermark bits w in the space saved from the remaining blocks in Class 3 and all blocks in Class 2 following all l bits. Yang et al. kept those x in Class 1 intact during the whole embedding process because they will surely overflow or underflow when tested with Eq. (3.52).

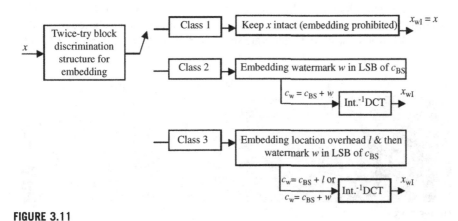

FIGURE 3.11

Embedding process of Yang et al.'s scheme [27].

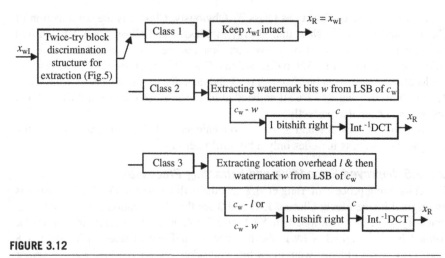

FIGURE 3.12

Extracting process of Yang et al.'s scheme [27].

The extracting process of Yang et al.'s scheme is illustrated in Fig. 3.12, from which we can see that it is virtually the inverse process of the embedding process in Fig. 3.11. We can use the twice-try-based block discrimination structure in Fig. 3.9 to retrieve data embedded in blocks of Classes 2 and 3 and then restore all original image blocks. Note that definitions of w, l, x_{wI}, c, and c_w are the same as in Figs. 3.10 and 3.11, and x_R is restored version of the original image block x.

3.3.2.6 Simulation Results

Yang et al. tested the above-mentioned reversible watermarking scheme on four 256 grayscale images with size 512×512: Lena, Barbara, Baboon, and Goldhill as shown in Fig. 3.13a–d. In all simulations, they selected N coefficients in one 8×8 coefficient block and obtained watermarked images with different qualities in terms of PSNR and different capacities (bits). The simulation results are presented in Table 3.1, where the N coefficients are selected in the order $i + j > M(M = 12, 11,$

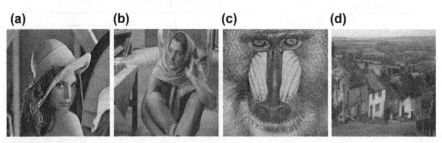

FIGURE 3.13

Test images. (a) Lena, (b) Barbara, (c) Mandrill, and (d) Goldhill.

Table 3.1 Simulation Results of Yang et al.'s Scheme [27] for Four 512 × 512 Grayscale Images

N		3	6	15	36	49	58	63
Lena	PSNR (dB)	49.645	46.765	42.852	38.188	36.106	34.665	31.847
	Capacity (bit)[a]	5192	14,432	41,834	103,616	138,053	156,158	150,758
Barbara	PSNR (dB)	49.419	45.979	39.136	33.046	31.917	30.669	30.098
	Capacity (bit)[a]	8003	20,012	55,334	119,852	146,922	161,088	139,670
Mandrill	PSNR (dB)	41.306	37.661	33.178	30.284	30.102	30.100	30.063
	Capacity (bit)[a]	7307	18,524	50,129	85,931	97,136	103,436	106,056
Goldhill	PSNR (dB)	48.523	45.438	41.196	35.336	32.495	30.302	28.158
	Capacity (bit)[a]	7484	19,004	53,309	131,444	174,509	192,930	173,123

PSNR, peak signal-to-noise ratio.
[a] The capacity is the lower limit. Actual capacity should be about 2000–4000 more than the images in Table 3.1.

6, 4, 2, 0), $0 \leq i \leq 7$, $0 \leq j \leq 7$, and i, j are the row and column numbers, respectively, in one coefficient block $c(i, j)$. Note that the capacity presented in this table is the lower limit number in light of the fact:

$$Capa. = Saved \ bits \ from \ bit - shift \ operation - location \ overhead$$

where the *location overhead* is calculated, for simplicity, as the maximum value (4096 binary bits, 1 bit for one block indicating embedded or not) in the simulations without any compression. The actual capacity is expected to be 2000−4000 more than the images in Table 3.1 if *location overhead* is appropriately losslessly compressed.

From Table 3.1 we can see that Yang et al.'s scheme shows advantage in capacity while good quality of watermarked image is maintained. Note that for simplicity, they omitted (1) the compressing process in companding (bit-shift operation remained) and (2) the losslessly compressing process for location overhead. On the other hand, IntDCT algorithms and overflow/underflow prevention method may be improved in the future. Considering these facts, they believed their scheme has potential in performance, which will be exploited in their future work.

3.3.3 HISTOGRAM SHIFT TECHNIQUE IN INTEGER DISCRETE COSINE TRANSFORM DOMAIN

In this section, we introduce Yang et al.'s another reversible watermarking scheme using histogram modification in the 8×8 IntDCT domain [19]. This scheme exploits the high-energy-concentrating property of IntDCT, allows fine coefficient selection for watermarking, and thus, shows equivalent or higher performance and wider quality (PSNR) ranges when compared with those in Refs. [31] and [32]. In Section 3.3.3.1, we first review the histogram modification technique for reversible watermarking. In Section 3.3.3.2, the histogram modification technique is introduced into the 8×8 IntDCT domain and Yang et al.'s scheme is introduced. Some experimental results are presented in Section 3.3.3.3.

3.3.3.1 Histogram Modification Technique for Lossless Information Hiding

The idea of histogram modification proposed in Refs. [31] and [32] is to exploit the redundancy of scale points in an image histogram. We illustrate this idea briefly in Fig. 3.14. After finding a peak point P and a zero point Z in the image's original histogram, the scale values in the range $[P, Z-1]$ shift to the right side by 1 unit to occupy the range $[P + 1, Z]$. This shifting operation is equivalent to adding 1 unit to all pixels with scale values originally in the range $[P, Z-1]$. Now we have artificially created a zero point at the scale value P and the original peak point at P has shifted to $P+1$. The watermark embedding process is performed by reassigning the peak-point-pixels' scale values to P or $P + 1$. For example, in Fig. 3.14, there are N peak-point-pixels at $P + 1$ (originally at P). During the embedding process, we embed "0" by keeping unaltered a pixel with scale value $P + 1$, or embed "1" by restoring it to P. Thus the embedding capacity in this example is N. In practical

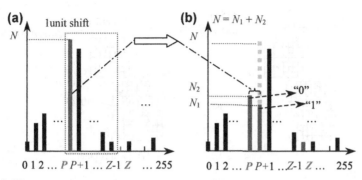

FIGURE 3.14

The idea of histogram modification technique. (a) Original histogram, and (b) modified histogram after embedding watermark.

applications, overhead information should be used to record the positions of the peak point and the zero point. If there is no zero point in the histogram, the minimum point (scale value with fewest pixels) can act as a zero point. In this case, more overhead bits are needed to differentiate the modified pixels from those original ones in the minimum point.

With the overhead bits to carry necessary information of the original histogram, this histogram modification technique is a reversible process. The reversible watermarking scheme in Ref. [31] uses this technique in the histogram of a whole image, so the performance depends on the peak point in the histogram. If the shape of the histogram is flat, the capacity will be limited. In addition, the distortion caused by the histogram shifting operation depends not only on the peak point but also on the zero or minimum point, or equivalently, on the size of the range $[P, Z-1]$. The scheme in Ref. [32] decreases the size of the histogram by dividing the whole image into small blocks and performs histogram modification on each block, thus reducing the distortion caused by histogram shifting operations. For each block, the scheme in Ref. [32] needs 1−2 bits as an overhead to store information of the original histogram, which makes the overhead reoccupy a large proportion of the total saved bits.

Note that the histogram modification techniques in both Refs. [31] and [32] are directly used in the spatial domain and the algorithms' performance is determined by the pixel distribution of the original image. Based on this fact, Yang et al. proposed using histogram modification in the IntDCT domain [19] in light of IntDCT's energy concentration property, and expected to heighten the amplitude of the peak point P and thus increase the capacity.

3.3.3.2 Yang et al.'s Scheme

Similar to a float-point DCT, an IntDCT has the energy concentration property, which can be used to improve the capacity of histogram modification scheme.

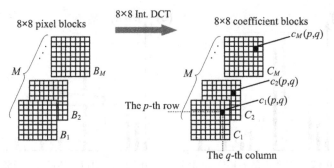

FIGURE 3.15

Coefficient grouping in 8 × 8 integer discrete cosine transform (DCT) domain.

Unlike the float-point DCT, the IntDCT is lossless and suitable for reversible watermarking. Besides, we require the IntDCT to satisfy the fact that (1) both input and output data are integers and (2) the transform is left-and-right invertible mapping. According to the two requirements, Yang et al. derived an 8 × 8 IntDCT from the 1D version proposed in Ref. [10] (algorithm A in Ref. [10]). It is easy to prove that this IntDCT satisfies the two requirements, and at the same time, possesses high-energy-concentrating efficiency. We explain Yang et al.'s whole watermarking process as follows.

The first step of Yang et al.'s scheme [19] is to generate the coefficient histograms in the IntDCT domain to perform histogram modification discussed in Section 3.3.3.1. Assume x is a gray-scale image with size at least 8 × 8. They divided the original x into M image blocks B_i ($i = 1, 2, ..., M$) with size 8 × 8, as shown in Fig. 3.15. Then Yang et al. performed 8 × 8 IntDCT on all M image blocks to obtain M coefficient blocks C_i ($i = 1, 2, ..., M$) with size 8 × 8, as shown in Fig. 3.15. To obtain a histogram for modification, we pick the coefficient in the position (p,q) ($1 \leq p, q \leq 58$) inside each coefficient block C_i ($i = 1, 2, ..., M$), where p and q are the row index and column index, respectively, in the 8 × 8 coefficient block. Thus for any coefficient position (p,q), totally M coefficients $c_i(p,q)$ ($i = 1, 2, ..., M$) can be collected to form a coefficient group $G(p,q)$. For each coefficient group $G(p,q)$, Yang et al. embedded the watermark reversibly by histogram modification in its histogram $H(p,q)$ ($1 \leq p, q \leq 8$), and there are totally 64 histograms formed by the 64 coefficient groups. Note that in the DCT domain, the AC coefficient group $G(p,q)$ ($1 \leq p, q \leq 8$, and $p + q > 2$) can be modeled with a general Gaussian distribution [11], with samples concentrated around "0," which is especially suitable for histogram modification. Since Yang et al.'s derived 8 × 8 IntDCT [27] has high compatibility with the float-point DCT in the sense of energy concentration, they assumed its AC coefficient groups are also distributed close to the general Gaussian model. So they considered only the AC coefficient groups $G(p,q)$ ($0 \leq p, q \leq 8, p + q > 2$) and their histograms for modification. In concrete applications, they utilized a secret key K_c to select $N(N \leq 63)$ coefficient groups for watermarking.

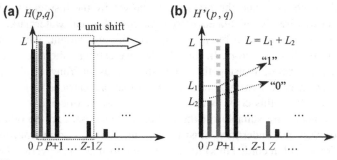

FIGURE 3.16

Histogram modification in the 8×8 integer discrete cosine transform domain. (a) Original histogram and (b) modified histogram after embedding watermark.

After the generation of the N coefficient groups and their histograms, Yang et al. performed the histogram modification scheme introduced in Section 3.3.3.1 on each of the N histograms. The watermark embedding process shown in Fig. 3.16 is similar to that in Fig. 3.14, except that the histogram is now calculated from the IntDCT coefficients instead of the original pixel values. Therefore the peak point P's amplitude is supposed to account for a higher proportion among the total number M than in the spatial domain (as in Fig. 3.14), whereas the size of range $[P, Z-1]$ is supposed to be shorter than in the spatial domain for the same reason. It is expected that the transform from the spatial domain to the IntDCT domain should improve the whole algorithm's capacity and image fidelity. Note that for each histogram of the total N coefficient groups, we must record the positions of the original peak point P and zero point Z as overhead information OH_{pz} to provide the synchronization information for watermark extraction. Where to store this overhead information later in this section.

Since both the histogram modification technique and the 8×8 IntDCT are reversible processes, the watermark extraction is just a reversed process of the embedding process. A problem we cannot neglect is the overflows (>255 for a 256 grayscale image) and underflows (<0) caused by histogram modification in the IntDCT domain. In the spatial domain, it is easy for us to predict the occurrence of over- and underflows, i.e., to see if the histogram shifting operation and the watermark embedding process involve any pixels with boundary scale values such as "0" and "255." If yes, we exclude these pixels from the histogram shifting operation, even with additional overhead bits to guarantee the reversibility of the whole algorithm, so that over- and underflows will not occur. However, for the case in the IntDCT domain, it is hard to know in advance which pixel will overflow or underflow as a result of embedding before we carry out a real embedding process. It is obvious that over- and underflows are related to two factors: the histogram shifting range $[P, Z-1]$ and the specific watermark bits. The range $[P, Z-1]$ is determined by the original image itself and the pixel errors caused by the histogram shifting in $[P, Z-1]$ can be directly calculated before we embed a real watermark, whereas the pixel errors caused by different watermark bits are variant, which makes it impossible to predict the errors. In this chapter, we estimate the errors caused by the watermark embedding using the same strategy as in Yang et al.'s previous work [27], which gave two maximum error estimation matrices to prevent over- and underflows. With this error estimation strategy, we can decide which original 8×8 image blocks are suitable for the embedding process, and the other blocks (possible to over- and underflow) must be kept unchanged during embedding and extraction. Yang et al. recorded this block decision information as overhead information, named as *location overhead* OH_L.

During extraction, with OH_L we can find out those image blocks embedded with watermark, and then with OH_{pz} we can find out the histogram shifting ranges on histograms of all coefficient groups $G(p,q)$ and finally restore the original image successfully. Now we consider where to store the overhead OH_{pz} and OH_L. In Yang et al.'s previous work [27], they stored the overhead information in the twice-embedding permitted blocks, which can be determined by a "twice-try" block discrimination scheme. Despite its high efficiency, this block discrimination scheme is complicated. Therefore, Yang et al. proposed a relatively simple scheme to store the overhead information, as shown in Fig. 3.17, an example of a gray-scale image with size 128×128. In this example, the original image can be divided into 16×16 blocks and we pick out some blocks $O_1, O_2, ..., O_H$ as overhead blocks according to a secret key K_o and then replace the LSBs of pixels in these blocks with the bits of the overhead OH_{pz} and OH_L. The original LSBs are embedded with watermark bits into the saved space from the histogram modification technique. During extraction, we can use K_o to find out these blocks and extract the overhead information OH_{pz} and OH_L. The total number of the overhead blocks H is decided by the length of all overhead bits and embedded in the first overhead block O_1.

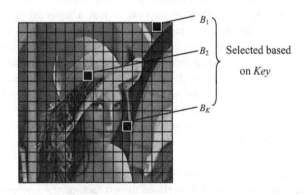

FIGURE 3.17

Block selection example for storage of overhead information.

FIGURE 3.18

Images for test: (a) Lena, (b) Bridge, (e) Barbara, (d) Airplane, (e) Baboon.

3.3.3.3 Experimental Results

Yang et al. tested their scheme using 5 grayscale images as shown in Fig. 3.18a—e, where Lena and Bridge are 256×256 in size, and Barbara, Airplane, and Baboon are 512×512 in size. In all experiments, Yang et al. selected N coefficients according to the key K_c in an 8×8 coefficient block and obtained watermarked images with different PSNR values compared with the original image and different capacities (bits). The results are presented in Table 3.2, where the N coefficients are selected in the order $p + q > A$ ($A = 15, 13, 11, 8, 6, 4$ corresponding to $N = 1$, 6, 15, 36, 49, 58, respectively), $1 \leq p \leq 8$, $1 \leq q \leq 8$, where N is the coefficient number selected for modification and p, q are the row and column indices, respectively, in an coefficient block. The capacity is obtained by $Capacity = Saved\ bits - OH_{pz} - OH_L$.

From Table 3.2 we can see Yang et al.'s scheme has relatively high capacity in the high PSNR range. Compared with other reversible image watermarking schemes [27,32,33], our scheme shows equivalent or higher performance, and particularly, capability of fine adjustment of the watermarked image's quality (PSNR) by selecting different numbers of coefficients. We notice that the experimental results, especially the capacities, are quite different for various tested images. This is related to Yang et al.'s special over- and underflow prevention measure [27].

Table 3.2 Experimental Results of the Proposed Scheme for Five Grayscale Images

Image	Size	N	1	6	15	36	49	58
Lena	256 × 256	PSNR (dB)	*	52.11	48.78	46.19	45.36	44.98
		Capacity (bits)	−750	573	2646	7230	9457	10,541
		Bit rate (bpp)	*	0.0087	0.0404	0.1103	0.1443	0.1608
Bridge	256 × 256	PSNR (dB)	*	*	48.74	46.36	45.56	45.199
		Capacity (bits)	−952	−508	165	1456	2099	2415
		Bit rate (bpp)	*	*	0.0025	0.0222	0.032	0.0368
Barbara	512 × 512	PSNR (dB)	59.428	51.84	48.49	45.83	44.95	44.50
		Capacity (bits)	1233	7265	17,708	39,103	49,489	54,494
		Bit rate (bpp)	0.0047	0.0277	0.0676	0.1492	0.1888	0.2079
Airplane	512 × 512	PSNR (dB)	60.25	52.43	48.78	45.957	45.06	44.62
		Capacity (bits)	1529	9438	22,292	47,288	59,282	65,433
		Bit rate (bpp)	0.0058	0.036	0.085	0.1804	0.2261	0.2496
Baboon	512 × 512	PSNR (dB)	*	51.39	48.27	45.76	44.99	44.60
		Capacity (bits)	−256	2003	5706	12,650	15,867	17,395
		Bit rate (bpp)	*	0.0076	0.0218	0.0483	0.0605	0.0664

PSNR, peak signal-to-noise ratio. * Cases in which Yang et al.'s scheme is infeasible because the overhead is higher than the saved space.

Note that the results given in Table 3.2 are obtained by just 1-unit shifting operation on the histograms. In Yang et al.'s experiments, they also tested their scheme by finding two highest peak points and shifting 2 units on each histogram, only to find that the capacity can be almost doubled and the PSNR can reach a lower end around 40 dB, but the performance in terms of PSNR and capacity remained close to the 1-unit shifting case.

3.3.4 LOSSLESS INFORMATION HIDING BY ADAPTIVE COEFFICIENT MODIFICATION IN INTEGER DISCRETE COSINE TRANSFORM DOMAIN

In Ref. [34], Yang et al. investigated several possible methods to improve the performance of the bit-shifting operation—based reversible image watermarking algorithm in the IntDCT domain. In view of the large distortion caused by the modification of high-amplitude coefficients in the IntDCT domain, several coefficient selection methods were proposed to provide the coefficient modification process with some adaptability to match the coefficient amplitudes' status of different 8×8 DCT coefficient blocks. Yang et al.'s adaptive modification methods include global coefficient-group distortion sorting (GCDS), zero-tree DCT prediction (ZTDCT), and a low-frequency-based coefficient prediction method for block classification. All these methods are supposed to optimize the bit-shifting-based coefficient modification process so as to improve the watermarking performance in terms of capacity/distortion ratio. They presented comparisons for these methods in aspects of performance in terms of capacity/distortion ratio, performance stability, performance scalability, algorithm complexity, and security. The following three subsections introduce Yang et al.'s three adaptive modification methods.

3.3.4.1 Global Coefficient-Group Distortion Sorting

The first idea that Yang et al. presented for coefficient adaptive modification is very simple: to collect all coefficients in the correspondent position (p,q) $(0 \leq p, q \leq 7)$ in all 8×8 coefficient block $c_l(l = 1, 2, ..., M, M$ is the total number of all coefficient blocks) into a group $AC_k(k = 8 \times p + q$ and $1 \leq k \leq 63)$, calculate the bit-shifting distortion D_k associated with each coefficient group AC_k, and then sort the AC_k in the ascending order of $D_k(1 \leq k \leq 63)$ values to obtain AC'_k, and tag the first N coefficient groups $AC'_1 \sim AC'_N$ as candidates for modification. An example of coefficient grouping and tagging process of GCDS is illustrated in Fig. 3.19, in which $N = 6$, that is, the six coefficient groups with the minimum six D_k are selected for bit-shifting, tagged by "×."

Considering that the general distortion measure PSNR is based on mean square error calculation, and the distortion caused by coefficient bit-shifting is directly related to the coefficients' original amplitudes $|AC_k(l)|$ $(1 \leq k \leq 63, l = 1, 2, ..., M)$, we realize D_k in the following form:

$$D_k = \sum_{l=1}^{M} |AC_k(l)|^2 \qquad (3.58)$$

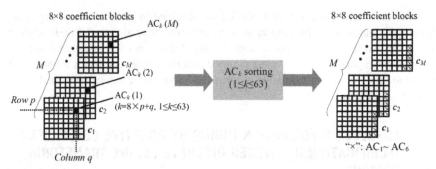

FIGURE 3.19

An example ($N = 6$) of coefficient grouping and sorting in global coefficient-group distortion sorting.

Once we obtain the sorted coefficient groups AC'_k, we can tag the first N coefficient groups $AC'_1 \sim AC'_N$ by "1" and other groups by "0" in the 8×8 coefficient block pattern, therefore totally 63 bits are stored as overhead to convey the information regarding which coefficient groups should be for watermarking. In Yang et al.'s experiments, they examined the coefficient-group distortion sorting process over two 512×512 grayscale images—Lena and Mandrill, and the two block patterns in Fig. 3.20 show the sorting results for the two images (the figures representing the order of the coefficient groups in the ascending order of D_k). Yang et al.'s experiments demonstrate that the N coefficient groups selected by the aforementioned GCDS method are always lower or equal in bit-shifting distortion compared with the scheme by the zigzag order used in their old scheme [27]. The associated

(a)

63	62	60	56	52	45	36	32
61	59	58	53	47	43	35	24
55	57	54	51	44	41	31	22
50	49	48	46	42	34	26	21
40	38	39	37	33	25	19	12
27	29	30	28	23	17	13	8
18	16	14	20	15	10	4	2
11	9	5	7	6	3	1	0

8×8 coefficient group sorting for Lena

(b)

63	61	56	46	36	26	17	8
62	59	53	45	34	27	16	7
60	57	52	43	33	24	15	6
58	54	49	42	30	22	14	5
55	51	44	38	28	20	9	2
50	47	41	32	25	18	10	1
48	40	37	29	21	13	12	3
39	35	31	23	19	11	4	0

8×8 coefficient group sorting for Mandrill

FIGURE 3.20

Coefficient-group distortion sorting results for 512×512 grayscale images, Lena and Mandrill. (a) 8×8 coefficient group sorting for Lena, (b) 8×8 coefficient group sorting for Mandrill.

capacity/distortion rate also has noticeable gain over the old scheme, and the price for this gain is low—just 63 bits, indicating which N coefficient groups are suitable for bit-shifting (by "1") and others are not (by "0"). Detailed results and comparisons are shown in Section 3.3.4.4.

3.3.4.2 Zero-Tree Discrete Cosine Transform Prediction

Similar to wavelet transform, the coefficients of DCT can be also structured in the form of a zero tree [35], considering the fact that the 8×8 DCT can be regarded as a 64-subband decomposition, which labels the coefficients' indices in a way presented in Fig. 3.21. The parent—children relationship in the tree structure is defined as follows:

$$\textit{The parent}: \quad i = floor(k/4)(1 \leq k \leq 63) \tag{3.59}$$

$$\textit{The children}: \quad j = \{4i, 4i + 1, 4i + 2, 4i + 3\} \tag{3.60}$$

In view of the correlation between the parent and children coefficients, the zero-tree embedded coding algorithm generally assumes that the significance of the children nodes can be predicted by their parent nodes. Intuitively, this assumption should also work if it is taken as an adaptive selection method for the coefficients generated in the IntDCT domain. In Yang et al.'s ZTDCT method, they set a threshold TH for all parent coefficients $(4 \leq k \leq 15)$ in the second layer in Fig. 3.21, and the coefficient selecting process can be formulated as

In the embedding process of Yang et al.'s reversible watermarking algorithm, they perform the aforementioned procedure for every 8×8 coefficient block of the original image. Yang et al. expected some improvements in performance using this tree structure for coefficient prediction and modification, but the experimental results are rather disappointing (refer to Section 3.3.4.4), showing even lower efficiency than that of the zigzag order—based selection method. This fact may be

0	1	4	5	16	17	20	21
2	3	6	7	18	19	22	23
8	9	12	13	24	25	28	29
10	11	14	15	26	27	30	31
32	33	36	37	48	49	52	53
34	35	38	39	50	51	54	55
40	41	44	45	56	57	60	61
42	43	46	47	58	59	62	63

FIGURE 3.21

Coefficient labeling in the form of a tree structure.

explained by DCT's high-energy-concentrating property, which has exploited the pixel correlation to a very high degree. A possibility for improvement is to select the coefficients by the original zigzag order but among the adopted coefficients collected by earlier mentioned procedure.

3.3.4.3 Low-Frequency Coefficients-Based Prediction (LFCP)

Both value expansion—based reversible watermarking algorithms and value addition—based algorithms face a problem: how to discriminate the modified values from the original ones if the two value sets have an overlap (actually in most cases this overlap is inevitable). Overhead information is a solution [28] but usually costly for the discrimination. The companding technique may also be a way [27] to achieve better rate of watermarking capacity versus overhead. Voigt et al. [36] proposed an AC coefficient addition scheme to obtain a clear discrimination for the three cases: exceptional, watermarked "1," and watermarked "0." The basic idea is to add an offset to the coefficients unsuitable for watermarking inside one 8-point data group. Note that this value addition operation is only for discrimination between the watermarked and the original case and has no watermark information involved in. This idea shares some similarities with the histogram shifting schemes used in Ref. [19] and the prediction-error expansion—based reversible watermarking algorithm [37], and in the spread spectrum—based algorithm [38], the authors name the result of this value addition operation as "pseudowatermark bit."

A possible reversible watermarking scheme is to adopt the value addition scheme similar to those in Refs. [37,38] over those IntDCT coefficients unsuitable for watermarking and perform bit-shifting over those coefficients to be watermarked. Accordingly, a threshold *BSTH* is preset to define which coefficients are suitable ones and which are not. Additionally, Yang et al. employed their algorithm [27] or the GCDS proposed in Section 3.3.4.1 to define the N coefficients to which the value addition scheme is applied. Based on this idea, they proposed a reversible image watermarking algorithm in the IntDCT domain, which can be simply viewed as a combination of GCDS proposed in Section 3.3.4.1 and the value addition scheme with a threshold *BSTH*. They named it as baseline algorithm (BA) for comparison with LFCP, which is based on BA and improved by referencing the 5 low AC coefficients' status for coefficient block classification. Details are presented as follows.

The adaptive block classification scheme that Yang et al. proposed for LFCP is based on an assumption: if the low-frequency coefficients are universally small in absolute value, in high probability the remaining coefficients are also small in absolute value. This assumption actually holds for most natural images. In Ref. [39], a DCT block classification scheme was proposed referencing low-frequency coefficients, but it was relatively complicated to use as many as 22 low-frequency coefficients for decision. Yang et al. proposed a simple but efficient low-frequency coefficient block classification scheme to predict the status of the remaining

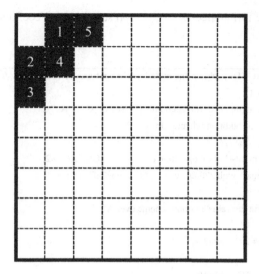

FIGURE 3.22

The 5 coefficients selected for block classification for LFCP.

coefficients, which uses only 5 lowest frequency coefficients shown in Fig. 3.22. The scheme checks if the absolute value of the maximum (denoted as AC_{max}) of the 5 lowest AC coefficients AC_1, AC_2, ..., AC_5 is larger than a preset threshold *TH* to classify all blocks into two classes. The classification rule and the detailed watermarking embedding process are formulated as follows (AC_{bk} represents the AC coefficient after bit-shifting and AC_{wk} represents the AC coefficient with the watermark bit embedded):

---

if $|ACmax| \leq TH$

　classified as "plane block";

　perform bit-shifting operation over all the other AC coefficients (AC_6~ AC_{63}): $AC_{bk}=AC_k \times 2$;

　watermark embedding: $ACwk= ACbk + w$("0" or "1")

　else

　classified as "complicated block";

　perform BA (Baseline Algorithm, the combination of GCDS and the value addition scheme with threshold *BSTH*);

　end

The BA can be formulated as (AC'_{ak} represents the AC coefficients after value addition):

Step 0 (GCDS): obtain the sorted coefficient groups $AC'k$ ($1 \leq k \leq 63$)(ref. to Section 3.3.4.1);

   Step 1: for an input coefficient number N, select $AC'_1 \sim AC'_N$;

   Step 2 (Value addition scheme): for $k=1:N$

     if $|AC'_k| \leq BSTH$

       perform bit-shifting operation over AC'_k: $AC'_{bk}=AC'_k \times 2$;

       watermark embedding: $AC'_{wk}= AC'_{bk} + w("0" \text{ or } "1")$

     else

       perform the value addition scheme over AC'_k:

     if $AC'_k > 0$

       $AC'_{ak}= AC'_k +BSTH$;

     else

       $AC'_{ak}= AC'_k -BSTH$;

     end

   end

   end

Compared with the BA, the low frequency coefficients based prediction (LFCP) efficiently exploits the capacity potential of those "plane blocks," and the experimental results in Section 3.3.4.4 demonstrate this improvement in performance in terms of capacity/distortion.

3.3.4.4 Experimental Results and Performance Analysis

Yang et al.'s experiments include tests on the five adaptive IntDCT coefficient modification—based reversible image watermarking algorithms proposed in this section: ZTDCT, GCDS, BA, LFCP1, and LFCP2 (different threshold settings for LFCP1 and LFCP2); and other three reversible image watermarking algorithms proposed in 2004: BS (Yang et al.'s old IntDCT-based bit-shifting algorithm) [27], the integer wavelet—based spread spectrum algorithm (SS) [38], and the prediction-error expansion based algorithm (PEE) [37]. The images for the testing are the 256-grayscale 512 × 512-sized Lena and Mandrill. The 8 × 8 IntDCT we used in all experiments is the same as in their old algorithm [27], which was proposed in Ref. [10] (algorithm A).

Another key problem to all reversible watermarking algorithms is the over- and underflows caused by the modification of those pixels close to the grayscale boundaries (such as 0 and 255 for 256-grayscale images) in the watermarked image. Yang et al. circumvented this problem in Ref. [27] by a pixel error estimation scheme to predict if a block will generate an overflow or underflow after bit-shifting and watermark embedding, which gave a guaranteed pixel range defined by two thresholds for the embedding process of any specific form of the watermark bits. In Ref. [34], instead, Yang et al. used an iteratively trying process to obtain the two thresholds, which are obviously (1) not so secured as the two obtained from the error estimation scheme in Ref. [27] and (2) depend on watermark bits, but permit more blocks to be watermarked and therefore higher capacity.

Yang et al. employed the same overhead recording scheme in Ref. [34] as in Ref. [19], in which the overhead bits can be stored in the LSB planes of some image blocks preselected by a secret key and the original LSB bits can be embedded together with watermark bits. Obviously, the selected blocks for storing the overhead information should not be modified in the later watermark embedding process. Yang et al. presented the experimental results and performance analysis in the following aspects.

3.3.4.4.1 Watermarking Capacity Versus Distortion

For most reversible image watermarking applications, we are interested in an algorithm's performance in terms of the capacity it is able to achieve [usually represented by bits-per-pixel (bpp)] and the distortion between the original image and its watermarked version [usually reflected by the fidelity index PSNR (dB)]. The experimental results are exhibited in Fig. 3.23 (for Lena) and Fig. 3.24 (for Mandrill)

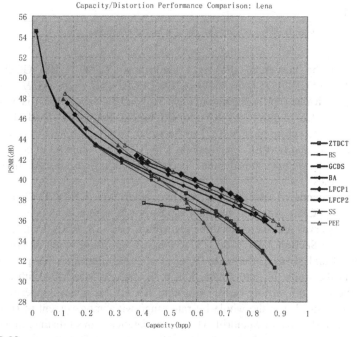

FIGURE 3.23

Capacity versus image quality comparison for the Lena image.

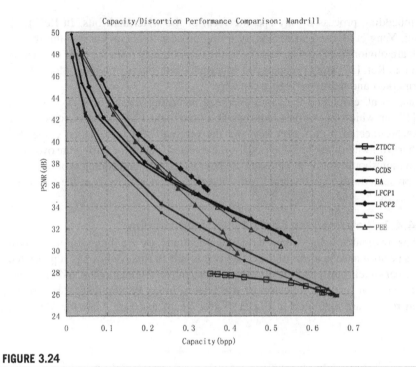

FIGURE 3.24

Capacity versus image quality comparison for the Mandrill image.

consisting of the curves of the eight algorithms: ZTDCT, BS, GCDS, BA ($BSTH = 10$), LFCP1 ($TH = 6$, $BSTH = 10$), LFCP2 ($TH = 20$, $BSTH = 5$), SS, and PEE. The bit-rate (bpp) adjusting in Figs. 3.23 and 3.24 for ZTDCT is by setting TH (Section 3.3.4.2) to different values: for BS, GCDS, BA, LFCP1, and LFCP2, by setting the coefficient number N ([27] or Sections 3.3.4.1 and 3.3.4.3); for SS, by threshold A [38]; and for PEE, by threshold T [37]. For convenience of comparison, for all algorithms, we only consider the one-time embedding case instead of multiple embedding cases.

For convenience of comparison, the five algorithms (ZTDCT, GCDS, BA, LFCP1, and LFCP2) proposed in this chapter are represented in Figs. 3.23 and 3.24 by bold curves and the other three algorithms (BS, SS, PEE), by thin curves. As analyzed in Section 3.3.4.2, the ZTDCT-based algorithm is not as efficient as we imagined and always inferior to Yang et al.'s old algorithm BS proposed in Ref. [27] in the whole bit-rate range, both for Lena and Mandrill. With a GCDS method, the new bit-shifting-based algorithm (GCDS) is always superior to the old algorithm BS [27] in the whole bit rate range with improvement of 0−0.8 dB for Lena and 0−1.4 dB for Mandrill. The preponderance is most distinct in the middle bit rate range (0.25−0.8 bpp for Lena and 0.1−0.6 bpp). The reason is, in low bit rate range, N (the number of coefficients selected for bit-shifting) is small and the coefficients selected by the zigzag order in BS are almost the same as those selected by GCDS, out of the highest frequency range, whereas in high bit-rate range, N is close to 63 (the highest number that can be selected) and distortion sorting results are also almost the same as the results by zig-zag ordering.

The BA for LFCP algorithms employs the value addition scheme (Section 3.3.4.3), which efficiently deduces the distortion caused by the high-amplitude (in absolute value) coefficients in the bit-shifting scheme. This can be verified by the curve of BA in both Figs. 3.23 and 3.24, from which we can see that the preponderance of BA over BS and GCDS is increasing with the improvement of capacity, due to the fact that the higher is N, the more are low-frequency coefficients are included for value addition and bit-shifting, and thus the more distinct is the advantage of the value addition scheme over bit-shifting for high-amplitude coefficients. In Yang et al.'s experiment, the threshold for the value addition scheme is set to $BSTH = 10$.

Compared with BA, the low-frequency coefficients prediction (LFCP)—based algorithms have an additional parameter TH to determine the statistical complexity status of the current image block. This preexamination process exploits the capacity potential, which is originally constrained by the coefficient number N. The argument is, in BS, GCDS, and BA, the same coefficient number N is imposed on all image blocks as the scope from which coefficient can be selected for bit-shifting, regardless of the statistical complexity of a specific image block. It is easily seen that for a plane block, N could be larger than the usual case, and in LFCP algorithms, TH takes this responsibility to determine if the current block is a plane block or not. If yes, N shall be counted as 58 (all the remaining AC coefficients except for the 5 lowest ones, which are references for the decision). In Yang et al.'s experiments, $TH = 6$ and $BSTH = 10$ is set for LFCP1 and $TH = 20$ and $BSTH = 5$ is set to LFCP2. From Figs. 3.23 and 3.24, we can see that LFCP-based algorithms exhibit preponderance of 0—1.7 dB over BA, around 1.0—4.0 dB over BS and GCDS for Lena, 0—4.0 dB over BA, and around 1.3—7.0 dB over BS and GCDS for Mandrill. These results demonstrate the effectiveness of the low-frequency coefficients prediction—based block classification scheme.

Compared with the spread spectrum based algorithm(SS) [38], for Lena, GCDS has no preponderance till after 0.5 bpp; BA and LFCP1 and LFCP2 have no preponderance till after 0.4 bpp. In the high-bit-rate range, GCDS, BA, and LFCP algorithms exhibit preponderance around 0—9.0 dB, and this can be explained by the fact that the IntDCT we used has higher energy-concentrating efficiency in the whole transformed domain than the integer wavelet CDF(2,2) used in SS. But the integer wavelet CDF(2,2) exhibits better scalability of energy concentration. That is, low-amplitude coefficients in CDF(2,2) are more efficiently distributed in high-frequency bands but globally less in amount than in the IntDCT used in Ref. [34]. For Mandrill, the case is similar, but the preponderance of BA and LFCP over SS in the high-bit-rate range is higher than the case of Lena. We note that LFCP2 even exhibits a preponderance of around 0.8—2.3 dB over SS in the whole bit-rate range that LFCP2 covers (0.08—0.35 bpp).

Compared with the PEE [37], only LFCP2 exhibits preponderance of around 0—0.4 dB in the bit-rate range 0.55—0.75 bpp for Lena. In all other cases, PEE exhibits absolute advantage over other algorithms. For Mandrill, LFCP2 exhibits a preponderance of around 0.8—1.8 dB over PEE in the whole bit-rate range that LFCP2 covers (0.08—0.35 bpp); BA and LFCP1 exhibit a preponderance of around 0—1.6 dB over PEE in the bit-rate range > 0.35 bpp.

In general, the algorithms GDCS, BA, and LFCP demonstrate distinct improvements in capacity/distortion performance compared with Yang et al.'s old algorithm [27] in almost all bit-rate ranges and exhibit noticeable preponderance over SS and PEE in high bit-rate ranges. This preponderance is especially distinct for the image Mandrill.

3.3.4.4.2 Performance Stability

From Figs. 3.23 and 3.24, we note that all algorithms exhibit relatively similar performance comparison results for the different images Lena and Mandrill, except that SS bears different performance compared with BS and GCDS in the high bit-rate ranges. LFCP2 is always the best in high-bit-rate ranges, and as a price the bit-rate range it covers is much constrained. PEE comprehensively bears an excellent performance in the whole bit-rate range, for both Lena and Mandrill. BS, GCDS, and BA cover the most comprehensive bit-rate ranges and PSNR ranges, for both Lena and Mandrill.

3.3.4.4.3 Performance Scalability

Algorithms based on N coefficient selection in the IntDCT domain (BS, GCDS, BA, LFCP) have better performance scalability than other algorithms in that the AC coefficients of the IntDCT bear a natural fine adjustability either by the zig-zag order or the GCDS order. For LFCP algorithms, threshold *TH* and *BSTH* are adjustable to achieve even higher performance than those exhibited in Figs. 3.23 and 3.24.

3.3.4.4.4 Algorithm Complexity

In terms of watermark embedding and extracting, the time complexity increases in the order PEE < SS < BS < ZTDCT < GCDS < BA < LFCP. Although for GCDS, BA, and LFCP algorithms, an extra storage of the distortion sorting results is needed, this information can be embedded together with other overhead information into the LSB planes of some preselected image blocks controlled by a secret key, and we do not need additional memory.

3.3.4.4.5 Algorithm Security

As mentioned earlier, for GCDS, BA, and LFCP algorithms, Yang et al. employed the same secret-key controlled overhead storing scheme as in Ref. [19]. The overhead information can be securely embedded into some preselected blocks whose positions (deciding the synchronization information) are encrypted by the secret key owned by authorized operators. In Yang et al.'s old algorithm BS, a twice-try scheme was used and they even do not need the secret key to position the blocks with overhead information embedded, but the security of the watermarking process is compromised. This problem is also with SS and PEE, in which where and how to securely embed such overhead bits has not been considered. Especially in PEE, the overhead bits for indication of block classification are closely embedded in the next embeddable location (refer to Ref. [37]), which is easy to recognize by positioning those pixels close to the grayscale boundaries. Aside from the security for the synchronization information, SS also has an artifact trace on the modified wavelet coefficients: there is no coefficient with "0" value (refer to Ref. [38]). This affects the undetectability of the watermarking process if we need to consider the steganography aspect in some applications.

3.4 INTEGER WAVELET TRANSFORM—BASED SCHEMES

In this section, we turn to integer wavelet transform—based lossless information hiding schemes, which adopt the so-called CDF(2,2) wavelet. Thus, we first introduce related concept of the CDF(2,2) wavelet.

The CDF(2,2) wavelet was proposed by Cohen, Daubechies, and Feauveau in 1992 [14]; it is a dual orthogonal (i.e., biorthogonal) (5,3) wavelet, whose low-pass and high-pass filters are with lengths of 5 and 3, respectively, both presenting symmetry. We can obtain an integer-to-integer bijective CDF(2,2) wavelet by lifting the original CDF (2,2) wavelet based on a certain lifting scheme, and this type of integer wavelet has been adopted in the JPEG2000 standard. Experiments have shown that, compared with other integer wavelets, the integer CDF (2,2) wavelet can get better performance in data capacity and distortion when it is used in reversible watermarking.

Assume that $x_i(0 \leq i \leq N)$ is a discrete integer signal sequence, then the forward and inverse transforms of CDF(2,2) can be defined as follows:

(1) Forward transform

Step 1: Grouping of the samples

$$s_i \leftarrow x_{2i}$$
$$d_i \leftarrow x_{2i+1} \tag{3.61}$$

Step 2: Prediction

$$d_i \leftarrow d_i - \left\lfloor \frac{1}{2}(s_i + s_{i+1}) + \frac{1}{2} \right\rfloor \tag{3.62}$$

Step 3: Updating

$$s_i \leftarrow s_i + \left\lfloor \frac{1}{4}(d_{i-1} + d_i) + \frac{1}{2} \right\rfloor \tag{3.63}$$

(2) Inverse transform

Step 1: Inverse updating

$$s_i \leftarrow s_i - \left\lfloor \frac{1}{4}(d_{i-1} + d_i) + \frac{1}{2} \right\rfloor \qquad (3.64)$$

Step 2: Inverse prediction

$$d_i \leftarrow d_i + \left\lfloor \frac{1}{2}(s_i + s_{i+1}) + \frac{1}{2} \right\rfloor \qquad (3.65)$$

Step 3: Sample recovery

$$\begin{aligned} x_{2i} &\leftarrow s_i \\ x_{2i+1} &\leftarrow d_i \end{aligned} \qquad (3.66)$$

These equations give the form of forward and inverse transforms only for one-dimensional integer CDF (2,2). However, the integer CDF (2,2) wavelet is separable, so we can easily obtain the 2D integer wavelet transform for natural images through the transforms in horizontal and vertical directions.

3.4.1 VALUE EXPANSION TECHNIQUE IN THE INTEGER WAVELET TRANSFORM DOMAIN

Conceptually, the integer Haar wavelet transform domain high-frequency coefficient expansion (i.e., the difference expansion) technique introduced in Section 2.3.1 of Chapter 2 also belongs to the integer transform domain value expansion technology. However, because the application of the difference expansion technique is confined in the pair of adjacent pixels, the effect is closer to the spatial domain prediction decorrelation approach, therefore we classify it as the spatial domain value expansion technology. This section describes Xuan et al.'s global integer wavelet transform (DWT) domain value expansion technique [40].

Based on Yang et al.'s bit-shift idea in the IntDCT domain, Xuan et al. tried to perform the companding and value expansion techniques on the integer CDF(2,2) transform coefficients, which are obtained from one-level integer CDF (2,2) wavelet decomposition (resulting in three high-frequency LH, HL, HH coefficients), achieving relatively good performance [40]. Note that, in this algorithm, the key problem to improving the performance is to design a suitable compression function. Next, we first introduce the compression function proposed by Xuan et al. Then, we discuss the calculation of the compression and expansion error and introduce a simplified method to record the error and give a more succinct form of the compression and expansion function.

3.4.1.1 The Compression Function Suitable for Value Expansion

To minimize the substantial distortion due to bit-shifting, Xuan et al. designed a compression function C according to the compression and expansion principles, and in this compression function, the amplitude distortion due to bit-shifting can be controlled by a preset threshold T, to obtain better balance between data capacity and distortion and improve the overall performance. The compression function C is designed as follows:

$$C(x) = \begin{cases} x, & |x| < T \\ \text{sign}(x) \cdot \left(\dfrac{|x| - T}{2} + T\right), & |x| \geq T \end{cases} \tag{3.67}$$

wherein the sign(x) denotes the sign of x, and the compression function and the error due to the compression and bit-shift operations are shown in Fig. 3.25. Fig. 3.25 shows that after the compression function C and the bit left shift operation (i.e., the amplitude is multiplied by 2) are performed on the original value x, the difference Δx is calculated as follows:

$$\Delta x = \begin{cases} x, & |x| < T \\ T, & |x| \geq T \end{cases} \tag{3.68}$$

That is, no matter how much the amplitude of the original value x is, after the compression process and the bit-shift operation, the absolute value of the magnitude of the error is always limited within the range T. This process can significantly reduce the image distortion caused by the reversible watermark embedding process. The digitized version $C_Q(x)$ of the compression function x is as follows:

$$C_Q(x) = \begin{cases} x, & |x| < T \\ \text{sign}(x) \cdot \left(\left\lfloor\dfrac{|x| - T}{2}\right\rfloor + T\right), & |x| \geq T \end{cases} \tag{3.69}$$

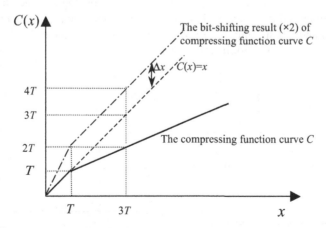

FIGURE 3.25

Compression function C and coefficient amplitude error analysis.

where x is an integer. Because of the rounding operation after being divided by 2, $C_Q(x)$ is unlikely to be a one-to-one mapping, which will inevitably bring the error to the expansion function. How to effectively record the error is also the key to improving the performance of the algorithm.

3.4.1.2 Recording of the Compression and Companding Error and Simplification of the Value Expansion

From Eq. (3.69), we can see that, if we keep the sign of x unchanged, $|x| = T + 2k$ with $|x| = T + 2k + 1$, $k \in \mathbf{N}$ will be compressed into the same value $\text{sign}(x) \times (k + T)$, so that the end of the extension function E_Q:

$$E_Q(x) = \begin{cases} x, & |x| \langle T \\ \text{sign}(x) \cdot (2x - T), & |x| \geq T \end{cases} \tag{3.70}$$

Thus, we will be unable to recover the original amplitude from $x = \text{sign}(x)(k + T)$, and we can only restore this value into the amplitude with the form $|x| = T + 2k$ but cannot restore to $|x| = T + 2k + 1$. That is, for all the original values with the amplitude form $|x| = T + 2k + 1$ value, after the compression and expansion, there is an error:

$$q[n] = x[n] - (E_Q C_Q x)[n] = \begin{cases} (T + 2k) - (T + 2k) = 0, & |x| = T + 2k \\ (T + 2k + 1) - (T + 2k) = 1, & |x| = T + 2k + 1 \end{cases}$$
$$\tag{3.71}$$

Obviously, no matter what the value of T is, the number of high-frequency coefficients of the integer CDF(2,2) whose amplitude is not less than T is always equal to the data capacity that these high-frequency coefficients can provide (assume that each coefficient can only be left-shifted by 1 bit), and is also equal to the number of resulting coefficients after compression and expansion that are required to be discriminated from their original magnitude. A relatively better method to record the error that is used to discriminate between the compressed and expanded amplitude and the original one is to use bits "0" and "1" to distinguish each coefficient error after compression and expansion, and this bit is stored in the vacated LSB after compression and left shifting. We illustrate the process with the example shown in Fig. 3.26, where $|x|$ is the original magnitude, $|C_Q(x)|$ is the magnitude compressed

$|x|$:	1	2	3	4	5	6	7	8	9	10...
$|C_Q(x)|$:	1	2	3	3	4	4	5	5	6	6 ...
$|2C_Q(x)|$:	2	4	6	6	8	8	10	10	12	12...
$|2C_Q(x)'|$:	2	4	6	7	8	9	10	1	12	13...
A:			0	1	0	1	0	1	0	1 ...
$|E_Q C_Q(x)|$:	1	2	3	3	5	5	7	7	9	9 ...

FIGURE 3.26

An example for value companding functions.

by the compression function C_Q, $|2C_Q(x)|$ is a 1-bit left-shifted magnitude, $|2C_Q(x)'|$ is the magnitude that contains the information to distinguish the original amplitude, A is the bit string for distinguishing the original amplitudes, $|E_Q C_Q(x)|$ is the expanded magnitude by the expansion function, and $T = 3$ is the threshold of the companding and compressing functions adopted in this example.

From Fig. 3.26, we can see that the companding error $|x| - |E_Q C_Q(x)|$ is even directly equal to the information A that is used to distinguish the original amplitude. The reason is that the error determined by Eqs. (3.69) and (3.70) is just the 0,1 interleaved situation Eq. (3.71). In this example, we use "0" to indicate the compression and expansion error 0, whereas "1" to represent the error 1, so the discrimination information A can be directly used to represent the companding error. Of course, you can change the way, saying that "0" indicates the companding error 1, and "1" represents the companding error 0. However, the experiment has proved that under this representation, the error between $|2C_Q(x)'|$ and the original amplitude $|x|$ becomes larger. The detailed analysis shows that, under the former representation, the error between $|2C_Q(x)'|$ and the original amplitude $|x|$ is T when $|x| \geq T$ (see Fig. 3.26), whereas under the latter representation, the corresponding error is $T + 1$ or $T - 1$. Since the distortion is calculated by using the square of the magnitude of the error, in the case that the distribution of adjacent original amplitudes is more balanced, obviously the former method can get smaller overall distortion.

From the above-mentioned analysis, we also find that if the first representation method is used, that is, the companding error 0 is denoted by "0", whereas the error 1 is denoted by "1.", we can always have the following relationship:

$$|2C_Q(x)'| = \begin{cases} 2 \cdot |x|, & |x| < T \\ |x| + T, & |x| \geq T \end{cases} \tag{3.72}$$

Thus, we can get a simplified form for value expansion—based watermark embedding:

$$X_W = \begin{cases} 2X + W, & |X| < T \\ X + \text{sign}(X) \cdot T, & |X| \geq T \end{cases} \tag{3.73}$$

It is easy to know that Eq. (3.73) is equivalent to Eq. (3.72) in terms of the magnitude distortion, and this value expansion—based watermark embedding method approximates Xuan et al.'s compressing and companding method in performance, but the form is more concise with less amount of calculation; hereinafter, it is referred to as the value expansion method within the threshold.

3.4.2 COEFFICIENTS' MAGNITUDE PREDICTION TECHNIQUE IN INTEGER WAVELET TRANSFORM DOMAIN

From the previous section, we can see that the coefficient companding and compression method in the integer DWT domain should consider further the selection of middle- and high-frequency coefficients. Obviously, if we need to perform the value expansion—based watermark embedding on N coefficients, the best way is to choose the N coefficients with the minimum absolute magnitude value, so as to make the watermark embedding algorithm bring the minimum distortion to the image quality. However, the problem is that once the N coefficients with minimum absolute magnitude values are performed with the expansion and watermark embedding operations, their resulting coefficients may not be the N coefficients with minimum absolute magnitude values; then during the watermark extraction and image recovery phase, we cannot recognize these N coefficients, and thus the image watermark extraction and recovery will be impossible.

According to the principle of selecting the coefficients with magnitude absolute values as small as possible, here we provide an adaptive selection scheme for integer CDF (2,2) wavelet coefficients, which can predict the magnitude distribution of co-efficient blocks or the positions of coefficients with small magnitudes by making use of the redundancy among the transform domain coefficients or bands. In theory, if the accuracy of this predictive method reaches 100%, then the correlation degree among coefficients must also reach 100%, which is not possible under the integer transform, which is clearly contrary to the decorrelation features of the original DWT. However, you can guess, the higher is the accuracy of this prediction, the less is the distortion that the watermark embedding method introduces, and the algorithm performance can be significantly improved.

Here, we provide a simple integer CDF (2,2) wavelet domain—based amplitude coefficient prediction method. For the integer CDF (2,2) wavelet, more redundancy exists between different frequency bands, and the corresponding coefficient positions reflect the similarity of the pixel distribution in the spatial domain. We can make use of the correlation between the high-frequency subbands HH_2, LH_2, and HL_2 in the second level and the high-frequency subbands HH_1, LH_1, and HL_1 in the first level to construct a tree structure similar to a zero tree, as shown in Fig. 3.27. Based on the $M-1$ thresholds TH_1, TH_2, ..., TH_{M-1}, which are set according to a certain parent node with the absolute magnitude value c_0 among HH_2, LH_2,

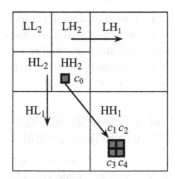

FIGURE 3.27

The space—frequency zero-tree structure.

and HL_2 subbands, we can classify their corresponding four child nodes $\{c_1,c_2,c_3,c_4\}$ into a certain class among M classes. Obviously, these M classes of high-frequency coefficients are with different expectation values, which are suitable for different watermarking algorithms to achieve improved performance.

3.4.3 COMPARISONS BETWEEN GENERALIZED LOSSLESS COMPRESSION–BASED AND VALUE EXPANSION–BASED SCHEMES

In this section, we compare the generalized lossless compression–based generalized LSB scheme [41], the integer DWT domain lossless bit-plane compression–based algorithm [31], the integer DWT domain coefficient compression- and expansion-based algorithm, and the integer DWT domain histogram shift–based algorithm. We will compare the performance of lossless compression–based methods in the spatial domain and in the integer DWT domain, as well as the performance of lossless compression–based methods and value expansion–based methods.

3.4.3.1 Generalized Least Significant Bit Lossless Compression Scheme

Celik et al. presented a kind of generalized LSB lossless compression (general LSB lossless compression)–based reversible watermarking technology in Ref. [41]. Unlike the traditional bit-plane lossless compression–based and value expansion–based schemes, Celik et al.'s method utilizes an efficient lossless compression algorithm CALIC [42] to losslessly compress the quantized residual, i.e., the lowest L amplitude levels (instead of the least n bit-planes), and embeds the watermark data and the compressed bit-planes into the original L minimum amplitude levels. In fact, the traditional LSB bit lossless compression method is a special case of $L = 2$. The performance and data capacity of this method are better than the original bit-plane lossless compression algorithm, and in theory, this method can embed $\log_2 L$ bit watermark data in each sample, representing the high level of generalized lossless compression–based methods. Therefore, we adopt it here as a reference for performance comparison, as shown in Table 3.3.

3.4.3.2 Integer Discrete Wavelet Transform Domain Lossless Bit-Plane Compression Scheme

Xuan et al.'s method perform the compression operation on the integer CDF(2,2) high-frequency subband bit-planes [31], with the performance shown in Table 3.4.

3.4.3.3 Integer Discrete Wavelet Transform Domain Coefficient Companding and Compression Scheme

Xuan et al. presented a lossless information hiding scheme based on coefficient companding and compression in the integer CDF(2,2) domain in Ref. [40], but they did

Table 3.3 Performance of Reversible Watermarking Based on General LSB Lossless Compression

Level L	2	3	4	5	6	8	10	12	14	16
Lena										
PSNR (dB)	51.1	46.9	44.2	42.1	40.5	38.0	36.0	34.4	33.0	31.9
Bit-rate (bpp)	0.018	0.047	0.087	0.131	0.180	0.285	0.387	0.481	0.584	0.675
Baboon										
PSNR (dB)	51.1	46.9	44.2	42.1	40.5	38.0	36.0	34.4	33.0	31.9
Bit-rate (bpp)	0.003	0.008	0.014	0.023	0.034	0.058	0.085	0.117	0.141	0.176

Table 3.4 Performance of Reversible Watermarking Based on Bit-Plane Lossless Compression in the Discrete Wavelet Transform Domain

Lena					
PSNR (dB)	41.0	39.0	38.0	35.6	34.1
Bit-Rate (bpp)	0.1	0.2	0.3	0.4	0.5
Baboon					
PSNR (dB)	32.5	29.4	27.6	25.3	
Bit-rate (bpp)	0.1	0.2	0.3	0.4	

PSNR, *peak signal-to-noise ratio.*

not provide the embedding scheme of the companding and compression errors. Thus, in the simulation, we adopt the value expansion method within the threshold as shown in Eq. (3.73), and the results are shown in Table 3.5, where T is the threshold in Eq. (3.73).

3.4.3.4 Integer Discrete Wavelet Transform Domain Histogram Shift Scheme

We can also perform the histogram shifting technique on the integer CDF(2,2) high-frequency coefficients to implement the lossless information hiding. In the simulation, we adopt the first N peak points with highest magnitude $P_i (i = 0, 1, ..., N-1)$ for histogram shifting, and the results are shown in Table 3.6, where N denotes the number of peaks.

Based on the results shown in Tables 3.3—3.6, we can give a comprehensive curve (PSNR-bit-rate) to show the performance for four different methods as given in Fig. 3.28 (Lena) and Fig. 3.29 (Baboon). In figures, GLSB denotes the generalized LSB lossless compression, DWTLC is the integer CDF(2,2) wavelet domain lossless bit-plane compression-based algorithm, DWTCP is the integer CDF(2,2) wavelet domain coefficient compression- and expansion-based algorithm, and DWTHS is the integer CDF(2,2) wavelet domain histogram shift—based algorithm.

From Figs. 3.28 and 3.29, we can obviously see that, the performance of DWTCP and DWTHS is much better than that of GLSB and DWTLC. Under the same data capacity, the improvement is nearly 5—8 dB (Lena) or 7—12 dB (Baboon). The performance of DWTLC is very close to that of GLSB, which indicates that, compared with the bit-planes in the spatial domain, the bit-planes in the integer wavelet domain are with much more unbalance of the "0" and "1" data, thus we can deeply compress them to embed more information without affecting the image quality. Furthermore, we can note that the performance advantage is much more obvious for the Baboon image, which indicates that the value expansion technique and the histogram shifting technique are much more suitable for images with high details.

Table 3.5 Performance of the Method Given in Eq. (3.73) to Simulate the Companding-Based Reversible Watermarking in the Integer Discrete Wavelet Transform Domain

T	1	2	3	4	5	6	7	8	9	10
Lena										
PSNR (dB)	48.054	44.46	42.413	41.175	40.299	39.638	39.117	38.68	38.307	37.995
Bit-rate (bpp)	0.114	0.314	0.465	0.563	0.625	0.661	0.684	0.699	0.709	0.717
Baboon										
PSNR (dB)	48.059	43.687	40.69	38.672	37.053	35.807	34.756	33.883	33.112	32.452
Bit-rate (bpp)	0.036	0.108	0.172	0.229	0.278	0.322	0.358	0.389	0.416	0.442

PSNR, *peak signal-to-noise ratio.*

Table 3.6 Performance of Histogram Shifting—Based Reversible Watermarking in the Integer Discrete Wavelet Transform Domain

N	1	2	3	4	5	6	7	8	9	10
Lena										
PSNR (dB)	48.705	45.322	42.413	41.175	40.299	39.638	39.117	38.68	38.307	37.995
Bit-rate (bpp)	0.2	0.351	0.465	0.563	0.625	0.661	0.684	0.699	0.709	0.717
Baboon										
PSNR (dB)	48.255	43.934	40.954	38.925	37.305	35.807	34.756	33.883	33.112	32.452
Bit-rate (bpp)	0.07	0.135	0.191	0.243	0.286	0.322	0.358	0.389	0.416	0.442

PSNR, *peak signal-to-noise ratio.*

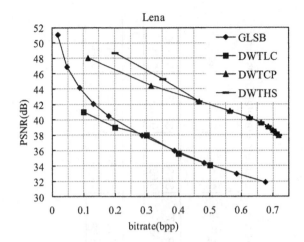

FIGURE 3.28

Performance of general lossless compression and discrete wavelet transform coefficient expansion–based reversible watermarking algorithms: Lena.

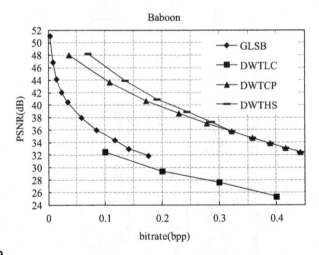

FIGURE 3.29

Performance of general lossless compression and discrete wavelet transform coefficient expansion–based reversible watermarking algorithms: Baboon.

3.5 SUMMARY

This chapter has discussed transform domain lossless information hiding schemes, including IntDCT-based schemes and integer DWT-based schemes. Before introducing then, we introduced some related concepts and requirements for lossless information hiding, and gave a brief overview of transform domain—based information hiding.

With regard to IntDCT-based schemes, we have introduced three Yang et al.'s schemes, i.e., the companding technique—based scheme, the histogram modification—based scheme, and the adaptive coefficient modification—based scheme. The first scheme takes advantage of the bit-shift operation in the companding process to achieve high watermarking capacity and good quality of watermarked images. To solve the over- and underflow problems caused by the coefficient modification, Yang et al. designed a twice-try-based block discrimination structure to find those twice-embedding permitted blocks to store overhead for block location information that reflects all blocks' over- and underflow situations. These twice-embedding permitted blocks can be recognized during extraction without any overhead for indication. The watermark bits can be reversibly embedded in the remaining twice-embedding permitted blocks and all once-embedding permitted blocks. In the second scheme, the histogram modification technique—based scheme is generalized into an 8×8 integer DCI' domain successfully and achieves high capacity and fine quality adjustment capability in relatively high PNSR ranges (about 40—60 dB) of the watermarked image. The experimental results demonstrate this scheme's competitive performance for general reversible image watermarking applications. In the third scheme, Yang et al. investigated three IntDCT coefficient selection methods to adapt the coefficient modification process to the current block's coefficients' amplitude status, and thus improved the watermarking performance in terms of the capacity/distortion rate. They integrated the GCDS technique, the value addition scheme, and a low-frequency coefficient-based block classification method and obtained satisfactory improvements in several performance aspects. Note that some coefficient adaptive modification ideas, such as the coefficient distortion sorting and the low frequency coefficient prediction, can be actually modified and migrated to other integer transform domains such as integer wavelet transform and achieve even greater improvements in some performance aspects.

With regard to integer DWT-based schemes, we introduce three schemes, i.e., the value expansion—based scheme, the histogram shift—based scheme, and the coefficient magnitude prediction—based scheme. The first scheme was originally proposed by Xuan et al. Based on Yang et al.'s bit-shift idea in the IntDCT domain, Xuan et al. tried to perform the companding and value expansion techniques on the integer CDF(2,2) transform coefficients, which are obtained from one-level integer CDF(2,2) wavelet decomposition (resulting in three high frequency LH, HL, HH coefficients), achieving relatively good performance. Note that, in this algorithm, the key problem to improving the performance is to design a suitable compression function. With regard to the second scheme, it is just a scheme to perform the histogram shifting technique on the integer CDF(2,2) high-frequency coefficients to implement the lossless information hiding. All these schemes are compared with the typical spatial domain—based schemes. With regard to the third scheme, we provide an adaptive selection scheme for integer CDF(2,2) wavelet co-efficients, which can predict the magnitude distribution of coefficient blocks or the positions of coefficients with small magnitudes by making use of the redundancy among the transform domain coefficients or bands redundancy. Finally, all the afore-mentioned methods are simulated and compared.

REFERENCES

[1] K. Komatsu, K. Sezaki, Reversible discrete cosine transform, Proceedings of IEEE ICASSP98 (1998) 1113–1772.
[2] W. Philips, Lossless DCT for combined lossy/lossless image coding, Proceedings of IEEE International Conference on Image Processing 3 (1998) 871–875.
[3] T. Tran, The BinDCT: fast multiplierless approximation of the DCT, IEEE Signal Processing Letters 7 (2000) 141–144.
[4] L. Cheng, H. Xu, Y. Luo, Integer discrete cosine transform and its fast algorithm, Electronics Letters 37 (2001) 64–65.
[5] Y. Zhang, L. Cheng, G. Bi, A.C. Kot, Integer DCTs and fast algorithms, IEEE Transactions on Signal Processing 49 (2001) 2774–2782.
[6] M.D. Adams, Reversible Integer-to-integer Wavelet Transforms for Image Coding (Ph.D. thesis), Department of Electrical and Computer Engineering, The University of British Columbia, 2002.
[7] M.D. Adams, F. Kossentini, Reversible integer-to-integer wavelet transforms for image compression: performance evaluation and analysis, IEEE Transactions on Image Processing 9 (6) (2000) 1010–1024.
[8] A.R. Calderbank, I. Daubechies, W. Sweldens, B.L. Yeo, Wavelet transforms that maps integers to integers, Applied and Computational Harmonic Analysis 5 (1998) 332–369.
[9] S. Dewitte, J. Cornelis, Lossless integer wavelet transform, IEEE Signal Processing Letters 4 (6) (1997) 158–160.
[10] G. Plonka, M. Tasch, Invertible integer DCT algorithms, Applied and Computational Harmonic Analysis 15 (2003) 70–88.
[11] G. Plonka, M. Tasche, Reversible Integer DCT Algorithms, Preprint, Gerhard-Mercator-University, Duisburg, 2002.
[12] G. Plonka, A Global Method for Invertible Integer DCT and Integer Wavelet Algorithms, Preprint, Gerhard-Mercator-University, Duisburg, 2004.
[13] W. Sweldens, The lifting scheme: a custom-design construction of biorthogonal wavelets, Applied and Computational Harmonic Analysis 3 (2) (1996) 186–200.
[14] A. Cohen, I. Daubechies, J.C. Feauveau, Biorthogonal bases of compactly supported wavelets, Communications on Pure and Applied Mathematics 45 (1992) 485–560.
[15] N. Ahmed, T. Natarajan, K.R. Rao, Discrete cosine transform, IEEE Transactions on Computers 32 (1974) 90–93.
[16] E. Koch, J. Zhao, Towards robust and hidden image copyright labeling, in: Proceedings of the IEEE Workshop on Nonlinear and Marmaras, Greece, 1995, pp. 1–4.

[17] I.J. Cox, J. Kilian, F.T. Leighton, et al., Secure spread spectrum watermarking for multimedia, IEEE Transactions on Image Processing 6 (12) (1997) 1673–1687.

[18] B. Tao, B. Dickinson, Adaptive watermarking in the DCT domain, in: Proceeding of the 1997 IEEE International Conference on Acoustics, Speech, and Signal Processing, 4 (4), 1997, pp. 2985–2988.

[19] B. Yang, M. Schmucker, X. Niu, C. Busch, S. Sun, Reversible image watermarking by histogram modification for integer DCT coefficients, in: IEEE 6th Workshop on Multimedia Signal Processing, September 29–October 1, 2004, 2004, pp. 143–146, http://dx.doi.org/10.1109/MMSP.2004.1436446.

[20] C.C. Chen, D.S. Kao, DCT-based reversible image watermarking approach, in: Third International Conference on Intelligent Information Hiding and Multimedia Signal Processing, November 26–28, 2007, Kaohsiung, 2007, pp. 489–492.

[21] S. Pereira, J.J.K. O'Ruanaidh, F. Deguillaume, et al., Template based recovery of Fourier-based watermarks using log-polar and log-log maps, in: Proceedings of the IEEE International Conference on Multimedia Computing and Systems. Florence, Italy, 1999, pp. 870–874.

[22] M. Corvi, G. Nicchiotti, Wavelet based image watermarking for Copyright Protection[C], in: Scandinavian Conference on Image Analysis. Lappeenranta,Finland, 1997, pp. 157–163.

[23] D. Kundur, D. Hatzinakos, A robust digital image watermarking method using wavelet-based fusion[C], in: Proceedings of the IEEE International Conference on Image Processing, 1997, pp. 544–547.

[24] G. Xuan, Y. Shi, P. Chai, et al., Optimum histogram pair based image lossless data embedding, in: Proceedings of Digital Watermarking, LNCS, 5041, 2008, pp. 264–278.

[25] Y.J. Chen, Integer discrete cosine transform (IntDCT), in: Presented at the Second International Conference on Information Communications and Signal Processing, Singapore, December 1999 (Invited paper).

[26] T.D. Tran. Fast multiplierless approximation of the DCT. (Online). Available: http://thanglong.ece.jhu.edu/Tran/Pub/intDCT.ps.gz.

[27] B. Yang, M. Schmucker, W. Funk, C. Busch, S. Sun, Integer DCT-based reversible watermarking for images using companding technique, in: Proc. SPIE, Security and Watermarking of Multimedia Content, Electronic Imaging, San Jose, USA, January 2004, pp. 405–415.

[28] A. Leest, M. Veen, F. Bruekers, Reversible image watermarking, in: IEEE Proceedings of ICIP'03, vol. 2, 2003, pp. 731–734.

[29] M. Veen, F. Bruekers, A. Leest, S. Cavin, High capacity reversible watermarking for audio, in: Proceedings of the SPIE, vol. 5020, 2003, pp. 1–11.

[30] E. Lam, J. Goodman, A mathematical analysis of the DCT coefficient distribution for images, IEEE Transactions on Image Processing 9 (10) (2000) 1661–1666.

[31] G. Xuan, J. Zhu, J. Chen, Y. Shi, Z. Ni, W. Su, Distortionless data hiding based on integer wavelet transform, IEE Electronics Letters 38 (25) (2002) 1646–1648.

[32] Z. Ni, Y.Q. Shi, N. Ansari, W. Suo, Reversible data hiding, in: IEEE Proceedings of/SCAS'03, vol.2, May 2003, pp. II·912–II-915.

[33] A. Leesl, M. Veen, E. Broekers, Reversible image watermarking, in: IEEE Proceedings of ICIP'03, vol. 2, September 2003, pp. 731–734.

[34] B. Yang, M. Schmucker, X. Niu, C. Busch, S. Sun, Integer DCT based reversible image watermarking by adaptive coefficient modification, in: SPIE-EI, Security and Watermarking of Multimedia Content, Proc. of SPIE-IS&T Electronic Imaging, SPIE, vol. 5681, Electronic Imaging, San Jose, USA, January, 2005, pp. 218–229.

[35] Z. Xiong, O.G. Guleryuz, M.T. Orchard, A DCT-based embedded image coder, IEEE Signal Processing Letters 3 (11) (1996) 289–290.

[36] M. Voigt, B. Yang, C. Busch, Reversible watermarking of 2D-vector data, in: Proceedings of the 2004 ACM International Workshop on Multimedia and Security, Magdeburg, Germany, 2004, pp. 160–165.

[37] M. Thodi, J.J. Rodríguez, Reversible watermarking by prediction-error expansion, in: The 6th IEEE Southwest Symposium on Image Analysis and Interpretation, Lake Tahoe, CA, USA, March 28–30, 2004, 2004, pp. 21–25.

[38] G. Xuan, C. Yang, Y. Zhen, Y. Shi, Z. Ni, Reversible data hiding based on wavelet spread spectrum, in: IEEE Proceedings of Multimedia Signal Processing Workshop, 2004. Siena, Italy.

[39] J. Nam, K. Rao, Image coding using a classified DCT/VQ based on two-channel conjugate vector quantization, IEEE Transactions on Circuits and Systems for Video Technology 1 (4) (1991) 325–336.

[40] G. Xuan, C. Yang, Y. Zhen, Y. Shi, Z. Ni, Reversible Data Hiding Using Integer Wavelet Transform and Companding Technique, IWDW, 2004.

[41] M.U. Celik, G. Sharma, A.M. Tekalp, E. Saber, Reversible data hiding, in: Proc. of International Conference on Image Processing, vol. II, September 2002, pp. 157–160.

[42] X. Wu, Lossless compression of coutinuous-tone images via context selection, quantization and modelling, IEEE Transactions on Image Processing 6 (5) (May 1997) 656–664.

Lossless Information Hiding in Vector Quantization Compressed Images

4.1 INTRODUCTION

4.1.1 BASIC FRAMEWORK OF LOSSLESS INFORMATION HIDING IN THE COMPRESSED DOMAIN

When we view the lossless information hiding problem in the compressed domain, such as vector quantization (VQ) [1] and block truncation coding (BTC) [2], the cover object becomes the compressed version of the original image—the code stream. For the change of information hiding from the pixel domain to the compressed domain the change of some requirements is necessary and information hiding algorithms are desired, which will be given afterward. Before that, we introduce a basic framework of lossy compression (encoding and decoding) and lossless information hiding [3] in the compressed domain presented by Yang et al. in Fig. 4.1, where I_o is supposed to be the original image, E is a lossy encoder containing a quantizer, and C is the code stream, resulting from E, as the exact cover object in the lossless information hiding model. D is a decoder corresponding to E, and Em. and Ex. are the embeddor and extractor, respectively.

From Fig. 4.1, we can see that the mapping from I_o to C is many-to-one because of the quantization operation in E. Thus, if we directly reversibly embed information in I_o, some distortion may be caused to the information embedded in I_o during the extraction process, which destroys the reversibility of the algorithm used in the pixel domain. So we change the cover object from I_o to C, which is the actual existing form of I_o for storing and transmission.

4.1.2 REQUIREMENTS OF LOSSLESS INFORMATION HIDING IN THE COMPRESSED DOMAIN

Now we prescribe some requirements in the definition of lossless information hiding in the aforementioned framework [3].

1. Reversibility

The perfect restoration of C and w after extraction without attacks, that is, $C = C_R$ and $w = w_r$.

Lossless Information Hiding in Images. http://dx.doi.org/10.1016/B978-0-12-812006-4.00004-8

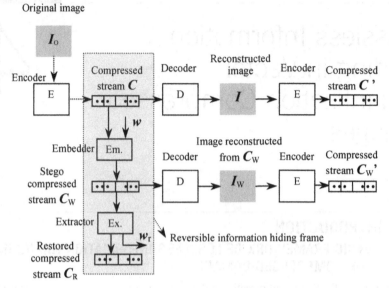

FIGURE 4.1

Framework of lossy compression and lossless information hiding in compressed domain.

2. Dispensability

The information w embedded in the C should be dispensable in format from the other part of C, which will guarantee the "invisibility" to the decoder. In other words, the decoder should be able to read the code stream C_w as smoothly as its normal version C without any "notice" that there is some information w embedded.

3. Fidelity

The embedding of w should not cause great perceptual distortion to the reconstructed image I_w compared with its original version I_o, which is decided by watermark's original intention.

4. Size preservation of the original image

The size of the reconstructed images I and I_w should be equal in the pixel domain. Note that this requirement is not necessary to the code stream as long as the change in code stream's size will not compromise the function of the decoder, although in many cases it is also desired that the code stream's size be preserved.

Aside from these requirements that are necessary for the general lossless information hiding algorithms in the compressed domain, there are also some desired properties of the algorithms from some practical views.

1. Compatibility

The lossless information hiding algorithm should be as compatible with existing lossy compression schemes as possible. No or least modification of existing encoders and decoders is preferred considering the convenience of algorithm implementation.

2. Size preservation of the code stream

This desired property has been explained in Requirement 4.

3. Clipping avoidance

Some modification due to lossless information hiding algorithms will be sensitive to pixel clipping (overflows and underflows), which will destroy the equality of C_w and C'_w in images' reconstruction, and accordingly, affect the inheritance of the information w from C_w to C'_w. Although the information extracted from C'_w is not a requirement for the general lossless information hiding scheme, in some cases, users may appreciate this virtue.

4. Separation of the encoder and the embeddor

This property facilitates the individual processing of encoder and information embeddor. From the previous discussion, we can see the difference between the pixel-domain lossless information hiding and the one performed in the compressed domain. In the VQ-compressed domain too, the requirements and desires apply in most cases.

4.1.3 VECTOR QUANTIZATION

VQ [1] has become an attractive *block-based encoding* method for image compression. It can achieve a high compression ratio. In environments such as image archival and one-to-many communications, the simplicity of the decoder makes VQ very efficient. In brief, VQ can be defined as a mapping from k-dimensional Euclidean space R^k into a finite subset $C = \{c_i | i = 0, 1, ..., N-1\}$ that is generally called a *codebook*, where c_i is a *codeword* and N is the *codebook size*, as shown in Fig. 4.2. Before compression, VQ generates a representative codebook from a training set consisting of a number of training vectors using, for example, the well-known iterative clustering algorithm [1] that is often referred to as the **generalized Lloyd algorithm**. In VQ, the image to be encoded is first decomposed into vectors and then sequentially encoded vector by vector. As shown in Fig. 4.3, in the *encoding* stage, each k-dimensional input vector $x = (x_1, x_2, ..., x_k)$ is compared with the codewords in the codebook $C = \{c_0, c_1, ..., c_{N-1}\}$ to find the best matching codeword $c_i = (c_{i1}, c_{i2}, ..., c_{ik})$ satisfying the following condition:

$$d(x, c_i) = \min_{0 \leq j \leq N-1} d(x, c_j) \tag{4.1}$$

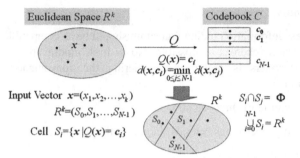

FIGURE 4.2

The principle of vector quantization.

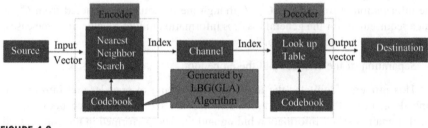

FIGURE 4.3

The encoding and decoding processes of vector quantization.

i.e., the distance between x and c_i is the smallest, where $d(x,c_j)$ is the distortion of representing the input vector x by the codeword c_j, which is often measured by the *squared Euclidean distance*, i.e.,

$$d(x, c_j) = \sum_{l=1}^{k} (x_l - c_{jl})^2 \qquad (4.2)$$

Then the *index i* of the best matching codeword assigned to the input vector x is transmitted over the channel to the decoder. The *decoder* has the same codebook as the *encoder*. In the *decoding* phase, for each index i, the decoder merely performs a simple table look-up operation to obtain c_i and then uses c_i to reconstruct the input vector x. The *compression ratio* is determined by the codebook size and the dimension of the input vectors, and the overall distortion depends on the codebook size and the selection of codewords.

4.2 OVERVIEW OF VECTOR QUANTIZATION—BASED INFORMATION HIDING

Since 2000, VQ has been successfully applied to digital image watermarking [21−31]. Since 2005, because of the emergence of lossless information hiding, several scholars have been dedicated to lossless information hiding in VQ-compressed images. In the following two subsections, we overview typical methods related to VQ-based watermarking and VQ-based lossless information hiding.

4.2.1 OVERVIEW OF VECTOR QUANTIZATION—BASED IMAGE WATERMARKING

Traditional digital watermarking schemes are mainly based on discrete cosine transform (DCT) and discrete wavelet transform. In the past 15 years, many robust image watermarking techniques based on VQ [21–31] have been presented. These algorithms can be mainly classified into three categories: codebook partition based, index properties based, and multipurpose methods. Refs. [21–26] embed the watermark information into the encoded indices under the constraint that the extra distortion is less than a given threshold. Ref. [27] embeds the watermark bit in the dimension information of the variable dimension reconstruction blocks of the input image. Refs. [28,29] embed the watermark information by utilizing the properties, such as mean and variance, of neighboring indices. Refs. [30,31] present multipurpose watermarking methods based on multistage VQ and DCT domain VQ, respectively. For example, in Ref. [30], the robust watermark is embedded in the first stage by using the embedding method presented in Ref. [28], and the semifragile watermark is embedded in the second stage by using index-constrained VQ. In the following two subsections, we introduce the main idea of the algorithms in the first two categories.

4.2.1.1 Watermarking Algorithms Based on Codebook Partition

The main idea of this kind of VQ-based digital watermarking schemes [21–26] is to carry secret copyright information by codeword indices. The aim of the codebook partition is to classify the neighboring codewords into the same cluster. Given a threshold $D > 0$, we denote by $S = \{S_1, S_2, ...,S_M\}$ a *standard partition* of the codebook $C = \{c_0, c_1, ..., c_{N-1}\}$ for the threshold D, if S satisfies the following four conditions:

1. $S = \bigcup_{i=1}^{M} S_i$;
2. $\forall i, j, 1 \leq i, j \leq M$, if $i \neq j$, then $S_i \cap S_j = \Phi$;
3. $\forall i, 1 \leq i \leq M$, if $c_i \in S_i$ and $c_j \in S_i$ ($0 \leq 1, j \leq N - 1$), then $d(c_1,c_j) \leq D$;
4. $\|S_i\| = 2^{n(i)}$, where $\|S_i\|$ denotes the number of codewords in S_i and $n(i)$ is a natural number.

Before the embedding process, the original image is first divided into blocks. For each block, the index of the best match codeword is found. The watermarked codeword index is then obtained by modifying the original codeword index according to the corresponding watermark bits. The modification is under the constraint that the modified index and the original one is in the same partition such that the introduced extra distortion is less than the given distortion threshold. In the decoding phase, not the original but the watermarked codeword is used to represent the input image block. Therefore, the VQ-based digital image watermarking will introduce some extra distortion. Whether the original image is required or not during the watermark extraction depends on the embedding method. In these algorithms, the codebook is open for users but the partition is the secret key. Experimental results show that these algorithms are robust to VQ compression with high-performance codebooks, JPEG compression, and some spatial image processing operations. However, these algorithms are fragile to rotation operations and VQ compression with low-performance codebooks.

4.2.1.2 Watermarking Algorithms Based on Index Properties

To enhance the robustness to rotation operations and VQ compression operations, some image watermarking algorithms [28,29] based on the properties of neighboring indices have been proposed. In Ref. [28], the original watermark W with size $A_w \times B_w$ is first permuted by a predetermined key, key_1, to generate the permuted watermark W_P for embedding. The original image X with size $A \times B$ is then divided into vectors $x(m,n)$ with size $(A/A_w) \times (B/B_w)$, where $x(m,n)$ denotes the image block at the position (m,n). After that, each vector $x(m,n)$ finds its best codeword c_i in the codebook C and the index i is assigned to $x(m,n)$; we can then obtain the indices matrix Y with elements $y(m,n)$, which can be represented by

$$Y = \mathrm{VQ}(X) = \bigcup_{m=0}^{\frac{A}{A_w}-1} \bigcup_{n=0}^{\frac{B}{B_w}-1} \mathrm{VQ}(x(m,n)) = \bigcup_{m=0}^{\frac{A}{A_w}-1} \bigcup_{n=0}^{\frac{B}{B_w}-1} y(m,n) \qquad (4.3)$$

For natural images, the VQ indices among neighboring blocks tend to be very similar, so we can make use of this property to generate the *polarities P*. After calculating the variances of $y(m,n)$ and the indices of its surrounding blocks with

$$\sigma^2(m,n) = \left(\frac{1}{9} \sum_{i=m-1}^{m+1} \sum_{j=n-1}^{n+1} y^2(i,j) \right) - \left(\frac{1}{9} \sum_{i=m-1}^{m+1} \sum_{j=n-1}^{n+1} y(i,j) \right)^2 \qquad (4.4)$$

We can obtain the polarities P as follows:

$$P = \bigcup_{m=0}^{\frac{A}{A_w}-1} \bigcup_{n=0}^{\frac{B}{B_w}-1} p(m,n) \qquad (4.5)$$

where

$$p(m,n) = \begin{cases} 1 & \text{if } \sigma^2(m,n) \geq T \\ 0 & \text{otherwise} \end{cases} \qquad (4.6)$$

For convenience, we set the threshold T to be half of the codebook size, $N/2$. We are then able to generate the final embedded watermark or the secret key, key_2, with the exclusive-or operation as follows:

$$key_2 = W_P \oplus P \qquad (4.7)$$

After the inverse VQ operation, both the reconstructed image, X', and the secret key, key_2, work together to protect the ownership of the original image.

In the extraction process, we first calculate the estimated polarities P' from X' and then obtain an estimate of the permuted watermark as follows:

$$W'_P = key_2 \oplus P' \tag{4.8}$$

Finally, we can perform the inverse permutation operation with key_1 to obtain the extracted watermark W'.

To embed multiple watermarks, Ref. [29] also uses the mean of indices to generate another polarities P_1 for embedding. Experimental results show that these algorithms are robust to many kinds of attacks, including JPEG, VQ, filtering, blurring, and rotation. However, these algorithms have the following two problems:

1. We can also extract the watermark from the original image that has no watermark embedded in it at all.
2. The codebook should be used as a key, because if the user possesses the same codebook, he can also embed his own watermark in the watermarked image without any modification.

In fact, unlike traditional watermarking methods, this kind of watermarking algorithm does not modify the VQ-compressed cover work at all. The term "fingerprint" or "secure fingerprint" may be more appropriate, and sometimes we can call this kind of watermark "zero-watermark."

4.2.2 OVERVIEW OF VECTOR QUANTIZATION–BASED LOSSLESS INFORMATION HIDING

As one of the most commonly studied image compression techniques, VQ has been widely applied in information hiding techniques because of its simplicity and cost-effective implementation. Promoted by the research works proposed by Chang et al. [32], Lu et al. [10], and Chen and Huang [16], VQ has been widely applied to information hiding. These schemes can be roughly classified into two categories: information hiding during VQ encoding and information hiding during VQ index coding.

For the first category, Yang et al. [3] proposed a lossless information hiding scheme based on modified fast correlation VQ (MFCVQ). Since the embeddable locations are determined by a predefined distance threshold, the hiding payload of the MFCVQ method is unstable and low. To improve the hiding payload, Chang et al. [4–7] proposed several information hiding algorithms based on side match VQ (SMVQ). The SMVQ algorithm [18–20] can achieve a lower bit rate; however, it brings relatively high computation cost.

In literatures, several lossless information hiding schemes based on VQ index coding have been proposed. Chang et al. proposed a lossless information embedding scheme [8] based on the VQ image compression technique, which emphasizes that the original VQ-compressed codes can be recovered after data extraction. Chang et al. [9] presented a lossless information hiding method based on the so-called joint neighboring coding (JNC) technique. This method embeds secret data by using the difference values between the current VQ-compressed index and left or upper neighboring indices. In 2013, Chu et al. [12] proposed a lossless information hiding scheme based on the difference coding technique, which achieves higher stego image quality and higher payload. However, the secret data are exposed in the output bitstream, and hence it is not safe enough. To enhance the security, Lu et al. [10] proposed a lossless information hiding algorithm based on the VQ-index residual value coding (VQIRVC). This algorithm can achieve higher peak signal-to-noise ratio (PSNR) and higher payload than the algorithms proposed by Yang et al. [3] and Chang et al. [6]. In 2009, a novel path optional lossless information hiding method [11] has been proposed with improvements on payload, stego image quality, transmission efficiency, and security. Lu et al. presented an improved JNC (IJNC) process [13] for both lossless information hiding and lossless index compression. The JNC process performs information hiding on each index outside the seed area, whereas the IJNC process performs information hiding on each 2×2 index block without any seed area. Wang et al. also proposed a novel lossless information hiding framework [14] to hide secret data into a binary codestream of VQ indices invertibly, in which matrix encoding is used to efficiently embed secret data, and error correction coding is employed for lossless restoration of the marked codestream at the receiver side. Zhao et al. [15] proposed a novel lossless information hiding scheme based on two-stage VQ (TSVQ), where the framework consists of three phases, TSVQ codebook generation, path selection and data embedding, and cover image reconstruction and secret data extraction.

In the following sections, we will introduce the aforementioned schemes in detail. We first introduce the MFCVQ-based scheme, the first VQ-based lossless information hiding algorithm. Then we introduce SMVQ-based schemes. Finally, we introduce VQ-index coding—based schemes.

4.3 MODIFIED FAST CORRELATION VECTOR QUANTIZATION—BASED SCHEME

Image blocks encoded by VQ are usually in the form of indices, which represent codewords' positions in a codebook C. The VQ encoder E quantizes the input image block x by selecting a best-matched code vector c_b [$c_b \in C = \{c_0, c_1, ..., c_{N-1}\}$, where N is the size of the codebook C]. Here, the Euclidean distance given in Eq. (4.2) is often employed as a metric for the best matching. It is obvious that this quantization might cause some distortion to the watermark information embedded in the pixel domain, if the embedding algorithms are sensitive to this operation, like most value expansion—based lossless information hiding algorithms [34—38]. So a lossless watermarking algorithm that works in the VQ indices is desired to circumvent the quantization operation. Many watermarking or information hiding algorithms have been proposed based on the VQ technique, which use VQ as a watermark embedding and extracting means based on the idea of *quantization index modulation*

(QIM) [33], which is a popular type of watermarking algorithm for VQ-compressed images. However, many VQ-based watermarking algorithms [22,25] by QIM just view VQ as a watermark embedding and extracting method for the original image. In Section 4.3.1, we review basic VQ (BVQ)—based watermarking algorithms from the view of the reversibility of the VQ indices in the compressed domain. Considering that the reversibility is usually traded with the compression performance of VQ, we first introduce the original fast correlation—based VQ (FCVQ) in Section 4.3.2 and then introduce the lossless information hiding algorithm based on MFCVQ in Section 4.3.3, where we give some simulation results and the advantages and disadvantages of the MFCVQ-based lossless information hiding algorithm.

4.3.1 LOSSLESS INFORMATION HIDING FOR BASIC VECTOR QUANTIZATION

Now we construct a lossless information hiding algorithm for BVQ indices based on the QIM idea [10], which has been implemented in [22,25] practically. Note the object of VQ-based watermarking techniques in [22,25] is to embed watermark information into the original image in the pixel domain. However, now for reversibility, we only need to fix the encoding results from one codebook as the original code stream, and the others for information hiding, then the whole schemes in [22,25] can be directly converted into lossless ones for indices. The whole scheme is illustrated as in Fig. 4.4 with a simple example containing two codebooks C_1 and C_2 with the same size N, where the indices encoded by C_1 represent the original set of indices (e.g., watermark bit "0"), and the indices encoded by C_2 represent the modified indices (e.g., watermark bit "1"). Note that all code vectors in C_1 and C_2 are grouped into pairs by two code vectors from C_1 and C_2, respectively, and each pair represents the two closest (in the Euclidean distance) code vectors of all code vectors out of C_1 and C_2. If we set the encoding results by C_1 as the original indices, we can then set C_2 for index modulation for watermark embedding. Thus whichever index we get, we can find its "partner" in the pair and their pertaining codebooks that modulate the watermark bit "0" and "1." After retrieval of the watermark, the indices can be perfectly restored to the original ones from C_1.

This basic lossless information hiding algorithm uses two N-sized codebooks to modulate the watermark bit "0" and "1," which has the watermarking capacity as

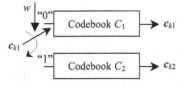

FIGURE 4.4

Basic index modulation based lossless information hiding: code vector c_{k1} and c_{k2} are in the same kth pair ($0 \le k \le N - 1$).

high as the amount of the indices. However, it is easily seen that this hiding algorithm trades compression performance with the watermarking performance and its bitrate nearly doubles at the similar encoding quality for the original VQ coding algorithm if we consider the desired properties (1) and (2) given in Section 4.1.2.

4.3.2 FAST CORRELATION VECTOR QUANTIZATION—BASED IMAGE COMPRESSION

Since the MFCVQ is derived from the original FCVQ [17], we introduce FCVQ before describing the lossless information hiding scheme based on MFCVQ.

The FCVQ predicts the current 4×4 pixel block x's state with its neighboring four encoded blocks c_a, c_b, c_c, and c_d, or the three encoded blocks c_a, c_b, and c_c for the last column of image blocks as shown in Fig. 4.5. An N-sized codebook C is used for encoding and decoding. The detailed encoding and decoding processes are described as follows with the example in Fig. 4.5a.

4.3.2.1 Encoding

Step 0: Encode the first row and the first column of original image blocks by full search in the codebook C.

Step 1: Calculate the distances between c_a, c_b, c_c, c_d, and the current bock x, respectively, as $d_a = \|c_a - x\|_2^2$, $d_b = \|c_b - x\|_2^2$, $d_c = \|c_c - x\|_2^2$, and $d_d = \|c_d - x\|_2^2$; find the smallest distance $d_m = \min\{d_a, d_b, d_c, d_d\}$.

Step 2: Compare d_m with the preset distance threshold TH, if $d_m \leq TH$, send a flag bit "0" to the code stream, and go to Step 3; otherwise, send a flag bit "1" to the code stream, and go to Step 5.

Step 3: Find the best-matched code vector c_{mb} out of $\{c_a, c_b, c_c, c_d\}$ as the encoded code vectors of the current block x and send the 2 bits' index of c_{mb} (indices of c_a, c_b, c_c, and c_d are 00, 01, 10, and 11 respectively) to the code stream, and go to Step 5.

Step 4: Find the best-matched code vector c_{mb} out of the whole codebook C as the current block x's encoded code vector and send its index in C to the code stream, and go to Step 5.

Step 5: Go to the next image block to be encoded and perform Steps 1 to 5 iteratively and only stop after all image blocks are encoded.

(a)   **(b)**

	c_b	c_c	c_d				c_b	c_c	
	c_a	x					c_a	x	

FIGURE 4.5

Correlation-based algorithms: (a) normal case of x's state prediction by c_a, c_b, c_c, and c_d and (b) last-column block case of x's state prediction by c_a, c_b, and c_c.

4.3.2.2 Decoding

The decoding process is actually the inverse of the embedding process since the flag bits can be explicitly used to guide the index selection.

4.3.3 MODIFIED FAST CORRELATION VECTOR QUANTIZATION– BASED LOSSLESS INFORMATION HIDING

Now we introduce MFCVQ, which satisfies both the desire of compression performance and the reversibility requirement of the watermarking algorithm for the indices. This MFCVQ is based on the aforementioned FCVQ [17] but modified in its index selection method to satisfy the reversibility but still exhibits higher compression ability than the ordinary VQ.

4.3.3.1 Encoding

Step 0: Encode the first row and the first column of original image blocks by full search in the codebook C.

Step 1: Calculate the distances between c_a, c_b, c_c, c_d, and the current bock x, respectively, as $d_a = \|c_a - x\|_2^2$, $d_b = \|c_b - x\|_2^2$, $d_c = \|c_c - x\|_2^2$, and $d_d = \|c_d - x\|_2^2$; find the smallest distance $d_m = \min\{d_a, d_b, d_c, d_d\}$.

Step 2: Compare d_m with the preset distance threshold TH; if $d_m \leq TH$ (information able to embed), send a flag bit "0" to the code stream, and go to Steps 3 and 4; otherwise, send a flag bit "1" to the code stream, and go to Step 5.

Step 3: Calculate the mean code vector $c_m = 1/4*(c_a + c_b + c_c + c_d)$.

Step 4: Find the best-matched (with the minimum Euclidean distance) code vector c_{mb} of c_m out of $\{c_a, c_b, c_c, c_d\}$ as the encoded code vectors of the current block x, and send the 2 bits' index of c_{mb} (indices of c_a, c_b, c_c, and c_d are 00, 01, 10, and 11 respectively) to the code stream, and go to Step 6.

Step 5: Find the best-matched code vector c_{mb} out of the whole codebook C as the current block x's encoded code vector, and send its index in C to the code stream, and go to Step 6.

Step 6: Go to the next image block to be encoded and perform Steps 1 to 6 iteratively and only stop after all image blocks are encoded.

4.3.3.2 Decoding

The decoding process is actually the inverse of the embedding process since the flag bits can be explicitly used to guide the index selection.

Note in the modified FCVQ mentioned earlier, when there is high correlation among adjacent blocks (in the case of $d_m \leq TH$), we use the closest encoded code vector c_{mb} to encode the current block x directly, which is different from original FCVQ's finding the code vector c_x with the minimum distance from the current block x because c_{mb} can be known to the decoder without any other knowledge about the original x except the retrievable flag bit in the code stream, and this provides the reversibility if we define c_{mb} as always the original indices.

Now we can go further to the lossless information hiding algorithm mentioned earlier. The embedding and extracting processes are quite simple: we embed all watermark bits by modulating the 2-bits indices in the high-correlation case to c_{mb-} or to the best-matched c_x out of $\{c_a, c_b, c_c, c_d\}$ while encoding. Specifically, for embedding, if the current watermark bit $w = 0$, we keep the original selected c_{mb} unchanged; if $w = 1$, we change c_{mb--} or to the best-matched 2-bits index c_x. Note that when the case $c_{mb} = c_x$ occurs, we choose the next best-matched code vector c_x' ($\neq c_{mb}$) to encode the current block x. For the decoder, first, know if all watermark bits have been embedded in the high-correlation structured image code vectors tagged with flag bit "0", and then check whether all the subsequent indices are c_{mb--} or not; if yes, the embedded watermark bit is "0," otherwise it is "1." Then all the embedded watermark bits can be retrieved without loss. To restore the original indices, just change all non-c_{mb---} indices back to c_{mb--}, and then the original MFCVQ-compressed indices can be perfectly restored. In addition, this lossless information hiding algorithm with MFCVQ satisfies the desired property (3) in Section 4.1.2.

We test two images sized 512×512 with 256 grayscales: Lena and Boat (Fig. 4.6), in the simulations, to compare the compression and the lossless information hiding performances, including PSNR between the original image and the reconstructed image without watermark embedded, PNSR between the original image and the reconstructed image with watermark embedded, the compression bitrates, encoding time of these two cases, and the watermarking capacity. Aside from these aspects, we also compare several desired properties given in Section 4.1.2. The algorithm testing is based on the basic lossless watermarking algorithm for VQ indices (BVQ) and the MFCVQ. Besides, the compression performance of the ordinary VQ and FCVQ is also presented for reference.

FIGURE 4.6

Two test images without vector quantization compression.

The simulation results of VQ compression performance are presented in Table 4.1, where N is the size of codebooks and TH is the distance threshold for FCVQ and MFCVQ. All codebooks are trained from the two images themselves, and the same 512-sized codebook is used for FCVQ and MFCVQ. From Table 4.1, although the compression performance of MFCVQ is lower than the original FCVQ, which is attributed to the suboptimal code vector selection method traded with hiding reversibility, it still shows preponderance over the

Table 4.1 Compression Performance of Different VQs

Algorithms	Parameter	Boat		Lena	
VQ	$N = 128$	PSNR (dB)	30.067	PSNR (dB)	31.426
		Bit rate (bpp)	0.438	Bit rate (bpp)	0.438
		Coding time (s)	1.9	Coding time (s)	1.9
	$N = 256$	PSNR (dB)	31.197	PSNR (dB)	32.506
		Bit rate (bpp)	0.500	Bit rate (bpp)	0.500
		Coding time (s)	3.7	Coding time (s)	3.8
	$N = 512$	PSNR (dB)	32.344	PSNR (dB)	33.664
		Bit rate (bpp)	0.563	Bit rate (bpp)	0.563
		Coding time (s)	7.5	Coding time (s)	7.7
FCVQ ($N = 512$)	$TH = 160$	PSNR (dB)	32.315	PSNR (dB)	33.632
		Bit rate (bpp)	0.400	Bit rate (bpp)	0.409
		Coding time (s)	1.6	Coding time (s)	1.7
	$TH = 320$	PSNR (dB)	32.214	PSNR (dB)	33.476
		Bit rate (bpp)	0.370	Bit rate (bpp)	0.371
		Coding time (s)	1.3	Coding time (s)	1.4
	$TH = 640$	PSNR (dB)	32.004	PSNR (dB)	33.117
		Bit rate (bpp)	0.347	Bit rate (bpp)	0.335
		Coding time (s)	1.1	Coding time (s)	1.1
MFCVQ ($N = 512$)	$TH = 320$	PSNR (dB)	32.244	PSNR (dB)	33.572
		Bit rate (bpp)	0.506	Bit rate (bpp)	0.543
		Coding time (s)	2.2	Coding time (s)	2.4
	$TH = 640$	PSNR (dB)	31.981	PSNR (dB)	33.380
		Bit rate (bpp)	0.457	Bit rate (bpp)	0.505
		Coding time (s)	1.9	Coding time (s)	2.2
	$TH = 2000$	PSNR (dB)	31.009	PSNR (dB)	32.205
		Bit rate (bpp)	0.408	Bit rate (bpp)	0.432
		Coding time (s)	1.6	Coding time (s)	1.7

PSNR, *peak signal-to-noise ratio*; VQ, *vector quantization*.

Table 4.2 Lossless Information Hiding Performance With MFCVQ

Method	Parameter	Boat		Lena	
Lossless information hiding on MFCVQ's indices ($N = 512$)	$TH = 320$	PSNR (dB)	32.27	PSNR (dB)	33.59
		Capacity (bits)	4570	Capacity (bits)	3075
	$TH = 640$	PSNR (dB)	32.13	PSNR (dB)	33.44
		Capacity (bits)	6363	Capacity (bits)	4556
	$TH = 2000$	PSNR (dB)	31.53	PSNR (dB)	32.52
		Capacity (bits)	8255	Capacity (bits)	7300

MFCVQ, *modified fast correlation vector quantization*; PSNR, *peak-signal-to-noise ratio*; VQ, *vector quantization.*

ordinary VQ in almost every aspect. Another performance is the encoding and decoding time, MFCVQ shows greater advantage in this aspect than the ordinary VQ.

The lossless hiding performance is presented in Table 4.2, where the PSNR is calculated between the original images and the reconstructed images by MFCVQ with watermark embedded. Note that, MFCVQ selects the best-matched code vector c_{mb} as a modulation of the watermark "1" out of the neighboring encoded blocks, which makes the PSNR (compared with the original images) even higher (0.1–0.5 dB improved in the simulations) than the typical compressing case (without watermark embedded). This may be a desired virtue for many applications. Another advantage of MFCVQ is that the code stream obtained by MFCVQ can be directly processed by the same decoder as the FCVQ, which is desired by compatibility prescribed in Section 4.1.2.

However, the lossless watermarking algorithm with MFCVQ has two problems. The first is related to the separation property in Section 4.1.2: the watermarking embedding process is inseparable from the encoding process because the best-matched code vector c_{mb} can only be found with the knowledge of the current pixel block x reachable while encoding. However, this deficiency can be easily removed by replacing the c_{mb-} (that depends on x) with another neighboring encoded code vector (independent from x) among c_a, c_b, c_c, c_d, e.g., the next closest code vector, except c_{mb}, compared with c_m. The encoding quality degradation by this replacement will not be high considering the fact the highest distortion has been bounded by the threshold TH. The second problem is related to the size preservation property: the compression bitrate change caused by the index modulation, which usually changes the candidate scope for the next image block's encoding. Fortunately, this bit rate variance is quite mild, and in the simulations, below 0.005 bpp.

4.4 SIDE MATCH VECTOR QUANTIZATION—BASED SCHEMES

From Section 4.3, we can see that the hiding capacity of the MFCVQ method is unstable and low. To improve the hiding capacity, Chang et al. proposed several information hiding algorithms [4–7] based on SMVQ. We first introduce SMVQ in Section 4.4.1, and then introduce Chang and Wu's information hiding algorithm [4] in Section 4.4.2, Chang and Lu's lossless information hiding algorithm [5] in Section 4.4.3, and Chang-Tai-Lin's lossless information hiding scheme [6] in Section 4.4.4.

4.4.1 SIDE MATCH VECTOR QUANTIZATION

VQ takes advantage of the high degree of correlation between individual pixels within a block without considering the similarity between neighboring blocks. In VQ, each block is coded independently and therefore tends to cause visible boundaries between blocks. The original SMVQ-based image coding scheme proposed by Kim [18] is designed to enhance the visual quality of VQ by reducing these visible boundaries. It employs the previous coded blocks, which are above and on the left-hand side of the current block, to help predict the current block so that the visible boundaries can be reduced. The SMVQ encoder first uses the master codebook C to encode the blocks in the first column and the blocks in the first row. Then all other image blocks are encoded from left to right row by row using the correlation of neighboring encoded blocks. Fig. 4.7 shows the SMVQ flowchart. Let x denote the current processing vector, and let u and l be the codewords of the upper and left neighboring blocks (Fig. 4.8), respectively. The side match distortion of a codeword c in C is defined as

$$smd(c) = vd(c) + hd(c) \tag{4.9}$$

where the vertical and horizontal distortions of c are defined as

$$vd(c) = \sum_{i=1}^{4} \left(u_{(4,i)} - c_{(1,i)} \right)^2 \tag{4.10}$$

and

$$hd(c) = \sum_{i=1}^{4} \left(l_{(i,4)} - c_{(i,1)} \right)^2 \tag{4.11}$$

where $x_{(i,j)}$ denotes the value of the jth pixel of the ith row in an image block x.

In SMVQ, a main codebook is required to encode the blocks in the first row and first column, and a state codebook is required to encode the rest of the blocks. The state codebook C_S is a subset of the main codebook. SMVQ is based on the concept that the pixels of the top row in the current block are correlated closely with those of the bottom row in the upper block, and the pixels of the first column in the current block are correlated closely with those of the right column in the left block. The gray

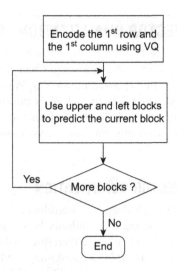

FIGURE 4.7

Flowchart of side match vector quantization (VQ).

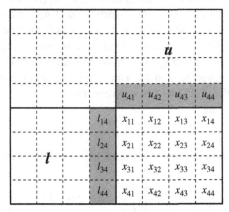

Current Block x

FIGURE 4.8

Neighboring blocks of the current block in side match vector quantization.

areas in Fig. 4.8 represent the upper and left blocks. These gray regions are used to choose codewords from the main codebook to create a state codebook.

The blocks in the first row and first column are encoded using VQ. During this process, the main codebook is fully searched to find the best representative codeword to replace the original blocks. The blocks of the first row and first column must be encoded accurately since these blocks are used to predict future blocks. If an error occurs in this encoding step, it propagates throughout the entire image.

In the state codebook generation procedure, the upper and left blocks previously encoded are used to generate the state codebook for the current block. The state codebook consists of N_s codewords, which are selected from the main codebook having the least side match distortion when compared with the side areas. The current block is encoded using VQ compression scheme with the state codebook of size N_s. This process is repeated for each block of the original image until all the blocks are encoded. This approach requires that only the codewords in the state codebook be searched, rather than all codewords in the main codebook, and the size of the state codebook is much smaller than that of the main codebook. Hence, the advantage of SMVQ is its significant saving in the number of bits required to encode blocks.

To decode a block, the previously encoded upper and left blocks are used to predict the state codebook with the least side match distortion for the current block. The generated state codebook is then searched to find the corresponding codeword to approximate the current block. Thus, SMVQ saves significant bits per pixel (bpp) without a significant reduction in the PSNR.

4.4.2 CHANG AND WU'S SCHEME

In 2005, Chang and Wu [4] proposed a steganographic scheme to hide secret data using SMVQ and VQ. Note that it is not a lossless information hiding scheme; however, it is the first information hiding algorithm using SMVQ, thus we briefly introduce it here. In their scheme, a random seed is generated and used to generate two mapping tables, list$_{SMVQ}$ and list$_{VQ}$, that contain half 0's and half 1's. The mapping table list$_{SMVQ}$ is with the same size as the state codebook C_S and the mapping table list$_{VQ}$ is with the same sizes as the main codebook C. Thereafter, VQ is used to encode the first row and the first column of the cover image. For the residual blocks, the corresponding state codebooks are created using SMVQ. The codewords in each state codebook are sorted in advance according to the similarity between the codewords and the corresponding blocks.

Because each state codebook is sorted in advance, the codewords are checked sequentially until the value in the mapping table that corresponds to the index value of the checked codeword is the same as the secret bit. However, if the Euclidean distance between the checked codeword and the current block exceeds the given threshold, VQ rather than SMVQ is used to hide secret data in the block.

The encoding steps using VQ are almost the same as the aforementioned steps. Since the main codebook is sorted in advance, the codewords are checked sequentially until the value in the mapping table for the index value of the checked codeword is the same as the secret bit. However, once the Euclidean distance between the checked codeword and the current block exceeds the given threshold, no secret is hidden in this block.

Chang and Wu's scheme does not achieve reversibility. To conquer this weakness, Chang et al. proposed two lossless information hiding schemes for SMVQ-based compressed images. We discuss them in Sections 4.4.3 and 4.4.4.

4.4.3 CHANG AND LU'S SCHEME

The diagram of Chang and Lu's scheme [5] is shown in Fig. 4.9, consisting of two phases: the embedding and the extraction phases. The embedding phase explains the procedure of hiding secret data in the cover image to generate the stego indices, whereas the extraction phase describes the procedure of extracting the hidden secret data and recovering the decoded image from the stego indices. These two phases are described in detail in the following sections.

4.4.3.1 The Embedding Phase

First, Chang and Lu's scheme encrypts the plaintext, which a sender wants to send to a receiver, by using a Data Encryption Standard (DES)-like method associated with the private key to form the secrete data. Next, this scheme divides a cover image into several nonoverlapping blocks. Let $x = \{x_1, x_2, ..., x_k\}$ be a block of size k, where $x_i \in [0, 255]$ and $1 \leq i \leq k$. Let $C = \{c_0, c_1, ..., c_{N-1}\}$ be the codebook that is generated by the Linde-Buzo-Gray (LBG) algorithm [1], and let the number of codewords

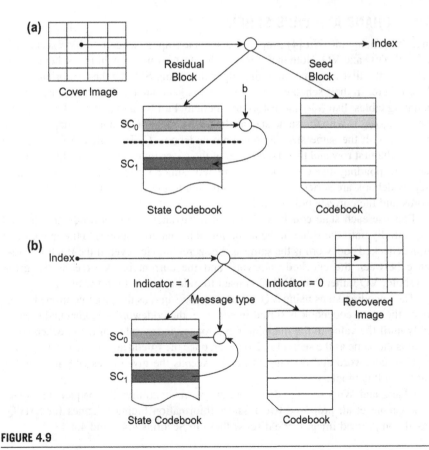

FIGURE 4.9

The diagram of Chang and Lu's scheme: (a) embedding phase and (b) extraction phase.

in the codebook be N. If the block is in the first row or the first column, which is called seed block, then this scheme matches the closest codeword for the block from the codebook. The measurement used to estimate the distance between the block x and the closest codeword c_i is

$$ED(x, c_i) = \sqrt{\sum_{p=1}^{k} (x_p - c_{ip})^2} \tag{4.12}$$

where c_{ip} is the pth component of c_i and x_p is the p-th component of x. The codeword with the least ED value is the closest codeword of x.

If the block is not the seed block, then the closest codeword is predicated by using SMVQ, and hide one secret bit b on it. Let $u = \{u_1, u_2, ..., u_k\}$ be the block in the upper of x, and $l = \{l_1, l_2, ..., l_k\}$ be the block in the left side of x. Chang and Lu's scheme uses the neighboring encoded pixels to predict the codeword of x. For $k = 16$, as shown in Fig. 4.8, $u = \{u_1, u_2, ..., u_{16}\} = \{u_{(1,1)}, u_{(1,2)}, ..., u_{(4,4)}\}$, $l = \{l_1, l_2, ..., l_{16}\} = \{l_{(1,1)}, l_{(1,2)}, ..., l_{(4,4)}\}$, then seven values $x'_1 = (u_{13} + l_4)/2$, $x'_2 = u_{14}$, $x'_3 = u_{15}$, $x'_4 = u_{16}$, $x'_5 = l_8$, $x'_9 = l_{12}$, $x'_{13} = l_{16}$ are used to find the closest codeword from the codebook. The measurement used to predict the closest codeword is given as

$$SED(x, c_i) = \sqrt{\sum_{p \in \{1,2,3,4,5,9,13\}}^{k} \left(x'_p - c_{ip}\right)^2} \tag{4.13}$$

Then, Chang and Lu's scheme sorts the codewords according to the SED values in the ascending order and selects the first N_s codewords from the sorted codebook to generate a state codebook $C_s = \{sc_0, sc_1, ..., sc_{N_s/2-1}\}$, where sc_i is the ith codedword in C_s and the SED value of sc_i is smaller than that of sc_{i+1}.

Chang and Lu's scheme equally divides the state codebook into two parts $C_{s0} = \{sc_0, sc_1, ..., sc_{N_s/2-1}\}$ and $C_{s1} = \{sc_{N_s/2}, sc_{N_s+1}, ..., sc_{N_s-1/2}\}$. Each part has its own message type, for example, the message type of C_{s0} is 0 and that of C_{s1} is 1. Next, they use the original block x to map the nearest codeword sc_j from C_{s0}. If the distance between sc_j and x is shorter than a predetermined threshold T, then x can be used to hide the secret bit. If the hidden secret bit matches with the message type of C_{s0}, then Chang and Lu's scheme uses sc_j to represent x. Otherwise, the codeword is used at the corresponding location of C_{s1} to represent x.

In short, for the block x of size $k = 16$ to hide the secret bit b, the embedding process can be depicted as follows:

Step 1: Let $x'_1 = (u_{13} + l_4)/2$, $x'_2 = u_{14}$, $x'_3 = u_{15}$, $x'_4 = u_{16}$, $x'_5 = l_8$, $x'_9 = l_{12}$, $x'_{13} = l_{16}$ be the neighboring pixels of x. Compute the distance between the neighboring pixels and the corresponding pixels of each codeword by using Eq. (4.13).

Step 2: Sort the codewords according to the distance value of each in the ascending order. Select the first N_s codewords to generate a state codebook $C_s = \{sc_0, sc_1, \ldots, sc_{N_s-1}\}$.

Step 3: Divide the state codebook into two parts $C_{s0} = \{sc_0, sc_1, \ldots, sc_{N_s/2-1}\}$ and $C_{s1} = \{sc_{N_s/2}, sc_{N_s+1}, \ldots, sc_{N_s-1}\}$, where each part has $N_s/2$ codewords, and give each part a distinct message type.

Step 4: Generate a random bit by using a random-number generator, which is only known by the sender and the receiver, and let it be the message type of C_{s0}. The message type of C_{s1} is the inverse value of the random bit.

Step 5: Find out the nearest codeword sc_j of x from C_{s0} by using Eq. (4.12), where sc_j is the jth codeword of the state codebook.

Step 6: If the distance between sc_j and x using Eq. (4.12) is shorter than the threshold T, then hide b in the compressed code of x. If the message type of C_{s0} is matched with b, then Chang and Lu's scheme uses an indicator "1," and the index of sc_j in the binary format to represent the stego block of x. If not, then an indicator "1" is used with the index of $sc_{j+N_s/2}$ in the binary format to represent the stego block of x.

Step 7: If the distance between sc_j and x using Eq. (4.12) is larger than the threshold T, then x is coded by VQ and the indicator of x is "0."

Now we give a concrete example to explain the hiding process. Assuming that we have a gray-level image of size 12×8. First, the scheme divides the image into 3×2 blocks. The size of the block used in this example is 4×4. Next, for the blocks in the first row and the first column, we find out the closest codewords from the codebook by using Eq. (4.12) and decode the blocks by using the closest codewords. Fig. 4.10 shows the example image where the blocks in the first row the first column have been decoded. Assume the threshold $T = 200$.

The fifth block is not the seed block. Thus, the scheme uses the neighboring encoded pixels $x_1' = (90 + 72)/2 = 81$, $x_2' = u_{14} = 15$, $x_3' = u_{15} = 53$, $x_4' = u_{16} = 34$, $x_5' = l_8 = 51$ $x_9' = l_{12} = 91$, $x_{13}' = l_{16} = 49$ to predict the codeword

11	63	91	90	54	88	49	26	2	88	0	69
4	50	23	62	17	2	5	19	52	19	25	79
58	53	34	85	16	51	52	50	88	96	73	35
53	59	94	12	90	15	53	34	37	61	73	6
56	20	61	72	78	10	30	25	70	25	76	90
6	33	77	51	13	78	58	10	7	41	96	63
22	33	5	91	22	100	43	39	27	41	6	113
83	1	99	49	15	13	15	3	103	1	123	61

FIGURE 4.10

An example image of size 12×8.

Table 4.3 The State Codebook of the Fifth Block in Fig. 4.10

Codeword No.	Codeword Value	SED
sc_0	(81,6,43,28,60,86,66,19,27,88,57,40,19,18,10,6)	72.76
sc_1	(78,42,14,63,54,66,54,39,27,54,68,98,40,70,28,4)	85.36
sc_2	(9,62,69,21,29,4,11,68,68,24,80,74,79,79,49,56)	98.65
sc_3	(99,78,28,14,77,58,24,60,29,87,24,77,35,73,38,48)	100.17
sc_4	(56,20,61,72,6,33,77,51,22,33,5,91,83,1,99,49)	100.50
sc_5	(54,88,49,26,17,2,5,19,16,51,52,50,90,15,53,34)	120.83
sc_6	(11,63,91,90,4,50,23,62,58,53,34,85,53,59,94,12)	122.87
sc_7	(2,88,0,69,52,19,25,79,88,96,73,35,37,61,73,6)	125.53

and generate the state codebook using SMVQ. Let N_s here be 8. The state codebook of the fifth block is shown in Table 4.3. Then, the scheme matches the closest codeword from codeword numbered 0 to the codeword numbered 3 in the state codebook The distances between the fifth block and sc_0, sc_1, sc_2, and sc_3 are 55.34, 125.29, 207.87, and 148.05, respectively. Hence, the nearest codeword of the fifth block is sc_0 and the distance is 55.34. Let the first random bit generated by random-number generator be 1. That is to say, the message type of $C_{s0} = \{sc_0, sc_1, sc_2, sc_3\}$ is 1 and that of $C_{s1} = \{sc_4, sc_5, sc_6, sc_7\}$ is 0. We assume that the hidden secret bit is 1, which is the same as the message type of C_{s0}. Therefore, the compressed code of the fifth block is composed by an indicator "1" followed with "000," which is the index of sc_0 in the binary format. Because the size of the state codebook is 8, $N_s = 8$, we use 3 bits to represent the index, since $\log_2 N_s = \log_2 8 = 3$.

For the sixth block, the sorted state codebook is shown in Table 4.4. The distances between the sixth block and sc_0, sc_1, sc_2, and sc_3 are 200.3, 149.5, 182.2, and 215.3, respectively, thus the nearest codeword is sc_1. Let the second random bit be 0 such that the message type of C_{s0} is 0 and that of C_{s1} is 1. We assume that the hidden secret bit is 1, which is not the same as the message type of C_{s0}.

Table 4.4 The State Codebook of the Sixth Block in Fig. 4.10

Codeword No.	Codeword Value	SED
sc_0	(9,62,69,21,29,4,11,68,68,24,80,74,79,79,49,56)	83.71
sc_1	(11,63,91,90,4,50,23,62,58,53,34,85,53,59,94,12)	85.36
sc_2	(54,88,49,26,17,2,5,19,16,51,52,50,90,15,53,34)	98.65
sc_3	(81,6,43,28,60,86,66,19,27,88,57,40,19,18,10,6)	100.17
sc_4	(56,20,61,72,6,33,77,51,22,33,5,91,83,1,99,49)	100.50
sc_5	(78,42,14,63,54,66,54,39,27,54,68,98,40,70,28,4)	120.83
sc_6	(2,88,0,69,52,19,25,79,88,96,73,35,37,61,73,6)	122.87
sc_7	(99,78,28,14,77,58,24,60,29,87,24,77,35,73,38,48)	125.53

Thus, the compressed code of the sixth block contains an indicator "1" followed with "101,", which is the index of sc_5 in the binary format, where $sc_{j+N_s/2} = sc_{1+8/2} = sc_5$.

4.4.3.2 The Extraction Phase

In this subsection, we introduce Chang and Lu's extraction process, which is used to extract the hidden information and recover the original indices of VQ-compressed image.

Step 1: If the indicator is "0," then the block is encoded by the traditional VQ. The following bitstream with length $\log_2 N$ is represented in decimal format to form an index i. Then, Chang and Lu's scheme uses the ith codeword c_i of the codebook to recover the block. After that, other blocks are continued to be decoded.

Step 2: If the indicator is "1," then the block is encoded by SMVQ, and the following bitstream with length $\log_2 N_s$ is represented in decimal format to form an index v.

Step 3: Use seven decoded pixels $x_1' = (u^*_{13} + l^*_4)/2$, $x_2' = u^*_{14}$, $x_3' = u^*_{15}$, $x_4' = u^*_{16}$, $x_5' = l^*_8$, $x_9' = l^*_{12}$, $x_{13}' = l^*_{16}$ to match the index of the block from the codebook, where u^*_p is the pth recovered pixel in the upper block, and l^*_p is the pth recovered pixel in the left block.

Step 4: Measure the distances between the seventh decoded pixel and the corresponding pixel of each codeword in the codebook using Eq. (4.13), and sort the codewords according to their distances in the ascending order.

Step 5: The first N_s codewords are selected to generate a state codebook, $C_s = \{sc_0, sc_1, ..., sc_{N_s-1}\}$, and the state codebook is divided into two parts $C_{s0} = \{sc_0, sc_1, ..., sc_{N_s/2-1}\}$ and $C_{s1} = \{sc_{N_s/2}, sc_{N_s+1}, ..., sc_{N_s-1}\}$.

Step 6: Generate a random bit as the message type of C_{s0} by using the random-number generator.

Step 7: If v is smaller than $N_s/2$ and the random bit is 0, then the hidden bit in the block is "0." Recover the block using the vth codeword of C_{s0}.

Step 8: If v is smaller than $N_s/2$ and the random bit is 1, then the hidden bit in the block is "1." Recover the block using the vth codeword of C_{s0}.

Step 9: If v is greater than $N_s/2$ and the random bit is 0, then the hidden bit in the block is "1." Recover the block using the $(v - N_s/2)$th codeword of C_{s1}.

Step 10: If v is greater than $N_s/2$ and the random bit is 1, then the hidden bit in the block is "0." Recover the block using the $(v - N_s/2)$th codeword of C_{s1}.

Step 11: Continue to decode the other blocks.

4.4.3.3 Experimental Results

As shown in Fig. 4.11, 6 gray-level images of the same size 512×512, Airplane, Baboon, Boat, Lena, Pepper, and Sailboat, were used as the host images to evaluate the performance of Chang and Lu's scheme. The sizes of the codebooks generated

FIGURE 4.11

Six test images.

by the LBG algorithm are 256, 512 and 1024. The system used the random function to generate pseudo random numbers and a secret data.

The PSNR, the hiding capacity $|H|$, and bpp are used to measure the stego image quality, the total number of the secret bits hidden in the stego image, and the compression rate of the stego image, respectively. The image with smaller bpp means that the compression performance of Chang and Lu's scheme on the image is higher. To determine the proper T for hiding information on the host image, Chang and Lu tested the host images with different T's. The experimental results are shown in Figs. 4.12–4.14. Chang and Lu's scheme with $T = 100$ and $N_s = 16$ obviously has the best performance for Lena, where 14,703 bits are hidden with image quality of 24.05 dB and compression rate of 0.34 bpp. As to Baboon, Chang and Lu's scheme is able to hide 11,513 bits with image quality of 21.97 dB and compression rate of 0.39 bpp. The stego image after the extraction phase can obtain the original indices to recover the image. The image quality of the recovered image is the same as that of the image after SMVQ compression. For example, the PSNR of the stego Lena with $T = 50$ is 26.43 dB, and the PSNR of the recovered Lena is 30.99 dB, which is just the same as that of Lena after SMVQ compression. The stego images of Lena and Baboon are shown in Fig. 4.15a and c, and the recovered images of Lena and Baboon are shown in Fig. 4.15b and d, respectively.

Next, Chang and Lu tested the host images with different N_s to measure the proper size of the state codebook. The results are shown in Table 4.5. From the results obtained, Chang and Lu's scheme with $N_s = 16$ and $T = 100$ apparently has the

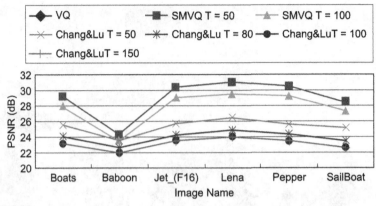

FIGURE 4.12

The image quality of Chang and Lu's scheme for the six host images. *PSNR*, peak signal-to-noise ratio; *SMVQ*, side match vector quantization; *VQ*, vector quantization.

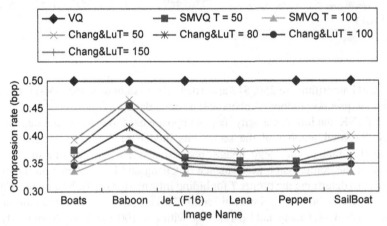

FIGURE 4.13

The compression rate of Chang and Lu's scheme for the six host images.

best performance. For example, although the system will decrease the image quality of Lena from 24.94 dB to 23.97 dB, $|H|$ can be increased from 14,348 to 14,654 bits. We can see that the hiding capacities of most images decrease when N_s increases from 64 to 128. That is because of the derailment phenomenon. In the embedding phase, if a secret bit b is not matched with the message type of the state codebook, then Chang and Lu's scheme encodes the block by using the index of the alternative codeword $sc_{j+N_s/2}$ instead of the index of the closest codeword sc_j. However, the distance between $sc_{j+N_s/2}$ and the block x is larger than that between sc_j and the block x, especially for a state codebook with greater value of N_s. In this case, if the scheme

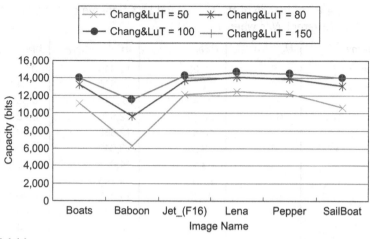

FIGURE 4.14

The hiding capacity of Chang and Lu's scheme for the six host images.

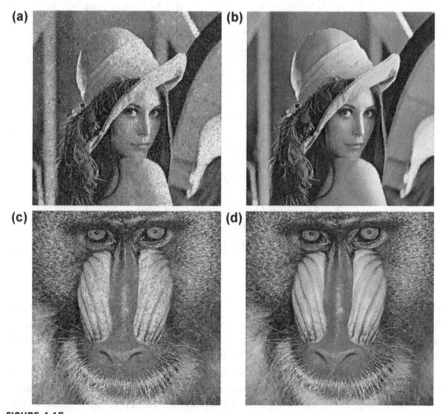

FIGURE 4.15

The stego images and recovered images of Lena and Baboon: (a) stego image Lena, (b) recovered image Lena, (c) stego image Baboon, and (d) recovered image Baboon.

Table 4.5 The Performance of the Chang and Lu's Scheme on Different Images With Different N_s's when $T = 100$

File Name	N_s	PSNR	$|H|$	bpp
Baboon	8	22.25	10,846	0.31
	16	21.92	11,500	0.34
	32	21.42	12,112	0.38
	64	20.43	12,580	0.42
	128	18.81	12,936	0.46
Boats	8	23.84	13,642	0.25
	16	23.17	14,075	0.29
	32	21.69	14,143	0.35
	64	20.10	14,272	0.40
	128	17.75	14,149	0.45
F16	8	24.46	13,945	0.24
	16	23.49	14,295	0.29
	32	21.47	14,194	0.35
	64	19.34	13,933	0.40
	128	17.14	13,772	0.46
Lena	8	24.94	14,348	0.23
	16	23.97	14,654	0.28
	32	22.73	14,851	0.34
	64	20.75	14,839	0.39
	128	18.54	14,767	0.45
Pepper	8	24.34	14,116	0.24
	16	23.51	14,485	0.29
	32	21.91	14,626	0.34
	64	20.07	14,599	0.40
	128	17.88	14,533	0.45
Sailboat	8	23.40	13,503	0.25
	16	22.68	13,984	0.30
	32	21.38	14,191	0.35
	64	19.67	14,159	0.40
	128	17.48	14,039	0.46

PSNR, *peak signal-to-noise ratio.*

continually uses the alternative codeword to predicate the closest codeword for the following blocks, more and more distortion will be made. Some valuable blocks, which originally can be used to hide a secret data, may become valueless. To avoid this problem, Chang and Lu set $N_s = 16$ in the following experiments.

The codebook size is an important factor that affects the efficiency and the effect of a compression algorithm. The following experiment examines whether the codebook size influences the performance of Chang and Lu's scheme. Fig. 4.16 shows the

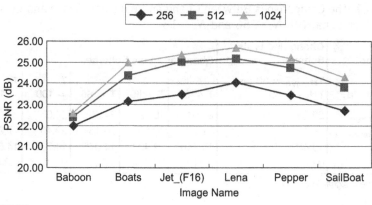

FIGURE 4.16

The image quality of Chang and Lu's scheme with different N's. *PSNR*, peak signal-to-noise ratio.

performance of Chang and Lu's scheme with different N. A larger codebook can obtain higher image quality. That is to say, N is a factor to judge the image quality, but it is not a factor to influence the capacity.

The execution times of VQ, SMVQ, and Chang and Lu's scheme are shown in Table 4.6. Because Chang and Lu's scheme is based on SMVQ, the execution time of Chang and Lu's scheme depends on the encoding and the extraction processes of SMVQ. According to the experimental results shown in Table 4.6, the hiding process of Chang and Lu's scheme only increases a few of the encoding and extraction times of SMVQ.

Now, we compare Chang and Lu's scheme with Chang and Wu's scheme. The comparisons are shown in Table 4.7. The thresholds used in Chang and Wu's scheme are $TH_{SMVQ} = 30$ and $TH_{VQ} = 50$. For example, when $T = 30$, the PSNR, hiding capacity, and compression rate of Chang and Lu's scheme for Lena are 27.64 dB, 10,246 bits, and 0.41 bpp, respectively, and the PSNR of the recovered image of Lena is 31.30 dB. On the contrary, those of Chang and Wu's scheme are

Table 4.6 The Execution Time Comparison Among VQ, Side Match VQ, and Chang and Lu's Scheme on Lena of Size 512×512 With Codebook Size $N = 256$, $T = 50$ and $N_s = 16$

	Methods		
Compare	**VQ**	**SMVQ**	**Chang and Lu's Scheme**
Time (s)	12.391	14.281	14.578
PSNR (dB)	31.348	30.99	26.32

PSNR, *peak signal-to-noise ratio;* SMVQ, *side match vector quantization;* VQ, *vector quantization.*

Table 4.7 The Comparisons Between Chang and Wu's and Chang and Lu's Scheme on Lena With $N = 256$ and $N_s = 16$

Method	Chang and Wu's Scheme	Chang and Lu's Scheme				
Threshold	$TH_{SMVQ} = 30$ and $TH_{VQ} = 50$	$T = 30$	$T = 50$	$T = 80$	$T = 100$	$T = 150$
$PSNR_{stego}$	29.25	27.64	26.43	24.85	24.05	24.03
$PSNR_{recovered}$	–	31.30	30.99	30.15	29.46	27.92
$|H|$	13.487	10.246	12.404	14.075	14.703	14.657
bpp	0.47	0.41	0.37	0.35	0.34	0.34

PSNR, *peak signal-to-noise ratio.*

29.25 dB, 13,487 bits, and 0.47 bpp, respectively. Although the PNSR of the stego images using Chang and Lu's scheme is lower than that of the stego images using Chang and Wu's schemes, Chang and Lu's scheme can recover the stego image to reconstruct the SMVQ-compressed image. Therefore, when given the same hiding capacity, the PSNRs of the recovered images using Chang and Lu's scheme are higher than those of the stego images of Chang and Wu's scheme. In addition, the compression performance of Chang and Lu's scheme is better than that of Chang and Wu's scheme. The comparison results demonstrate that Chang and Lu's scheme indeed outperforms Chang and Wu's scheme.

From these data, we can see that Chang and Lu's scheme is a lossless index-domain information hiding scheme based on SMVQ for gray-level images. This scheme not only conceals information on the indices of SMVQ-compressed image with low image distortion but also recovers the original indices to reconstruct the SMVQ-compressed image from the hidden indices without any loss. As proved by the experiments, Chang and Lu's scheme obviously outperforms Chang and Wu's scheme. In terms of security problem, the scheme sets the message type of C_{s0} by using a random-number generator in the embedding phase to ensure the security of the hidden secret data. Hence, illegal people cannot correctly extract the secret data, except for those who know the random-number generator. In addition, the secret data are encrypted by using a DES-like method. Only legal people who own the private key have the ability to decrypt the original plaintext from the secret data.

4.4.4 CHANG–TAI–LIN'S SCHEME

Both Chang and Wu's scheme and Chang and Lu's scheme require additional information to indicate that the current block is encoded using VQ or SMVQ, and the additional indicators will yield a low compression rate. To conquer this weakness, Chang et al. [6] proposed a lossless information hiding scheme (we call it Chang–Tai–Lin's scheme) for SMVQ-based compressed images that do not require the use of additional indicators. To ensure that the original compression codes can be recovered directly during the extracting phase and stored for later use, Chang—Tai—Lin's scheme modified the codeword selection strategy of SMVQ and developed an information hiding scheme with the property of reversibility. To achieve this goal, Chang—Tai—Lin's scheme was broken into three phases: the preprocessing phase, the hiding phase, and the extracting and reversing phase. These phases are described in greater detail in the following subsections.

4.4.4.1 Preprocessing Phase

Secret data must be preprocessed for security reasons. Encrypting the hidden data prevents them from being illegally accessed or unscrambled. Some existing encryption techniques, such as DES and RSA others can be used to encrypt hidden data. Secret data also can be compressed in advance using lossless compression techniques to reduce the amount of hidden data and increase the visual quality of stego-image, and thus deceive potential grabbers.

After preprocessing in Chang—Tai—Lin's scheme, the cover image is encoded using SMVQ and the SMVQ-compressed image is created. The preprocessed secret data are then hidden in the SMVQ-compressed image using Chang—Tai—Lin's scheme. The stego image is thus generated, ready for transmission to a receiver. Receivers can extract the secret data from the stego image using Chang Tai—Lin's extracting and reversing scheme. In addition, receivers can restore the original SMVQ—compressed codes completely. The reconstructed SMVQ-compressed codes can be stored directly to save storage space. The hiding, extracting, and reversing phases are described in detail in the following subsections.

4.4.4.2 The Hiding Phase

Fig. 4.17 shows the flowchart of Chang—Tai—Lin's hiding procedure. To better explain this phase, they defined the symbols to be used in hiding phase as follows: the main codebook $C = \{c_0, c_1, ..., c_{N-1}\}$, the SMVQ-compressed cover image I, the subindices $D = \{d_0, d_1, ..., d_r\}$, and the secret data $B = \{b_0, b_1, ..., b_r\}$, where $b_i \in \{0, 1\}$ and $0 \leq i \leq r$. The hiding phase consists of the following steps.

Step 1: The SMVQ-compressed cover image I is divided into nonoverlapping blocks. Because the blocks in the first row and first column are encoded by VQ, the secret data B are hidden in the residual blocks.

Step 2: For each residual block, the upper and left encoded blocks in I are used to generate the state codebook $C_s = \{sc_0, sc_1, ..., sc_{N_s-1}\}$, where sc_i is the ith codeword and $0 \leq i \leq N_s - 1$. The subindex d_i is used to find the corresponding codeword sc_a from the state codebook C_s.

Step 3: If the secret bit b_i is equal to 0, then the codeword sc_a becomes the content of the stego image.

Step 4: If the secret bit b_i is equal to 1, then we search the codeword sc_b from the state codebook C_s so that the codeword sc_b is the closest to the codeword sc_a.

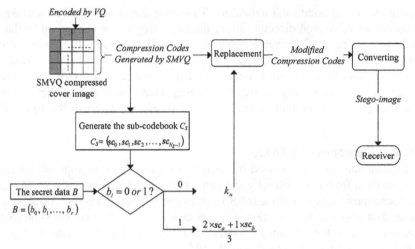

FIGURE 4.17

Flowchart showing the steps in the hiding phase. *SMVQ,* side match vector quantization; *VQ,* vector quantization.

The approximate codeword $c*$ becomes the content of the stego image and is defined as

$$c^* = \left\lfloor \frac{2sc_a + sc_b}{3} \right\rfloor \qquad (4.14)$$

where $\lfloor v \rfloor$ stands for the operation of obtaining a different but closest vector with integer components to v.

Step 5: Steps 2–4 are repeated until the whole stego image is generated.

In Chang–Tai–Lin's lossless information hiding scheme, the modified SMVQ compression codes are converted into a stego image. The stego image must be transmitted without extra messages being required to achieve reversibility.

4.4.4.3 Extracting and Reversing Phases

Once the stego image is received, the receiver can extract the secret data without having to refer to the original cover image. The steps for extracting and reversing follow.

Step 1: The stego image is divided into nonoverlapping blocks. The first row and first column blocks are encoded using VQ and the indexes are generated.

Step 2: For each residual block, the previously reconstructed upper and left blocks are used to generate a state codebook $C_s = \{sc_0, sc_1, ...sc_{N_s-1}\}$, where sc_j is the jth codeword and $0 \le j \le N_s - 1$. The codeword sc_a is selected from the state codebook C_s such that the Euclidean distance between the current block x and the codeword sc_a is the shortest.

Step 3: If the Euclidean distance $ED(x,sc_a)$ is equal to 0, then the secret bit $b_i = 0$. The index a of the codeword sc_a is output to restore the original state.

Step 4: If the Euclidean distance $ED(x,sc_a)$ does not equal 0, then the secret bit $b_i = 1$. The index a of the codeword sc_a is output to restore the original state.

Step 5: Steps 2–4 are repeated until all the secret data are extracted and all the original indices are generated.

After all five steps in the extracting and reversing phases have been performed, the secret data can be accurately extracted and the output indexes should equal the original SMVQ-compressed codes. The reconstructed compressed codes can now be stored directly to save storage space and can be reused repeatedly for a variety of applications.

4.4.4.4 Experimental Results

In this subsection, we test the effectiveness and feasibility of Chang–Tai–Lin's scheme. The experiments use five 512×512 gray-level test images: Lena, F16, Boat, Peppers, and Baboon. These standard gray-level images are compressed as the cover images using SMVQ with a main codebook of 256 codewords and a state codebook of 128 codewords. The secret data are a randomly generated bitstream. The relative PSNRs for Chang–Tai–Lin's SMVQ-compressed cover images (without hidden data) are shown in Table 4.8.

Hiding the secret data in the compressed information certainly creates larger distortions in stego images. However, Chang–Tai–Lin's lossless information hiding scheme shows its ability to hide the secret data in a low bit rate (0.438 bpp) compressed cover image that achieves a very high hiding capacity and keeps the

Table 4.8 PSNRs for SMVQ-Compressed Cover Image With/Without Hidden Data

Images	Bit Rate 0.438 bpp	PSNR (dB)
Lena	With hidden data	30.7746
	Without hidden data	31.0487
F16	With hidden data	29.9363
	Without hidden data	30.2280
Boat	With hidden data	28.7849
	Without hidden data	29.0712
Peppers	With hidden data	29.0675
	Without hidden data	30.1798
Baboon	With hidden data	22.6614
	Without hidden data	22.8004

PSNR, *peak signal-to-noise ratio;* SMVQ, *side match vector quantization.*

(a) (b)

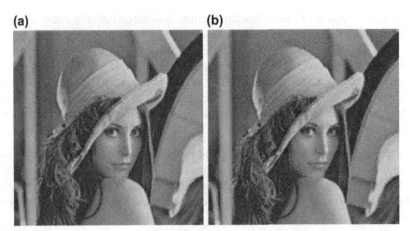

FIGURE 4.18

Compressed and stego Lena images. (a) Original compressed image (PSNR: 31.0487 dB). (b) Stego image (PSNR: 30.7746 dB). *PSNR*, peak signal-to-noise ratio.

distortion low. Fig. 4.18 illustrates the hiding results using 16K bits of secret data. As Fig. 4.18 shows, Chang–Tai–Lin's scheme keeps the hiding distortion low and achieves very high visual quality. Table 4.8 shows the PSNRs with and without hidden data at the same bit rate (0.438 bpp) for various images. This table also shows that the average PSNR of the five stego images is about 29 dB. In the best case, the PSNR is still 30.7746, which is close to that of the SMVQ-compressed cover images.

Table 4.9 gives additional hiding results for the Lena image at a range of sizes for the main codebook and the state codebook. The average PSNR of Lena is 29.0686 dB, which is quite close to that of SMVQ-compressed Lena without the secret data embedded but with the same compression rate and a main codebook of 512 codewords. All this shows that Chang–Tai–Lin's scheme guarantees not only that

Table 4.9 Hiding Results of Lena for Various Main Codebook Sizes and State Codebook Sizes

State Codebook Size	Main Codebook Size					
	128		256		512	
	PSNR	bpp	PSNR	bpp	PSNR	bpp
16	26.37	0.252	26.54	0.253	25.73	0.254
32	27.92	0.314	28.42	0.315	27.81	0.316
64	28.67	0.375	29.85	0.377	29.52	0.377
128			30.77	0.438	31.06	0.439
256					31.21	0.501

PSNR, *peak signal-to-noise ratio.*

Table 4.10 Comparisons Between Chang—Tai—Lin's Scheme and Chang and Wu's Scheme

Images	Chang and Wu's Scheme			Chang-Tai-Lin's Scheme		
	Payload (bits)	PSNR (dB)	Bit Rate (bpp)	Payload (bits)	PSNR (dB)	Bit Rate (bpp)
Lena	13,487	29.25	0.47	16,129	30.78	0.44
F16	13,914	29.15	0.45	16,129	29.94	0.44
Boat	13,246	28.12	0.46	16,129	28.79	0.44
Peppers	13,984	29.07	0.45	16,129	30.18	0.44
Baboon	8794	22.43	0.61	16,129	22.66	0.44

PSNR, *peak signal-to-noise ratio.*

the receiver can accurately extract the hidden secret data but also that the SMVQ-compressed codes can be recovered and reused after the secret data are extracted.

Table 4.10 compares Chang—Tai—Lin's scheme and Chang and Wu's scheme by size of secret data, visual quality, and compression rate. In Chang and Wu's scheme, $TH_{SMVQ} = 30$ and $TH_{VQ} = 50$ and a state codebook of size 16 is used to maintain a lower bit rate. The main codebook with a size of 256 is adopted in all schemes for this comparison. As the table shows, Chang—Tai—Lin's hiding capacity is larger and the visual quality is still better than Chang and Wu's scheme. In addition, Chang—Tai—Lin's scheme can preserve the high compression rate because additional indicators are not needed. Thus, the compression rate of Chang—Tai-Lin's scheme is superior to that of Chang and Wu's scheme. Most important, Chang—Tai—Lin's scheme maintains the high hiding capacity and compression rate while achieving reversibility. This superior performance enables the receiver to use the reconstructed compression codes as cover media, hide secret data, and send back the SMVQ stego image to make communication between parties more efficient.

From this discussion, we can see that hiding data in SMVQ-compressed codes originally caused a large distortion in stego images because SMVQ is a low-bitrate compression scheme. To maintain the advantages of SMVQ and make sure the original compression indexes can be successfully reconstructed after secret data are extracted, Chang—Tai—Lin's scheme hides the secret data in the compressed cover image and achieves the property of reversibility. The procedures for hiding and extracting and reversing are straightforward. Being lossless, the original compressed codes can be completely reconstructed after hidden secret data extraction, and the original compressed codes can be stored directly and used repeatedly. In addition, Chang—Tai—Lin's scheme can simply hide or extract the secret data and restore the SMVQ-compressed codes without complex computations. The hidden secret data can also be extracted from the stego image without referencing the original compressed cover image. In terms of secret data size, visual quality, and compression rate, the performance of Chang—Tai—Lin's scheme is superior to that of Chang and Wu's hiding scheme.

However, the main drawback of SMVQ-based hiding methods is that the PSNR value of the stego image is much less than that of the original VQ-compressed image. Thus, improving the stego image quality while maintaining high hiding capacity is the main goal of VQ-based lossless information hiding. Next, we introduce VQ-index-coding—based schemes, which can achieve this goal.

4.5 VECTOR QUANTIZATION—INDEX CODING—BASED SCHEMES

Achieving low image distortion (i.e., it reduces the suspicion of adversaries), high data embedding capacity, reversibility, and efficiency are desired by most information hiding system designers. Since no method is capable of achieving all these goals, a class of information hiding schemes is needed to span the range of possible applications. With the purpose of improving the visual quality of reconstructed images and achieving high embedding capacity and fast execution speed at the cost of a little higher bit rate, Chang et al., Wang et al., and Lu et al. propose a kind of lossless information embedding schemes for the steganographic application (i.e., secret communications) by using index coding for VQ-compressed images. These methods embed secrets into VQ-compressed indices by using the difference values between the current index and left or upper neighboring indices. Next, we will introduce seven typical index coding—based methods in detail.

4.5.1 JOINT NEIGHBORING CODING—BASED SCHEME

JNC was first proposed by Chang et al. [9]. In their article, as a lossless coding algorithm, JNC is used to encode VQ indices and hide secret data during the encoding process. Compared with the traditional method to transform each VQ index directly into the binary format with the preset number of bits, JNC of the VQ index table efficiently takes advantage of the correlation between the adjacent indices. In the JNC scheme, the VQ-compressed indices located in the first row and the first column of the index table P (as shown in Fig. 4.19) are kept unchanged during the data

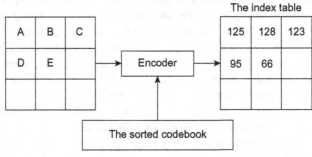

FIGURE 4.19

The generation process of the index table.

embedding process. This means that there is no data embedding in this area (called the seed area). Embedding the secret data into the index table P (i.e., into VQ indices) is started from the VQ-compressed index located at the second row and the second column of the index table P.

For the security purpose, the secret data B is encrypted before embedding by using a *pseudo random number generator* with a seed z, which is known by the sender and the receiver only, to generate a bitstream U. Next, the new bitstream Z is created by $Z = B \oplus U$, where $\oplus$ is the exclusive OR operator. Then, Z is embedded into the index table P. The detailed embedding process of the JNC scheme can be represented as follows.

4.5.1.1 The Embedding Process

Given an $A \times B$-sized cover image I and the N-sized codebook C containing N k-dimensional codewords c_i's, where $c_i = (c_{i1}, c_{i2}, ..., c_{ik})$ and $i = 0, 1, ..., N - 1$. First, compute the sum S_i of each codeword c_i in the codebook C by $S_i = c_{i1} + c_{i2} + ... + c_{ik}$. Second, sort the codebook C according to S_i in ascending order: $S_0 < S_1 < ... < S_{N-1}$. The purpose of sorting the codebook C in this way is to make neighboring codewords c_i's in the sorted codebook C close to each other. Consequently, the difference values d's, where d means the distance between two neighboring VQ-compressed indices, are very small. The set of VQ-compressed indices is called the index table P as shown in Fig. 4.19. For $k = 4 \times 4$, the index table P is $(A/4) \times (B/4)$-sized matrix containing VQ-compressed indices $p_{a,b}$, where $a = 0, 1, ..., (A/4) - 1$ and $b = 0, 1, ..., (B/4) - 1$. The secret data are then embedded by encoding the current VQ-compressed index. One secret bit is embedded into the current VQ-compressed index at a time during the embedding process. More specifically, encoding the current index $p_{a,b}$ is performed by encoding the difference values d's between the left neighboring index $p_{a,b-1}$ or the upper neighboring index $p_{a-1,b}$ and the index $p_{a,b}$ as shown in Fig. 4.20. The embedding strategy is based on two embedding rules as follows.

> Rule 1: If the secret bit is 1, then the difference value d between the left neighboring index $p_{a,b-1}$ and the current VQ-compressed index $p_{a,b}$ is computed by $d = p_{a,b-1} - p_{a,b}$.
> Rule 2: If the secret bit is 0, then the difference value d between the upper neighboring index $p_{a-1,b}$ and the current VQ-compressed index $p_{a,b}$ is computed by $d = p_{a-1,b} - p_{a,b}$.

The JNC technique is really affected by various amplitudes of the difference values d's. The amplitude variation of the difference values d's depends on the image content (i.e., smooth images or complex images). The various amplitudes of the difference values d's are represented with various number of bits. The d's absolute value $|d|$ ranges from 0 to $N - 1$ (i.e. $0 \leq |d| \leq N - 1$). Thus, the binary representation of d needs m bits, where $1 \leq m \leq \text{Ceil}(\log_2 N)$ and the notation $\text{Ceil}(x)$ denotes the ceiling function returning the smallest integer not less than x. The possible amplitudes of d are represented as $2^m - 1$. The dynamic values of m used

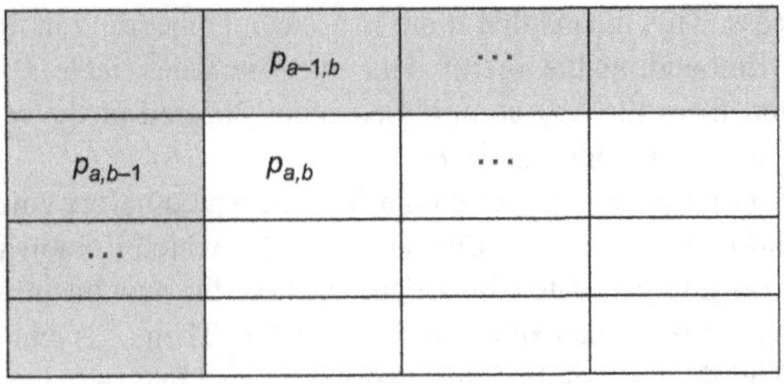

	$p_{a-1,b}$	$\cdots$	
$p_{a,b-1}$	$p_{a,b}$	$\cdots$	
$\cdots$			

FIGURE 4.20

Left and upper joint neighboring indices $p_{a,b-1}$ and $p_{a-1,b}$.

Table 4.11 m's Dynamic Values Used Corresponding to the d's Dynamic Ranges

M	1	2	3	4	...	m	...	Ceil($\log_2 N$)
D	1	3	7	15	...	2^m-1	...	$N-1$

correspondingly to the dynamic values of d during the embedding process of the JNC scheme are shown in Table 4.11. Note that d equals 0 is the typical case and it is considered in detail in Case 3.

For the sake of convenience, the binary representation of d is denoted as $d_{(2)} = g_0 g_1 \cdots g_{m-1}$, where $g_j \in \{0, 1\}$ and $0 \leq j \leq m - 1$. Two prefix bits 00, 01, 10, and 11 used for four different cases of the various amplitudes of d are represented as follows. Note that, in Cases 1 and 2 (called normal cases), and Case 3(called zero case), m bits are needed to represent $d_{(2)}$. So the $(2 + m)$-bit code is concatenated with the binary code stream for each case. For example, if $15 < |d| \leq 31$ then 5 bits (i.e., $m = 5$) are needed to represent $d_{(2)}$ and the 7-bit code is concatenated with the binary codestream.

> **Case 1:** $0 < d \leq 2^m - 1$. The current VQ-compressed index $p_{a,b}$ is encoded into binary form as $11|d_{(2)}$ or $01|d_{(2)}$, where | denotes the concatenation operation, to represent embedding the secret bit 1 or 0, respectively.
>
> **Case 2:** $(2^m - 1) \leq d < 0$. The current VQ-compressed index $p_{a,b}$ is encoded into binary form as $10|d_{(2)}$ or $00|d_{(2)}$ to represent embedding the secret bit 1 or 0, respectively.
>
> **Case 3:** $d = 0$. The current VQ-compressed index $p_{a,b}$ is encoded into binary form as $11|d_{(2)}$ or $01|d_{(2)}$, where $d_{(2)}$ is represented with m digits "0," to represent embedding the secret bit 1 or 0, respectively.
>
> **Case 4:** $|d| > 2^m - 1$. The current VQ-compressed index $p_{a,b}$ is encoded into binary form as $10|00...0| (p_{a,b})_{(2)}$, ($m$ digits "0"), or $00|00...0|(p_{a,b})_{(2)}$, ($m$ digits "0"), to represent embedding the secret bit 1 or 0, respectively, where $(p_{a,b})_{(2)}$ is

Table 4.12 Summary of the Embedding Process

Secret Bit	Case 1	Case 2	Case 3	Case 4
1	$11\|d_{(2)}$	$10\|d_{(2)}$	$11\|00...0$	$10\|00...0\|(p_{a,b})_{(2)}$
0	$01\|d_{(2)}$	$00\|d_{(2)}$	$01\|00...0$	$00\|00...0\|(p_{a,b})_{(2)}$

the binary representation of $p_{a,b}$, $(p_{a,b})_{(2)} = g_0 g_1 ... g_{Ceil(log2N)-1}$ ($g_j \in \{0, 1\}$, $0 \le j \le Ceil(log_2N)-1$). Note that, in this case, $Ceil(log_2N)$ bits are needed to represent $(p_{a,b})_{(2)}$. So the $(2 + m + Ceil(log_2N))$-bit code is concatenated with the binary code stream. The embedding process of the JNC scheme is summarized in Table 4.12.

4.5.1.2 The Extracting Process

When the data embedding process is done, the sender sends the binary code stream to the receiver, the N-sized sorted codebook C, and the seed area to the receiver via a secure channel. The extracting process used to extract the embedded secret data and recover the original VQ-compressed indices is represented in the following description.

Step 1: Read the next $(2 + m)$ bits into p from the binary code stream.
Step 2: Get the first bit of p to be the secret bit.
Step 3: If the last m bits of p are $00...0$, (m digits "0"), then

    If the second bit of p is 1 (i.e. $d = 0$), then
        If the secret bit is 1, then
            The original VQ index is decoded by $p_{a,b}=p_{a,b-1}$.
        Otherwise
            The original VQ index is decoded by $p_{a,b}=p_{a-1,b}$.
    Otherwise, (i.e. $|d| > 2^m-1$)
        Read next $Ceil(log_2N)$ bits into $q_{(2)}$ from the binary code stream.
        Convert $q_{(2)}$ into the decimal value q.
        The original VQ index is decoded by $p_{a,b}=q$.
    Otherwise, (i.e. $-(2^m-1) \le d < 0$ or $0 < d \le 2^m-1$)
        Assign the last m bits of p to the difference value $d_{(2)}$.
        Convert $d_{(2)}$ into the decimal difference value d.
        If the second bit of p is 0 (i.e. $-(2^m-1) \le d < 0$), then $d=-d$.
        If the secret bit is 1, then
            The original VQ index is decoded by $p_{a,b}= p_{a,b-1}-d$.
        Otherwise
            The original VQ index is decoded by $p_{a,b}= p_{a-1,b}-d$.

Step 4: Repeat Steps 1–3 until all bits of the binary code stream are read.

The main drawback of JNC-based hiding method is that the bit rate of the stego image is a bit larger than that of the original VQ-compressed image, which will be tested in the following subsections.

4.5.2 VECTOR QUANTIZATION–INDEX RESIDUAL VALUE CODING–BASED SCHEME

The main idea of the VQIRVC-based lossless information hiding scheme [10] is to encode the cover image with an index table and then utilize the relationship between the neighboring four indices of the current index and their mean values to hide the secret bit; finally the index difference is encoded by the proper bitstream to reduce the bit rate. This algorithm consists of three phases as follows.

4.5.2.1 The Preprocessing Phase

During the preprocessing phase, a sorted VQ codebook is generated to encode the original cover image as follows:

Step 1: The original cover image is divided into nonoverlapping blocks of size 4×4.

Step 2: A codebook of size N is generated by the well-known LBG algorithm [1] based on the training set consisting of all blocks of the cover image.

Step 3: For each codeword vector c_i, add up the values of its components to obtain its sum value $S_i = c_{i1} + c_{i2} + \ldots + c_{ik}$. Sort the codewords in the codebook in the ascending order of their sum values.

Step 4: Encode each image block with the sorted codebook, obtaining the index table of the cover image, as shown in Fig. 4.19.

Here, the purpose of using a sorted codebook is to make the VQ indices of adjacent blocks as close to each other as possible.

4.5.2.2 The Information Hiding Phase

The secret data are hidden based on the index table obtained in the preprocessing phase. The indices of the first row and the leftmost and rightmost columns of the index table are selected as the seed area and kept unchanged during the information hiding process. This means that no data are hidden in these locations. The information hiding process is performed from the second to the last row and from the second to the second last column of the VQ index table. The hiding process consists of the following steps. The form of the resulting codestreams is shown in Table 4.13, where $(**)^1$ and $(**)^2$ denote two different 2-bit flag numbers.

Step 1: For each index i_{cur} that is not in the seed area, mark its adjacent indices i_l, i_{lu}, i_u, and i_{ru} with 2-bit flag numbers "00," "01," "10," and "11," respectively, as shown in Fig. 4.21. Then we calculate the approximate mean value of these

Table 4.13 The Final Codestreams for Different Cases

Secret Bit	Case 1	Case 2	Case 3	Case 4
1	$(**)^1\|11\|(d)_2$	$(**)^1\|10\|(-d)_2$	$(**)^1\|01\|(d)'_2$	$(**)^1\|00\|(-d)'_2$
0	$(**)^2\|11\|(d)_2$	$(**)^2\|10\|(-d)_2$	$(**)^2\|01\|(d)'_2$	$(**)^2\|00\|(-d)'_2$

i_{lu} (01)	i_u (10)	i_{ru} (11)
i_l (00)	i_{cur}	

FIGURE 4.21

The flag numbers of the neighboring indices related to the current index.

indices by $i_m = \text{Floor}((i_l + i_{lu} + i_u + i_{ru})/4)$, where $\text{Floor}(a)$ denotes the largest integer that is not greater than a.

Step 2: Compute the absolute value of the difference between each adjacent index and the approximate mean calculated in Step 1, i.e., $d_l = |i_l - i_m|$, $d_{lu} = |i_{lu} - i_m|$, $d_u = |i_u - i_m|$, $d_{ru} = |i_{ru} - i_m|$.

Step 3: Judge if the four difference values obtained in Step 2 are equal. If they are identical, the current index is jumped over and the secret data are not embedded into it, and then go to Step 8. Otherwise, if at least two of them are different, secret data can be embedded into the current index, and then go to Step 4.

Step 4: Find the smallest value $d_{min} = \min\{d_l, d_{lu}, d_u, d_{ru}\}$ and then find a different second smallest value d_{min2} among $\{d_l, d_{lu}, d_u, d_{ru}\}$ to ensure that d_{min2} is not equal to d_{min}.

Step 5: Input 1 bit of secret data w. If $w = 1$, go to Step 6. Otherwise, go to Step 7.

Step 6: Get the two flag bits of the adjacent index i_{min} that are closest to the approximate mean i_m (their distance is d_{min}) and then append the two flag bits to the resulting code stream. Finally, the index residual value $d = i_{cur} - i_{min}$ is calculated, and then go to Step 9.

Step 7: Get the two flag bits of the adjacent index i_{min2} that are second closest to the approximate mean i_m (their distance is d_{min2}) and then append the two flag bits to the resulting code stream. Finally, the index residual value $d = i_{cur} - i_{min2}$ is calculated, and then go to Step 9.

Step 8: Out of the four adjacent indices, find the adjacent index i_{clo} that is closest to i_{cur} and send the corresponding two flag bits to the output codestream. Finally, the index residual value $d = i_{cur} - i_{clo}$ is calculated.

Step 9: To decrease the bit rate of the output code stream, we choose a fixed appropriate integer s, which is unchanged for all the indices in the information hiding phase and can be acquired through the experiments mentioned in Section 4.5.2.4, i.e., the number of bits required to represent the absolute value of each residual value can be denoted in the binary form. For a codebook of size N, the residual value d ranges from $-(Ni - 1)$ to $(N - 1)$. Thus the integer s ranges from 1 to Ceil($\log_2 N$), where Ceil(a) denotes the least integer not less than a.

Step 10: With the integer s determined in the previous step and the obtained index residual value d, we can encode d according to one of the four following different cases and concatenate the binary encoding result right after the two flag bits to form the final resulting codestream.

Case 1: If $0 \le d \le 2^s - 1$, the current index residual value d is encoded into the binary form $11 |(d)_2$, where $|$ denotes the concatenation operation.

Case 2: If $-(2^s - 1) \le d < 0$, the current index residual value d is encoded into the binary form $10|(-d)_2$.

Case 3: If $|d| > 2^s - 1$ and $d > 0$, the current index residual value d is encoded into the binary form $01 |(d)'_2$, where $(d)'_2 = g_0 g_1 ... g$Ceil($\log_2 N$) $- 1$, $g_i \in \{0, 1\}$, $0 \le i \le$ Ceil($\log_2 N$) $- 1$, and N is the size of the codebook.

Case 4: If $|d| > 2^s - 1$ and $d < 0$, the current index residual value d is encoded into the binary form $00 |(-d)'$

Step 11: Repeat Steps 1–10 to encode the following index in the raster-scan order until all the indices except for the indices in the seed area are encoded.

4.5.2.3 The Decoding and Extracting Phase

In the VQIRVC-based scheme, the decoder used to reconstruct the stego image is the same as the one used to restore the original image and extract the secret data. The detailed decoding and extracting process can be described as follows.

Step 1: Read the first two flag bits at the proper position from the code stream (started from the second block in the second row of the stego image) to find the corresponding adjacent index i_{adj}, and then compute the mean value i_m of the four adjacent indices.

Step 2: Whether the four adjacent indices are with the same distance from i_m is judged. If the result is true, then no secret data are embedded into the index. Go to Step 5. Otherwise, go to Step 3.

Step 3: Find the index i_{clo} closest to i_m among the four adjacent indices.

Step 4: If $i_{adj} = i_{clo}$, then the hidden secret bit is "1." Otherwise, the secret bit is "0."

Step 5: Read the next 2 bits. If they are "'11," go on with reading the following s bits and convert them into the decimal difference value d; then the original VQ index is recovered as $i_{adj} + d$. If the 2 bits are "'10," go on with the similar operation and recover the original VQ index as $i_{adj} - d$. If the 2 bits are "'01,'" continue to read the next Ceil($\log_2 N$) bits and change them into the decimal form d', and the original VQ index is recovered as $i_{adj} + d'$. If the 2 bits are "'00,'" perform the same operation to get d' and restore the original VQ index as $i_{adj} - d'$.

Step 6: Repeat Steps 1 to 4 to extract other secret data from the next index in the raster-scan order until all indices are processed.

Step 7: According to the restored VQ indices and the sorted codebook, we can reconstruct the VQ-compressed original image. In this way, the whole lossless process is realized.

4.5.2.4 Experimental Results

To evaluate the VQIRVC-based scheme, we use six test images, Lena, Peppers, Mandrill, Boat, Goldhill, and Jet_F16, of the same size 512×512 with 256 gray-scales, as shown in Fig. 4.22. The VQIRVC scheme, the MFCVQ-based scheme [3], and the SMVQ-based scheme [6] are compared (i.e., Chang—Tai—Lin's scheme). Three aspects are assessed in the experiment to evaluate an information hiding scheme, i.e., the capacity representing the maximum amount of information that can be hidden, the PSNR representing the quality of the stego image, and the bit rate representing the performance of the compression efficiency whose unit is bpp.

Lena   Peppers   Mandrill

Boat   Goldhill   Jet_F16

FIGURE 4.22

Six test images.

Table 4.14 Comparisons of the VQIRVC-Based, MFCVQ-Based, and SMVQ-Based Algorithms

Algorithm	Parameters	Lena	Peppers	Mandrill	Boat	Goldhill	Jet_F16
VQIRVC	VQ (dB)	31.216	30.561	23.887	30.038	31.230	31.608
($N = 512$)	PSNR (dB)	31.216	30.561	23.887	30.038	31.230	31.608
	Capacity	15,319	15,590	15,829	15,537	15,395	14,631
	Bit rate (bpp)	0.635	0.626	0.684	0.664	0.662	0.649
MFCVQ	PSNR (dB)	29.831	29.072	23.229	27.002	28.135	26.879
($N = 512$,	Capacity	7512	6995	969	7155	2317	8283
$TH = 18$)	Bit rate (bpp)	0.424	0.438	0.599	0.431	0.566	0.406
SMVQ	PSNR (dB)	28.192	28.747	21.542	26.681	27.322	28.032
($N = 512$,	Capacity	16,129	16,129	16,129	16,129	16,129	16,129
$N_s = 128$)	Bit rate (bpp)	0.44	0.44	0.44	0.44	0.44	0.44

MFCVQ, *modified fast correlation vector quantization*; PSNR, *peak signal-to-noise ratio*; SMVQ, *side match vector quantization*; VQ, *vector quantization*; VQIRVC, *vector quantization–index residual value coding*.

To ensure that all the algorithms can be fairly compared, the sizes of codebooks adopted in all algorithms are 512. The VQIRVC-based algorithm is performed with the appropriate *s* values. The comparisons are shown in Table 4.14. From Table 4.14, we can see that the PSNR in the VQIRVC-based scheme is much larger than that of the other two methods, which indicates that the quality of the stego image is much better. This is because in the VQIRVC-based scheme the secret data are hidden in the flag bits of the codestream rather than in the index residual values. In fact, the reconstructed image itself does not contain any secret information, whereas its codestream does. The information hiding capacity has evidently been increased in comparison with the MFCVQ-based scheme. In the VQIRVC-based scheme, we can nearly hide 1 bit secret data per index. Unlike the MFCVQ-based method, there is no need to judge whether a location is fit for information hiding. Compared with the SMVQ-based scheme, the capacity of the VQIRVC-based scheme is a little lower than that of the SMVQ-based method. However, the PSNRs of the stego images in the VQIRVC-based algorithm are significantly higher than those of the SMVQ-based scheme. Obviously, the two parameters have a relationship of mutual restriction. The more secret data are embedded in the cover image, the lower the PSNR of the stego image obtained.

To take the two attributes into comprehensive consideration, 3000, 6000, 9000, 12,000 and the embedding capacity (i.e., the number of maximum bits that can be embedded) are embedded in the test images to measure the PSNRs of the stego images. Based on test images of Lena and Peppers, the comparison results in Fig. 4.23 show that the performance curve of the VQIRVC-based scheme is greater than that of the SMVQ-based method, which means when the number of embedded bits is the same, the PSNRs of the VQIRVC-based method are much higher. Therefore, these experiments demonstrate the superiority of the VQIRVC-based

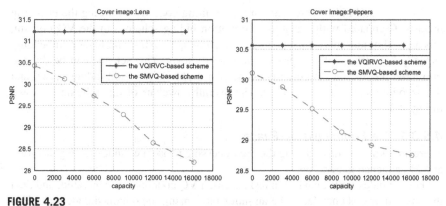

FIGURE 4.23

Comparisons of the capacity and peak signal-to-noise ratio (PSNR) of vector quantization–index residual value coding (VQIRVC)–based and side match vector quantization (SMVQ)–based schemes.

algorithm. As to the bit rate, it is a bit larger in the VQIRVC-based algorithm. This is because we have introduced two flag bits for each index. However, taking the three attributes into comprehensive consideration, the VQIRVC-based scheme is a more effective method for its high capacity, high PSNR, and an acceptable bit rate.

From this, we can see that the main advantages of the VQIRVC-based lossless information hiding scheme are as follows. (1) This algorithm achieves higher PSNR and higher information hiding capacity than the MFCVQ- and the SMVQ-based schemes. (2) This scheme can be separated into the VQ encoding process for generating the VQ index table and the information hiding process to embed secret data into the codestream. Obviously, this algorithm realizes the desired "separation of the encoder and the embedder" requirement stated in Section 4.1.2, which facilitates the individual processing of the encoder and the watermark embedder and the controlling of the corresponding performance. (3) It is obvious that whether the secret data are embedded or not, the composition of the output codestream is the same. The only difference lies in the flag bits for each index. This characteristic makes unauthorized users not perceive the existence of the secret data and thus makes the VQIRVC-based scheme meet the requirement of "distinguishability" described in Section 4.1.2, which is important for the application of information hiding.

4.5.3 PATH OPTIONAL LOSSLESS INFORMATION HIDING SCHEME

In the applications of lossless information hiding techniques, the stego image quality, the embedding capacity, and the security level are the three main aspects to be considered. To improve the performance of previous algorithms, Wang and Lu proposed a novel path optional lossless information hiding scheme [11]. This method encodes the VQ indices of the cover image into the binary codestream using the

JNC scheme and hides secret data in the resulting codestream during the encoding process. Compared with previous information hiding schemes in the VQ domain, this algorithm not only achieves higher stego image quality and higher embedding capacity but also greatly improves the security level. This scheme can be divided into three phases, i.e., the preprocessing phase, the information hiding phase, and the decoding and extraction phase. The overall flowchart of this scheme is shown in Fig. 4.24.

4.5.3.1 The Preprocessing Phase

There are two main tasks during the preprocessing phase, i.e., index table generation and M-sequence generation.

For the index table generation task, a sorted VQ codebook is generated, and then the cover image is encoded to be an index table using the obtained codebook. This task can be described in detail as follows:

Step 1: The cover image is divided into nonoverlapping blocks of size 4×4.
Step 2: The codebook is generated by the well-known LBG algorithm based on the training set composed of all cover image blocks. And then according to Eq. (2), the codewords are sorted in the ascending order of their sum values.
Step 3: The sorted codebook is utilized to encode each block, generating the VQ index table, as described in Section 4.5.2.1.

For the second task, the M-sequence is generated according to the selected path and an initial key. Wang and Lu's scheme provides users with two optional paths. When the amount of secret data is huge, Path 2 in Fig. 4.25b is suggested to reach higher transmission efficiency. When the amount of secret data is not large, Path 1 in Fig. 4.25a is proposed to reduce the length of the output codestream. This task is performed by the M-sequence generator, where the length of the M-sequence is determined according to the selected path in the following two cases:

Case 1: When Path 1 is selected, 2-bit secret data are hidden in each block on an average, and the number of bits of the output M-sequence is twice as large as the number of blocks in the cover image to ensure that almost each block can be distributed with 2-bit data from the M-sequence.
Case 2: When Path 2 is selected, 3-bit secret data are hidden in each block on an average, and then the number of bits of the output M-sequence is three times as large as the number of blocks in the cover image to ensure that almost each block can be distributed with 3-bit data from the M-sequence.

4.5.3.2 The Hiding Phase

During the information hiding phase, Wang and Lu employ two different implementation processes, i.e., Path 1—based and Path 2—based schemes corresponding to the two different paths. When the amount of secret data is huge, Path 2—based method is suggested to almost embed 3-bit secret data in each block to achieve high embedding capacity and transmission efficiency. When the purpose is to reduce the length of the output codestream, Path 1—based scheme is proposed to nearly embed 2 bits secret data in each block. These two processes can be expressed in detail as follows.

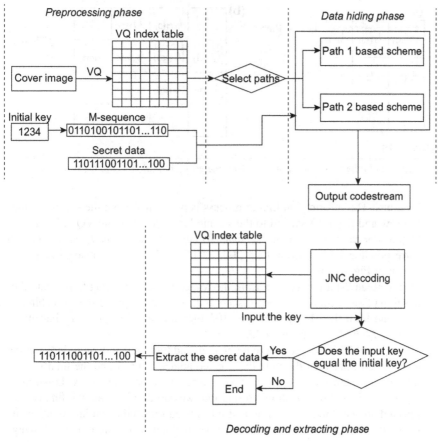

Preprocessing phase

VQ index table

Cover image — VQ → [grid]

Initial key
1234

M-sequence
0110100101101...110

Secret data
110111001101...100

Select paths

Data hiding phase

Path 1 based scheme

Path 2 based scheme

Output codestream

VQ index table

JNC decoding

Input the key

110111001101...100 ← Extract the secret data ← Yes — Does the input key equal the initial key?

End ← No

Decoding and extracting phase

FIGURE 4.24

The overall flow chart of Wang and Lu's scheme [11].

4.5.3.2.1 Path 1–Based Scheme

Input: the VQ index table, secret data, the M-sequence (or initial key)
Output: the output JNC codestream

Step 1: Two parameters m and n are preset, which indicate the number of bits required to represent each absolute residual value between the current index and the selected adjacent index and the number of the adjacent indices to be searched, respectively. The parameter m is a randomly selected integer value between 1 and $\mathrm{Ceil}(\log_2 N)$, where N is the codebook size, whereas the parameter n is set to be 4.

Step 2: The indices in the first row and the leftmost and rightmost columns of the index table are selected as seed area, in which the indices are kept unchanged during the information hiding process. It means that no data are hidden in these

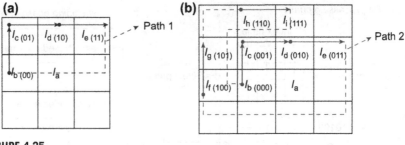

FIGURE 4.25

The flag bits of adjacent indices and the two related paths, (a) $n = 4$ and (b) $n = 8$.

locations. The information hiding process is performed from the second to the last row and from the second to the second last column of the VQ index table.

Step 3: For each current index I_a, mark its adjacent indices I_b, I_c, I_d, and I_e with corresponding 2-bit position flags "00," "01," "10," and "11," respectively, as shown in Fig. 4.25a.

Step 4: Read 2-bit binary data from the M-sequence as the flag to indicate the position of an initially selected adjacent index. For example, if the 2 bits binary data read from the M-sequence are "10," then the initially selected adjacent index is I_d, as shown in Fig. 4.25a.

Step 5: Read 2 bits secret data to be hidden, and then utilize them to indicate the location shift between the initially selected adjacent index and the finally selected adjacent index in the clockwise direction along Path 1, as shown in Fig. 4.25a. Based on the shift information, we can easily locate the finally selected adjacent index. Assume that d has been selected as an initial adjacent index; then the final adjacent index can be obtained according to the following four cases:

Case 1: If the 2 bits secret data are "00," then the location shift is 0, and thus the finally selected adjacent index is I_d.

Case 2: If the 2 bits secret data are "01," then the location shift is 1, and thus the finally selected adjacent index is I_e.

Case 3: If the secret data are "10," then the final selected adjacent index is I_b.

Case 4: If the secret data are "11," then the final selected adjacent index is I_c.

Step 6: Based on the finally selected adjacent index, we can perform the JNC-encoding process to encode the current index I_a as follows:

$$d = index_a - index_{final} \tag{4.15}$$

where d is the residual value and $index_a$ and $index_{final}$ are the current index and the finally selected adjacent index, respectively.

Step 6.1: The position flag of the finally selected adjacent index is appended to the output codestream.

Table 4.15 Forms of the JNC Codestream for Each Index in Different Cases

Cases	Case 1: $0 \leq d \leq 2^m - 1$	Case 2: $-(2^m - 1) \leq d < 0$	Case 3: $d > 2^m - 1$	Case 4: $d < -(2^m - 1)$
Forms	$(**/***)_2\|11\|(d)_2$	$(**/***)_2\|10\|(-d)_2$	$(**/***)_2\|01\| (d)'_2$	$(**/***)_2\|00\|(-d)'_2$

JNC, *joint neighboring coding.*

> Step 6.2: According to the preset parameter n in Step 1, for the current index I_a, a search set composed of four neighboring indices is determined.
> Step 6.3: The residual value between the finally selected adjacent index and the current index is calculated as follows:
> Step 6.4: According to the preset parameter m, the decimal residual value d is transformed into the binary form in one of four cases mentioned in Table 4.15, and then the resulting binary form is appended to the output codestream.
> Step 7: Repeat Steps 3 to 6 for all the indices except the indices in the seed area.

Obviously, when the parameter m is set to be different values, the length of the output codestream may be different. To decrease the length of the output codestream, we should test all possible m values and select the optimal case. In this chapter, the parameter m is set to the integer value from 1 to Ceil(log$_2 N$) successively, where N is the codebook size. The appropriate m value is selected by finding the case in which the resulting length of the output codestream is minimal.

It is obvious that the form of the output codestream obtained through the Path 1–based scheme for each index is similar to that obtained through the basic JNC scheme as shown in Table 4.15, where (**/***) for the output codestream of the Path 1–based scheme represents the position flag of the finally selected adjacent index.

Let us give a concrete example as shown in Fig. 4.26. The indices in the gray blocks are selected as the seed area, and thus no secret data are hidden there. Assume that the codebook size N is 256, and the parameters $m = 2$ and $n = 4$. In Fig. 4.26, the first index to be encoded is "138." The 2-bit "10" in the M-sequence indicates that the initially selected adjacent index is "136," and "00" in the secret data denotes that the location shift is 0. So the finally selected adjacent index is still "136," and the residual value $d = 138 - 136 = 2$. According to the relationship between d and m, we know that d can be denoted as $(10)_2$ satisfying Case 1. Thus, the index "138" can be finally encoded as "10||11||10." Now, the following index to be encoded is "133." The 2-bit "11" in the M-sequence indicates that the initially selected adjacent index is "129," and then that based on "10" in the secret data, i.e., the location shift is 2, the finally selected adjacent index is "136" and $d = 133 - 136 = -3$. Obviously, because m and d satisfy the relationship $-(2^m - 1) = -3 \leq d = -3 < 0$, we have $(-d) = (11)_2$ based on Case 2. Therefore, the index "133" is finally encoded as "01||10||11." Similarly, for the index "137," the 2-bit "01" in the M-sequence

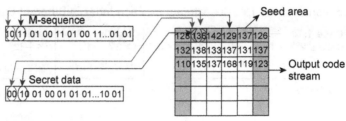

FIGURE 4.26

A concrete example for the Path 1—based scheme.

denotes that the initially selected adjacent index is "142" and the final selected adjacent index is "129" based on "01" in the secret data; then we have $d = 137 - 129 = 8$. Because m and d satisfy Case 3 and $\log_2 N = 8$, we have $d = (00,001,000)_2$. Finally, the index "137" can be encoded as "10||01||00001000." For the following index "131," based on the following 2-bits data in the M-sequence and secret data, the initially and finally selected adjacent indices are both 137. Thus we have $d = 131 - 137 = -6$ which can be denoted as $(-d) = (00000110)_2$ satisfying Case 4. Therefore, the encoded binary form for the index "131" is "00||00||00000110.". Obviously, the final output codestream for the index sequence "138 133 137 131" is "10||11||10 01||10||11 10||01||00001000 00||00||00000110".

4.5.3.2.2 Path 2—Based Scheme

Input: the VQ index table, secret data, the M-sequence.

Output: the output JNC codestream

The implementation of the Path 2—based scheme is similar to that of the Path 1—based scheme, which can be described as follows:

Step 1: Two parameters m and n are preset. The parameter m is a randomly selected integer value between 1 and Ceil($\log_2 N$), where N is the codebook size, while the parameter n is set to be 8.

Step 2: The indices in the first and second rows, the leftmost, the second leftmost, and rightmost columns of the index table are selected as seed area. The information hiding process is performed from the third to the last row and from the third to the second last column of the VQ index table.

Step 3: For each current index I_a, mark its adjacent indices I_b, I_c, I_d, I_e, I_f, I_g, I_h, and I_i with three-bit position flags "000," "001," "010" "011," "100," "101," "110," and "111," respectively, as shown in Fig. 4.25b.

Step 4: Read 3-bit binary data from the M-sequence as the flag to indicate the position of an initially selected adjacent index.

Step 5: Read 3-bit secret data to be hidden, and then utilize them to indicate the location shift between the initially selected adjacent index and the finally selected adjacent index in the clockwise direction along Path 2, as shown in

Fig. 4.25b. Based on the shift information, we can easily locate the finally selected adjacent index.

For example, if the 3-bit binary data read from M-sequence are "100," the initially selected adjacent index of I_a is I_f. Then, if the secret data are "000," the location shift is 0 and thus the finally selected adjacent index is I_f. If the secret data are "010," the finally selected adjacent index should be I_h. If the secret data are "100," the finally selected adjacent index is I_b.

Step 6: Based on the finally selected adjacent index, we can perform the JNC encoding process to encode the current index I_a similar to the Path 1—based scheme.

Step 7: Repeat Steps 3—6 for all the indices except the indices in the seed area.

Similar to the Path 1—based scheme, the appropriate m value should also be selected by finding the case in which the resulting length of the output codestream is minimal.

4.5.3.3 The Decoding and Extraction Phases

The codestream decoding and secret data extraction are two separate tasks. The codestream decoding algorithm is open to all users to ensure that anyone who receives the codestream can reconstruct the VQ index table of the cover image. Moreover, the secret data extraction algorithm can also be publicized, since the security of secret data only depends on the initial key.

4.5.3.3.1 The Codestream Decoding Process

The codestream decoding algorithm is the same as the JNC decoding process, which can be described in detail as follows:

Input: the received codestream, the seed area, parameters m and n, the codebook size N.

Output: the VQ index table.

Step 1: When Path 1 is selected, the first 2-bit binary data are read from the codestream as the position flag to indicate the finally selected adjacent index $index_{final}$ for the current index. Similarly, if Path 2 is selected, the first 3-bit binary data are read to indicate $index_{final}$.

Step 2: The next 2-bit binary data are read from the codestream to denote the case in which the residual value d is encoded into the binary form. Here, 2-bit binary data "11," "10," "01," and "00" indicate Cases 1, 2, 3, and 4, respectively, as described in Table 4.15.

Step 3: The residual result d is calculated according to the following four cases:

Case 1: If the 2-bit data read in Step 2 are "11," then Case 1 described in Section 2.2 is satisfied. Therefore, the following m-bit binary data are read and then transformed into the decimal value d.

Case 2: If the 2-bit data read in Step 2 are "10," then Case 2 is indicated. Therefore, the following m-bit binary data are read and then transformed into the decimal value $-d$.

Case 3: If the 2-bit data read in Step 2 are "01," then Case 3 is indicated. The following Ceil($\log_2 N$)-bit binary data are read and then transformed into the decimal value d.

Case 4: If the 2-bit data read in Step 2 are "00," then Case 4 is indicated. The following Ceil($\log_2 N$)-bit binary data are read and then transformed into the decimal value $-d$.

Step 4: The original VQ index $index_a$ is recovered according to Eq. (4.15).

Step 5: Repeat Steps 1–4 to recover all VQ indices.

4.5.3.3.2 The Secret Data Extracting Process

Input: the received codestream, the seed area, parameters m and n, the codebook size N, the initial key.

Output: Secret data.

Step 1: According to the selected path, the corresponding M-sequence is generated using the initial key. The detailed process can be referred to the preprocessing phase.

Step 2: For each index, its finally selected adjacent index is recorded during the codestream decoding process.

Step 3: When Path 1 is selected, the following 2-bit binary data from the M-sequence are read to indicate the position of the initially selected adjacent index. When Path 2 is selected, the following 3-bit binary data from the M-sequence are read to indicate the position of the initially selected adjacent index.

Step 4: According to positions of the initially and finally selected adjacent indices, the location shift in the anticlockwise direction along the path is calculated and then transformed into the binary form as the output secret data previously hidden in the current index.

Step 5: Repeat Steps 2–4 to extract other secret data until all the indices are processed.

4.5.3.4 Experimental Results

To evaluate the performance of Wang and Lu's scheme, we compared it with another two algorithms. Six general test images, Lena, Peppers, Mandrill, Boat, Goldhill, and Jet_F16, of size 512×512 with 256 grayscales, were adopted as shown in Fig. 4.22. Five aspects of performance, i.e., the hiding capacity, the stego image quality, the bit rate of the output codestream, the transmission efficiency, and the security are discussed. In the experiment, the parameter *capacity* denoting the number of secret bits hidden in each test image with the same size is utilized to estimate the hiding capacity. The PSNR is used to evaluate the image quality. The parameter *bit_rate* defined as follows is used to estimate the compression performance of the output codestream.

$$bit\_rate = \frac{L}{P \times Q} \tag{4.16}$$

where L is the number of total bits in the output codestream and $P \times Q$ is the test image size. The unit of the parameter *bit_rate* is bpp. Besides, the parameter e is introduced to denote the transmission efficiency that represents the cost of bandwidth for transmitting the same secret data. Namely, the parameter e denotes how many bits of secret data can be carried when the output codestream of the same length is transmitted. Therefore, the parameter e is defined as:

$$e = \frac{capacity}{bit\_rate \times P \times Q} \tag{4.17}$$

where $P \times Q$ is the size of test images. Obviously, when e is higher, the transmission efficiency is also higher and the corresponding algorithm is more applicable.

To demonstrate the superiority of Wang and Lu's algorithm, we compared it with the MFCVQ-based algorithm proposed by Yang et al. [3] and the SMVQ-based algorithm proposed by Chang et al. [6]. To ensure all of them can be fairly compared, the codebook size for all the algorithms is fixed to be 512. Wang and Lu's algorithm is performed with the appropriate m values. The comparisons are shown in Table 4.16.

Based on Table 4.16, we can see that the PSNR values of Wang and Lu's scheme are much larger than those of the other two methods, which indicates that the method can obtain stego images with much higher quality. This is because in this scheme a lossless index coding method is adopted and the secret data are hidden in the position flags in the codestream. The reconstructed image based on the output codestream does not contain any secret information.

Table 4.16 also shows that, based on the same test image size, the method can evidently increase the hiding capacity. In this scheme, we nearly hide 2-bits (or 3-bits) secret data per index based on Path 1 (or Path 2), whereas the hiding capacity of other two algorithms is not more than 1 bit per index on an average. And unlike the MFCVQ-based method, there is no need to judge whether a location is fit for information hiding or not in the scheme.

In terms of bit rate, it is somewhat larger in this algorithm. That is because the 2-bit or 3-bit position flag is introduced for each index. However, when taking the three attributes (capacity, quality, and bit rate) into comprehensive consideration, Wang and Lu's scheme is more effective for its high capacity, high PSNR, and an acceptable bit rate. According to the transmission efficiency e shown in Fig. 4.27, the effectiveness of Wang and Lu's method can be further proved. The results in Fig. 4.27 show that the method can hide many more bits of secret data than other two methods if the length of the output codestream is the same. In addition, it is true that the transmission efficiency of the Path 2—based scheme is much higher than that of the Path 1—based scheme in the same case.

Finally, the security issue is discussed. Compared with the MFCVQ-based algorithm and the SMVQ-based algorithm, Wang and Lu's scheme has improved the security level because of the following two main characteristics. One is that the JNC encoding process and the secret information hiding algorithm can be publicized over the Internet and the security of secret data only depends on the unique initial key that

Table 4.16 Comparisons of Wang and Lu's, MFCVQ-Based and SMVQ-Based Schemes

Algorithm	Parameter	Lena	Peppers	Mandrill	Boat	Goldhill	Jet_F16
Wang and Lu's ($N = 512$, the initial key: 3387)	m (Path 1)	5	5	6	5	5	5
	VQ (dB)	31.216	30.561	23.887	30.038	31.231	31.608
	Stego image quality (dB)	31.216	30.561	23.887	30.038	31.231	31.608
	Capacity (Path 1)	32,004	32,004	32,004	32,004	32,004	32,004
	Bit rate (bpp, Path 1)	0.641	0.632	0.691	0.665	0.664	0.649
	m (Path 2)	5	5	6	6	6	5
	Capacity (Path 2)	47,250	47,250	47,250	47,250	47,250	47,250
	Bit rate (bpp, Path 2)	0.706	0.701	0.751	0.732	0.731	0.722
MFCVQ-based ($N = 512$, $TH = 18$)	Stego image quality (dB)	29.831	29.072	23.300	27.002	28.135	26.879
	Capacity	7512	6995	969	7155	2317	8283
	Bit rate (bpp)	0.424	0.438	0.599	0.431	0.566	0.406
SMVQ-based ($N = 512$, $N_s = 128$)	Stego image quality (dB)	28.192	28.747	21.542	26.681	27.322	28.032
	Capacity	16,129	16,129	16,129	16,129	16,129	16,129
	Bit rate (bpp)	0.44	0.44	0.44	0.44	0.44	0.44

MFCVQ, *modified fast correlation vector quantization*; SMVQ, *side match vector quantization*; VQ, *vector quantization*.

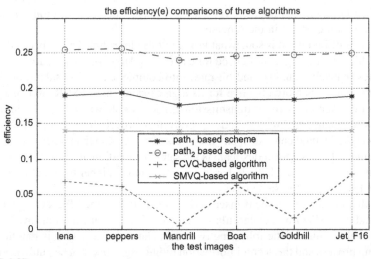

FIGURE 4.27

Transmission efficiency comparisons of Wand and Lu's, modified fast correlation vector quantization—based and side match vector quantization—based schemes.

is known to authorized users. The other is that the secret data extraction process and the cover image recovering process are separated, as shown in Fig. 4.24. These features enable all users (even malicious attackers) to reconstruct the cover image according to the received codestream using the open JNC algorithm, while only enabling the authorized users to extract secret data using the unique initial key and the publicized data extraction algorithm. Wang and Lu's algorithm enables all users to deal with the output codestream without noticing the existence of the secret data and thus improves the security, whereas the MFCVQ-based algorithm and the SMVQ-based algorithm do not possess these two features. Obviously, the excellent characteristics can be efficiently utilized in covert communication systems. To hide secret data, a content-related cover image, which maybe represents the opposite meaning, is used to transmit the secret data. As a result, when a certain segment of data are intercepted by a malicious eavesdropper, based on the given decoder, a cover image carrying the opposite information can be reconstructed to mislead the malicious eavesdropper and consequently conceal the real content of secret data.

Experimental results demonstrate that Wang and Lu's scheme achieves several improvements: (1) to achieve a higher PSNR and a higher information hiding capacity compared with the algorithms proposed by Yang et al. and Chang et al., respectively; (2) to realize the desired separation of the secret data extraction process and the cover image recovering process; and (3) to meet the desired requirement of algorithm openness by adopting the JNC algorithm and the proposed secret information hiding algorithm. In addition, it is important that a path optional scheme be offered to users who can choose an appropriate path based on various actual requirements.

4.5.4 DIFFERENCE CODING–BASED SCHEME

The main shortcomings of SMVQ and MFCVQ-based schemes are low hiding capacity and low stego image quality. To partially solve these problems, Chu et al. proposes a novel lossless information hiding scheme for VQ-compressed images by performing a special difference coding operation on the VQ indices [12]. During the hiding process, the difference between the current index and its neighboring ones is computed and encoded based on four cases in view of the current watermark bits to be embedded. In the decoding phase, not only the original watermark bits but also the original indices can be losslessly recovered if the codestream of the stego image is under no attacks. This scheme includes two opposite processes, i.e., hiding and extracting processes, which can be described in detail as follows.

4.5.4.1 The Hiding Process

In this subsection, we provide Chu et al.'s hiding process. Based on a pretrained codebook, we first perform the VQ compression operation on the original image blocks to generate the corresponding index table and then hide secret bits based on the obtained index table. The VQ indices located in the first row and the leftmost and rightmost columns of the index table remain unchanged during the hiding process, i.e., no secret bits are hidden in these locations. This unchanged special area is called the seed area. Chu et al.'s hiding process is started from the VQ index located in the second row and the second column to the index located in the last row and the second last column. Assuming that the input image is of size $R \times R$ and the block size is 4×4, the detailed process can be illustrated as follows:

> Step 1: Offline step. The mean value $V_i = (c_{i1} + c_{i2} + ... + c_{ik})/k$ of each code-word $c_i(i = 0, 1, ..., N - 1)$ is computed and all the codewords in the codebook are sorted in the ascending order of their mean values. The purpose of this offline step is to make neighboring codewords in the sorted codebook C close to each other. Therefore, the difference values between two neighboring VQ indices are relatively small.
>
> Step 2: VQ index table generation. The input original image is segmented into nonoverlapping 4×4 blocks to form input vectors, and then each input vector is encoded based on the sorted codebook C to obtain its corresponding index. Thus a $(R/4) \times (R/4)$-sized index table can be generated. Obviously, the index table is an $(R/4) \times (R/4)$-sized matrix with elements $p_{i,j}$, where $i = 0, 1, ..., (R/4) - 1$ and $j = 0,1, ..., (R/4) - 1$.
>
> Step 3: Index difference calculation. According to the secret bits, the residual value of the current index is calculated based on the following rule. The secret bits can be hidden into a new code stream by encoding the difference value d between the current VQ index $p_{i,j}$ and an optional neighboring VQ index, $p_{i-1,j-1}, p_{i-1,j}, p_{i,j-1},$ or $p_{i-1,j+1}$. During the hiding process, two secret bits are hidden in the current VQ index $p_{i,j}$ at a time. If the two secret bits to be hidden are "00," d is defined as the difference between the left neighboring index $p_{i,j-1}$ and the current index $p_{i,j}$, i.e., $d = p_{i,j-1} - p_{i,j}$. If the 2 bits to be hidden are "01," d is defined as the difference between the upper left index $p_{i-1,j-1}$ and $p_{i,j}$, i.e., $d = p_{i-1,j-1} - p_{i,j}$. If the 2 bits to be hidden are "10," d is defined as the difference between the upper neighboring index $p_{i-1,j}$ and $p_{i,j}$, i.e., $d = p_{i-1,j} - p_{i,j}$. Similarly, if the 2 bits to be hidden are "11," d is defined as $d = p_{i-1,j+1} - p_{i,j}$.
>
> Step 4: Difference coding. According to the distribution of difference values, an appropriate integer m is chosen to record the number of bits required to represent each difference value. Namely, the difference d can be denoted as the binary form $(d)_2 = a_0a_1...a_{m-1}$, where $a_i \in \{0, 1\}$. Since Chu et al.'s hiding process is affected by the amplitude range of the difference values, which depends on the image content, various amplitudes should be represented with various numbers of bits. Obviously, the amplitude of the absolute difference value s from 0 to $N - 1$, thus m ranges from 1 to Ceil($\log_2 N$), where Ceil(z) is a function to get the smallest integer not less than z.
>
> Step 5: Codestream generation. According to the obtained difference and the chosen m, the hiding process is performed based on the following rule: if $0 < d < 2^m - 1$, $p_{i,j}$ is encoded as $001||(d)_2, 011||(d)_2, 101||(d)_2,$ or $111||(d)_2$ to represent hiding the secret bits 00,01,10, or 11, respectively, where $||$ denotes the concatenation operation. If $-(2^m - 1) < d < 0$, $p_{i,j}$ is encoded as $000||(d)_2,$

$010||(d)_2, 100||(d)_2$, or $110||(d)_2$ to represent hiding the secret bits 00,01,10, or 11, respectively. If $d = 0$, $p_{i,j}$ is encoded as $001||(d)_2$, $011||(d)_2, 101||(d)_2$, or $111||(d)_2$, where $(d)_2$ equals m bits of "0" (000...0), to represent hiding the secret bits 00,01,10, or 11, respectively. If $|d| > 2^m - 1$, $p_{i,j}$ is encoded as $000||00...0||(p_{i,j})_2$, $010||00...0||(p_{i,j})_2$, $100||00...0||(p_{i,j})_2$, or $110||00...0||(p_{i,j})_2$, to represent hiding the secret bits 00,01,10, or 11, respectively, where $(p_{i,j})_2 = g_0 g_1...g_{\log_2 N-1}$ $(g_i \in \{0, 1\}, 0 \le i \le \log_2 N - 1)$, and there are m bits of "0" in the middle part. Obviously, if the difference values satisfy the first two cases (called normal case) and the third case (called zero case), m bits are required to represent $(d)_2$. Thus $(3 + m)$ bits are required to form a new codestream for each case. If the difference values satisfy the last case (called special case), Ceil($\log_2 N$) bits are required to represent $(p_{i,j})_2$, thus $(3 + m + \text{Ceil}(\log_2 N))$ bits are concatenated to form a new codestream for this case.

4.5.4.2 The Extracting Process

Chu et al.'s extracting process is just the opposite process of the hiding process, and this process can recover the original VQ-compressed image. That is, Chu et al.'s extracting process is a lossless process. Assume we have the stego VQ-compressed image whose binary codestream is possibly hidden with secret bits, and then we can extract the secret bits and recover the VQ index table by following steps:

Step 1: $(3 + m)$ bits are read from the bitstream and stored into a register p.
Step 2: p's first 2 bits are directly extracted to be the two secret bits.
Step 3: If p's last m bits are all 0 and p's third bit is 1, then the following cases are judged: If the secret bits are "00," then the original VQ index is recovered as $p_{i,j} = p_{i,j-1}$; else if the secret bits are "01," then the original VQ index is recovered as $p_{i,j} = p_{i-1,j-1}$; if the secret bits are "10," then the original VQ index is recovered as $p_{i,j} = p_{i-1,j}$; else the original VQ index is recovered as $p_{i,j} = p_{i-1,j+1}$. Go to Step 6.
Step 4: If p's last m bits are all 0 and p's third bit is 0, then we read the next $\lceil \log_2^N \rceil$ bits into a temporary register q_2 from the code stream and convert q_2 into the decimal value q; then the recovered VQ index is computed by $p_{i,j} = q$. Go to Step 6.
Step 5: If p's last m bits are not all 0, then we compute the p's last m bits as the difference value d_2 and convert d_2 into the decimal value d. If p's third bit is 0, then we set $d = -d$. The following cases are judged: If the secret bits are "00," then the VQ index is recovered as $p_{i,j} = p_{i,j-1} - d$; else if the secret bits are "01," then $p_{i,j} = p_{i-1,j-1} - d$; if the secret bits are "10," then $p_{i,j} = p_{i-1,j} - d$; else $p_{i,j} = p_{i-1,j+1} - d$. Go to Step 6.
Step 6: Repeat Steps −5 until all the codestream are read.

4.5.4.3 Experimental Results

To evaluate performance of Chu et al.'s scheme, three 256 grayscale images (Lena, Pepper, and Baboon) of size 512×512 are adopted as test images, and then Chu et al.'s algorithm is compared with the MFCVQ-based algorithm proposed by Yang et al. [3] and the SMVQ-based algorithm proposed by Chang et al. [6]. The codebook C of size 512 is pregenerated before hiding. To measure the performance of a lossless information hiding algorithm, we choose three parameters: payload capacity representing the maximal amount of information can be hidden, the PSNR representing the quality of the image with hidden data, and the bit rate representing the number of bits required to transmit during the lossless process in the experiment.

In Chu et al.'s algorithm, we should first choose an appropriate integer m to make the number of transmitted bits as less as possible. Namely, we should make the bit rate as less as possible. The results are shown in Table 4.17 for the test image Lena. From this table, we can see that we should select $m = 6$ for the test image Lena.

To show the superiority of Chu et al.'s algorithm, we compare it with the MFCVQ-based algorithm and the SMVQ-based algorithm. The results are shown in Table 4.18. Obviously, Chu et al.'s algorithm uses the ordinary VQ and actually hides the secret bits into a new codestream, and therefore the quality of the stego image is better than that generated by the algorithms in Refs. [3,6]. From the performance in hiding capacity, we can see that Chu et al.'s algorithm outperforms the other two algorithms, which makes Chu et al.'s algorithm have more application foreground. In view of the bit rate, Chu et al.'s algorithm is a little worse than other algorithms; however if we take both the capacity and bit rate into account, the performance of Chu et al.'s algorithm is much better.

From this, we can conclude that the lossless information hiding scheme based on the difference coding of VQ indices has a higher greater role in the stego image's quality and hiding capacity, thus it will have a wider application area.

Table 4.17 The Performance of the Test Image Lena

m	2	3	4	5	6	7	8	9
bpp	0.744	0.740	0.703	0.670	0.654	0.654	0.666	0.727
Blocks in normal case	1086	2949	5787	8526	10,767	12,511	13,928	13,928
Blocks in zero case	1948	1948	1948	1948	1948	1948	1948	1948
Blocks in special case	12,842	10,979	8141	5402	3161	1417	0	0

Table 4.18 Comparison Results Among Chu et al.'s and Existing Algorithms

Algorithm	Parameter	Lena	Pepper	Baboo
Chu et al.'s scheme ($m = 6$)	PSNR	31.2804	30.6384	23.8881
	Capacity	31,752	31,752	31,752
	Bit rate (bpp)	0.6535	0.6246	0.7392
SMVQ-based scheme ($N_s = 128$)	PSNR	28.1923	28.7471	21.5422
	Capacity	13,487	13,984	8794
	Bit rate (bpp)	0.539	0.528	0.692
MFCVQ-based scheme ($TH = 18$)	PSNR	29.8311	29.0723	23.2998
	Capacity	7512	6995	969
	Bit rate (bpp)	0.424	0.438	0.599

MFCVQ, *modified fast correlation vector quantization;* PSNR, *peak signal-to noise ratio;* SMVQ, *side match vector quantization.*

4.5.5 IMPROVED JOINT NEIGHBORING CODING–BASED SCHEME

From the previous sections, we can see that MFCVQ, SMVQ, and JNC-based information hiding methods do not embed secret bits in the seed area. Furthermore, they perform the information hiding process in embeddable blocks one by one. In order to embed more secret bits, Lu et al.' presented an IJNC scheme [13]. In this scheme, the first strategy is to cancel the seed area and make all blocks embeddable. To reduce the coding bit rate, the second strategy is to perform the index coding process on each 2×2 index block rather than one by one. The main idea of the IJNC scheme is to first vector-quantize the cover image, obtaining an index table, and then divide the index table into nonoverlapping 2×2 index blocks. Finally, we encode the indices in each 2×2 index block according to four input secret bits and the dynamic range is evaluated by the difference between the maximal index value and the minimal index value in the index block. The IJNC algorithm consists of three stages, i.e., the VQ encoding stage, the information hiding and index coding stage, and the data extraction and decoding stage, which can be illustrated as follows.

4.5.5.1 The Vector Quantization Encoding Stage
This stage is a preprocessing stage before information hiding and index coding. The aim of this stage is to obtain the index table for later use. Given a $P \times Q$-sized 256 grayscale host image I and the codebook C with N 16-dimensional codewords c_i, $i = 0, 1, \ldots, 511$ (here, we adopt $k = 4 \times 4$ and $N = 512$), this stage can be expressed as follows:

Step 1: For each codeword c_i, compute its sum value by
$s_i = c_{i1} + c_{i2} + \ldots + c_{i16}$, $i = 0, 1, \ldots, 511$.
Step 2: Sort the codebook C according to s_i in the ascending order,
$s_0 \le s_1 \le \cdots \le s_{511}$, obtaining the sorted codebook C_s.

Step 3: The original cover image I is divided into nonoverlapping 4×4-sized blocks $b_{i,j}$, $i = 0, 1, ..., P/4 - 1, j = 0,1,...,Q/4 - 1$.

Step 4: Encode each image block $b_{i,j}$ with the sorted codebook C_s, obtaining the index of its best matched codeword, $p_{i,j}$. All these indices compose the index table $\mathbf{P} = \{p_{i,j} \,|i = 0,1,...,P/4 - 1; j = 0,1,...,Q/4 - 1\}$.

4.5.5.2 The Information Hiding and Index Coding Stage

With the index table $\mathbf{P}$ in hand, now we can introduce IJNC-based lossless information hiding and index coding algorithm. Before embedding, we perform the permutation operation on the secret bit sequence to enhance the security. The IJNC embedding method is performed not index by index but on each 2×2 index block to make full use of the correlation between neighboring indices, and thus the encoding bit rate can be reduced. Assume the index table $\mathbf{P}$ is segmented into nonoverlapping 2×2 index blocks, $q_{h,l}$, $h = 0,1,...,P/8 - 1$; $l = 0,1,...,Q/8 - 1$. Here, $q_{h,l} = \{p_{2h,2l}, p_{2h,2l+1}, p_{2h+1,2l}, p_{2h+1,2l+1}\}$, and we adopt $\{$"00," "01," "10," "11"$\}$ to denote their locations accordingly. For each 2×2 index block $q_{h,l}$, assume the corresponding four secret bits to be embedded are $\{w_1, w_2, w_3, w_4\}$; the information hiding and index coding process can be illustrated in detail as follows.

Step 1: Find the maximal and minimal indices $p_{\max}$ and $p_{\min}$ in $q_{h,l}$, and record their location bits $w_{\max} \in \{$"00," "01," "10," "11"$\}$ and $w_{\min} \in \{$"00," "01," "10," "11"$\}$.

Step 2: Calculate the dynamic range $r = p_{max} - p_{min}$. For $N = 512$, based on the dynamic range r, consider eight cases as shown in Table 4.19. Obviously, it requires 3 bits to denote each case. Append these 3 bits (they are called range bits w_{ran} in this chapter) to the codestream. (If $N = 256$, we may consider four cases, and thus each case requires 2 bits.)

Step 3: Viewing the first two secret bits w_1 and w_2 as the location bits, find the reference index p_{ref} in $q_{m,n}$ (e.g., if the first two secret bits are "01," then $p_{ref} = p_{2h,2l+1}$). Append the two secret bits $w_{ref} = w_1\|w_2$ (they are called reference location bits) followed by the 9 bits $(p_{ref})_2$ (since the codebook size $N = 512$) to the codestream. Here, $\|$ denotes the concatenation operation, and $(\ )_2$ denotes the operation to get the binary description of a number.

Step 4: According to the third secret bit w_3, select the comparison index p_{com} out of $\{p_{\max}, p_{\min}\}$. If $w_3 = 1$, then set $p_{com} = p_{\max}$ and $w_{com} = w_{\max}$; Otherwise, if $w_3 = 0$, then set $p_{com} = p_{\min}$ and $w_{com} = w_{\min}$. Here we should consider two cases. In Case 1, the reference index and the comparison index are located at the same position, i.e., $p_{ref} = p_{com}$ and $w_{ref} = w_{com}$. Denote the remainder three indices in $q_{h,l}$ as p_A, p_B, and p_C (in the raster-scan order). In Case 2, the reference index and the comparison index are located at different positions, i.e., $w_{ref} \neq w_{com}$. Except for p_{com}, define $p_A = p_{ref}$ and denote the remainder two indices in $q_{h,l}$ as p_B and p_C (in the raster-scan order). Append the third secret bit w_3 followed by the two comparison location bits w_{com} to the codestream.

Table 4.19 Eight Cases Considered for Coding the Index Differences ($N = 512$)

Case	Dynamic Range r $= p_{max} - p_{min}$	Range Bits w_{ran}	m (Number of Bits Required to Code Each Difference)
Case 1	$0 \leq r < 2$	"000"	1
Case 2	$2 \leq r < 4$	"001"	2
Case 3	$4 \leq r < 8$	"010"	3
Case 4	$8 \leq r < 16$	"011"	4
Case 5	$16 \leq r < 32$	"100"	5
Case 6	$32 \leq r < 64$	"101"	6
Case 7	$64 \leq r < 128$	"110"	7
Case 8	$r \geq 128$	"111"	9

Step 5: According to the secret bits w_3 and w_4, calculate the differences among p_{com}, p_A, p_B, and p_C. If $w_4 = 0$ and $w_3 = 0$, then $d_A = p_A - p_{com}$, $d_B = p_B - p_{com}$, and $d_C = p_C - p_{com}$. If $w_4 = 0$ and $w_3 = 1$, then $d_A = p_{com} - p_A$, $d_B = p_{com} - p_B$, and $d_C = p_{com} - p_C$. If $w_4 = 1$ and $w_3 = 0$, then $d_A = p_{com} - p_A$, $d_B = p_{com} - p_B$, and $d_C = p_{com} - p_C$. If $w_4 = 1$ and $w_3 = 1$, then $d_A = p_A - p_{com}$, $d_B = p_B - p_{com}$, $d_C = p_C - p_{com}$. We easily find that w_4 can indicate the sign of the differences, i.e., if $w_4 = 0$, the sign is positive; otherwise, the sign is negative.

Step 6: According to the dynamic range r given in Table 4.19 look up the number of bits (it is denoted by m) required to encode each difference. If $w_4 = 0$, $3m$ bits are used to denote $(d_A)_2$, $(d_B)_2$, and $(d_C)_2$. Otherwise, if $w_4 = 1$, $3m$ bits are used to denote $(-d_A)_2$, $(-d_B)_2$, and $(-d_C)_2$. Append the fourth secret bit w_4 followed by the $3m$ bits of d_A, d_B, and d_C to the codestream.

Perform Steps 1–6 for each 2×2 index block $q_{h,l}$; we can hide 4 bits in each index block and output a bit string of length $18 + 3m$, as given in Fig. 4.28. Here, m is different from block to block. If most of the index blocks are with $m < 6$, then the bit rate can be reduced compared to the original index table that requires 36 bits to denote four indices in each index block ($N = 512$). An index coding and information hiding example for a typical 2×2 index block is shown in Fig. 4.29.

4.5.5.3 The Decoding and Extracting Stage

The IJNC-based information hiding scheme is lossless because we can recover the original index table after data extraction, and thus the original VQ-compressed image can be losslessly recovered. The input is the IJNC codestream, and the purpose is to extract the secret bit sequence and recover the original VQ-compressed image.

Three range bits w_{ran}	Two reference location bits $w_{ref}=w_1\|w_2$	9-bit reference index p_{ref}	The third secret bit w_3	Two comparison location bits w_{com}	The fourth secret bit w_4	$3m$ bits for coding d_A, d_B and d_C

FIGURE 4.28

The bit string structure for encoding each index block ($N = 512$).

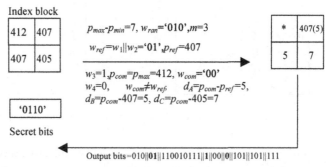

Index block

412	407
407	405

$p_{max}\text{-}p_{min}=7$, $w_{ran}=$'010', $m=3$

$w_{ref}=w_1\|w_2=$'01', $p_{ref}=407$

$w_3=1$, $p_{com}=p_{max}=412$, $w_{com}=$'00'
$w_4=0$, $w_{com}\neq w_{ref}$ $d_A=p_{com}\text{-}p_{ref}=5$,
$d_B=p_{com}\text{-}407=5$, $d_C=p_{com}\text{-}405=7$

*	407(5)
5	7

'0110'

Secret bits

Output bits=010‖01‖110010111‖1‖00‖0‖101‖101‖111

FIGURE 4.29

A detailed example to hide 4 bits and encode an index block.

Assume $N = 512$, the detailed decoding and extracting process can be described as follows.

Step 1: Read the next 3 bits into w_{ran} from the codestream, find the corresponding case in Table 4.19, and look up the value m in Table 4.19.

Step 2: Read the next 11 bits from the codestream. Get the first 2 bits w_1 and w_2 as the reference location bits w_{ref}, append them to the output secret bit sequence. Transform the last 9 bits into the reference index p_{ref}, and put this index in the current index block according to the location bits w_{ref}.

Step 3: Read the next 3 bits from the codestream. Get the first bit w_3, append it to the output secret bit sequence. Get the last 2 bits as the comparison location bits w_{com}.

Step 4: Read the next $1 + 3m$ bits from the codestream. Get the first bit w_4, append it to the output secret bit sequence. Transform the following three m bits into three positive difference values d_{A+}, d_{B+}, and d_{C+}. If $w_4 = 0$, $d_A = d_{A+}$, $d_B = d_{B+}$, and $d_C = d_{C+}$; otherwise, $d_A = -d_{A+}$, $d_B = -d_{B+}$, and $d_C = -d_{C+}$.

Step 5: Except for the reference index, recover the other three indices in the current 2×2 index block. Here, we should consider two cases:

Case 1: $w_{ref} = w_{com}$. In this case, the reference index is just the comparison index, and thus $p_{com} = p_{ref}$. If $w_4 = 0$ and $w_3 = 0$, then $p_A = d_A + p_{com}$, $p_B = d_B + p_{com}$, and $p_C = d_C + p_{com}$. If $w_4 = 0$ and $w_3 = 1$, then $p_A = p_{com} - d_A$, $p_B = p_{com} - d_B$, and $p_C = p_{com} - d_C$. If $w_4 = 1$ and $w_3 = 0$, then $p_A = p_{com} - d_A$, $p_B = p_{com} - d_B$, and $p_C = p_{com} - d_C$. If $w_4 = 1$ and $w_3 = 1$, then $p_A = d_A + p_{com}$, $p_B = d_B + p_{com}$, and $p_C = d_C + p_{com}$. Put p_A, p_B, and p_C at the remainder three locations in the raster-scan order.

Case 2: $w_{ref} \neq w_{com}$. In this case, p_A is the difference between p_{com} and p_{ref}. If $w_4 = 0$ and $w_3 = 0$, then $p_{com} = d_A - p_{ref}$. If $w_4 = 0$ and $w_3 = 1$, then $p_{com} = p_{ref} + d_A$. If $w_4 = 1$ and $w_3 = 0$, then $p_{com} = p_{ref} + d_A$. If $w_4 = 1$ and $w_3 = 1$, then $p_{com} = d_A - p_{ref}$. Put p_{com} in the current 2×2 index block according to the location bits w_{com}. Now turn to recover left two indices. If $w_4 = 0$ and $w_3 = 0$, then $p_B = d_B + p_{com}$ and $p_C = d_C + p_{com}$. If $w_4 = 0$ and $w_3 = 1$, then $p_B = p_{com} - d_B$ and $p_C = p_{com} - d_C$. If $w_4 = 1$ and $w_3 = 0$, then $p_B = p_{com} - d_B$ and $p_C = p_{com} - d_C$. If $w_4 = 1$ and $w_3 = 1$, then $p_B = d_B + p_{com}$ and $p_C = d_C + p_{com}$. Put p_B and p_C at the remainder two locations in the raster-scan order.

Repeatedly perform Steps 1–5 for all 2×2 index blocks; we can recover the original VQ index table and output the whole secret bit sequence. Fig. 4.30 gives an example to show the decoding and data extraction process for an index block. According to the restored VQ indices and the sorted codebook, we can reconstruct the original VQ-compressed image. In this way, the whole lossless process is realized.

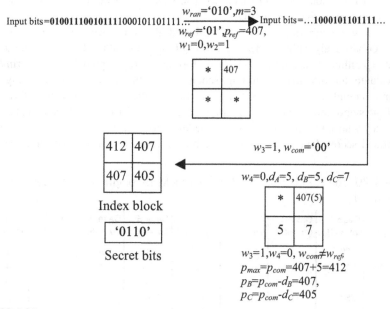

FIGURE 4.30

A detailed example to extract secret data and decode an index block.

4.5.4.4 Experimental Results

To evaluate the IJNC-based scheme, we use six test images, Lena, Peppers, Mandrill, Boat, Goldhill, and Jet_F16, of the same size 512×512 with 256 gray-scales. The 512-sized master codebook C is generated by the LBG algorithm based on two training images, Lena and Peppers, where the dimension of each codeword is 4×4. Comparisons among the IJNC-based algorithm, the MFCVQ-based algorithm [13], the SMVQ-based algorithm [17], and the JNC-based algorithm [19] are performed. For SMVQ, we set the state codebook size to be 128. For MFCVQ, we set the threshold to be 324 (in this chapter we use the squared Euclidean distance; if the normal Euclidean distance is used then the threshold is 18). For JNC, we adopt $m = 6$ as given in Ref. [19].

To show the distribution of 2×2 index blocks for different images, Table 4.20 lists the number of index blocks belonging to each case of Table 4.19. Because the total number of bits required to encode an index block based on the IJNC-based algorithm is $18 + 3m$, whereas the number of bits required to encode four indices based on the BVQ ($N = 512$) is 36; to reduce the bit rate, we expect to have $18 + 3m \leq 36$, i.e., $m \leq 6$, for most index blocks. From Table 4.20, we can see that, for all images except for the Mandrill image, most index blocks belong to the first 6 cases, thus the IJNC-based scheme can reduce the bit rate as shown in Table 4.21. The Mandrill image is very complex with high detail and is outside the training set, which makes the variation of indices in most index blocks to be large, and thus most index blocks belong to Case 7 and the bit rate is somewhat larger than that of the normal VQ.

To show the superiority of the IJNC-based algorithm, we compare it with the MFCVQ-based algorithm [13], the SMVQ-based algorithm [17], and the JNC-based algorithm [19]. Four aspects of performance are adopted in the experiments to evaluate an information hiding scheme, i.e., the capacity representing the maximum number of secret bits that can be hidden, the PSNR representing the quality of the stego image, the bit rate representing the performance of the compression efficiency whose unit is bpp, and the embedding efficiency indicating the number of embedded secret data when a bit of the binary code stream has been transmitted.

Table 4.20 The Number of 2×2 Index Blocks Belonging to Each Case in Table 4.19

Image	Case 1 ($m = 1$)	Case 2 ($m = 2$)	Case 3 ($m = 3$)	Case 4 ($m = 4$)	Case 5 ($m = 5$)	Case 6 ($m = 6$)	Case 7 ($m = 7$)	Case 8 ($m = 9$)
Lena	162	51	362	782	890	738	622	489
Peppers	211	147	376	756	928	599	505	574
Mandrill	2	2	55	216	597	1216	1502	506
Boat	283	70	217	698	887	843	638	460
Glodhill	227	42	140	474	1010	1189	812	202
Jet_F16	678	286	638	512	402	438	591	551

Table 4.21 Comparisons of IJNC-Based, MFCVQ-Based, SMVQ-Based, and JNC-Based Algorithms

Algorithm	Performance	Lena	Peppers	Mandrill	Boat	Goldhill	Jet_F16
VQ ($N = 512$)	PSNR (dB)	30.860	30.428	22.070	28.184	29.618	28.014
	Bit rate (bpp)	0.563	0.563	0.563	0.563	0.563	0.563
IJNC-based ($N = 512$)	PSNR (dB)	30.860	30.428	22.070	28.184	29.618	28.014
	Capacity	16,384	16,384	16,384	16,384	16,384	16,384
	Bit rate (bpp)	0.534	0.528	0.583	0.532	0.537	0.498
	Efficiency	0.117	0.118	0.107	0.117	0.116	0.126
JNC-based ($N = 512$, $m = 6$)	PSNR (dB)	30.860	30.428	22.070	28.184	29.618	28.014
	Capacity	16,129	16,129	16,129	16,129	16,129	16,129
	Bit rate (bpp)	0.574	0.573	0.606	0.567	0.567	0.572
	Efficiency	0.107	0.107	0.102	0.109	0.109	0.108
MFCVQ-based ($N = 512$, $TH = 324$)	PSNR (dB)	28.443	28.139	21.412	26.148	27.823	26.079
	Capacity	7435	6875	957	7107	2304	8175
	Bit rate (bpp)	0.425	0.440	0.599	0.434	0.563	0.406
	Efficiency	0.067	0.059	0.006	0.062	0.016	0.076
SMVQ-based ($N = 512$, $N_s = 128$)	PSNR (dB)	28.192	27.947	21.042	25.881	27.422	25.832
	Capacity	16,129	16,129	16,129	16,129	16,129	16,129
	Bit rate (bpp)	0.44	0.44	0.44	0.44	0.44	0.44
	Efficiency	0.140	0.140	0.140	0.140	0.140	0.140

IJNC, *improved joint neighboring coding;* JNC, *joint neighboring coding;* MFCVQ, *modified fast correlation vector quantization;* PSNR, *peak signal-to-noise ratio;* SMVQ, *side match vector quantization;* VQ, *vector quantization.*

Obviously, the embedding efficiency can be calculated as capacity/(bit rate $\times P \times Q$). Because the VQ codebook is generated from the Lena and Peppers images, their PSNRs based on any scheme are much higher than those of other test images outside the training set. Because the Mandrill image is a high-detail image outside the training set, its encoding quality is far worse than any other image. As shown in Table 4.21, the PSNRs of stego images in the IJNC-based scheme and the JNC-based method are exactly equal to those of the original VQ-compressed images; the reason is that the IJNC-based scheme and the JNC-based scheme reversibly hide data during the coding of the VQ index table and no distortions are introduced in the index coding and information hiding process. The MFCVQ-based and SMVQ-based methods reversibly hide data during the VQ encoding, no operations are performed on the consequent VQ-index coding process, and their reversibility means that they can recover the original MFCVQ-encoded image and the SMVQ-encoded image, respectively. However, the MFCVQ- and SMVQ-based encoding methods obtain worse image quality by around 2 dB, although they obtain relatively lower bit rates.

With respect to the embedding capacity, the IJNC-based scheme achieves the highest embedding capacity. Compared with the SMVQ-based scheme and the

JNC-based scheme, the IJNC-based scheme embeds information in all indices without the seed area, so we can embed 255 more bits in the index table. The IJNC-based scheme achieves significantly better embedding capacity compared with the MFCVQ-based method. The embedding capacity of the MFCVQ-based method is quite low because this method just embeds the secret data into smooth image blocks outside the seed area.

With regard to the bit rate, from Table 4.21, we can see that the MFCVQ- and SMVQ-based methods obtain relatively lower bit rates, whereas the IJNC-based scheme and the JNC-based scheme achieve relatively higher bit rates. This is because the MFCVQ scheme only uses 3 bits to encode one embeddable VQ-compressed index, whereas the SMVQ only uses 7 bits ($N_s = 128$) to denote each index outside the seed area. Anyhow, compared with the ordinary VQ, the IJNC-based scheme not only can hide information but also can compress indices, because the IJNC-based scheme can get lower bit rates by around 0.02 bpp for most images except the Mandrill image. Compared with the JNC-based scheme, the IJNC-based scheme can achieve lower bit rates for all test images by around 0.04 bpp.

In terms of embedding efficiency, the SMVQ-based scheme has the highest efficiency values, and the MFCVQ-based method has the lowest efficiency values. This means that the SMVQ can transmit the most number of embedded secret data when a bit of the binary code stream has been transmitted, whereas the MFCVQ-based method can transmit the least number of embedded secret data. The IJNC-based scheme has the second highest efficiency values, which are higher than those of the JNC-based scheme by around 0.01.

With regard to the embedding and extracting speed, because the IJNC-based scheme and the JNC-based scheme are based on the index table, if we ignore the VQ encoding process, the IJNC-based scheme and the JNC-based scheme are much faster than the MFCVQ-based and SMVQ-based schemes. Taking the aforementioned five attributes into comprehensive consideration, the IJNC-based scheme is a more effective method for its high capacity, high PSNR, high embedding efficiency, and low bit rate.

From this discussion, we can conclude that the main features of the IJNC-based scheme are as follows: (1) The IJNC-based scheme can obtain the same PSNR values as the JNC-based scheme. (2) The IJNC-based scheme does not need the seed area, so it can achieve higher information hiding capacity compared with other algorithms that require the seed area. (3) The IJNC-based scheme is based on 2×2 index blocks, which can make full use of the correlation between indices, thus it can reduce the bit rate compared with the ordinary VQ. (4) The IJNC-based scheme is separated into the VQ encoding process for generating the index table and the information hiding process to embed secret data into the output codestream. Obviously, the IJNC-based algorithm realizes the desired "separation of the encoder and the embedder" requirement stated in Ref. [3], which facilitates the individual processing of the encoder and the watermark embedder and the controlling of the corresponding performance.

4.5.6 LOSSLESS HIDING SCHEME FOR TWO-STAGE VECTOR QUANTIZATION COMPRESSED IMAGES

The BVQ system has a simple decoding structure but the encoding complexity is high. To release the complexity, *multistage vector quantization* (MSVQ) is introduced to divide the encoding task into successive stages, where the first stage performs a relatively crude quantization of the input vector using a small codebook. Then, a second stage quantizer operates on the error vector between the original and quantized first stage output. The quantized error vector then provides a second approximation to the original input vector thereby leading to a refined or more accurate representation of the input. A third stage quantizer may then be used to quantize the second stage error to provide a further refinement, and so on. Here, each stage generates its codebook based on the corresponding training vectors in advance. As shown in Fig. 4.31, VQ_i ($i = 1, 2,..., p$) represents the ith VQ operation. Source $S^{(0)}$ denotes the input image, and p is the total number of stages. $D^{(i)}$ ($i = 1, 2,..., p - 1$) denotes the ith version encoded image. $S^{(i)}$ ($i = 2, 3,..., p - 1$) is the residue of $S^{(i-1)}$ subtracting $D^{(i)}$. $I^{(i)}$ ($i = 1, 2,..., p$) is the ith output index table.

Compared with the traditional VQ, MSVQ is a more attractive data compression scheme with lower complexity and less encoding time due to the reduced codebook size. TSVQ with two codebooks is the simplest MSVQ. Based on TSVQ, Zhao et al. proposed a lossless information hiding scheme [15] in 2014 as illustrated in Fig. 4.32. This scheme can be divided into three stages, namely, the preprocessing stage, the data embedding stage, and the decoding and extraction stage, which can be expressed in detail as follows.

4.5.6.1 The Preprocessing Stage

The aim of this step is to obtain the cover image to be embedded with secret data. First, the two-stage codebooks, N_1-sized C_1 and N_2-sized C_2, with 4×4-dimensional codewords, are generated offline based on the TSVQ codebook generation algorithm. Second, the codewords in each VQ stage are sorted in the ascending order of their mean values to make neighboring codewords close to each other. Third, based on the sorted TSVQ codebooks, the $P \times Q$-sized original image is encoded as two $(P/4) \times (Q/4)$-sized index matrices $\mathbf{I}^{(s)}$ ($s = 1$ or two) for the first and second VQ stages, respectively. With these two-stage index tables in hand, the secret data can then be hidden by encoding $\mathbf{I}^{(s)}$ jointly to achieve a high payload

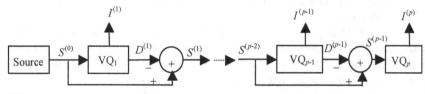

FIGURE 4.31

The flowchart of the multistage vector quantization.

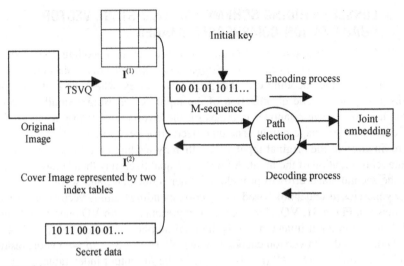

FIGURE 4.32

The flowchart of the two-stage vector quantization–based algorithm.

and obtain a more secure bitstream. The bitstream of Zhao et al.'s algorithm consists of three parts including the head information HI, the bitstream CS_1 of the first stage, and the bitstream CS_2 of the second stage. CS_1 and CS_2 are generated from the index tables $\mathbf{I}^{(1)}$ and $\mathbf{I}^{(2)}$, respectively. HI provides the basic information of the bitstream, such as the length of CS_1, the length of CS_2, the length of the secret data, the parameters m and n, and the cover image sizes.

4.5.6.2 The Data Embedding Process

For the sake of convenience, the parameter set $\{m, n\}$ is adopted, where the values of m and n have the same meaning as that in Section 4.5.3.2. Given the TSVQ codebooks, the current indices to be encoded in the index tables $\mathbf{I}^{(1)}$ and $\mathbf{I}^{(2)}$ are denoted as I_{c1} and I_{c2}, respectively. Similarly, the reference indices to predict I_{c1} and I_{c2} in the index tables $\mathbf{I}^{(1)}$ and $\mathbf{I}^{(2)}$ are denoted as I_{r1} and I_{r2}, respectively. Since the initial location bits of the indices used to predict I_{c1} and I_{c2} are the same, the term b_i is not changed and it plays the same role as that in Section 4.5.3.2. However, b_o and b_r have to be changed into $b_o^{(s)}$ and $b_r^{(s)}$, respectively, where $s = 1$ or 2. The differences between the current index and the reference index for $\mathbf{I}^{(1)}$ and $\mathbf{I}^{(2)}$ are denoted as E_1 and E_2, respectively.

Suppose an M-sequence is generated with an initial key in advance. Its length should be not less than twice the length of secret data, since Zhao et al.'s scheme needs exactly twice the length as long as that of the secret data for encoding. During the embedding stage, the input are two index tables $\mathbf{I}^{(1)}$ and $\mathbf{I}^{(2)}$, the M-sequence, and the secret data, while the output is the stego bitstream. Zhao et al.'s data embedding process can be illustrated in detail as follows.

Step 1: Parameter selection. Before embedding, $\{m, n\}$ should be appropriately selected. Here, we adopt two optional paths, namely, $n = 8$ and $n = 4$. Usually, the larger the n value is, the higher is the payload. If $n = 4$, then the topmost row and the leftmost and right-most columns in the index tables $\mathbf{I}^{(1)}$ and $\mathbf{I}^{(2)}$ are viewed as the seed area and kept unchanged. If $n = 8$, then the topmost two rows and the leftmost and rightmost two columns in the index tables $\mathbf{I}^{(1)}$ and $\mathbf{I}^{(2)}$ are viewed as the seed area and kept unchanged. Suppose r is defined as the number of bits read from the M-sequence or secret data each time. Obviously, the r value can be computed as

$$r = \log_2 n \tag{4.18}$$

That is, r is set as 2 for $n = 4$, whereas $r = 3$ for $n = 8$.

Step 2: Difference computation. From this step on, we turn to encoding the current indices I_{c1} and I_{c2} in the index tables $\mathbf{I}^{(1)}$ and $\mathbf{I}^{(2)}$, respectively. First, we get r bits from the M-sequence as the initial location bits b_i of the reference indices in the $\mathbf{I}^{(1)}$ and $\mathbf{I}^{(2)}$, respectively. Second, we get $2r$ bits from the secret data, where the first r bits are adopted as the offset bits $b_o^{(1)}$ for $\mathbf{I}^{(1)}$ and the second r bits $b_o^{(2)}$ for $\mathbf{I}^{(2)}$. Third, we compute $b_r^{(1)} = b_i + b_o^{(1)}$ for $\mathbf{I}^{(1)}$ and $b_r^{(2)} = b_i + b_o^{(2)}$ for $\mathbf{I}^{(2)}$. Fourth, according to $b_r^{(1)}$ and $b_r^{(2)}$, we find the neighboring reference indices I_{r1} and I_{r2} in $\mathbf{I}^{(1)}$ and $\mathbf{I}^{(2)}$, respectively. Finally, we compute the differences $E_1 = I_{c1} - I_{r1}$ and $E_2 = I_{c2} - I_{r2}$, respectively.

Step 3: E_2 encoding. Obviously, E_2 takes values in the interval $[-N_2 + 1, N_2 - 1]$, and there are four cases to encode E_2 into E_2' according to either Eq. (4.19) or Eq. (4.20). If $E_1 \neq 0$, we encode E_2 into

$$E_2' = \begin{cases} 11 \big\| (E_2)_2^{(m)} & \text{if } 0 \leq E_2 \leq (2^m - 1) \\ 10 \big\| (E_2)_2^{(m)} & \text{if } -(2^m - 1) \leq E_2 < 0 \\ 01 \big\| (E_2)_2^{(\lceil \log_2 N_2 \rceil)} & \text{if } E_2 > (2^m - 1) \\ 00 \big\| (-E_2)_2^{(\lceil \log_2 N_2 \rceil)} & \text{if } E_2 < -(2^m - 1) \end{cases} \tag{4.19}$$

If $E_1 = 0$, we encode E_2 as

$$E_2' = \begin{cases} (11)_2 & \text{if } 0 \leq E_2 \leq (2^m - 1) \\ (10)_2 & \text{if } -(2^m - 1) \leq E_2 < 0 \\ (01)_2 & \text{if } E_2 > (2^m - 1) \\ (00)_2 & \text{if } E_2 < -(2^m - 1) \end{cases} \tag{4.20}$$

Step 4: E_1 encoding. In this chapter, we consider five cases for E_1 encoding as follows.

Case 1: $E_1 = 0$. In this case, E_1 is not encoded in CS_1, whereas E_2 is encoded in CS_1. In the first stage of VQ, there is high correlation among the neighboring indices. Accordingly, it is reasonable that $E_1 = 0$ for most I_{c1} indices. This property can be employed to reduce the length of output bitstream. Here, we use 3 bits to encode this case as $(100)_2$. If E_2 belongs to its Case 1 or Case 2, 3 bits are used to represent the case of E_1 and m bits are used to represent E_2. Thus, the binary stream is encoded as $100||(|E_2|)_2$, where $|\bullet|$ denotes the absolute value of its element. If E_2 belongs to its Case 3 or Case 4, 3 bits are used to represent the case of E_1 and Ceil($\log_2 N_2$) bits are used to represent E_2. Thus, the binary stream is encoded as $100||(|E_2|)_2$. This case can be summarized as Eq. (4.21), where E_1' represents the encoded version of E_1, $(X)_2$ denotes the binary code of X, and A$||$B stands for the concatenation of A and B.

$$E_1' = \begin{cases} (100)_2 \left|\left| (E_2)_2^{(m)} \right.\right. & \text{if } 0 \le E_2 \le (2^m - 1) \\ (100)_2 \left|\left| (-E_2)_2^{(m)} \right.\right. & \text{if } -(2^m - 1) \le E_2 < 0 \\ (100)_2 \left|\left| (E_2)_2^{(\lceil \log_2 N_2 \rceil)} \right.\right. & \text{if } E_2 > (2^m - 1) \\ (100)_2 \left|\left| (-E_2)_2^{(\lceil \log_2 N_2 \rceil)} \right.\right. & \text{if } E_2 < -(2^m - 1) \end{cases} \qquad (4.21)$$

Cases 2–5: For $E_1 \ne 0$, we can classify E_1 into four cases and encode E_1 as follows:

$$E_1' = \begin{cases} (011)_2 \left|\left| (E_1)_2^{(m)} \right.\right. & \text{if } 0 < E_1 \le (2^m - 1) \\ (010)_2 \left|\left| (-E_1)_2^{(m)} \right.\right. & \text{if } -(2^m - 1) \le E_1 < 0 \\ (001)_2 \left|\left| (E_1)_2^{(\lceil \log_2 N_1 \rceil)} \right.\right. & \text{if } E_1 > (2^m - 1) \\ (000)_2 \left|\left| (-E_1)_2^{(\lceil \log_2 N_1 \rceil)} \right.\right. & \text{if } E_1 < -(2^m - 1) \end{cases} \qquad (4.22)$$

Step 5: CS_1 encoding. To encode CS_1, we just append E_1' to $b_r^{(1)}$. For example, assume $b_r^{(1)} = (01)_2$, $E_1 = 0$ and the case of E_2 is $(11)_2$, then the final bitstream for the current index is $01||000||(|E_2|)_2$.

Step 6: CS_2 encoding. To encode CS_2, we just append E_2' to $b_r^{(2)}$. For example, assume $b_r^{(2)} = (00)_2$, $E_1 = 0$ and the case of E_2 is $(11)_2$, then the final bitstream for the current index is $00||11$. If $E_1 \ne 0$, and the case of E_2 is $(11)_2$, then the final bitstream for the current index is $00||11||(|E_2|)_2$.

Step 7: If all secret data have been embedded or all the indices outside the seed area have been processed, we append CS_1 and CS_2 to the head information HI to obtain the final bitstream. Otherwise, we go to Step 2.

In sum, the final bitstream consists of three parts, namely, the head information of the stream, the first encoded index table (bitstream1, CS_1) and the second encoded index table (bitstream2, CS_2). The head information of the stream embodies the size of the original image, the length of the secret data, $\{m, n\}$, and the lengths of second and third parts sequentially. CS_1 is encoded as the binary form "$b_r^{(1)}\|\text{case}\|(|E_1|)_2$" or "$b_r^{(1)}\|\text{case}\|(|E_2|)_2$" depending on whether E_1 equals 0 or not. If $E_1 \neq 0$, CS_1 is encoded as the former, otherwise as the latter. CS_2 is encoded as the binary form "$b_r^{(2)}\|\text{case}\|(|E_2|)_2$" or "$b_r^{(2)}\|\text{case}$" depending on whether E_1 equals 0 or not. If $E_1 \neq 0$, CS_2 is encoded as the former, otherwise as the latter.

Here, we take a concrete example as shown in Fig. 4.33 to explain Zhao et al.'s embedding scheme. Suppose $N_1 = 16$, $N_2 = 32$, $n = 4$, and $m = 2$. At each time, we read 2 bits from the M-sequence while obtaining 4 bits from the secret data. To deal with the index $I_{c1} = $ "12" $=$ in the second row and the second column of $\mathbf{I}^{(1)}$, the four neighbors $(14)_{00}$, $(13)_{01}$, $(12)_{10}$, and $(14)_{11}$ are taken into account. At the same time, the index $I_{c2} = $ "26" in the second row and the second column of $\mathbf{I}^{(2)}$ is also processed. "00" Is first read from the M-sequence as b_i, and then four bits "1000" are obtained from the secret data, where $b_o^{(1)} = $ "10" and $b_o^{(2)} = $ "00". Then we compute $b_r^{(1)} = $ "00" $+$ "10" $=$ "10" and $b_r^{(2)} = $ "00" $+$ "00" $=$ "00" and locate the reference indices $I_{r1} = $ "12" and $I_{r2} = $ "30" respectively. Thus, we can compute $E_1 = 12 - 12 = 0$ and $E_2 = 26 - 30 = -4$. Since $E_1 = 0$, according to Eqs. (4.20) and (4.21), CS_1 and CS_2 can be encoded as $10\|100\|00,100$ and $00\|00$, respectively.

4.5.6.3 The Decoding and Extraction Process

Assume that the bitstream received by the decoder does not suffer any attack, then the original TSVQ-compressed image can be completely recovered without the aid of the input M-sequence. Here, the input is the received bitstream, which can be

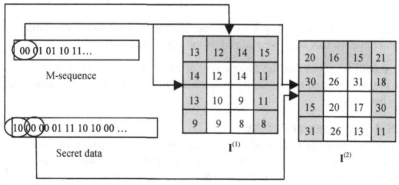

FIGURE 4.33

An example to explain the two-stage vector quantization—based data embedding scheme.

divided into three parts, namely, HI, CS_1, and CS_2, whereas the output is the two TSVQ index tables. The decoding process can be illustrated in detail as follows.

Step 1: Obtain the head information HI from the bitstream to get the cover image size, the length of CS_1, the length of CS_2, and the values of n and m.

Step 2: Input r bits from CS_1 to obtain $b_r^{(1)}$, and input r bits from CS_2 to get $b_r^{(2)}$. Based on $b_r^{(1)}$ and $b_r^{(2)}$, we obtain their corresponding indices I_{r1} and I_{r2}, respectively.

Step 3: Obtain the case information from CS_1 and CS_2, and get the difference values E_1 and E_2 from CS_1 and CS_2 based on the case information.

Step 4: Compute the current two-stage indices I_{c1} and I_{c2} as follows.

$$\begin{cases} I_{c1} = I_{r1} + E_1 \\ I_{c2} = I_{r2} + E_2 \end{cases} \tag{4.23}$$

Step 5: Perform Steps 2 to 4 over and over again until two index tables are generated.

With regard to extracting the secret data, one input is the received bitstream, which can be divided into three parts, namely, HI, CS_1, and CS_2, and the other input is the key for generating the same M-sequence as used in the embedding process, while the output is the secret data. The same key as used in the embedding process is applied to generate the M-sequence, and the secret data can be obtained as follows.

Step 1: Read the head information HI from the received bitstream.

Step 2: Input r bits of the M-sequence to obtain the initial location bits b_i.

Step 3: Input r bits of CS_1 to get $b_r^{(1)}$, and input r bits of CS_2 to obtain $b_r^{(2)}$. Then retrieve the corresponding indices I_{r1} and I_{r2}, respectively. Then, compute the offset bits $b_o^{(1)} = b_r^{(1)} - b_i$ and $b_o^{(2)} = b_r^{(2)} - b_i$. Append $b_o^{(1)}$ and $b_o^{(2)}$ to the extracted secret data.

Step 4: Perform Steps 2 and 3 over and over again until two index tables are generated. In this way, we can obtain the final secret data.

It should be noted that the complexity of Zhao et al.'s decoding and extraction stage is very low, and the decoding process and the extraction process can be absolutely detached.

4.5.6.4 Experimental Results

A set of experiments is carried out to evaluate the performance of Zhao et al.'s scheme. The performance indicators used include PSNR, payload, bit rate (bit_rate), and transmission efficiency. A higher PSNR indicates a better image quality. The bit_rate means the average number of bits required for representing one pixel. Payload stands for the maximum number of secret bits that can be embedded in the cover image. Transmission efficiency is defined as the ratio of payload to the bitstream length. For the TSVQ-based scheme (i.e., Zhao et al.'s scheme), we take $m = 2$ in comparisons with previous algorithms, namely, the path optional lossless information hiding scheme [11] and the VQIRVC-based lossless information hiding scheme [10]. The TSVQ-based algorithm adopts the codebook size $N = (32,64)$, whereas the two previous algorithms have the codebook size 512.

Based on six test images of size 512×512 as given in Fig. 4.22, Table 4.22 lists the comparison results of PSNR, payload, bit rate, and efficiency among Zhao et al.'s [15], Wang and Lu [11], and Lu et al.'s [10] schemes. From Table 4.22, we can see that Zhao et al.'s scheme can obtain larger PSNR values. Also, the payload and bit rate of Zhao et al.'s algorithm are improved to some extent. Especially, Zhao et al.'s scheme achieves the payload twice larger than Wang et al.'s scheme and nearly four times larger than Lu et al.'s scheme. From Table 4.22, we can also see that Zhao et al.'s scheme obtains higher efficiency values than Wang et al.'s and Lu et al.'s schemes for both $n = 4$ and $n = 8$. In a word, Zhao et al.'s scheme can not only improve the payload with a higher PSNR but also enhance the transmission efficiency.

From this, we can conclude that the TSVQ-based algorithm enhances the performance in three aspects. (1) Since Zhao et al.'s scheme can losslessly recover the original index tables and secret data from the bitstream, the process of encoding and decoding is lossless. (2) Given the two index tables, double payload of Wang

Table 4.22 Comparison of Zhao et al.'s, Wang et al.'s, and Lu et al.'s Schemes for Six Test Images

Scheme	N	n	Indicators	Lena	F16	Peppers	Baboon	Boat	Goldhill
Zhao et al.'s	(32,64)	4	Payload	64,008	64,008	64,008	64,008	64,008	64,008
			Bit rate	0.979	0.956	0.965	1.049	0.996	0.994
			Efficiency	0.249	0.256	0.253	0.233	0.245	0.246
		8	Payload	93,744	93,744	93,744	93,744	93,744	93,744
			Bit rate	1.093	1.067	1.079	1.151	1.105	1.108
			Efficiency	0.327	0.335	0.332	0.311	0.324	0.323
		—	PSNR_v	32.26	31.62	31.74	24.73	30.14	31.28
			PSNR_e	32.26	31.62	31.74	24.73	30.14	31.28
Wang et al.'s	512	4	Payload	32,004	32,004	32,004	32,004	32,004	32,004
			Bit rate	0.641	0.649	0.632	0.691	0.665	0.644
			Efficiency	0.188	0.173	0.181	0.188	0.163	0.173
		8	Payload	47,250	47,250	47,250	47,250	47,250	47,250
			Bit rate	0.706	0.722	0.701	0.751	0.732	0.731
			Efficiency	0.251	0.249	0.250	0.252	0.241	0.248
		—	PSNR_v	31.22	31.61	30.56	23.89	30.04	31.23
			PSNR_e	31.22	31.61	30.56	23.89	30.04	31.23
Lu et al.'s	512	—	Payload	14,954	13,588	14,784	15,662	14,785	15,104
			Bit rate	0.569	0.589	0.632	0.691	0.665	0.664
			Efficiency	0.100	0.088	0.089	0.086	0.084	0.086
			PSNR_v	31.22	31.61	30.56	23.89	30.04	31.23
			PSNR_e	31.22	31.61	30.56	23.89	30.04	31.23

PSNR, *peak signal-to-noise ratio.*

et al.'s scheme and more than four times payload of Lu et al.'s scheme can be obtained in Zhao et al.'s scheme. (3) The transmission efficiency is greatly enhanced with the strategy of embedding secret data in two index tables.

4.6 SUMMARY

This chapter discusses lossless information hiding schemes for VQ-compressed image. These schemes can be broadly classified into two categories, i.e., information hiding during VQ encoding and information hiding during VQ-index coding. The first category mainly includes MFCVQ-based and SMVQ-based schemes. The first category embeds information during VQ encoding, which can recover the VQ-compressed version after extraction of the embedded information. The second category views the index table as the cover object and embeds information during lossless index coding. In general, the schemes in the first category obtain worse stego images than index coding–based schemes. Furthermore, most of the index coding–based schemesnot only can further compress the bit rate but also can embed larger amount of secret information. In a word, index coding–based schemes perform better than the algorithms in the first category. In the second category, the TSVQ-based scheme can embed large amount of data in the cost of a bit worse stego image quality. Since VQ is not a compression standard for images, the application field of VQ-based lossless information hiding may be very limited.

REFERENCES

[1] Y. Linde, A. Buzo, R.M. Gray, An algorithm for vector quantizer design, IEEE Transactions on Communications 28 (1) (1980) 84–95.
[2] E.J. Delp, O.R. Mitchell, Image compression using block truncation coding, IEEE Transactions on Communications 27 (9) (1979) 1335–1342.
[3] B. Yang, Z.M. Lu, S.H. Sun, Lossless watermarking in the VQ-compressed domain, in: Proceedings of the 5th IASTED International Conference on Visualization, Imaging, and Image Processing(VIIP'2005), Benidorm, Spain, September 7–9, 2005, pp. 298–303.
[4] C.C. Chang, W.C. Wu, A steganographic method for hiding secret data using side match vector quantization, IEICE Transactions on Information and Systems E88-D (9) (2005) 2159–2167.
[5] C.C. Chang, T.C. Lu, Lossless index-domain information hiding scheme based on side-match vector quantization, Journal of Systems and Software 79 (8) (2006) 1120–1129.
[6] C.C. Chang, W.L. Tai, C.C. Lin, A lossless information hiding scheme based on side match vector quantization, IEEE Transactions on Circuits and Systems for Video Technology 16 (10) (2006) 1301–1308.
[7] C.C. Chang, C.Y. Lin, Lossless steganography for VQ-compressed images using side matching and relocation, IEEE Transactions on Information Forensics and Security 1 (4) (2006) 493–501.

[8] C.C. Chang, W.C. Wu, Y.C. Hu, Lossless recovery of a VQ index table with embedded secret data, Journal of Visual Communication and Image Representation 18 (3) (2007) 207–216.

[9] C.C. Chang, T.D. Kieu, W.C. Wu, A lossless data embedding technique by joint neighboring coding, Pattern Recognition 42 (7) (2009) 1597–1603.

[10] Z.M. Lu, J.X. Wang, B.B. Liu, An improved lossless information hiding scheme based on image VQ-index residual value coding, Journal of Systems and Software 82 (6) (2009) 1016–1024.

[11] J.X. Wang, Z.M. Lu, A path optional lossless information hiding scheme based on VQ joint neighboring coding, Information Sciences 179 (19) (2009) 3332–3348.

[12] D.H. Chu, Z.M. Lu, J.X. Wang, A high capacity lossless information hiding algorithm based on difference coding of VQ indices, ICIC Express Letters, Part B: Applications 3 (4) (2012) 701–706.

[13] Z.M. Lu, H. Chen, F.X. Yu, Lossless information hiding based on improved vq index joint neighboring coding, International Journal of Innovative Computing, Information and Control 9 (9) (2013) 3851–3861.

[14] J.X. Wang, J.Q. Ni, Z.M. Lu, Hybrid matrix coding and error-correction scheme for lossless information hiding in binary VQ index codestream, International Journal of Innovative Computing, Information and Control 9 (6) (2013) 2021–2031.

[15] D.-N. Zhao, W.-X. Xie, Z.-M. Lu, High efficiency lossless information hiding for two-stage vector quantization compressed images, Journal of Information Hiding and Multimedia Signal Processing 5 (4) (2014) 625–641.

[16] W.J. Chen, W.T. Huang, VQ indexes compression and information hiding using hybrid lossless index coding, Digital Signal Processing 19 (3) (2009) 433–443.

[17] Z.M. Lu, S.H. Sun, Image coding using fast correlation based VQ, Chinese Journal of Image and Graphics 5A (6) (2000) 489–492.

[18] T. Kim, Side match and overlap match vector quantizers for images, IEEE Transactions on Image Processing 1 (2) (1992) 170–185.

[19] Z.M. Lu, J.S. Pan, S.H. Sun, Image coding based on classified side-match vector quantization, IEICE Transactions on Information and Systems E83-D (12) (2000) 2189–2192.

[20] Z. Sun, Y.N. Li, Z.M. Lu, Side-match predictive vector quantization, in: Lecture Notes in Artificial Intelligence, 2005 International Workshop on Intelligent Information Hiding and Multimedia Signal Processing, September 14–16, 2005, vol. 3683, Hilton Hotel, Melbourne, Australia, August 2005, pp. 405–410.

[21] Z.M. Lu, S.H. Sun, Digital image watermarking technique based on vector quantisation, Electronics Letters 36 (4) (2000) 303–305.

[22] Z.M. Lu, J.S. Pan, S.H. Sun, VQ-based digital image watermarking method, Electronics Letters 36 (14) (2000) 1201–1202.

[23] Z.M. Lu, C.H. Liu, S.H. Sun, Digital image watermarking technique based on block truncation coding with vector quantization, Chinese Journal of Electronics 11 (2) (2002) 152–157.

[24] Y. Bao, Z.M. Lu, D.G. Xu, A tree-structured codebook partitioning technique for VQ-based image watermarking, in: The 5th International Symposium on Test and Measurement (ISTM'2003), Shenzhen, China, June 1–5, 2003, pp. 2541–2544.

[25] Z.M. Lu, W. Xing, D.G. Xu, S.H. Sun, Digital image watermarking method based on vector quantization with labeled codewords, IEICE Transactions on Information and Systems E86-D (12) (2003) 2786–2789.

[26] J. Minho, K. HyoungDo, A digital image watermarking scheme based on vector quantisation, IEICE Transactions on Information and Systems E85-D (6) (2002) 1054−1056.

[27] A. Makur, S.S. Selvi, Variable dimension vector quantization based image watermarking, Signal Processing 81 (4) (2001) 889−893.

[28] H.C. Huang, F.H. Wang, J.S. Pan, A VQ-based robust multi-watermarking algorithm, IEICE Transactions on Fundamentals E85-A (7) (2002) 1719−1726.

[29] H.C. Huang, F.H. Wang, J.S. Pan, Efficient and robust watermarking algorithm with vector quantisation, Electronics Letters 37 (13) (2001) 826−828.

[30] Z.M. Lu, D.G. Xu, S.H. Sun, Multipurpose image watermarking algorithm based on multistage vector quantization, IEEE Transactions on Image Processing 14 (6) (2005) 822−831.

[31] W. Xing, Z.M. Lu, Multipurpose image watermarking based on vector quantization in DCT domain, in: The 5th International Symposium on Test and Measurement (ISTM'2003), Shenzhen, China, June 1−5, 2003, pp. 2057−2061.

[32] C.C. Chang, Y.C. Chou, Y.P. Hsieh, Search-order coding method with indicator-elimination property, Journal of Systems and Software 82 (2009) 516−525.

[33] B. Chen, G.W. Wornell, Quantization index modulation: a class of provably good methods for digital watermarking and information embedding, IEEE Transactions on Information Theory 47 (4) (2001) 1423−1443.

[34] J. Tian, Lossless watermarking by difference expansion, in: Proceedings of Workshop on Multimedia and Security, Dec. 2002, pp. 19−22.

[35] B. Yang, M. Schmucker, W. Funk, C. Busch, S. Sun, Integer DCT-based lossless watermarking for images using companding technique, in: Proc. SPIE-EI, San Jose, USA, 2004.

[36] G. Xuan, C. Yang, Y. Zhen, Y. Shi, Z. Ni, Lossless information hiding using integer wavelet transform and companding technique, IWDW (2004).

[37] M. Thodi, J.J. Rodríguez, Lossless watermarking by prediction-error expansion, in: The 6th IEEE Southwest Symposium on Image Analysis and Interpretation, Lake Tahoe, USA, March 2004.

[38] B. Yang, M. Schmucker, X. Niu, C. Busch, S. Sun, Approaching optimal value expansion for lossless watermarking, in: ACM Multimedia and Security Workshop 2005, New York, USA, 2005.

Lossless Information Hiding in Block Truncation Coding–Compressed Images

5.1 BLOCK TRUNCATION CODING

5.1.1 ORIGINAL BLOCK TRUNCATION CODING ALGORITHM

Block truncation coding (BTC) is a simple lossy image compression technique to compress monochrome image data, originally introduced by Delp and Mitchell [1]. It achieves 2 bits per pixel (bpp) with low computational complexity. The key idea of BTC is to perform moment-preserving quantization for each nonoverlapping block of pixels so that the image quality will remain acceptable and simultaneously the demand for the storage space will decrease. The quantizer of the original algorithm of BTC retains standard arithmetic mean and standard deviation for each nonoverlapping block as 1-bit quantized output. The statistical overhead is that each block needs to keep mean and standard deviation. The BTC algorithm can be illustrated as follows:

After dividing a 256-grayscale image into blocks of size $\times n$ (typically $n = 4$), the blocks are coded individually, each into a two-level signal. The levels for each block are chosen such that the first two sample moments are preserved. Let $m = n^2$ and let $x_1, x_2, \ldots, x_m$ be the values of the pixels in a block of the original image.

Then the first moment $\bar{x}$, the second moment $\overline{x^2}$ and the variance σ^2 can be calculated as follows:

$$\bar{x} = \frac{1}{m} \sum_{i=1}^{m} x_i \tag{5.1}$$

$$\overline{x^2} = \frac{1}{m} \sum_{i=1}^{m} x_i^2 \tag{5.2}$$

$$\sigma^2 = \overline{x^2} - (\bar{x})^2 \tag{5.3}$$

Lossless Information Hiding in Images. http://dx.doi.org/10.1016/B978-0-12-812006-4.00005-X
Copyright © 2017 Zhejiang University Press Co., Ltd., published by Elsevier Inc. All rights reserved.

As with the design of any 1-bit quantizer, we find a threshold, x_{th}, and two output levels, a and b, such that

$$\begin{cases} \text{if } x_i \geq x_{th} \quad \text{output} = b \\ \text{if } x_i < x_{th} \quad \text{output} = a \end{cases} \tag{5.4}$$

In the original BTC, we set $x_{th} = \bar{x}$, then the output levels a and b are found by solving the following equations. Let $q = $ number of x_i's greater than $x_{th}(= \bar{x})$, to preserve $\bar{x}$ and $\overline{x^2}$, we have

$$\begin{cases} m\bar{x} = (m-q)a + qb \\ m\overline{x^2} = (m-q)a^2 + qb^2 \end{cases} \tag{5.5}$$

Solving for a and b:

$$\begin{cases} a = \bar{x} - \sigma\sqrt{\dfrac{q}{m-q}} \\ b = \bar{x} + \sigma\sqrt{\dfrac{m-q}{q}} \end{cases} \tag{5.6}$$

Each block is then described by the values of a, b and an $n \times n$ bitplane P consisting of 1s and 0s indicating whether the pixels are above or below x_{th}. For $n = 4$, assigning 8 bits each to a and b results in a data rate of 2 bits per pixel. The receiver reconstructs the image block by calculating a and b from Eq. (5.6) and assigning these values to pixels in accordance with the code in the bitplane. An example of coding a 4×4 image block is presented in Fig. 5.1.

From this description, we can see that, in the original BTC, for each block we have to compute the value of a and b. So it is time consuming. To overcome the this problem, Lema and Mitchell introduced the concept of absolute moment block truncation as given in the next subsection.

Original   Bitplane   Reconstructed

$$x = \begin{bmatrix} 121 & 114 & 56 & 47 \\ 37 & 200 & 247 & 255 \\ 16 & 0 & 12 & 169 \\ 43 & 5 & 7 & 251 \end{bmatrix} \quad P = \begin{bmatrix} 1 & 1 & 0 & 0 \\ 0 & 1 & 1 & 1 \\ 0 & 0 & 0 & 1 \\ 0 & 0 & 0 & 1 \end{bmatrix} \quad \hat{x} = \begin{bmatrix} 204 & 204 & 17 & 17 \\ 17 & 204 & 204 & 204 \\ 17 & 17 & 17 & 204 \\ 17 & 17 & 17 & 204 \end{bmatrix}$$

$\bar{x} = 98.75, \sigma = 92.95, q = 7$ $a = 16.7 \cong 17, b = 204.2 \cong 204$

FIGURE 5.1

Block truncation coding by the triple (a, b, P).

5.1.2 ABSOLUTE MOMENT BLOCK TRUNCATION CODING

In the original absolute moment block truncation coding (AMBTC) method, the image is first divided into blocks of size $m = 4 \times 4$. The pixels in each block are individually quantized into two-level outputs in such a way that the mean value and the first absolute central moment are preserved in the reconstructed block. The mean value of pixels in each block x is taken as the 1-bit quantizer threshold x_{th}, i.e.,

$$x_{th} = \frac{1}{m} \sum_{i=1}^{m} x_i \tag{5.7}$$

The two output quantization level values are directly calculated from

$$a = \frac{1}{m-q} \sum_{x_i \leq x_{th}} x_i \tag{5.8}$$

$$b = \frac{1}{q} \sum_{x_i > x_{th}} x_i \tag{5.9}$$

where a and b denote the lower and higher means of block x, respectively and q stands for the number of pixels having value higher than the mean value. If $q = 0$, one can define $a = b = x_{th}$. Then a two-level quantization is performed for all the pixels in the block to form a bitplane so that "0" is stored for the pixels with values not larger than the mean and the rest of the pixels are presented by "1." The image is reconstructed at the decoding phase from the bitplane by assigning the value a to "0" and b to "1." Thus a compressed block appears as a triple $(a, b, \mathbf{P})$, where a, b, and $\mathbf{P}$ denote the lower mean, the higher mean, and the bitplane, respectively. Fig. 5.2 shows an example of a compressed image block by AMBTC, and Fig. 5.3 shows the AMBTC-compressed Lena image with peak signal-to-noise ratio (PSNR) = 32.041 dB.

AMBTC is very fast, is easy to implement, and has low computational demands. It preserves the quality of the reconstructed image and retains the edges. However, in the AMBTC, the lower and higher means are coded separately with 8 bits each, and the bitplane needs 16 bits, so the bit rate of AMBTC is 2 bits/pixel. How to reduce

$$x = \begin{bmatrix} 121 & 114 & 56 & 47 \\ 37 & 200 & 247 & 255 \\ 16 & 0 & 12 & 169 \\ 43 & 5 & 7 & 251 \end{bmatrix} \quad P = \begin{bmatrix} 1 & 1 & 0 & 0 \\ 0 & 1 & 1 & 1 \\ 0 & 0 & 0 & 1 \\ 0 & 0 & 0 & 1 \end{bmatrix} \quad \hat{x} = \begin{bmatrix} 194 & 194 & 25 & 25 \\ 25 & 194 & 194 & 194 \\ 25 & 25 & 25 & 194 \\ 25 & 25 & 25 & 194 \end{bmatrix}$$

Original — Bitplane — Reconstructed

$\bar{x} = 98.75, q = 7$ $a = 24.78 \cong 25, b = 193.86 \cong 194$

FIGURE 5.2

Absolute moment block truncation coding by the triple (*a*, *b*, *P*).

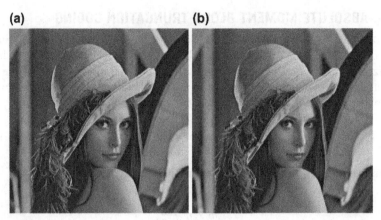

FIGURE 5.3

Absolute moment block truncation coding (AMBTC) on Lena image. (a) Original image and (b) AMBTC-reconstructed image.

the bit rate and at the same time losslessly embed secret information is our main concern in this chapter.

5.2 OVERVIEW OF BLOCK TRUNCATION CODING—BASED INFORMATION HIDING

In the 2000s, several watermarking and data hiding schemes for BTC-compressed gray-level images have been proposed. We overview them in two categories, i.e., watermarking schemes and lossless information hiding schemes.

5.2.1 OVERVIEW OF BLOCK TRUNCATION CODING—BASED IMAGE WATERMARKING

The first watermarking method [3] based on BTC was proposed by Lu et al. in 2002, where the robust watermark is embedded by modifying the vector quantization (VQ)-BTC encoding process according to the watermark bits. In 2004, Lin and Chang [4] proposed a data hiding scheme for BTC-compressed images by performing least significant bit (LSB) substitution operations on BTC high and low means and performing the minimum distortion algorithm on BTC bitplanes. In 2006, Chuang and Chang proposed a hiding scheme to embed data in the BTC bitplanes of smooth regions [5]. In 2011, Yang and Lu proposed a fragile image watermarking scheme [6] whose main idea is to apply VQ or BTC to encode each block according to the watermark bit. In the same year, Yang and Lu also proposed another blind semifragile image watermarking scheme [7] by using BTC to guide the watermark embedding and extraction processes. The central idea is to force the number of "1s" (or "0s") in each bitplane to be odd for the watermark bit "1" or to be even for the watermark bit "0." In 2012, Zhang et al. proposed an oblivious image watermarking scheme [8] by exploiting BTC bitmaps. Unlike the traditional schemes, this approach does not really perform the BTC compression on images during the embedding process but utilizes the parity of the number of horizontal edge transitions in each BTC bitmap to guide the watermark embedding and extraction processes. In the following subsections, we introduce several typical BTC-based watermarking schemes.

5.2.1.1 Chuang and Chang's Scheme

It is well known that for the smooth block x_i whose a_i and b_i are highly close, its bitplane p_i will be less significant in the AMBTC decoding process. In this case, some suitable locations in p_i may be replaced with the secret bit. Based on this idea, Chuang and Chang [5] proposed the data hiding scheme for BTC-compressed images that embeds data in the smooth blocks' bitplanes.

The embedding process can be divided into two steps. The first step segments the image into blocks and computes the quantized data for each block, and the second step embeds the secret data in the bitplanes of smooth blocks that are determined by the difference between b_i and a_i. If $b_i - a_i$ is not greater than the preset threshold TH, then the block x_i is classified as a smooth block; otherwise, the block is a complex block. The embedding method is very simple, i.e., a suitable location in the smooth block's bitplane p_i is selected to be replaced with the secret bit. The smooth blocks are selected because even after the bit replacement in their bitplanes, less distortion will be introduced in the BTC-compressed image.

The extraction process is also very simple. From each compressed BTC block, the difference $b_i - a_i$ is first calculated, and then whether the difference is less than TH or not is determined. Once confirmed, the secret bit in the bitplane p_i is extracted. One obvious drawback of Chuang and Chang's scheme is that the capacity is determined by the number of smooth blocks. In the embedding process, the threshold TH is used to select the embeddable locations. The higher the threshold value is, the more data may be hidden, but the more distortion will be introduced.

5.2.1.2 Yang and Lu's Method 1

Yang and Lu [6] proposed a very simple BTC-domain watermarking scheme. Let $\mathbf{X}$ be a 512×512-sized original image, and $\mathbf{W}$ be a 128×128-sized binary watermark, which can be viewed as a 16,384-lengthed binary string $\mathbf{W} = \{w_i, i = 1,2,\ldots,16,384\}$. The VQ codebook C contains 1024 codewords c_i, $i = 1, 2,\ldots,1024$, each being a 4×4-sized block. Their embedding procedure can be detailed as follows: the original image $\mathbf{X}$ is first divided into non-overlapping blocks of size 4×4, denoted as x_i, $i = 1, 2,\ldots,16,384$. For each image block x_i, if the watermark bit to be embedded $w_i = 1$, then VQ is used to encode the block x_i by searching its best-matched codeword c_j in the codebook C, satisfying

$$d(x_i, c_j) = \min_{1 \leq l \leq 1024} d(x_i, c_l) \tag{5.10}$$

where $d(x_i, c_l)$ denotes the Euclidean distance between the input vector x_i and the codeword c_l. If the watermark bit to be embedded $w_i = 0$, then the AMBTC is used to encode the block x_i by replacing the pixels that are not less than the mean value m_i with the high mean b_i and replacing the pixels that are smaller than the mean value m_i with the low mean a_i. Finally, all encoded image blocks are pieced together to obtain the final watermarked image $\mathbf{X}^w$.

The extraction process is just the reverse process of the embedding process. Let $\mathbf{Y}$ be a 512×512-sized suspicious image to be detected, and C contain 1024 codewords c_i, $i = 1, 2,\ldots,1024$, each being a 4×4-sized block. The extraction procedure can be described in detail as follows: the suspicious image $\mathbf{Y}$ is first divided into nonoverlapping blocks of size 4×4, denoted as y_i, $i = 1, 2,\ldots,16{,}384$. For each image block y_i, it is encoded with VQ and BTC to obtain their corresponding mean squared error (MSE) MSE_{VQ} and MSE_{BTC}, respectively. If $\mathrm{MSE}_{VQ} < \mathrm{MSE}_{BTC}$, then the extracted watermark $w_i = 1$. If $\mathrm{MSE}_{VQ} > \mathrm{MSE}_{BTC}$, then the extracted watermark bit $w_i = 0$. If $\mathrm{MSE}_{VQ} = \mathrm{MSE}_{BTC}$, then w_i is randomly set to be 0 or 1. All obtained watermark bits are pieced together to obtain the final extracted watermark $\mathbf{W}_e$.

5.2.1.3 Yang and Lu's Method 2

From the previous sections, we saw that Chuang and Chang's scheme [5] and Yang and Lu's method 1 [6] actually embed the watermark or hide the information in the BTC-compressed image or VQ-compressed image. Thus, the stego image or the watermarked image is usually of a poor quality. To improve the image quality while preserving the embedding capacity, Yang and Lu (the author of this book) provide a new train of thought [7], where we still utilize the BTC, but we do not perform the watermark embedding on the BTC-compressed image. Here, BTC is only used to guide the watermark embedding and extraction process. Yang and Lu's method 2 consists of three processes, i.e., the preprocessing stage, the watermark embedding stage, and the watermark extraction stage.

5.2.1.3.1 Preprocessing

The preprocessing stage is the common stage for watermark embedding and extraction processes. The aim of this stage is to obtain the BTC bitplanes as the control parameter. To explain the watermarking scheme more intuitively, assume the input image $\mathbf{X}$ (or $\mathbf{Y}$) is 512×512 sized, the block size is 4×4, and the watermark $\mathbf{W}$ is 128×128-sized binary image. Thus, the preprocessing stage is just a BTC coding process as follows:

Step 1: The input image $\mathbf{X}$ (or $\mathbf{Y}$) is divided into nonoverlapping 4×4-sized blocks x_i (or y_i), $i = 1, 2,\ldots,16{,}384$.
Step 2: Each image block x_i (or y_i) is encoded by AMBTC, obtaining its bitplane p_i.
Step 3: All bitplanes are composed to obtain the bitplane sequence
$\mathbf{P} = \{p_i \,|\, i = 1,2,\ldots,16{,}384\}$.

5.2.1.3.2 Watermark Embedding

With the bitplanes $\mathbf{P} = \{p_i \,|i = 1,2,\ldots,16{,}384\}$ in hand as the guider, now we turn to the watermark embedding process. Before embedding, the raster scanning is performed on the original watermark $\mathbf{W}$, obtaining the watermark bit sequence $\mathbf{W} = (w_1, w_2,\ldots,w_{16{,}384})$. The purpose of this embedding process is to ensure the blind extraction such that we can extract the watermark from the watermarked image only based on its bitplane information. The central idea is to force the number of "1s" (or "0s") in each bitplane to be odd for the watermark bit "1" or to be even for the watermark bit "0." The embedding process can be illustrated in detailed as follows:

> Step 1: The original image $\mathbf{X}$ is divided into nonoverlapping 4×4-sized blocks x_i, $i = 1, 2,\ldots,16{,}384$.
>
> Step 2: The embedding process is performed block by block. For each block x_i, the embedding procedure is controlled by the bitplane p_i as the following substeps.
>
> Step 2.1: The number of "1s" in p_i is counted and denoted as q_i. Obviously, according to the definition of q_i as mentioned in Eqs. (5.7) and (5.8), for a $k = 4 \times 4$-sized block, we have $1 \le q_i \le 16$.
>
> Step 2.2: We find all the pixels in x_i that correspond to "1" in the bitplanes, and then arrange them in descending order, obtaining a "high: set H. In the set H, we denote the last element as $\min_1$. That is, $\min_1$ is the minimal pixel that is not less than the mean value m_i of x_i.
>
> Step 2.3: Similarly, we find all the pixels in x_i that correspond to "0s" in the bitplanes, and then arrange them in descending order, obtaining a "low" set L. In the set L, we denote the first element as $\max_0$ and the last element as $\min_0$. That is, $\max_0$ is the maximal pixel that is less than the mean value m_i, whereas $\min_0$ is the minimal pixel that is less than the mean value m_i.
>
> Step 2.4: We check the parity of q_i and compare it with the watermark bit w_i. Here, we define $\text{Parity}(q_i) = 1$ if q_i is an odd number and $\text{Parity}(q_i) = 0$ if q_i is an even number. If $\text{Parity}(q_i) = w_i$, we do not change any pixel in the block x_i, which can be summarized as Eq. (5.11), and go to Step 3. Otherwise, we go to Step 2.5.

$$x_i \text{ is not changed} \quad (\text{Parity}(q_i) = w_i) \tag{5.11}$$

> Step 2.5: We change some pixels in x_i to force the number of "1s" (or "0s") in the renewed bitplane to be odd for the watermark bit "1" or to be even for the watermark bit "0." There are two cases:
>
> Case 1: $q_i = 16$. In this case, $\text{Parity}(q_i) = 0$ and $w_i = 1$. In fact, this case corresponds to a block with uniform pixel values. Thus, we only need to randomly select a pixel and modify it. If the selected pixel is larger than u, we subtract a proper positive integer u from this pixel. Otherwise, we add a proper positive integer u to this pixel. Here, we adopt $u = 4$. Assume we select the first pixel

(this process can be determined by a key), then we can summarize the modification rule for this case as:

$$\begin{cases} x_{i1} \leftarrow x_{i1} + u & x_{i1} \leq u \\ x_{i1} \leftarrow x_{i1} - u & x_{i1} > u \end{cases} \quad (q_i = 16, w_i = 1) \tag{5.12}$$

Case 2: $q_i < 16$. In this case, we should consider two subcases according to the sum "$min_1 + max_0$." In the first subcase, $Parity(min_1 + max_0) = 0$, we perform the following modification rule:

$$min_1, max_0 \leftarrow (min_1 + max_0)/2$$
$$(q_i < 16 \text{ and } Parity(q_i) \neq w_i \text{ and } Parity(min_1 + max_0) = 0) \tag{5.13}$$

That is, we replace the original min_1 and max_0 in the block x_i with their mean value (here, if there is more than one pixel with the same value of min_1 or max_0, then we can randomly select one among them by a key). By this way, we do not change the mean value m_i of the block x_i, but the number of "1s" in the renewed bitplane will either increase or decrease by 1. In the second subcase, $Parity(min_1 + max_0) = 1$; in order not to change the mean value m_i of x_i, we perform the following modification rule:

$$\begin{cases} min_1, max_0 \leftarrow (min_1 + max_0 - 1)/2 \\ min_0 \leftarrow min_0 + 1 \end{cases} \tag{5.14}$$
$$(q_i < 16 \text{ and } Parity(q_i) \neq w_i \text{ and } Parity(min_1 + max_0) = 1)$$

From Eq. (5.14), we can see that the sum "$min_1 + max_0 + min_0$" is not changed after modification, thus the mean value m_i is unchanged, but the number of "1s" in the renewed bitplane will either increase or decrease by 1.

Step 3: Steps 2.1–2.5 are performed on following blocks. If all blocks have been embedded with watermark bits, then the algorithm is terminated. Otherwise, go to Step 2.1.

From these steps, we can see that the embedding process modifies at most three pixels in each original image block, thus the watermarked image should be very similar to the original one.

5.2.1.3.3 Watermark Extraction
The watermark extraction process is a blind process such that we do not require the original image in the extraction process. It is very simple because we can get the watermark bit only based on checking the parity of q_i (the number of "1s" in each bitplane p_i). Before extraction, the same preprocessing step is performed on the suspicious image Y to obtain its bitplane sequence $P = \{p_i \mid i = 1,2,\ldots,16,384\}$. For each block y_i, If the number of "1s" in the bitplane p_i is odd, then we can extract

the watermark bit "1." Otherwise, we can extract the watermark bit "0." This rule can be described as follows:

$$\begin{cases} w_{ei} = 1 & \text{Parity}(q_i) = 1 \\ w_{ei} = 0 & \text{Parity}(q_i) = 0 \end{cases} \tag{5.15}$$

After all blocks are performed, we piece these bits together to obtain the final extracted watermark $\mathbf{W}^e = \{w_{e1}, w_{e2}, \ldots, w_{e16,384}\}$.

5.2.1.4 Zhang et al.'s Method

The existing BTC-based watermarking or hiding approaches essentially embed the secret data in the BTC-compressed image. Thus, the watermarked image usually has a poor quality, at most the same as the BTC-compressed image. To increase the image quality while preserving the embedding capacity, Yang and Lu [7] have provided a new train of thought. That is, we still apply the BTC technique. However, instead of embedding the watermark in the BTC compressed image, similar to Yang and Lu's method [7], Zhang et al. [8] also exploited the BTC bitmap to guide the watermark embedding and extraction process as follows.

5.2.1.4.1 Watermark Embedding

Assume the cover image $\mathbf{X}$ consists of N blocks and the watermark is a binary image $\mathbf{W}$ with N bits. Before embedding, we perform the following preprocessing steps:

Step 1: Perform the raster scanning on the original watermark $\mathbf{W}$ to obtain the watermark bit sequence $\mathbf{W} = (w_1, w_2, \ldots, w_{2N})$.

Step 2: Divide the input image $\mathbf{X}$ (or $\mathbf{Y}$) into nonoverlapping k-dimensional blocks x_i (or y_i), $i = 1, 2, \ldots, N$.

Step 3: Encode each image block x_i (or y_i) by AMBTC to obtain its mean value m_i and its bitmap b_i.

Step 4: All bitmaps are composed of the bitmap sequence $\mathbf{B} = \{b_i | i = 1, 2, \ldots, N\}$.

With the bitmaps $\mathbf{B} = \{b_i \,| i = 1, 2, \ldots, N\}$ in hand as the guider, now we can describe the watermark embedding process. The purpose of the embedding process is to ensure blind extraction so that we can extract the watermark from the watermarked image only based on its bitmap. The central idea is to force the parity of the number of horizontal edge transitions in b_i to be equal to the watermark bit. That is, we embed one watermark bit in each block.

The embedding process can be illustrated in detail as follows:

Step 1: The original image $\mathbf{X}$ is segmented into nonoverlapping k-dimensional blocks x_i, $i = 1, 2, \ldots, N$.

Step 2: The embedding process is performed block by block. For each block x_i, the watermark bit to be embedded is w_i, and the embedding procedure is controlled by the bitmap b_i in following substeps.

Substep 2.1: Count the number of horizontal edge transitions (from 0 to 1 or from 1 to 0) in b_i, and denote it by n_i. For example, for the block in Fig. 5.1, we have

$n_i = 4$. Define Parity(n_i) = 1 if n_i is an odd number and Parity(n_i) = 0 if n_i is an even number. Count the number of pixels corresponding to "1" and denote it by q_i; thus the number of pixels corresponding to "0" is k-q_i. Obviously, we have $1 \leq q_i \leq k$.

Substep 2.2: If Parity(n_i) = w_i is satisfied, we do not change any pixel in the block x_i, and go to Step 3. Otherwise, go to Substep 2.3.

Substep 2.3: If $l_i < h_i$, go to Substep 2.4. Otherwise, we have a special case $l_i = h_i = m_i$ (equivalently, $q_i = k$). In fact, this case corresponds to a block with uniform pixel values. Simply select the first pixel x_{i1} and modify it based on Eq. (5.16), and go to Step 3.

$$\begin{cases} \widehat{x}_{i1} = x_{i1} + 4 & x_{i1} \leq 4 \\ \widehat{x}_{i1} = x_{i1} - 4 & x_{i1} > 4 \end{cases} \tag{5.16}$$

Substep 2.4: It is well known that if we increase or decrease the number of horizontal edge transitions by 1, then the parity of n_i will be changed. Based on this idea, we only need to scan the block x_i row by row to find a suitable row in which the modification of pixels will introduce less distortion. For $k = 4 \times 4$, there are 16 row patterns as shown in the first column of Table 5.1. To increase or decrease the number of horizontal edge transitions by 1, the candidate resulting patterns are shown in the second column of Table 5.1. From each case

Table 5.1 The Candidate Changes in Edge Transitions for the 16 Row Patterns for $k = 4 \times 4$

The Original Row Pattern	The Candidate Resulting Row Patterns
0000	1000,0001
0001	1001,0000
0010	1010,0011
0011	1011,0010
0100	1100,0101
0101	1101,0100
0110	1110,0111
0111	1111,0110
1000	0000,1001
1001	0001,1000
1010	0010,1011
1011	0011,1010
1100	0100,1101
1101	0101,1100
1110	0110,1111
1111	0111,1110

in Table 5.1, we can find that we only need to change the first bit or the last bit in a row to achieve our goal. For example, for "0000," we only need to change it into "1000" or "0001" to increase the number of edge transitions by 1. Based on this idea, we first find all the rows whose first and last bits are different, i.e., whose row pattern is "$0\times\ldots\times1$" or "$1\times\ldots\times0$," where "x" denotes the bit we do not care about. For the first and last pixels in the row with pattern "$0\times\ldots\times1$" or "$1\times\ldots\times0$," we denote the pixel value corresponding to 1 by v_1 and the pixel value corresponding to 0 by v_0. If we can find one or more such rows, then we select the row with the least value of v_1-v_0, and we change this row based on either of the following two rules Eqs. (5.17) and (5.18):

$$\begin{cases} \widehat{v}_1 = \widehat{v}_0 = (v_1 + v_0)/2 & \text{if } v_1 + v_0 \text{ is even} \\ \widehat{v}_1 = \widehat{v}_0 = (v_1 + v_0 + 1)/2, \widehat{v}_{\max 0} = v_{\max 0} - 1 & \text{if } v_1 + v_0 \text{ is odd and } v_{\max 0} > 0 \\ \widehat{v}_1 = \widehat{v}_0 = (v_1 + v_0 + 1)/2 & \text{if } v_1 + v_0 \text{ is odd and } v_{\max 0} = 0 \end{cases}$$

$$(5.17)$$

or

$$\begin{cases} \widehat{v}_1 = \widehat{v}_0 = (v_1 + v_0)/2 & \text{if } v_1 + v_0 \text{ is even} \\ \widehat{v}_1 = \widehat{v}_0 = (v_1 + v_0 - 1)/2, \widehat{v}_{\min 1} = v_{\min 1} + 1 & \text{if } v_1 + v_0 \text{ is odd and } v_{\min 1} < 255 \\ \widehat{v}_1 = \widehat{v}_0 = (v_1 + v_0 - 1)/2 & \text{if } v_1 + v_0 \text{ is odd and } v_{\min 1} = 255 \end{cases}$$

$$(5.18)$$

where $v_{\max 0}$ denotes the maximal pixel value corresponding to "0" in the block x_i excluding v_0, while $v_{\min 1}$ denotes the minimal pixel value corresponding to "1" in the block x_i excluding v_1. If we cannot find the pattern "$0\times\ldots\times1$" or "$1\times\ldots\times0$," we must have found the pattern "$0\times\ldots\times0$" or "$1\times\ldots\times1$." In this case, assume we can find a row with a bit in the middle different from the first bit, and then denote the corresponding pixel value by v_m, the first pixel value by v_f, and the last pixel value by v_l. Then we just exchange v_f with v_m or exchange v_l with v_m, depending on which exchange will result in less distortion. On the other hand, if we cannot find these kinds of rows, we must have met the extreme case where each row is either "00…00" or "11…11," and then we select two pixels: one is the first pixel v_0 from one of the rows with pattern "00…00," and the other is the first pixel v_1 from one of the rows with pattern "11…11." Finally, we use Eq. (5.17) or Eq. (5.18) to modify them.

Step 3: If every block has been embedded with one watermark bit, then the algorithm is terminated with the watermarked image $\mathbf{X}^w$. Otherwise, go to Step 2.1 for next block.

5.2.1.4.2 Watermark Extraction

Our watermark extraction process is very simple. Before extraction, we perform the following preprocessing steps:

Step 1: The suspicious image $\mathbf{Y}$ is divided into nonoverlapping k-dimensional blocks y_i, $i = 1, 2,\ldots,N$.

Step 2: Each image block y_i is encoded by AMBTC, obtaining its mean value m_i and its two quantization levels l_i and h_i.

Step 3: All bitmaps are composed of the bitmap sequence $\mathbf{B} = \{b_i | i = 1, 2, ..., N\}$.

With the bitmaps $\mathbf{B} = \{b_i | \ i = 1,2,...,N \ \}$ in hand as the guider, now we can describe our watermark extraction process. The watermark extraction process is an oblivious process and therefore we no longer require the original image during the extraction process. For each block y_i, if the number of horizontal edge transitions (from 1 to 0 or from 0 to 1) n_i in b_i is odd, then we can extract the watermark bit $w_i = 1$. Otherwise, we can extract the watermark bit $w_i = 0$. After all the blocks are performed, we piece these bits together to obtain the final extracted watermark $\mathbf{W}^e = \{w_{e1}, w_{e2}, ..., w_{eN}\}$.

5.2.2 OVERVIEW OF BLOCK TRUNCATION CODING—BASED LOSSLESS INFORMATION HIDING

The first reversible data hiding scheme for BTC-compressed gray-level images was proposed in 2008 by Hong et al. [9]. In their work, the secret data are embedded by toggling or preserving the BTC bitplane according to the secret bit and the relationship between the high mean and low mean. Although this scheme is reversible, when the high mean equals the low mean, there will be some problem in secret data extraction. To overcome this problem, Chen et al. [10] has recently proposed an improved reversible hiding scheme. In their work, the difference between the high mean and low mean for each block is used to determine whether only to hide 1-bit secret bit for the block or to toggle bits in the bitplane to hide more bits.

To improve the hiding capacity, in 2011, Chen et al. proposed two high-capacity reversible data hiding scheme for BTC-compressed color images [11,12]. In the same year, Li et al. proposed a reversible data hiding scheme [13] for BTC-compressed images based on bitplane flipping and histogram shifting of mean tables and Luo et al. proposed a joint secret sharing and data hiding for BTC-compressed image transmission [14]. In 2012, Wang et al. presented a reversible data hiding scheme for BTC-compressed images based on prediction-error expansion [15]. In 2013, Zhang et al. proposed a reversible data hiding scheme for BTC-compressed images based on lossless coding of mean tables [16]. In the same year, Sun et al. proposed a high-performance reversible data hiding for BTC-compressed images [17].

From next section, we will introduce the aforementioned techniques in detail, which are divided into three classes, bitplane flipping—based schemes for BTC compressed grayscale images, mean coding—based schemes for BTC-compressed grayscale images, and lossless data hiding in BTC-compressed color images.

5.3 BITPLANE FLIPPING—BASED LOSSLESS HIDING SCHEMES

In this section, we introduce the first reversible data hiding scheme for BTC-compressed gray-level images proposed by Hong et al. [9], and its improved scheme by Chen et al. [10]. Then, the reversible data hiding scheme [13] for BTC-compressed images based on bitplane flipping together with histogram shifting of mean tables is introduced, which is proposed by the author of this book.

Here, the original AMBTC method is used in all these methods, assuming that the $M \times N$-sized 256-gray-level image $\mathbf{X}$ is divided into nonoverlapping $m \times n$-sized blocks, i.e., $\mathbf{X} = \{x^{(ij)}, 1 \leq i \leq M/m, 1 \leq j \leq N/n\}$. The pixels in each block are individually quantized into two-level outputs in such a way that the mean value and the first absolute central moment are preserved in the reconstructed block. The mean value of pixels in each block $x^{(ij)} = \left\{x_{uv}^{(ij)}, 1 \leq u \leq m, 1 \leq v \leq n\right\}$ is taken as the 1-bit quantizer threshold t_{ij}, i.e.,

$$t_{ij} = \frac{1}{m \times n} \sum_{u=1}^{m} \sum_{v=1}^{n} x_{uv}^{(ij)} \tag{5.19}$$

The two output quantization level values are calculated as

$$l_{ij} = \begin{cases} \dfrac{1}{m \times n - q_{ij}} \displaystyle\sum_{x_{uv}^{(ij)} < t_{ij}} x_{uv}^{(ij)} & q_{ij} < m \times n \\[2ex] t_{ij} & q_{ij} = m \times n \end{cases} \tag{5.20}$$

$$h_{ij} = \frac{1}{q_{ij}} \sum_{x_{uv}^{(ij)} \geq t_{ij}} x_{uv}^{(ij)} \tag{5.21}$$

where l_{ij} and h_{ij} denote the low and the high means of block $x^{(ij)}$, respectively, and q_{ij} stands for the number of pixels having a value not less than the mean value t_{ij}. If $q_{ij} = m \times n$, we have $l_{ij} = h_{ij} = t_{ij}$. Then a two-level quantization is performed for all the pixels in the block to form a bitplane p_{ij} such that "0" is stored for the pixels with values less than the mean and the rest of the pixels are presented by "1." The image is reconstructed at the decoding phase from the bitplane by assigning the value l_{ij} to "0" and h_{ij} to "1." Thus a compressed block appears as a triple (l_{ij}, h_{ij}, p_{ij}), where l_{ij}, h_{ij} and p_{ij} denote the low mean, the high mean, and the bitplane of block $x^{(ij)}$, respectively. In fact, if we gather all high means of all blocks, we can obtain a matrix that is called high mean table $\mathbf{H} = \{h_{ij}, 1 \leq i \leq M/m, 1 \leq j \leq N/n\}$ in this chapter. Similarly, we can obtain the low mean table $\mathbf{L} = \{l_{ij}, 1 \leq i \leq M/m, 1 \leq j \leq N/n\}$ by gathering all low means, whereas all bitplanes can construct a bitplane sequence $\mathbf{P} = \{p_{ij}, 1 \leq i \leq M/m, 1 \leq j \leq N/n\}$.

5.3.1 ORIGINAL BITPLANE FLIPPING—BASED SCHEME

As we know, if we exchange l_{ij} and h_{ij} in the compressed triple of block $x^{(ij)}$, we only need to flip the bitplane p_{ij} into $\bar{p}_{ij}$ to obtain the same reconstructed block. Based on this idea, Hong et al. proposed a reversible data hiding scheme [10] based on bitplane flipping according to the corresponding secret bit.

The embedding process of Hong et al.'s scheme can be illustrated as follows. First, each image block is compressed by AMBTC resulting in the compressed codes $(l_{ij}, h_{ij}, \boldsymbol{p}_{ij})$. Second, all embeddable blocks with $l_{ij} < h_{ij}$ are found, that is to say, the block with $l_{ij} = h_{ij}$ is nonembeddable. Third, for each embeddable block, if the bit to be embedded is "1," then the compressed code is changed from $(l_{ij}, h_{ij}, \boldsymbol{p}_{ij})$ into $\left(h_{ij}, l_{ij}, \overline{\boldsymbol{p}}_{ij}\right)$. Otherwise, if the bit to be embedded is "0," then no operation is required. In other words, the secret bit "0" corresponds to the code $(l_{ij}, h_{ij}, \boldsymbol{p}_{ij})$ and the secret bit "1" corresponds to the code $\left(h_{ij}, l_{ij}, \overline{\boldsymbol{p}}_{ij}\right)$.

The secret data extraction process is very simple. Assume we receive the code $(l'_{ij}, h'_{ij}, \boldsymbol{p}'_{ij})$, then we only need to judge the relationship between l'_{ij} and h'_{ij}. If $l'_{ij} > h'_{ij}$, then the secret bit is 1; if $l'_{ij} < h'_{ij}$, the secret bit is 0; otherwise, no secret bit is embedded. Although Hong et al.'s scheme [10] is reversible, it does not consider hiding data in the blocks with $l_{ij} = h_{ij}$.

5.3.2 IMPROVED BITPLANE FLIPPING–BASED SCHEME

To embed secret data in the blocks with $l_{ij} = h_{ij}$, Chen et al. proposed an improved reversible data hiding algorithm [11] by introducing Chuang and Chang's bitplane replacement idea to deal with the case $l_{ij} = h_{ij}$ in Hong et al.'s bitplane flipping scheme. The purpose of this scheme is to increase the payload compared with Hong et al.'s bitplane flipping scheme while improving the stego image quality compared with Chuang and Chang's scheme.

The embedding process of Chen et al.'s scheme can be illustrated as follows: each image block is compressed by AMBTC resulting in the compressed codes $(l_{ij}, h_{ij}, \boldsymbol{p}_{ij})$. For each block with $l_{ij} < h_{ij}$, if the bit to be embedded is "1," then the compressed code is changed from $(l_{ij}, h_{ij}, \boldsymbol{p}_{ij})$ into $\left(h_{ij}, l_{ij}, \overline{\boldsymbol{p}}_{ij}\right)$. Otherwise, if the bit to be embedded is "0," then no operation is required. For the block with $l_{ij} = h_{ij}$, since the bitplane has no use in the reconstruction process, the whole bitplane can be replaced with $m \times n$ secret bits.

The secret data extraction process is also very simple. Assume we receive the code $(l'_{ij}, h'_{ij}, \boldsymbol{p}'_{ij})$, we only need to judge the relationship between l'_{ij} and h'_{ij}. If $l'_{ij} > h'_{ij}$, then the secret bit is 1; if $l'_{ij} < h'_{ij}$, the secret bit is 0; otherwise, all $m \times n$ bits in the bitplane $\boldsymbol{p}'_{ij}$ are extracted as the secret bits. Obviously, the improved scheme can increase the payload compared with the original scheme.

5.3.3 BITPLANE FLIPPING–BASED SCHEME WITH HISTOGRAM SHIFTING OF MEAN TABLES

From the previous section, we can see that Hong et al.'s bitplane flipping scheme and Chen et al.'s scheme can embed 1-bit information per block if there is no block with $l_{ij} = h_{ij}$. To embed more secret bits, after using Chen et al.'s scheme, we can further compose all high/low means as a high/low mean table and then introduce the histogram shifting technique to high and low mean tables. Our algorithm [13] consists of three stages, i.e., the AMBTC compression stage, the data hiding stage, and the data extraction and image recovery stage, which can be illustrated as follows.

5.3.3.1 The Absolute Moment Block Truncation Coding Compression Stage

This stage is a preprocessing stage before data hiding. The aim of this stage is to obtain the two mean tables and the bitplane sequence for later use. Given an $M \times N$-sized 256-grayscale original image $\mathbf{X}$, this stage can be expressed as follows:

Step 1: The original image $\mathbf{X}$ is divided into nonoverlapping $m \times n$-sized blocks $x^{(ij)}$, $i = 1, 2,..., M/m$, $j = 1, 2, ..., N/n$.

Step 2: Encode each image block $x^{(ij)}$ by AMBTC, obtaining the compressed triple (l_{ij}, h_{ij}, p_{ij}).

Step 3: Compose all high and low means to obtain the high mean table $\mathbf{H} = \{h_{ij} \mid i = 1,2,...,M/m; j = 0,1,...,N/n\}$ and the low mean table $\mathbf{L} = \{l_{ij} \mid i = 1,2,...,M/m; j = 0,1,...,N/n\}$, respectively. Similarly, compose all bitplanes to obtain the bitplane sequence $\mathbf{P} = \{p_{ij} \mid i = 1,2,...,M/m; j = 0,1,...,N/n\}$.

5.3.3.2 The Data Hiding Stage

With the mean tables $\mathbf{H}$ and $\mathbf{L}$ and the bitplane sequence $\mathbf{P}$ in hand, now we can introduce our reversible data hiding algorithm. Assume the secret bit sequence to be embedded is $\mathbf{W} = \{w_1, w_2, ...\}$. Before embedding, we perform the permutation operation on the secret bit sequence to enhance the security. Our embedding method is performed in two main steps, i.e., bitplane flipping and histogram shifting, which can be illustrated in detailed as follows:

Step 1: We first perform the bitplane flipping technique on $\mathbf{H}$, $\mathbf{L}$, and $\mathbf{P}$ to embed the first part of secret bits. For each image block with $l_{ij} < h_{ij}$, if the bit to be embedded is "1," then the element h_{ij} in $\mathbf{H}$ and the element l_{ij} in $\mathbf{L}$ are swapped, and the bitplane p_{ij} in $\mathbf{P}$ is replaced by $\bar{p}_{ij}$. Otherwise, if the bit to be embedded is "0," then no operation is required. For the block with $l_{ij} = h_{ij}$, since the bitplane has no use in the reconstruction process, the whole bitplane p_{ij} in $\mathbf{P}$ can be replaced with $m \times n$ secret bits. After this step, we get the modified mean tables and bitplane sequence denoted as $\mathbf{H}'$, $\mathbf{L}'$, and $\mathbf{P}'$, respectively.

Step 2: We further perform the histogram shifting technique on $\mathbf{H}'$ and $\mathbf{L}'$, respectively, to embed the second part of secret bits. The detailed substeps can be illustrated as follows:

Step 2.1: Generate the histogram from $\mathbf{H}'$.

Step 2.2: In the histogram, we first find a zero point and then a peak point. A zero point corresponds to the grayscale value v, which does not exist in the given image. A peak point corresponds to the grayscale value u, which has the maximum number of pixels in the given image.

Step 2.3: The whole mean table is scanned in a sequential order. Assume $u < v$, the grayscale value of pixels between u (including u) and v (including v) is incremented by "1." This step is equivalent to shifting the range of the histogram, $[u, v]$, to the right-hand side by 1 unit, leaving the grayscale value u empty.

Step 2.4: The whole mean table is scanned once again in the same sequential order. Once a pixel with grayscale value of u is encountered, we check the secret bit to be embedded. If this bit is binary "1," the pixel value is incremented by 1. Otherwise, the pixel value remains intact.

Step 2.5 After above substeps, we can get the final marked high mean table $\mathbf{H}''$. Similarly, perform above substeps on the low mean table $\mathbf{L}'$ to get the final marked low mean table $\mathbf{L}''$. Note that we should record the u, v values for $\mathbf{H}$ and $\mathbf{L}$, respectively, as the overhead information.

5.3.3.3 The Decoding and Extracting Stage

Our data hiding scheme is reversible because we can recover the original mean tables and the bitplane sequence after data extraction, and thus the original BTC-compressed image can be losslessly recovered. Given the marked mean tables $\mathbf{H}^w$ and $\mathbf{L}^w$ and the marked bitplane sequence $\mathbf{P}^w$, our purpose is to extract the secret bit sequence and recover the original BTC-compressed image, the extraction process as follows:

Step 1: Perform the reverse histogram shifting technique on $\mathbf{H}^w$ and $\mathbf{L}^w$ to extract the second part of secret bits and get the intermediate result $\mathbf{H}^r$ and $\mathbf{L}^r$, respectively. The detailed substeps can be illustrated as follows:

Step 1.1: Scan the marked table $\mathbf{H}^w$ in the same sequential order as that used in the embedding procedure. If a pixel with its grayscale value $v + 1$ is encountered, the secret bit "1" is extracted. If a pixel with its value v is encountered, a secret bit "0" is extracted.

Step 1.2: Scan the image again, for any pixel whose grayscale value is in the interval $[u, v]$, the pixel value is subtracted by 1.

Step 1.3: After these substeps, we can get the intermediate high mean table $\mathbf{H}^r$. Similarly, perform these substeps on the marked low mean table $\mathbf{L}^w$ to get the intermediate low mean table $\mathbf{L}^r$.

Step 2: Perform the reverse bitplane flipping technique on $\mathbf{H}^r$, $\mathbf{L}^r$, and $\mathbf{P}^w$ to extract the first part of secret bits and recover the BTC-compressed image data. For each triple $(l^r_{ij}, h^r_{ij}, p^w_{ij})$, we only need to judge the relationship between l^r_{ij} and h^r_{ij}. If $l^r_{ij} > h^r_{ij}$, then the secret bit is 1, and l^r_{ij} and h^r_{ij} are swapped and the bitplane p^w_{ij} is replaced by $\bar{p}^w_{ij}$; if $l^r_{ij} < h^r_{ij}$, the secret bit is 0; otherwise, all $m \times n$ bits in the bitplane p^w_{ij} are extracted as the secret bits. Replace the bitplane p^w_{ij} with $m \times n$ '1's.

Based on these two steps, we can extract all secret bits and reconstruct the original BTC-compressed image, thus the whole reversible process is realized. Obviously, the improved scheme can increase the payload compared with Chen et al.'s scheme.

5.3.3.4 *Experimental Results and Discussion*

To evaluate our scheme, we use six test images, Lena, Peppers, Bridge, Boat, Goldhill, and Jet_F16, of the same size 512×512 with 256 grayscales, as shown in Fig. 5.4. Comparisons among our algorithm, Hong et al.'s algorithm, and Chen et al.'s algorithm are performed under the same block size 4×4. Table 5.2 lists the number of image blocks whose low mean equals its high mean (i.e., $l_{ij} = h_{ij}$) for different images. From Table 5.2, we can see that, for Lena, Boat, Goldhill, and Jet_F16 images, there is no image block with $l_{ij} = h_{ij}$, thus both Hong et al.'s

FIGURE 5.4

Six test images.

Table 5.2 The Number of 4×4 Pixel Blocks Whose High Mean Equals its Low Mean (*EB*)

Image	EB
Lena	0
Peppers	285
Bridge	54
Boat	0
Goldhill	0
Jet_F16	0

algorithm and Chen et al.'s algorithm can embed 16,384 bits in each 512×512 image. However, for the Bridge image and the Peppers image, since there are some blocks with $l_{ij} = h_{ij}$, Chen et al.'s algorithm can embed more bits, whereas Hong et al.'s algorithm can embed less bits.

To show the superiority of our proposed algorithm, we compare it with Hong et al.'s scheme and Chen et al.'s scheme. Three aspects of performance are adopted in the experiments to evaluate a data hiding scheme, i.e., the capacity representing the maximum number of secret bits that can be hidden, the PSNR representing the quality of the stego image, and the embedding efficiency indicating the number of embedded secret data when a bit of the binary code stream has been transmitted. Obviously, the embedding efficiency can be calculated as Capacity/(bit rate $\times M \times N$). As shown in Table 5.3, the PSNRs of stego images based on our, Hong et al.'s, and Chen et al.'s schemes are exactly the same as those of the original AMBTC-compressed images, the reason being that these three schemes are reversible.

With respect to the embedding capacity, our scheme achieves the highest embedding capacity. Compared with the other two schemes, our scheme can embed more secret bits because we adopt the histogram shifting technique in addition to Chen et al.'s scheme. The capacity of Hong et al.'s and Chen et al.'s schemes is normally 1 bit in each 4×4 pixel block. However, if there are some blocks with the same high and low means, then Hong et al.'s scheme will have less capacity and Chen et al.'s scheme will have more capacity. As shown in Tables 5.2 and 5.3, for the Peppers image, because $EB = 285$, Hong et al.'s scheme can only embed $16,384 - 285 = 16,099$ bits, whereas Chen et al.'s scheme can embed $16,384 - 285 + 285 \times 4 \times 4 = 20,659$ bits.

In terms of embedding efficiency, our scheme has the highest efficiency values. Our scheme can transmit the most number of embedded secret data when a bit of the

Table 5.3 Comparisons of Our, Hong et al.'s, and Chen et al.'s Schemes ($m \times n = 4 \times 4$)

Algorithm	Performance	Lena	Peppers	Bridge	Boat	Goldhill	Jet_F16
AMBTC	PSNR (dB)	32.041	31.595	28.585	31.151	33.163	31.033
	Bit rate (bpp)	2.000	2.000	2.000	2.000	2.000	2.000
Proposed	PSNR (dB)	32.041	31.595	28.585	31.151	33.163	31.033
	Capacity (bits)	16,684	21,969	17,548	17,061	16,770	17,375
	Efficiency	0.032	0.042	0.034	0.033	0.032	0.033
Hong et al.'s	PSNR (dB)	32.041	31.595	28.585	31.151	33.163	31.033
	Capacity (bits)	16,384	16,099	16,330	16,384	16,384	16,384
	Efficiency	0.031	0.030	0.031	0.031	0.031	0.031
Chen et al.'s	PSNR (dB)	32.041	31.595	28.585	31.151	33.163	31.033
	Capacity (bits)	16,384	20,659	17,194	16,384	16,384	16,384
	Efficiency	0.031	0.039	0.033	0.031	0.031	0.031

AMBTC, *absolute moment block truncation coding*; PSNR, *peak signal-to-noise ratio*.

binary code stream has been transmitted. Taking these three attributes into comprehensive consideration, our scheme is a more effective method because of its high capacity, high PSNR, and high embedding efficiency.

5.4 MEAN CODING–BASED LOSSLESS HIDING SCHEMES

The aforementioned data hiding schemes in the BTC domain modify either the BTC encoding stage or the BTC-compressed data according to the secret bits, and they have no ability to reduce the bit rate but may reduce the image quality. To reduce the bit rate and increase the hiding capacity, this section introduces our three reversible data hiding schemes for BTC-compressed images, which can further losslessly encode the BTC-compressed data according to secret data.

5.4.1 PREDICTION-ERROR EXPANSION–BASED SCHEME

In 2012, we proposed a reversible data hiding scheme for BTC-compressed images by introducing the prediction-error expansion technique [15]. For the purpose of increasing the capacity, all high and low mean values are composed as a low and a high mean table, respectively. Then prediction-error expansion is applied on these two tables. This operation enables one block of the image to embed two secret bits.

However, as mentioned in Chapter 2, it also may lead to the overflow or underflow of mean values. To solve this problem, the original low and high mean values are swapped and the binary bitmap is flipped, i.e., the original AMBTC code turns into $(l', h', B') = (h, l, \overline{B})$, where $\overline{B}$ is the result of performing a logical NOT operation on binary bitmap B. Reconstruction of this image block will remain the same for the inherent property of AMBTC decompression procedure [9]. Thus, whether certain blocks have hidden bits or not can be determined by comparing the modified low and high mean values and no additional overflow/underflow location map is required.

For some cases the new low mean value is greater than the new high mean value after prediction-error expansion; we also keep the original mean values and apply the previously mentioned mean value swapping and bitmap flipping operations. To further increase the capacity, prediction-error expansion would not be applied to those blocks with equal values of low and high means. Instead, $n \times n$ secret bits are directly embedded into the binary bitmap B by replacing bits, since the bitmap is of no use for reconstruction in the decompression process [10]. Take this into consideration, it may cause the conflict in the data extracting phase. Therefore, blocks with same new mean values need keeping original mean values and applying mean value swapping and bitmap flipping operations as well.

Our algorithm can be divided into two phases: the data hiding phase and the data extracting and image restoring phase, which are illustrated in the following subsections.

5.4.1.1 Data Hiding Phase

The detailed data hiding phase is given step by step as follows.

Step 1: Decode the original $M \times N$-sized BTC-compressed image to get all BTC codes (l, h, B) of nonoverlapping $n \times n$-sized blocks.

Step 2: Compose all low and high mean values to obtain the low mean table $L = \{L(i, j) \,|\, i = 1, 2,...,M/n; \, j = 1, 2,...,N/n\}$ and the high mean table $H = \{H(i, j) \,|\, i = 1, 2,...,M/n; \, j = 1, 2,...,N/n\}$, respectively.

Step 3: Encrypt the secret data, then start to hide secret bits.

Step 3.1: Scan two mean tables in right-to-left and bottom-to-top manner with an eye on the property of the predictor. For each block, go to Step 3.2 if $L(i, j)$ is not equal to $H(i, j)$; otherwise go to Step 3.3.

Step 3.2: Apply prediction-error expansion as described in Section 2.3.1 to $L(i, j)$ and $H(i, j)$, and then embed 2 bits into current block if the prediction-error p_e^l for $L(i, j)$, p_e^h for $H(i, j)$, the new low mean value $L'(i, j)$ and high mean value $H'(i, j)$ satisfy the following requirements:

$$\begin{cases} |p_e^l| + |p_e^h| \leq TH \\ 0 \leq L'(i,j) < H'(i,j) \leq 255 \end{cases} \tag{5.22}$$

where TH represents a threshold balancing the embedding capacity and image quality of the output image; or else no bit could be embedded and label the block as no hidden data block $(h, l, \overline{B})$. Repeat Step 3.1 until every block is scanned.

Step 3.3: Directly embed $n \times n$ bits into the bitmap B of the current block by replacing bits. Repeat Step 3.1 until every block is scanned.

5.4.1.2 Data Extracting and Image Restoring Phase

Data extracting and image restoring phase is the inverse process of data hiding phase and described as follows:

Step 1: Decode the received BTC-compressed image to get all BTC codes of blocks.

Step 2: Compose all low and high mean values to obtain the low mean table L' and the high mean table H', respectively.

Step 3: Scan two mean tables in left-to-right and top-to-bottom manner. For each block, go to Step 3.1 if $L'(i, j)$ is smaller than $H'(i, j)$, go to Step 3.2 if $L'(i, j)$ is equal to $H'(i, j)$, otherwise go to Step 3.3.

Step 3.1: Extract two secret bits from the prediction- error $p_e^{\prime l}$ for $L''(i, j)$ and $p_e^{\prime h}$ for $H'(i, j)$ by applying prediction-error expansion technique and restore the original mean values. Repeat Step 3 until every block is scanned.

Step 3.2: Directly extract $n \times n$ bits of secret data from the bitmap B' of the current block and set all elements of bitmap B' to 1 for restoring. Repeat Step 3 until every block is scanned.

Step 3.3: No bit is hidden for this case. Apply mean value swapping and bitmap flipping operations $\left(h', l', \overline{B}'\right)$ to restore the original BTC codes. Repeat Step 3 until every block is scanned.

Step 4: Rearrange the secret bits in reverse order because the scan orders of data hiding phase and data extracting and image restoring phase are reversed. Then decrypt the secret bits to obtain the original secret data.

5.4.1.3 Experimental Results

In this section, six grayscale test images of size 512×512 shown in Fig. 5.5 are used to evaluate the performance of our scheme. The block size of AMBTC compression is 4×4. We analyze the properties of it and compare it with other scheme. Two aspects, image quality and capacity, are discussed. Here, PSNR is adopted to measure the impact of data hiding on image quality.

Experimental results of our scheme with threshold $TH = 12$ are shown in Table 5.4, which also contains the result of Li et al.'s scheme [13]. As shown in Table 5.4, the proposed scheme has a higher capacity when compared with Li et al.'s. Even though the PSNR values of the proposed scheme are lower than those of Li et al.'s, they are still very closed to those of original BTC-compressed images and the image quality is acceptable. The prediction-error expansion technique enables the proposed scheme to hide two secret bits into one block, which improves the capacity significantly. Images F16 and Tiffany have higher capacity than other test images for the proposed scheme, since the prediction-error expansion takes

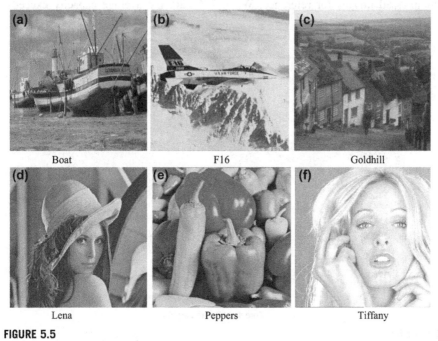

Boat   F16   Goldhill

Lena   Peppers   Tiffany

FIGURE 5.5

Six grayscale test images.

Table 5.4 Comparison of Algorithm Performance

Image	AMBTC	Li et al.'s [13]		Proposed (TH = 12)	
	PSNR (dB)	Capacity (Bit)	PSNR (dB)	Capacity (Bit)	PSNR (dB)
Boat	31.14	17,089	31.13	18,490	30.63
F16	31.02	22,656	31.01	24,620	30.67
Goldhill	33.10	16,883	33.09	19,386	32.18
Lena	33.91	16,968	33.90	22,062	33.14
Peppers	33.63	16,826	33.62	22,230	32.78
Tiffany	35.08	19,878	35.08	24,878	33.93

PSNR, *peak signal-to-noise ratio.*

advantage of the correlation of adjacent blocks and smooth blocks help to increase the capacity. Image F16 and Tiffany have more smooth blocks.

The superiority of the proposed scheme lies in the capacity and the tuning parameter *TH*. *TH* could be set to a smaller value when data that need hiding are less and better image quality could be achieved; when the data that need hiding are more, *TH* could be set to a larger value, which satisfies the embedding requirement. Fig. 5.6 demonstrates the average capacity and PSNR across six test images with different thresholds *TH*; the dotted line is the average PSNR value of six original BTC-compressed images for reference. When *TH* = 20, the average capacity exceeds

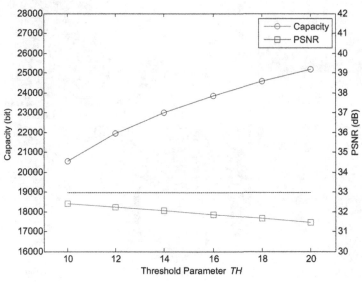

FIGURE 5.6

Average capacity and peak signal-to-noise ratio (PSNR) with different thresholds *TH*.

25,000 bits, whereas the average PSNR is still greater than 31 dB. Fig. 5.6 reveals that the capacity becomes higher with the increase of *TH*, and the decrease of PSNR value is slow and acceptable.

5.4.2 JOINT NEIGHBORING CODING–BASED SCHEME

5.4.2.1 Brief Introduction to Joint Neighboring Coding

The joint neighboring coding (JNC) data hiding algorithm used here is derived from the VQ-based data hiding algorithm in Section 4.5.1 in Chapter 4. In short, the VQ algorithm divides the input image into nonoverlapping blocks, and each block is substituted by the matched block in a designated codebook. In this way the output data for the input image are just the indices of the matched blocks. The indices are nearly the same for the neighboring blocks and they are the embedding objects of the JNC-based data hiding algorithm.

Fig. 5.7 shows the composition of neighboring indices with location bits marked as darker areas around the center index I_{cur}. Here, I_{cur} is the current index to be encoded. Evidently, there are four neighboring indices as shown in Fig. 5.7 that are selected to encode I_{cur}, and their location bits are denoted as $(00)_2$, $(01)_2$, $(10)_2$ and $(11)_2$, respectively. Given the secret data, an M-sequence is generated with the same length as that of the secret data for encoding. Here, M-sequence is a kind of pseudorandom sequence, which plays an important role in keeping the security of secret data.

To describe the encoding process clearly, we give some definition of the terms used in the following illustration: (1) b_i Stands for the initial location of the reference index for encoding I_{cur}, and it is read from the M-sequence. (2) b_o Denotes the offset of the reference index used to encode I_{cur}, and it is read from the secret data. (3) b_r Denotes the actual location of the reference index to encode I_{cur}, and we have $b_r = b_i + b_o$. (4) n denotes the number of neighboring indices considered, and thus the number of bits in b_i, b_o, and b_r are all $\log_2 n$. (5) I_{ref} Stands for the index corresponding to b_r, and it is the reference index used to encode I_{cur}. (6) D denotes the difference between I_{cur} and I_{ref}, i.e., $D = I_{cur} - I_{ref}$. (7) N Is defined as the codebook size. (8) The function $\lceil x \rceil$ denotes the least integer not less than x. (9) m ($1 \leq m \leq \lceil \log_2 N \rceil$) is defined as the truncation integer that is used to distinguish the range of D.

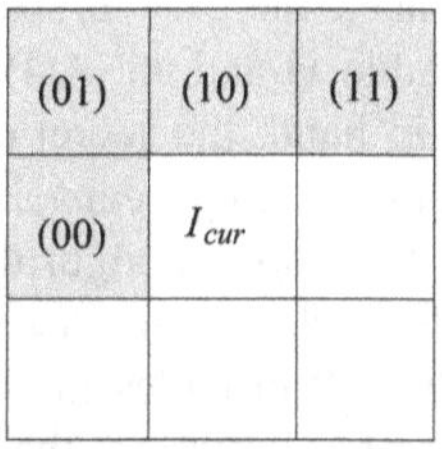

(01)	(10)	(11)
(00)	I_{cur}	

FIGURE 5.7

The neighboring indices of the current index I_{cur}.

With these definitions in hand, the JNC encoding process can be described as follows. First, 2 bits from the M-sequence and 2 bits from the secret data are read as b_i and b_o, respectively. Next, they are added together to determine b_r, and thus I_{ref} can be found. Second, D is calculated as $D = I_{cur} - I_{ref}$. Here, the encoding mode for D is classified by the parameter m $(1 \leq m \leq \lceil \log_2 N \rceil)$ into four cases. Next, D is encoded into its binary form D' by one of four cases, which can be summarized as follows.

$$D' = \begin{cases} (11)_2 \big\| \left(D^{(m)} \right)_2 & \text{case"11"} \quad 0 \leq D \leq (2^m - 1) \\ (10)_2 \big\| \left(-D^{(m)} \right)_2 & \text{case"10"} \quad -(2^m - 1) \leq D < 0 \\ (01)_2 \big\| \left(D^{(\lceil \log_2 N \rceil)} \right)_2 & \text{case"01"} \quad D > (2^m - 1) \\ (00)_2 \big\| \left(-D^{(\lceil \log_2 N \rceil)} \right)_2 & \text{case"00"} \quad D < -(2^m - 1) \end{cases} \tag{5.23}$$

where "U||V" stands for the concatenation of U and V and $(D^{(m)})_2$ denotes the m bits binary code of D. Finally, the output codestream for the current index is encoded into the binary form as "$(b_r)\|$case$\|(|D|)_2$." Repeat the this process for all the indices outside the seed area (here the seed area includes the first row and the first column in the index table) and the final output codestream can be produced.

5.4.2.2 The Hiding Scheme

As we know, the existing data hiding schemes in the BTC domain modify either the BTC encoding stage or the BTC-compressed data according to the secret bits, and they are weak to embed more secret data and may reduce the image quality. To improve the embedding capacity and image quality, we proposed a novel reversible data hiding for AMBTC-compressed image by further losslessly encoding the AMBTC-compressed data according to the relation among neighboring mean values in the high and low mean tables. First, one high mean table, one low mean table, and one bitplane sequence are generated by performing the AMBTC method on the input image. The high and low mean tables are used for hiding information, whereas the bitplane sequence is reserved unchanged. Second, the M-sequence is generated with the double length of secret data. Third, the high and low mean tables are embedded with secret data by the JNC technique and the bitplane sequences are added to the end of the stream. For instance, the $A \times B$-sized image is encoded as an $(A/4) \times (B/4)$-sized high mean table **H** and an $(A/4) \times (B/4)$-sized low mean table **L**. With these two mean tables in hand, the secret data can then be embedded by encoding **H** and **L** jointly to achieve a high capacity and generate a more secure codestream. The codestream of the proposed algorithm is composed of three parts, i.e., the head information HI, the codestream CS_H and CS_L of the two embedded mean tables, and the bitplane BP. HI provides the basic information of the codestream, such as the total lengths of codestream, the length of the secret data, CS_H and CS_L, and the cover image size. The flowchart of our scheme is shown in

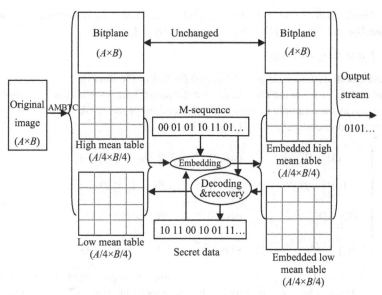

FIGURE 5.8

The flow chart of the proposed algorithm.

Fig. 5.8. We can see clearly that not only the encoding and decoding processes are reversible but also the mean tables and the secret data can be retrieved accurately. The proposed scheme is illustrated in the following two subsections.

5.4.2.2.1 Embedding Process

Suppose the high mean table, low mean table, and bitplane sequence are obtained by compressing the original image based on the AMBTC method. An M-sequence is generated with an initial key in advance. For clarity, some terms used in the embedding process are defined in advance. The current high and low mean values in **H** and **L** to be encoded are denoted as h_{cur} and l_{cur}, respectively. The initial location read from the M-sequence is denoted as b_i. The offsets read from the secret data for encoding h_{cur} and l_{cur} are denoted as $b_o^{(H)}$ and $b_o^{(L)}$, respectively. The final reference locations for encoding h_{cur} and l_{cur} are denoted as $b_r^{(H)}$ and $b_r^{(L)}$, respectively. Here, $b_r^{(H)} = b_i + b_o^{(H)}$ and $b_r^{(L)} = b_i + b_o^{(L)}$. D_H is the difference between h_{cur} and h_{ref}, that is, $D_H = h_{cur} - h_{ref}$. Similarly, D_L is the difference between l_{cur} and l_{ref}, that is, $D_L = l_{cur} - l_{ref}$. The detailed data embedding process can be described by the following steps.

Step 1: Difference calculation.

First, read 2 bits from the M-sequence as b_i. Second, read 4 bits from the secret data, where the first 2 bits serves as $b_o^{(H)}$ for h_{cur} and the latter 2 bits as $b_o^{(L)}$ for l_{cur}. Third, calculate the reference location $b_r^{(H)} = b_i + b_o^{(H)}$ for h_{cur} and $b_r^{(L)} = b_i + b_o^{(L)}$ for l_{cur}.

Fourth, based on $b_r^{(H)}$ and $b_r^{(L)}$, find h_{ref} and l_{ref} in **H** and **L,** respectively. Finally, calculate D_H and D_L, i.e., $D_H = h_{cur} - h_{ref}$ and $D_L = l_{cur} - l_{ref}$.

Step 2: D_H and D_L encoding.

Obviously, both dynamic ranges of D_H and D_L fall in the interval $[-N + 1, N - 1]$. The embedding process for D_H and D_L are the same, hence we take the D_H embedding process as the example to illustrate the encoding process. We can classify it into four cases, and encode D_H into D_H' as follows:

$$D_H' = \begin{cases} 11 \| \left(D_H^{(m)}\right)_2 & \text{case"11"} \quad 0 \le D_H \le (2^m - 1) \\ 10 \| \left(-D_H^{(m)}\right)_2 & \text{case"10"} \quad -(2^m - 1) \le D_H < 0 \\ 01 \| \left(D_H^{(\lceil \log_2 N \rceil)}\right)_2 & \text{case"01"} \quad D_H > (2^m - 1) \\ 00 \| \left(-D_H^{(\lceil \log_2 N \rceil)}\right)_2 & \text{case"00"} \quad D_H < -(2^m - 1) \end{cases} \tag{5.24}$$

That is, for $0 \le D_H \le (2^m - 1)$, the case is represented by $(11)_2$ and $D_H' = 11 \| (D_H)_2$, where D_H requires m bits to represent. For $-(2^m-1) \le D_H < 0$, the case is represented by $(10)_2$ and $D_H' = 10 \| (-D_H)_2$, where $-D_H$ requires m bits. For $D_H > (2^m - 1)$, the case is represented by $(01)_2$ and $D_H' = 01 \| (D_H)_2$, where D_H requires $\lceil \log_2 N \rceil$ bits. For $D_H < -(2^m - 1)$, the case is represented by $(00)_2$ and $D_H' = 00 \| (-D_H)_2$, where D_H requires $\lceil \log_2 N \rceil$ bits. Similarly, the same process is performed on D_L to obtain D_L'.

Step 3: CS_H and CS_L encoding.

Append D_H' and D_L' to the reference index location bits $b_r^{(H)}$ and $b_r^{(L)}$, respectively. For example, assuming $b_r^{(H)} = (01)_2$, the case of D_H is $(11)_2$, then the final codestream of CS_H for the current high mean is $01 \| 11 \| (D_H)_2$, where D_H requires m bits.

Step 4: CS combination.

If all the secret data or all indices outside the seed area have been processed, append CS_H and CS_L and the bitplane sequence **P** to the head information HI to obtain the final codestream. Otherwise, go to step 1.

We take an example to illustrate the embedding process as shown in Fig. 5.9, where we suppose $m = 4$. Each time, we obtain 2 bits from the M-sequence and 4 bits from the secret data. To encode the high mean $h_{cur} = $ "251" located in the second row and the second column of **H**, its four neighbors, $(254)_{00}$, $(255)_{01}$, $(242)_{10}$, and $(251)_{11}$ are considered. Meanwhile, the low mean $l_{cur} = $ "57" located in the second row and the second column of **L** is also encoded. "00" in the M-sequence is first read as b_i, and then "1000" is read from the secret data, where $b_0^{(H)} = $ "10" and $b_0^{(L)} = $ "00". Next, we calculate the reference location bits $b_r^{(H)} = $ "00" $= +$"10" $= $ "10" and $b_r^{(L)} = $ "00" $= +$"00" $= $ "00," and then we can find the reference indices

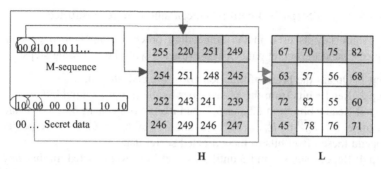

FIGURE 5.9

An example to explain our data embedding scheme.

$h_{ref} = $ "242" and $l_{ref} = $ "63", respectively. Thus, we can obtain $D_H = 251 - 242 = 9 < 2^4$, $D_L = 57 - 63 = -6 > -2^4$. Obviously, D_H and D_L belong to their corresponding Case "11" and Case "10," respectively. Therefore, CS_H and CS_L can be encoded as 10||11||1001 and 00||10||0110, respectively. For the next high and low means to be encoded, i.e., $h_{cur} = $ "248" in **H** and $l_{cur} = $ "56" in **L**, we read the initial location bits $b_i = $ "01" the offset bits $b_o^{(H)} = $ "00" $b_o^{(L)} = $ "01", respectively. By calculating $b_r^{(H)} = $ "01"+"00" $= $ "01" and $b_r^{(L)} = $ "01"+"01" $= $ "10", we can find $h_{ref} = $ "220" and $l_{ref} = $ "75", respectively. Thus, we have $D_H = 248 - 220 = 28$ and $D_L = 56 - 75 = -19$, and D_H and D_L belong to their corresponding Case "01" and Case "00", respectively. Consequently, CS_H and CS_L are encoded as 01||01||10 and 10||00||10,000, respectively.

5.4.2.2.2 Decoding and Extraction Process

Suppose the codestream obtained by the decoder suffers no alterations, then the AMBTC-compressed image can be precisely recovered without the M-sequence. The detailed decoding operations can be described as follows.

Step 1: Read the head information *HI* of the codestream. From *HI*, we can get the cover image size, the lengths of CS_H and CS_L, and the value of m.

Step 2: Read r bits from CS_H as $b_r^{(H)}$ and r bits from CS_L as $b_r^{(L)}$. Then retrieve the corresponding high and low means h_{ref} and l_{ref}, respectively.

Step 3: Read the case information from CS_H and CS_L. Also, read D_H and D_L from CS_H and CS_L according to the case information.

Step 4: Calculate the current high and low means h_{cur} and l_{cur} as follows:

$$\begin{cases} h_{cur} = h_{ref} + D_H \\ l_{cur} = l_{ref} + D_L \end{cases} \tag{5.25}$$

Step 5: Repeat Steps 2—4 until two mean tables are reconstructed.

The same key as used in the embedding process is applied to generate the M-sequence, and the secret data can be extracted with the following steps.

Step 1: Obtain the head information HI of the codestream.
Step 2: Read r bits from the M-sequence as the initial location bits b_i.
Step 3: Read r bits from CS_H as $b_r^{(H)}$ and r bits from CS_L as $b_r^{(L)}$. Then calculate the offset bits $b_o^{(H)}$ by $b_o^{(H)} = b_r^{(H)} - b_i$ and $b_o^{(L)}$ by $b_o^{(L)} = b_r^{(L)} - b_i$, respectively. Append these offset bits to the extracted secret data.
Step 4: Repeat Steps 2 and 3 until all secret bits are extracted. In this way, the secret data can be finally obtained.

Obviously, the complexity of the decoding and extraction process is quite low, and these two processes can be detached if necessary.

5.4.2.3 Experimental Results

Now we turn to evaluate the proposed scheme using six test images, Lena, Peppers, Mandrill, Boat, Goldhill, and Jet_F16, of the same size 512×512 with 256 grayscales, as shown in Fig. 5.10. First, we test the performance of our algorithm under different m values. Afterward, under the same block size 4×4, we compare our algorithm with Chuang and Chang's algorithm [5], Hong et al.'s algorithm [9], and Chen et al.'s algorithm [10].

FIGURE 5.10

Six test images.

The performance indicators used in this chapter include PSNR, hiding capacity, bit rate (bit_rate) and transmission efficiency. For an $A \times B$-sized 256 gray-level image, the PSNR is defined as Eq. (5.26), where the MSE is computed by Eq. (5.27) and the bit rate is computed by Eq. (5.28). The higher the PSNR value is, the better quality the stego image has. The bit_rate indicator means the number of bits required for encoding one pixel. Hiding capacity denotes the length of the binary secret data that can be hidden in the host media. Transmission efficiency stands for the ratio of capacity to codestream length.

$$\text{PSNR} = 10 \log_{10} \frac{255 \times 255}{\text{MSE}} \qquad (5.26)$$

$$\text{MSE} = \frac{1}{A \times B} \sum_{i=1}^{A} \sum_{j=1}^{B} \left(x_{i,j} - x'_{i,j} \right)^2 \qquad (5.27)$$

$$\text{bit\_rate} = \frac{L}{A \times B} \qquad (5.28)$$

where $x_{i,j}$ and $x'_{i,j}$ are the original and stego grayscale pixel values located at (i,j) respectively, and L is the codestream length.

5.4.2.3.1 Performance of Our Algorithm

To evaluate the average performance of our scheme, a set of experiments are performed on six test images as shown in Fig. 5.10. In the experiments, the block size is set to be 4×4, and four aspects of performance are adopted to evaluate a data hiding scheme, i.e., the capacity, representing the maximum number of secret bits that can be hidden; the PSNR, representing the quality of the stego image; the bit rate, representing the performance of the compression efficiency whose unit is bpp; and the embedding efficiency, indicating the amount of embedded secret data when a bit of the binary code stream has been transmitted. Obviously, the embedding efficiency can be obtained by Capacity/(bit rate $\times A \times B$).

In fact, m is the only parameter that affects the performance of our scheme, hence we just test the performance indicators for different m values. As shown in Fig. 5.11, the PSNR value does not change with m ($m = 1,2,\ldots,7$), while the capacity remains the same (64,008 bits) for all test images with different m values. Hereby, the parameter m does not affect the PSNR and capacity, and the capacity only relates to the image size, which can also be inferred from the method itself. The bit_rate values with different m values are shown in Fig. 5.12. The bit rate when $m = 3$ or 4 is much lower than that with other m values. Similarly, $m = 3$ or 4 brings the highest efficiency performance, as shown in Fig. 5.13. Lower bit_rate and higher efficiency indicate better performance. We should note that the optimal value $m = 3$ or 4 is obtained based on a number of experimental results, which show that for most natural images the difference between the neighboring pixels mainly falls into $[-8, 8]$ or $[-16, 16]$. If we adopt a large value of $m > 4$, then we will waste much more bits to describe the difference, resulting in a higher bit rate. On the other hand, if we

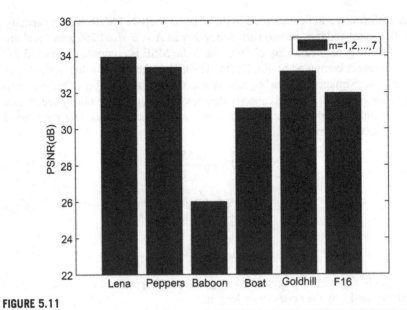

FIGURE 5.11

Peak signal-to-noise ratio (PSNR) values under different *m* values for six test images.

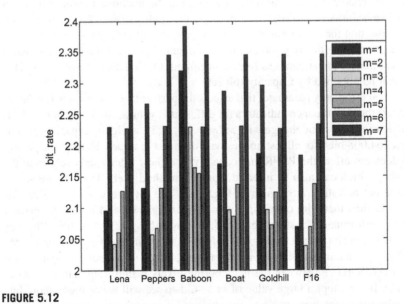

FIGURE 5.12

Bit_rate values under different *m* values for six test images.

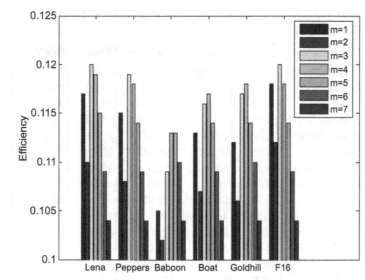

FIGURE 5.13

Efficiency values under different *m* values for six test images.

use a small value of $m = 1$ or 2, then many differences will be out of the range $[-(2^m - 1), (2^m - 1)]$, which also results in a higher bit rate. Since we cannot confirm under which *m* value ($m = 3$ or $m = 4$) our scheme can obtain the best performance from Fig. 5.12, we have to calculate the mean bit_rate value and the mean efficiency value over all test images to achieve the best *m* value, and the result shows that our algorithm can obtain a better performance when $m = 4$.

5.4.2.3.2 Comparison of Our Algorithm With Those of Others

To show the superiority of our proposed algorithm, we compare it with Chuang and Chang's scheme [5], Hong et al.'s scheme [9], and Chen et al.'s scheme [10]. As shown in Table 5.5, the PSNRs of stego images based on our, Hong et al.'s, and Chen et al.'s schemes are exactly the same as those of the original AMBTC-compressed images, since these three schemes do not change the AMBTC-compressed image quality during the data hiding process. However, Chuang and Chang's method obtains worse image quality as it is not a reversible data hiding scheme.

With respect to the embedding capacity, the proposed scheme achieves the highest embedding capacity. Compared with other three schemes, our scheme embeds 2 bits in each mean value, including the low and high mean tables, so we can embed 4 bits in each 4×4 pixel block. The capacity of Chuang and Chang's scheme is determined by the number of smooth blocks. The capacity of Hong et al.'s and Chen et al.'s schemes is normally 1 bit in each 4×4 pixel block. However, if there are some blocks with the same high and low mean, then Hong et al.'s scheme will

Table 5.5 Comparisons of the Proposed, Chuang and Chang's, Hong et al.'s, and Chen et al.'s Schemes ($a \times b = 4 \times 4$)

Algorithm	Performance	Lena	Peppers	Baboon	Boat	Goldhill	Jet_F16
AMBTC	PSNR (dB)	33.971	33.400	25.995	31.147	33.161	31.949
	Bit rate (bpp)	2.000	2.000	2.000	2.000	2.000	2.000
Proposed	PSNR (dB)	33.971	33.400	25.995	31.147	33.161	31.949
	Capacity (bits)	64,008	64,008	64,008	64,008	64,008	64,008
	Bit rate (bpp)	2.060	2.067	2.164	2.086	2.072	2.069
Chuang and Chang's	PSNR (dB)	31.659	31.233	25.912	30.789	32.534	30.849
	Capacity (bits)	13,048	13,464	5168	11,981	12,487	12,631
	Bit rate (bpp)	2.000	2.000	2.000	2.000	2.000	2.000
Hong et al.'s	PSNR (dB)	33.971	33.400	25.995	31.147	33.161	31.949
	Capacity (bits)	16,384	16,099	16,384	16,384	16,384	16,384
	Bit rate (bpp)	2.000	2.000	2.000	2.000	2.000	2.000
Chen et al.'s	PSNR (dB)	33.971	33.400	25.995	31.147	33.161	31.949
	Capacity (bits)	16,384	20,944	16,384	16,384	16,384	16,384
	Bit rate (bpp)	2.000	2.000	2.000	2.000	2.000	2.000

AMBTC, *absolute moment block truncation coding*; PSNR, *peak signal-to-noise ratio*.

have less capacity and Chen et al.'s scheme will have more capacity. As shown in Table 5.5, the capacity in our scheme is nearly twice higher than that in the other schemes, with a bit higher bit_rate. With high capacity and acceptable bit_rate, our scheme has much higher efficiency, as shown in Fig. 5.14. We can see that the efficiency of our scheme is nearly four times larger than that of the other schemes.

5.4.3 BLOCKWISE CODING–BASED SCHEME

As we know, Chuang and Chang's scheme is not a reversible scheme, while Hong et al.'s bitplane flipping scheme and Chen et al.'s scheme can embed 1 bit information per block if there is no block with $l_{ij} = h_{ij}$. To both embed more secret bits and reduce the coding bit rate, we can view all high/low means as a high/low mean table and then make full use of the correlation among the neighboring high/low means to encode the high/low mean table with less bits based on the secret data. To make use of the correlation among neighboring high/low means, we can perform the high/low mean table coding process on each 2×2 high/low mean block rather than one by one. Based on these considerations, we proposed a novel data hiding scheme for BTC-compressed images based on lossless encoding of the high and low mean tables [16]. The main idea of our scheme is to first perform AMBTC on the original image, obtaining one high mean table, one low mean table, and one bitplane sequence, and then divide the high and low mean tables into nonoverlapping 2×2 blocks. Finally, we encode the mean values in each 2×2 block according

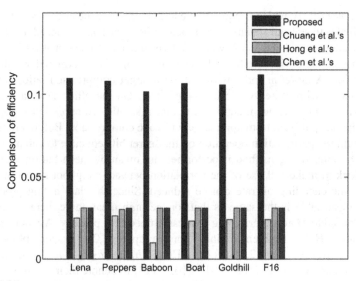

FIGURE 5.14

Comparisons of the proposed, Chuang and Chang's, Hong et al.'s, and Chen et al.'s schemes in terms of efficiency ($a \times b = 4 \times 4$).

to four input secret bits and the dynamic range evaluated by the difference between the maximal mean value and the minimal mean value in the mean block. The proposed algorithm consists of three stages, i.e., the AMBTC compression stage, the data hiding & mean table coding stage and the data extraction and decoding stage, which can be illustrated as follows:

5.4.3.1 The Absolute Moment Block Truncation Coding Compression Stage
This stage is a preprocessing stage before data hiding and mean table coding. The aim of this stage is to obtain the two mean tables for later use. Given an $M \times N$-sized 256 grayscale original image **X**, this stage can be expressed as follows:

Step 1: The original image **X** is divided into nonoverlapping $m \times n$-sized blocks $x^{(ij)}$, $i = 1, 2,...,M/m, j = 1, 2,...,N/n$.
Step 2: Encode each image block $x^{(ij)}$ by AMBTC, obtaining the compressed triple $(l_{ij}, h_{ij}, \boldsymbol{p}_{ij})$.
Step 3: Compose all high means and low means to obtain the high mean table $\mathbf{H} = \{h_{ij} \mid i = 1,2,...,M/m; j = 0,1,...,N/n\}$ and the low mean table $\mathbf{L} = \{l_{ij} \mid i = 1,2,...,M/m; j = 0,1,...,N/n\}$, respectively. Compose all bitplanes to obtain the bitplane sequence $\mathbf{P} = \{\boldsymbol{p}_{ij} \mid i = 1,2,...,M/m; j = 0,1,...,N/n\}$.

5.4.3.2 The Data Hiding and Mean Table Coding Stage
With the mean tables **H** and **L** in hand, now we can introduce our reversible data hiding and mean table coding algorithm. Assume the secret bit sequence is of length

$2 \times M \times N/(m \times n)$, which is equal to the total number of mean values in two mean tables. That is to say, our scheme can embed 2 bits in each $m \times n$-sized image block. Here, we adopt $m = 4$ and $n = 4$, which is derived from conventional BTC compression schemes. The visual effect of the stego image is determined by the BTC compression. A larger m and n will result in a larger compression ratio, but worse image quality with more visible blocking effect. On the other hand, a smaller m and n will result in better image quality, but a smaller compression ratio, which will further keep it back from application in image compression. Before embedding, we perform the permutation operation on the secret bit sequence to enhance the security. Our embedding method is performed not mean by mean but on each 2×2 mean block to make full use of the correlation between neighboring mean values, and thus the encoding bit rate can be reduced. Since the data hiding process for the low mean table is the same as that for the high mean table, here we take the high mean table **H** to describe the lossless embedding process. Assume the high mean table **H** is segmented into nonoverlapping 2×2-sized blocks, h_{uv}, $u = 1, 2, \ldots, M/(2m)$; $v = 1, 2, \ldots, N/(2n)$. Here, $h_{uv} = \{h_{2u,2v} \quad h_{2u,2v+1}, \quad h_{2u+1,2v}, h_{2u+1,2v+1}\}$, and we adopt $\{\text{"00," "01," "10," "11"}\}$ to denote their locations accordingly. For each 2×2 high mean block h_{uv}, assume the corresponding four secret bits to be embedded are $\{w_1, w_2, w_3, w_4\}$; the data hiding and high mean table coding process can be illustrated in detailed as follows.

> Step 1: Find the maximal and minimal mean values h_{max} and h_{min} in h_{uv}, and record their location bits $w_{max} \in \{\text{"00," "01," "10," "11"}\}$ and $w_{min} \in \{\text{"00,"}$ "01," "10," "11"}\}$, respectively.
>
> Step 2: Calculate the dynamic range $r = h_{max} - h_{min}$. For 256-gray-level images, since the dynamic range r belongs to the interval $[0, 255]$, we consider eight cases as shown in Table 5.6. Obviously, it requires 3 bits to denote each case.

Table 5.6 Eight Cases Considered for Coding the Mean Differences

Case	Dynamic Range r ($r = h_{max} - h_{min}$ for High Means, Whereas $r = l_{max} - l_{min}$ for Low Means)	Range Bits w_{ran}	c (Number of Bits Required to Code Each Difference)
1	$0 \leq r < 2$	"000"	1
2	$2 \leq r < 4$	"001"	2
3	$4 \leq r < 8$	"010"	3
4	$8 \leq r < 16$	"011"	4
5	$16 \leq r < 32$	"100"	5
6	$32 \leq r < 64$	"101"	6
7	$64 \leq r < 128$	"110"	7
8	$r \geq 128$	"111"	8

Append these 3 bits (they are called range bits w_{ran} in this chapter) to the codestream.

Step 3: Viewing the first two secret bits w_1 and w_2 as the location bits; find the reference high mean h_{ref} in $\mathbf{h}_{uv}$. (e.g., if the first two secret bits are "01," then $h_{ref} = h_{2u,2v+1}$). Append the two secret bits $w_{ref} = w_1 \| w_2$ (they are called reference location bits) followed by the 8 bits $(h_{ref})_2$ to the codestream. Here, $\|$ denotes the concatenation operation and $(\cdot)_2$ denotes the operation to get the binary description of a number.

Step 4: According to the third secret bit w_3, select the comparison high mean h_{com} out of $\{h_{max}, h_{min}\}$. If $w_3 = 1$, then set $h_{com} = h_{max}$ and $w_{com} = w_{max}$; otherwise, if $w_3 = 0$, then set $h_{com} = h_{min}$ and $w_{com} = w_{min}$. Here we should consider two cases. In Case 1, the reference high mean and the comparison high mean are located at the same position, i.e., $h_{ref} = h_{com}$ and $w_{ref} = w_{com}$. Denote the remainder three high mean values in $\mathbf{h}_{uv}$ as h_A, h_B, and h_C (in the raster-scan order). In Case 2, the reference high mean and the comparison high mean are located at different positions, i.e., $w_{ref} \neq w_{com}$. Except for h_{com}, we define $h_A = h_{ref}$ and denote the remainder two high mean values in $\mathbf{h}_{uv}$ as h_B and h_C (in the raster-scan order). Append the third secret bit w_3 followed by the two comparison location bits w_{com} to the codestream.

Step 5: According to the secret bits w_3 and w_4, calculate the differences among h_{com}, h_A, h_B and h_C. If $w_4 = 0$ and $w_3 = 0$, then $d_A = h_A - h_{com}$, $d_B = h_B - h_{com}$, and $d_C = h_C - h_{com}$. If $w_4 = 0$ and $w_3 = 1$, then $d_A = h_{com} - h_A$, $d_B = h_{com} - h_B$, and $d_C = h_{com} - h_C$. If $w_4 = 1$ and $w_3 = 0$, then $d_A = h_{com} - h_A$, $d_B = h_{com} - h_B$, and $d_C = h_{com} - h_C$. If $w_4 = 1$ and $w_3 = 1$, then $d_A = h_A - h_{com}$, $d_B = h_B - h_{com}$, and $d_C = h_C - h_{com}$. We easily find that w_4 can indicate the sign of the differences, i.e., if $w_4 = 0$, the sign is positive; otherwise, the sign is negative.

Step 6: According to the dynamic range r given in Table 5.6, look up the number of bits (it is denoted by c) required to encode each difference. If $w_4 = 0$, $3c$ bits are used to denote $(d_A)_2$, $(d_B)_2$, and $(d_C)_2$. Otherwise, if $w_4 = 1$, $3c$ bits are used to denote $(-d_A)_2$, $(-d_B)_2$, and $(-d_C)_2$. Append the fourth secret bit w_4 followed by the $3c$ bits of d_A, d_B, and d_C to the codestream.

Perform Steps 1–6 for each 2×2 high mean block $\mathbf{h}_{uv}$; we can hide 4 bits in each high mean block and output a bit string whose length is $17 + 3c$. Similarly, by performing Steps 1–6 for each low mean block $\mathbf{l}_{uv}$, we can also hide 4 bits in each low mean block. Here, c is different from block to block. If most of the mean blocks are with $c \leq 5$, then the bit rate can be reduced compared with the original mean table that requires 32 bits to denote four mean values in each mean block. An example of high mean coding and data hiding for a typical 2×2 high mean block is shown in Fig. 5.15.

5.4.3.3 The Decoding and Extracting Stage
Our data hiding scheme is reversible because we can recover the original mean tables after data extraction, and thus the original BTC-compressed image can be

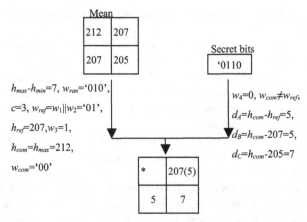

FIGURE 5.15

An example to hide 4 bits and encode a high mean block.

losslessly recovered. Given the codestream, our purpose is to extract the secret bit sequence and recover the original BTC-compressed image. Since the reconstruction process for the low mean table is the same as that for the high mean table, here we take the reconstruction process for the high mean table to describe the extraction process as follows.

Step 1: Read the next 3 bits into w_{ran} from the codestream of the high mean table, find the corresponding case and look up the value c in Table 5.6.
Step 2: Read the next 10 bits from the codestream of the high mean table. Get the first 2 bits w_1 and w_2 as the reference location bits w_{ref}, and append them to the output secret bit sequence. Transform the last 8 bits into the reference high mean h_{ref}, and put this mean in the current mean block according to the location bits w_{ref}.
Step 3: Read the next 3 bits from the codestream of the high mean table. Get the first bit w_3, and append it to the output secret bit sequence. Get the last 2 bits as the comparison location bits w_{com}.
Step 4: Read the next $1 + 3c$ bits from the codestream of the high mean table. Get the first bit w_4, append it to the output secret bit sequence. Transform the following three c bits into three positive difference values d_{A+}, d_{B+}, and d_{C+}. If $w_4 = 0$, $d_A = d_{A+}$, $d_B = d_{B+}$, and $d_C = d_{C+}$; otherwise, $d_A = -d_{A+}$, $d_B = -d_{B+}$ and $d_C = -d_{C+}$.
Step 5: Except for the reference high mean, recover the other three mean values in the current 2×2 high mean block. Here, we should consider two cases:
Case 1: $w_{ref} = w_{com}$. In this case, the reference high mean is just the comparison high mean, and thus $h_{com} = h_{ref}$. If $w_4 = 0$ and $w_3 = 0$, then $h_A = d_A + h_{com}$, $h_B = d_B + h_{com}$, and $h_C = d_C + h_{com}$. If $w_4 = 0$ and $w_3 = 1$, then $h_A = h_{com} - d_A$,

$h_B = h_{com} - d_B$, and $h_C = h_{com} - d_C$. If $w_4 = 1$ and $w_3 = 0$, then $h_A = h_{com} - d_A$, $h_B = h_{com} - d_B$, and $h_C = h_{com} - d_C$. If $w_4 = 1$ and $w_3 = 1$, then $h_A = d_A + h_{com}$, $h_B = d_B + h_{com}$, and $h_C = d_C + h_{com}$. Put h_A, h_B, and h_C at the remainder three locations in the raster-scan order.

Case 2: $w_{ref} \neq w_{com}$. In this case, d_A is the difference between h_{com} and h_{ref}. If $w_4 = 0$ and $w_3 = 0$, then $h_{com} = d_A - h_{ref}$. If $w_4 = 0$ and $w_3 = 1$, then $h_{com} = h_{ref} + d_A$. If $w_4 = 1$ and $w_3 = 0$, then $h_{com} = h_{ref} + d_A$. If $w_4 = 1$ and $w_3 = 1$, then $h_{com} = d_A - h_{ref}$. Put h_{com} in the current 2×2 high mean block according to the location bits w_{com}. Now turn to recover left two indices. If $w_4 = 0$ and $w_3 = 0$, then $h_B = d_B + h_{com}$ and $h_C = d_C + h_{com}$. If $w_4 = 0$ and $w_3 = 1$, then $h_B = h_{com} - d_B$ and $h_C = h_{com} - d_C$. If $w_4 = 1$ and $w_3 = 0$, then $h_B = h_{com} - d_B$ and $h_C = h_{com} - d_C$. If $w_4 = 1$ and $w_3 = 1$, then $h_B = d_B + h_{com}$ and $h_C = d_C + h_{com}$. Put h_B and h_C at the remainder two locations in the raster-scan order.

Repeatedly perform Steps 1–5 for all 2×2 high mean blocks; we can recover the original high mean table and output the first half sequence of secret bits. Similarly, by performing Steps 1– for all 2×2 low mean blocks, we can recover the original low mean table and output the second half sequence of secret bits. Fig. 5.16 gives an example to show the decoding and data extraction process for a

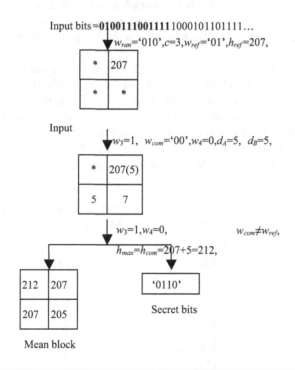

FIGURE 5.16

An example to extract secret data and decode a mean block.

high mean block. Based on the two decoded mean tables together with the unchanged bitplane sequence, we can reconstruct the original BTC-compressed image. In this way, the whole reversible process is realized.

5.4.3.4 Experimental Results

To evaluate the proposed scheme, we use six test images, Lena, Peppers, Mandrill, Boat, Goldhill, and Jet_F16, of the same size 512×512 with 256 grayscales. Comparisons among our algorithm, Chuang and Chang's algorithm [5], Hong et al.'s algorithm [9], and Chen et al.'s algorithm [10] are performed under the same block size 4×4. Besides BTC-based schemes, we also compare our scheme with a JPEG-based lossless data hiding scheme presented in 2012 [18] with $QF = 50$. Because the total number of bits required to encode a mean block based on our algorithm is $17 + 3c$, whereas the number of bits required to encode four mean values based on the original AMBTC is 32, to reduce the bit rate, we expect to have $17 + 3c \leq 32$, i.e., $c \leq 5$, for most mean blocks. To explain the capacity of three existing schemes more clearly, for six test images, we list the number of 4×4 pixel blocks whose high mean equals its low mean and the number of 4×4 smooth pixel blocks with $|h_{ij} - l_{ij}| \leq TH$ in Table 5.7. In our experiment, we can find that, for all images except for the Mandrill image, most high/low mean blocks belong to the first 4 cases, thus our scheme can reduce the bit rate as shown in Table 5.8. The Mandrill image is very complex with high detail, which makes the variation of mean values in most mean blocks be large, and thus most mean blocks belong to cases 5 and 6 and the bit rate is a bit larger than that of the original AMBTC.

To show the superiority of our proposed algorithm over the other BTC-based methods, we compare it with Chuang and Chang's scheme [5], Hong et al.'s scheme [9], and Chen et al.'s scheme [10]. Five aspects of performance are adopted in the experiments to evaluate a data hiding scheme, i.e., the capacity, representing the maximum number of secret bits that can be hidden; the PSNR, representing the quality of the stego image; the bit rate, representing the performance of the compression efficiency whose unit is bpp; the embedding efficiency, indicating the number of

Table 5.7 The Number of 4×4 Pixel Blocks Whose High Mean Equals Its Low Mean (Denoted by *EB*) and the Number of 4×4 Smooth Pixel Blocks With $|h_{ij} - l_{ij}| < TH$ (Denoted by *SB*, *TH* = 20)

Image	SB	EB
Lena	13,048	0
Peppers	13,464	285
Mandrill	5168	0
Boat	11,981	0
Goldhill	12,487	0
Jet_F16	12,631	0

Table 5.8 Comparisons of the Proposed, Chuang and Chang's, Hong et al.'s, and Chen et al.'s Schemes ($m \times n = 4 \times 4$) and the JPEG-Based Scheme (QF = 50)

Algorithm	Performance	Lena	Peppers	Mandrill	Boat	Goldhill	Jet_F16
AMBTC	PSNR (dB)	32.034	31.595	25.995	31.147	33.162	31.031
	Bit rate (bpp)	2.000	2.000	2.000	2.000	2.000	2.000
	Complexity	1.000	1.000	1.000	1.000	1.000	1.000
Proposed	PSNR (dB)	32.034	31.595	25.995	31.147	33.162	31.031
	Capacity (bits)	32,768	32,768	32,768	32,768	32,768	32,768
	Bit rate (bpp)	1.917	1.916	2.009	1.934	1.932	1.892
	Efficiency	0.065	0.065	0.062	0.065	0.065	0.066
	Complexity	1.010	1.011	1.014	1.011	1.011	1.012
Chuang and Chang's	PSNR (dB)	31.659	31.233	25.912	30.789	32.534	30.849
	Capacity (bits)	13,048	13,464	5168	11,981	12,487	12,631
	Bit rate (bpp)	2.000	2.000	2.000	2.000	2.000	2.000
	Efficiency	0.025	0.026	0.010	0.023	0.024	0.024
	Complexity	1.000	1.001	1.001	1.000	1.001	1.001
Hong et al.'s	PSNR (dB)	32.034	31.595	25.995	31.147	33.162	31.031
	Capacity (bits)	16,384	16,099	16,384	16,384	16,384	16,384
	Bit rate (bpp)	2.000	2.000	2.000	2.000	2.000	2.000
	Efficiency	0.031	0.030	0.031	0.031	0.031	0.031
	Complexity	1.000	1.001	1.000	1.000	1.001	1.000
Chen et al.'s	PSNR (dB)	32.034	31.595	25.995	31.147	33.162	31.031
	Capacity (bits)	16,384	20,944	16,384	16,384	16,384	16,384
	Bit Rate(bpp)	2.000	2.000	2.000	2.000	2.000	2.000
	Efficiency	0.031	0.040	0.031	0.031	0.031	0.031
	Complexity	1.001	1.001	1.002	1.001	1.002	1.001
JPEG-based method	PSNR (dB)	35.235	35.077	28.426	34.433	36.429	34.034
	Capacity (bits)	364	389	1080	522	810	760
	Bit rate (bpp)	1.654	1.656	3.109	1.811	1.750	1.597
	Efficiency	0.0008	0.0009	0.0013	0.0011	0.0020	0.0018
	Complexity	18.231	18.874	30.012	19.245	20.532	19.429

AMBTC, *absolute moment block truncation coding;* PSNR, *peak signal-to-noise ratio.*

embedded secret data when a bit of the binary code stream has been transmitted; and the time complexity, indicating the ratio of the time cost by a data hiding scheme to the time cost by the standard BTC compression. Obviously, the embedding efficiency can be calculated as Capacity/(bit rate $\times M \times N$). As shown in Table 5.8, the PSNRs of stego images based on our, Hong et al.'s, and Chen et al.'s schemes are exactly the same as those of the original AMBTC-compressed images, the reason being is that these three schemes are reversible. However, Chuang and Chang's method obtains worse image quality, because it is not a reversible data hiding scheme. Fig. 5.17 shows the original Lena image, BTC-compressed Lena image and stego Lena images by various BTC-based methods.

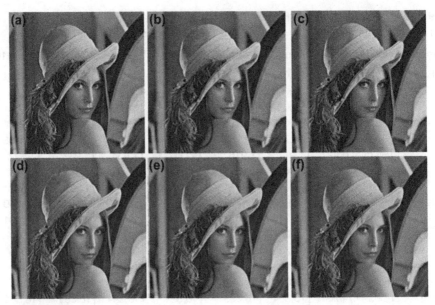

FIGURE 5.17

The original Lena image, the AMBTC-compressed image, and stego images by various hiding schemes. (a) The original image; (b) the AMBTC-compressed image, PSNR = 32.034 dB; (c) the stego image by our scheme, PSNR = 32.034 dB; (d) the stego image by Chuang and Chang's scheme, PSNR = 31.659 dB; (e) the stego image by Hong et al.'s scheme, PSNR = 32.034 dB; (f) the stego image by Chen et al.'s scheme, PSNR = 32.034 dB. *AMBTC*, absolute moment block truncation coding; *PSNR*, peak signal-to-noise ratio.

With respect to the embedding capacity, the proposed scheme achieves the highest embedding capacity. Compared with other three schemes, our scheme embeds information in all mean values, so we can embed 2 bits in each 4×4 pixel block. The capacity of Chuang and Chang's scheme is determined by the number of smooth blocks as given in Table 5.7. The capacity of Hong et al.'s and Chen et al.'s schemes is normally 1 bits in each 4×4 pixel block. However, if there are some blocks with the same high and low means, then Hong et al.'s scheme will have less capacity and Chen et al.'s scheme will have more capacity. As shown in Table 5.7, for the Peppers image, because $EB = 285$, Hong et al.'s scheme can only embed $16,384 - 285 = 16,099$ bits, whereas while Chen et al.'s scheme can embed $16,384 + 285 \times 4 \times 4 = 20,944$ bits. In fact, the reason why our scheme can embed more bits is that our scheme further losslessly compresses the BTC data and releases room for data hiding. In other words, Hong et al.'s method and Chen et al.'s method only exploit the BTC data (that is, they retain the bit rate 2.0 bpp), whereas our method further losslessly compresses the BTC data based on the correlation between neighboring high and low means, and thus we have more room for data hiding.

With regard to the bit rate, from Table 5.8, we can see that only our scheme can reduce the bit rate by around 0.1 bpp, whereas the other three BTC-based schemes have the same bit rate as the original AMBTC scheme. That is to say, our scheme can not only hide information but also further compress BTC-compressed data for most images. However, for the Mandrill image, because it is too complex, our scheme gets a bit higher bit rate of 2.009 bpp.

In terms of embedding efficiency, our scheme has the highest efficiency values, and Chuang and Chang's method has the lowest efficiency values among various BTC-based schemes. This means that our scheme can transmit the most amount of embedded secret data when a bit of the binary code stream has been transmitted, whereas Chuang and Chang's scheme can transmit the least amount of embedded secret data. Our scheme has the efficiency values that are approximately one time higher than those of Hong et al.'s and Chen et al.'s schemes.

In terms of time complexity, we can see that all BTC-based schemes have very low complexity since the BTC compression process is very fast, and the hiding procedure is relatively simple. Compared with the two existing BTC-based reversible data hiding schemes, our scheme has a bit higher complexity since our hiding procedure is a bit more complicated.

We also compared our scheme with the JPEG-based reversible data hiding scheme [18] when QF $= 50$. From Table 5.8, we can see that the JPEG-based scheme can only hide few bits, whereas our algorithm can hide 32—90 times as many secret bits as the JPEG-based scheme. Thus, although the bit rate of the JPEG-based scheme is less than our scheme, the resulting embedding efficiency of the JPEG-based scheme is much less than ours. On the other hand, the time complexity of the JPEG-based scheme is about 18—30 times as high as that of our scheme. However, the image quality of the JPEG-based scheme is much higher than ours.

Taking the above five attributes into comprehensive consideration, compared with other BTC-based schemes, the proposed scheme is a more effective method for its high capacity, high PSNR, high embedding efficiency, low bit rate, and relatively low complexity. In addition, our scheme is also superior to the JPEG-based scheme in terms of embedding efficiency and complexity. Since our scheme is very fast and its capacity is high, it can be used to transmit a great deal of secret information real time by embedding them in images, which has a potential value in military and business fields.

5.5 LOSSLESS DATA HIDING IN BLOCK TRUNCATION CODING—COMPRESSED COLOR IMAGES

As we know, BTC [1] is a lossy compression technique that can significantly reduce the size of digital images with acceptable visual quality. The traditional color BTC method compresses each color image block (typically 4×4) into three high means, three low means, and three bitplanes. To conceal secret data into color BTC compression codes as well as reducing the number of bitplanes, Chang et al. [5] used the genetic algorithm (GA) to generate an optimal common bitplane (replacing the traditional three bitplanes) to reduce the bit rate, and then utilized the side match distortion concept to increase the embedding capacity. However, Chang et al.'s method is time consuming for generating a common bitplane. Recently, Chou and Chang [6] proposed an improved data hiding method to save the computation cost during common bitplane generation. However, Both Chang et al.'s algorithm and Chou and Chang's scheme increase the bit rate because of the additional bits required to recognize the irreplaceable blocks. To both increase the hiding capacity and reduce the bit rate, this section introduces two reversible data hiding for BTC-compressed color images, one is to further losslessly encoding the high mean tables and low mean tables based on the secret data, and the other is using the difference expansion (DE) technique. Before introducing these two methods, we first introduce the BTC compression technique for color images.

5.5.1 BLOCK TRUNCATION CODING COMPRESSION FOR COLOR IMAGES

5.5.1.1 Traditional Color Block Truncation Coding

The traditional color BTC applies the grayscale BTC three times on *red*, *green*, and *blue* planes. Therefore, every compressed color image block requires three bitplanes together with three high means and three low means. The key steps of the color BTC compression are as following. First, a color image $\mathbf{I}$ is divided into nonoverlapping blocks of size 4×4. For each block $\mathbf{B}_i$, the mean values $M_{i,r}$, $M_{i,g}$, and $M_{i,b}$ are calculated for *red*, *green*, and *blue* components, respectively. After that, $M_{i,r}$ is compared with every *red* component in $\mathbf{B}_i$; if a *red* component is not less than $M_{i,r}$, then the corresponding element in the *red* bitplane $\mathbf{BP}_{i,r}$ is set to "1," otherwise it is set to "0." At the same time, the high mean $H_{i,r}$ and the low mean $L_{i,r}$ are obtained by calculating the mean value for all *red* components not less than $M_{i,r}$ and the mean value for all *red* components less than $M_{i,r}$, respectively. Similarly, the *green* bitplane $\mathbf{BP}_{i,g}$ and the *blue* bitplane $\mathbf{BP}_{i,b}$ can be also obtained, together with the *green* mean pair ($H_{i,g}$, $L_{i,g}$) and the *blue* mean pair ($H_{i,b}$, $L_{i,b}$). Thus, the compressed code for each block $\mathbf{B}_i$ can be represented as ($\mathbf{BP}_{i,r}$, $H_{i,r}$, $L_{i,r}$, $\mathbf{BP}_{i,g}$, $H_{i,g}$, $L_{i,g}$, $\mathbf{BP}_{i,b}$, $H_{i,b}$, $L_{i,b}$).

5.5.1.2 Common Bitplane Color Block Truncation Coding

The traditional color BTC method encodes each block with three bitplanes ($\mathbf{BP}_{i,r}$, $\mathbf{BP}_{i,g}$, $\mathbf{BP}_{i,b}$) together with three mean pairs. To reduce the bit rate, a good way is to find an optimal common bitplane $\mathbf{BP}_{i,c}$ to replace the original three bitplanes, i.e., $\mathbf{BP}_{i,r} = \mathbf{BP}_{i,g} = \mathbf{BP}_{i,b} = \mathbf{BP}_{i,c}$. Thus, in this case, the compressed code for each block $\mathbf{B}_i$ can be represented as ($\mathbf{BP}_{i,c}$, $H_{i,r}$, $L_{i,r}$, $H_{i,g}$, $L_{i,g}$, $H_{i,b}$, $L_{i,b}$). Now the remaining problem is how to find the optimal common bitplane. A natural idea is to use an optimization technique. In Chang et al.'s method [19], they adopted the GA to find the approximate optimal bitplane. In fact, there are only 16 pixels in each block, we can absolutely use an exhausted search algorithm to find the optimal bitplane. Based on this simple idea, Chou and Chang's scheme [20] generated the optimal common bitplane $\mathbf{BP}_{i,c} = \{y_1, y_2,...,y_{16}\}$ from the block $\mathbf{B}_i = \{x_1, x_2, ..., x_{16}\}$ by Eq. (5.29).

$$y_k = \begin{cases} 1 & \text{if} |x_k - p_H| \leq |x_k - p_L| \\ 0 & \text{otherwise} \end{cases}, \quad k = 1, 2, ..., 16 \qquad (5.29)$$

where, $p_H = (H_{i,r}, H_{i,g}, H_{i,b})$ and $p_L = (L_{i,r}, L_{i,g}, L_{i,b})$ are two virtual color pixels.

5.5.2 DIFFERENCE EXPANSION–BASED SCHEME

5.5.2.1 The Difference Expansion Technique

The DE technique for reversible data hiding was first proposed by Tian [21]. Given a pair of 256-grayscale image pixel values (x, y), $0 \leq x, y \leq 255$, their integer average c and difference d are computed as

$$c = \left\lfloor \frac{x+y}{2} \right\rfloor, d = x - y \qquad (5.30)$$

where $\lfloor z \rfloor$ denotes the floor function that seeks the greatest integer less than or equal to z. The inverse transform of Eq. (5.30) is

$$x = c + \left\lfloor \frac{d+1}{2} \right\rfloor, y = c - \left\lfloor \frac{d}{2} \right\rfloor \qquad (5.31)$$

The reversible transforms denoted by Eqs. (5.30) and (5.31) are called the integer Haar wavelet transform. Tian [21] embedded a binary bit b into d based on the following rule:

$$d' = 2d + b \qquad (5.32)$$

For both $b = 0$ and $b = 1$, if the difference value d satisfies Eq. (5.33), it is a changeable difference value

$$\left| 2 \cdot \left\lfloor \frac{d}{2} \right\rfloor + b \right| \leq \min(2 \cdot (255 - c), 2c + 1) \qquad (5.33)$$

Furthermore, for both $b = 0$ and $b = 1$, if the difference value d satisfies Eq. (5.34), it is an expandable difference value

$$|2d + b| \leq \min(2 \cdot (255 - c), 2c + 1) \qquad (5.34)$$

In the DE method, data embedding and extraction rely on expendable and changeable differences. The expandable differences provide space for data embedding, and the changeable differences are used to guarantee blind data extraction. All difference values in the difference image are classified into three categories: expandable, changeable but nonexpandable, and nonchangeable. For a pure payload (the secret bits to be hidden), a number of expandable differences should be selected and their locations should be stored into a binary-type location map, which can be losslessly compressed by run-length coding. All the LSBs of changeable but nonexpandable differences are recorded as an original bitstream. The compressed location map, the original bitstream, and the pure payload are embedded into the difference image together.

The secret data extraction process is simple. The LSBs of all changeable differences in the image compose a bitstream, from which we can extract the location map, the original bitstream, and the pure payload. To restore the image, all previous expandable differences divide by two integrally. The LSBs of all changeable but not expandable differences are reset with the original bitstream.

5.5.2.2 The Proposed Scheme

For convenience, let $\mathbf{X}$ be the color image with M rows and N columns:

$$
\begin{aligned}
\mathbf{X} &= \{\mathbf{R}, \mathbf{G}, \mathbf{B}\} \\
\mathbf{R} &= \{r_{ij} | 1 \le i \le M, 1 \le j \le N\} \\
\mathbf{G} &= \{g_{ij} | 1 \le i \le M, 1 \le j \le N\} \\
\mathbf{B} &= \{b_{ij} | 1 \le i \le M, 1 \le j \le N\}
\end{aligned}
\tag{5.35}
$$

where $\mathbf{R}$, $\mathbf{G}$, and $\mathbf{B}$ denote as the three components of the RGB color space of the $\mathbf{X}$. In our scheme, we perform the same process on $\mathbf{R}$, $\mathbf{G}$, and $\mathbf{B}$ separately. Without loss of generality, we take the $\mathbf{R}$ channel, for example, to illustrate the data hiding and extraction processes. The data hiding process consists of two main steps, one is to obtain the BTC-compressed image data, and the other is to perform the DE technique on the obtained compressed data, which can be illustrated as follows:

Step 1. Perform AMBTC on the $\mathbf{R}$ component.
Step 1.1. The $\mathbf{R}$ image is divided into nonoverlapping $m \times n$-sized blocks $r^{(uv)}$, $1 \le u \le M/m$, $1 \le v \le N/n$.
Step 1.2. Encode each block $r^{(uv)}$ by AMBTC to obtain the compressed triple (l_{uv}, h_{uv}, p_{uv}).
Step 1.3. Collect all high means and low means to obtain the high mean table $\mathbf{H_r} = \{h_{uv}, 1 \le u \le M/m, 1 \le v \le N/n\}$ and the low mean table $\mathbf{L_r} = \{l_{uv}, 1 \le u \le M/m, 1 \le v \le N/n\}$. Finally, compose all bitplanes to obtain the bitplane sequence $\mathbf{P_r} = \{p_{uv}, 1 \le u \le M/m, 1 \le v \le N/n\}$.
Step 2. Hide data in $(\mathbf{H_r}, \mathbf{L_r})$ using the DE technique.
Step 2.1: Encode each pair $(h_{uv}, l_{uv}) \in (\mathbf{H_r}, \mathbf{L_r})$ by the integer Haar transform to obtain the difference sequence $\mathbf{D_r} = \{d_{uv}, 1 \le u \le M/m, 1 \le v \le N/n\}$ and the mean sequence $\mathbf{E_r} = \{e_{uv}, 1 \le u \le M/m, 1 \le v \le N/n\}$.
Step 2.2. Embed the secret data into the difference sequence $\mathbf{D_r}$ by the DE technique as described in Section 2.2 to obtain the watermarked compressed data $\left(\mathbf{H_r^w}, \mathbf{L_r^w}, \mathbf{P_r^w}\right)$ which can be used to reconstruct the watermarked $\mathbf{R}$ image. Here, $\mathbf{P_r^w} = \mathbf{P_r}$, which means that the bitplane is unchanged during the data hiding process.

Assume we have received the watermarked compressed data $\left(\mathbf{H}_r^w, \mathbf{L}_r^w, \mathbf{P}_r\right)$ of the **R** image; our data extraction and image recovery process is very simple, which can be illustrated as follows.

Step 1. Perform the integer Haar transform on each pair $\left(h_{uv}^w, l_{uv}^w\right) \in \left(\mathbf{H}_r^w, \mathbf{L}_r^w\right)$ to obtain the difference sequence $\mathbf{D}_r^w = \left\{d_{uv}^w \mid u = 1, 2, ..., M/m; v = 1, 2, ..., N/n\right\}$ and the mean sequence $\mathbf{E}_r^w = \left\{e_{uv}^w \mid u = 1, 2, ..., M/m; v = 1, 2, ..., N/n\right\}$.
Step 2. Extract the pure payload from $\mathbf{D}_r^w$ by the DE technique as shown in Section 2.2. Meanwhile, $\mathbf{H}_r$ and $\mathbf{L}_r$ can be also losslessly recovered from $\mathbf{D}_r^w$ and $\mathbf{E}_r^w$.
Step 3. Reconstruct the **R** component of the BTC-compressed color image from $\left(\mathbf{H}_r, \mathbf{L}_r, \mathbf{P}_r\right)$.

Based on these steps, we can extract all secret data and reconstruct the original BTC-compressed color image, thus the whole reversible hiding process is realized.

5.5.2.3 Experimental Results

To evaluate the performance of the proposed scheme, we use six test color images, Lena, Peppers, Sailboat, Goldhill, Zelda, and Jet_F16, of the same size 512×512, as shown in Fig. 5.18. We choose three aspects of performance in the experiments to evaluate our data hiding method, i.e., the capacity, representing the maximum number of secret bits that can be hidden; the PSNR, representing the quality of the stego image; and the number of secret bits per pixel on average. In DE, a number of

FIGURE 5.18

Six test images.

Table 5.9 Number of Overflow Differences in Each Image

Image	Number of Overflow
Lena	669
Peppers	3496
Sailboat	1628
Goldhill	24
Zelda	135
Jet_F16	736

changeable but nonexpendable differences should be recorded to avoid the overflow. This recording information reduces the capacity for secret data. Table 5.9 shows the number of this kind of differences in each image. Table 5.10 shows the evaluation results.

5.5.3 BLOCKWISE CODING—BASED SCHEME

To both embed more secret bits and reduce the coding bit rate, we can piece all high (low) means as a high(low) mean table and then make full use of the correlation among the neighboring high (low) means to encode the high (low) mean table with less bits based on the secret data. The main idea of our blockwise scheme is to first perform the common bitplane color BTC on the original color image, obtaining three high mean tables $(\mathbf{H_r}, \mathbf{H_g}, \mathbf{H_b})$, three low mean tables $(\mathbf{L_r}, \mathbf{L_g}, \mathbf{L_b})$, and one bitplane sequence $\mathbf{BP_c}$, and then divide each mean table into nonoverlapping 2×2 blocks. Here, $\mathbf{BP_c} = \{\mathbf{BP}_{i,c}\}$, $\mathbf{H_t} = \{H_{i,t}\}$, and $\mathbf{L_t} = \{L_{i,t}\}$, where t = r,g,b. Finally, we encode the mean values in each 2×2 block according to four input secret bits and the dynamic range evaluated by the difference between the maximal mean value and the minimal mean value in the mean block. The proposed data embedding scheme and extraction process can be illustrated in Sections 5.5.3.1 and 5.5.3.2, respectively.

Table 5.10 Evaluation Results

Image	Capacity (Bits)	AMBTC Compressed (dB)	Watermarked (dB)	Recovered (dB)	SBPP
Lena	37,955	33.22	26.94	33.22	0.14
Peppers	21,772	32.82	27.20	32.82	0.08
Sailboat	28,012	29.62	23.98	29.62	0.10
Goldhill	45,680	32.29	25.84	32.29	0.17
Zelda	44,377	35.56	29.42	35.56	0.17
Jet_F16	40,744	32.68	26.12	32.68	0.16

AMBTC, *absolute moment block truncation coding*; SBPP, *secret bits per pixel*.

5.5.3.1 Data Embedding Process

With the six mean tables ($\mathbf{H_r}$, $\mathbf{H_g}$, $\mathbf{H_b}$, $\mathbf{L_r}$, $\mathbf{L_g}$, $\mathbf{L_b}$) in hand, now we can introduce our reversible data hiding algorithm. Assume the secret bit sequence has length $6 \times M \times N/(4 \times 4)$, which is equal to the total number of mean values in six mean tables, where $M \times N$ denotes the image size. That is to say, our scheme can embed 6 bits in each 4×4-sized color image block. Before embedding, we perform the permutation operation on the secret bit sequence to enhance the security. Our embedding method is performed not mean by mean but on each 2×2 mean block to make full use of the correlation between neighboring mean values, and thus the encoding bit rate can be reduced. Since the data hiding process for each mean table is the same, here we take the high mean table $\mathbf{H_r}$ to describe the lossless embedding process. For convenience, we let $\mathbf{H} = \mathbf{H_r}$ in the following description. Assume the high mean table $\mathbf{H}$ is segmented into nonoverlapping 2×2-sized blocks, $\mathbf{h}_{uv}$, where $u = 1, 2,...,M/8$ and $v = 1, 2,...,N/8$. Here, $\mathbf{h}_{uv} = \{h_{2u,2v}, h_{2u,2v+1}, h_{2u+1,2v}, h_{2u+1,2v+1}\}$, and we adopt {"00," "01," "10," "11"} to denote their locations accordingly. For each 2×2 high mean block $\mathbf{h}_{uv}$, assume the corresponding four secret bits to be embedded are $\{w_1, w_2, w_3, w_4\}$, the data hiding process can be illustrated in detail as follows.

> Step 1: Find the maximal and minimal mean values h_{max} and h_{min} in $\mathbf{h}_{uv}$, and record their location bits $w_{max} \in \{$"00," "01," "10," "11"$\}$ and $w_{min} \in \{$"00," "01," "10," "11"$\}$.
>
> Step 2: Calculate the dynamic range $r = h_{max} - h_{min}$. Since the dynamic range r belongs to the interval $[0,255]$, we consider eight cases as shown in Table 5.11. Obviously, it requires 3 bits to denote each case. Append these 3 bits (called range bits w_{ran}) to the codestream.
>
> Step 3: Viewing the first two secret bits w_1 and w_2 as the location bits, find the reference high mean h_{ref} in $\mathbf{h}_{uv}$. (e.g., if the first two secret bits are "01," then $h_{ref} = h_{2u,2v+1}$). Append the two secret bits $w_{ref} = w_1 \| w_2$ (called reference

Table 5.11 Eight Cases Considered for Coding the Mean Differences

Case	Dynamic range r ($r = h_{max} - h_{min}$ for High Means, While $r = I_{max} - I_{min}$ for Low Means)	Range Bits w_{ran}	c (Number of Bits Required to Code Each Difference)
Case 1	$0 \leq r < 2$	"000"	1
Case 2	$2 \leq r < 4$	"001"	2
Case 3	$4 \leq r < 8$	"010"	3
Case 4	$8 \leq r < 16$	"011"	4
Case 5	$16 \leq r < 32$	"100"	5
Case 6	$32 \leq r < 64$	"101"	6
Case 7	$64 \leq r < 128$	"110"	7
Case 8	$r \geq 128$	"111"	8

location bits) followed by the eight bits $(h_{ref})_2$ to the codestream. Here, $\|$ denotes the concatenation operation and $(\cdot)_2$ denotes the operation to get the binary description of a number.

Step 4: According to the third secret bit w_3, select the comparison high mean h_{com} out of $\{h_{max}, h_{min}\}$. If $w_3 = 1$, then set $h_{com} = h_{max}$ and $w_{com} = w_{max}$; otherwise, if $w_3 = 0$, then set $h_{com} = h_{min}$ and $w_{com} = w_{min}$. Here we should consider two cases. In Case 1, the reference and comparison high means are located at the same position, i.e., $h_{ref} = h_{com}$ and $w_{ref} = w_{com}$. Denote the remainder three high mean values in $\boldsymbol{h}_{uv}$ as h_A, h_B, and h_C, respectively (in the raster-scan order). In Case 2, the reference and comparison high means are located at different positions, i.e., $w_{ref} \neq w_{com}$. Except for h_{com}, we define $h_A = h_{ref}$ and denote the remainder two high mean values in $\boldsymbol{h}_{uv}$ as h_B and h_C, respectively (in the raster-scan order). Append the third secret bit w_3 followed by the two comparison location bits w_{com} to the codestream.

Step 5: According to the secret bits w_3 and w_4, we calculate the differences among h_{com}, h_A, h_B, and h_C. If $w_4 = 0$ and $w_3 = 0$, then $d_A = h_A - h_{com}$, $d_B = h_B - h_{com}$, and $d_C = h_C - h_{com}$. If $w_4 = 0$ and $w_3 = 1$, then $d_A = h_{com} - h_A$, $d_B = h_{com} - h_B$, and $d_C = h_{com} - h_C$. If $w_4 = 1$ and $w_3 = 0$, then $d_A = h_{com} - h_A$, $d_B = h_{com} - h_B$, and $d_C = h_{com} - h_C$. If $w_4 = 1$ and $w_3 = 1$, then $d_A = h_A - h_{com}$, $d_B = h_B - h_{com}$, and $d_C = h_C - h_{com}$. We easily find that w_4 can indicate the sign of the differences, i.e., if $w_4 = 0$, the sign is positive; otherwise, the sign is negative.

Step 6: According to the dynamic range r given in Table 5.11, we look up the number of bits (denoted by c) required to encode each difference. If $w_4 = 0$, $3c$ bits are used to denote $(d_A)_2$, $(d_B)_2$, and $(d_C)_2$. Otherwise, if $w_4 = 1$, $3c$ bits are used to denote $(-d_A)_2$, $(-d_B)_2$, and $(-d_C)_2$. Append the fourth secret bit w_4 followed by the $3c$ bits of d_A, d_B, and d_C to the codestream.

Performing Steps 1–6 for each 2×2 high mean block $\boldsymbol{h}_{uv}$, we can hide 4 bits in each high mean block and output a bit string whose length is $17 + 3c$, as given in Fig. 5.19. Similarly, by performing Steps 1–6 for each low mean block $\boldsymbol{l}_{uv}$, we can also hide 4 bits in each low mean block. Here, we should note that c is different from block to block. If most of the mean blocks are with $c \leq 5$, then the bit rate can be reduced compared to the original mean table where 32 bits are required to denote four mean values in each mean block.

Three range bits w_{ran}	Two reference location bits $w_{ref}=w_1\|w_2$	8-bit reference mean h_{ref} (or l_{ref})	The third secret bit w_3	Two comparison location bits w_{com}	The fourth secret bit w_4

FIGURE 5.19

The bit string structure for encoding each mean block.

5.5.3.2 The Data Extraction Process

Our data hiding scheme is reversible because we can recover the original mean tables after data extraction, and thus the original BTC-compressed image can be losslessly recovered. Given the codestream, our purpose is to extract the secret bit sequence and recover the original BTC-compressed image. Since the reconstruction process for each mean table is the same, here we take the reconstruction process for each high mean table $\mathbf{H}$ to describe the extraction process as follows.

Step 1: Read the next 3 bits into w_{ran} from the codestream of the high mean table $\mathbf{H}$, find the corresponding case in Table 5.11, and look up the value c in Table 5.11.

Step 2: Read the next 10 bits from the codestream of the high mean table. Get the first 2 bits w_1 and w_2 as the reference location bits w_{ref}, append them to the output secret bit sequence. Transform the last 8 bits into the reference high mean h_{ref}, and put this mean in the current mean block according to the location bits w_{ref}.

Step 3: Read the next 3 bits from the codestream of the high mean table. Get the first bit w_3, and append it to the output secret bit sequence. Get the last 2 bits as the comparison location bits w_{com}.

Step 4: Read the next $1 + 3c$ bits from the codestream of the high mean table. Get the first bit w_4, append it to the output secret bit sequence. Transform the following three c bits into three positive difference values d_{A+}, d_{B+}, and d_{C+}. If $w_4 = 0$, $d_A = d_{A+}$, $d_B = d_{B+}$, and $d_C = d_{C+}$; otherwise, $d_A = -d_{A+}$, $d_B = -d_{B+}$, and $d_C = -d_{C+}$.

Step 5: Except for the reference high mean, recover the other three mean values in the current 2×2 high mean block. Here, we should consider two cases:

Case 1: $w_{ref} = w_{com}$. In this case, the reference high mean is just the comparison high mean, and thus $h_{com} = h_{ref}$. If $w_4 = 0$ and $w_3 = 0$, then $h_A = d_A + h_{com}$, $h_B = d_B + h_{com}$, and $h_C = d_C + h_{com}$. If $w_4 = 0$ and $w_3 = 1$, then $h_A = h_{com} - d_A$, $h_B = h_{com} - d_B$, and $h_C = h_{com} - d_C$. If $w_4 = 1$ and $w_3 = 0$, then $h_A = h_{com} - d_A$, $h_B = h_{com} - d_B$, and $h_C = h_{com} - d_C$. If $w_4 = 1$ and $w_3 = 1$, then $h_A = d_A + h_{com}$, $h_B = d_B + h_{com}$, and $h_C = d_C + h_{com}$. Put h_A, h_B, and h_C at the remainder three locations in the raster-scan order.

Case 2: $w_{ref} \neq w_{com}$. In this case, h_A is the difference between h_{com} and h_{ref}. If $w_4 = 0$ and $w_3 = 0$, then $h_{com} = d_A - h_{ref}$. If $w_4 = 0$ and $w_3 = 1$, then $h_{com} = h_{ref} + d_A$. If $w_4 = 1$ and $w_3 = 0$, then $h_{com} = h_{ref} + d_A$. If $w_4 = 1$ and $w_3 = 1$, then $h_{com} = d_A - h_{ref}$. Put h_{com} in the current 2×2 high mean block according to the location bits w_{com}. Now turn to recover left two indices. If $w_4 = 0$ and $w_3 = 0$, then $h_B = d_B + h_{com}$ and $h_C = d_C + h_{com}$. If $w_4 = 0$ and $w_3 = 1$, then $h_B = h_{com} - d_B$ and $h_C = h_{com} - d_C$. If $w_4 = 1$ and $w_3 = 0$, then $h_B = h_{com} - d_B$ and $h_C = h_{com} - d_C$. If $w_4 = 1$ and $w_3 = 1$, then $h_B = d_B + h_{com}$ and $h_C = d_C + h_{com}$. Put h_B and h_C at the remainder two locations in the raster-scan order.

By repeatedly performing Steps 1—5 for all 2 × 2 high mean blocks, we can recover three high mean tables and output the half secret bit sequence. Similarly, by performing Steps 1—5 for all 2 × 2 low mean blocks, we can recover three low mean tables and output another half secret bit sequence.

5.5.3.3 Experimental Results

To evaluate the proposed scheme, we use six color images, i.e., Lena, Baboon, Jet_F16, Goldhill, Sailboat, and Zelda of the same size 512 × 512. Comparisons among our algorithm, Chang et al.'s algorithm [19], and Chou and Chang's algorithm [20] are performed under the same block size 4 × 4. Four aspects of performance are adopted in the experiments to evaluate a data hiding scheme, i.e., the capacity representing the maximum number of secret bits that can be hidden; the PSNR, representing the quality of the stego image; the bit rate, representing the performance of the compression efficiency whose unit is bpp; and the embedding efficiency, indicating the number of embedded secret data when a bit of the binary code stream has been transmitted. Obviously, the embedding efficiency can be calculated as Capacity/(bit rate $\times M \times N$). As shown in Table 5.12, the PSNRs of stego images based on our, Chang et al.'s, and Chou and Chang's schemes are exactly the same as those of the common bitplane color BTC-compressed images, the reason being that these three schemes are reversible. From Table 5.12, we can obviously see that the proposed scheme is a more effective method for its high capacity, high embedding efficiency, and low bit rate.

Table 5.12 Comparisons of the Proposed, Chang et al.'s, and Chou and Chang's Schemes

Algorithm	Performance	Lena	Baboon	F16	Goldhill	Sailboat	Zelda
Common bitplane color BTC	PSNR (dB)	31.52	22.88	31.99	31.50	27.71	34.81
	Bit rate (bpp)	4.000	4.000	4.000	4.000	4.000	4.000
Proposed	PSNR (dB)	31.52	22.88	31.99	31.50	27.71	34.81
	Capacity (bits)	98,304	98,304	98,304	98,304	98,304	98,304
	Bit rate (bpp)	3.500	3.828	3.433	3.619	3.625	3.604
	Efficiency	0.107	0.098	0.109	0.104	0.103	0.104
Chang et al.'s	PSNR (dB)	31.52	22.79	31.93	31.50	27.69	34.81
	Bit rate (bpp)	4.162	4.291	4.141	4.169	4.150	4.061
	Capacity (bits)	60,771	59,265	62,493	62,209	62,420	63,926
	Efficiency	0.056	0.053	0.058	0.0570	0.057	0.060
Chou and Chang's	PSNR (dB)	31.52	22.88	31.99	31.50	27.71	34.81
	Bit rate (bpp)	4.351	4.375	4.257	4.281	4.378	4.445
	Capacity (bits)	57,876	58,072	60,778	60,574	58,887	57,834
	Efficiency	0.051	0.051	0.055	0.054	0.051	0.050

BTC, *block truncation coding;* PSNR, *peak signal-to-noise ratio.*

5.6 SUMMARY

This chapter discusses lossless information hiding schemes for BTC-compressed image. These schemes can be broadly classified into three categories, i.e., bitplane flipping—based schemes for BTC-compressed grayscale images, mean coding—based schemes for BTC-compressed grayscale images, and lossless data hiding schemes in BTC-compressed color images.

The first category includes three schemes, i.e., original bitplane flipping—based scheme, improved bitplane flipping—based scheme, and bitplane flipping—based scheme with histogram shifting of mean tables. The third method is proposed by us. Through histogram shifting of mean tables, our scheme can maintain the same PSNR values as the original AMBTC technique. We embed secret bits in two mean tables, and also more secret bits in bitplanes if there are some blocks whose high mean equals its low mean; thus our scheme can obtain higher capacity. Furthermore, our scheme is separated into the AMBTC compression process for generating two mean tables together with one bitplane sequence and the data hiding process to embed secret data into the output codestream, which facilitates the individual processing of the encoder and the watermark embedder and the controlling of the corresponding performance.

The second category includes three methods, i.e., prediction-error expansion—based scheme, JNC-based scheme, and blockwise coding—based scheme, and all of them are proposed by us. All these methods are separated into the AMBTC compression process for generating two mean tables and the data hiding process to embed secret data into the output codestream, which facilitates the individual processing of the encoder and the watermark embedder and the control of overall performance. In the first method, by introducing the prediction-error expansion technique, both high and low means of one BTC image block could hide one secret bit, thus one block could hide 2 bits. Moreover, additional overflow/underflow location map, which is generally needed in other algorithms is not required. Furthermore, the blocks whose high and low means are equal can embed much more secret bits. Through tuning parameter the proposed scheme balances the embedding capacity and image quality of the output image. In the second method, we embed secret data in two mean tables and each value in the table can embed two secret data, thus our scheme can obtain capacity four times as large as the number of blocks in the input image. In the decoding part, the AMBTC-compressed image and the secret data can be recovered separately, which not only can further protect the secret data but also makes the decoding of the compressed image public. The third method is based on 2×2 mean blocks, which can make full use of the correlation among mean values, thus it can reduce the bit rate compared with the original AMBTC. On the other hand, we embed secret data in two mean tables, thus our scheme can obtain double capacity.

The third category includes DE-based scheme and blockwise coding—based scheme. The main idea of the first scheme is to apply the DE technique to BTC-compressed data. Experimental results demonstrate that the first scheme can embed a large amount of secret data reversibly while maintaining perfect visual quality. The main idea of the second scheme is to encode the mean values in each 2×2 block according to four input secret bits and the dynamic range evaluated by the difference between the maximal mean value and the minimal mean value in the mean block. Experimental results demonstrate that the second scheme can embed a large amount of secret data reversibly while reducing the bit rate.

REFERENCES

[1] E.J. Delp, O.R. Mitchell, Image compression using block truncation coding, IEEE Transactions on Communications 27 (9) (1979) 1335–1342. COM.

[2] M.D. Lema, O.R. Mitchell, Absolute moment block truncation coding and its application to color images, IEEE Transactions on Communications 32 (10) (1984) 1148–1157. COM.

[3] Z.M. Lu, C.H. Liu, S.H. Sun, Digital image watermarking technique based on block truncation coding with vector quantization, Chinese Journal of Electronics 11 (2002) 152–157.

[4] M.H. Lin, C.C. Chang, A novel information hiding scheme based on BTC, in: Proceedings of the 4th International Conference on Computer and Information Technology, Wuhan, China, 2004.

[5] J.C. Chuang, C.C. Chang, Using a simple and fast image compression algorithm to hide secret information, International Journal of Computers and Applications 28 (2006) 329–333.

[6] C.N. Yang, Z.M. Lu, Blind fragile image watermarking based on vector quantization and block truncation coding, ICIC Express Letters Part B: Applications 2 (4) (2011) 905–910.

[7] C.N. Yang, Z.M. Lu, A blind image watermarking scheme utilizing BTC bitplanes, International Journal of Digital Crime and Forensics 3 (4) (2011) 42–53.

[8] Y. Zhang, Z.M. Lu, D.N. Zhao, An oblivious fragile watermarking scheme for images utilizing edge transitions in BTC bitmaps, Science China Information Sciences 55 (11) (2012) 2570–2581.

[9] W. Hong, T.S. Chen, C.W. Shiu, Lossless steganography for AMBTC compressed images, in: Proceedings of the First International Congress on Image and Signal Processing, vol. 2, 2008, pp. 13–17.

[10] J. Chen, W. Hong, T.S. Chen, C.W. Shiu, Steganography for BTC compressed images using no distortion technique, The Imaging Science Journal 58 (4) (2010) 177–185.

[11] Z.F. Chen, Z.M. Lu, Y.X. Su, High-capacity reversible data hiding scheme for optimal common-bitplane BTC-compressed color images, ICIC Express Letters 5 (12) (2011) 4251–4256.

[12] Z.F. Chen, Y.X. Su, Z.M. Lu, Reversible data hiding for BTC-compressed color images using difference expansion, ICIC Express Letters Part B: Applications 2 (5) (2011) 1213–1218.

[13] C.H. Li, Z.M. Lu, Y.X. Su, Reversible data hiding for BTC-compressed images based on bitplane flipping and histogram shifting of mean tables, Information Technology Journal 10 (3) (2011) 1421–1426.

[14] H. Luo, Z.F. Zhao, Z.M. Lu, Joint secret sharing and data hiding for block truncation coding compressed image transmission, Information Technology Journal 10 (3) (2011) 681–685.

[15] K. Wang, Y.J. Hu, Z.M. Lu, Reversible data hiding for block truncation coding compressed images based on prediction-error expansion, in: The 2012 Eighth International Conference on Intelligent Information Hiding and Multimedia Signal Processing (IIH-MSP 2012), July 18–20, 2012, pp. 317–320. Piraeus-Athens, Greece.

[16] Y. Zhang, S.Z. Guo, Z.M. Lu, H. Luo, Reversible data hiding for BTC-compressed images based on lossless coding of mean tables, IEICE Transactions on Communications E96-B (2) (2013) 624–631.

[17] W. Sun, Z.M. Lu, Y.C. Wen, F.X. Yu, R.J. Shen, High performance reversible data hiding for block truncation coding compressed images, Signal, Image and Video Processing 7 (2) (2013) 297–306.

[18] Z. Qian, X. Zhang, Lossless data hiding in JPEG bitstream, The Journal of Systems and Software 85 (2) (2012) 309–313.

[19] C.C. Chang, C.Y. Lin, Y.H. Fan, Lossless data hiding for color images based on block truncation coding, Pattern Recognition 41 (7) (2008) 2347–2357.

[20] Y.C. Chou, H.H. Chang, A data hiding scheme for color image using BTC compression technique, in: Proceedings of the 9th IEEE International Conference on Cognitive Informatics, 2010, pp. 845–850.

[21] J. Tian, Reversible data embedding using a difference expansion, IEEE Transactions on Circuits System for Video Technology 13 (8) (2003) 890–896.

Lossless Information Hiding in JPEG- and JPEG2000-Compressed Images

6

6.1 INTRODUCTION

6.1.1 JPEG

In this section, a brief introduction to the JPEG concept and the JPEG compression process is given. JPEG is a common lossy compression method for digital images. The JPEG standard consists of two types of compression methods, i.e., discrete cosine transform (DCT)—based methods and prediction-based methods given by Wallace [3]. The former are designed for lossy compression, whereas the latter are designed for lossless compression. JPEG features a simple lossy mode known as the baseline method, which is a subset of the other DCT-based modes of operation. The baseline method has been the most widely used JPEG method so far, thus this chapter focuses on the baseline method.

Fig. 6.1 shows the main steps of the baseline method. An input image is first divided into 8×8 nonoverlapping blocks, and then each block is applied by the forward DCT (FDCT) to get a set of 64 DCT coefficients. Mathematical definitions of 8×8 FDCT and 8×8 inverse DCT (IDCT) are as follows:

$$F(u, v) = \frac{1}{4} C(u)C(v) \left[\sum_{x=0}^{7} \sum_{y=0}^{7} f(x, y) \cos \frac{(2x+1)u\pi}{16} \cos \frac{(2y+1)v\pi}{16} \right] \quad (6.1)$$

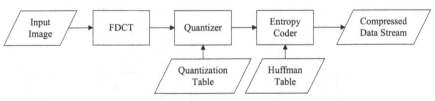

FIGURE 6.1

The block diagram of the JPEG encoder. *FDCT*, forward discrete cosine transform.

Lossless Information Hiding in Images. http://dx.doi.org/10.1016/B978-0-12-812006-4.00006-1

$$f(x,y) = \frac{1}{4}\left[\sum_{u=0}^{7}\sum_{v=0}^{7} C(u)C(v)F(u,v)\cos\frac{(2x+1)u\pi}{16}\cos\frac{(2y+1)v\pi}{16}\right] \quad (6.2)$$

$$\text{where: } C(u) = \begin{cases} \dfrac{1}{\sqrt{2}} & u = 0 \\ 1 & \text{otherwise} \end{cases}$$

To compress the image data, these coefficients are then quantized by using a quantization table with 64 entries. The standard quantization table is shown in Fig. 6.2. The quantized coefficients are all integers, which are obtained by dividing each DCT coefficient by its corresponding value in the quantization table and rounding to the nearest integer as follows:

$$D(u,v) = \text{IntegerRound}\left(\frac{F(u,v)}{Q(u,v)}\right) \quad (6.3)$$

where $F(u,v)$ means the original DCT coefficient, $Q(u,v)$ means the corresponding value in the quantization table, and $D(u,v)$ means the quantized DCT coefficient. Because of the rounding loss, the quantization step is not lossless. The final data stored in the JPEG file are the quantized DCT coefficients, which are entropy coded and saved in the entropy-coded segment of the JPEG file. The quantization table is stored in the Define Quantization Table (DQT) segment. In this chapter, our experiment is done with the JPEG library "Libjpeg" developed by the Independent JPEG Group (IJG) (http://www.ijg.org/). The quantization table in Libjpeg is controlled by

16	11	10	16	24	40	51	61
12	12	14	19	26	58	60	55
14	13	16	24	40	57	69	56
14	17	22	29	51	87	80	62
18	22	37	56	68	109	103	77
24	35	55	64	81	104	113	92
49	64	78	87	103	121	120	101
72	92	95	98	112	100	103	99

FIGURE 6.2

The JPEG standard quantization table.

the quality factor (QF), which is an integer in the interval [1 100]. Libjpeg adopts the following transformation to get the scale factor to form a new quantization table:

$$ScaleFactor = \begin{cases} \dfrac{5000}{QF} & QF < 50 \\ 200 - 2QF & \text{otherwise} \end{cases} \qquad (6.4)$$

Then it multiplies every entry of the standard quantization table by ScaleFactor/100 and then rounds the resulting value to its nearest integer. If the result is smaller than 1, then it is set to 1.

$$Q_{new}(u, v) = \max\left(\text{IntegerRound}\left(\frac{Q_{standard}(u, v) \cdot ScaleFactor}{100}\right), 1\right) \qquad (6.5)$$

From Eqs. (6.4) and (6.5), we can see that when the image QF equals 50, the standard quantization table is used.

The final step is the lossless step called entropy coding. The quantized coefficients are first scanned in the zigzag manner as shown in Fig. 6.3. For natural images, there are a lot of consecutive zeros in the high-frequency portion, which helps to further compress the image using entropy coding. Thus, AC (alternating current) coefficients can be encoded by zero run length coding (ZRLC). The DC (direct current) coefficient corresponds to the lowest frequency in an 8×8 block, which is the average value over the 64 pixels. Usually there is a very close correlation between the DCT coefficients of adjacent blocks, thus the encoding of the quantized DC coefficient is performed on the difference between the quantized DC

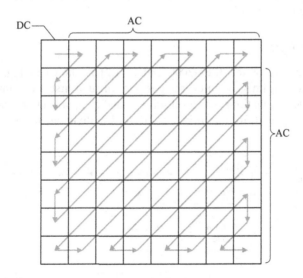

FIGURE 6.3

The zigzag sequence.

coefficients of the two consecutive blocks. Finally, the intermediate sequence of symbols is converted to a data stream by Huffman coding.

The JPEG decoding process shown in Fig. 6.4 is the inverse process of JPEG encoding. The decoding process mainly consists of three steps, i.e., entropy decoding, dequantization, and IDCT. The decoder reads the quantization table and the quantized DCT coefficients from the DQT segment and entropy-coded segment, respectively. The decoder then multiplies the quantized DCT coefficients by corresponding elements in the quantization table and applies IDCT to the results to obtain uncompressed image.

If an input grayscale image is compressed into the JPEG format by the JPEG encoder, it is saved in the form of bitstream. Fig. 6.5 shows the structure of the JPEG bitstream. It starts with an SOI (start of image) marker and ends with an EOI (end of image) marker. There is one frame containing several segments between the two markers. Among these segments, the DHT (Define Huffman Table) and SOS (start of scan) segments are shown in Fig. 6.5. The data in the DHT segment are used to generate the Huffman table. For example, the AC coefficients are coded in a specific run length encoding (RLE) format as intermediate symbols (variable length code (*VLC*), variable length integer (*VLI*)). Each *VLC* is defined as (*run, size*) and encoded by a Huffman code. Here, *run* denotes the zero run length, and each nonzero AC coefficient can be obtained by its corresponding *size* and *VLI* values. L_i in the DHT segment stands for the number of VLCs whose code length is i, and $V_{i,j}$ is the (*run, size*) value of the jth code whose code length is i. According to a specific rule, the Huffman table can be established itself with these aforementioned data. The SOS segment has a scan header and an entropy-coded segment. The image content is saved in the entropy-coded segment, and particularly the AC coefficients are represented in the form of several (*VLC, VLI*)s. More details can be seen in the JPEG guidelines [4].

6.1.2 JPEG2000

The block diagram of the JPEG2000 codec [1,2] is shown in Fig. 6.6. In the JPEG2000 encoder, image preprocessing is performed at first. Here, image preprocessing includes image tiling, DC level shifting, and component transformation. Image tiling is applied to the original image by dividing it into rectangular

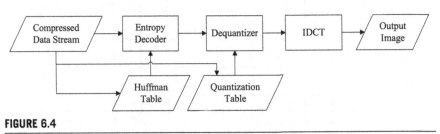

FIGURE 6.4

The block diagram of the JPEG decoder. *IDCT*, inverse discrete cosine transform.

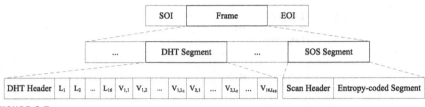

FIGURE 6.5

JPEG bitstream structure. *DHT*, Define Huffman Table; *EOI*, end of image; *SOI*, start of scan; *SOS*, start of scan.

nonoverlapping blocks (tiles). These blocks can be processed independently. DC level shifting can ensure that the input sample data has a nominal dynamic range that is approximately centered about 0. Then component transformation or color transformation is performed on the tile-component data. Only two component transformations are defined in the baseline JPEG2000 codec, i.e., irreversible component transform (ICT) and reversible component transform (RCT). Both of them can map the image data from the RGB color space to the YCbCr color space. Next, these tiles are decomposed into different decomposition levels by the forward discrete wavelet transform (FDWT). After N levels of discrete wavelet transform (DWT), we can get the decomposed image, which is made up of a low-frequency subband called LL_N and $3 \times N$ high-frequency subbands referred to as HL_i, LH_i, HH_i, where $i = 1, 2, ...N$. Fig. 6.7 shows the subband structure after three levels of DWT. Then the resulting wavelet coefficients in all subbands are quantized. Next, entropy coding including tier-1 coding and tier-2 coding is applied to the quantized blocks to generate JPEG2000-ompressed bitstream. With this step, the encoding process is finished. The decoding process of the JPEG2000 codec is just the reverse of the encoding process.

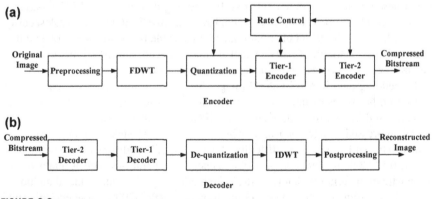

FIGURE 6.6

Block diagram of JPEG2000 codec. *FDWT*, forward discrete wavelet transform; *IDWT*, inverse discrete wavelet transform.

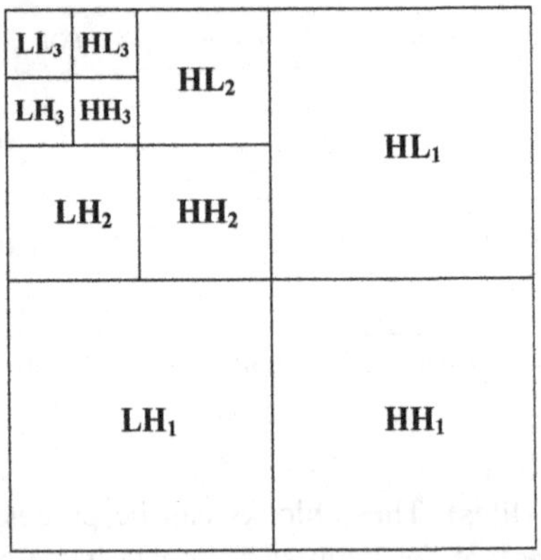

FIGURE 6.7

The subband structure.

6.1.3 CHALLENGES

Among various data hiding techniques, the reversible ones for the JPEG domain are still only a few and there is a huge margin for improvement in both the stego image quality and the capacity. For the purpose of making the influence caused by data hiding as small as possible, the selection of embedding positions should be carefully considered. As Huang et al. [5] said, traditional data hiding techniques tended to choose the midfrequency DCT coefficients in the DCT transform domain. However, when considering the quantization stage, things may be different. Thus, the earlier techniques might affect the researchers' choice on embedding positions in the JPEG-compressed domain. Most existing lossless data hiding techniques increase the file size after embedding the secret data, which negates the advantages of the lossless data hiding scheme. Lossless data hiding with file size preservation is now a new important research subarea. Embedding data into the JPEG bitstream, which is one of the open compression standards, has two limitations of weak security and fragility [6]. The JPEG bitstream must be viewable by normal viewers, and it is also available for the third party. Attackers may reencode the JPEG image to erase the embedded data or replace it using the open algorithm.

Embedding data into JPEG2000 images has some differences from embedding data into other types of images. The differences will lead to some difficulties. As a compressed image, the redundancy of a JPEG2000 image is smaller than that of an uncompressed image such as a BMP image. So the space for data hiding is limited. This will increase the difficulty of data hiding. In addition, the encoding process of JPEG2000 is more complex. Some encoding operations such as quantization and bitstream layering probably destroy the hidden data. It requires that data hiding should be coordinated with the encoding process of JPEG2000. So selecting a suitable embedding position is important and difficult.

6.2 LOSSLESS INFORMATION HIDING IN JPEG IMAGES
6.2.1 OVERVIEW OF INFORMATION HIDING IN JPEG IMAGES

The JPEG image format is a widely used compressed format. For JPEG images, as early as in 1997, Upham [7] first developed a famous hiding tool for JPEG images named Jpeg-Jsteg, where the secret data are embedded into the least significant bits (LSBs) of the quantized DCT coefficients whose values are not 0, 1 or -1. Westfeld [8] developed the so-called F5 algorithm, which implements matrix encoding to improve the embedding efficiency. In addition, F5 also employs permutative straddling to uniformly spread out the changes over the whole steganogram. Both these methods are irreversible with a low capacity. In the same year, Fridrich et al. [9] presented for the first time two invertible watermarking methods for authentication of digital images in the JPEG domain, where they modified the quantization matrix to enable lossless embedding of 1 bit per DCT coefficient. Fridrich et al. [10] proposed a new idea to losslessly compress the LSB plane of some selected JPEG mode coefficients to make space for reversible data embedding. Later, Chang et al. [11] presented a reversible hiding scheme to modify the quantization table and hide the secret data in the cover image based on the midfrequency-quantized DCT coefficients. Iwata et al. [12] proposed a hiding scheme by modifying the boundaries between zero and nonzero quantized DCT coefficients in each block. However, it is irreversible with a low capacity. Inspired by Iwata et al.'s scheme, Chang et al. [13] proposed a lossless steganography scheme to hide secret data in the quantized DCT coefficients of each block in JPEG images. In the same year, Xuan et al. [14] proposed a scheme to shift the quantized DCT coefficient histogram and then embed data based on histogram pairs. Later, Sakai et al. [15] improved Xuan et al.'s scheme and yielded better image quality by judging whether a block is suitable for embedding data or not. Almohammad et al. [16] extended the method of Chang et al. [11] by using an optimized 16×16 quantization table and improved the stego image quality and the embedding capacity. Later, Cheng and Yoo [17] proposed a reversible scheme, which is similar to the schemes of Iwata and Chang et al. [13], and performed multilevel embedding to reach a higher capacity. Zhang et al. [18] proposed a reversible data hiding method to carry the watermark for JPEG image authentication.

With regard to existing reversible data hiding techniques for JPEG domain, the stego image quality and the capacity should be further improved. The method of Fridrich et al. [10] divided some elements of the quantization table by a factor; at the same time, the corresponding quantized DCT coefficients were simply multiplied by the same factor to make space for embedding. Lin and Chan [19] proposed an invertible secret image sharing with a steganography scheme. The secret pixels are first transformed into k-ary notational numbers, then encrypted into shared data, and finally shared along with the information data based on the (t,n)-threshold sharing scheme with a modulo operation.

Most existing lossless data hiding techniques, including those mentioned previously, increase the file size after embedding the secret data, which negates the advantages of the lossless data hiding scheme. Lossless data hiding with file size preservation is now a new important research subarea. In 2004, Fridrich et al. [20] introduced a lossless watermarking technique that preserves the file size for the first time. In their work, the watermark is embedded into the VLI codes of AC coefficients encoded by RLE. Mobasseri et al. [6] proposed an algorithm to embed data directly into the bitstream of JPEG image by flipping 1 bit of the VLC or the appended bits and applying an error concealment technique to minimize the image quality loss. Inspired by Mobasseri et al.'s method, Qian and Zhang [21] presented a method to embed the secret data into the JPEG bitstream by Huffman code mapping, guaranteeing no quality distortion while providing more embedding capacity. Their method maps several unused codes to one used code instead of flipping bits and concealing errors in the used codes.

In the following six subsections, seven typical methods (note that Fridrich et al. presented two schemes for image authentication) including two schemes from the authors are introduced. For the first five schemes, we only introduce the basic ideas, whereas for the schemes from the authors, we provide a detailed introduction with experimental results.

6.2.2 FRIDRICH ET AL.'S INVERTIBLE WATERMARKING METHODS FOR IMAGE AUTHENTICATION

Fridrich et al. presented two reversible watermarking methods for JPEG image authentication in 2001 [9]. The first one is based on lossless compression of biased bitstreams of the quantized coefficients. The second one modifies the quantization matrix to enable lossless embedding of 1 bit per DCT coefficient. Both methods are fast and can be used for general lossless data embedding. They provide information assurance tools for integrity protection of sensitive imagery, such as medical images or military images.

6.2.2.1 Method 1

Assume that there is a JPEG file X represented in a discrete form using bits. Let us identify a subset $E \subset X$ that can be randomized without changing the essential properties of X. For authentication, the subset E needs to have enough structure to allow lossless compression by at least 128 bits (e.g., the hash of X). We can then authenticate X in a lossless manner by replacing the subset E with an encrypted version of its compressed form concatenated with the hash H(X).

Note that if the set E is easily compressible, we do not need to work with the whole set E but only with a smaller portion of it, which would give us enough space for the hash after lossless compression. Fridrich et al. used this general authentication principle to develop lossless authentication of JPEG files. JPEG compression starts with dividing the image into disjoint blocks of 8×8 pixels. For each block, DCT is performed, obtaining 64 DCT coefficients. Let us denote the (i, j)th DCT coefficient of the kth block as $d_k(i, j)$, $0 \le i, j \le 7$, $k = 1, 2, ..., B$, where B is the total number of blocks in the image. In each block, all 64 coefficients are further quantized to integers $D_k(i, j)$ with a JPEG quantization matrix Q:

$$D_k(i,j) = \text{IntegerRound}\left(\frac{d_k(i,j)}{Q(i,j)}\right) \tag{6.6}$$

The quantized coefficients are arranged in a zigzag manner and then compressed using the Huffman coder. The compressed stream together with a header forms the final JPEG file. The largest DCT coefficients occur for the lowest frequencies (small i and j). Owing to properties of typical images and due to quantization, the quantized DCT coefficients corresponding to higher frequencies have a large number of zeros or small integers, such as 1s or -1s. For example, for the classical grayscale image "**Lena**" of size 256×256, the DCT coefficient in the position $(5, 5)$ is 0 in 94.14% blocks. For 2.66% cases, it is equal to 1, and for 2.81% cases, it is equal to -1, with less than 1% of 2s and -2s. Thus, the sequence $D_k(5, 5)$ forms a subset E that is easily compressible with a simple Huffman or arithmetic coder. Furthermore, if the message bits (the hash) are embedded into the LSBs of the coefficients $D_k(5,5)$, we only need to compress the original LSBs of the sequence $D_k(5,5)$ instead of the whole sequence. The efficiency of the algorithm can be further improved if the LSB of negative integers $D_k < 0$ is defined as $\text{LSB}(D_k) = 1 - (|D_k| \bmod 2)$. Thus, $\text{LSB}(-1) = \text{LSB}(-3) = 0$, and $\text{LSB}(-2) = \text{LSB}(-4) = 1$, etc. Because DCT coefficients D_k have a symmetrical distribution with zero mean, this simple measure will increase the bias between 0s and 1s in the LSB bitstream of original DCT coefficients.

DCT coefficients $D_k(i, j)$ corresponding to higher frequencies will produce a set E with a larger bias between 0s and 1s, but because the quantization factor $Q(i,j)$ is also higher for such coefficients, the distortion in each modified block will also be higher. To obtain the best results, we should use different DCT coefficients for different JPEG QFs to minimize the overall distortion and avoid introducing easily detectable artifacts.

Following is the pseudocode for lossless authentication of grayscale JPEG files.

6.2.2.1.1 Algorithm for Lossless Authentication of JPEG Files

Step 1. According to the JPEG QF, select the set of L authentication pairs (i_1, j_1), (i_2, j_2), ..., (i_L, j_L), $0 \le i_l, j_l \le 7$, $1 \le l \le L$, in middle frequencies.

Step 2. Parse the JPEG file and adopt the Huffman decompressor to obtain the quantized DCT coefficients, $D_k(i, j)$, $0 \le i, j \le 7$, $k = 1, 2, ..., B$, where B is the total number of blocks in the image.

Step 3. Calculate the hash H of the Huffman decompressed stream $D_k(i, j)$.

Step 4. Seed a pseudo-random number generator (PRNG) with a secret key and follow a random nonintersecting walk through the set $E = \{D_1(i_1, j_1), ..., D_B(i_1, j_1), D_1(i_2, j_2), ..., D_B(i_2, j_2), ..., D_1(i_L, j_L), ..., D_B(i_L, j_L)\}$. There are $L \times B$ elements in the set E.

Step 5. While following the random walk, run the adaptive context-free lossless arithmetic compression algorithm for the LSBs of the coefficients from E. While compressing, check for the difference between the length of the compressed bitstream C and the number of processed coefficients. Once there is enough space to insert the hash H, stop running the compression algorithm. Denote the set of visited coefficients as E_1, $E_1 \subseteq E$.

Step 6. Concatenate the compressed bitstream C and the hash H and insert the resulting bitstream into the LSBs of the coefficients from E_1. Compress all DCT coefficients $D_k(i,j)$ including the modified ones using the Huffman coder and store the authenticated image as a JPEG file on a disk.

6.2.2.1.2 Algorithm for Integrity Verification Process

Step 1. According to the JPEG QF, find the set of L authentication pairs (i_1,j_1), (i_2,j_2), ..., (i_L,j_L), where $0 \le i_l, j_l \le 7$, $1 \le l \le L$.

Step 2. Parse the JPEG file and adopt the Huffman decompressor to obtain the quantized DCT coefficients $D_k(i,j)$, where $0 \le i, j \le 7$, $k = 1, 2, ..., B$.

Step 3. Seed a PRNG with a secret key and follow a random nonintersecting walk through the set $E = \{D_1(i_1,j_1), ..., D_B(i_1,j_1), D_1(i_2,j_2), ..., D_B(i_2,j_2), ..., D_1(i_L,j_L), ..., D_B(i_L,j_L)\}$.

Step 4. While following the random walk, run the context-free lossless arithmetic decompression algorithm for the LSBs of the coefficients visited during the random walk. Once the length of the decompressed bitstream reaches B |H| (that is, the number of 8×8 blocks in the image plus the hash length), stop the procedure.

Step 5. Separate the decompressed bitstream into the LSBs of visited DCT co-efficients and the extracted candidate for hash H'. Replace the LSBs of all visited coefficients with the decompressed bitstream and compute the hash H of the resulting stream of all quantized DCT coefficients $D_k(i,j)$, $0 \le i, j \le 7$, $k = 1, 2, ..., B$.

Step 6. Compare H' with H. If they are the same, the JPEG file is authentic and the original JPEG image is obtained. If $H \ne H'$, the image is deemed nonauthentic.

The selection of the L authentication coefficients can be adjusted according to the QF to minimize the distortion and other artifacts. For example, for L = 3, using coefficients (5,5), (4,6), and (6,3) in a random fashion will contribute to the overall security of the scheme because the statistical artifacts due to lossless authentication will be more difficult to detect.

6.2.2.2 Method 2

The idea of the second method of Fridrich et al. is simple. For a given DCT coefficient position (i,j), if the corresponding quantization factor $Q(i,j)$ is even, it can be divided by 2 and all coefficients $D_k(i,j)$ can be multiplied by 2 without changing the visual appearance of the image at all. Because now all $D_k(i,j)$ are even, any binary message can be embedded into the LSBs of $D_k(i,j)$ and this LSB embedding is obviously reversible.

If $Q(i,j)$ is odd, it is replaced with floor $(Q(i,j)/2)$ and all $D_k(i,j)$ are multiplied by 2. In this case, it is required to include a flag in the hash to indicate that $Q(i,j)$ was originally odd in order that the original JPEG stream can be reconstructed during verification. Because this method uses a nonstandard quantization table, this table should be included in the header of the authenticated image. Because the table entry $Q(i,j)$ is not compatible with the rest of the table, this authentication method is steganographically obvious.

In fact, we can have several other possible realizations of the aforementioned idea. For example, $Q(i,j)$ could be replaced with 1 instead of its half and each $D_k(i,j)$ is multiplied by $Q(i,j)$. This version may introduce very small distortion since the DCT coefficients used for embedding have a quantization factor equal to 1. On the other hand, the modified stream will be less compressible using the Huffman code and thus reduce the overall compression ratio.

6.2.3 FRIDRICH ET AL.'S LOSSLESS EMBEDDING METHOD WITH FILE SIZE PRESERVATION

The aforementioned two lossless embedding schemes for JPEG images do not preserve the JPEG file size, and in some cases the file size increase can be quite disproportional to the embedded message size. This partially negates the advantages of embedding data rather than appending. In this subsection, we introduce Fridrich et al.'s another scheme to address this issue, which is a lossless embedding technique for sequentially encoded JPEG images that preserves their file size [20] (within a few bytes).

The JPEG encoder consists of three fundamental components (see Fig. 6.8): FDCT, a scalar quantizer, and an entropy-encoder. After the DCT is applied to a block of 8×8 pixels to transform it from the spatial domain to the frequency domain, DCT coefficients are quantized according to the quantization table. The quantized coefficients are arranged in a zigzag order and precompressed by performing the differential pulse code modulation (DPCM) on DC coefficients and RLE on

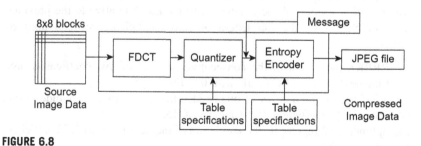

FIGURE 6.8

Lossless embedding in JPEG files. *FDCT*, forward discrete cosine transform.

AC coefficients. Finally, the symbol string is Huffman-coded to obtain the final compressed bitstream. After prepending the header, the final JPEG file is obtained.

The lossless embedding scheme with file size preservation works with the Huffman-decompressed stream of intermediate symbols. This bitstream is modified in a careful manner to guarantee that the final file size after Huffman compression keeps the same within a few bytes. To understand the embedding principles, we first describe the lossless part of JPEG compression in more detail.

6.2.3.1 The JPEG Entropy Coder

The entropy coder is composed of two steps: (1) DPCM encoding of the DC term and RLE of the AC coefficients and (2) Huffman coding. The purpose of the DPCM is to decorrelate the DC term because DC coefficients from neighboring blocks still have significant local correlations. The AC coefficients, on the other hand, contain long runs of 0s because of the quantization. Thus, AC coefficients are conveniently encoded using the RLE. The DPCM coding of DC coefficients and the run length coding of AC coefficients produce a sequence of intermediate symbols, which is finally entropy-coded to a data stream in which the symbols no longer have externally identifiable boundaries. The embedding technique works with the sequence of intermediate symbols and usually ignores the DC coefficients because their modifications may lead to visible artifacts. To explain how to modify the run length−encoded AC coefficients, it is required to describe run length coding in more detail.

6.2.3.2 Run Length Encoding of AC Coefficients

RLE is a simple lossless compression technique that assigns short codes to long runs of identical symbols. As mentioned earlier, the majority of quantized AC coefficients in each block are usually 0s. To efficiently utilize this fact, the AC coefficients are coded in a special RLE format as pairs of intermediate symbols (S1, S2). The codeword S1 represents both the number of zeros before the next nonzero DCT coefficient and the *category* (the number of bits required to represent its amplitude). The symbol S2 defines the amplitude and sign of the nonzero coefficient. The symbol S1, S1 = (Run/Category) is a composite 8-bit value of the form S1 = binary "RRRRCCCC." The four LSBs, "CCCC," define a category for the amplitude of the next nonzero coefficient in the block. The four most significant bits (MSBs), "RRRR," give the position of the coefficient in the block relative to the previous nonzero coefficient (i.e., the run length of zero coefficients between nonzero coefficients):

1. Run (RRRR): the length of the consecutive zero-valued AC coefficients preceding the next nonzero AC coefficient, $0 \leq \text{Run} \leq 15$.
2. Category (CCCC): the number of bits needed to represent the amplitude of the next nonzero AC coefficient, $0 \leq \text{Category} \leq 15$.
3. S2 (amplitude): S2 represents the amplitude of the next nonzero AC coefficient by a signed integer.

Once the quantized coefficient data from each 8×8 block is represented in the intermediate symbol sequence described earlier, variable-length codes are assigned. Each S1 (Run/Category) is encoded with a VLC from a Huffman table. Each S2 (amplitude) is encoded with a VLI code, which is an index into the amplitude value field whose length in bits is given in the second column of Fig. 6.9.

Both VLCs (S1) and VLIs (S2) are codes with variable lengths, but VLIs are not Huffman coded. They are appended to the Huffman coded S1 to form the final JPEG bitstream. Thus, we can change a particular VLI as long as the modified value is from the same category (has the same length) without changing the JPEG file size. Consequently, if all the embedding changes have this property, the JPEG file size will be preserved.

6.2.3.3 Lossless Embedding With File Size Preservation
As explained in the previous subsection, to preserve the file size, a given DCT coefficient d from the category C can only be changed to another coefficient d' from the same category C. To minimize the embedding distortion, this change should be as small as possible. Also, changes to DC coefficients usually introduce visible distortion, so we only perform the embedding modifications on AC coefficients.

Considering these requirements, we further limit the embedding changes to the same category, swapping values of AC coefficients within the following pairs: $(-2,-3)$, $(2,3)$ from the category 2, $(-7,-6)$, $(-5,-4)$, $(4,5)$, $(6,7)$ from the category 3, etc. During the embedding process, one value from the pair may be changed to another from the same pair. The value pairs are called embedding pairs. If we assign the parity 0 to all even-valued coefficients and the parity 1 to odd-valued

Amplitude value field	Category	AC size
0	0	N/A
−1, 1	1	1
−3, −2, 2, 3	2	2
−7,...,−4, 4,..., 7	3	3
−15,...,−8, 8,..., 15	4	4
−31,...,−16, 16,..., 31	5	5
−63,...,−32, 32,..., 63	6	6
−127,...,−64, 64,..., 127	7	7
−255,...,−128, 128,..., 255	8	8
−511,...,−256, 256,..., 511	9	9
−1023,...,−512, 512,..., 1023	10	A
−2047,...,−1024, 1024,..., 2047	11	B
−4095,...,−2048, 2048,..., 4095	12	C
−8191,...,−4096, 4096,..., 8191	13	D
−16383,...,−8192, 8192, 16383	14	E
−32767,...,−16384, 16384, 32767	15	N/A

FIGURE 6.9

Run length coding category and amplitude of AC coefficients.

coefficients, then the parities of the DCT coefficients that participate in embedding pairs in the original JPEG file is a binary sequence T that is losslessly compressible. This is because in natural images the distribution of DCT coefficients is generalized Gaussian centered at 0 and thus the sequence T contains more 0's in T than 1's.

The rest of the embedding process follows the RS method. We first losslessly compress the sequence T, obtaining the compressed bitstream $C(T)$, $|C(T)| < |T|$; append the message bits M to the compressed bitstream, $C(T)\&M$; and embed this composite message as the parities of DCT coefficients participating in embedding pairs (the capacity of this scheme is $|T| - |C(T)|$). Due to the generalized Gaussian distribution of DCT coefficients, the coefficients occur with highly uneven probabilities. Thus, to obtain a more efficient lossless compression result of the sequence T, we divide T into several subsequences (each subsequence corresponding to one category) and perform the arithmetic compression technique on the coefficients from each category separately.

6.2.3.3.1 Encoder

Step 1. Huffman-decode the original JPEG file.
Step 2. Either sequentially, or along a key-dependent path, read all DCT coefficients d_i belonging to embedding pairs from all Huffman-decoded data. Form the sequence $T = \{t_i\}$, $t_i = \text{parity}(d_i)$.
Step 3. Compress T using the arithmetic encoder to obtain the compressed bitstream $C(T)$.
Step 4. Concatenate m message bits M, $m < |T| - |C(T)|$, to the compressed bitstream, obtaining $T' = C(T)\&M$.
Step 5. For each i, if $t_i \neq \{t_i'\}$, modify d_i to d_i', where (d_i, d_i') is an embedding pair.
Step 6. Using the same Huffman code table, reencode the modified Huffman-decoded data to obtain the embedded JPEG file.

6.2.3.3.2 Decoder

Step 1. Perform the Huffman decoder on the JPEG file.
Step 2. Either sequentially, or along a key-dependent path, read all DCT coefficients d_i' belonging to embedding pairs from all Huffman-decoded data, obtaining the sequence $T' = \{t_i'\}$, where $\{t_i'\} = \text{parity}(d_i')$.
Step 3. Read the message M from T' and decompress $C(T)$.
Step 4. Either sequentially, or along a key-dependent path, modify all DCT coefficients d_i' belonging to the embedding pairs so that their parities match the decompressed sequence T, i.e., $\text{parity}(d_i) = t_i$. After reencoding the modified Huffman-decompressed coefficients, the original JPEG file can be obtained.

6.2.4 XUAN ET AL.'S HISTOGRAM PAIR–BASED LOSSLESS DATA EMBEDDING SCHEME

Xuan et al. presented a technique based on histogram pairs applied to some mid- and low-frequency JPEG quantized 8×8 block DCT coefficients for reversible data hiding [14]. The block diagram of data embedding and extraction is shown in Fig. 6.10. The data embedding capacity ranges from 0.0004, to 0.001, 0.1, up to 0.5 bpp for one-time (or, one-loop) reversible data hiding, whereas the visual quality of images with hidden data measured by both subjective and objective ways remains high. The increase in the size of image file due to data hiding is not noticeable, and the shape of histogram of the mid- and lower frequency DCT coefficients keeps similar. This technique can work for various Q-factors. In the following parts, we first introduce the principle of the histogram pair−based lossless data hiding scheme, and then the concept of thresholding is discussed. The lossless data embedding and extraction algorithm is finally described.

6.2.4.1 Principles
6.2.4.1.1 Definitions
Histogram $h(x)$ is the number of occurrences of feature x within a set of samples X. Here the samples X are some selected JPEG-quantized 8×8 DCT coefficients, and the feature x is one of the JPEG coefficient values. The x is either positive, or negative integer, or 0, such as $x \in \{-2, -1, 0, 1, 2, 3\}$.

A histogram pair is defined as a part of the histogram, denoted by $h = [m, n]$, where m and n are, respectively, the occurrences of two immediately neighboring feature values $x \in \{a, b\}$ with $a < b$, i.e., $b = a + 1$, and one of the two frequencies (m and n) is 0. The histogram pair can be formulated by *histogram expansion*. For example, the histogram pair $h = [\underline{m}, \underline{0}]$ can be produced by expanding. Here, the underline is used to mark the histogram pair. The feature value whose occurrence (h value) is not 0 is called the feature's original position. The feature value whose h value is 0 is called the feature's expansion position. Here, it is defined that

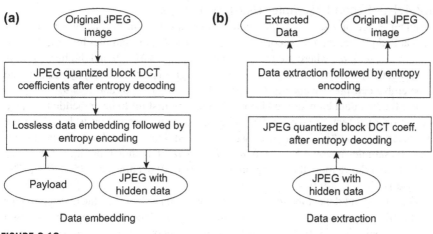

(a) Data embedding

(b) Data extraction

FIGURE 6.10

Block diagram of the lossless data embedding for JPEG image. *DCT*, discrete cosine transform.

when the feature value x is greater or equal to 0, the histogram pair is of the format $h = [m, 0]$, which means $h(a) = m$ and $h(b) = 0$; when the feature value x is less than 0, the histogram pair is of $h = [0, n]$, which means $h(a) = 0$ and $h(b) = n$.

After the histogram pair is produced, lossless data embedding can be developed. We can use the following data embedding rule. If the bit to be embedded is 0, the feature's original position is used. If the bit to be embedded is 1, the feature's expansion position is used. It is observed that after data embedding the histogram becomes more flat. When the histogram is completely flat, it is impossible to further embed data.

6.2.4.1.2 First Example: Using Single Histogram Pair

Assume the samples are $X = [a, a, a, a]$, i.e., the number of samples is $M = 4$, and the feature values $x \in \{a, b\}$ are greater than 0. There is one histogram pair $h = [4, 0]$. Assume the bit sequence to be embedded is $D = [1, 0, 0, 1]$ whose length $L = 4$. During data embedding, we scan the sequence $X = [a, a, a, a]$ in a certain order. When we meet the first "a," since we need to embed the bit "1," we change it to its expansion position "b." For the next 2 bits to be embedded, since they are bit "0," we keep it in its original position as "a." For the last bit to be embedded "1," we change "a" to "b." Therefore, after the embedding process, we obtain $X = [b, a, a, b]$ with the new histogram $h = [2, 2]$. Obviously, the embedding capacity is $C = L = 4$. Data extraction or the histogram pair recovery is the reverse process of the aforementioned data embedding process. After extracting the data $D = [1, 0, 0, 1]$, the histogram pair becomes [4, 0] and we can recover $X = [a, a, a, a]$ losslessly. Note that after data embedding, the histogram is changed from $h = [4, 0]$ to $h = [2, 2]$, since the histogram is completely flat and hence we cannot embed data any more.

6.2.4.1.3 Second Example: Using Two Loops

Given an image of size 3×3, the feature values are $x \in \{a, b, c, d\}$, where the features are all greater than 0. According to the scan order, the samples become $X = [a, a, a, a, a, a, a, a, a]$, where the total number of samples $M = 9$ and the histogram is $h = [9, 0, 0, 0]$, as shown in Fig. 6.11a. The histogram pair is $h = [9, 0]$. Assume the to-be embedded bit sequence is $D = [0, 1, 0, 0, 1, 0, 1, 1, 0]$ and $L = 9$.

For the first data embedding "Loop 1," since the first bit to be embedded is 0, we use the original feature position "a," whereas since the second bit is 1, we use the expansion position "b." In this way, we can embed 9 bits in total; after data embedding, the samples become $X = [a, b, a, a, b, a, b, b, a]$ as shown in Fig. 6.11b. After the first embedding loop, the histogram $h = [9, 0, 0, 0]$ becomes $h = [5, 4, 0, 0]$. The payload is $C_1 = L = 9$ bits.

For the second data embedding "Loop 2," we expand first, i.e., the histogram pair $h = [4, 0]$ is right shifted by one position, thus producing the histogram with two histogram pairs $h = [5, 0, 4, 0]$, and the samples become $X = [a, c, a, a, c, a, c, c, a]$; refer to Fig. 6.11c. Thus, the second embedding loop will separately use the two histogram pairs in $h = [5, 0, 4, 0]$, $x \in \{a, b, c, d\}$ to avoid confliction. That

(a) Original histogram			(b) Histogram after 1st embedding			(c) Histogram after expansion			(d) Histogram after 2nd embedding		
[9,0,0,0]			[5,4,0,0]			[5,0,4,0]			[2,3,3,1]		
a	a	a	a	b	a	a	c	a	b	c	a
a	a	a	a	b	a	a	c	a	b	d	b
a	a	a	b	b	a	c	c	a	c	c	a

FIGURE 6.11

Bit sequence $D = [0, 1, 0, 0, 1, 0, 1, 1, 0]$ embedded in two loops.

is, it first uses the histogram pair with larger absolute feature values, and then uses the histogram pair with smaller absolute feature values. In this example, we first embed data into the right histogram pair, and then into the left histogram pair. The to-be-embedded bit sequence $D = [0, 1, 0, 0, 1, 0, 1, 1, 0]$ is separated into two parts accordingly. That is, we first embed the front portion of data $D_1 = [0, 1, 0, 0]$ into the histogram pair at the right side $h = [\underline{4, 0}]$, $x \in \{c, d\}$, resulting in the corresponding samples $X_1 = [c, d, c, c]$. Then, we embed the remaining data $D_2 = [1, 0, 1, 1, 0]$ into the left histogram pair $h = [\underline{5, 0}]$, $x \in \{a, b\}$, resulting in the corresponding samples $X_2 = [b, a, b, b, a]$. After Loop2, the histogram becomes $h = [2, 3, 3, 1]$ and the samples become $X = [b, c, a, b, d, b, c, c, a]$ as given in Fig. 6.11d. Thus the embedding capacity in Loop 2 is $C_2 = L = 9$ bits.

The total capacity after two embedding loops is $C = 18$ bits. After two embedding loops, histogram changes from $h = [9, 0, 0, 0]$ to $h = [2, 3, 3, 1]$. It is observed that the histogram has changed from rather sharp ([9, 0, 0, 0]) to relatively flat ([2, 3, 3, 1]).

6.2.4.2 Thresholding

The histogram pair—based lossless data hiding scheme seeks for not only a higher embedding capacity but also a higher visual quality of stego images. For example, we may embed data with sufficient payload for annotation or for security with reversibility as well as the highest visual quality of the stego image with respect to the cover image.

To obtain the optimal performance, we need the so-called thresholding technique. The thresholding method involves first setting a threshold T, and then embedding data into those JPEG coefficients x with $|x| \leq T$. That is, it does not embed data into the JPEG coefficients with $|x| > T$. In addition, it makes sure that the small JPEG coefficients after data embedding will not conflict with the large JPEG coefficients with ($|x| > T$). That is, for the JPEG coefficients satisfying $|x| \leq T$, the histogram pair—based data embedding is applied. It requires that after data embedding, the coefficients between $-T \leq x \leq T$ will be separable from the coefficients with $|x| > T$. The *simple* thresholding will divide the whole histogram into two parts: (1) the data-to-be embedded region, where the JPEG coefficients' absolute value is small and (2) no data-to-be embedded region named end regions, where the JPEG coefficients' absolute value is large.

In fact, the smallest threshold T does not necessarily lead to the highest PSNR for a given data embedding capacity. Instead, it is found that for a given data embedding capacity there is an optimum value of T. This can be justified as follows. If a smaller threshold T is selected, the number of coefficients with $|x| > T$ will be larger. This implies that more coefficients with $|x| > T$ need to be moved away from 0 to create histogram pair(s) to losslessly embed data. This may lead to a lower PSNR and more side information. Therefore the best threshold T for a given data embedding capacity is selected to achieve the highest PSNR.

6.2.4.3 Hiding Algorithm
6.2.4.3.1 Data Embedding
Assume the length of the data to be embedded is L. The data embedding steps are listed below (see Fig. 6.12a).

1. Select a threshold $T > 0$, to make sure that the number of the mid- and low-frequency JPEG coefficients within $[-T, T]$ is greater than L, and $P \leftarrow T$.
2. In the JPEG coefficient histogram, move the portion of histogram with the coefficient value greater than P to the right-hand side by one unit to make the histogram at $P + 1$ equal to 0 (call $P + 1$ as a zero-point). Then embed data into P and $P + 1$ according to the bit to be embedded (0 or 1).
3. If some of the bits to be embedded have not been embedded at this point, let $P \leftarrow (-P)$, and move the histogram (less than P) to the left-hand side by one

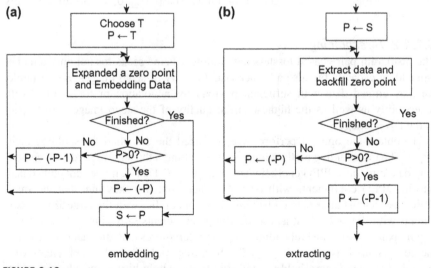

FIGURE 6.12

Flowchart of proposed lossless data embedding and extracting. (a) embedding, (b) extracting

unit to leave a zero-point at the value $(P - 1)$. Embed data into P and $(P - 1)$ according to the bit to be embedded (0 or 1).

4. If all data have been embedded, then stop the embedding process and record the P value as the stop value S. Otherwise, $P \leftarrow (-P - 1)$; go back to Step (2) to continue to embed the remaining data to be embedded.

6.2.4.3.2 Data Extraction

The data extraction process is the reverse process of the data embedding process. Without loss of generality, assume the stop position of data embedding is S (positive). The data extraction steps are as follows (Refer to Fig. 6.12b).

1. Set $P \leftarrow S$.
2. Decode with the stopping value P and the value $(P + 1)$. Extract all the data until $P + 1$ becomes a zero-point. Move all the DCT coefficients' histogram (greater than $P + 1$) toward the left-hand side by one unit to eliminate the zero-point.
3. If the amount of extracted data is less than C, set $P \leftarrow (-P - 1)$. Continue to extract data until $(P - 1)$ becomes a zero-point. Then move the histogram (less than $P - 1$) to the right-hand side by one unit to eliminate the zero-pint.
4. If all the hidden bits have been extracted, stop the process. Otherwise, set $P \leftarrow -P$, go back to Step 2 to continue to extract the following data.

6.2.4.3.3 Formulae of Lossless Data Hiding Based on Histogram Pairs

In summary, the aforementioned method divides the whole histogram into three parts: the part where data are to be embedded; the central part, where no data are embedded and the absolute value of coefficients is small; and the end part, where no are data embedded and the absolute value of coefficients is large. The whole embedding and extraction procedure can be expressed by the formulae in Fig. 6.13, where T is the selected threshold, i.e., the start position, S is the stop position, x is the feature value before embedding, x' is the feature value after

parts of histogram	Embedding		Recovering	
	after embedding	condition	after recovering	condition
Data to be embedded region (right side) (positive or zero)	$x'=2x+b-|S|$	$|S| \leq x \leq T$	$x=\lfloor (x'+|S|)/2 \rfloor, b$ $=x'+|S|-2x$	$|S| \leq x' \leq 2T-1-|S|$
Data to be embedded region (left side) (negative)	$x'=2x-b$ $+|S|+u(S)$	$-T \leq x \leq -|S|-u(S)$	$x=$ $\lfloor (x'-|S|-u(S)+1)/2 \rfloor$ $b=x'-|S|-u(S)-2x$	$-2T-1+|S|+u(S)$ $\leq x' \leq -|S|-u(S)$
Central part (small absolute value)	$x'=x$	$-|S|-u(S)<x<|S|$	$x=x'$	$-|S|-u(S)<x'<|S|$
Right edge part (positive)	$x'=x+T+1-|S|$	$x>T$	$x=x'-T-1+|S|$	$x'> 2T+1-|S|$
Left edge part (negative)	$x'=x-T-1$ $+|S|+u(S)$	$x<-T$	$x=x'+T+1-|S|-u(S)$	if $x'<-2T-1$ $+|S|+u(S)$

FIGURE 6.13

Formulae of lossless data hiding based on histogram pairs.

embedding, u(S) is unit step function (when $S \geq 0$, u(S) = 1, when $S < 0$, u(S) = 0), and $\lfloor x \rfloor$ rounds x to the largest integer not larger than x.

6.2.5 QIAN AND ZHANG'S SCHEME

Qian and Zhang found that, in Mobasseri et al.'s method [6], flipping one or more bits of VLC in a JPEG image to hide secret bits usually would cause collision in the decoding process and thus error concealment steps are required to minimize the decrease of output JPEG image quality. Therefore, they mapped VLCs by direct VLC replacement in the JPEG bitstream and the image quality can be kept the same as the original [21]. Their scheme can be described as follows.

Step 1: Parse the JPEG bitstream and read all the VLCs to get the used and unused ones.
Step 2: Establish mapping relationships based on the number of the used VLCs and the number of the unused VLCs.
Step 3: Modify the $V_{i,j}$ value in the file header according to the mapping relationships.
Step 4: Replace the VLCs in the bitstream to embed the secret data.

All the VLCs can be classified into 16 categories $\{C_1, C_2, ..., C_{16}\}$ and Category C_i has L_i codes of length $i(i = 1, 2, ..., 16)$. Thus, the used and unused VLCs in each category C_i can be expressed as follows:

$$C_i = \left\{ VLC_{i,1}^{(u)}, ..., VLC_{i,p_i}^{(u)}; VLC_{i,1}^{(n)}, ..., VLC_{i,q_i}^{(n)} \right\} \tag{6.7}$$

where $VLC_{i,1}^{(u)}, ..., VLC_{i,p_i}^{(u)}$ are p_i used codes, $VLC_{i,1}^{(n)}, ..., VLC_{i,q_i}^{(n)}$ are q_i unused codes, and $p_i + q_i$ L_i. Here we briefly introduce the method they adopted to establish the mapping relationships. If $p_i \geq q_i > 0$, VLCs in each category are mapped by a one-to-one manner:

$$M_i = \left\{ \left\{ VLC_{i,1}^{(u)} \leftrightarrow VLC_{i,1}^{(n)} \right\}, ..., \left\{ VLC_{i,q_i}^{(u)} \leftrightarrow VLC_{i,q_i}^{(n)} \right\} \right\} \tag{6.8}$$

where "$\leftrightarrow$" stands for the mapping relationship. If $0 < p_i < q_i$, VLCs are mapped by one-to-many manner for each category:

$$M_i = \left\{ \begin{array}{l} \left\{ VLC_{i,1}^{(u)} \leftrightarrow \left\{ VLC_{i,1}^{(n)}, ..., VLC_{i,k_i}^{(n)} \right\} \right\}, ..., \\ \left\{ VLC_{i,p_i}^{(u)} \leftrightarrow \left\{ VLC_{i,(p_i-1) \times k_i+1}^{(n)}, ..., VLC_{p_i \times k_i}^{(n)} \right\} \right\} \end{array} \right\} \tag{6.9}$$

where $k_i = 2^{\lfloor \log_2(q_i/p_i+1) \rfloor} - 1$ and $\lfloor x \rfloor$ stands for the floor function. For Eq. (6.8), each code in the mapping relationship presents one secret bit "0" or "1", and for Eq. (6.9) each code can present $\lfloor \log_2(q_i/p_i + 1) \rfloor$ secret bits.

For example, assume there are four VLCs (VLC_m, VLC_n, VLC_k, and VLC_l) and they are listed in the order in which they appear in the DHT segment. If the three unused VLCs (VLC_n, VLC_k, and VLC_l) are mapped to the same used VLC_m, then the mapping set is $\{\text{VLC}_m \leftrightarrow \{\text{VLC}_n, \text{VLC}_k, \text{VLC}_l\}\}$. To map codes, the (*run, size*) values of VLC_n, VLC_k, and VLC_l are all modified to that of VLC_m, then the four VLCs present secret bits "00," "01," "10," and "11," respectively. When scanning the entropy-coded segment in the data hiding phase, if VLC_m is met and the secret bits to be embedded are "01,", then VLC_m is replaced with VLC_n.

Qian and Zhang successfully hide data into the JPEG bitstream by VLC mapping and replacement. After data are embedded, both the image quality and the file size of the stego image are kept the same as the original JPEG image. However, the statistical results of the used and unused codes are not made full use of. Thus, the code mapping relationships could be able to be better explored to further increase the capacity.

6.2.6 JOINT MODIFICATION OF QUANTIZATION TABLE AND DISCRETE COSINE TRANSFORM COEFFICIENTS—BASED SCHEME

To make the distortion smaller, the authors of this book proposed a high-capacity reversible data hiding scheme utilizing the k-ary—based modulo operation [22]. The data are hidden in the space made by lowering certain quantization table entries and lifting the corresponding quantized DCT coefficients with an adjustment value added. The embedding strategy and sequence are optimized to get a better stego image. In our scheme, a cover JPEG image is first decoded to get the quantization table and quantized DCT coefficients; then some entries of the quantization table are divided by an integer and the corresponding quantized DCT coefficients are multiplied by the same integer and added by an adjustment value to make space for embedding the data. After extracting secret bits from the stego image, the original JPEG image can be recovered at the same time. Our algorithm can be divided into two phases: the data hiding phase and the extracting and restoring phase, which are illustrated in the following subsections. To reduce the distortion caused by embedding and control the increase of the file size, the selection of embedding positions should be discussed first.

6.2.6.1 The Selection of Embedding Positions

For the purpose of making the influence caused by data hiding as small as possible, the selection of embedding positions should be carefully considered. As Huang et al. [5] said, traditional data hiding techniques tended to choose the midfrequency DCT coefficients in the DCT transform domain. However, when considering the quantization stage, things may be different. Thus, the earlier techniques might affect the researchers' choice on embedding positions in the JPEG-compressed domain. Xuan et al. [14] did some simple experimental investigation to decide their optimum parameters. To test the effect of every single quantized DCT coefficient on image quality in much more detail, theoretical analysis and experimental investigation are done in this chapter. Here the peak signal-to-noise ratio (PSNR) is adopted to evaluate the impact:

$$\text{PSNR} = 10 \log_{10}\left(\frac{255^2}{\text{MSE}}\right) \tag{6.10}$$

where mean squared error (MSE) for an $M \times N$ grayscale image is defined as:

$$\text{MSE} = \frac{1}{M \cdot N} \sum_{x=0}^{M-1} \sum_{y=0}^{N-1} [\Delta f(x, y)]^2 = \frac{1}{M \cdot N} \sum_{x=0}^{M-1} \sum_{y=0}^{N-1} [f'(x, y) - f(x, y)]^2 \quad (6.11)$$

where $f'(x,y)$ and $f(x,y)$ are the pixel values of the distorted image and the original image, respectively.

In fact, the data stored in the JPEG image are the quantization table and quantized DCT coefficients; thus we can calculate the reconstructed DCT coefficient by $\widetilde{F}(u, v) = D(u, v) \cdot Q(u, v)$. When we add a number a to the quantized DCT coefficient $D(u,v)$, it is equivalent to adding the number a multiplied by the corresponding quantization table entry to $\widetilde{F}(u, v)$. From the JPEG standard quantization table shown in Fig. 6.2, we can see the entries vary a lot. The low-frequency entries are smaller than the midfrequency ones, which in turn are smaller than the high-frequency ones. For example, when adding 2 to $D(i,j)$ $(0 \leq i,j < 8)$, we have $\widetilde{F}'(i,j) = \widetilde{F}(i,j) + 2Q(i,j)$. In this case, from Eq. (6.2), we can see that the difference $\Delta f(x, y) = f'(x, y) - f(x, y)$ can be uniquely determined by the difference $\Delta \widetilde{F}(i,j) = \widetilde{F}'(i,j) - \widetilde{F}(i,j)$ since $\Delta \widetilde{F}(u, v) = 0$ for $u \neq i$ or $v \neq j$. Based on this fact, the impact of every single DCT coefficient can be tested as follows.

In one block, if we add 1 to $D(i,j)$ and keep other $D(u,v)$ the same as its original value, then we can obtain the introduced error as below:

$$\Delta f(x, y) = f'(x, y) - f(x, y)$$

$$= \frac{1}{4} \left[\sum_{u=0}^{7} \sum_{v=0}^{7} C(u)C(v)\Delta \widetilde{F}(u, v) \cos \frac{(2x+1)u\pi}{16} \cos \frac{(2y+1)v\pi}{16} \right]$$

$$= \frac{1}{4} C(i)C(j)Q(i,j) \cos \frac{(2x+1)i\pi}{16} \cos \frac{(2y+1)j\pi}{16} \quad (6.12)$$

Theoretical results are calculated according to Eqs. (6.10)–(6.12) on condition that the standard quantization table is used. Substitute $\Delta f(x,y)$ into Eq. (6.11) and set $M = N = 8$ to get the MSE value and then get the corresponding PSNR value. The experiments for real cases are also performed, where six test images Baboon, Boat, F16, Goldhill, Lena, and Pepper, of size 512×512 with 256 grayscales are adopted, as shown in Fig. 6.14. In real cases, to test the impact of quantized DCT coefficient $D(i,j)$, the LSB of $D(i,j)$ in every block of the image is flipped. The corresponding experimental results calculated between original JPEG images and stego JPEG images are shown in Fig. 6.15. Every DCT coefficient is tested in the zigzag sequence. In Fig. 6.15, the blue solid line with circles is the theoretical results and other colorful solid lines are the results for real cases.

From Fig. 6.15 we can see that the results for the real cases are almost the same and overlap with each other. The theoretical result is very similar in general trends to the ones for the real cases. The little difference is introduced by fast implementations of FDCT and IDCT rather than the mathematical definitions. Fig. 6.16 shows the

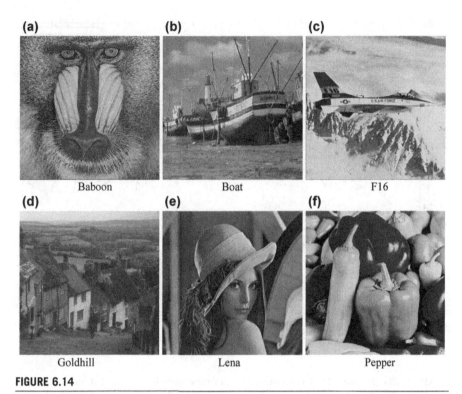

FIGURE 6.14

Six grayscale test images. (a) Baboon, (b) Boat, (c) F16, (d) Goldhill, (e) Lena, (f) Pepper.

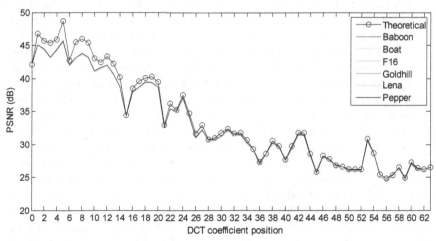

FIGURE 6.15

The impact of every quantized discrete cosine transform (DCT) coefficient in zigzag sequence on peak signal-to-noise transform (PSNR) calculated between original JPEG images and stego JPEG images.

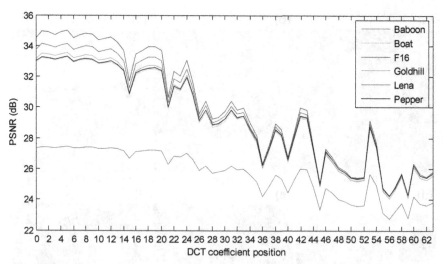

FIGURE 6.16

The impact of every quantized discrete cosine transform (DCT) coefficient in zigzag sequence on peak signal-to-noise ratio (PSNR) calculated between the original uncompressed images and stego JPEG images.

PSNR results calculated between original uncompressed images and stego JPEG images. The PSNR results of original JPEG images for Baboon, Boat, F16, Goldhill, Lena, and Pepper are 27.4883, 33.4953, 35.3906, 33.7908, 34.4441, and 33.5518 dB, respectively. Fig. 6.16 has the similar trends with Fig. 6.15. Because of the complex texture, the image Baboon has a lower PSNR than others. Based on these charts, we can conclude that quantized low-frequency DCT coefficients, even the quantized DC coefficient, have less influence on the image quality than quantized midfrequency and high-frequency DCT coefficients when considering the quantization process. Since the quantized DC coefficient is encoded based on the difference between the one in the current block and the one in the previous block, when the quantized DC coefficient is modified, the file size after data hiding will not increase too much. However, since quantized AC coefficients in a block are encoded by ZRLC, when the change is performed on the quantized midfrequency and high-frequency AC coefficients, things may be totally different, i.e., the file size may increase a lot along with the increase of nonzero AC coefficients. Therefore, when high capacity is required, it is recommended to give priority to hiding data in the quantized DC coefficient and low-frequency coefficients in the zigzag order, which will also help to achieve higher image quality and less file size. Based on the previous experiment and the actual visual effect by comparing images between the original image and stego image, we choose the third to the fourteenth (zero-based) quantized DCT coefficients to embed data.

6.2.6.2 The Data Hiding Phase

To make space for embedding the data into quantized DCT coefficients, some quantization table entries are divided by an integer and the quantized DCT coefficients are lifted correspondingly. When an integer number M is multiplied by an integer k, the result is the multiple of k that allows secret data and additional information (k-ary: 0, 1, ..., $k-1$) to be embedded into and to be extracted from by applying the modulo operation: M mod k.

Assume the original quantization table entry at (u,v) is $Q(u,v)$, we divide it by k to get a new quantization entry. For the reason that the entry is an integer, to make the variation as small as possible, we take the largest integer not greater than it, i.e.,

$$Q'(u, v) = \lfloor Q(u, v)/k \rfloor \tag{6.13}$$

where $\lfloor \cdot \rfloor$ stands for the floor function. Then the quantized DCT coefficient $D(u,v)$ is multiplied by k, i.e., $D'(u, v) = k \cdot D(u, v)$, and thus the embedding space is made. Note that this may result in more information loss because of the floor function; an adjustment value X should be added to make $D'(u,v)*Q'(u,v)$ as close as possible to the original reconstructed DCT coefficient $\widetilde{F}(u, v)$. Assuming that $r(u,v)$ is the remainder of the expression $Q(u,v)/k$, we have $r(u, v) = Q(u, v) - k \cdot \lfloor Q(u, v)/k \rfloor$. To obtain the relationship $\widetilde{F}(u, v) = D(u, v) \cdot Q(u, v) = D'(u, v) \cdot Q'(u, v)$, we should let $D(u, v) \cdot [k \cdot Q'(u, v) + r(u, v)] = [k \cdot D(u, v) + X] \cdot Q'(u, v)$, which results in $X = \frac{r(u,v) \cdot D(u,v)}{Q'(u,v)}$. However, this X may not be the multiple of k. To obtain a multiple of k, we set $X = k \cdot \text{round}\left(\frac{r(u,v) \cdot D(u,v)}{k \cdot Q'(u,v)}\right)$. Finally, we have $D'(u,v)$ as follows:

$$D'(u, v) = k \cdot D(u, v) + k \cdot \text{round}\left(\frac{r(u, v) \cdot D(u, v)}{k \cdot Q'(u, v)}\right) \tag{6.14}$$

A block diagram illustrating this phase is shown in Fig. 6.17, and the detailed data hiding phase is given step by step as follows.

Step 1: Partially decode the original JPEG image I to get the quantization table and quantized DCT coefficients, as well as get the width and height of the image so that the total number of 8 × 8 blocks N_I can be calculated.

Step 2: Encrypt the original secret data and then convert them into a series of k-ary digits. In fact, the embedding capacity increases a lot because of this step. Count the total number of digits N_D after conversion.

Step 3: Calculate the number of elements in the quantization table N_Q which we need to apply Eq. (6.13) to. A quantized DCT coefficient can embed one k-ary digit, and an element of the quantization table corresponds to N_I-quantized DCT coefficients. N_Q can be calculated by $N_Q = \lceil (N_D + 24)/N_I \rceil$, where $\lceil \cdot \rceil$ is the ceiling function that maps a real number to the smallest following integer and 24 is the number of digits for additional information to be mentioned later. Then apply Eq. (6.13) to the quantization table in the zigzag sequence, starting from the third coefficient till N_Q elements of the quantization table are applied. The

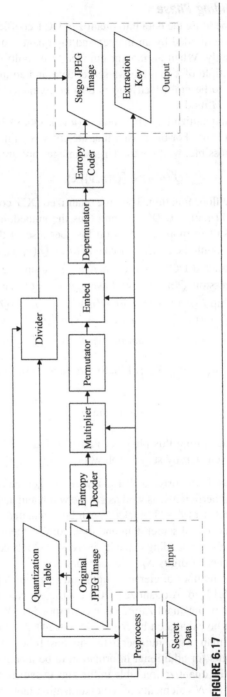

FIGURE 6.17

The block diagram of our data hiding phase.

remainder $r(u,v)$ needs to be recorded as additional information for the restoring step, which occupies 12 digits. Sometimes the result is 0, the element should be skipped and kept as its original value and a flag also should be recorded as additional information to tell that this element is not modified, which also occupies 12 digits. The first modified quantization table entry position should be saved and can be regarded as an extraction key. Fig. 6.18 shows two examples of modifying the quantization tables. Fig. 6.18a is the original quantization table for $QF = 70$ and we need to modify nine elements with $k = 2$. We apply Eq. (6.13) from the third element in the zigzag sequence and get the modified

(a)

10	7	6	10	14	24	31	37
7	7	8	11	16	35	36	33
8	8	10	14	24	34	41	34
8	10	13	17	31	52	48	37
11	13	22	34	41	65	62	46
14	21	33	38	49	62	68	55
29	38	47	52	62	73	72	61
43	55	57	59	67	60	62	59

Original quantization table (QF= 70)

(b)

10	7	3	5	14	24	31	37
7	3	4	11	16	35	36	33
4	4	10	14	24	34	41	34
4	5	13	17	31	52	48	37
5	13	22	34	41	65	62	46
14	21	33	38	49	62	68	55
29	38	47	52	62	73	72	61
43	55	57	59	67	60	62	59

Modified quantization table (QF= 70)

(c)

3	2	2	3	5	8	10	12
2	2	3	4	5	12	12	11
3	3	3	5	8	11	14	11
3	3	4	6	10	17	16	12
4	4	7	11	14	22	21	15
5	7	11	13	16	21	23	18
10	13	16	17	21	24	24	20
14	18	19	20	22	20	21	20

Original quantization table (QF= 90)

(d)

3	2	2	1	5	8	10	12
2	2	1	4	5	12	12	11
1	1	3	5	8	11	14	11
1	3	4	6	10	17	16	12
1	4	7	11	14	22	21	15
5	7	11	13	16	21	23	18
10	13	16	17	21	24	24	20
14	18	19	20	22	20	21	20

Modifiedquantizationtable(QF= 90)

FIGURE 6.18

The examples of modifying the quantization tables. (a) Original quantization table (QF = 70), (b) modified quantization table (QF = 70), (c) original quantization table (QF 90), and (d) modified quantization table (QF = 90). *QF*, quality factor.

quantization table in Fig. 6.18b. Fig. 6.18c is the original quantization table for $QF = 90$ and we need to modify six elements with $k = 3$. For the fourth and fifth elements, the results of applying Eq. (6.13) are 0. Thus, they are skipped and kept as their original value and we continue to modify elements from the sixth one.

Step 4: Permute the DCT blocks (each 8×8 DCT block is regarded as a whole, no permutation is applied inside it) and then embed the additional information generated in Step 3 together with the converted secret digits block by block. Permutation shuffles the blocks, and then data are embedded into the permuted sequence. After blocks are permuted back to original positions, the changes could be distributed over the whole image. The straddling mechanism scatters the changes and avoids concentrating changes in certain part of the image. Quality degradation concentrating in certain part of the image may make the image look strange. That is, we first embed one secret digit into the ith quantized DCT coefficient of the jth block and then embed the next digit into the ith quantized DCT coefficient of the $(j + 1)$th block. After all the ith quantized DCT coefficients from every block have been embedded, we start to embed secret digits into the $(i + 1)$th quantized DCT coefficient of each block.

Fig. 6.19 illustrates the embedding sequence of a 16×16 JPEG image, starting

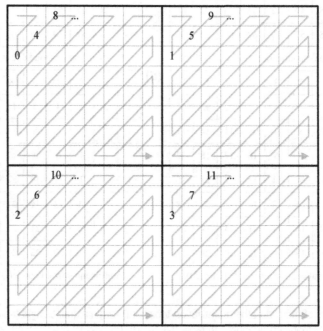

FIGURE 6.19

An example of embedding sequence for a 16×16 JPEG image.

from Position 3 of the first block. The converted digit W is a k-ary number (i.e., $W \in \{0, 1, ..., k-1\}$), and to make the distortion smaller, the embedding rule is as follows:

$$D''(u, v) = \begin{cases} D'(u, v) + W & W \leq k/2 \\ D'(u, v) + W - k & \text{otherwise} \end{cases} \tag{6.15}$$

After embedding, all blocks are permuted back to their original positions.

Step 5: Save the modified quantization table in the header of the JPEG file and apply entropy coding to the modified quantized DCT blocks, obtaining the stego JPEG image.

6.2.6.3 The Extraction and Restoration Phase

Fig. 6.20 illustrates the block diagram of extraction and restoration phase. The detailed steps of this phase can be described as follows:

Step 1: Decode the stego JPEG image to get the quantization table and quantized DCT blocks.

Step 2: Permute the quantized DCT blocks by the same key as used in the embedding phase, and then use the extraction key to determine the first entry for extraction. The Mod function is applied to extract the secret digits:

$$W = D''(u, v) \bmod k \tag{6.16}$$

The additional information (flags and $r(u,v)$) is extracted first, and then followed by the secret data. At the same time, the quantized DCT coefficients are restored using the equations below:

$$D'(u, v) = \begin{cases} D''(u, v) - W & W \leq k/2 \\ D''(u, v) - W + k & \text{otherwise} \end{cases} \tag{6.17}$$

$$D(u, v) = \text{round}\left(\frac{D'(u, v)}{k + r(u, v)/Q'(u, v)}\right) \tag{6.18}$$

The proof of Eq. (6.18) is as follows: From Eq. (6.14) and the definition of round function we have $D'(u, v) = k \cdot D(u, v) + \frac{r(u,v) \cdot D(u,v)}{Q'(u,v)} + k \cdot R$, where $R \in \left(-\frac{1}{2}, \frac{1}{2}\right)$.

Namely, $D(u, v) = \frac{D'(u,v) - k \cdot R}{k + r(u,v)/Q'(u,v)}$. This equation is equivalent to $D(u, v)$

$+ \frac{k \cdot R}{k + r(u,v)/Q'(u,v)} = \frac{D'(u,v)}{k + r(u,v)/Q'(u,v)}$ because $\frac{k \cdot R}{k + r(u,v)/Q'(u,v)} \in \left(-\frac{1}{2}, \frac{1}{2}\right)$, that is to say

$D(u, v) - \frac{1}{2} < \frac{D'(u,v)}{k + r(u,v)/Q'(u,v)} < D(u, v) + \frac{1}{2}$. Note that the definition of the rounding function is $\text{round}(x) = n \Leftrightarrow n - \frac{1}{2} \leq x < n + \frac{1}{2}$, hence Eq. (6.18) is finally established.

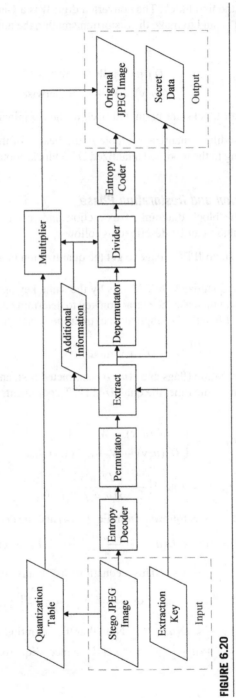

FIGURE 6.20

The block diagram of our extraction and restoration phase.

Step 3: Convert each k-ary secret digit extracted in Step 2 to the binary bits and decrypt them back to achieve the original secret data. Thus the extraction part is complete.

Step 4: Utilize the additional information $r(u,v)$ to restore the quantization table as follows:

$$Q(u, v) = k \cdot Q'(u, v) + r(u, v) \tag{6.19}$$

Step 5: Save the recovered quantization table in the header of the JPEG file and apply entropy coding to the restored quantized DCT blocks; then the original JPEG image is restored.

6.2.6.4 Experimental Results

To evaluate the performance of our scheme, we analyze properties of our scheme and compare it with those of other schemes. Six test images mentioned in Section 6.2.6.1 are shown in Fig. 6.14. In the experiment, the JPEG library Libjpeg developed by IJG is utilized. The three aspects, namely, the stego JPEG image quality, hiding capacity, and file size are discussed. The PSNR, which has been mentioned in Section 6.2.6.1, is used as a measure to evaluate the quality of stego JPEG images. PSNR is calculated between the original uncompressed image and the stego JPEG image.

6.2.6.4.1 The Performance of Our Algorithm

Since the conversion of secret data into a series of k-ary digits makes the capacity increase significantly, thus the performance for different k may vary largely. The experiments are performed based on different values of k. For $k = 3$, we take three binary bits to convert them into two ternary digits, that is to say, embedding 1 ternary digit is equivalent to embedding 1.5 binary bits. For $k = 4$, 1 quaternary digit is equivalent to 2 binary bits for the same reason. Similar explanations can be given for other values of k.

Table 6.1 shows the performance of capacity, distortion, and file size under different k values. The experiments are tested on the JPEG image Lena with the $QF = 70$. Observing the maximum capacity, as k becomes larger, the capacity increases at the beginning. However, when k is larger than 6, the capacity does not increase with the increasing k value, and even fluctuates instead. For some entries of the quantization table, they are not large enough to apply Eq. (6.13) if k is too large, and thus they are kept as their original values. These unaltered entries result in that the corresponding quantized DCT coefficients are unaltered and the corresponding space cannot be made to hide the data. Thus, the choice of k cannot be too large, and thus we select 2, 3, and 4 as the possible values of k to test in the following experiments. The deep explanation about the effect of different k values on the performance is provided later.

Table 6.1 Performance for Lena Image With Quality Factor QF = 70 Under Different Values of k

k	Capacity (bit)	PSNR (dB)		File Size (KB)	
		0.125 bpp	Fully Embedded	0.125 bpp	Fully Embedded
2	49,128	35.61	35.39	38.2	40.4
3	73,692	35.80	35.64	39.0	45.0
4	98,256	35.80	35.58	40.9	49.6
5	112,000	35.82	35.60	39.8	52.9
6	126,252	35.83	35.63	40.4	55.1
7	113,477	35.84	35.60	38.5	53.5
8	122,808	35.82	35.63	39.0	52.8

PSNR, *peak signal-to-noise ratio.*

The experimental results tested on the JPEG image Lena with different embedding rates and QFs are listed in Tables 6.2–6.4. The left slash (/) in the tables means that the corresponding embedding rate cannot be reached because some quantization table entries are not large enough to apply Eq. (6.13). The results of all test images

Table 6.2 PSNRs Tested on Lena Image With Different Embedding Rates and QFs ($k = 2$)

QF	Embedding Rate (×1 bpp)					
	0.031	0.062	0.094	0.125	0.156	0.187
50	34.32	34.20	34.07	33.90	33.74	33.48
60	34.97	34.89	34.80	34.69	34.55	34.37
70	35.84	35.76	35.70	35.63	35.53	35.39
80	37.00	36.97	36.93	36.89	36.83	36.73
90	39.43	39.41	39.39	39.36	39.34	39.29

PSNR, *peak signal-to-noise ratio;* QF, *quality factor.*

Table 6.3 PSNRs Tested on Lena Image With Different Embedding Rates and QFs ($k = 3$)

QF	Embedding Rate (× 1.5 bpp)					
	0.031	0.062	0.094	0.125	0.156	0.187
50	34.38	34.31	34.24	34.14	34.06	33.89
60	35.01	34.96	34.92	34.87	34.80	34.68
70	35.86	35.82	35.80	35.76	35.71	35.64
80	37.02	37.00	36.98	36.96	36.92	36.88
90	39.43	39.42	39.40	39.39	39.36	/

PSNR, *peak signal-to-noise ratio;* QF, *quality factor.*

Table 6.4 PSNRs Tested on Lena Image With Different Embedding Rates and QFs ($k = 4$)

QF	Embedding Rate (×2 bpp)					
	0.031	0.062	0.094	0.125	0.156	0.187
50	34.36	34.26	34.19	34.09	33.97	33.77
60	35.00	34.94	34.90	34.83	34.75	34.62
70	35.85	35.80	35.75	35.71	35.66	35.58
80	37.00	36.98	36.94	36.90	36.86	36.79
90	39.41	/	/	/	/	/

PSNR, *peak signal-to-noise ratio;* QF, *quality factor.*

with $QF = 70$ and different embedding rates are displayed in Fig. 6.21. From Tables 6.2–6.4, it can be seen that the bigger the embedding rate is or the smaller the QF is, the lower the PSNR is. Upon Comparison between these tables, it is observed that the PSNRs of the stego images obtained by modifying the same amount of digits are similar, while the embedding rates are multiplied for the existence of the parameter k. To check the impact of the parameter k on the image quality, we test on the JPEG image Lena with $QF = 70$ and the PSNR trends with the increases in embedding rate are illustrated in Fig. 6.22. When the embedding rate is the same, the results of $k = 3$ and $k = 4$ are better than that of $k = 2$.

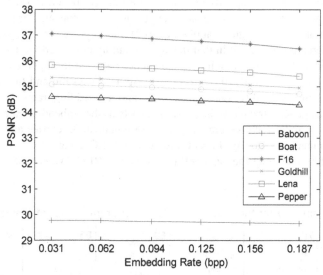

FIGURE 6.21

The performance of all test images with quality factor (QF) = 70. *PSNR,* peak signal-to-noise ratio.

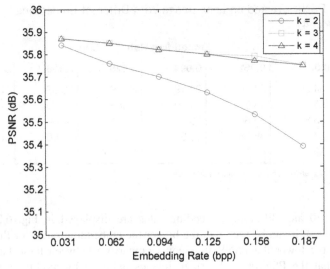

FIGURE 6.22

The peak signal-to-noise ratio (PSNR) trends of the Lena image with quality factor (QF) = 70.

Table 6.5 and Fig. 6.23 present the embedding capacity for the Lena image with different values of k and QFs. Obviously, the embedding capacity for higher value of k is larger. However, the capacity decreases when the QF becomes very big. When the QF becomes bigger, the quantization table entries become smaller so that some entries are not large enough to apply Eq. (6.9) and kept as their original values. These unaltered entries result in that the corresponding quantized DCT coefficients are unaltered and the corresponding space cannot be made to hide the data.

The comparison between the size of the original JPEG file and the size of the stego JPEG file with different values of k and embedding rates is shown in Fig. 6.24. The general trends are increasing linearly as the embedding rate increases. In general, the more data we embed, the more quantization entries and quantized DCT coefficients we modify. In fact, the size of JPEG image file is significantly compressed by encoding the AC coefficients using ZRLC. We choose the third to

Table 6.5 Capacity for the Lena Image With Different Values of k and QFs

QF	70	75	80	85	90
$k = 2$	49,128	49,128	49,128	49,128	49,128
$k = 3$	73,692	73,692	73,692	73,692	61,404
$k = 4$	98,256	98,256	98,256	90,064	24,528

QF, quality factor.

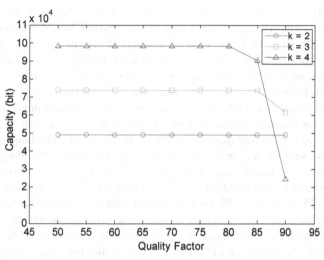

FIGURE 6.23

The capacity of the Lena image with different values of k and quality factors.

the fourteenth (zero based) quantized DCT coefficients to embed data, therefore the consecutive zero AC coefficients of midfrequency and high-frequency will not be broken. The file size growth is acceptable when the embedding rate is not too high.

From this discussion, we can see that the bigger the parameter k is, the better the stego image quality is, and the more capacity can be achieved under the same

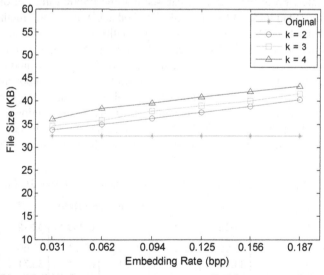

FIGURE 6.24

Comparison between the original JPEG file size and the stego file size with QF = 70. *QF*, quality factor.

conditions. However, the file size increases more when k is bigger. Thus, the choice of k needs to balance the image quality and file size growth. Note that k cannot be too large or the capacity will decrease when the cover JPEG image has a very high QF.

Table 6.6 shows the improvement of our method in image quality. However, Fridrich et al.'s method embedded only 4000-bit message in a certain high-frequency quantized DCT coefficient and did not offer the choice of the quantized DCT coefficients for high-capacity embedding. Here, we test their method in the same quantized DCT coefficients as our method. From Table 6.6, we can see that the optimization of multiplying quantized DCT coefficients and embedding rule makes the distortion smaller and improves the image quality after embedding the same amount of data. To directly display the subjective quality, we give two stego Lena images of our method and Fridrich et al.'s method with $QF = 70$, $k = 4$, and embedding rate 0.125 in Fig. 6.25. We observe that both stego images are almost identical with the original one. Moreover, ours is close to the original one on comparing both stego images with the original one. It can be seen more clearly from the areas near the hair and the brim of Lena's hat in Fig. 6.25d–f; the corresponding areas of Fridrich et al.'s are coarser than those of ours.

6.2.6.4.2 Comparisons Between Our Method and Former Methods

To demonstrate that our method is superior to some existing methods, we compare our proposed method with the methods of Chang et al. [13] and Xuan et al. [14] in terms of stego image quality and file size. To ensure that all schemes can be fairly compared, the test JPEG image Lena is used and the QF for both algorithms is fixed to 70. Our algorithm is performed with $k = 2$.

Fig. 6.26 shows the comparison of the stego image quality under different embedding rates. From Fig. 6.26, we can see that the PSNR values of our method are much larger than those of Chang et al.'s method and Xuan et al.'s method, which means that our scheme has a better stego image quality. One reason is that the actual variation of the original DCT coefficient will not be larger than $\frac{1}{2}Q(u, v)$, whereas the variations of both Chang et al.'s method and Xuan et al.'s method are $Q(u,v)$. Another reason is that zero coefficients of the midfrequency components in each block are used to hide the secret data in Chang et al.'s method, whereas our method embeds data in low-frequency components. As analyzed in Section 6.2.6.1, the change of low-frequency quantized DCT coefficients have less influence on the image quality than the change of midfrequency and high-frequency coefficients.

Table 6.6 PSNR Results Tested on the Lena Image With QF = 70 ($k = 4$)

PSNR	Embedding Rate					
	0.062	0.125	0.187	0.250	0.312	0.375
Proposed method	35.85	35.80	35.75	35.71	35.66	35.58
Fridrich et al.'s method	34.72	33.98	33.91	33.84	33.71	33.54

PSNR, *peak signal-to-noise ratio*; QF, *quality factor*.

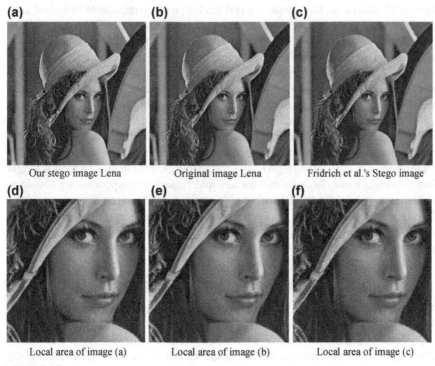

(a) Our stego image Lena **(b)** Original image Lena **(c)** Fridrich et al.'s Stego image

(d) Local area of image (a) **(e)** Local area of image (b) **(f)** Local area of image (c)

FIGURE 6.25

The results of stego images of our method and Fridrich et al.'s method. (a) Our stego image Lena, (b) original image Lena, (c) Fridrich et al.'s stego image, (d) local area of image (a), (e) local area of image (b), and (f) local area of image (c).

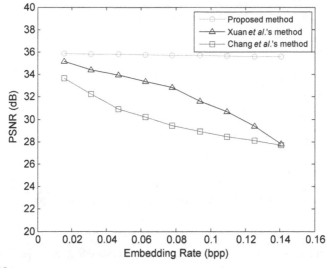

FIGURE 6.26

Comparison of the stego image quality with quality factor (QF) = 70 and $k = 2$. *PSNR,* peak signal-to-noise ratio.

Xuan et al. also chose low-frequency and midfrequency components to embed data. However, they need to modify more components because of the histogram pairs expanding technique. When a high embedding rate is required, their method makes more histogram pairs which causes the fast decrease of image quality.

Fig. 6.27 shows the comparison of the file size among the stego images obtained by our method, by Xuan et al.'s method, and by Chang et al.'s method and the original JPEG image on the condition that the embedding rate is 0.125 bpp. For $QF = 70$, the original and modified quantization tables in the experiment are shown in Fig. 6.18a and b. For different QFs, the file size of the stego images obtained by our method and Xuan et al.'s method are much closer to the original one. By contrast, the file size of the stego image obtained by Chang et al.'s method is bigger than the original one. Because the low and midfrequency components are chosen to embed data, our method and Xuan et al.'s method could restrain the growth of file size. However, the file sizes obtained by the three methods and the file size of the original image tend to be equal when the QF becomes very high. High QF means less compression ratio, which leads to the aforementioned results.

6.2.7 VARIABLE LENGTH CODE MAPPING—BASED SCHEME

Although Qian and Zhang [21] have made use of the little redundancy existing in the JPEG bitstream, there is still potential free space that can be explored to hide data. In this section, the authors improve their scheme and provide a lossless data hiding scheme in the JPEG bitstream that improves the hiding capacity. By analyzing the

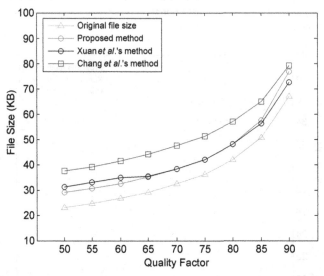

FIGURE 6.27

Comparison of the stego image file size with $k = 2$ and embedding rate 0.125 bpp.

statistics of both used and unused VLCs, a specific mapping strategy is produced and the unused VLCs can be taken full advantage of. The code mapping relationships are well designed, and the unused VLCs can be properly utilized. The optimization of mapping relationships can further increase the capacity. The detailed optimization algorithm as well as embedding and extracting procedures are presented in the following subsections.

6.2.7.1 Optimization Algorithm to Establish Mapping Relationships

Take AC coefficients for instance; there are 162 predefined VLCs in total. However, not all the codes are used in a normal JPEG image. For this reason, the unused VLCs can be mapped to the used VLCs to present secret bits. Mapping codes must observe certain rules, else the standard JPEG image viewers used by normal users will be unable to decode and display the stego image properly. As mentioned in Section 6.1.1, VLC corresponds to the (*run, size*) value, which means one VLC indicates the current zero run length and the size of appending VLI. The arbitrary mapping VLC may lead to the misunderstanding of zero run length or the incorrect reading of appending VLI. To preserve the file size, we adopt the following code mapping rules: (1) the length of every code in the mapping set {VLC_m, VLC_n, ..., VLC_l} should be the same and (2) all codes should correspond to the same (*run, size*) value. Thus, the mapping relationships can be established inside each category C_i.

These rules are the same as those used in Qian and Zhang's scheme. Now we turn to explain our optimization scheme for establishing optimal mapping relationships. We notice that the statistics of both used and unused VLCs can help design the mapping relationships to increase the capacity. Thus, the JPEG bitstream is parsed and the number of occurrences of every VLC is recorded first. A zero number of occurrences means that the corresponding VLC is unused. The VLCs in each category C_i are then sorted in the descending order according to their numbers of occurrences, which can be presented in the following form:

$$C_i = \left\{ VLC_{i,1}^{(u)'}, ..., VLC_{i,p_i}^{(u)'}; VLC_{i,1}^{(n)}, ..., VLC_{i,q_i}^{(n)} \right\} \qquad (6.20)$$

where $VLC_{i,1}^{(u)'}, ..., VLC_{i,p_i}^{(u)'}$ are p_i-sorted used codes, $VLC_{i,1}^{(n)}, ..., VLC_{i,q_i}^{(n)}$ are q_i unused codes, and $p_i + q_i = L_i$.

If we go along with Qian and Zhang's way of thinking, we can develop a mapping method that takes the above statistics into consideration and call it *mapping method 1*. For the case $0 < q_i \leq p_i$, the VLCs in each category are mapped by a one-to-one manner similar to Eq. (6.8) as follows:

$$M_i = \left\{ \left\{ VLC_{i,1}^{(u)'} \leftrightarrow VLC_{i,1}^{(n)} \right\}, ..., \left\{ VLC_{i,q_i}^{(u)'} \leftrightarrow VLC_{i,q_i}^{(n)} \right\} \right\} \qquad (6.21)$$

In this case, not all used VLCs could be utilized for the reason $p_i \geq q_i$, thus the sorting keeps the q_i frequently appearing used VLCs and abandons the ($p_i - q_i$) relatively seldom appearing used VLCs. It avoids easily abandoning the last ($p_i - q_i$)

used VLCs in the original order, which may contain the frequently- appearing ones, and therefore helps to increase the capacity.

For the case $0 < p_i < q_i$, VLCs are mapped by the combination of one-to-many manner and one-to-one manner. One-to-k manner, for example, can present $\log_2(k + 1)$ secret bits, where k satisfies the restrictive condition that $\log_2(k + 1)$ is a positive integer. In other words, one-to-$(2^j - 1)$ manner can present j secret bits. For AC coefficients, there are 162 VLCs in total, and the largest category is C_{16}, which has 125 VLCs, i.e., $L_{16} = 125$. The maximum j that satisfies $2^j - 1 \leq 125$ is 6, thus j could be 1, 2, 3, 4, 5, and 6, which means the parameter of one-to-k manner could be 1, 3, 7, 15, 31, and 63, respectively. In each category C_i, assuming the number of one-to-$(2^j - 1)$ manner mapping sets is $m_{i,j}$ $(1 \leq j \leq 6)$. To efficiently utilize the unused VLCs in this case, the selection of $m_{i,j}$ should satisfy the following condition:

$$\text{maxZ} = \sum_{j=1}^{6} j \cdot m_{i,j}$$

$$\text{s.t.} \begin{cases} \sum_{j=1}^{6} m_{i,j} \leq p_i \\ \sum_{j=1}^{6} (2^j - 1) \cdot m_{i,j} \leq q_i \\ m_{i,j} \geq 0, j = 1, 2, ..., 6 \\ m_{i,j} \text{ integer}, j = 1, 2, ..., 6 \end{cases} \tag{6.22}$$

This is an integer linear programming problem. After Eq. (6.22) is solved, all code mapping relationships can be expressed as:

$$M_i = \begin{cases} \left\{ \text{VLC}_{i,1}^{(u)'} \leftrightarrow \left\{ \text{VLC}_{i,1}^{(n)}, ..., \text{VLC}_{i,63}^{(n)} \right\} \right\}, ..., \\ \left\{ \text{VLC}_{i,m_{i,6}}^{(u)'} \leftrightarrow \left\{ \text{VLC}_{i,63 \cdot (m_{i,6}-1)+1}^{(n)}, ..., \text{VLC}_{i,63 \cdot m_{i,6}}^{(n)} \right\} \right\}, \\ \left\{ \text{VLC}_{i,m_{i,6}+1}^{(u)'} \leftrightarrow \left\{ \text{VLC}_{i,63 \cdot m_{i,6}+1}^{(n)}, ..., \text{VLC}_{i,63 \cdot m_{i,6}+31}^{(n)} \right\} \right\}, ..., \\ \left\{ \text{VLC}_{i,\sum_{j=1}^{6} m_{i,j}}^{(u)'} \leftrightarrow \text{VLC}_{i,\sum_{j=1}^{6} [(2^j-1) \cdot m_{i,j}]}^{(n)} \right\} \end{cases} \tag{6.23}$$

That is to say, the first $m_{i,6}$ sorted used VLCs are mapped by the one-to-63 manner, the next $m_{i,5}$ sorted used VLCs are mapped by the one-to-31 manner, and so on, and the last $m_{i,1}$ sorted used VLCs are mapped by the one-to-one manner.

This mapping method only makes the unused VLCs be able to be mapped to as many used VLCs as possible. In fact, there is still certain potential space to further increase the capacity. In real cases, some used VLCs may appear with a very high frequency. Thus, it is even worth abandoning parts of the used VLCs and mapping more unused VLCs to the frequently used VLCs, which can help to carry more secret bits. The following method, which considers these situations, is called *mapping method 2*. For the case $p_i > 0$ and $q_i > 0$, VLCs are mapped by the combination of one-to-many manner and one-to-one manner. Thus, in *mapping method 2*, we adopt the same code mapping relationships as given in Eq. (6.23); however the selection of $m_{i,j}$ should satisfy the following condition:

$$
\begin{aligned}
\max Z = {} & 6 \cdot \sum_{v=1}^{m_{i,6}} \text{count}(i, v) + 5 \cdot \sum_{v=m_{i,6}+1}^{m_{i,6}+m_{i,5}} \text{count}(i, v) \\
& + 4 \cdot \sum_{v=m_{i,6}+m_{i,5}+1}^{m_{i,6}+m_{i,5}+m_{i,4}} \text{count}(i, v) + 3 \cdot \sum_{v=m_{i,6}+m_{i,5}+m_{i,4}+1}^{m_{i,6}+m_{i,5}+m_{i,4}+m_{i,3}} \text{count}(i, v) \\
& + 2 \cdot \sum_{v=m_{i,6}+m_{i,5}+m_{i,4}+m_{i,3}+1}^{m_{i,6}+m_{i,5}+m_{i,4}+m_{i,3}+m_{i,2}} \text{count}(i, v) + \sum_{v=m_{i,6}+m_{i,5}+m_{i,4}+m_{i,3}+m_{i,2}+1}^{m_{i,6}+m_{i,5}+m_{i,4}+m_{i,3}+m_{i,2}+m_{i,1}} \text{count}(i, v)
\end{aligned}
$$

$$
\text{s.t.} \begin{cases}
\displaystyle\sum_{j=1}^{6} m_{i,j} \le p_i \\[3mm]
\displaystyle\sum_{j=1}^{6} (2^j - 1) \cdot m_{i,j} \le q_i \\[3mm]
m_{i,j} \ge 0, j = 1, 2, \dots, 6 \\[2mm]
m_{i,j} \text{ are integers}, j = 1, 2, \dots, 6
\end{cases}
$$

$$(6.24)$$

where the function *count(i,v)* presents the number of times that the vth sorted used code in category C_i appears in the entropy-coded segment. After Eq. (6.24) is solved, by substituting them into Eq. (6.23), we can get the optimal code mapping relationships.

6.2.7.2 Extension to the Application Case Where File Size Increase is Acceptable

From Section 6.2.7.1, we establish the mapping relationships inside each category C_i to preserve the original file size. In fact, we can extend the earlier scheme to the situations where slight file size increase is allowed. In this case, the mapping relationships are not required to be established inside each category. They can be established among all categories. The file size increase is induced by mapping the short used VLCs to long unused VLCs, and a threshold *TH* could be set to constrain the selection of used VLCs. The search of used VLCs can be performed among a limited number of categories, i.e., those categories C_i whose index i is not smaller than *TH*, so that certain shortest VLCs will not be chosen. However, the selection of unused VLCs is not restrained. Suppose the number of selected used VLCs is p and the number of unused ones is q. For the case $0 < p \le q$, VLCs can be mapped by the combination of one-to-many manner and one-to-one manner. However, for the case $p > q > 0$, even all unused codes are mapped by one-to-one manner, and no more than q used codes will be utilized. Thus, p' used codes and q unused codes will be chosen. The definition of p' is as follows:

$$p' = \begin{cases} p, 0 < p \le q \\ q, p > q > 0 \end{cases} \tag{6.25}$$

The first p' most frequently appearing used codes are selected and sorted. Likewise, the q unused codes are sorted in the ascending order of their lengths for the purpose that the shorter unused codes could be mapped to the more frequently appearing used codes:

$$C = \left\{ \text{VLC}_1^{(u)'}, \dots, \text{VLC}_{p'}^{(u)'}; \text{VLC}_1^{(n)'}, \dots, \text{VLC}_q^{(n)'} \right\} \tag{6.26}$$

It helps to control the increase of file size. Note that all VLCs are taken here, i.e., there are 162 VLCs in total for AC coefficients. Hence, the maximum j that satisfies $2^j - 1 \le 162$ is 7 and we suppose the number of one-to-(2^j-1) manner mapping sets is m_j $(1 \le j \le 7)$. The rest part is similar to *mapping method 2* as depicted in Section 6.3.1. The selection of m_j should satisfy the following condition:

$$\text{maxZ} = 7 \cdot \sum_{v=1}^{m_7} \text{count}(v) + 6 \cdot \sum_{v=m_7+1}^{m_7+m_6} \text{count}(v) + 5 \cdot \sum_{v=m_7+m_6+1}^{m_7+m_6+m_5} \text{count}(v)$$

$$+ 4 \cdot \sum_{v=m_7+m_6+m_5+1}^{m_7+m_6+m_5+m_4} \text{count}(v) + 3 \cdot \sum_{v=m_7+m_6+m_5+m_4+1}^{m_7+m_6+m_5+m_4+m_3} \text{count}(v)$$

$$+ 2 \cdot \sum_{v=m_7+m_6+m_5+m_4+m_3+1}^{m_7+m_6+m_5+m_4+m_3+m_2} \text{count}(v) + \sum_{v=m_7+m_6+m_5+m_4+m_3+m_2+1}^{m_7+m_6+m_5+m_4+m_3+m_2+m_1} \text{count}(v)$$

$$\text{s.t.} \begin{cases} \sum_{j=1}^{7} m_j \le p' \\ \\ \sum_{j=1}^{7} (2^j - 1) \cdot m_j \le q \\ \\ m_j \ge 0, j = 1, 2, \dots, 7 \\ \\ m_j \text{ are integers}, j = 1, 2, \dots, 7 \end{cases} \tag{6.27}$$

where the function count(v) stands for the number of times that the vth sorted used code appears in the entropy-coded segment. After Eq. (6.27) is solved, the code mapping relationships can be expressed as:

$$M_i = \begin{cases} \left\{ \text{VLC}_1^{(u)'} \leftrightarrow \left\{ \text{VLC}_1^{(n)}, \dots, \text{VLC}_{127}^{(n)} \right\} \right\}, \dots, \\ \left\{ \text{VLC}_{m_7}^{(u)'} \leftrightarrow \left\{ \text{VLC}_{127 \cdot (m_7-1)+1}^{(n)}, \dots, \text{VLC}_{127 \cdot m_7}^{(n)} \right\} \right\}, \\ \left\{ \text{VLC}_{m_7+1}^{(u)'} \leftrightarrow \left\{ \text{VLC}_{127 \cdot m_7+1}^{(n)}, \dots, \text{VLC}_{127 \cdot m_7+63}^{(n)} \right\} \right\}, \dots, \\ \left\{ \text{VLC}_{\sum_{j=1}^{7} m_j}^{(u)'} \leftrightarrow \text{VLC}_{\sum_{j=1}^{7} [(2^j-1) \cdot m_j]}^{(n)} \right\} \end{cases} \tag{6.28}$$

That is to say, the first m_7 sorted used VLCs are mapped by the one-to-127 manner, the next m_6 sorted used VLCs are mapped by the one-to-63 manner, and so on, and the last m_1 sorted used VLCs are mapped by the one-to-one manner.

6.2.7.3 Data Embedding and Extracting Procedures

Our scheme embeds data into the bitstream of JPEG images based on VLC mapping and replacing. Our scheme can be divided into two procedures: the data embedding procedure and the data extracting procedure. After collecting the VLC statistical information and establishing optimization mapping relationships, our scheme embeds data into the VLCs in the entropy-coded segment. Fig. 6.28 shows how secret bits are embedded by replacing VLCs. The detailed data embedding steps are as follows:

Step 1: Parse the JPEG bitstream, read all the VLCs in the entropy-coded segment, and get statistical results of the number of occurrences for every used VLC.

Step 2: According to the statistical results, establish the mapping relationships based on the mapping method mentioned in Sections 6.2.7.1 and 6.2.7.2.

Step 3: Encrypt the original secret data and then modify the $V_{i,j}(run, size)$ value in the DHT segment in accordance with the mapping relationships.

Step 4: Replace the VLCs in the entropy-coded segment to embed secret bits.

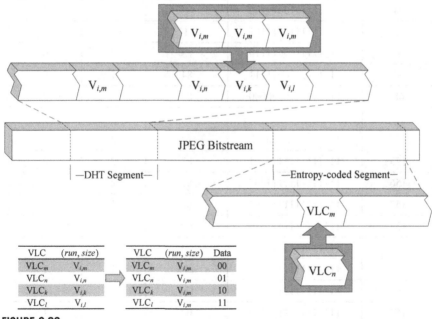

FIGURE 6.28

The sketch map of our data hiding scheme by replacing VLCs. *DHT*, Define Huffman Table; *VLC*, variable length code.

Because the data embedding procedure will keep the original image content without impacting the image quality, no restoring procedure is required. The data hidden in the entropy-coded segment can be extracted according to a lookup table, which is generated by scanning the Huffman table. Fig. 6.29 shows an example of creating a lookup table. The VLCs with the same (*run, size*) value are divided into groups, and the bits that each VLC could present can be calculated by counting the number of occurrences of the same (*run, size*) value, i.e., the binary logarithm of the number of occurrences. Four rows with gray background in Fig. 6.29 are the VLCs with the same (*run, size*) value 83. Therefore each of them can present $\log_2 4 = 2$ bits and the data are listed in the column *Value* and recorded in decimal

No.	VLC	(*run, size*)	Bits	Value
1	00	1	0	-
2	01	2	0	-
3	100	3	0	-
4	1010	0	0	-
...	...	...	...	...
64	1111111110011100	147	4	3
65	1111111110011101	147	4	4
66	1111111110011110	83	2	0
67	1111111110011111	84	1	0
68	1111111110100000	85	3	0
...	...	...	...	...
154	1111111111110110	83	2	1
155	1111111111110111	83	2	2
156	1111111111111000	83	2	3
157	1111111111111001	84	1	1
158	1111111111111010	99	1	1
159	1111111111111011	23	1	1
160	1111111111111100	115	1	1
161	1111111111111101	131	1	1
162	1111111111111110	67	1	1

FIGURE 6.29

An example of creating a lookup table in the extracting phase. *VLC*, variable length code.

numbers. After a stego JPEG image is received, secret data can be extracted by the following steps:

Step 1: Read the DHT segment of the stego JPEG image to reconstruct the Huffman table.

Step 2: Scan the Huffman table and find the VLC mapping sets with the same (*run, size*) value to create a lookup table containing VLCs and corresponding secret bits.

Step 3: Parse the JPEG bitstream, read the VLCs in the entropy-coded segment to extract secret bits according to the lookup table, and then decrypt them back to achieve original secret data.

6.2.7.4 Security Analysis

In our scheme, the mapping relationships are established by modifying the DHT segment of the JPEG header. Because the JPEG bitstream must be viewable by common viewers, the mapping relationships cannot be concealed. The modified Huffman table is viewable by the third party, thus careful observation may lead to the identification of the existence of mapping relationships. However, it could be encrypted to further improve the security of embedded information. For example, there is a mapping set $\{VLC_m, VLC_n, VLC_k, VLC_l\}$ and the four VLCs are listed in the order of their appearance in the DHT segment; they present secret bits "00," "01," "10," and "11," respectively. If we use a secret key to shuffle the order of the whole predefined VLCs and generate a new order list, which leads to a different lookup table, then VLC_m, VLC_n, VLC_k, and VLC_l may present "10," "00," "11," and "01" according to the lookup table. The shuffle is equivalent to encrypting the mapping relationships. On the receiver side, the same secret key is used to get the shuffled order and extract the secret data.

In the data embedding phase, a secret key k_1 encrypting the secret information and another secret key k_2 encrypting the mapping relationships guarantee the security of the embedded data. In some situations, attackers may even erase the embedded data and replace them with other information. Thus, we can add the secret information authentication part to the scheme by computing the message integrity code (MIC) and storing it in the user fields of JPEG header. MIC is computed by hashing the original embedded data with a secret key k_3. For example, MD2 is one of the useful hashing functions [11,12]. The receiver extracts the embedded data and calculates the new MIC from them. By comparing the calculated and stored MICs, the receiver can authenticate the embedded data.

6.2.7.5 Experimental Results

To evaluate the performance of our scheme, 10 test images obtained from the USC-SIPI image database [14] are used. These images are the same as those are used in Ref. [12] and provided in 512×512 TIFF format, which are further converted to grayscale JPEG images with different QFs using the Netpbm image format conversion program [15]. Comparisons of hiding capacity and embedding efficiency between Qian and Zhang's scheme and our scheme are discussed. Experimental results tested on 10 test images with different QFs are listed in Table 6.7, where the results of Qian and Zhang's method [12] are also listed. From Table 6.7, we can see that the capacities of both our method 1 and method 2 are larger than those of Qian and Zhang's method and the capacity of our method 2 is larger than that of our method 1. To demonstrate the capacity increase of our methods compared with Qian's methods more clearly, Table 6.8 presents the comparison results from the perspective of average capacity across all QFs. Our method 1 increases the embedding bits by 28–43% compared with Qian and Zhang's method, whereas our method 2 by 31–63%.

The capacities of our methods and Qian and Zhang's method are not fixed, and they depend on the statistical results of the used and unused VLCs. Different image contents lead to different statistical results. Table 6.8 reveals that the image with more similar content blocks usually has higher capacity. Take the test JPEG image F16 with QF = 70, for example; there are 22 used VLCs and 103 unused VLCs in Category C_{16}. The occurrence distribution of the used VLCs in Category C_{16} appearing in the entropy-coded segment is given in Fig. 6.30. The left blue bar in each bin is in the original order (12, 4, 14, 1, 20, 3, 13, 1, 5, 5, 11, 5, 2, 4, 22, 4, 18, 33, 1, 36, 12, and 2) and the right red one (36, 33, 22, 20, 18, 14, 13, 12, 12, 11, 5, 5, 5, 4, 4, 4, 3, 2, 2, 1, 1, and 1) is in the sorted order. For Qian and Zhang's method, VLCs are mapped in the original order, whereas they are mapped in the sorted order for our methods. Priority in mapping by the one-to-many manner with higher capacity will be given to those with larger occurrence, which helps to increase the embedding capacity. In Qian and Zhang's scheme, every used VLC in Category C_{16} can carry $k_{16} = \lfloor \log_2(q_{16}/p_{16} + 1) \rfloor = \lfloor \log_2(103/22 + 1) \rfloor = 2$ bits, thus all VLCs in Category C_{16} in the entropy-coded segment can carry 456 bits. For our method 1, $m_{16,1}$, $m_{16,2}$, $m_{16,3}$, $m_{16,4}$, $m_{16,5}$, and $m_{16,6}$ are 0, 13, 9, 0, 0, and 0, respectively, thus all VLCs in Category C_{16} can carry 636 bits. For our method 2, $m_{16,1}$, $m_{16,2}$, $m_{16,3}$, $m_{16,4}$, $m_{16,5}$, and $m_{16,6}$ are 6, 1, 7, 3, 0, and 0, respectively, thus all VLCs in Category C_{16} can carry 699 bits. From Fig. 6.30 it can be seen that the values of first several red bars are much higher those of the last several ones, therefore our method 2 abandons the last several ones and thus more unused VLCs can be mapped to the first several ones.

The numbers of VLC mapping sets generated by Qian and Zhang's method and our method 2 are compared in Fig. 6.31. Since the number of our method 1 is similar to that of Qian and Zhang's method, we do not present it in Fig. 6.31. The abandoning of the last several sorted used VLCs and the mapping of more unused VLCs to first several sorted used VLCs makes the number of sets by our method 2 below that of Qian and Zhang's. Fig. 6.32 shows the comparison results of the embedding efficiency, which is defined as the capacity divide by the number of mapping sets. It can be seen that our method 2 has higher efficiency for it can achieve higher capacity with the lower number of mapping sets.

Table 6.9 lists the performance of our method in terms of the image file size when the file size change is allowed. Experiments are performed on five test images with

Table 6.7 Comparison of Embedding Capacity (bits) Between Qian and Zhang's Method and Our Methods With Different Quality Factors

Image	Method	Quality Factor								
		10	20	30	40	50	60	70	80	90
Baboon	Qian and Zhang's	4954	2263	1278	1588	1080	1005	1082	615	346
	Our method 1	6569	3463	1692	1746	1204	1172	1219	669	518
	Our method 2	6576	3478	1758	1790	1268	1304	1353	757	681
Boat	Qian and Zhang's	484	388	522	481	522	714	370	510	978
	Our method 1	950	551	680	548	633	782	572	725	1408
	Our method 2	950	551	691	571	687	811	679	1000	1929
Bridge	Qian and Zhang's	733	675	614	755	781	501	436	306	350
	Our method 1	1802	996	699	833	912	599	635	446	491
	Our method 2	1802	999	713	860	1035	714	817	596	615
Elaine	Qian and Zhang's	116	142	177	328	402	218	272	576	1002
	Our method 1	341	264	200	414	531	302	365	662	1328
	Our method 2	341	264	200	414	553	326	409	788	1745
F16	Qian and Zhang's	615	639	722	737	760	536	487	404	464
	Our method 1	791	729	865	881	812	763	678	507	493
	Our method 2	791	764	904	961	886	860	741	553	595
Gray21	Qian and Zhang's	201	447	694	640	767	796	913	1286	2154
	Our method 1	235	502	865	987	900	897	1463	1616	2868
	Our method 2	235	502	904	987	900	929	1510	1675	3207
Lena	Qian and Zhang's	261	210	250	291	364	188	204	249	294
	Our method 1	565	326	257	296	368	198	256	316	436
	Our method 2	565	326	259	296	369	204	286	351	576

Continued

Table 6.7 Comparison of Embedding Capacity (bits) Between Qian and Zhang's Method and Our Methods With Different Quality Factors—cont'd

Image	Method	Quality Factor								
		10	20	30	40	50	60	70	80	90
Peppers	Qian and Zhang's	391	380	491	383	389	473	295	280	768
	Our method 1	567	513	698	487	534	616	415	280	1065
	Our method 2	567	517	717	493	557	652	455	374	1562
Splash	Qian and Zhang's	330	481	632	724	871	1112	653	714	284
	Our method 1	497	581	967	1147	1273	1334	979	953	566
	Our method 2	497	597	1064	1345	1382	1547	1180	1147	710
Tiffany	Qian and Zhang's	4404	500	345	485	467	563	724	590	256
	Our method 1	4721	1138	663	888	705	803	920	742	506
	Our method 2	4721	1153	681	907	786	875	1002	956	720

Table 6.8 Comparison of Average Capacity (bits) Between Qian and Zhang's Method and Our Methods Across JPEG Quality Factors From 10 to 90

		Our Method 1		Our Method 2	
Image	Qian and Zhang's Method	Capacity	Increase (%)	Capacity	Increase (%)
Baboon	1579.00	2028.00	28.44	2107.22	33.45
Boat	552.11	761.00	37.83	874.33	58.36
Bridge	572.33	823.67	42.91	905.67	58.24
Elaine	359.22	489.67	36.31	560.00	55.89
F16	596.00	724.33	21.53	783.89	31.52
Gray21	877.56	1148.11	30.83	1205.44	37.36
Lena	256.78	335.33	30.59	359.11	39.85
Peppers	427.78	575.00	34.42	654.89	53.09
Splash	644.56	921.89	43.03	1052.11	63.23
Tiffany	926.00	1231.78	33.02	1311.22	41.06

$QF = 70$. The capacities are not fixed, either. The image content will affect the capacity and file size. From Table 6.9 we can see that as the threshold TH increases, the capacity decreases and so does the file size. For small THs, the capacity is very high. Nonetheless, the file size growth after hiding data is not acceptable. Large THs result

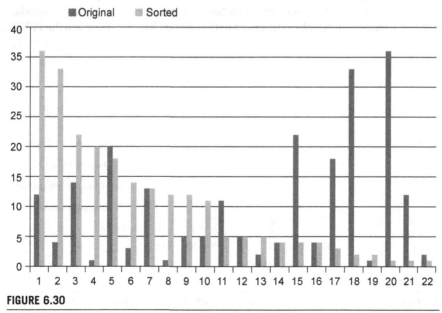

FIGURE 6.30

Statistical results of 22 used VLCs in Category C16 (for the test image F16 with quality factor 70). *VLC*, variable length code.

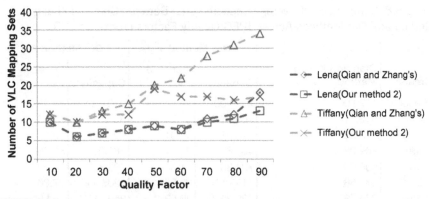

FIGURE 6.31

Comparisons of the number of VLC mapping sets between our method 2 and Qian and Zhang's method with different quality factors. *VLC*, variable length code.

in a satisfactory file size growth at the expense of lowing capacity. A proper threshold balances the capacity and the file size. Threshold could be selected according to the data to be hidden. Suppose we need to hide 32,768 bits into the JPEG image Lena, i.e., the embedding rate is 0.125 bpp, *TH* is recommended to be set to 4.

Fig. 6.33 compares our method with Chang et al.'s method [11] in terms of the image file size and PSNR when the file size change is allowed. Experiments are performed on the test image Lena with QFs ranging from 10 to 90. Fig. 6.33 shows the results when hiding 32,768 bits. For each case, the file size of our method is similar to that of Chang et al.'s and a little closer to the original file size. Note that the PSNR

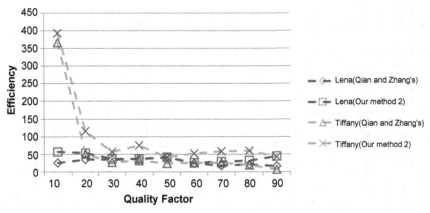

FIGURE 6.32

Comparisons of embedding efficiency between Qian and Zhang's method and our method 2 with different quality factors.

Table 6.9 Performance of Our Scheme in the Application Case Where the File Size Increase is Allowed (Quality Factor = 70)

Image	Original File Size (KB)	Evaluation Criteria	4	5	6	TH 7	8	9	10
Baboon	61.0	Capacity (bit)	119,513	56,672	31,421	21,176	12,486	8436	3493
		File size (KB)	113.0	84.6	73.0	68.6	65.1	63.6	61.9
Boat	36.6	Capacity (bit)	73,174	33,552	18,891	12,223	7223	5347	2925
		File size (KB)	69.1	50.8	44.1	41.3	39.0	38.2	37.2
F16	30.0	Capacity (bit)	64,676	27,829	13,987	8252	3969	2520	1470
		File size (KB)	58.6	41.6	35.3	33.0	31.3	30.7	30.3
Lena	28.6	Capacity (bit)	65,325	29,198	15,976	8879	4874	3010	1557
		File size (KB)	56.7	40.4	34.6	31.8	30.1	29.5	28.9

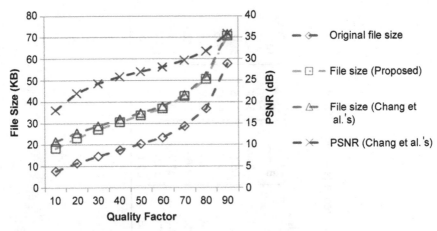

FIGURE 6.33

Comparisons of image file size and PSNR between our method and Chang et al.'s method when the file size change is allowed. *PSNR*, peak signal-to-noise ratio.

of Chang et al.'s changes from 18 to 36 dB, whereas our method can keep the original image's content and quality. Therefore, our method can provide high capacity, acceptable file size growth, and image quality preservation.

6.3 LOSSLESS INFORMATION HIDING IN JPEG2000 IMAGES

As an important branch of information security, information hiding in images has been extensively studied in recent years. However, most schemes will introduce irreversible distortion to the original image. It is unallowable in some special applications such as legal imaging and medical imaging. So reversible information hiding deserves us to study. In addition, most existing information hiding schemes are for BMP and JPEG images. There are few related schemes for JPEG2000 images. So it is very necessary for us to study reversible information hiding for JPEG2000 images.

6.3.1 OVERVIEW

To understand the following schemes better, we introduce the JPEG2000 codec first. The block diagram of the JPEG2000 codec is shown in Fig. 6.34. In the JPEG2000 encoder, image preprocessing is performed at first. Here, image preprocessing includes image tiling, DC level shifting, and component transformation. Image tiling is applied to the original image by dividing it into rectangular nonoverlapping blocks (tiles). These blocks can be processed independently. DC level shifting can ensure that the input sample data has a nominal dynamic range that is approximately centered about 0. Then component transformation or color transformation is

(a)

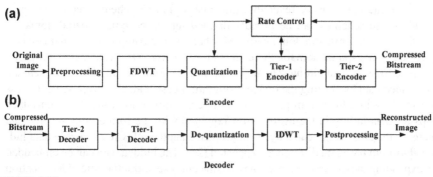

FIGURE 6.34

The block diagram of JPEG2000 codec. (a) Encoder, (b) Decoder

performed on the tile-component data. Only two component transformations are defined in the baseline JPEG2000 codec, i.e., ICT and RCT. Both of them can map the image data from the RGB color space to the YCbCr color space. Next, these tiles are decomposed into different decomposition levels by the FDWT. After N levels of DWT, we can get the decomposed image, which is made up of a low-frequency subband called LL_N and $3 \times N$ high-frequency subbands referred to as HL_i, LH_i, HH_i, where $i = 1, 2, \ldots N$. Fig. 6.35 shows the subband structure after three levels of DWT. Then the resulting wavelet coefficients in all subbands are quantized. Next, entropy coding including tier-1 coding and tier-2 coding is applied to the quantized blocks to generate JPEG2000-compressed bitstream. Up to this point, the encoding process is finished. The decoding process of the JPEG2000 codec is just the reverse of the encoding process.

LL_3	HL_3	HL_2	HL_1
LH_3	HH_3		
LH_2		HH_2	
LH_1			HH_1

FIGURE 6.35

The subband structure.

In the literature, many reversible information hiding schemes have been proposed. These schemes can be broadly divided into three types: spatial domain—based schemes, transform domain—based schemes, and compressed domain—based schemes. In the spatial domain, there are many effective schemes. Ni et al. proposed a classic lossless data hiding scheme based on histogram shifting [24]. The scheme can embed data by shifting the image histogram. Leest et al. also proposed a lossless scheme based on histogram [25]. They utilize a compression function to introduce gaps for data hiding in the histogram. Compared with the former, this scheme can increase the embedding capacity. Tian proposed another classic reversible data hiding algorithm based on difference expansion [26]. The hidden data can be embedded by expanding the difference between two adjacent pixels. But the embedded location map takes up much space. In addition, in recent years, Wu et al. proposed a novel data hiding algorithm with the property of contrast enhancement [27]. Luo et al. proposed a scheme based on hybrid prediction and interleaving histogram modification with single-seed pixel recovery [28]. Shin et al. proposed a lossless data hiding technique using a reversible function and a pattern table [29]. In the transform domain, Yang et al. proposed a good reversible watermarking scheme [30]. This scheme takes advantage of integer DCT coefficients' Laplacian-shape-like distribution and chooses AC coefficients for the bit shift operation. In the compressed domain, with regard to vector quantization (VQ)—compressed images, Chu et al. proposed a high-capacity reversible information hiding algorithm based on difference coding of VQ indices [31]. Zhao et al. proposed a high-efficiency reversible data hiding scheme for two-stage VQ-compressed images [32]. With regard to block truncation coding—compressed images, Li et al. proposed a reversible data hiding scheme based on bit-plane flipping and histogram shifting of mean tables [33]. With regard to JPEG-compressed images, Hu et al. proposed a lossless data hiding scheme based on improved VLCs) [23]. Jung proposed a new data hiding algorithm of embedding filter coefficients in JPEG bitstream [34]. With regard to JPEG2000 compressed images, Ohyama et al. proposed a lossless data hiding scheme using bit-depth information embedding [35].

6.3.2 CHEN ET AL.'S IRREVERSIBLE WATERMARKING SCHEME

Before introducing lossless data hiding schemes for JPEG2000 images, we first introduce an irreversible watermarking scheme proposed by Chen et al. [36]. This scheme embeds and extracts information based on the JPEG2000 Codec process. It applies the torus automorphisms (TA) technique to break up the watermark, which are then embedded into the bitstreams after the JPEG2000 quantization step but prior to entropy coding. During quantization, all the coefficients would have been normalized and easy to manipulate. Distortion reduction technique is used on the compressed image to lessen image degradation caused by embedding. It is simple and easy to implement. Furthermore, it is robust to attacks like blurring, edge enhancement, and mosaic. In JPEG2000, we can use either 16 or 32 bits to be the binary length for the coefficients [1]. For convenience, this scheme uses 32 bits.

The MSB is the signed bit, and the remaining would be the absolute magnitude of the coefficient where embedding takes place (starting from the nonsigned high-magnitude bits). This scheme is divided into the embedding and extracting processes. More details are presented in the following subsections.

6.3.2.1 Embedding the Watermark

First, scattering is performed on a 32×32 binary watermark using the TA technique. The aim of this action is to cause the embedded watermark to be imperceptible. Assume that $(x_0, y_0)^T$ represents the original coordinate of the watermark and $(x_1, y_1)^T$ denotes the coordinate after scattering. Assume that N is the breadth size for the watermark and n is the overlap frequency for the transform matrix $\begin{pmatrix} 1 & 1 \\ k & k+1 \end{pmatrix}$ and $(x_0, y_0)^T$, where the value of n is the private scattering key. Then, using the single parameter TA, the scattering is performed according to

$$\begin{pmatrix} x_1 \\ y_1 \end{pmatrix} = \begin{pmatrix} 1 & 1 \\ k & k+1 \end{pmatrix}^n \begin{pmatrix} x_0 \\ y_0 \end{pmatrix} \bmod N \tag{6.29}$$

For example, to scatter a 32×32 watermark we have

$$\begin{pmatrix} x_1 \\ y_1 \end{pmatrix} = \begin{pmatrix} 1 & 1 \\ 1 & 2 \end{pmatrix}^n \begin{pmatrix} x_0 \\ y_0 \end{pmatrix} \bmod 32 \tag{6.30}$$

Here, for $n = 24$, we have an image similar to that of the original. At this point we say it has reached a cycle C. Therefore, by subtracting C from n we will get the overlap frequency needed for restoring the watermark. This is the private restore key.

The scattered watermark will be embedded in the subbands after quantization. The number of subbands used depends on the size of the watermark. The embedding process is in the sequence of LL, LH_j, HL_j, HH_j where $j = J, J-1, \ldots, 1$ (J is the integer number of frequency of decomposition in DWT). For example, in an image of size 512×512 pixels, after being decomposed 5 times, the subbands LH_j, HL_j, and HH_j are of the size $\frac{512}{2^j} \times \frac{512}{2^j}$ where $j = 5, 4, 3, 2, 1$. The size of LL is $\frac{512}{2^5} \times \frac{512}{2^5} = 16 \times 16$. Thus, a 32×32 watermark requires four subbands: LL, LH_5, HL_5, and HH_5 to embed.

After quantization, all coefficients are normalized in JPEG2000 as shown in Fig. 6.36. The MSB is the sign bit and will not be used for embedding. The rest

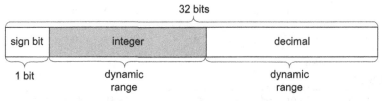

FIGURE 6.36

Coefficient after normalization.

is the nonsigned absolute coefficient used for embedding. The watermark is embedded into the nondecimal integer portion of the coefficient, whereas its decimal fraction portion is discarded as insignificant. Next, embedding process begins by inserting a value of either 0 or 1 into the M_b bit as follows:

$$M_b = \lfloor I_n \times \alpha_b \rfloor \quad \text{where} \quad \alpha_b \in [0, 1] \tag{6.31}$$

where I_n are the nondecimal integer bits with the dynamic range as given in Fig. 6.36 and α_b is the predefined threshold value. The bigger the threshold is, the more robust the embedding watermarks are. For example, when $I_n = 7$ and $\alpha_b = 0.6$, then $M_b = \lfloor 9 \times 0.6 \rfloor = 5$. Based on the embedding value, either 0 or 1 will be embedded into the fifth bit location. Thus, if the threshold α_b is larger, the embedding position is in the higher magnitude bit, implying stronger image robustness.

Since the watermark is embedded in the significant subband (for example, LL), this will affect the quality of the image. For this reason, the distortion reduction technique should be applied to help reduce the damage from image distortion. Assume that there is a coefficient with a whole number value of $(314)_{10}$. Its binary form is shown in Fig. 6.37. The LSB is the zeroth bit. The MSB is the eighth bit (excluding the sign bit and the left 0-padded bits that make up 32 bits). The watermark is also converted into the binary form. For this example, we will not use the M_b rule and threshold α_b to simplify the analysis process to choose the embedded value for the coefficient that is closest to the original value. Next, we introduce embedding 0 and 1.

6.3.2.1.1 Embedding Value 0

Suppose 0 is embedded into the fifth bit of the coefficient, the modified value and original coefficient might have the difference of $2^5 = 32$. As shown in Fig. 6.38, value 1 is equal to $(282)_{10}$. To lower the image distortion, a value 0 is chosen to replace the fifth bit. Since there are too many values to choose from, only three conditions are considered as shown in Fig. 6.38. The first one is value 1. The second one is to change the sixth bit into 1 in Value 2, whereas the fourth, third, and second bits are changed to 0 with the first and zeroth bits flipped from 0 to 1, or vice versa, depending on its original value. Value 2 is equal to $(321)_{10}$. The third one is to change the fourth, third, and second to 1 with the first and zeroth bits flipped as

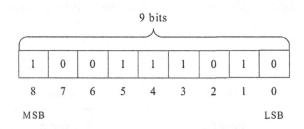

FIGURE 6.37

$(314)_{10}$ In the binary form. *LSB*, least significant bit; *MSB*, most significant bit.

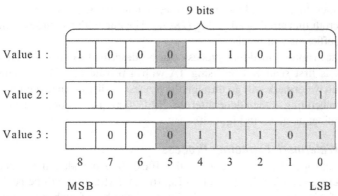

FIGURE 6.38

The three candidate conditions for embedding 0. *LSB*, least significant bit; *MSB*, most significant bit.

in Value 2. Here, Value 3 is equal to $(317)_{10}$. Finally, a value closest to the original coefficient from those three conditions is chosen to replace and to get the smallest image distortion possible.

6.3.2.1.2 Embedding Value 1

The rules for modifications here are similar to Eq. (6.30), as shown in Fig. 6.39. For Value 1, it is embedded into the fifth bit giving $(314)_{10}$. It is coincidental that the embedded value happens to be the original value. The test performs well for other test data, too. The sixth bit in Value 2 is modified to 0 and the fifth to second bits are modified to 1 with the first and zeroth bits flipped between 0 and 1 depending on its original values. This give the value $(317)_{10}$. On the contrary, in Value 3, the

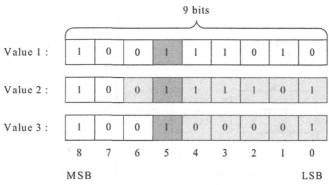

FIGURE 6.39

The three candidate conditions for embedding 1. *LSB*, least significant bit; *MSB*, most significant bit.

fifth bit is modified to 1 and the fourth to second bits are modified to 0, whereas the first and zeroth bits are flipped giving $(289)_{10}$. The one with the closest value to the original coefficient will be chosen.

Thus the whole embedding process can be described as follows. The original watermark is first scattered by using TA with a private key. Before embedding, the scattered watermark will go through the process of distortion reduction to reduce the loss. Embedding is then done after the JPEG2000 quantization stage and before entropy coding, as given in Fig. 6.40.

6.3.2.2 Watermark Extraction Process

After the entropy decoding stage of the JPEG2000 decoder, the watermark is extracted using the M_b rule as given in Eq. (6.31). Extraction will be performed in the order of embedding in the subbands. The total number of subbands extracted represents the size of the watermark. Restoring is performed using TA and the private restore key. Fig. 6.41 illustrates the flowchart of the watermark extraction process.

6.3.3 BIT-DEPTH EMBEDDING—BASED SCHEME

In 2007, Tanaka et al. proposed a reversible information hiding for binary images [37]. Based on this article, Ohyama et al. presented a lossless data hiding method for JPEG2000-compressed data based on the reversible information hiding [35]. In JPEG2000 compression, wavelet coefficients of an image are quantized, therefore, the LSB plane can be extracted. Ohyama et al.'s method recovers the quantized wavelet coefficients of cover images from stego images. To realize this, Ohyama et al. embedded not only secret data and the JBIG2 bitstream of a part of the LSB

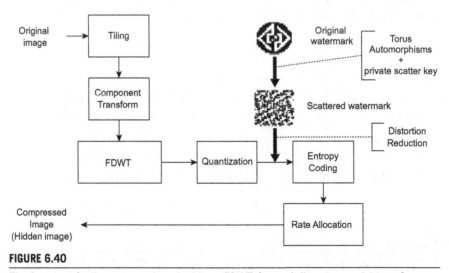

FIGURE 6.40

The flowchart for the watermark embedding. *FDWT*, forward discrete wavelet transform.

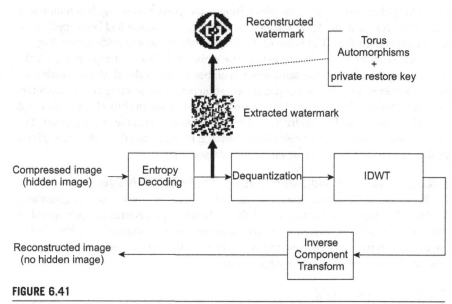

FIGURE 6.41

Flowchart for watermark extraction. *IDWT*, inverse discrete wavelet transform.

plane but also the bit-depth of the quantized coefficients on some code-blocks. Experimental results demonstrate the feasibility of application of this method to image alteration detection for JPEG2000-compressed data.

6.3.3.1 Reversible Information Hiding for Binary Images

In Tanaka et al.'s scheme [37], the data to be embedded is hidden into the noisy blocks on cover binary images. The noisy blocks are extracted by the simple thresholding with threshold α_{TH} of the measure called complexity defined for binary images. Only half of the pixels in noisy blocks are replaced with the bitstream of embedded data. Pixels used in the embedding are corresponding to white pixels (or block pixels) on checkerboard patterns. In other words, cover binary images are regarded as consisting two types of pixels: replaceable pixels and unusable pixels which correspond to white pixels and black pixels on checkerboard patterns, respectively.

In order to recover original images, it is required to embed the original information of replaceable pixels and make space for secret data, therefore cover binary images are compressed that all unusable pixels are set to 0 (or one) using the JBIG2 compression scheme. The compressed data and secret data are embedded into cover binary images.

The embedding process of this method is performed by replacing replaceable pixels with the embedded bitstream. The complexity of the noisy block may become smaller than α_{TH} by the embedding. In that case, the conjugate operation is applied to it to keep the complexity of the block from being greater than α_{TH}. It is required to keep track, for each block, of whether the conjugate operation had been applied using a conjugation flag. The value of 1 of replaceable pixels is made to the flag.

At the receiver side, one can extract the embedded bitstream from noisy blocks by scanning the image in the same order in embedding. For the blocks to which conjugate operation applied, the conjugate operation prior to extracting embedded information is applied. The extracted bitstream is separated into the bits of secret data and the JBIG2 bitstream. The bitstream is decompressed to reveal the original pixel. The original binary image can be completely restored by replacing the replaceable pixels of the stego image with one of the decompressed image.

6.3.3.2 Reversible Information Hiding for JPEG2000 Images

In Ohyama et al.'s method, they assume that the data of cover image is given as a JPEG2000-compressed bitstream and the embedding procedures are performed to the bitstream; as a consequence of this, stego images are produced as a JPEG2000-compressed bitstream. The quantized wavelet coefficients in the cover image are completely recovered from the stego image.

6.3.3.2.1 Embedding

The block diagram of the encoding in Ohyama et al.'s method is illustrated in Fig. 6.42. In JPEG2000, the bit-depth to represent quantized wavelet coefficients is allowed for code-blocks to vary within 32 bits including plus minus sign, and this depth is determined after the tier-2 encoding. Therefore, by using the bit-depth information, we can extract the LSB from each wavelet coefficient encoded in the JPEG2000 bitstream.

Basically, Ohyama et al.'s method applies Tanaka et al.'s reversible information hiding method for binary images described before to the LSB plane extracted from quantized wavelet coefficients, which is regarded as a binary image. However, Tanaka et al. have found a problem that the bit-depth of code-blocks containing wavelet coefficients value of 0, 1 or -1 increases by the embedding through several experiments. This makes us to extract embedded information incorrectly. To solve the problem, it is required to embed not only JBIG2 bitstream and secret data but also the bit-depth of the code-blocks. The embedding procedures in detail are as follows. Firstly, the bit-depth information of code-blocks on all resolution of subbands

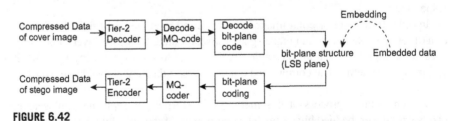

FIGURE 6.42

The flowchart for watermark extraction. *LSB*, least significant bit; *MQ-coder*, binary adaptive multiplication-free arithmetic entropy coder used in JPEG2000.

except for the lowest one is collected, and then it is embedded into the region where code-blocks are on the lowest resolution of subbands. For the rest of pixels, the JBIG2 bitstream and secret data are embedded.

6.3.3.2.2 Extraction and Recovering Original Wavelet Coefficients

After tier-1 decoding, quantized wavelet coefficients are reconstructed, and then the coefficients are divided into code-blocks with the same size as in encoding. From the code-blocks that are on the lowest resolution of subbands, the original bit-depth information of the rest of code-blocks is extracted, and then, by using the bit-depth information, the embedded bitstream consisting of secret data and JBIG2 bitstream is extracted. The recovering of the original wavelet coefficients is as follows. The extract JBIG2 bitstream is first decoded, and then the pixel value located on changeable pixels of the decoded image is replaced. After this replacement, the original quantized wavelet coefficients are completely reconstructed.

6.3.3.3 Experimental Results

Ohyama et al. have implemented their algorithm in the JJ2000 software. To illustrate the performance of Ohyama et al.'s method, they embedded four JPEG2000 test images Airplane, Bridge, Barbara, and Lena (8 bpp, 512 × 512) with 8 × 8 block size used to calculate the complexity of binary images, 5/112 complexity threshold ($=\alpha_{TH}$), and a random bit sequence embedded as a secret data. A 5-scale wavelet transform with the Daubechies 9/7 filter was applied to the images, therefore 64 × 64 and 32 × 32 of code-blocks in size were selected. The number of code-blocks on the images was 70. The four code-blocks on the lowest resolution of subband were used to embed the bit-depth of the rest of code-blocks. Therefore, it is required to embed 330 bits ($= 66 \times 5$ bits) to keep the depth information.

Table 6.10 shows the results obtained by the experiment. PSNRc and PSNRs represent PSNR of cover image and that of the stego image with the JPEG2000 compression, respectively. The quality of the whole image is almost acceptable for the test images that Ohyama et al. used in the experiments. However, uniform regions could be slightly distorted with sandy noise added. In addition, the image degradation of zoomed regions may be recognized. The embedded information

Table 6.10 Experimental Results for Five Test Images

Image	Cover Size (byte)	Stego Size (byte)	PSNRc (dB)	PSNRs (dB)	JBIG2 of LSB Plane (byte)	Secret Data (bit)	Hiding Rate (%)
Airplane	33,467	49,394	41.39	36.84	6230	9166	22.16
Bridge	32,604	49,394	30.53	27.02	8276	9502	29.15
Barbara	32,641	49,014	37.96	33.61	7294	4198	24.08
Lena	33,150	50,471	40.43	36.38	6195	11,814	23.26

LSB, *least significant bit;* PSNRc, *peak signal-to-noise ratio of cover image;* PSNRs, *peak signal-to-noise ratio of stego image with JPEG compression.*

used in the experiments is quite large compared with the number of bits to represent hash value, such as SHA-1, which produces a message digest that is 160 bits long. Because whole LSB plane was used in the experiments, Ohyama et al. certainly avoid the image degradation by using only a part of the LSB plane for the embedding.

6.3.4 REVERSIBLE INFORMATION HIDING BASED ON HISTOGRAM SHIFTING FOR JPEG2000 IMAGES

6.3.4.1 Introduction

Recently, the authors of this book have proposed a reversible information hiding scheme for JPEG2000-compressed images. In our scheme, high-frequency subbands of the cover image are divided into blocks. In each block, the histogram generated by the quantized wavelet coefficients of the block is shifted to create gaps for embedding data. Experimental results show that our scheme has satisfactory performance. Compared with other schemes, our scheme has higher embedding capacity and better visual quality of the stego image.

Embedding data into JPEG2000 images has some differences from embedding data into other types of images. The differences will lead to some difficulties. As a compressed image, the redundancy of a JPEG2000 image is smaller than that of an uncompressed image such as a BMP image. So the space for data hiding is limited. This will increase the difficulty of data hiding. In addition, the encoding process of JPEG2000 is more complex. Some encoding operations such as quantization and bitstream layering probably destroy the hidden data. It requires that data hiding should be coordinated with the encoding process of JPEG2000. So selecting suitable embedding position is important and difficult. To realize reversible data hiding, our scheme utilizes histogram shifting technique to embed data into quantized wavelet coefficients in high-frequency subbands of the cover image. Our shifting scheme is different from Ni et al.'s scheme [24]. In Ref. [24], the histogram is generated from the pixel values in the image. However, in our scheme, the histogram is generated from the quantized wavelet coefficients in the small block. In addition, the way we shift the histogram is also different. In their scheme, the histogram is always shifting toward the zero-point. However, in our scheme, we introduce a direction sign first. The value of the sign depends on the distribution of the histogram. Then the histogram of the block is shifted to the left or right adaptively according to the value of the direction sign. This can reduce the impact of histogram shifting on image visual quality to some extent. Moreover, the histogram will be shifted by three units in our work instead of one unit in their scheme. So every coefficient that is associated with the peak point can embed 2 bits instead of 1 bit. This can increase the embedding capacity.

To embed data into a JPEG2000 image and recover the image without any distortion, a reversible information hiding scheme based on histogram shifting is presented. Our scheme is different from Ohyama et al.'s scheme [35]. In their scheme, the low-frequency subband is also used for embedding data. However, we embed data into the high-frequency subbands only. In addition, they utilize the LSB plane of wavelet coefficients to embed data, whereas we adopt a method different from theirs. We use a new histogram shifting method to create space for embedding data. In our scheme, we introduce a direction sign first. The value of the sign depends on the distribution of the local histogram. Then the local histogram is shifted to the left or right adaptively according to the direction sign. Every coefficient that is associated with the peak point of the histogram can embed 2 bits. The detailed procedure of our scheme is described as follows.

6.3.4.2 Data Embedding

The block diagram of data embedding is shown in Fig. 6.43. In the embedding process, high-frequency subbands of the cover image are divided into blocks. For each block, a new histogram shifting method is applied to the local histogram generated from all quantized wavelet coefficients in the block. The detailed embedding process is described as follows.

Step 1: The original JPEG2000 image is partially decoded first. The decoding process stops before the dequantization stage. So we can get the quantized wavelet coefficients of all subbands.

Step 2: Divide the high-frequency subbands into $m \times m$ blocks. The number of the blocks is denoted by N.

Step 3: For each block B_i ($i = 1, 2, ..., N$), all coefficients in B_i are used to generate the local histogram of the block. Denote the peak point in the histogram as P_i. The number of times P_i occurs in the block is denoted by C_i. Then calculate T (the number of blocks that need to be used for embedding data) according to the number of hidden data bits and the values of C_i.

Step 4: For each needed block B_i ($i = 1, 2, ..., T$), calculate L_i (the number of values that are distributed in the left side of P_i) and R_i (the number of values that are distributed in the right side of P_i). Define a direction sign S_i to mark the direction that the histogram shifts toward: $S_i = 1$ denotes that the histogram shifts to the right, whereas $S_i = 0$ denotes that the histogram shifts to the left. Then compare L_i with R_i. If $L_i \geq R_i$, $S_i = 1$; otherwise, $S_i = 0$.

Step 5: If $S_i = 1$, shift the right side of P_i to the right by three units. It means that all coefficients in the right side of P_i are added by 3. If $S_i = 0$, shift the left side of P_i to the left by three units. It means that all coefficients in the left side of P_i are subtracted by 3. This step is used to create gaps for embedding data.

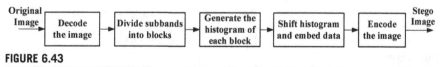

FIGURE 6.43

The block diagram of data embedding.

Step 6: Scan the coefficients of each block B_i ($i = 1, 2, ..., T$) in a sequential order (row by row, from top to bottom). Once we encounter the coefficient whose value is P_i, check the hidden binary sequence and perform embedding operations until all data bits are embedded. There are four possible cases as follows:

> Case 1: If the hidden bit string is "00," the coefficient remains unchanged.
> Case 2: If the hidden bit string is "01," 1 is added to the coefficient while $S_i = 1$ or 1 is subtracted from the coefficient while $S_i = 0$.
> Case 3: If the hidden bit string is "10," 2 is added to the coefficient while $S_i = 1$ or 2 is subtracted from the coefficient while $S_i = 0$.
> Case 4: If the hidden bit string is "11", 3 is added to the coefficient while $S_i = 1$ or 3 is subtracted from the coefficient while $S_i = 0$.

Step 7: After all data bits have been embedded, perform encoding operations to generate the stego JPEG2000 image.

The values of P_i and S_i of block B_i ($i = 1, 2, ..., T$) and the size of hidden data serve as a key. The sender can send the stego JPEG2000 image to the receiver in the public channel. Only on getting the key can the receiver extract the hidden data from the image and recover the image.

6.3.4.3 Data Extraction and Original Image Restoration

The block diagram of data extraction and image restoration is shown in Fig. 6.44. The detailed process can be described as follows.

Step 1: At first, decode the stego JPEG2000 image partially. The decoding process stops before the dequantization stage. So the modified quantized wavelet coefficients can be obtained.

Step 2: Divide the high-frequency subbands into $m \times m$ blocks. For each block B_i ($i = 1, 2, ..., T$), scan the coefficients of the block in the same sequential order as that used in the aforementioned embedding process and perform the corresponding operations according to the value of S_i. If all hidden data bits have been extracted, stop extracting data and just shift the histogram of the block back. The corresponding operations are as follows.

(1) If $S_i = 1$, perform the following operations:

Scan the block. Once the coefficient between P_i and $P_i + 3$ is encountered (including P_i and $P_i + 3$), extract data from this coefficient. There are also four possible cases as follows:

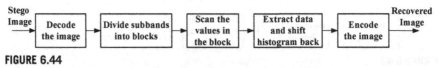

FIGURE 6.44

The block diagram of data extraction and image restoration.

Case 1: If the coefficient is equal to P_i, extract bit string "00." The coefficient remains unchanged.

Case 2: If the coefficient is equal to $P_i + 1$, extract bit string "01" and set it to P_i.

Case 3: If the coefficient is equal to $P_i + 2$, extract bit string "10" and set it to P_i.

Case 4: If the coefficient is equal to $P_i + 3$, extract bit string "11" and set it to P_i.

Scan the block again. If a coefficient is below $P_i - 3$, add 3 to it. The goal is to shift the histogram back. Other coefficients remain unchanged.

(2) If $S_i = 0$, perform the following operations:

Scan the block. If the coefficient is between $P_i - 3$ and P_i (including $P_i - 3$ and P_i), extract data from the value. In this case, P_i corresponds to "00," $P_i - 1$ corresponds to "01," $P_i - 2$ corresponds to "10," and $P_i - 3$ corresponds to "11." After the bit string is extracted from the coefficient, the coefficient will be set to P_i.

Scan the block again. If a coefficient is above $P_i + 3$, subtract 3 from it. The goal is to shift the histogram back. Other coefficients remain unchanged.

Step 3: After all data bits have been extracted, perform encoding operations to reconstruct the original image.

6.3.4.4 Experimental Results

In this section, some experimental results are given to evaluate the performance of our scheme. The implementation of our scheme is based on JasPer [16] and Visual Studio 2010. The JasPer software is specified by the JPEG2000 standard. It can provide the implementation of the JPEG2000 codec. Some 512×512 JPEG2000 grayscale images are used as test images, as shown in Fig. 6.45. The hidden data are a block of secret text. The text will be converted to a binary sequence. The number of levels of DWT we performed is five. To evaluate the similarity between the original image and the stego image, we choose their PSNR as the indicator. A larger PSNR value indicates a higher similarity and less image distortion. Generally, the stego image with 30 dB PSNR or above will be regarded as visually acceptable.

In our scheme, high-frequency subbands are divided into $m \times m$ blocks. The choice of the block size is an important issue. So we need to analyze the relationship between the block size and the embedding capacity first. The block size is typically set to a power of 2. The results are shown in Table 6.11.

From Table 6.11, we can find that the embedding capacity of the scheme decreases with the increase of block size on the one hand. On the other hand, for convenience, the block size should not be too small. So a good choice is 8×8. In the following experiments, the block size is 8×8.

For information hiding, the embedding capacity and the visual quality of stego image are both important indicators to measure the performance of the scheme. Table 6.12 shows the PSNR values of stego images after embedding different amounts of data. From Table 6.12, we can see that our scheme achieves satisfactory PSNR values. In addition, in the experiments, the hidden data can be exactly

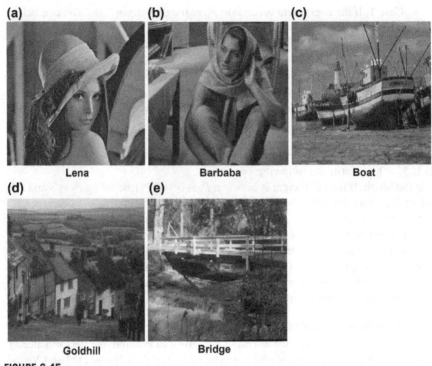

FIGURE 6.45

Five test images. (a) Lena, (b) Barbara, (c) Boat, (d) Goldhill, (e) Bridge.

extracted and the PSNR between the recovered image and the original image is infinite, which means that the cover image can be totally restored.

Next, we compare our scheme with the scheme proposed by Ohyama et al. [35]. The results of the comparison are shown in Table 6.13. From the table we can see that our scheme can embed more secret data bits for the same image.

Then we further compare our scheme with the scheme proposed by Chen et al. [36]. The results of the comparison with their scheme are shown in Table 6.14

Table 6.11 The Relationship Between Block Size and Embedding Capacity

Image	Capacity (bit) (Block Size = 8 × 8)	Capacity (bit) (Block Size = 16 × 16)	Capacity (bit) (Block Size = 32 × 32)
Lena	95,172	82,052	77,288
Barbaba	79,662	67,084	61,948
Boat	66,824	53,788	48,454
Goldhill	68,246	55,038	49,632
Bridge	53,118	40,494	35,632

Table 6.12 PSNR Values After Embedding Different Amounts of Data

Image	PSNR (dB) (0.5 KB)	PSNR (dB) (1.0 KB)	PSNR (dB) (1.5 KB)
Lena	59.05	55.59	53.67
Barbaba	57.96	55.16	53.19
Boat	56.39	53.36	51.92
Goldhill	58.65	54.56	52.44
Bridge	55.62	53.07	51.59

PSNR, *peak-signal-to-noise ratio.*

Table 6.13 The Results of the Comparison

Image	Embedded Secret Data Bits of Our Scheme (bit)	Embedded Secret Data Bits of Reference [35] (bit)
Lena	95,172	11,814
Barbaba	79,662	4198
Bridge	53,118	9502

Table 6.14 The Comparison of PSNR

Image	Embedded Bits (bit)	PSNR of Our Scheme (dB)	PSNR of Ref. [36] (dB)
Lena	1024	66.03	45.23
Boat	1024	62.76	44.80
Goldhill	1024	65.83	43.90

PSNR, *peak-signal-to-noise ratio.*

Compared with their scheme, we can see that our scheme has higher PSNR value after embedding equivalent amounts of data into the same image. It proves that our scheme has better invisibility of hidden data.

6.4 SUMMARY

This chapter focuses on the lossless information hiding in JPEG and JPEG2000 images.

For JPEG images, seven typical methods including two schemes from the authors were introduced. For the first five schemes, we introduced the basic ideas, whereas for the schemes from the authors, we provided a detailed introduced detail with experimental results. In the first method of ours, our high-capacity reversible JPEG-to-JPEG data hiding scheme is introduced. Through lowering certain quantization table entries and lifting corresponding quantized DCT coefficients, space is made for embedding data. Using the proposed embedding strategy, our scheme can achieve high embedding capacity and keep the distortion introduced by embedding very low; meanwhile the original cover JPEG image can be restored after the secret data are extracted. Experiments results demonstrate that the proposed scheme maintains the image quality of a stego JPEG image when the embedding capacity is high. Besides, the file size after embedding with not too huge data is acceptable. Compared with Chang et al.'s method and Xuan et al.'s method, the proposed method is superior in terms of the image quality, hiding capacity, and file size. Our scheme is very practical for image files stored and transmitted in the JPEG format. In the second method of ours, a lossless data hiding scheme with file size preservation is proposed. Through analyzing the code space and the statistics of both used and unused VLCs, we find there is still potential free space in the JPEG bitstream that can be explored to hide data. The best of unused VLCs are made and mapped to the used VLCs in specific mapping manners. The proposed scheme embeds data into the VLC codes and whatever mapped VLCs are present are not changed, therefore the image content after data hiding is exactly the same as the original one. Experimental results demonstrate that the proposed scheme can reach better performance irrespective of whether file size preservation is required or not.

For JPEG2000 images, we first introduced two schemes from the literature, and then introduce our scheme. In our scheme, high-frequency subbands of the cover image are divided into blocks. In each block, a new histogram shifting method is applied to the histogram of the block for embedding data. Every coefficient that is associated with the peak point embeds 2 bits of data. In addition, we shift the histogram to the left or right adaptively according to a direction sign. Experimental results show that the proposed scheme has high embedding capacity and good invisibility of hidden data.

REFERENCES

[1] ISO/JEC FCD 15444-1, JPEG2000 Part 1, Final Committee Draft Version1.0, 2000.

[2] ISO/JEC FCD 15444-2, JPEG2000 Part 2, Final Committee Draft, 2000.

[3] G.K. Wallace, The JPEG still picture compression standard, Communications of the ACM 34 (4) (1991) 30−44.

[4] International Telecommunication Union, CCITT Recommendation T.81, Information Technology- Digital Compression and Coding of Continuous-Tone Still Images- Requirements and Guidelines, 1992.

[5] J. Huang, Y.Q. Shi, Y. Shi, Embedding image watermarks in DC components, IEEE Transactions on Circuits and Systems for Video Technology 10 (6) (2000) 974−979.

[6] B.G. Mobasseri, R.J. Berger, M.P. Marcinak, Y.J. NaikRaikar, Data embedding in JPEG bitstream by code mapping, IEEE Transactions on Image Processing 19 (4) (2010) 958−966.

[7] D. Upham, JPEG-JSteg, 1997. http://www.funet.fi/pub/crypt/steganography/jpeg-jsteg-v4.diff.gz.

[8] A. Westfeld, F5-a steganographic algorithm: high capacity despite better steganalysis, in: Proceedings of the 4th International Workshop on Information Hiding, Pittsburgh, PA, USA, 2001, pp. 289–302.

[9] J. Fridrich, M. Goljan, R. Du, Invertible authentication watermark for JPEG images, in: Proceedings of IEEE International Conference on Information Technology: Coding and Computing, Las Vegas, Nevada, USA, 2001, pp. 223–227.

[10] J. Fridrich, M. Goljan, R. Du, Lossless data embedding for all image formats, in: Proceedings of SPIE, Electronic Imaging 2002, Security and Watermarking of Multimedia Contents IV, San Jose, California, vol. 4675, 2002, pp. 572–583.

[11] C.C. Chang, T.S. Chen, L.Z. Chung, A steganographic method based upon JPEG and quantization table modification, Information Sciences 141 (1–2) (2002) 123–138.

[12] M. Iwata, K. Miyake, A. Shiozaki, Digital steganography utilizing features of JPEG images, IEICE Transactions on Fundamentals of Electronics, Communications and Computer Sciences E87-A (4) (2004) 929–936.

[13] C.C. Chang, C.C. Lin, C.S. Tseng, W.L. Tai, Reversible hiding in DCT-based compressed images, Information Sciences 177 (13) (2007) 2768–2786.

[14] G.R. Xuan, Y.Q. Shi, Z.C. Ni, P.Q. Chai, X. Cui, X.F. Tong, Reversible data hiding for JPEG images based on histogram pairs, in: Proceedings of International Conference on Image Analysis and Recognition, Montreal, Canada, 2007, pp. 715–727.

[15] H. Sakai, M. Kuribayashi, M. Morii, Adaptive reversible data hiding for JPEG images, in: Proceedings of International Symposium on Information Theory and Its Applications, Auckland, New Zealand, 2008, pp. 1–6.

[16] A. Almohammad, G. Ghinea, R.M. Hierons, JPEG steganography: a performance evaluation of quantization tables, in: Proceedings of IEEE International Conference on Advanced Information Networking and Applications, Bradford, United Kingdom, 2009, pp. 471–478.

[17] Z. Cheng, K.Y. Yoo, A reversible JPEG-to-JPEG data hiding technique, in: Proceedings of 2009 Fourth International Conference on Innovative Computing, Information and Control, Kaohsiung, Taiwan, 2009, pp. 635–638.

[18] X. Zhang, S. Wang, Z. Qian, G. Feng, Reversible fragile watermarking for locating tampered blocks in JPEG images, Signal Processing 90 (12) (2010) 3026–3036.

[19] P. Lin, C. Chan, Invertible secret image sharing with steganography, Pattern Recognition Letters 31 (13) (2010) 1887–1893.

[20] J. Fridrich, M. Goljan, Q. Chen, V. Pathak, Lossless data embedding with file size preservation, in: Proceedings of SPIE, Security and Watermarking of Multimedia Contents VI, San Jose, California, vol. 5306, 2004, pp. 354–365.

[21] Z. Qian, X. Zhang, Lossless data hiding in JPEG bitstream, The Journal of Systems and Software 85 (2) (2012) 309–313.

[22] K. Wang, Z.M. Lu, Y.J. Hu, A high capacity lossless data hiding scheme for JPEG images, Journal of Systems and Software 86 (7) (2013) 1965–1975.

[23] Y.J. Hu, K. Wang, Z.M. Lu, An improved VLC-based lossless data hiding scheme for JPEG images, Journal of Systems and Software 86 (8) (2013) 2166–2173.

[24] Z. Ni, Y.Q. Shi, N. Ansari, W. Su, Reversible data hiding, in: Proceedings of 2003 International Symposium on Circuits and Systems, Bangkok, Thailand, vol. 2, 2003, pp. 912–915.

[25] A. Leest, M. Veen, F. Bruekers, Reversible image watermarking, in: Proceedings of 2003 International Conference on Image Processing, vol. 2, 2003, pp. 731–734.

[26] J. Tian, Reversible data embedding using a difference expansion, IEEE Transactions on Circuits and Systems for Video Technology 13 (8) (2003) 890–896.

[27] H.T. Wu, J.L. Dugelay, Y.Q. Shi, Reversible image data hiding with contrast enhancement, IEEE Signal Processing Letters 22 (1) (2015) 81–85.

[28] H. Luo, F.X. Yu, Z.L. Huang, H. Chen, Z.M. Lu, Reversible data hiding based on hybrid prediction and interleaving histogram modification with single seed pixel recovery, Signal, Image and Video Processing 8 (1) (2014) 813–818.

[29] S.H. Shin, J.C. Jeon, Lossless data hiding technique using reversible function, International Journal of Security and Its Application 8 (1) (2014) 389–400.

[30] B. Yang, M. Schmucker, W. Funk, C. Busch, S. Sun, Integer DCT-based reversible watermarking for image using companding technique, Proceedings of the SPIE 5306 (2004) 405–415.

[31] D.H. Chu, Z.M. Lu, J.X. Wang, A high capacity reversible information hiding algorithm based on difference coding of VQ indices, ICIC Express Letters, Part B: Applications 3 (4) (2012) 701–706.

[32] D.N. Zhao, W.X. Xie, Z.M. Lu, High efficiency reversible data hiding for two-stage vector quantization compressed images, Journal of Information Hiding and Multimedia Signal Processing 5 (4) (2014) 625–641.

[33] C.H. Li, Z.M. Lu, Y.X. Su, Reversible data hiding for BTC-compressed images based on bitplane flipping and histogram shifting of mean tables, Information Technology Journal 10 (3) (2013) 1421–1426.

[34] S.W. Jung, Adaptive post-filtering of JPEG compressed images considering compressed domain lossless data hiding, Information Sciences 281 (2014) 355–364.

[35] S. Ohyama, M. Niimi, K. Yamawaki, H. Noda, Lossless data hiding using bit-depth embedding for JPEG2000 compressed bit-stream, in: International Conference on Intelligent Information Hiding and Multimedia Signal Processing, 2008, pp. 151–154.

[36] T.S. Chen, J. Chen, J.G. Chen, A simple and efficient watermarking technique based on JPEG2000 codec, Multimedia Systems 10 (1) (2004) 16–26.

[37] S. Tanaka, M. Niimi, H. Noda, A study on reversible information hiding using complexity measure for binary images, in: Proceedings of Intelligent Information Hiding and Multimedia Signal Processing, vol. II, 2007, pp. 29–32.

Index

'*Note*: Page numbers followed by "f" indicate figures, "t" indicate tables.'

Printed in the United States
By Bookmasters